Region, Race, and Reconstruction

Region, Race, and Reconstruction

Essays in Honor of
C. Vann Woodward

Edited by
J. MORGAN KOUSSER
and
JAMES M. McPHERSON

New York   Oxford
OXFORD UNIVERSITY PRESS
1982

Library of Congress Cataloging in Publication Data
Main entry under title:
Region, race, and Reconstruction.
"Writings of C. Vann Woodward—a bibliography"—p.
1. Southern States—History—1865-   —Addresses, essays, lectures.
2. United States—Race relations—Addresses, essays, lectures.
3. Reconstruction—Addresses, essays, lectures.
4. Woodward, C. Vann (Comer Vann), 1908-   .
I. Woodward, C. Vann (Comer Vann), 1908-   .
II. Kousser, J. Morgan.   III. McPherson, James M.
F215.R43   975'.04   81-16965
ISBN 0-19-503075-3   AACR2

Printing (last digit): 9 8 7 6 5 4 3 2 1

Printed in the United States of America

To Glenn
and to the memory
of Peter

Preface

This book has been a long time in the making. During the spring of 1971, several of C. Vann Woodward's former students discussed informally the possibility of producing a *festschrift* to be published at the time of Woodward's retirement from Yale in 1977. From 1973 to 1976, plans for such a volume went forward in a less than systematic fashion. Then the usual procrastinating proclivities of scholars, along with a hesitancy to seem to sum up the career of a still active scholar, caused the project to lapse for several years. In 1979 the present editors revived it. Exchanges of correspondence with other Woodward students, all of whom expressed enthusiasm for the proposal, convinced us that arrangements for the volume should proceed, even though Woodward's continued productivity might suggest themes that we had neglected in constructing the framework of this book. Sheldon Meyer of Oxford University Press shared our enthusiasm for the project and has given it his indispensable support at every stage of preparation.

We made three decisions at the outset. First, since Woodward's influence and circle of friendships among fellow scholars are so broad, there would be no way to decide whom to ask and whom to exclude unless we limited the contributions to his former students. Because we knew that the quality of his students' work is high, we believed that this limitation would still allow us to put together a series of first-rate papers, a decision that the finished product justifies. Second, after inviting all those who earned their Ph.D.s under Woodward to submit essay proposals, we wanted to avoid a pitfall of many *festschriften*—disparate essays that fail to cohere in a thematic structure. In order, therefore, to produce a volume whose contributions would reflect the main themes of Woodward's work, we reluctantly turned down proposed essays from several people because their inclusion would have made the book either less cohesive or less related to Woodward's scholarship than we desired. Third, we hoped that, if at all possible, the project could be kept a secret from Woodward until publication. A great many people have assisted us in this aim, and we believe that we have succeeded.

The topics of "Region, Race, and Reconstruction" represent, alliteratively, the mainstream of Woodward's work, but unfortunately preclude exploration of major tributaries in military and literary history. Rather than summarize the essays or demonstrate their connections with the Woodward corpus, we shall let their authors speak for themselves. It should be emphasized that each author *does* speak for himself or herself and not necessarily for the editors or for the other contributors as a collective entity. Although the editors felt free to criticize or challenge the arguments or analyses of essay drafts, we have not tried to impose our viewpoints on the authors and we by no means agree with every point made in the published essays. Such diversity is the essence of the historical enterprise, and is fittingly consistent with Woodward's own nonprescriptive style as a teacher and adviser.

The editors wish to acknowledge the assistance of many people, in addition to Sheldon Meyer, who have contributed to the fruition of this project. Louis Masur devoted a great deal of time and care to the preparation of the bibliography of Woodward's writings. Loueva F. Pflueger at Yale and Sharon Widomski and Betty Whildin at Johns Hopkins helped us compile a list of Woodward students and supplied useful biographical data. Robert W. Fogel offered encouragement at an early stage of the project. William G. Rose and William W. Freehling provided crucial advice and support. Judith and Otto Sonntag accomplished with skill and good humor the task of copy editing the prose of seventeen authors in a manner to create some consistency of style without violating individuality of expression. Finally, on behalf of all his students, we wish to thank Vann himself for the precepts and example that have helped shape our careers.

December 1981

J. MORGAN KOUSSER
JAMES M. MC PHERSON

Contents

The Contributors

Vincent P. DeSantis is Professor of History at the University of Notre Dame. He is the author of *Republicans Face the Southern Question, 1877–1897*, and of other books and articles on United States history since 1865.

Charles B. Dew is Professor of History at Williams College. He is the author of *Ironmaker to the Confederacy: Joseph R. Anderson and the Tredegar Iron Works*, and he is currently at work on a study of the slave ironworkers of Buffalo Forge, Virginia.

Tilden G. Edelstein is Professor of History at Rutgers University. He is the author of *Strange Enthusiasm: A Life of Thomas Wentworth Higginson*. He is completing a book of essays about race and gender concentrating upon American policies and attitudes toward miscegenation and racial intermarriage.

Robert F. Engs is Associate Professor of History at the University of Pennsylvania. He is the author of *Freedom's First Generation: Black Hampton, 1861–90*, and is now working on a biography of Samuel Chapman Armstrong.

Barbara J. Fields is Assistant Professor of History at the University of Michigan and currently serving as associate editor at the Freedmen and Southern Society Project at the University of Maryland. She is the author of the forthcoming book, *The Maryland Way from Slavery to Freedom*.

Steven Hahn is Assistant Professor of History at the University of California at San Diego. He is the author of the forthcoming book, *The Roots of Southern Populism: Yeomen Farmers and the Transformation of Georgia's Upper Piedmont, 1850–1899*.

Louis R. Harlan is Professor of History at the University of Maryland and editor of *The Booker T. Washington Papers*. He is author of *Separate and Unequal* and of *Booker T. Washington: The Making of a Black Leader*.

THOMAS C. HOLT is Associate Professor of History and Afro-American Studies at the University of Michigan. He is author of *Black Over White: Negro Political Leadership in South Carolina During Reconstruction*, and is currently working on a comparative study of emancipation in South Carolina and Jamaica.

J. MORGAN KOUSSER is Professor of History and Social Science at the California Institute of Technology. He is the author of *The Shaping of Southern Politics: Suffrage Restriction and the Establishment of the One-Party South*, and is now working on a study of the legal history of segregation and desegregation.

WILLIAM S. McFEELY is Rodman Professor of History at Mount Holyoke College. He is the author of *Yankee Stepfather: General O. O. Howard and the Freedmen* and of *Grant: A Biography*.

JAMES M. McPHERSON is Professor of History at Princeton University. He is the author of *The Struggle for Equality*, of *The Abolitionist Legacy*, and of *Ordeal By Fire: The Civil War and Reconstruction*.

ROBERT DEAN POPE has a J. D. from Yale Law School and a Ph.D. in History from Yale University. He is currently a partner in the law firm of Hunton and Williams in Richmond, Virginia.

LAWRENCE N. POWELL is Associate Professor of History at Tulane University and co-editor of *The Papers of Frederick Douglass*. He is the author of *New Masters: Northern Planters During the Civil War and Reconstruction*, and is currently working on a study of Southern Republicans during Reconstruction.

DANIEL T. RODGERS is Associate Professor of History at Princeton University. He is the author of *The Work Ethic in Industrial America, 1850–1920*, and is currently engaged in a study of political ideas in nineteenth-century Britain and America.

WILLIE LEE ROSE is Professor of History at the Johns Hopkins University. She is the author of *Rehearsal for Reconstruction: The Port Royal Experiment* and of *Slavery and Freedom*.

J. MILLS THORNTON III is Professor of History at the University of Michigan. He is the author of *Politics and Power in a Slave Society: Alabama, 1800–1860*, and is currently working on a study of Southern taxation during Reconstruction.

BERTRAM WYATT-BROWN is Professor of History at Case Western Reserve University. He is the author of *Lewis Tappan and the Evangelical War Against Slavery*, and of the forthcoming books *Southern Honor: Ethics and Behavior in the Old South*, and *Yankee Saints and Southern Sinners*.

C. Vann Woodward:
An Assessment of His Work and Influence

J. MORGAN KOUSSER
JAMES M. McPHERSON

C. VANN WOODWARD was born in 1908 in the Arkansas hamlet of Vanndale and grew up in Morrilton, a small town on the Arkansas River fifty miles above Little Rock. His family was rooted several generations deep in Southern soil; his father was a public-school administrator and later a college dean; during his high-school and college years Woodward knew Rupert Vance, Howard Odum, and Will Alexander, intellectuals and liberals who were trying to push the South in the direction of greater cosmopolitanism and racial tolerance. From these associations Woodward absorbed influences that were to help shape the course and concerns of his career.

After graduating from Emory University in 1930 and teaching for a year at Georgia Tech, Woodward journeyed to New York, where he earned an M.A. in political science from Columbia University in 1932. Returning to Atlanta, he taught for another year at Georgia Tech until a depression-induced layoff of thirty faculty members jettisoned him into the ranks of unemployed academics, in 1933. Woodward had by then achieved a reputation as a young radical and dissenter from Southern folkways, a reputation that did not increase his popularity with Georgia legislators who controlled the purse strings of Georgia Tech. Woodward had formed friendships with black as well as white intellectuals in Atlanta; he had visited the Soviet Union; and, worst of all, he became vice-chairman of a committee to protest the conviction for "insurrection" of Angelo Herndon, a black Communist who had spoken with bitter eloquence at a relief demonstration outside an Atlanta courthouse.

Woodward's sympathies both as a scholar and as an activist were enlisted in behalf of justice for the downtrodden. He wanted to write history "from the bottom up," and fastened on agrarian radicals in general and on Tom Watson in particular as a subject for research. Obtaining access to Watson's papers and armed with a fellowship from the Rockefeller Foundation (one of the earliest ironies in the career of an ironist), Woodward moved to Chapel Hill in 1934 to begin graduate study in history. He probably learned less from his classes and seminars at Chapel Hill than he did from his associations with other liberals and radicals at Milton Abernathy's bookstore, from his research in the Watson papers and his independent reading in Southern history, and from his friendship with the young history professor Howard K. Beale. Studying with Beale and reading Charles A. Beard helped to shape in Woodward's mind a concept of American history as a conflict between classes and economic interest groups. These concepts, reinforced by his sympathy for the underdog, formed the framework for the interpretation of Southern history between the Civil War and World War I that he put forward in his first three books: *Tom Watson: Agrarian Rebel* (1938); *Reunion and Reaction: The Compromise of 1877 and the End of Reconstruction* (1951); and *Origins of the New South, 1877–1913* (1951).

After receiving the Ph.D. in 1937 for his dissertation on Watson, Woodward took jobs as an assistant professor at the University of Florida from 1937 to 1939, a visiting assistant professor at the University of Virginia in 1939–1940, and an associate professor at Scripps College in Claremont, California, from 1940 until he entered the navy in 1943 for three years' of service as a lieutenant in the Office of Naval Intelligence and the Naval Office of Public Information. His naval career included the writing of an outstanding book about the largest naval engagement in history, *The Battle for Leyte Gulf* (1947).

After the war Woodward joined the Johns Hopkins faculty. During his fifteen years in Baltimore, he published four books (plus a large number of articles and reviews, listed in the bibliography at the end of this volume) that reshaped the field of Southern history: *Reunion and Reaction* and *Origins of the New South* in 1951; *The Strange Career of Jim Crow* (1955); and *The Burden of Southern History* (1960). *Strange Career* alone has reached a huge reading audience in its four editions; it is unquestionably the single most influential book ever written on the history of American race relations.

The Woodward bibliography testifies to the continued volume of his writings since he joined the Yale faculty as Sterling Professor of History in 1961. Most of these writings have taken the form of essays, reviews, and introductions to books written by important figures in Southern history, the most recent being his definitive edition of Mary Boykin Chesnut's Civil War diary. These shorter pieces, several of which were published together in the book *American Counterpoint: Slavery and Racism in the North–South Dialogue* (1971), have done almost as much to fashion our perception of the Civil War/Reconstruction era and of the second Reconstruction as Woodward's earlier books did for the post-Reconstruction South. In addition, Woodward has delivered an enormous number of invitational lectures in the United States and abroad and has held various fellowships and visiting professorships or lectureships in three countries. Since his retirement from Yale in 1977, he has resided in Hamden, Connecticut, where he continues his numerous scholarly activities, including the editorship of the forthcoming eleven-volume Oxford History of the United States.

How can one gauge a scholar's influence? Some relatively superficial means are readily quantified: book sales, citations to his or her work, awards, elections to office in professional associations, and incorporation of his or her views into leading textbooks. Measured by these tests, C. Vann Woodward is surely among the most important historians of his time. Several of his books have gone into multiple printings, and, cumulatively, have sold approximately a million copies. His entries in published citation indexes and in the footnotes of historical monographs must be counted by the column foot. *Origins of the New South* won a Bancroft Prize. He has been elected to the presidencies of the Southern and American historical associations and to that of the Organization of American Historians. Nearly all American history texts written in the last generation adopt his views on Southern and post-Reconstruction history, and he is the author of the section covering those years in one of the most widely used and respected texts.

Less easily measured, but more important, is the impact of one thinker's work on that of others. Influence may be transmitted through direct teaching, through private, as well as public, critiques of manuscripts and books, through setting an example for emulation, through offering ideas or observations of sufficient originality and inherent interest that others feel compelled either to attack or to extend them, or, to put the point in its most general terms, through framing the agenda for a field of study. Woodward has directed some forty Ph.D. dissertations, and, as the essays in this book show, he has attracted some of the best students in the discipline during his career. On each of them, as well as on numerous other graduate and undergraduate students who have taken his courses, he has had a considerable, often a profound, effect. Industrious without being joyless, politically active without compromising his scholarly integrity, friendly but not hovering, never patronizing, Woodward by his personal example has affected many friends and colleagues, in addition to his students. The qualities of his written scholarship—clarity, comprehensiveness, subtlety, and lightness of tone coating an obvious seriousness of purpose—have pleased and affected more.

Woodward's chosen period and region have become "his" in much more than the usual sense for a historian. It is hard to think of a serious book or an important scholarly article written on the post-Reconstruction South or on modern American race relations in the last generation which does not repeat, take issue with, flesh out, test on other data, or carry out the implications of some idea first adumbrated or at least first fully enunciated by Woodward. No other recent American historian has so dominated an area of study. Indeed, Woodward has become a sort of one-man establishment, an idol to be chipped away at, a landmark to be assaulted and defended in scholarly frays—a curious position for a born dissenter who is no doubt more comfortable, as he himself observed about Tom Watson, in the role of a rebel.

Solid research and a felicitous writing style account only partially for Woodward's present ironic position. More important considerations are that he has attacked problems of profound and lasting importance and that he has propounded compelling and original interpretations. What were those problems, what central empirical propositions has he advanced, and how have they been received?

In his famous attack on "consensus history," John Higham singled out one historian of the 1950s for retaining the "progressive historians' " stress on socioeconomic and ideological conflict, their sympathy for the underdog, and their self-consciously moral stance, and for emphasizing, as the progressives had, discontinuity over continuity.[1] It was not mere chance that this one historian was Woodward, for he had set out from the beginning not only to re-evaluate and reorder Southern history—indeed, with respect to many issues, to impose order for the first time—but also to attack the prevailing consensus view of the South's experience. For a Southern "consensus school" long predated its national counterpart, and the Dixie branch was at the height of its influence in the 1930s and 1940s.

After all, more than a decade before Higham's bête noire Daniel Boorstin looked into the American political mind and found it empty, W. J. Cash had noted a similarly incogitant and undifferentiated genius in the Southern intellect.[2] Nor were the North Carolina journalist's flat and timeless generalizations about the region typical only of the gifted amateur. To economist Broadus Mitchell, the South in 1880 had been "homogeneous . . . one family, knit together and resolute through sufferings"; its leaders were "far-seeing, public-minded, generous-natured . . . true patriots"; and even so notorious an evil as child labor in the textile mills had initially represented "philanthropy; not exploitation, but generosity and cooperation and social-mindedness."[3] In one of the then standard histories of the post-Reconstruction South, Philip A. Bruce viewed the region's two chief strengths as a belief in white racial "superiority" and the Southerners' "complete homogeneity as a people." In his short chapter on the politics of the 1880s and 1890s, Bruce did not mention Populism.[4] While strenuously denying national uniformity in thought and culture, the Nashville Agrarians, furthermore, implied that nearly all Southerners took the same stand as they did. And Ulrich B. Phillips's works, with their climatic determinism, their rosy view of race relations during and after slavery, and their racist "central theme," dominated professional historians' views of the section.[5]

Tom Watson was, among other things, an attack on the myth of an everlastingly solid South. "What [needed] proof and demonstration at that time," Woodward later noted, "was that there were ever any exceptions, any evidence against the once prevalent . . . assumption that 'things have always been the same!' "[6] Originally conceived as part of a collective biography of seven tribunes of the common people, *Watson* presented a most imperfect hero whose stark change from racial egalitarian to race-baiting, religiously bigoted demagogue emphasized the discontinuity of Southern history at the same time it created, in Watson's Populist phase, a usable past for Southern liberals and radicals. Breaking points and disconnections were similarly main themes of *Reunion and Reaction,* with its story of a corrupt bargain that ended Reconstruction; of *Origins of the New South,* which painted the "New Departure Democrats" as strikingly different in character from the South's pre-war rulers and, in general, described the period between Reconstruction and the First World War as one of transition, contradiction, class and race conflicts, and unfulfilled possibilities; and of *The Strange Career of Jim Crow,* a demonstration that absolute segregation was not a "natural," unchangeable condition, since there had been a time when significant exceptions existed.

Nor did Woodward abandon his anticonsensus theme in later publications. His editions of the works of three extraordinary Southern dissenters, Lewis Harvey Blair, George Fitzhugh, and Mary Boykin Chesnut; his harsh critique, in *American Counterpoint,* of Cash's "two fundamental theses . . . of unity and . . . of continuity"; and his anxiety that such recent books as those by Carl Degler, Jonathan M. Wiener, and Dwight B. Billings, Jr., represent a recrudescence of consensus theories of Southern history—all indicate the persistence of Woodward's concern with this issue.[7]

Yet Woodward did not invariably highlight discontinuity and dissent. In fact, he seemed to take considerable glee in pointing to connections as well as disconnections that differed from those which previous observers had noticed or owned up to. For example, the pro-industrial and pro–Northern-capital policies of the New Departure Democrats appeared to him more like those of the antebellum Whigs, and, of all people, the Reconstruction Radicals, than most previous historians, who had usually referred to the New South Conservatives as "Bourbons," had noted or been willing to admit. Even their extensive defalcations, mention of which had previously been taboo, and their notorious ballot-box machinations, for which most previous observers had offered racist defenses, identified the Conservatives as close kin of the Radicals. And although John D. Hicks and most other historians had seen Progressivism as a fulfillment of many Populist impulses and programs, Woodward viewed the two movements, or at least their Southern branches, as much less similar.[8]

While always attentive to class, race, and geographical divisions within the South, Woodward also forcefully reminded Southerners of the aspects of historical experience that all groups in the region shared. Whites or their ancestors had a common heritage of military defeat, occupation, and forced reconstruction; blacks had been subjected to the illiberal "peculiar institution" and whites had betrayed Locke to defend slavery; and majorities of both whites and blacks had had to live with "un-American" poverty. In stressing these facets of sectional identity, Woodward neatly turned on its head the then conventional Yankee contrast between a backward-looking, problem-laden South and a more moral, generally prosperous, invincible nation, as well as the Fugitives' conception of a nobler, less materialistic Dixie.

But despite his implied rejection of the "American South" school's denial of Southern exceptionalism, Woodward was more open to notions of consensus, and the motivation for his views was perhaps less different from those of certain "consensus historians," than is sometimes noted.[9] In fact, his openly presentist purpose in the essays "The Search for Southern Identity" and "The Irony of Southern History" was not entirely unlike Boorstin's policy-related reading of the American mind in *The Genius of American Politics*. "Historical circumstances," not adherence to a political theory, Boorstin believed, accounted for America's prosperity and freedom and explained why "nothing could be more un-American than to urge other countries to imitate America." Likewise, Woodward hoped that an America attentive to the lessons that he drew from Southern—and Northern—history would be less likely to try to enforce conformity in thought and actions at home and abroad, to stake all on the defense of a single institution, such as slavery, segregation, or laissez-faire capitalism, or to engage in "the fallacy of a diplomacy based on moral bigotry" or even "preventive war."[10] Varying purposes and alterations in focus from one to another aspect of Southern and American society, then, have led Woodward to emphasize consensus or disunity, stability or change, as the situation and his aims required.

The conflicts that Woodward highlighted were more complex than the liberal-conservative, realty-personalty, or frontier-seaboard clashes of Parrington, Beard, and Turner, or the pietist-liturgical dichotomy of those more recent opponents of the political-consensus view, the "ethnocultural" political historians. Thus, Populism, in Woodward's eyes, was not merely a conflict of sections, of farmers and city dwellers, of ideologies, of economic interests, of classes, of competing elites, but all of these and more. Anyone who comes to grips with *Watson* and *Origins* and *Strange Career* can never again describe racial conflicts and alliances, the racial ideologies of men and women of both races, and the behavior of people of different groups toward each other so starkly and simply as he was able to do before. And as committed as Woodward at times seemed in some battles—for example, in those over charges that the Populists were antidemocratic and backward-looking and over the timing of the adoption of segregation—he maintained a degree of skepticism, an air of detachment and ironic distance that freed his vision from the constraints of blind partisanship. While Woodward shared many characteristics with the "progressive historians," then, he largely avoided their over-simplification and their restrictive biases.

Woodward's influence stems in part from his mastery of the ironic technique.[11] There are two basic ironic categories—situational irony and verbal irony—and Woodward employs both with consummate skill. Situational irony is an ironic state of affairs or an event viewed as ironic; verbal irony is an ironic style of speaking or writing. The latter is a means of communication; the former is the thing communicated. The essence of situational irony lies in an apparent contradiction or incongruity between two events or meanings, a contradiction resolved when the literal or surface meaning turns out to be one of appearance only, while the initially incongruous meaning turns out to be the reality. Those who hold or perpetrate the plausible but false meaning are thereupon revealed as hypocritical and self-serving, or naive and comic in their smug self-assurance. Verbal irony shares this incongruity between appearance and reality. The author of an ironic passage intends something quite different from the literal meaning of his words; the reader must reject the surface meaning and reconstruct the passage to find the hidden and incongruous "real" meaning.

Verbal irony can be either satiric or comic. Satiric irony is a form of blame by means of apparent praise, of deliberate overstatement to lampoon the object of such overstatement. Comic irony is a form of praise through apparent blame, of understatement in order to lead the reader to sympathize with the subject of the irony. Woodward employs both satiric and comic irony, though like most ironists he relies mainly on the former. Consider, for example, this description in *Origins of the New South* of Francis Dawson, a transplanted Englishman who became editor of the Charleston *News and Courier* and a zealous advocate of Southern salvation through Yankee-style capitalism and industrialism: "In Dawson's metropolitan and unprejudiced eyes there was nothing in old Charleston that could not be improved with an eye to Pittsburgh."[12] Only the dullest of readers will fail to recognize that Dawson is the object of satirical irony and that the words "unprejudiced" and "improved" must be translated into something close to their opposites in order to reconstruct the sentence's real meaning—a meaning shared by the author and reader but not by Dawson. The following example of comic irony illustrates Woodward's occasional use of this technique. Describing the political machinations of the Louisiana Lottery Company, he refers to its successful effort in 1879 to write the company charter into the new state constitution, "where it would be beyond the reach of fickle legislatures and ungrateful governors."[13] The reader, having already learned of the lottery's attempts to corrupt public officials, and of "reformers' " attempts to curb it, understands that the words "fickle" and "ungrateful" are doubly intended criticisms both of the lottery and of its critics, who were often merely politicians who refused to stay bought.

Verbal irony can be broad and obvious, as in much of Mark Twain's writing, or subtle and ambiguous, as in Henry James's. Although the examples of irony cited in the previous paragraph are fairly obvious to anyone familiar with the general theme of *Origins of the New South,* Woodwardian irony often lies closer to the subtle end of the scale. Consider this sentence from the preface to the 1971 edition of *Origins,* a sentence about historians rather than about history: referring to scholarly developments during the twenty years since publication of the first edition, Woodward noted that if he were to rewrite *Origins* in 1971 "it is even possible that I should have been able to make use of some of the new historical techniques, methods, and insights that have matured in the last two decades to improve the quality of scholarship."[14] The irony here is so subtle that some readers might insist that the sentence should be read "straight." If pressed, even Woodward might claim that he meant it straight. But to those familiar with Woodward's skepticism about the claims of some proponents of the "new historical techniques," the reference to improving the quality of scholarship carries at least faint overtones of satiric irony. At the same time, Woodward's open-mindedness toward new methods and new interpretations—many of them practiced and advanced by his own students—gives the self-deprecating tone or the phrase "even possible" in this sentence a quality of comic irony. An ironic reading of the sentence, then, uncovers a genuine ambiguity on Woodward's part, a mixed feeling that results from his ability to see through—or, perhaps, his constitutional inability to avoid penetrating—the starkly contrasting opinions of those on each side of a hotly controverted question.[15] It also demonstrates that the reader must often read between the lines for the hidden meaning in Woodward's subtle irony, and that to do that he must be familiar with the larger context of the author's work and ideas.

Woodward's technique of verbal irony includes the skillful use of quotations. After devoting several pages to a description of embezzlements, defalcations, and other peccadilloes by post-Reconstruction Southern officials, he quotes a statement by an early historian of this era: "The incredible waste and robbery of the Reconstruction Era was followed as soon as that era ended by the most careful handling of the public funds. Nowhere has there been so little peculation and defalcation on the part of officials in charge of the public treasuries."[16] This vivid satire, accomplished by the quotation of filiopietistic historiography following evidence of Redeemer roguery, makes Woodward's point more effectively than any other rhetorical device could have done. Or consider the following quoted assertions by spokesmen for the

Southern textile industry, juxtaposed with data showing that the annual profits of the industry averaged 22 percent while the workers' wages averaged three dollars per week: the mill owners professed to be motivated by a "philanthropic incentive" to provide "employment to the necessitous masses of poor whites," which offers them "elevating social influences, encourages them to seek education, and improves them in every conceivable respect."[17] Finally, let us examine the following quotation from the New York *Tribune* in 1879 criticizing movements in Southern states for repudiation or readjustment of state debts: "Wherever slavery existed," declared the *Tribune,* "the moral sense was so blunted and benumbed that the white people as a whole is to this day incapable of that sense of honor which prevails elsewhere."[18] Coming from a city that had produced Boss Tweed, Jim Fisk, Jay Gould, and other assorted rascals, this was delicious irony indeed. It struck one of Woodward's favorite targets—the Yankee self-image of superior virtue.

This image, especially with regard to the antislavery movement and race relations, is the subject of Woodwardian irony in several essays in *The Burden of Southern History* and *American Counterpoint* as well as in *The Strange Career of Jim Crow.* In two essays whose titles contain the word "Irony," the national myths of innocence, virtue, and success become the topic for sober analysis by the ironist whose Southern perspective provides the detachment that allows him to deflate those myths.[19] Like all examples of irony, these essays have a moral purpose; they are intended to expose fallacies in the American self-image with the hope that a more realistic perception will nudge national behavior a step or two closer to national ideals.

Apart from these essays, the most powerful and sustained applications of Woodwardian irony occur in *Origins of the New South,* particularly in the earlier chapters. Even more unforgettable than the examples of verbal irony already cited from the book are Woodward's ironic portraits of the leading actors of the New South, which establish the book's thematic framework. Democrats who are really Whigs in disguise busily demolish the traditional principles of Jacksonian democracy. "Redeemers" implant the very Yankee institutions and values against which the antebellum South had fought. "Bourbons" celebrate the past while embracing a laissez-faire version of the future. The Reconstruction settlement involves a sacrifice of Reconstruction's ostensible purpose—black rights—to obtain its "real" purpose of Yankee capitalist domination. The Democratic party of white supremacy maintains itself in power against challenges by white dissidents by manipulating black votes or collaborating with black voters, while the Republican party of hard money and Negro rights allies itself with agrarian antimonopolists, repudiationists, and rednecks. The spokesman for black upward mobility through hard work allies himself with the economic elite, North and South, whose enterprises benefit from a docile, static, low-wage Southern labor force. A gospel of economic progress and prosperity produces educational regression and poverty for the rural masses, and a colonial relationship with the North. "Progressives" preside over a massive retrogression in the political and legal rights of black people. In each of these ironic contradictions, the context makes clear the real meaning Woodward intends to convey. The reader is subtly led to agree with the author's perception of the self-interest, hypocrisy, arrogance, or naiveté of his subjects.

The evocative power of the ironic contrasts is enhanced by the sudden shift from an ironic to a straight style when the author is dealing with the aspirations and activities of poor whites and blacks. While the values and programs of Bourbons, Redeemers, Democrats, Republicans, industrialists, and New South propagandists are to be viewed with ironic detachment, the values and programs of their opponents and critics—above all the Populists —are to be taken literally. The incongruity between Tom Watson's Populist support for black rights and his later racist demagoguery is not irony but rather tragedy, a microcosm of the Populist tragedy brought about by the frustration and bitterness of unjust defeat. As in a Bach fugue, a distinct and compelling theme emerges from this Woodwardian counterpoint of irony and tragedy.

Other historians present their interpretations by explicit assertion, by statistical demonstration, by the piling up of examples or quotations, by carefully selecting evidence, by rhetoric or argument. While not necessarily shunning these devices, Woodward relies on irony to a greater extent than does perhaps any other historian. The influence of his work is testimony to the power of the method. Woodward's students could hardly escape the healthy contagion of this approach. Alert readers will discover numerous instances of irony among the essays in this volume as well as in other writings by the same authors. This is a function not only of the teacher's precept and example, but also of the subjects he and his students have chosen to write about, for the complexities and contradictions of the South, of race relations, and of Reconstruction offer more scope for irony than do most other topics in American history.

Woodward's range of knowledge and the flexibility and sheer playfulness of his mind have cast up so many new and striking ideas that there are many "Woodward theses"—some merely accepted, some repeatedly confirmed, some extended, some challenged, some forcefully disputed, some discarded, some (in our view, unfortunately) ignored. Probably the most familiar of these hypotheses are the two that have been most disputed—the "Jim Crow thesis" and his depiction of the background of the Compromise of 1877.

Strange Career contains, as it were, three related but separable arguments of different levels of generality. The broadest is that there is no "natural" form to relationships between people of different races. Unless bound by laws, people will intermingle, separate, or do each simultaneously in different social spheres or each sequentially at different times in their lives. Only legal regulations can enshrine strict segregation and/or the relatively unbroken subordination of one group to another. The second theme, in its most general statement, is that there have been temporal variations in Southern race relations. The politician's cry of the 1950s and early 1960s—"Segregation forever!"—ignored the past as surely as it failed to hold back the future. The third contention was that Reconstruction was succeeded by a transitional era in race relations which was much less uniform and at least somewhat less harsh than that which began in the last decade of the nineteenth century. The position of blacks deteriorated around the turn of the century, and the possibilities for interracial social contact on anything like an equal basis were almost wholly cut off.

That segregation and other forms of racial discrimination were highly but not perfectly correlated in the South necessarily complicated Woodward's treatment of the subject and made the evaluation of evidence relevant to his thesis a very tricky matter indeed. Did voluntary segregation by blacks in churches, lodges, and businesses, much of which developed during Reconstruction, a time when blacks wielded considerable political influence, indicate that Woodward was wrong? Did the fact that black political power declined, but was by no means extinguished, in the post-Reconstruction South support or damage his case? Did the patterns of legal and private segregation of antebellum urban free people of color and often their exclusion from services otherwise open to the public, which Richard C. Wade and Howard N. Rabinowitz found, disprove or replace the "Jim Crow thesis"? Could state studies, such as those by Charles E. Wynes on Virginia, Joel Williamson on South Carolina, or John W. Graves on Arkansas, validate or invalidate Woodward's theory?[20]

Such questions suggest a further ambiguity in Woodward's notion, which may best be illustrated with the elementary statistical concepts of mode, mean, and variance. In examining Jim Crow's life span, should one focus in each period on the dominant tendency (the mode), the average circumstance (the mean), or the extent of the divergencies (the variance)? If the mode is the proper object of attention, and if one ignores the possibility that there may be more than one important facet to an era, then Woodward's case is lost, as he, of course, realized from the beginning. For although segregation was rarely the prime method of social control under slavery, after 1865 segregation and racial discrimination have been and in many respects still are the dominant features of the historical picture in every era. If, at the other extreme, it is the temporal or spatial variance or the variation across different social institutions at the same time which is at issue, then the simultaneous emergence of voluntary separation and political potency, the replacement of exclusion with largely private, imperfectly enforced segregation and subsequently with strict legal Jim Crow, and the different political and social experiences of blacks across the Southern states all buttress Woodward's contention. If the mean is the crucial statistic, then assessing the surviving data becomes much more difficult—does the fact that integration in nineteenth-century first-class railroad cars is rarely mentioned, for example, prove that it was so conventional as not to attract attention, or, rather, that it rarely occurred? —and the problem of weighing the relevant situations in different social institutions becomes virtually intractable.

Although Woodward did not formulate the "Jim Crow thesis"

in exactly this manner, our reading of *Strange Career* convinces us that he was more interested in variation than in averages, and much less concerned with mere predominant trends than with either of the other parameters. Surely this is one implication of his discussion of the "paternalistic" and "competitive" models of race relations and of the variation in patterns in different countries in "The Strange Career of a Historical Controversy." If our reading is correct, then in spite of attacks, the career of the thesis still flourishes. In any case, despite its tentative and heavily qualified statement and the passage, with the decline in legal segregation and expressions of virulent racism, of the conditions of rigid and unbroken racial separation in the South which gave rise to the argument in the first place, the notion stimulated a great deal of research that has added, and continues to add, both depth and breadth to our knowledge of race relations.[21]

If "Jim Crow" suggested both more intensive examinations of subsets of the Southern universe to which it was originally applied and the extension of the same or similar theories in studies of patterns of race relations outside that time and place, the plot of *Reunion and Reaction* could be tested only by logic and by minute and painstaking analyses, mostly of the same documents Woodward had used. It seems curious, therefore, that major assaults on this interpretation of Woodward's were so long in coming, for these tasks required less additional research than did studies of race relations in previously unexamined cities or states, and the open Beardianism of the "Compromise thesis" was generally under much more serious attack during the 1950s and 1960s than was the social theory underlying "Jim Crow."

Critics have made four major points against *Reunion and Reaction:* that evidence for the economic part of the Compromise is sparse; that the fact that major parts of it were not carried out casts doubt on whether a deal was actually cut; that Woodward's account overestimated the importance of certain behind-the-scenes participants and of the Southern Democrats in particular, and of the financial segment of the understanding in general; and that the whole election settlement was "insignificant," since black civil rights would have been abandoned by either Democrats or Republicans anyway and since there was never any chance that Whiggish Southerners would bolt in sufficient numbers to rejuvenate the Southern Republicans.[22]

No one of these arguments is entirely persuasive. First, conspirators destroy evidence, and many of those involved in the events of 1876 and 1877, such as Major E. A. Burke of Louisiana, undoubtedly did so in this case. The surprising thing is not that there is so little but that there is so much surviving evidence. Second, as Woodward pointed out in his reply to Peskin, many political agreements have been violated, and, in any case, some of the most important provisions of the 1877 understanding were kept. The third and fourth contentions are more serious, but both rely too much on hindsight to be entirely convincing. Benedict fails to take sufficient account of how contingent the situation must have seemed to Hayes and his entourage, how desirous they must have been to ensure against failure or continued deadlock, and therefore how important they must have considered every vote that might potentially contribute to the Ohioan's slim margin. By neglecting to consider the overwhelmingly negative Republican reaction to Hayes's Southern policy, when the policy became clear, as well as the continuation, through at least 1890, of Republican efforts to build a Southern Republican party and to safeguard the Negro's constitutional liberties, Gillette writes off the GOP's commitment to black rights and the possibility of a biracial Southern coalition too early and too absolutely, and therefore underestimates at least the temporary importance of the Compromise.

A third idea central to Woodward's work has been his attempt to draw from the general pattern of American and particularly Southern experience chastening and moderating lessons for the present. A recognition of the South's past burden—sin, defeat, occupation, and poverty—would, he hoped, save the nation from stifling dissent at home and from engaging in misadventures, bred by hubris, abroad. The historian thus became not only a moralist but also society's psychoanalyst, seeking to eradicate "childish" behavior and to avoid future traumas by bringing past experiences to consciousness. No doubt this is a difficult undertaking, for as Robert B. Westbrook has pointed out, societies are prone to "cultural amnesia," particularly when less scrupulous analysts purvey quicker and less painful nostrums.[23] Perhaps the chief irony for the historian who points out ironies is that the demonstration is likely to be largely futile, for more conventional maxims are much easier for the public to accept.

Although Woodward concentrated on the South in this endeavor, the principles he deduced from Northern history were not so different from the ones he derived from the Southern experience.[24] After all, he realized that the components of the historical Northern self-image are "myths," that they represent only what he termed "the illusion of pretended virtue," that no part of the nation has been entirely innocent, invincible, and prosperous, that America's overweening self-confidence and optimism are not justified. Even many in the antislavery movement were not fully egalitarian or entirely free from racist sins. The Civil War was less than the moral crusade sometimes hazily remembered. The Yankees' failure to reconstruct the South in the image of New England and the rapid disillusionment of many of them with the attempt hardly augured well for American attempts to impose this country's will on others. Prosperity has always been unevenly distributed. The point is not that Northern history validates American myths, but that Southern history so much more obviously does not that it provides a superior vantage point for attacking a set of historically inaccurate self-conceptions which are used to buttress what Woodward believes are misconceived present policies.

Much of the rest of his work may be considered under the rubric of his characterization of the post-Reconstruction South's political forces and its economic development. His portrait of the New South regimes as largely morally bankrupt, politically vacuous, dominated by opportunistic politicians who employed neo-Whig policies to enrich themselves and to turn large parts of the Southern economy over to Yankee capitalists, who used a laissez-faire ideology to starve social services, and who allied at times with blacks and nearly always with the relatively conservative Eastern United States rather than with the potentially more liberal Western states, was strikingly revisionist when it was first offered. But it has since been more often confirmed than revised. Thomas B. Alexander's study of "persistent Whiggery," for example, brought more extensive quantitative support to Woodward's views on that antebellum party's postbellum importance. Paul M. Gaston's detailed exposition of the "New South Creed" generally substantiated Woodward's briefer examination. And attacks on the novelty and pervasiveness of the creed, and the behavior it justified, by John M. Cooper, Jr., Jonathan M. Wiener, and Dwight B. Billings, Jr., entail serious difficulties of their own.[25] Although Carl Harris has made some dents in the East-West or right fork–left fork thesis and although the seriousness of the black-Redeemer coalition has been questioned, few historians have arisen to defend the New Departurites' morality or policies. Indeed, some recent views of them are harsher than Woodward's.[26]

His emphasis on the importance of the Southern branch of Populism and his image of the Populists as political, economic, and racial radicals have also stood up well. Heirs of the agrarian tradition of Jefferson, Jackson, the Granger-independents, and the Greenbackers, the small farmers who were the backbone of the movement and their usually wealthier leaders accepted capitalism as a system, according to Woodward, but "formed the vanguard against the advancing capitalistic plutocracy."[27] Monographs by Lawrence C. Goodwyn, Robert C. McMath, Jr., and Michael Schwartz agree with him on the significance of the Southern branch of the movement, though they characterize its leadership somewhat differently—McMath and Schwartz to a large extent because they concentrate on its Alliance, not its Populist, phase.[28] Goodwyn, Norman Pollock, and Bruce Palmer, a Woodward student, all emphasize the anticapitalist facet of Populist ideology more than Woodward did, but the difference is primarily one of degree.[29]

Another Woodward student, Sheldon Hackney, has presented the Alabama Populists as more opportunistic and backward-looking than his adviser did. Woodward's assertion that the Populists were uniquely nonracist among nineteenth-century white Southern politicians and that they were singularly successful in appealing for black votes has been directly denied by some critics and indirectly contradicted by studies of Reconstruction and post-Reconstruction scalawags.[30] Still, the most that these arguments show, even if one accepts them at close to face value, is that the Populists were less unconventional politicians than Woodward contended, that his generalizations do not hold everywhere equally, and that he may have somewhat exaggerated the Populists' racial idealism. Henry Demarest Lloyd's "cowbird thesis" about a conspiracy by national Populist free-silverite leaders to force fusion with the Bryanite Democrats in 1896, which Woodward endorsed and embellished, has been disputed by Robert F. Durden but supported by Pollack and Goodwyn, and currently seems basically secure.[31] Even Woodward himself has largely withdrawn his suggestion that "soured Populists," angry at the use of black votes to beat them and generally frustrated, were especially important in the moves toward Jim Crow and disfranchisement, and others have firmly rejected the notion, which in any case seemed somewhat out of harmony with Woodward's more general portrait of the Populists.[32]

If he was concerned in *Origins* to demonstrate that the South did have a "Progressive Movement," Woodward succeeded in keeping its limitations at the forefront of his readers' consciousness, entitling his chapter "Progressivism—For Whites Only" and highlighting the break between Populist agrarianism and the later middle-class movement, with its largely urban leadership, and the anti-"foreign" nature of many of the specific crusades. Integrally connected with the restriction of the suffrage and the extension of Jim Crow, Southern Progressivism did little to assist the small white farmer and in general "no more fulfilled the political aspirations and deeper needs of the mass of people than did the first New Deal administration."[33]

Much of the scholarship since 1951 on Southern progressivism has taken the form of biography, and since most biographers develop a good deal of sympathy with their subjects, their portraits tend to be less critical of the Progressives than Woodward's synthesizing work was. Nor have such authors as Dewey W. Grantham, Jr., Oliver H. Orr, William E. Larsen, and William D. Miller, the authors of four of the five best of these biographies, felt much compelled to take specific exception to Woodward's conclusions.[34] While two implications of William F. Holmes's perceptive study of James K. Vardaman are that the connection between agrarian reform and progressivism may have been closer than Woodward thought, and that Vardaman did, in the later years of his career at least, accurately represent many small white farmers' material interests, the fact that Vardaman came from overwhelmingly rural Mississippi detracts from the generalizability of the example.[35] Two state studies view progressivism as, in turn, somewhat more reactionary and somewhat more forward-looking than Woodward did, but do not sharply dissent from his analysis.[36] As the author of one of them remarked a decade ago, "*Origins of the New South* has survived relatively untarnished through twenty years of productive scholarship."[37] The only major emendation now necessary in that statement is a change to "thirty years."

Woodward's picture of the postbellum Southern economy as a slowly developing one that, concentrated in extractive industries, remained tributary to Northern capital, shattered Broadus Mitchell's then conventional wisdom, but it has itself suffered from few challenges since. Not only does recent cliometric work on Southern agriculture not undermine Woodward's cautious and evenhanded generalizations, but the concentration on that sector, at the expense of more comprehensive investigations of regional economic development as a whole, leaves his "industrial evolution" and "colonial economy" notions largely untested by the systematic methods of the "new economic history."[38] Even if the neoclassical economists' neglect of these hypotheses can be explained by their desire to work on smaller, more tractable problems and by the underdeveloped state of neoclassical development theory, the lack of attention given Woodward's conclusions by Marxists, whose "dependency theory" seems strongly related to the Southern case as he describes it, is most surprising.[39]

Two other major avenues of research toward which Woodward pointed the way either have not been much traveled or have only begun to attract other scholars. Although David Potter believed that Woodward's 1960 "Age of Reinterpretation" essay was "widely regarded as his most significant single piece of work and as one of the major contributions to the interpretation of American history," others have not elaborated on the implications of his "age of free security" thesis for American economic and intellectual history.[40] Turner's frontier thesis, on which Woodward's was patterned and to which it was comparable in scope, decreased in plausibility as increasing urbanization was accompanied by no noticeable decline in political democracy or individualism. But Woodward's assertion that nineteenth-century American economic growth was quickened by the country's low level of military expenditures, as well as his notion that our earlier comparative freedom from the threat of foreign attack encouraged a careless optimism and a penchant for "demagogic diplomacy," should have appeared even more likely as the 1960s and 1970s wore on, for the postwar disarmed Japanese and German economies sustained much higher growth rates than our garrison-state economy did, and worldwide nuclear anxiety and economic trauma brought malaise even to America. In fact, it may be that, as Woodward remarked about the theme of irony, history "had caught up with" the historian "or gone him one better"—that, whereas the Turner thesis attracted attention because post-1893 conditions made it seem open to attack, the "free security" contention appeared too obviously correct to deserve rebuttal or require support.

The second intellectual pathway, that of comparative history, and particularly of comparative Reconstruction, is a road that has not as yet been taken very far by very many American historians, except those studying slavery and antislavery. In organizing a series of lectures by twenty-two historians for the Voice of America in the mid-1960s, as well as in drafting general comparative essays and delivering three stimulating public lectures on comparative Reconstruction (only one of which has yet been published), Woodward perhaps more than any other American historian helped to make the profession aware of the comparative approach. Although the demands of mastering languages and sources in two or more countries, as well as the academic depression of the 1970s, have no doubt impeded the growth of the field, incisive studies, including Thomas Holt's essay in this volume, are beginning to appear.[41]

Ideas are a scholar's world and his legacy. Woodward's have already had an enormous influence on both the professional and the lay audience. His books, essays, lectures, and editions do not merely delight passive readers; they stimulate them to intellectual action. And in his case, the legacy, far from being exhausted, is still being built up. The endowment will last for many years to come.

NOTES

1. Higham, "The Cult of the 'American Consensus': Homogenizing Our History," *Commentary*, 27 (1959), 93–100; idem, "Beyond Consensus: The Historian as Moral Critic," in Higham, *Writing American History: Essays on Modern Scholarship* (Bloomington & London, 1970), 138–56 (originally pub-

lished in the *American Historical Review*, 67 (1962), 609–25). The reference to Woodward appears on p. 146 of the second article.

2. Cash, *The Mind of the South* (New York, 1941).

3. Broadus Mitchell, *The Rise of Cotton Mills in the South* (Baltimore, 1921), pp. 90, 95, 104, for the quotations; and, similarly, pp. 161, 163.

4. Philip Alexander Bruce, *The Rise of the New South* (Philadelphia, 1905), pp. 4, 437–53. Holland Thompson's *The New South* (New Haven, 1920) was a partial exception to the consensus theme, and, of course, the serious study of Southern Populism had begun by the time Woodward started working on *Watson*. Especially important in this regard was Alex M. Arnett's *The Populist Movement in Georgia* (New York, 1922).

5. Phillips, *Life and Labor in the Old South* (Boston, 1929), p. 3 and passim; "The Central Theme of Southern History," reprinted in E. Merton Coulter, ed., *The Course of the South to Secession* (New York, 1964), pp. 151–66.

6. John Herbert Roper, "C. Vann Woodward's Early Career—The Historian as Dissident Youth," *Georgia Historical Quarterly*, 64 (1980), 14.

7. Degler, *Place over Time: The Continuity of Southern Distinctiveness* (Baton Rouge & London, 1977); Wiener, *Social Origins of the New South: Alabama, 1860–1885* (Baton Rouge & London, 1978); Billings, *Planters and the Making of a 'New South': Class, Politics, and Development in North Carolina, 1865–1900* (Chapel Hill, 1979).

8. For a review and listing of these studies, see Allen J. Going, "The Agrarian Revolt," in Arthur S. Link and Rembert W. Patrick, eds., *Writing Southern History: Essays in Historiography in Honor of Fletcher M. Green* (Baton Rouge, 1965), pp. 364–66.

9. Michael O'Brien, "C. Vann Woodward and the Burden of Southern Liberalism," *American Historical Review*, 78 (1973), 589–604, stresses the anti-consensus theme but also notes that Woodward attempted to tie Southern identity to what O'Brien calls "one sensation . . . the experience of poverty and defeat." Calling this regional consensus theme "as much of a half-truth as Phillips' belief that white supremacy made the South," O'Brien charges that Woodward's "Southern Liberalism" accounts for this assertedly flawed hypothesis and implies that there is necessarily something contradictory about simultaneously holding consensus and conflict views, as Woodward undoubtedly did. It seems to us that the wellspring of the "Search" and "Irony" essays is nationally, not just regionally, focused political values and that the view that people are united by some things and divided over other, perhaps equally fundamental issues, creates no logical difficulties. Sheldon Hackney deals with several of the same issues in *"Origins of the New South* in Retrospect," *Journal of Southern History*, 38 (1972), 191–216.

10. Boorstin, *The Genius of American Politics* (Chicago, 1953), p. 1; Woodward, *Burden*, pp. 193–210.

11. Among the many scholarly studies of the use of irony in literature, we found the following to be the most useful: Wayne C. Booth, *A Rhetoric of Irony* (Chicago, 1974); and Douglas C. Muecke, *The Compass of Irony* (London, 1969).

12. *Origins of the New South* (Baton Rouge, 1951), p. 146.

13. Ibid., p. 12.

14. Ibid., 2nd ed. (1971), p. viii.

15. See his "History and the Third Culture," *Journal of Contemporary History*, 3, no. 2 (1968), 23–36.

16. *Origins of the New South*, pp. 73–74.

17. Ibid., pp. 134, 222, 224.

18. Ibid., p. 88.

19. "The Irony of Southern History" and "A Second Look at the Theme of Irony," in *The Burden of Southern History, rev. ed.* (Baton Rouge, 1968), pp. 187–211 and 213–33.

20. Wade, *Slavery in the Cities: The South, 1820–1860* (New York, 1964), pp. 266–77; Wynes, *Race Relations in Virginia, 1870–1902* (Charlottesville, 1961); Williamson, *After Slavery: The Negro in South Carolina during Reconstruction, 1861–1877* (Chapel Hill, 1965); Graves, "The Arkansas Negro and Segregation, 1890–1903" (M.A. thesis, University of Arkansas, 1967); Williamson, ed., *The Origins of Segregation* (Lexington, Mass., 1968); Woodward's "Strange Career of a Historical Controversy," in *American Counterpoint*, and Howard N. Rabinowitz's *Race Relations in the Urban South, 1865–1890*, paperback ed. (Urbana & London, 1980), refer to, summarize, and analyze nearly all the literature.

21. For instance, chapter 6 of George M. Fredrickson's *White Supremacy: A Comparative Study in American and South African History* (New York, 1981) is entitled "Two Strange Careers: Segregation in South Africa and the South."

22. Thomas B. Alexander, "Persistent Whiggery in the Confederate South, 1860–1877," *Journal of Southern History*, 27 (1961), 324–25; Allan Peskin, "Was There a Compromise of 1877?" *Journal of American History*, 60 (1973), 63–75, and Woodward's response, "Yes, There Was a Compromise of 1877," ibid., 215–23; Michael Les Benedict, "Southern Democrats in the Crisis of 1876–1877: A Reconsideration of *Reunion and Reaction*," *Journal of Southern History*, 46 (1980), 489–524; William Gillette, *Retreat from Reconstruction, 1869–1879* (Baton Rouge and London, 1979), pp. 333–34, 449–50.

23. Robert B. Westbrook, "C. Vann Woodward: The Southerner as Liberal Realist," *South Atlantic Quarterly*, 77 (1978), 54–71.

24. Several of Woodward's essays, including "The Age of Reinterpretation," "The Northern Crusade against Slavery," "Seeds of Failure in Radical Race Policy," "A Second Look at the Theme of Irony," and "The Aging of America," undercut Michael O'Brien's contention in "Woodward and the Burden of Southern Liberalism" (p. 601) that Woodward "accepted the homogenized version of the American past" contained in the writings of national-consensus scholars.

25. For much more extensive reviews, see Paul M. Gaston, "The New South," in Link and Patrick, eds., *Writing Southern History*, pp. 316–36, and Hackney, "*Origins of the New South* in Retrospect." On Wiener's *Social Origins of the*

New South, see Kousser's review in *American Historical Review,* 84 (1979), 1482–83. Billings's *Planters and the Making of a 'New South'* repeatedly flogs a straw man. Compare, e.g., his treatment of quotations from Woodward on pp. 39 and 219 with their statement in the original context. See also the review of Billings's book by Peter Kolchin in *Agricultural History,* 54 (1980), 252–54.

26. Harris, "Right Fork or Left Fork? The Section-Party Alignments of Southern Democrats in Congress, 1873–1897," *Journal of Southern History,* 42 (1976), 471–506; J. Morgan Kousser, *The Shaping of Southern Politics: Suffrage Restriction and the Establishment of the One-Party South, 1880–1910* (New Haven, 1974), pp. 14–18, 36–38.

27. *Tom Watson,* pp. 217–19.

28. Goodwyn, *Democratic Promise: The Populist Moment in America* (New York, 1976); McMath, *Populist Vanguard: A History of the Southern Farmers' Alliance* (Chapel Hill, 1975); Schwartz, *Radical Protest and Social Structure* (New York, 1976).

29. Pollack, *The Populist Response to Industrial America* (Cambridge, Mass., 1962); Palmer, *'Man over Money': The Southern Populist Critique of American Capitalism* (Chapel Hill, 1980).

30. Hackney, *Populism to Progressivism in Alabama* (Princeton, 1969); Robert Saunders, "Southern Populists and the Negro, 1893–1895," *Journal of Negro History,* 54 (1969), 240–61; Charles Crowe, "Tom Watson, Populists, and Blacks Reconsidered," ibid., 55 (1970), 99–116; Lawrence J. Friedman, *The White Savage: Racial Fantasies in the Postbellum South* (Englewood Cliffs, N.J., 1970), pp. 77–98. That scalawags were seldom paragons of antiracist virtue does not negate the fact that they successfully appealed to blacks, and, in office, delivered on the most important of the promises they had made to their black constituents. See, e.g., Nelson M. Blake, *William Mahone of Virginia: Soldier and Political Insurgent* (Richmond, Va., 1935); Lillian A. Pereyra, *James Lusk Alcorn: Persistent Whig* (Baton Rouge, 1966); Jeffrey J. Crow and Robert F. Durden, *Maverick Republican in the Old North State: A Political Biography of Daniel L. Russell* (Baton Rouge, 1977).

31. Durden, *The Climax of Populism: The Election of 1896* (Lexington, Ky., 1965). Woodward's concept of "Pseudo-Populism" (*Watson,* p. 330), developed in Goodwyn's "shadow movement" thesis, is key to the debate over the specific instance of the conflict between Populism and its paler twin in 1896.

32. For Woodward's original view, see *Watson,* p. 419, and for his more recent qualifications, see *Burden* (1968 ed.), p. 163, and "The Ghost of Populism Walks Again," New York *Times Magazine,* June 4, 1972, p. 66. On the connection between Populism and suffrage restriction, see Kousser, *Shaping of Southern Politics,* pp. 5–6, 161, 195, 220–21, 246, 259.

33. *Origins,* p. 395.

34. Grantham, *Hoke Smith and the Politics of the New South* (Baton Rouge, 1958); Orr, *Charles Brantley Aycock* (Chapel Hill, 1961); Larsen, *Montague of Virginia: The Making of a Southern Progressive* (Baton Rouge, 1965); Miller, *Mr. Crump of Memphis* (Baton Rouge, 1964).

35. Holmes, *The White Chief: James Kimble Vardaman* (Baton Rouge, 1970).

36. Raymond H. Pulley, *Old Virginia Restored: An Interpretation of the Progressive Movement* (Charlottesville, 1968); Hackney, *Populism to Progressivism in Alabama.*

37. Hackney, "*Origins of the New South* in Retrospect," p. 213.

38. Stephen J. DeCanio, *Agriculture in the Postbellum South: The Economics of Production and Supply* (Cambridge, Mass., and London, 1974); Roger L. Ransom and Richard Sutch, *One Kind of Freedom: The Economic Consequences of Emancipation* (Cambridge, 1977); Robert Higgs, *Competition and Coercion: Blacks in the American Economy, 1865–1914* (Cambridge, 1977); Gavin Wright, *The Political Economy of the Cotton South: Households, Markets, and Wealth in the Nineteenth Century* (New York, 1978).

39. Actually, Billings's view of the Southern economy in *Planters and the Making of a 'New South'* is closer to Woodward's than Billings contends.

40. Potter, "C. Vann Woodward," in Marcus Cunliffe and Robin W. Winks, eds., *Pastmasters: Some Essays on American Historians* (New York, 1969), p. 388.

41. E.g., George M. Fredrickson's "After Emancipation: A Comparative Study of the White Responses to the New Order of Race Relations in the American South, Jamaica, and the Cape Colony of South Africa," in David G. Sansing, ed., *What Was Freedom's Price?* (Jackson, Miss., 1978), pp. 71–92; and his book *White Supremacy.*

Region

Regionalism and the Burdens
of Progress

DANIEL T. RODGERS

I

To predict the staying power of an idea is always a treacherous enterprise. But rarely has the prudent investor in intellectual fashion been more rudely tricked than in the 1930s' South. Who, as he read his way through the decade's barrage of social manifestoes, foresaw the immense future reputation of *I'll Take My Stand*—who, that is, outside Agrarianism's own handful of converts and those foolhardy enough to assume that literary style is the essential determinant of endurance? The Agrarians were obviously long in talent, in furious antipathy to industrialism, and in nuisance value. But Agrarianism had all the earmarks of an intellectual fad, destined for the same brief notoriety and hasty burial that befell the rest of the now forgotten varieties of antimodern thought with which Agrarianism in its day kept company.

The idea to bet on, certainly, was Regionalism. Unlike Agrarianism, in the 1930s' South it stood for an academic empire to conjure with. Chapel Hill was the hub of its kingdom, and there it could count on the best of the Southern universities, the most fertile and aggressive of the Southern university presses, a social-research institute with an open pipeline to foundation support, and, at the center of it all, the South's leading social scientist, Howard W. Odum. Out of this apparatus poured as monumental a pile of books and reports as the South has ever produced in a decade. Regionalism stood not only for a powerful academic empire, however; it was an equally expansive intellectual construct as well. Regionalism began in Odum's hands as a descriptive term

3

for a massive factual reinventory of the South's assets. It grew into an agenda for the social reconstruction of the South, then into a scheme for national planning, and finally into a theory of social change that Odum thought was as sweeping as the general theories of a Max Weber or a Talcott Parsons.

And then the whole enterprise vanished with scarcely a trace. While the study of *I'll Take My Stand* expanded into a bustling industry, Odum's name dropped abruptly out of the sociological texts. Even in the sociological journal Odum founded, his name and his ideas have hardly been mentioned since his death in 1954. Odum's consummate skills as an academic entrepreneur have been brought back to the historical record. His *Southern Regions* still holds a place on the lists of Southern classics which historians like to compile, even though its sociological reputation has long since evaporated. But Odum's grand designs, his troubled relationship with the South, his long and increasingly anxious wrestlings with the nature of social change, the whole unwieldy assortment of ideas he tried to stuff into the term "Regionalism" have all been reduced to those pat phrases used to bury ideas long past their time. Odum was a "liberal" and a "modernizer"; or perhaps, to the contrary, he was an old-fashioned, positivistic Victorian. But always he and the Agrarians have been seen as poles apart, his once born social scientific confidence set against their twice born broodings over time and progress.[1]

For a man who in his day had good claim to be ranked among the South's leading intellectuals, it is a meager lot. But if Odum's ideas were not better than his reputation admits, they were bigger, messier, and more tension filled. Odum was a social scientist and a modernizer increasingly possessed by ideas that did not reduce to either science or straightforward modernity. He was an empiricist who could write in sprawling, Whitmanesque prose of the "folk-soul." He was the pre-eminent cataloguer of the South's backwardness, who ended up as troubled by change and progress as any of the professed reactionaries at Vanderbilt. The contradictions were no private possession. As much as were any of the Agrarians, Odum was caught up in the South's complex and uneasy relationship with progress. And if Odum's accent was not quite the familiar one, that was because, for a moment in the 1930s and 1940s, that troubled reckoning with progress was not only the South's, but the nation's as well.

II

In the intellectual genesis of Regionalism, empiricism came first, for Regionalism took shape as part of the zeal for factual rediscovery that swept over the South in the 1930s. Realism was the Regionalists' initial battle cry, and it was a set of big, encyclopedic, regional inventories that first announced the stirrings of something new in Chapel Hill. From 1929 to 1945 a shelf-full of such volumes rolled out of the University of North Carolina's sociology department under Odum's patronage. Rupert B. Vance's social and economic geography of the cotton South, *Human Factors in Cotton Culture,* was the first of them, in 1929, the work of Odum's best and most loyal graduate student and his principal collaborator in shaping regional sociology. The other volumes followed rapidly: Vance's still broader-gauged *Human Geography of the South,* in 1932; Arthur F. Raper's intensive study of two black-belt Georgia counties, *Preface to Peasantry,* and Odum's own huge inventory of regional resources and poverty, *Southern Regions of the United States,* both in 1936; Margaret J. Hagood's study of sex roles and childbearing among white tenant farm women, *Mothers of the South,* in 1939; and finally, after the war's interruption, Vance's inquiry into the crisis of the South's expanding population, *All These People,* in 1945.[2] By 1939 Maury Maverick could write that while everywhere else in the South the universities trafficked in magnolia blossoms, at Chapel Hill you could get facts, reams of them.[3]

The tribute exaggerated somewhat, for the South had had fits of empiricism before the thirties. E. C. Branson, who dominated University of North Carolina sociology before Odum arrived at Chapel Hill in 1920, had sent his students throughout the state on a good many county-by-county fact-collecting expeditions. Odum, too, had gathered his share of facts since absorbing the empirical creed from the most statistical of the founders of American sociology, Franklin H. Giddings, at Columbia University in 1910. He had, moreover, spent a good deal of the 1920s gently but pointedly chiding his fellow Southerners for their weakness for illusion and their inability to stomach straightforward unsettling fact.[4] But Odum's work had been on the fairly restricted canvas of social work and Negro folklore. Those twin preoccupations had helped produce the most ambitious sociological undertaking generated at Chapel Hill in the 1920s: a large-scale investigation of Negro life on the coastal island of St. Helena, South Carolina, designed to demonstrate the effects of intensive uplift efforts on a highly isolated black population.[5] But by the time the last volume of the St. Helena study appeared, in 1932, that out-of-the-way island and the issues it represented had grown much too cramped for the rapidly expanding ambitions of the Chapel Hill sociologists. "Regionalism," when they seized on the term in the last year of the twenties, signified a massive growth in their empirical appetites and a new determination to take the South in its entirety as their subject.

Those Chapel Hill ambitions were of a piece with a dramatic rise in interest in the factual South in the 1930s, only some of it the result of the work of Odum and his associates. Through Charles S. Johnson and his students at Fisk, the omnivorous interests of Chicago sociology penetrated the region in the 1930s. From Yale, Harvard, and the University of Chicago, half a dozen social anthropologists descended on the South to pry even more rudely than the Fisk investigators did into the region's racial mores and class structures. The University of North Carolina Press not only actively fostered the genre of regional assessment but by the middle of the decade had also weighed in with its own encyclopedic inventory of Southern civilization, *Culture in the South*.[6] All of this was augmented by the streams of facts and documentary photos that began to pour out of the New Deal research agencies in the mid-1930s, and swollen still more by the journalistic attention stirred up by such startling goings-on in the South as the TVA, the cotton plow-up, and the Southern Tenant Farmers' Union. Yet even if the Chapel Hill sociologists could not claim exclusive credit for the Depression rediscovery of the South, the prevailing inventory style was to a great extent theirs; and more than any of the other empiricists they helped to make regional stock taking a bustling enterprise among Southern writers, some of the best of whom, such as W. J. Cash and Jonathan Daniels, did their work with a copy of *Southern Regions* propped up at their elbows.[7]

The Chapel Hill Regionalists heralded all of this with the encomiums of hardheaded science. They praised the "new disposition to probe ruthlessly for the truth" and to "face facts realistically [and] with courage." Their own "stark realism" was at war, as they saw it, with all the varieties of Southern romanticism: the ghosts still at large in the antebellum mansions, the daydreams of a New South, or the Agrarians' fatal weakness for metaphor and poetry.[8] But empiricism has never, of course, been a straight-forward business. Which facts matter? On the usual tangle of the roadmap, which avenues lead to the land of the stark reality? The Regionalists' answers on both counts were a measure of how deeply their empirical agendas were shaped by the old, troubling idea of progress. Not that Odum and his circle proposed to invoke the future in the tradition of North Carolina boosterism. Their at-tachment to the idea of progress was different from that, though no less strong. Rather, amid the furious debate over the impact of progress on the South, the Regionalists set out, essentially, to measure it—to count schools and tally agricultural returns, to plot the region's wealth, and, in short, to bring the South's relationship with progress to an empirical test at last.

That ambition not only led them to prefer facts of the hard, statistical, and, they hoped, uncontrovertible sort. What was more striking was their impact on the geography of the South, for when the Regionalists had finished their work the generally perceived map of the South was no longer what it had been. No one could deny that the map the Chapel Hill sociologists inherited—propor-tioned to a scale of public attention to Southern places in the late 1920s—bore a curious resemblance to what an empiricist might have been inclined to call reality. North Carolina easily over-whelmed the rest; its central, textile-mill-lined axis was the ac-knowledged main street of the late-1920s' South, and it ran straight and quickly to places like Atlanta and Birmingham that bustled with similar energy. A picturesque and well-beaten path ran off toward Dayton, Tennessee, and another toward the real-estate meccas of Florida, but the cotton fields were not well posted and were hard to find. In their search for stark reality, however, the sociologists of the 1930s took all of this and swept it into the corners. Their essential statistical South—the place where the progress and tendencies of the region were to be most accurately measured—was the deep rural South. W. J. Cash might still write of North Carolina and the South as if they were one, but his gesture breasted a tremendous tide of interest south toward Ala-bama, Georgia, and Mississippi and the baked earth of their cotton fields.

Sharecropping, soil erosion, credit, out-migration, and above all cotton—these were the essential facts in the regional inventories. To find them the Chapel Hill sociologists plunged into the study of human geography, agriculture, and ecology, in search of what Arthur Raper called the essential "man-land relation." They also converged on certain places in the South. Raper's own boll-weevil-devastated, population-depleted Greene County, Georgia, was the most heavily traveled by both sociologists and documentary photographers.[9] From there the counties intensively studied spread in a line east toward Erskine Caldwell's Jefferson County, Georgia, and west to James Agee and Walker Evans's Hale County, Alabama, and then in a second line running north along the Mississippi River from Natchez to Memphis, forming two arcs that represented almost precisely the domain of the Southern black belt and Delta—those parts of the South, in short, that had once been thickest with slaves, cotton, and plantations.[10]

That this narrow slice of the South *was* the South represented no less partial a statement, of course, than the one it so quickly replaced, and it bleached out almost as many of the region's complexities and contradictions. The Yankee woman Jonathan Daniels found on a palm-lined Florida byway lamenting the accident that had brought her there instead of to Pasadena; the Virginia entrepreneur who stood ready to sell Daniels antiques with "curb service"; the cousins passing furtively into white society who eluded J. Saunders Redding in Kentucky; the Southerners locked in fierce battles over TVA power and CIO unionism—none of them had much of a place in the sociological South. But cotton had made and unmade the South's economy. And the convergence on its collapsing Deep South kingdom reflected a conviction, with a good deal of newfound statistical truth to it, that the region's well-being was still inextricably tangled in the crop—that the South's real progress was to be measured by the social. economic, and ecological ramifications of cotton.[11]

Yet even to say that the South slid precipitously down the map in the 1930s still oversimplifies the geography of social discovery. The sociological South was not one kingdom but two. The particular domain of the Chapel Hill–influenced sociologists was the Georgia Alabama black belt. That represented a handy choice but not an entirely obvious one, for in Georgia, in particular, by 1930 the structure of cotton and tenancy had been in peculiarly rapid flux for almost a decade. If one wanted to see cotton and its economic encumbrances at their clearest, the obvious place was the Mississippi Delta. Nowhere else were farm-tenancy rates so high, the legacies of slavery more visible, or cotton itself more thickly planted.[12]

But in the sociological division of the South, the delta belonged not to Chapel Hill but to the anthropologists. They came to Mississippi's Natchez and Claiborne County and Indianola by way of New Guinea, the Berlin Psychoanalytical Institute, or W. Lloyd Warner's Yankee City project—Northern-trained, many of them black, and bearing an outsider's capacity for shock unusual in Chapel Hill. They came, moreover, with an empirical agenda quite different from that of the Regionalists. Race and class were their essential facts, and it was the delta's exaggerations—its blackness, its terrific inequalities of power and wealth, its apparent timelessness, all, in short, that tended to make the delta seem too outlandish at Chapel Hill—that drew them there. They were not much interested in progress; they eschewed statistics in favor of personal observation and in-depth interviews. And in the end they came back with one of the most powerful books of social observation to come out of the 1930s, John Dollard's *Caste and Class in a Southern Town*, with a set of graphic pictures of Southern class and racial behavior, and with a new sense of how deeply race was embedded in the region's culture and psyche.[13]

That the Regionalists' inventories by and large skirted these issues to focus on such matters as schools, incomes, and soil fertility provides an important measure of their empiricism and the assumptions behind it. For all the Regionalists' liberalism on the issue of race, they were wary of the subject, and it caught them in one of Southern liberalism's particular dilemmas. To treat their mounds of data without regard to race was to cut themselves off from precisely those facts that others were beginning to see as central to understanding the South. To segregate their data by race, on the other hand, was to lay their conclusions about the region's backwardness and poverty open to the well-rehearsed retort that there was nothing the matter with the South that could not be explained by the downward drag of its Negro population.

In the end, most of the Chapel Hill Regionalists resolved the dilemma by lumping their data together without regard to race.[14] In doing so they emphasized the fact that ultimately mattered to

them more than all the rest, the fact of poverty. Odum's very
definition of the region—his attempt to pin down the boundaries
of the South not by the outlines of another generation's Confederacy, but on the basis of present-day statistical homogeneity—
turned on that fact. His raft of socioeconomic indices was most
heavily weighted by measures of poverty, and essentially on that
basis he insisted that such comparatively wealthy fragments of the
old slave South as Texas and Maryland were no longer effectively
Southern at all.[15]

Out of their selective though indisputable facts of cotton and
poverty the Chapel Hill Regionalists and their allies ultimately
constructed a picture of the South almost as unsettling as that of
the anthropologists. They took hold of the tenancy-ladder idea,
with its comforting assumption that sharecropper and tenant alike
were slowly working their way toward independent farm status,
and broke it in pieces. They dramatized the ecological catastrophe
taking place in the Southeast under the impact of tenancy and
careless soil management. They raised the alarm of an impending
collision between a peculiarly high birth rate and a regional economy peculiarly meager in means of livelihood. The South was
progress's stepchild, they insisted, technologically backward, and
"very poor."

No volume argued the point more effectively than Odum's own
Southern Regions. Odum intended the book to be a sequel to the
Hoover-commissioned Recent Social Trends, an attempt at a comprehensive empirical survey of the state of American society on
which Odum had been one of the major collaborators between
1929 and 1932.[16] It was the hardheaded empiricism of the project's
director, William F. Ogburn, that turned Odum to the persuasive
power of unadorned facts, just as it was the publicity Ogburn
organized that gave Odum the model for the tremendous ballyhoo
he arranged for Southern Regions when it appeared in 1936. But
the key to the impact of Southern Regions probably lay simply
in Odum's decision to present most of its data in the form of
hundreds of national maps, shaded to represent the quartile rank-
ing of each state in measures of economic and social well-being.
Nothing could have made Odum's central point more dramatic
than the parched white spaces and black smears that marked off
the Southeast from the rest of the nation in everything from
libraries and milk production per capita, to wealth, lynchings,

and radios. Even Odum's turgid prose could not significantly reduce the visual impact. The South's poverty, the maps in *Southern
Regions* proclaimed, was older than the national Depression and
vastly deeper.

Not everyone swallowed that conclusion easily, or was as ready
to dismiss the proud lights of Atlanta and Birmingham. But such
gestures as the Georgia state board of education's decision to ban
Southern Regions from the schools of Odum's home state did not
appreciably diminish the book's impact. By the mid-1930s even
the Agrarians had capitulated, shucking off their early embarrassing talk of "happy farmers" and joining the outcry over agricultural poverty. Regionalism's first project was to bring Southern
progress to a test, and the result was as bleak a picture of poverty
and backwardness as the South had seen in a long while.

III

What had caused progress to skip so rudely over the South? In
answer to that question, big with implications, Odum and his
co-workers made the usual pro forma references to slavery, Reconstruction, and single-crop agriculture. But Chapel Hill was of
the present and the future, and its sociologists were in fact not
very much interested in the past. Rupert Vance lent his considerable weight to the argument that stressed the long-standing
drain of resources northward out of the South's staple-dominated
"colonial" economy—a theme familiar in the South at least since
the 1890s and with a good deal of life left in it. But Odum, always more cautious than his students, was much more hesitant;
and when the National Emergency Council's report on the economic conditions of the South made headlines out of the colonial-
economy idea in 1938, with rhetoric lifted from Walter Prescott
Webb's *Divided We Stand* and facts lifted from *Southern Regions,*
Odum backed away from the idea altogether.[17] The angriest furor
over Northern economic domination, in any event, came from
places other than Chapel Hill; and, for all their omnivorous
factual appetites, none of the Regionalists, including Vance, bothered to bring the argument to an empirical test.

What little sense of history Regionalism had, in fact, tended
toward some confusion. Arthur Raper's *Preface to Peasantry,* for
example, argued in *Tobacco Road* fashion that the South was a

degenerate society in the process of senescent decay. Charles S. Johnson, on the other hand, saw in Macon County, Alabama, the outlines of a region slowly emancipating itself from the grip of the past. Odum himself preferred the language of arrested development. *Southern Regions* was full of appeals to the South's "chronological lags," its anachronistic frontier mores, and its retarded growth. Overflowing in natural resources, it had not yet gone to school in the scientific attitudes and technological skills necessary to harness them. The South was not an exhausted region, Odum insisted, but an "immature" one—yet why, being so old, it had failed to grow up, he never made very clear.

For the most part the Regionalists were content to leave the past to those, like the Agrarians, who cared about it more deeply than they did. What Odum and his co-workers had in place of history was a set of audacious plans for the future. By the mid-1930s, social planning had moved into the heart of what they meant by Regionalism. The upshot of their "colossal" factual preliminary work, Odum was ready to insist by 1935, was planning on a scale that amounted to nothing less than a "new social reconstruction."[18] Not having found progress in the South, the Regionalists proposed to construct it.

The nation was alive with plans and the heady rhetoric of planning in the mid-1930s, of course, and everywhere in the region social tinkerers were drawing blueprints of brave new Souths to replace the one that Southerners had somehow muddled into. To the right, as the landscape appeared from Chapel Hill, the Agrarians had turned to what looked suspiciously like social planning by the mid-1930s. Several of them, at any rate, had moved from *I'll Take My Stand*'s rhetorical appeal to the South's anti-industrial conscience to much more drastic measures: massive federal repurchase of the region's absentee-owned lands and their redivision among actual farmers on terms forfeitable by speculation, bad soil management, or the planting of too much cotton; the strangulation of absentee-owned corporations by new tax measures; and a wholesale revision of the Constitution on regional and corporatist lines.[19] To the left a group loosely tied together through H. C. Nixon's Southern Policy Committee was calling for a very different social reconstruction in the form of a massive farm-village construction program designed to stamp a new and much more collective environmental pattern on the rural South—and with it, they hoped, a far more collective set of social ideals than had flourished on the region's strung-out and isolated farms.[20] Neither group, for all the shouting that erupted between them, thought that the second reconstruction of the South was going to be an easy affair or accomplished without an unprecedented amount of coercion. Even the Agrarian economists, dedicated as they were to the restoration of small proprietorships and the family farm, left their new-model yeoman farmers with startlingly few of the familiar rights of property, once they were through sealing off such farmers from the temptations of soil mining, land speculation, and commercial agriculture.

In this respect Odum and his co-workers, with their insistent talk of voluntarism, were much the more cautious planners. Odum's prose was saturated with the bloodless language of "waste," "deficiencies," and "chronological lag," and with cautious, if not downright vague, appeals to "balance" and "equilibrium." There were hardly any villains in the Regionalists' South, and no conflicts that dispassionate reason could not resolve into harmonies. Vance could be tempted into debate, but Odum cultivated an indistinctness that sometimes left all sides of the battle convinced they had his support.[21]

But for all the Regionalists' cautious approach to issues of human conflict, their plans were in many ways the most audacious of them all. On their preferred terrain of resource management, in particular, their proposals had a sweep to them that none of the others could equal. The Appalachian highlands and the piney woods were finished as crop lands, they insisted, and were salvageable only by a wholesale return to forest and a wholesale dispersion of their populations. The South's cotton did not need price supports as much as it needed massive plowing up and replacement by forage crops, livestock, and diversified farming. A cheese and dairy region to rival Wisconsin lay ready to be carved out of the piedmont crescent. Everywhere there was need for detailed planning for new industries carefully chosen to mesh with local markets and resources. The Regionalists were ready to sweep the South's people across the map with the same grand gestures. Between 1.5 million and 6 million of them needed planned relocation off the South's exhausted soils, Vance wrote, into newly designed city neighborhoods, into Northern industries, or, if necessary, into a brand-new network of cooperative subsistence colonies independent of the overloaded cash economy. In the same vein, Odum, worried about the approaching conflict between hardening Southern resistance on racial matters and escalating Negro ambitions, wrote of a planned exodus northward of fully half the South's black population as the only answer with a glint of hope to it. In these moods the Regionalists resembled nothing so much as Southern Rexford Tugwells, ready to rearrange the South's clumsily scattered pieces with sublime confidence.[22]

Nor were their other proposals any less large in scope. Odum wrote of a national equalization fund to restore regional parity in wealth and help the South catch up to the living standards of the nation, of a huge twelve-year public-works program, of the massing of all the South's progressive forces into a single unit, of regional university building on a grand scale, and of a flowering of social experiments and social research. By the end of the decade he was deep into proposals for a structure of state, regional, and national planning boards that would add up to a fourth, expert branch of government—a permanent version of the Committee on Recent Social Trends, isolated from the emotionalism of politics and charged with the long-term, scientifically based planning that was society's only preserve against chaos.[23]

It was no wonder that no other Southern voices were more strongly identified with planning than those at Chapel Hill. Regionalism stood for facts, for social science, for advance, for brave, newly designed worlds. "Instead . . . of becoming alarmed at the processes of social change or of fearing dire results, the student should glory in the opportunity to live and work in an age of rapid change," Odum had written in 1927.[24] That was the authentic accent of a man of progress, and no one in the South knew, or seemed to know that accent better.

IV

But as the thirties slid toward war and a growing recognition of the intractability of the Depression, progress was no easy faith to hang on to—even the rationally designed progress that Regionalism stood for. Even as early as 1934, Odum had fallen prey to doubts. He had begun to worry about the technological fruits of science, about planning, and about change itself. Whence had come the modern cry for "speed, bigness . . . technology, and change?" Whence had come the rage for the "mechanized perfections" of moving pictures and automobiles at the expense of the slowly built equilibrium of societies? Whence, to come closest to the bone, had come the new "ideological dictators," the "playboys, supertechnologists, who seek new experimentation every morning, new games of human direction every night?"[25] If anyone in the South stood for technocratic experiment and games of human direction it was Odum, but even before *Southern Regions* had come off the press his call for social reconstruction concealed some complex doubts.

Those doubts were still small enough to brush aside in the mid-1930s. Within a decade, however, the doubts had all but swallowed up the confidence and propelled Odum into a radically different sort of sociological endeavor. While his Chapel Hill co-workers continued to delve for facts and weave their plans, Odum grew increasingly dissatisfied with empirical sociology. The "extreme of isolated, unrelated, nonphilosophical fact finding" began to seem to him less important than sociological theory.[26] As pressing as the planning needs of the South were, they gave place in Odum's mind to the bigger and more worrisome task of puzzling out the "way of all culture." By the mid-1940s, Odum had left behind fact-dominated Regionalism for a grand theory he called Folk Sociology. Odum's habit of recycling his old words and paragraphs obscured the magnitude of the break. But there was no disguising the fact that Odum's writings had taken a distinctly new turn in the late 1930s, or that what impelled the shift was above all an avalanche of second thoughts about progress.

Of the concepts out of which Odum struggled to construct a sweeping theory of social change, the most fundamental was the concept of the "folk." The term had been part of Odum's vocabulary for a long time; indeed, it would have been a very difficult idea for any eager graduate student in sociology to miss in 1909, particularly one who, like Odum, arrived at graduate school with his pockets stuffed full of scraps of Negro folklore. He quickly picked up something of the busy German industry of *Völkerpsychologie* from G. Stanley Hall at Clark University. Still deeper in its impact was William Graham Sumner's *Folkways,* still new in 1909, with its impressive catalogue of the tenacity and variety of cultural mores. In the 1920s Odum merged these early fragments of cultural anthropology with the literary cult of the primitive then in vogue to produce a set of popular books on Negro folk-lore which veered back and forth between romantic evocation of the spirit of the black folk ("Sing, Africans, sing . . . dig under our cities with singing / Into the primitive earth . . . show us where we came from," he repeated the chant of his friend Howard Mumford Jones) and the social-scientific language of family and social disorganization that came more properly to a professor of sociology and social work.[27]

For all the massive ambivalence Odum's folklore series dis-played on the issue of race, however, his initial conception of the "folk" was limited, static, and relatively undisturbing. The blues-singing, tale-telling roustabout at the center of his Black Ulysses series was a figure outside of time and change. He was a picturesque fixture of the South; and like the folk he represented, he endured. At Columbia, Franklin Giddings had distilled this assumption of stasis into the maxim that the folkways always defeat the state-ways, that is, social mores inevitably triumph over legislation that tries to cross them—a piece of conventional laissez-faire wisdom that Odum clung to throughout his career, however much it some-times jarred against his social-planning designs. When Odum's election to the presidency of the American Sociological Society in 1930 stirred him into his first foray into high theory, he used the occasion to elaborate on the endurance of the folkways, fleshing out Giddings's dictum with the Reconstruction examples that came naturally to a Southerner.[28]

But what if outside forces, stronger than mere legislation, *could* overpower the folkways? In the 1930s Odum suddenly came alive to that possibility, and the villain that loomed up awesomely in his mind was technology. Exactly what triggered Odum's sudden awakening to the disruptive power of technology is not easy to pinpoint. His experience on the Recent Social Trends project holds a share of the responsibility, for no one was better prepared to demonstrate the far-reaching effects of technology than the project's director, William F. Ogburn. Ogburn had made a career out of the subject of the social impact of technology since the early 1920s, when his *Social Change* had injected the notion of cultural lag into the working vocabularly of sociology; and as fellow Georgians and fellow Giddings students Ogburn and his associate director had much to draw them into discussion. Still more responsibility probably lay with the Depression itself or, rather, with the way in which Odum, like so many others, tended to see it: as a result of reckless, unplanned industrial expansion and consequent overproduction, as a matter of machines left to their own devices, like those which tore through the Great Plains in Pare Lorenz's imagination or, in Charlie Chaplin's, swallowed workers whole.

For whatever combination of reasons, at any rate by the end of the decade Odum's writings were aboil with alarm at the impact of "supertechnology"—at the onslaught not only of machines but of those technology-generated mores he had begun to call collectively the "technicways." Had Odum stopped there, his troubled prose would not have amounted to much more than another demonstration of the ability of the idea of maladjustment between machines and society to make sense out of the confusions of the 1930s. But Odum did not stop; and Ogburn's conclusion, that, technological innovation being irresistible, the sociologist's task lay in assisting people over the most acute manifestations of cultural lag, offered Odum no satisfactory resting place.[29] The heart of the problem, as Odum increasingly saw it, seemed to lie not in faulty adjustments but in change itself. "Faster, faster, faster; more, more, more; bigger, bigger, bigger; new, new, new," he complained of the "overpowering mode of the age" in 1937. "How much speed, bigness, science, technology for bigness' sake, for speed's sake, for science's sake, for technology's thrills can society stand and survive?"[30]

The question went to the heart of Odum's faith in modernism, but he could not let it go. Nor could he reduce it, layman fashion, to the simpler statement that in the South he was so freely redesigning, some things were worth preserving. The question was that of a society's tolerance for change; and increasingly it seemed to him not only the biggest of sociological questions but the only one worth asking. "When the demands and sweep of artificial society and of supertechnological processes exceed the natural capacity of the people or of a living culture to absorb and adjust . . . there must inevitably be crisis, maladjustment; and if the process goes on long enough, disintegration." Folk Sociology, as Odum struggled to put its pieces together, turned on the effort to measure those processes of absorption and disintegration, to observe the technicways and folkways in collision, and, out of their smash-up, to calculate the tolerable rate of change itself. What he was after, Odum wrote, was a "theory of limits." What was the "shock-tolerance" of a culture? How much progress could a society take before shattering under the impact?[31]

As Odum's worries about the whirlwinds unleashed by science and invention intensified, the old idea of the changeless folk grew larger and more alluring. By the end of the decade, when Odum landed on Spengler's *Decline of the West* and its stark dichotomy between technological "civilization" and folk "culture," he was more than ready for it. Civilization was the extrapolation into the future of the present rage for change; it was chronological lag overcome; and as Odum's and Spengler's fears fused it became a nightmare. Civilization, Odum wrote at the culmination of this pessimistic mood, was artificial, machine dominated, and megalopolitan. Its people lived in a ceaseless whirl of change, soul-stripped intellectualism, and mass confusions. Civilization represented science, bigness, concentration, and the superstate. New York and Washington were civilization; so was Nazi Germany and the mechanized blitzkrieg, the atomic bomb, and the dark and menacing skyscrapers that now shadowed Odum's social-problem texts.

But cultures, as Odum elaborated the contrast that had taken hold of his imagination, were natural, stable, and organic. Their folk lived close to the earth and the region, the emotions, and the primary human group. Amid the wrecks of experiments in bigness, cultures were small and decentralized. Civilization meant "merely progress and decline," but cultures evolved slowly and in balance.[32] Odum was too good a sociologist not to know an ideal type when he helped construct one. Folk culture and state civilization were sociological ciphers at opposite ends of a continuum, somewhere in the midst of which real societies could be found, pushed hard by the technicways toward civilization. Odum would have made his sociological endeavor simpler had he left it at that. But Odum could not resist turning the dichotomy into a moral imperative—"What shall it profit to gain a world of civilization and lose the folk-soul?"—that virtually cut all the remaining ground out from under his modernizing faith.[33] Nor could he any more successfully resist the suggestion that something like cultures really existed. Walt Whitman had been of a culture, Odum wrote of his favorite poet. The small cooperative democracies of Denmark and Holland were cultures, and so—there could be no mis-taking the implication—was Odum's own rural South.

The Agrarians, long since retired from the contest with indus-trialization, had scattered far beyond the South by the mid-1940s, but had any of them looked back they could hardly have missed the irony of the spectacle. For none of them, even at the height of their indignation, had produced a harsher assessment of modernity than could be found in the dark and angry words tumbling out of the South's pre-eminent spokesman for progress; nor had any of them written with more romantic affection for the premachinery world than Odum poured into the idea of the "folk." It would not be exactly fair to say that Odum had worked his way through his massive pile of facts only to offer the South a magnolia blossom, its tatters disguised by its new sociological label. But something of the sort had indeed taken place.

Certainly there could be no missing the Southern accents of Folk Sociology. When Odum wrote of a folk living close to nature, it was a Southern landscape he found it most natural to evoke in his Whitmanesque "roll-calls" of longleaf and loblolly pines, mockingbirds and warblers. "In the South the folk were Nature-folk longer than in the rest of the nation," he maintained. More-over, when Odum wrote of the Southern folk in the 1940s, in-creasingly it was in defense, not in criticism, of their slowly evolved peculiarities, and in mounting apprehension of yet an-other Yankee crusade to reconstruct them. In the 1930s, Regional-ism had stood squarely against all the narrow forms of sectionalism, but if it was not a sectional tone that had crept into Odum's voice it was something suspiciously like it.[34]

In Odum's furious efforts of the 1940s, in fact, there was a good deal that was reminiscent of nothing so much as of that other explicitly Southern sociologist George Fitzhugh, a century before. There was the same restless gathering in of evidence of a botched civilization, the same ransacking of the social sciences for anti-types to progress. Still more, there was the same heroic effort to build not merely a defense but a sociology in itself out of the South's very backwardness. What else could explain the spectacle of a man, in a setting so deeply affected by "chronological lag," writing so feverishly about the threats of modernity, were it not that some of the ghosts of the South's long-troubled quarrel with progress—those same ancients that had haunted Fitzhugh's Port Royal and swarmed over Nashville—had taken up residence even in Chapel Hill?

But if Odum was of the South, his armor of facts incapable of warding off all its hoary dreams and rhetoric, it is as important to insist that he was of the thirties as well—of a particularly vulnerable moment in the faith in the extrapolated future. Odum gathered in the pieces of Folk Sociology from places far beyond the South, with a good eye for his intellectual surroundings. The antitypes of modern civilization and pre-modern culture were not only Spengler's; they were at virtually every hand in the thirties, from Robert Redfield's studies of peasant Mexico to the revival of Ferdinand Tönnies's reputation. The idea of the natural region and of the organic culture it might nurture was Patrick Geddes's as filtered through Lewis Mumford, and mixed with borrowings from the burgeoning new sciences of human geography and ecology. Odum's tormented vision of impending megalopolitan civilization drew as much from Mumford's *Culture of Cities* as from Spengler. And Odum's hunger for a theoretical structure to make sense out of the whipsawing processes of social change was palpable everywhere in sociological circles—though it was Talcott Parsons's work, not the scraps of gathered ideas Odum was trying to shape together, that eventually completed it.[35]

Above all it was Odum's affection for the "folk" that echoed most widely beyond Chapel Hill. It was of a piece with a yearning, unmistakable by the end of the 1930s, for places outside the straightforward course of progress: machineless Mexico, perhaps, or the medieval townscapes Mumford had begun to celebrate, or those islands of earthy human strength toward which the Farm Security Administration photographers were ever more rapidly tending. James Agee's descent on Hale County, Alabama, as he worked that experience into words, partook of the mood. So did Saunders Reddings's still more affecting journey, through the economic flotsam of the Depression and his own ambivalent feelings about race, deep into the slow-moving bayous of Louisiana.[36] Earlier in the 1930s one had scoured such places for hints of change and mapped their futures. But increasingly they seemed to offer lessons in equilibrium and balance for an age in which progress had played out its hand.

There was nothing new about that mood, of course, except its urgency, and the feeling not simply that progress was a mistake to be fled by acts of individual desertion, but that progress had literally gone to smash in a great terminal debauch of war, squandered resources, and the manic gestures of fascism. Growth was over, at least in the linear sense of the past, Mumford insisted. It was time, Aldo Leopold had begun to write, to try to learn to think in a plane perpendicular to that of evolution. For all its Southern accents, Odum's troubled recantation of his earlier, simpler faith in progress belonged in that company.[37]

The effort to think not nostalgically but at cross-purposes to progress did not fit well into the American political or sociological vocabulary. Nor was it always very clear how that society which lay neither in the line of retreat nor of straightforward advance was to be gained. Leopold and Mumford ultimately looked to some form of moral renewal. Others poured their energies into the cooperative movement, into the dreams of social ecology that hung for a moment over the TVA, or into planned communities, whose closed greenbelt rings proclaimed an end to old-fashioned linear progress.

Odum, for all his alarm at the misuses of science, clung to the last to planning. If technological "superachievement" was at the heart of the contemporary crisis, the answer must lie in still more strenuous efforts to bring the whirl of change under control, to design a set of "social technicways" that would arrest the drift toward civilization and provide, somehow, the equilibrium that "intellectualism" had destroyed. Perhaps that was enough to account for the tenacity of Odum's reputation as a man of social science and progress, whose facts still supplied Southern liberals with their basic ammunition in their assault on the mummies of Southern tradition. But the reputation his students sustained disguised the deep strains in Odum's own sociological endeavor. The big question on which Odum wanted to hang the whole sociological enterprise—how much change a people could stand—was far removed from the Southern liberals' straightforward confidence in modernity. And Odum, as he wrestled with the question in the mid-1940s, had good reason to believe that he, not they, were at the cutting edge of social thought.

V

In the end, the grand theory Odum thought was so close never cohered. He set his students to computing rates of technological impact, but nothing permanent came of it, or of his visions of a regional laboratory in which to test the impact of technics-generated change. Folk Sociology remained a set of fragments, increasingly badly written and then quickly forgotten. Perhaps there was no putting them together, and probably Odum was not the man to try.

The South too forgot Odum, almost as fast as the sociologists did. Within a generation the region had abandoned his plea for planned equilibrium and cast its lot with the more familiar temptress of unplanned progress. By 1960 even Rupert Vance was ready to admit that she had served the region well. Of the terrific backwardness and poverty of the 1930s, Vance wrote, there was little left. What made the South different from the rest of the nation had shriveled to the one factor the Chapel Hill Regionalists had found most awkward to deal with, that of race.[38] The main roads of the South begin in the Golden Triangle once again, and it is once more hard to find the fields where the cotton once grew.

But in the 1930s, when the goddess of progress jilted the nation more rudely than usual, it was different. That decade's facts and plans, epitomized in *Southern Regions,* command easy recognition from a society awash in empirical endeavors. But Regionalism's peculiar anxieties—Odum's Spenglerian nightmares, his hopes of calculating the shock-tolerance of cultures, his struggle to articulate a kind of planning at cross-purposes to time—all these were part of the 1930s too, before progress grandly swept back in and, for a moment, quieted the doubts and the discord.

NOTES

1. George B. Tindall, "The Significance of Howard W. Odum to Southern History: A Preliminary Estimate," *Journal of Southern History,* 24 (1958), 285–307; Harvey A. Kantor, "Howard W. Odum: The Implications of Folk, Planning, and Regionalism," *American Journal of Sociology,* 79 (1973), 278–

95; Morton Sosna, *In Search of the Silent South: Southern Liberals and the Race Issue* (New York, 1977); Michael O'Brien, *The Idea of the American South, 1920–1941* (Baltimore, 1979); Richard H. King, *A Southern Renaissance: The Cultural Awakening of the American South, 1930–1955* (New York, 1980).

2. Rupert B. Vance, *Human Factors in Cotton Culture: A Study in the Social Geography of the American South* (Chapel Hill, 1929); idem, *Human Geography of the South: A Study in Regional Resources and Human Adequacy* (Chapel Hill, 1932); Arthur F. Raper, *Preface to Peasantry: A Tale of Two Black Belt Counties* (Chapel Hill, 1936); Howard W. Odum, *Southern Regions of the United States* (Chapel Hill, 1936); Margaret J. Hagood, *Mothers of the South: Portraiture of the White Tenant Farm Woman* (Chapel Hill, 1939); Rupert B. Vance, *All These People: The Nation's Human Resources in the South* (Chapel Hill, 1945). The full range of Chapel Hill sociology is laid out in "Institute for Research in Social Science: Publications and Manuscripts," *Social Forces,* 23 (1945), 309–28.

3. Maury Maverick, "Let's Join the United States," *Virginia Quarterly Review,* 15 (1939), 65.

4. Dewey W. Grantham, "The Regional Imagination: Social Scientists and the American South," *Journal of Southern History,* 34 (1968), 3–32; Willard B. Gatewood, Jr., "Embattled Scholar: Howard W. Odum and the Fundamentalists, 1925–1927," ibid., 31 (1965), 375–92; Howard W. Odum, *An American Epoch: Social Portraiture in the National Picture* (New York, 1930).

5. T. J. Woofter, Jr., who directed the St. Helena project, summarized its findings in *Black Yeomanry: Life on St. Helena Island* (New York, 1930).

6. *Culture in the South,* ed. W. T. Couch (Chapel Hill, 1934).

7. W. J. Cash, *The Mind of the South* (New York, 1941); Jonathan Daniels, *A Southerner Discovers the South* (New York, 1938).

8. Gerald W. Johnson, *The Wasted Land* (Chapel Hill, 1937), p. 6; Lee M. Brooks, *Manual for "Southern Regions"* (Chapel Hill, 1937), p. xi; Odum, *Southern Regions,* p. 231.

9. Raper himself wrote two books about Greene County: *Preface to Peasantry* (1936) and his partisan account of New Deal agricultural reconstruction work there, *Tenants of the Almighty* (New York, 1943). Dorothea Lange and Paul S. Taylor visited the county in the making of *An American Exodus: A Record of Human Erosion* (New York, 1939); and Charles S. Johnson surveyed its black adolescents in the preparation of his *Growing Up in the Black Belt: Negro Youth in the Rural South* (Washington, D.C., 1941).

10. The major Southern community studies were Charles S. Johnson, *Shadow of the Plantation* (Chicago, 1934), set in Macon County, Alabama; Waller Wynne, *Culture of a Contemporary Rural Community: Harmony, Georgia,* U.S. Bureau of Agricultural Economics, Rural Life Studies no. 6 (Washington, D.C., 1943); John Dollard, *Caste and Class in a Southern Town* (New Haven, 1937), and Hortense Powdermaker, *After Freedom: A Cultural Study in the Deep South* (New York, 1939), both set in Indianola, Mississippi; and Allison

Davis, Burleigh B. Gardner, and Mary R. Gardner, *Deep South: A Social Anthropological Study of Caste and Class* (Chicago, 1941), an offshoot of W. Lloyd Warner's Yankee City study set in Natchez and Claiborne County, Mississippi.

11. Charles S. Johnson, Edwin R. Embree, and W. W. Alexander, *The Collapse of Cotton Tenancy: Summary of Field Studies and Statistical Surveys, 1933–35* (Chapel Hill, 1935); Southern Regional Committee, *Problems of the Cotton Economy: Proceedings of the Southern Social Science Research Conference, New Orleans, 1935* (Dallas, 1936).

12. Charles S. Johnson, *Statistical Atlas of Southern Counties* (Chapel Hill, 1941).

13. Dollard, *Caste and Class in a Southern Town;* Powdermaker, *After Freedom;* Davis et al., *Deep South;* Allison Davis and John Dollard, *Children of Bondage: The Personality Development of Negro Youth in the Urban South* (Washington, D.C., 1940). Hortense Powdermaker recalled the shock of encounter in *Stranger and Friend: The Way of an Anthropologist* (New York, 1966).

14. Arthur Raper's *Preface to Peasantry,* with its powerful description of the peculiar barriers in the way of black farm ownership, was the major exception.

15. Odum, *Southern Regions,* pp. 4–11.

16. Barry D. Karl, "Presidential Planning and Social Science Research: Mr. Hoover's Experts," *Perspectives in American History,* 3 (1969), 347–409.

17. George B. Tindall, "The 'Colonial Economy' and the Growth Psychology: The South in the 1930's," *South Atlantic Quarterly,* 64 (1965), 465–77; Vance, *Human Geography,* pp. 467–76; Howard W. Odum, *The Way of the South: Toward the Regional Balance of America* (New York, 1947), pp. 231, 334.

18. Howard W. Odum, "Promise and Prospect of the South: A Test of American Regionalism," *Proceedings of the Eighth Annual Session of the Southern Political Science Association,* 1935, p. 17.

19. Frank L. Owsley, "The Pillars of Agrarianism," *American Review,* 4 (1935), 529–47; Troy J. Cauley, *Agrarianism: A Program for Farmers* (Chapel Hill, 1935).

20. W. T. Couch, "An Agrarian Programme for the South," *American Review,* 3 (1934), 313–26; Herman C. Nixon, *Forty Acres and Steel Mules* (Chapel Hill, 1938).

21. The Agrarian Donald Davidson claimed Odum as an ally in "Howard Odum and the Sociological Proteus," *American Review,* 8 (1937), 385–417; so did Arthur F. Raper and Ira De A. Reid in the angriest book to come out of the Chapel Hill connection, their left-leaning manifesto *Sharecroppers All* (Chapel Hill, 1941).

22. Vance, *Human Geography,* chap. 18; Rupert B. Vance, "The Economic Future in the Old Cotton Belt," *Southern Workman,* 65 (1936), 85–92; idem, "How Can the Southern Population Find Gainful Employment?" *Journal of*

Farm Economics, 22 (1940), 198–205; Odum, *Southern Regions,* chaps. 6–7; Howard W. Odum, "The Regional Quality and Balance of America," *Social Forces,* 23 (1945), 283.

23. Odum, *Southern Regions,* chap. 11; *Folk, Region, and Society: Selected Papers of Howard W. Odum,* ed. Katharine Jocher et al. (Chapel Hill, 1964), pp. 403–26.

24. Howard W. Odum, *Man's Quest for Social Guidance: The Study of Social Problems* (New York, 1927), p. 101; Edwin R. Embree, *Prospecting for Heaven: Some Conversations about Science and the Good Life* (New York, 1932), pp. 135–61.

25. Howard W. Odum, "The Case for Regional-National Social Planning," *Social Forces,* 13 (1934), 12; idem, "Promise and Prospect of the South," p. 15; idem, "Orderly Transitional Democracy," *Annals of the American Academy of Political and Social Science,* 180 (1935), 38.

26. Howard W. Odum, "The State of Sociology in the United States and Its Prospects in the South," *Social Forces,* 17 (1938), 12.

27. Howard W. Odum, *Rainbow Round My Shoulder: The Blue Trail of Black Ulysses* (Indianapolis, 1928), pp. 271–72 and passim.

28. Howard W. Odum, "Folk and Regional Conflict as a Field of Sociological Study," *Publications of the American Sociological Society,* 25 (1931), 1–17.

29. William F. Ogburn, *Social Change, with Respect to Culture and Original Nature* (New York, 1922); William F. Ogburn and Meyer F. Nimkoff, *Sociology* (Boston, 1940), chap. 28.

30. Howard W. Odum, "The Errors of Sociology," *Social Forces,* 15 (1937), 337.

31. Howard W. Odum and Harry E. Moore, *American Regionalism: A Cultural-Historical Approach to National Integration* (New York, 1938), p. 629; Howard W. Odum, *Understanding Society: The Principles of Dynamic Sociology* (New York, 1947), p. 514; Hope T. Eldridge, "The Implications of Regionalism to Folk Sociology with Illustrations from the Southern Regions," *Social Forces,* 22 (1943), 41.

32. *Folk, Region, and Society,* p. 443; Howard W. Odum, "Folk Sociology as a Subject Field for the Historical Study of Total Human Society and the Empirical Study of Group Behavior," *Social Forces,* 31 (1953), 192–223; idem, *American Social Problems: An Introduction to the Study of the People and Their Dilemmas* (New York, 1939), chap. 5 and passim; idem, *Understanding Society,* p. 284 and passim.

33. Ibid., p. 522.

34. Odum, *Way of the South,* p. 15 and passim.

35. Oswald Spengler's *The Decline of the West* (New York, 1926–28); Lewis Mumford's *The Culture of Cities* (New York, 1938); and Robert Redfield's *The Folk Culture of Yucatan* (Chicago, 1941) all made a particularly profound impact. The ties to geography were largely through Vance; those to ecology were through Odum's sons, Eugene P. and Howard T. Odum.

36. James Agee and Walker Evans, *Let Us Now Praise Famous Men* (Boston, 1941); J. Saunders Redding, *No Day of Triumph* (New York, 1942).

37. Lewis Mumford, "Social Purposes and New Plans," *Survey Graphic,* 29 (1940), 119ff; Aldo Leopold, *Round River* (New York, 1953), p. 159.

38. Rupert B. Vance, "The Sociological Implications of Southern Regionalism," *Journal of Southern History,* 26 (1960), 44–56.

Modernizing Southern Slavery: The Proslavery Argument Reinterpreted

BERTRAM WYATT-BROWN

HISTORIANS of the proslavery argument have generally treated the topic with self-conscious distaste. No scholar today wants to be called a friend of slavery. As a result, most interpretations assume that the antebellum apologizers were just as ill at ease in the undertaking as later writers are in assessing the results. Thus Louis Hartz dismisses Old South polemics as troubled anti-quarianism, out of place in a dullish America where the dollar, not a Virginia pedigree, was king.[1] Wilbur J. Cash and a number of more recent authors have argued that proslaveryism barely masked pangs of guilt, fear, and anxiety over denying rights to restless blacks and poor whites.[2] In an ingenious argument, David Donald suggests that the propagandists sought to elevate sagging reputations by telling Southerners about what they already knew —the benefits of slavery. More recently Drew Faust in a skillful study has disagreed with David Donald's thesis, but she too por-trays the Deep South intellectuals as culturally (rather than socially) alienated from crude surroundings. For all its persuasive-ness, her argument fails to show the crucial relation between the writers and the audience that they sought to cultivate. The pro-slavery thinkers of Faust's "Sacred Circle" were not solely devoted to shoring up their sagging egos and creating a literary culture on the foundations of slavery.[3] They genuinely thought that they had a special message. They were no less self-confident than any

The author wishes to thank the following for financial assistance in the preparation of this paper: The John Simon Guggenheim Foundation; the Woodrow Wilson International Center for Scholars; the Shelby Cullom Davis Center for Historical Studies, Princeton University.

cluster of intellectuals of an underdeveloped but awakening land. They were aware of Southern vulnerability but were convinced that time would not betray them. The future for bondage could be bright. However distasteful their arguments, Southern intellectuals did more than jab episodically at free-labor hypocrisies, and they were no more alienated from their surroundings than such writers as Nathaniel Hawthorne, Henry Thoreau, and Herman Melville. They, too, disputed the vulgarities of an unthinking, hedonistic public.

Of course, the morality of justifying slavery belongs on the trash heap of history, as Eugene Genovese has correctly observed.[4] But conservative thought, though based on race prejudice in this context, had an integrity of its own. What must be grasped is that the proslavery vindication had a genuine audience. It was designed not solely to rally nonslaveholders to planter leadership or to calm the morally perplexed and fearful in slaveholding ranks themselves. These factors all played a part.[5] The first aim was to convince the Christian and conservative elite of both Great Britain and the free states that the Southern way was honorable, God sanctioned, and stable. The second objective, with which this study is chiefly concerned, was hortatory and instructional, as most appeals to one form of "right thinking" or another usually are. In the words of Henry Hughes of Mississippi, "The young men must be taught to reason the matter. They must learn why our home system is *not* wrong: why it *is* right: and be able to give the reasons for it."[6]

Intermingled with the declamations of regional glories was an important corollary: the desire to modernize, to improve the "home system," so that its foundations were no less secure, no less progressive than those on which free labor rested. In this context, modernization scarcely implies a wholehearted Southern endorsement of all the democratic and urban tendencies of the age.[7] Believing that there was nothing inevitable or even desirable in marching to Yankee or British drums, the Southern intelligentsia repudiated middle-class hedonism and lamented the decline of gallantry. Nostalgia for lost virtues and hatred of modern cant and grubbiness were not themselves peculiar to plantation dreamers. British self-criticism, as Marcus Cunliffe has pointed out, supplied them with ample means to catalogue the wrongs of industrialization. Thomas Carlyle, Charles Kingsley,

Sir Walter Scott, and other luminaries whom Southern literati admired offered the same kinds of ambivalent responses to modernity and the overthrow of ancient custom that they themselves felt. In fact, Scott's popularity extended far beyond his romantic Waverley novels with their sentimentality and derring-do in battle regalia. For Scott, as for most of his Southern readers, there existed side by side a revulsion against the primitivism of warrior honor (duels were constantly, if ineffectively, deplored on every hand) and an antipathy to the impersonality of modern trends. Yet Scott's "elegy on the passing of the old Highland order comes not from a sitter-on-the-fence," as one recent critic has noted, "but from the fair-minded man who knows that history cannot stand still, that there can be no change, even for the better without loss, suffering, and waste."[8] Since so many Southerners were themselves of Celtic ancestry, they found in him the spokesman for the world that they were losing even as they gloried in its alleged strengths of intense family life, intimacy with wild nature, and simple if bloody principles and passions.

However much defiance of Yankeedom may have masked inner doubts, Southern intellectuals sought to combine the best of two worlds rather than merely storm ineffectually in the manner of Don Quixote. Without relinquishing the supposed virtues of forefathers, whether Celtic, English, or Revolutionary American, they were determined to move forward. "Twenty years ago," declared George Fitzhugh in 1857, "the South had no thought— no opinion of her own." At that time, the region "stood behind all christendom, admitted her social structure, her habits, her economy, and her industrial pursuits to be wrong, deplored them as a necessity, and begged pardon for their existence." But, he boasted, a new order of things prevailed as other nations found "wage slavery" to be a system with grave defects and looked enviously upon the Southern mode. "This, of itself, would put the South at the lead of modern civilization," he insisted.[9] Thus, literary justifications of slavery were not just hymns of praise for a changeless, primordial society, but rather a stirring appeal to place the South in the forefront of modern life itself, an effort that required not only a new regional self-consciousness but also concrete demonstration of just, humane, and morally uplifting techniques of patriarchal management.[10]

The basis of this effort lay in the evolutionary nature of the

institution itself, for slavery changed as society changed. In a
crude way, one may trace a progression from the beginning to the
end of slavery. Three ways existed whereby masters could perceive
the system: (1) as crude chattel bondage, wherein slaves were more
or less beasts of burden to meet the possessors' needs and whims;[11]
(2) as familial proprietorship, in which reciprocal, parent-child
obligations and affections gave meaning to those involved, a system
that required a deeper appreciation of the psychology and wants
of the dependent class but still required that those beneath were
obliged to give more in love and service than those who ruled;
(3) as state racial regulation, an interposition of government between white and black, setting limits upon proprietary powers and
strictly defining proper racial boundaries. None of these perspectives was ever exclusive to one era or another. Roughly speaking,
however, "chattel bondage" was rather characteristic of colonial
thralldom. Slaves were part of the household and its possessions,
but they were not often regarded as family members. Stage two,
the familial concept, became more prominent in early national
years, largely as an outgrowth of Christian evangelicalism.[12] Slaveholding benevolence never achieved more than spotty success. The
ideal of Christian slave stewardship was established as a way to
distinguish respectability from churlishness.[13] Stage three, state
racial interposition, based on the growing use of civil bureauc-
racies and legal professionalization, had made only limited progress
prior to 1861.

Sketchy though this description is, it helps to explain the point
from which proslavery vindicators departed and the direction in
which they were heading. Willie Lee Rose, one of our most perceptive Southern scholars, has already observed a "common tendency" among historians to treat slavery—250 years old in America
—"as though it were the same institution from start to finish."[14]
Proslavery authors did not make that mistake. They repudiated
chattel bondage but extolled the merits of patriarchal or "Bible
slavery," as one apologist called it.[15] James L. Petigru, lawyer and
planter of South Carolina, for instance, recognized the distinction
in 1835 when he boasted, "The only thing to flatter my vanity
as a proprietor is the evident and striking improvement in the
moral and physical conditions of the negroes since they have been
under my administration. When I took them, they were naked

and destitute, now, there is hardly one that has not a pig at least. . . ." His Christian bounty left something to be desired. Yet, like most planters of the benevolent persuasion, Petigru judged his performance against the grim squalor of forefathers and unenlightened neighbors.[16] Professors Engerman and Fogel may have exaggerated the universality of Squire Allworthys like Petigru, but it stands to reason that advances in wealth and human sensibilities ameliorated plantation conditions, if only because whites were becoming mindful of the comforts of general tidiness.[17]

The proslavery argument was largely based upon the familial solicitudes that Petigru represents, but a complementary development, stage three, was also emerging. State legislators passed laws that intervened in the personal relationships of master and subject. To safeguard the public against insurrection, masters lost the discretionary right to train slaves in literacy, to permit autonomous black assembly, even to use their property as clerks in stores.[18] Setting boundaries around various work specialties, excluding blacks, bond and free, from public places, and other forms of racial discrimination were already appearing on statute books long before 1865.[19] At the same time, some slave states were enacting protective laws for the slave criminal and the slave victim of white crime as well.[20] These efforts at rationalizing the racial system not only conferred protections upon slaves and took privileges away from them too; they also infringed upon the traditional options that chattel bondage had granted masters.

Likewise in jurisprudence, judges and lawyers sought to formalize the standards of admissible evidence, procedures, and resorts to appeal. Moreover, the penalties assigned to both white and black criminals were becoming more uniform and penitential rather than corporal in nature.[21] This transition may have influenced plantation justice, though hardly enough to mean much. The Reverend Charles C. Jones, an earnestly Christian master, was not a typical planter, but in 1859 he turned over to Georgia authorities a case of plantation thievery, an offense usually handled at an owner's discretion. For lack of sufficient evidence, the case was dismissed. Jones was delighted. "It is my impression," he said, "that if owners would more frequently refer criminal acts of their servants to the decision of the courts, they would aid in establishing different kinds of crimes committed by Negroes, give better

support to their own authority, and restrain the vices of the
Negroes themselves." His son, a forward-looking lawyer, naturally
agreed with pleasure.[22]

The point of stressing the evolutionary character of slave culture is not to argue that the system would have died peacefully in
a gush of Victorian sentiment but for Yankee intervention and
war. Far from it. Establishing the ideal of Christian masterhood
and strengthening state controls fell short of genuine black autonomy of any kind. The evolutionary process was not toward freedom but rather toward more refined means of perpetuating black
dependency, either through acts of personal benefaction or
through state regulations that also ensured white rule.[23] One
could argue that in fact patriarchal slavery was more psychically
damaging in fashioning the "Sambo" personality than was chattel
bondage. Under the latter formula, there was no reason to pene-
trate the slave's soul in order to save it, only to extract his labor.
In any case, the evolution of slavery—"the domestication of
domestic slavery," as Willie Rose calls it—was the chief point of
departure for Southern antebellum polemics.[24]

There is little need to explain the attractiveness of the domestic
analogy. Not only was it an obvious contrast to the chattel servitude associated with the squalid foreign slave trade, outlawed
since 1808, but it also was intimately connected with evangelical
and indeed scriptural reverence for familial government.[25] As
Frank Vandiver bluntly stated, "God counted in Dixie," especially so when it came to defending Southern arrangements.[26] The
ordinary slaveholder, seldom a reading man, appreciated the domestic imagery and paternal authoritarianism that he heard from
the pulpit. According to Southern church fathers, slavery was a
condition, not a moral evil.[27] As such it resembled the family,
civil government, hierarchies, all elements of social organization
with which God had forever equipped his fallen, self-seeking
creatures.[28] To be sure, some advocates of slavery, mostly politicians, called the institution a "positive good," but the Southern
preacher generally claimed that it was only potentially so, according to the moral fiber of those involved. Like the Southern lawyers,
the professional clergy admired uniformity, rational objectives, in
the evangelical assumption that what was truly practical and
profitable was also divinely blessed. Therefore they championed a

form of slaveholding that extended the protective authority of a loving father over the entire household of whites and blacks.[29] Self-disciplined reciprocations of loyalty and duty bound the organic plantation community. Thus, in a vigorous attack on abolitionist "disorganization," Lucy Kenny, a Virginia churchwoman, declared "it is in the interest of the master to observe to his slave that kind of love which makes" the slave rejoice "to serve and obey his master; not with eye-service," but with heartfelt, Christian "willingness."[30] This appeal, with its familiar overtones of the Golden Rule, made better sense to the planter than did the esoteric examinations of George Fitzhugh or the Bible-challenging scientific racisms of Josiah Nott.[31] To live up to the Christian proposition, however, was quite another matter, and the clergy, aware of human depravity, knew it.[32]

Religious simplicities not only established Abrahamic ideals of slaveholding fatherhood, they also implicitly defined what was ungodly, disreputable. Without the domestic feature, declared one pious writer, "Negroes are herded on the plantation and propagate as mere animals."[33] In contrast to unfeeling masterhood, Christopher Memminger, a Charleston layman, offered the ideal, which steadily became the most popular rendering of regional self-congratulation: "The Slave Institution at the South increases her tendency to dignify the family. Each planter in fact is a Patriarch—his position compels him to be a ruler in his household," guiding children, female dependents, and slaves alike with steady hand and loving voice. Like the image of the Southern lady, gracious and ethereal, the model of Christian slaveholder was a stereotype that served a cultural function. It celebrated the alleged disappearance of old barbarisms and offered a standard of behavior to which respectable folk were to aspire.[34] The lines between what was and what ought to be were sadly blurred, but the instructional function remained.

Just as there was an outpouring of advice literature to parents and young people, so too advice on Christian masterhood flowed from busy Southern pens.[35] The duty of religious instruction to slaves was a chief concern, but particularly revealing was an emphasis on the need for moving slaves in moral paths by internal mechanisms of control.[36] Godly writers urged owners to reach for the Bible, not the lash.[37] Like Northern reformers, Southern

thinkers had begun to question old-fashioned corporal penalties
in the handling of prisoners, schoolchildren, and youngsters in
the home. Application to slave management was not surprising.[38]
The transition symbolized a growing awareness of new psychological techniques that encouraged self-discipline, inner moral
consciousness, and a sense of individual dignity. Thomas Clay of
Bryan County, Georgia, and Calvin Wiley, a noted advocate of
white common schools in North Carolina, both advised masters
to apply rational systems of rewards and nonphysical punishments
to uplift slave morality. They and others also stressed that every
proprietor should know his hands as individuals and select those
disciplinary means suited to the abilities and characters of each.
Moreover, the Christian planter was supposed to follow scriptural
injunctions about the material wants of his people, provisions for
decent housing, clothing, food, and sense of privacy that would
promote the moral welfare of the whole plantation.[39] This humanitarian advice, though seldom followed in its totality, embraced
these attributes of Victorian modernity: self-control, rationality,
practical consistency.[40] One might agree with Kenneth Stampp
that this missionary effort to masters was largely designed to make
slave property more efficient and secure.[41] So it was. But the aim
was also to achieve the Christian order—conceived in the primitive style of personal, immediate religion—that proslavery clergymen and laymen envisioned.[42]

When writing for Northern audiences, proslavery thinkers
grandly pronounced that moral slaveholding was as modern as
any organic system, true to nature and to God. Yet in preaching
at home, there was room for more cautionary evaluations. Calvin
Wiley, the North Carolina educator, for instance, directed his
fury at those hypocrites who treated slaves "as chattel for profit
and comfort," yet, to avoid masters' responsibilities, called the
institution "an evil, a curse," in the manner of Thomas Jefferson.
"This is not merely unchristian philosophy," he said; "it is supreme selfishness."[43] Sophisticated deism, such as Jefferson represented, was ungodly; likewise, attacks on God's natural order of
master over slave were impious and dangerous. Attacks on planter
misbehavior were rare, but some clergy who lamented the imperfections of the "domestic" slavery they cherished were sometimes
outspoken.[44] A few even called for state interposition in behalf of
slave rights. The Reverend W. T. Hamilton of Mobile, Alabama,

denounced the failure to recognize slave matrimony in law—"an outrage to humanity . . . an insult to God!"[45] Perplexity over the principle of church-state separation, fear, complacency, religious and political conservatism—all these factors prevented a use of political means.[46] Moral suasion was supposedly more Christian anyhow.

As a result, proslavery writers relied upon the drift of events, whose charitable direction was assumed to be in God's hands. George F. Simmons, another minister of Mobile, believed, for instance, that the progress of Christian refinement was sufficiently powerful to "eat the heart of slavery even as slavery continues." In his opinion, "the servitude" of the future "will not be grinding bondage, but a mutual and fraternal dependence."[47] The words of Simmons, a Unitarian and Yankee, were misapprehended. He was forced to leave Mobile under threat of lynch law. Nevertheless, his message, had it come from a familiar, native source, would have passed without comment, so unexceptional were such pulpit counselings. The Reverend James Thornwell, leader of South Carolina's wealthy Presbyterians, for instance, proclaimed the immediacy of Christian triumph, calling the Southern system "regulated liberty," a discipline that opposed both "the despotism of the masses on the one hand and the supremacy of a single will on the other." Likewise, Woodrow Wilson's father, the Reverend Joseph Wilson, presented ameliorative slavery as a topic in a pulpit series on "family government." God, the North Carolina Presbyterian exclaimed in 1859, "included slavery as an organizing element in that family order which lies at the Foundation of Church and State." What other way, he argued, could blacks advance? The institution of bondage was "that scheme of politics and morals, which by saving a lower race from the destruction of heathenism, has under divine management, contributed to refine, exalt, and enrich its superior race!"[48]

Moving in religious and respectable circles, the clerical ideologues romanticized what they saw and ignored the unpleasant.[49] Scores of thousands of newcomers to slaveholding ranks were pushing their way up the social ladder with little regard for the niceties of Christian slaveholding, a chiefly upper-class posture. The advice literature aimed at the new additions as well as at those whose experience with ownership entitled them to set community standards. Yet, the slavery advocate seldom acknowledged that his idealizations soothed more than they uplifted the savage heart. Compared with Yankee evangelical zeal, the fires of Southern missionary fervor flickered rather unevenly.[50]

For all its manifold weaknesses, Christian patriarchalism remained the keystone of proslavery thought. In the last pre-war decade, however, a new doctrine made an appearance. Though too exotic and academic to gain popularity, the approach was based on an idealization of actual changes in civil and legal conventions. Henry Hughes, a lawyer of Port Gibson, Mississippi, who had studied under Auguste Comte in Paris, proposed a rationale in which the state replaced the familial arrangement as the foundation of overlordship. As romantically antinomian as any Yankee prophet, Hughes was only twenty-five when he published his *Treatise on Sociology* in 1854.[51] Intrigued with European positivism and learned in both ancient and modern literature, he was an unusually gifted thinker, but, judging from his diary, the young visionary suffered acutely in handling inmost feelings: "Let me shuffle of[f] this mortal coil, and burst forth into unpenetrated regions of space where God dwells in solitude and rush around the Circuit infinety [*sic*]," an extraordinary reference to his occupation of following the state judge from one county seat to another. "Am I a man, an angel, God, Devil. Is there a God or Devil. Why then do I not fear & shrink from. O, I feel like I could drive Satan from Hell. Down, down, thoughts, I am weary, O God let me die."[52] Aspiring to ambitions greater than those of Calhoun, Caesar, and Napoleon, the trinity he worshiped, Hughes set before himself the task of planning what he grandly called "A Universal Republic, Ultimum Organum, Longitude, Slavery Perfect Society; Myself the God-beloved, the human supreme of Earth's Politics, Society, Philosophy, Economics, Religion & Aesthetics."[53] This kind of exuberant self-fascination matched similar introspections of such youthful romantics as Stephen Pearl Andrews, John Humphrey Noyes, and Henry C. Wright, among many other Yankee idealists.[54] In the Southern locale, among the trees and spacious houses of Port Gibson on the cliffs above the Mississippi, the intellectual ruminations of Henry Hughes led to different plans for human improvement from the dreams of reform that a Transcendental New Englander might entertain.

If, as one suspects, there is a relation between even the most antinomian prophecy and actual tendencies and social values in a society, then Hughes's writings deserve a serious reading.[55] They help to point the direction in which slave culture was heading. Certainly Hughes saw matters in an evolutionary context. "We know that our peculiar establishment is with a rapidity unparalled [sic] and marvelous perfecting itself; and hastening to set before civilized nations . . . a labor system . . . they must copy . . . to prevent pestilence, starvation and countless crimes."[56] A believer in earthly perfection that any good Calvinist like Thornwell would consider blasphemous, Hughes announced the total withering away of a savage bondage just as the Unitarian Simmons did. That form of slavery, "a system of inhumanity and injustice," he confessed, had once existed, at the time of the Revolution.[57] Its horrors had moved the Northern Founding Fathers to emancipate Northern slaves, even as Southern heroes, like Washington and Jefferson, despaired that the system could ever be reformed. Knowing only the polarities of free and slave arrangements, they failed to see, Hughes claimed, the potentiality for another mode of labor discipline. But, he continued, this third form had evolved in the nineteenth-century South, a system that Hughes called "liberty labor" or "warranteeism."[58] By these terms, Hughes meant a labor-capital association, ruled by "moral duty, civilly enforced."[59] The young American positivist made no direct attack on Christian patriarchalism, but, like many other Victorian intellectuals, he entertained severe doubts about revealed religion. Yet, out of duty he held religious classes for blacks in Port Gibson, and later for Confederate soldiers under his command in Virginia. For himself, however, he reserved a faith in the absolutes of morality, not enjoined by divinity but by the state.[60] Thus, "moral duty, civilly enforced" became the instrument of his slave millennium. Strangely enough, his disposition, his search for a utopia divorced from church institutions, resembled some features of William Lloyd Garrison's theology of moral absolutism. Hughes, an ardent secessionist, raised the figurative banner: "No Union with *Non*-Slaveholders."

Unlike most Southerners, Hughes admired the power and uses of the state, which he defined as "the economic sovereign. It is the supreme orderer. The capitalist [or slave master] is its deputy orderer." Thus, he maintained, slavery was an agency of the state, though management was delegated to owners. In this reading, the planter was a state functionary, a lay magistrate, exercising powers for the benefit of the commonwealth. To be sure, Hughes granted the familial concept a place in the scheme, describing the laborer and capitalist as members of "the same family," with the head of the household warranting "subsistence to all." Yet, the planter's motives were neither personal profit nor paternal solicitude; instead, he undertook slaveholding responsibilities out of a sense of "civil duty."[61]

Whereas the proslavery clergy generally offered specific Biblical texts, practical plans for Christian masters to administer, and comparative statistics and illustrations to contrast labor conditions at home and abroad, Hughes operated in the realm of pure abstraction.[62] As a result, he was able to insist that his "warrantees" or "simple-laborers" enjoyed the "judicial rights" of trials by jury, petition, habeas corpus, appeal, free counsel, and even freedom from some white felonies such as bigamy.[63] Also, they had material support for life, backed by law, whereas free laborers possessed the liberty to starve. Hughes thought that slave protective legislation had already reached near-perfection. He ridiculed those legislators—"the good, the wise, and the wealthy"—who persistently offered "some minor betterment" for the benefit of Mississippi's blacks.[64]

However eccentric and blind to realities Hughes was, his dreams illustrated the tendencies of the age. For example, slave ownership was still a commonplace, but the trend seemed to be toward some concentration of slaves into fewer hands.[65] Hughes was no egalitarian. Yet, he sought to bring slave mastership into every home, a program requiring the reopening of trade with Africa. The advantages, he thought, were compelling: a lessening of white class antagonisms; the reorientation of the Upper South toward slaveholding neighbors; increased regional prosperity; greater congressional representation.[66] Other zealots were making similar expansionary pleas in the 1850s, but Hughes had something more in mind than simply alleviating problems of labor shortage.[67]

In speeches and newspaper columns, Hughes championed what he called African contract labor, whereby imported blacks would serve fifteen-year apprenticeships. The numbers, he believed, should be so massive that their presence would alter existing slave arrangements. Gradually the contract form would apply universally, perhaps within twenty years. Careful not to appear subversive of perpetual bondage, Hughes left unclear whether the African coolies would subsequently become permanent slaves or resident slaves would merge into semi-autonomous peonage.[68] So long as whites retained control of black destiny, it probably mattered very little to him.

Intrigued with the possibilities of civil bureaucracy as a source for progress and internal security, Hughes envisioned new regulations under state auspices. Through the taxing power, for instance, the state could ensure a safe proportion of whites to blacks, native or otherwise, in any region. Furthermore, even prior to the reintroduction of African workers, there had to be new laws restricting the subservient race to noncompetitive, unskilled employments, thereby enabling poor whites to fill the positions that an expanding, diversified economy created.[69] At the same time, Hughes told a commercial convention at Vicksburg in 1859, the state must regulate "the negroes' hours of service, holidays, and food, raiment, habitation and peculium, and the other elements of their wages."[70] Satisfied though he was that slave criminals had already gained sufficient protections, he offered a few "minor betterments" of his own. The state, he suggested, ought to pay full, not partial, compensation to owners of convicted slaves in order to encourage masters to surrender suspects instead of running them off to another state for sale. Also, he urged Mississippi legislators to provide penitentiary sentences for slave convicts to replace some capital and corporal mandates. All these plans required an expanded public service to rationalize race controls.[71] Like T. R. Dew and other proslavery thinkers, Hughes believed that the expansion of Southern population, newspaper networks, education, and transportation systems had made it easier, not harder, to control the underclass.[72]

In October 1862 Henry Hughes, a colonel at the head of the Twelfth Mississippi Regiment, died from a war-related illness at his home in Port Gibson. He lived to see neither the defeat of the nation of which he had dreamed as the "Ultimum Organum" nor the enactment of the Black Codes of 1865. These fiercely suppressive laws to subvert Yankee-imposed emancipation came closer to what Hughes had in mind than any arrangement in the slave

regime for which his schemes were designed. An earnest advocate
of Christian masterhood preached the funeral oration at the
Methodist Church of Port Gibson. The Reverend W. D. Moore
could scarcely conceal his distress that Hughes had lived a life of
religious doubt.[73] Though disturbed at Hughes's admiration for
"the socialistic writers" of Paris, Moore took solace in his friend's
search for truth. As a Christian, Moore was proud of his opposition to Hughes's plan for contract African labor, given the dismal
record of the old trade and the continued imperfections of men.[74]

For those who believed in the more familiar, domestic vision of
servitude, Henry Hughes had pushed too far ahead, toward the
bureaucratic impersonality of an industrial apartheid.[75] By the
time that system of exploitation was adopted, and not just in the
Southern states, the proslavery argument was thoroughly repudiated and Hughes long since consigned to oblivion. Fortunately,
Yankees had intervened before the modernizing of slavery was
complete. At least, in a manner of speaking, Jim Crow at the
turn of the nineteenth century was not literally a ward of the
state, as Hughes had planned, or a possession of a condescending,
Bible-toting patrician, as the clergy and pious laymen had sought
to fashion. If Hughes, the most forward-looking of the proslavery
zealots, had had his way, corporate servitude would have developed out of chattel bondage, a new system conferring some
nominal liberties as modern means of ultimate control fed Southern self-confidence.[76] Yet, the suffocation of the black soul would
have continued as inexorably as ever. In the latter part of the
Victorian age, as evangelical enthusiasms declined and the tenets
of racial Darwinism, industrial boosterism, and imperial destiny
arose, what room would there have been for the flowering of sentimental Christian mastery in the Southern states? The speculation
that the country, spared both war and emancipation, might well
have become a richer, more powerful version of South Africa may
be fanciful. C. Vann Woodward has already called attention to
the parallels between the two biracial societies during the post-
Reconstruction years, but, as he said, their paths "diverged" after
World War I, a change that surely would have been severely
limited in a South free to pursue its own fate.[77] In this grim
context, the Union dead, it seems, had not bled in vain.

Visionary and inward-looking to the very end, Henry Hughes
whispered to his Methodist friend three deathbed words: "Nos

sumus purificate." Perhaps as the Reverend W. D. Moore intoned from the pulpit, "A few moments after he was indeed purified forever from earthly sins and sorrows."[78] The same could not be said for the South he died to save.

NOTES

1. Louis Hartz, *The Liberal Tradition in America: An Interpretation of American Political Thought since the Revolution* (New York, 1955), pp. 145–77.

2. Wilbur J. Cash, *The Mind of the South* (New York, 1941), p. 63; Ralph Morrow, "The Proslavery Argument Revisited," *Mississippi Valley Historical Review*, 48 (1961), 79–94; William W. Freehling, *Prelude to Civil War: The Nullification Controversy in South Carolina, 1816–1836* (New York, 1965), pp. 79–82, 327–34, 377; Steven A. Channing, *Crisis of Fear: Secession in South Carolina* (New York, 1970), esp. pp. 58–93; William B. Hesseltine, "Some New Aspects of the Pro-Slavery Argument," *Journal of Negro History*, 21 (1936), 1–5; Charles G. Sellers, "The Travail of Slavery," in Sellers, ed., *The Southerner as American* (Chapel Hill, 1960), pp. 40–71; and, for a skillful overview, see James M. McPherson, "Slavery and Race," *Perspectives in American History*, 3 (1969), 463–67. On the interaction of fear and pride, see Robert E. Shalhope, "Race, Class, and the Antebellum Southern Mind," *Journal of Southern History*, 37 (1971), 557–74.

3. David Donald, "The Proslavery Argument Reconsidered," *Journal of Southern History*, 37 (1971), 3–18; Drew G. Faust, *A Sacred Circle: The Dilemma of the Intellectual in the Old South, 1840–1860* (Baltimore, 1977); Faust, "A Southern Stewardship: The Intellectual and the Proslavery Argument," *American Quarterly*, 31 (1979), 63–80. See also George M. Fredrickson, *The Black Image in the White Mind: The Debate on Afro-American Character and Destiny, 1817–1914* (New York, 1971).

4. Eugene D. Genovese, *The World the Slaveholders Made: Two Essays in Interpretation* (New York, 1969), p. 119. Aileen S. Kraditor has shrewdly written: "To exclude from our definition of past reformisms the movement to humanize slavery, or the movement to bar Catholics from office-holding during the nineteenth century, is to distort our image of the past by depicting it in the image of the present. . . ." Kraditor, "American Radical Historians on Their Heritage," *Past & Present*, no. 56 (1972), 145.

5. There were, of course, some Southerners opposed to slavery, and the major denominations had at one time considered it a moral evil; declensions from Revolutionary zeal and Enlightenment principles, however, were at least partly a result of an appearance of evangelical practice in slave management, not just crass expediency. On Southern antislavery, see Carl N. Degler, *The Other South: Southern Dissenters in the Nineteenth Century* (New York, 1974); idem, *Memoir of Samuel N. Janney* (Philadelphia, 1881), pp. 28–29, 92.

Admissions of "guilt" sometimes appeared in proslavery writings, but usually as a rhetorical device; see, for instance, Albert T. Bledsoe, *An Essay on Liberty and Slavery* (Philadelphia, 1857), p. 12. This issue is well explored in two works: Genovese, *World the Slaveholders Made*, pp. 144–50, and Dickson D. Bruce, Jr., *Violence and Culture in the Antebellum South* (Austin, Tex, 1979), pp. 114–36.

6. Henry Hughes, "New Duties of the South," Port Gibson (Miss.) *Southern Reveille,* November 18, 1854, clipping, Henry Hughes Scrapbook, Mississippi Department of Archives and History (hereafter MDAH), Jackson, Mississippi. Ideological instruction of young people was a universal concern in the Victorian era: see also William A. Smith, *Lectures on the Philosophy and Practice of Slavery* (Nashville, 1856), pp. 15, 17, 18, 26. The best summary, though largely uninterpretive, is William S. Jenkins, *Pro-Slavery Thought in the Old South* (Chapel Hill, 1935).

7. A very suggestive analysis of Alabama's ambivalent response to institutional modernization is found in J. Mills Thornton III, *Politics and Power in a Slave Society: Alabama, 1800–1860* (Baton Rouge, 1978); also see the persuasive reinterpretation of Jacksonian politics in William J. Cooper, Jr., *The South and the Politics of Slavery, 1828–1856* (Baton Rouge, 1978).

8. Quotation from Robin Mayhead, *Walter Scott* (Cambridge, 1973), p. 43; see also David Daiches, "Scott's Achievement as a Novelist," in D. D. Devlin, ed., *Walter Scott: Modern Judgements* (Nashville and London, 1970, 1st ed., 1969), p. 37; Grace W. Landrum, "Sir Walter Scott and His Literary Rivals in the Old South," *American Literature,* 2 (1930), 256–76; *Southern Literary Messenger,* 22 (1856), 291–94, and ibid., 23 (1856), 247–48. David Daiches, "Scott and Scotland," in Alan Bell, ed., *Scott Bicentenary Essays: Selected Papers at the Sir Walter Scott Bicentenary Conference, Edinburgh, 1971* (Edinburgh, 1973), pp. 38–60. On Scots-Irish ethnicity, see George Tucker, *The Valley of the Shenandoah . . .* (Chapel Hill, 1970, 1st ed., 1824), pp. 47–58. Marcus Cunliffe, *Chattel Slavery and Wage Slavery: The Anglo-American Context 1830–1860* (Athens, Ga., 1979).

9. George Fitzhugh, "Southern Thoughts," *DeBow's Review,* 23 (1857), 337. See "Harper on Slavery," in *The Pro-Slavery Argument, As Maintained by the Most Distinguished Writers of the Southern States . . .* (Philadelphia, 1853), pp. 1–2, passim; see also James H. Hammond, "Slavery in the Light of Political Science," in E. N. Elliott, ed., *Cotton Is King . . .* (Augusta, Ga.: 1860), p. 647; cf. Genovese, *World the Slaveholders Made*, p. 158. Genovese claims that proslavery writers had to justify the system against "the whole social, ethical, political, and economic philosophy of the day." Victorian philosophies were very wide-ranging, and one could argue that authoritarianism and conservatism were as much a part of intellectual baggage as democracy and liberalism. After all, the South did not lack for defenders, who admired the policing, curfew, antiliquor regulations, and other suppressions of Southern blacks that contrasted with the "chaos" and degradation of the urban poor elsewhere. See Nehemiah Adams, *A Southside View of Slavery; Or Three Months at the South in 1854* (Boston, 1854), and consider, too, the observations of British travelers like Sir Charles Lyell and others, conveniently summarized in J. D. B. DeBow, *The Industrial Resources, Etc. of the Southern and Western States . . .,* 3 vols. (New Orleans, 1853), III, 62–70.

10. Edward J. Pringle of South Carolina put the matter in these words: "One object in this [essay] has been not so much to answer the objections of the opponents of slavery, as to prove for the slaveholder that his dependent laborer is capable of better things than the world would have him believe, and especially to remind him that whatever arguments he urges in favor of the slave's position are all of necessity so many pledges for the faithful discharge of his own duties." Pringle, *Slavery in the Southern States* (Cambridge, Mass., 1853, 3rd ed.), p. 43.

11. For example, David M. Erskine, an English visitor, reported that in Norfolk in 1798, "it is not at all uncommon for a white to keep blacks to let out as horses are in England." Quoted in Robert McColley, *Slavery and Jeffersonian Virginia* (Charlottesville, 1964), p. 58.

12. Gerald W. Mullin, *Flight and Rebellion: Slave Resistance in Eighteenth-Century Virginia* (New York, 1972); Peter H. Wood, *Black Majority: Negroes in Colonial South Carolina from 1670 through the Stono Rebellion* (New York, 1974); Richard B. Sheridan, *Sugar and Slavery: An Economic History of the British West Indies, 1623–1775* (Baltimore, 1973), and Winthrop D. Jordan, *White over Black: American Attitudes toward the Negro 1550–1812* (Chapel Hill, 1968). For an historiographical overview of early black history see Peter H. Wood, " 'I Did the Best I Could for My Day': The Study of Early Black History during the Second Reconstruction, 1960 to 1976," *William and Mary Quarterly*, 3rd ser., 35 (1978), 185–225, and Allan Kulikoff, "The Origins of Afro-American Society in Tidewater Maryland and Virginia, 1700 to 1790," ibid., 226–59.

13. The negative reference approach to self-identity is evident in the Christian slaveholder as well as in the teetotaler: Charles C. Jones, Jr., for instance, wrote his pious father of a decision not to settle his blacks in Bryan County owing to "the character of the region, the semi-barbaric tone in morals and religion, the character of the treatment to which Negroes are there subjected, the esteem in which they are held." Jones to Charles Colcock Jones, December 26, 1859, Robert M. Myers, ed., *Children of Pride: A True Story of Georgia and the Civil War* (New Haven, 1972), p. 551.

14. Professor Rose kindly lent me a draft of her paper "The Domestication of Domestic Slavery," an address delivered at the Charles Warren Center, Harvard University, spring 1974. This interesting essay clarifies the whole issue of slavery's evolution.

15. The Reverend R. G. Grundy, "Thoughts for the People—No. 9," Memphis *Bulletin*, October 19, 1862, a reference to which was given me by John Cimprich of Ohio State University.

16. James L. Petigru to his daughter Jane North, December 24, 1835, transcription, James L. Petigru MSS, Library of Congress. Like H. B. Stowe's Shelby family in *Uncle Tom's Cabin*, however, Petigru was classically improvident, which led to the breakup of slave families, a situation Southern pietists invariably lamented as a fall from God's grace. See William R. Taylor, *Cavalier and Yankee: The Old South and American National Character* (New York, 1961), pp. 285–94.

17. Emmet F. Horine, ed., *Dr. Daniel Drake's Letters on Slavery to Dr. John C. Warren, of Boston* . . . (New York, 1940 ed. [1851]), p. 7; Robert W. Fogel and Stanley L. Engerman, *Time on the Cross: The Economics of American Negro Slavery* (Boston, 1974); cf. Bertram Wyatt-Brown, essay rev. in *Reviews in American History*, 2 (1974), 457–65. "Practicality" was a key word in the proslavery lexicon; see Smith, *Lectures*, p. 26.

18. John C. Hurd, *The Law of Freedom and Bondage in the United States*, 2 vols. (Boston, 1862), II, 94, 98, 107. See also Edward R. Laurens, *A Letter to the Hon. Whitemarsh Seabrook of St. John's, Colleton; in Explanation and Defence of 'An Act to Amend the Law in Relation to Slaves and Free Persons of Color'* (Charleston, S.C., 1835), pp. 9–10; Rosser H. Taylor, "Humanizing the Slave Code of North Carolina," *North Carolina Historical Review*, 2 (1925), 323–31.

19. Dale A. Somers, "Black and White in New Orleans: A Study in Urban Race Relations, 1865–1900," *Journal of Southern History*, 40 (1974), 19; Richard C. Wade, *Slavery in the Cities: The South 1820–1860* (New York, 1964), pp. 97–110.

20. For examples, see Hurd, *Law of Freedom and Bondage*, II, 85, 91, 104, 106–7; Ivan E. McDougle, *Slavery in Kentucky, 1792–1865* (Lancaster, Pa., 1918), p. 36; Engene D. Genovese, *Roll, Jordan, Roll: The World the Slaves Made* (New York, 1974), pp. 37–39, 42.

21. Daniel J. Flanigan, "Criminal Procedure in Slave Trials in the Antebellum South," *Journal of Southern History*, 40 (1974), 537–64; and Flanigan, "The Criminal Law of Slavery and Freedom 1800–1868" (Ph.D. diss., Rice University, 1973). The author points out in "Criminal Procedure," loc. cit., 546 n26, that slaves had better rights of appeal than an Englishman convicted of a felony (until 1907). The legal situation, in the total context of Southern justice, was much more complex than Genovese indicates in his otherwise admirable *Roll, Jordan, Roll* (see esp. pp. 43–49). On the professionalizing of Southern legal life, see the most provocative chapter, "Branding Iron and Retrospect: Lawyers in the Cumberland River Country," by Daniel H. Calhoun, *Professional Lives in America: Structure and Aspiration 1750–1850* (Cambridge, Mass., 1965), pp. 59–87.

22. Charles C. Jones to Charles C. Jones, Jr., December 10, 1859, Myers, ed., *Children of Pride*, p. 545; Jones, Jr., to Jones, Sr., December 12, 1859, ibid., p. 546.

23. Genovese, *World the Slaveholders Made*, pp. 228–34.

24. See Bertram Wyatt-Brown, "The Ideal Typology and Ante-Bellum Southern History: A Testing of a New Approach," *Societas*, 5 (1975), 16–22.

25. The closing of the foreign slave trade on January 1, 1808, by the Act of 1807, granted a boon to the development of proslavery thought by removing an indefensible aspect of the system.

26. Frank E. Vandiver, "The Southerner as Extremist," in Vandiver, ed., *The Idea of the South: Pursuit of a Central Theme* (Chicago, 1964), p. 45.

27. A good summary, despite the obvious bias, of ordinary planter understanding of slavery, is found in the Reverend James H. McNeilly, D.D., *Religion and Slavery: A Vindication of the Southern Churches* (Nashville, 1911), pp. 12–14; for a contemporary summary, see Natchez (Miss.) *Courier*, September 3, 1835, and Albert G. Seal, ed., "Notes and Documents: Letters from the South, A Mississippian's Defense of Slavery," *Journal of Mississippi History*, 2 (1940), 212–31.

28. B. M. Palmer, as quoted in Jenkins, *Pro-Slavery Thought*, p. 216; David Ewart, *A Scriptural View of the Moral Relations of African Slavery* (Charleston, S.C., 1859), pp. 9, 11; The Reverend W. T. Hamilton, D.D., *The Duties of Masters and Slaves Respectively: Or Domestic Servitude as Sanctioned by the Bible: A Discourse Delivered in the Government-Street Church, Mobile, Ala.* (Mobile, 1845), p. 14; James H. Thornwell, *The Rights and the Duties of Masters. A Sermon Preached at the Dedication of a Church Erected in Charleston for the Benefit and Instruction of the Coloured Population* (Charleston, 1850), p. 31. See Larry E. Tise, "Proslavery Ideology: A Social and Intellectual History of the Defense of Slavery in America, 1790–1840" (Ph.D. diss., University of North Carolina, 1974). Tise argues that most spokesmen for slavery were Yankee or Yankee-trained clergymen. The point demonstrates that slavery was so ingrained in white mores that it required little rationalization until the more literate culture of the North influenced Southern styles of thinking and argumentation. Yale and other schools trained students in rhetoric; that such techniques would be applied in such conservative causes at proslavery polemics is not as surprising as it might appear.

29. Charles C. Jones, *Religious Instruction of the Negroes in the United States* (Savannah, Ga., 1842), p. 227: "The churches are composed of households: parents and children, masters and servants. . . ."

30. "A Lady of Fredericksburg, Virginia" [Lucy Kenny], *A Death Blow to the Principles of Abolition* (Washington, D.C., 183?), p. 4; see also Nathaniel Bowen, D.D., *A Pastoral Letter on the Religious Instruction of Slaves, at the Request of the Convention of the Churches of the Diocese . . .* (Charleston, 1835), pp. 4, 6–7; Jones, *Religious Instruction*, p. 110.

31. Pringle, *Slavery in the Southern States*, p. 17.

32. Patricia Hickin, " 'Situation Ethics' and Antislavery Attitudes in the Virginia Churches," in John B. Boles, ed., *America, The Middle Period: Essays in Honor of Bernard Mayo* (Charlottesville, 1973), pp. 188–215.

33. Grundy, Memphis *Bulletin*, October 19, 1862.

34. Christopher G. Memminger, *Lecture delivered before the Young Men's Library Association of Augusta, April 10, 1851* (Augusta, Ga., 1835), p. 14.

35. Philip Greven, ed., *Child-Rearing Concepts, 1628–1861: Historical Sources* (Itasca, Ill., 1973); Ronald G. Walters, *Primers for Prudery: Sexual Advice to Victorian America* (Englewood Cliffs, N.J., 1974); Bernard Wishy, *The Child and the Republic: The Dawn of Modern American Child Nurture* (Philadelphia, 1972).

36. Of course this advice was not confined to pietists: see Charles D. Lowery, "James Barbour, A Progressive Farmer of Antebellum Virginia," in Boles, ed., *America, the Middle Period*, pp. 178–79, for example.

37. Jones, *Religious Instruction*, pp. 241–42: "*Punishments* should be inflicted upon those *proven guilty* (neither in *anger, nor out of proportion to the offence,*) with as little resort to *corporal chastisement* as possible."

38. Legal and social changes in attitudes about corporal penalties were much slower in the South than in the North, but the disciplinary transition was underway before 1861.

39. William G. Sims, "The Morals of Slavery," in *The Pro-Slavery Argument*, p. 275; Thomas S. Clay, *Detail of a Plan for the Moral Improvement of Negroes on Plantations, Read before the Georgia Presbytery* (n.p., 1833), pp. 10–21; Calvin H. Wiley, "The Art of Governing," a chapter in "The Christian Duty of Masters," unpublished work, Calvin H. Wiley MSS, Southern Historical Collections, University of North Carolina Library; Horine, ed., *Drake's Letters*, p. 17.

40. See Ralph T. Parkinson, "The Religious Instruction of Slaves, 1820–1860" (M.A. thesis, University of North Carolina, 1948), pp. 13–15.

41. Kenneth M. Stampp, *The Peculiar Institution: Slavery in the Antebellum South* (New York, 1956), pp. 156–62.

42. See Donald G. Mathews, "Reform in the Old South: Charles Colcock Jones and the Southern Evangelical Crusade To Form a Biracial Community," *Journal of Southern History*, 41 (1975), 299–320; see also Mathews's *Religion in the Old South* (Chicago, 1977), 137–50. Charles C. Jones, *The Religious Instruction of the Negroes in the United States* (New York, 1969, 1st ed., 1842); David Christy, *Pulpit Politics* . . . (New York, 1969, 1st ed., 1862).

43. Wiley, "Christian Duty of Masters," Wiley MSS, Southern Historical Collections, University of North Carolina Library; the Reverend Thornton Stringfellow, "The Bible Argument," in Elliott, ed., *Cotton Is King*, p. 522; George F. Holmes, in *Southern Literary Messenger*, 19 (1853), 324; [Edwin C. Holland], *A Refutation of the Calumnies Circulated against the Southern & Western States* . . . (Charleston, 1822), p. 46.

44. Jones, *Religious Instruction of the Negroes*, pp. 175–205; Frances A. Cabaniss and James A. Cabaniss, "Religion in Ante-Bellum Mississippi," *Journal of Mississippi History*, 2 (1944), 221–22; Clay, *Moral Improvement of Negroes*, p. 20; C. F. Sturgis, *Melville Letters; or, Duties of Masters to Their Servants* (Charleston, 1851), p. 54.

45. Hamilton, *Duties of Masters and Slaves*, pp. 22, 23; Reverend James A. Lyon, in *Southern Presbyterian Review*, 16, 35–36, as quoted in James J. Pilar, "Religious and Cultural Life, 1817–1860," in Richard A. McLemore, ed., *A History of Mississippi*, 2 vols. (Jackson, Miss., 1973), I, 409: "There is a natural repugnance in the breast of civilized men against *tyranny;* but there is none against the *domestic* relations. Let us, therefore, make slavery, by law, the patriarchal institution that is recognized and sanctioned in the Bible, and it will appear in entirely a different light to the eyes of the civilized

world than that which it now appears." See also Pringle, *Slavery in the Southern States,* p. 34.

46. See James H. Otey, "The Duty of Ministers of the Gospel to their People, Considered in their Civil Relations, Primary Charge to the Clergy, October 11, 1837, Nashville Diocesan Convention," in appendix of Reverend William M. Green, *Memoir of Rt. Rev. James Hervey Otey, D.D., LL.D., the First Bishop of Tennessee* (New York, 1885), pp. 194–210; see also Jenkins, *Pro-Slavery Thought,* pp. 208–10.

47. George F. Simmons, *Two Sermons on the Kind Treatment and on the Emancipation of Slaves. Preached at Mobile, on Sunday the 10th and Sunday the 17th of May, 1840* (Boston, 1840), p. 23. Simmons overstepped the bounds of propriety; and townsfolk, but not the congregation present at the delivery, forced him to leave Mobile. A victim of what Joseph Fletcher calls "situation ethics," Simmons was antislavery but still believed that slavery was redeemable under Christian evolution.

48. Thornwell, *Rights and Duties of Masters,* p. 12. Freehling, *Prelude to Civil War,* pp. 80–81, suggests that in the 1820s there was hesitation at calling slavery a "positive good," a posture that died out in South Carolina, he says, later on. But Presbyterians, particularly, had to be careful to avoid labeling any human institution perfect; otherwise the doctrine of Adamic sin would be lost. Thus, one continues to find qualifications. Wiley, in his lengthy essay on Christian slaveholding, Wiley MSS, Southern Historical Collection, devoted a chapter to the origins of slavery in "sin." See Theodore D. Bozeman, "Science, Nature and Society: A New Approach to James Henley Thornwell," *Journal of Presbyterian History,* 50 (1972), 307–25; also, Drew G. Faust, "Evangelicalism and the Meaning of the Proslavery Argument: The Reverend Thornton Stringfellow of Virginia," *Virginia Magazine of History and Biography,* 75 (1977), 3–17; William B. Gravely, "Methodist Preachers, Slavery and Caste: Types of Social Concern in Antebellum America," *Duke Divinity School Review,* 34 (1969), 209–29; Anne C. Loveland, "Richard Furman's 'Questions on Slavery,'" *Baptist History and Heritage,* 10 (1975), 177–81, and Jack P. Maddex, "Proslavery Millennialism: Social Eschatology in Antebellum Southern Calvinism," *American Quarterly,* 31 (1979), 46–62, and Thomas V. Peterson, *Ham and Jepheth: The Mythic World of Whites in the Antebellum South* (Metuchen, N.J., 1978), 111–14. Wilson is quoted in Robert Bober, "The Young Woodrow Wilson, A Study of the Formative Years," (Ph.D. diss., Case Western Reserve University, 1980).

49. Morrow, "Proslavery Argument Revisited," *Mississippi Valley Historical Review,* 48 (1961), 88, considers the ameliorative impulse an escapist device.

50. See Donald G. Mathews, *Slavery and Methodism: A Chapter in American Morality, 1780–1845* (Princeton, 1965), pp. 67–87; Donald G. Mathews, "Charles Colcock Jones and the Southern Evangelical Crusade to Form a Biracial Community," *Journal of Southern History,* 41 (1975), 299–320. McNeilly, *Religion and Slavery,* pp. 34–37; Jones, *Religious Instruction to the Negroes,* pp. 1–110; H. Shelton Smith, *In His Image, But . . .: Racism in Religion, 1780–1910* (Durham, N.C., 1972), pp. 153–54, wrongly, I think, causally connects the mission to slaves with the tightening of controls, whereas

the religious effort reflected a growing institutionalization of Southern life, a transformation that was underway in many other areas of regional experience.

51. *Dictionary of American Biography*, 20 vols. (New York, 1932), IX, 350; Henry Hughes, *Treatise on Sociology: Theoretical and Practical* (Philadelphia, 1854).

52. Henry Hughes Diary (transcription), January 28, 1849, p. 56, MDAH. Except for this early diary, January 1, 1848–May 1, 1853, and a scrapbook, all of Hughes's papers have disappeared.

53. Ibid., October 24, 1852, p. 220. Hughes studied architecture, sculpture, painting, social science, anatomy, chemistry, ancient and modern languages and literature, and moral philosophy, in France and Italy, as well as law, in New Orleans.

54. See Bertram Wyatt-Brown, "Conscience and Career: Young Abolitionists and Missionaries," in Seymour Drescher and Christine Bolt, eds., *Religion, Reform, and Anti-Slavery: Essays in Memory of Roger Anstey* (Folkstone, Eng., 1980), 183–203; and "John Brown and Weathermen: The Antinomian Impulse in American Radicalism," *Soundings*, 58 (1975), 417–40; Michael Fellman, *The Unbounded Frame: Freedom and Community in Nineteenth Century American Utopianism* (Westport, Conn., 1973), pp. 42–61.

55. Kraditor, "American Radical Historians," *Past & Present*, no. 56 (1972), 136–52.

56. Hughes, "New Duties of the South," Port Gibson *Southern Reveille*, November 18, 1854, Hughes scrapbook, MDAH.

57. *Southern Commercial Convention, Vicksburg, Miss. A Report on the African Apprenticeship System, Read at the Southern Commercial Convention by Henry Hughes. Held at Vicksburg, May 10th, 1859* (Vicksburg, 1859), p. 2.

58. Ibid., pp. 2–3, 12.

59. Hughes, *Treatise on Sociology*, p. 91.

60. Reverend W. D. Moore, *The Life and Works of Col. Henry Hughes; A Funeral Sermon, Preached in the Methodist Episcopal Church, Port Gibson, Miss., October 26th, 1862* (Mobile, 1863), pp. 28–31. Josiah Nott of Mobile, exponent of "scientific" explanations for black inferiority, also opposed revealed religion, but for quite different reasons. See William Stanton, *The Leopard's Spots: Scientific Attitudes toward Race in America, 1815–59* (Chicago, 1960), pp. 120–21; Ronald T. Takaki, *A Pro-Slavery Crusade: The Agitation to Reopen the African Slave Trade* (New York, 1971).

61. *Treatise on Sociology*, pp. 110, 113, 256. See also, Genovese, *World the Slaveholders Made*, p. 167.

62. An example of his Positivist style, much resembling the French tradition of epigrammatic abstractionism, is: "Subordination is not slavery; ethical segregation is not ethical degradation. For the duties coupled to the relation of races, must be actualized. Purity of race, is right." Hughes, *Treatise on Sociology*, p. 243.

63. Ibid. pp. 350–55.

64. Hughes, in *Southern Reveille*, July 30, 1859, clipping, Hughes scrapbook, MDAH; *Treatise on Sociology*, pp. 69, 73, 258.

65. Otto H. Olsen, "Historians and the Extent of Slave Ownership in the Southern United States," *Civil War History*, 18 (1972), 101–17; Gavin Wright, *The Political Economy of the Cotton South* (New York, 1978), pp. 83–84.

66. Hughes, "Warranteeism and Free Labor," Jackson, Miss., *Eagle of the South*, March 28, 1859, and "Re-Opening of the Slave Trade," *Southern Reveille*, July 30, 1859, Hughes scrapbook, MDAH. Strangely, Robert E. May, *The Southern Dream of a Caribbean Empire, 1854–1861* (Baton Rouge, 1973), fails to mention this "coolie" scheme, which was another answer to the same issue of labor shortage.

67. William L. Yancey of Alabama and John A. Quitman of Mississippi were two other leaders in the African scheme. Hughes admired them both. See Hughes, "Letter from Montgomery," New Orleans *Delta*, May 19, 1858, and "Eulogy of Quitman . . . August 26, 1858" [*Southern Reveille?*], Hughes Scrapbook, MDAH.

68. Hughes, "A Quartette of Objections to African Labor Immigration," March 9, 1858, ibid. See also Stella Herron, "The African Apprentice Bill," in *Proceedings of the Mississippi Valley Historical Association, for the Year 1914–15* (Cedar Rapids, 1916), pp. 135–45.

69. Hughes, "Negro Mechanics," *Eagle of the South*, October 16, 1858, Hughes scrapbook, MDAH; *Treatise on Sociology*, p. 112; *Southern Commercial Convention*, p. 14; "Large Slaveholders and the African Immigration Scheme," New Orleans *Delta*, February 14, 1858, Hughes scrapbook, MDAH.

70. *Treatise on Sociology*, pp. 199–200, 233–34; under his scheme, slaves would have been "warranted" a sufficiency of household utensils, furniture, medicines, medical services, religious and educational opportunities, entertainments and recreational activity, as well as the additional legal right to sue for damages. Quotation from *Southern Commercial Convention*, p. 12.

71. Hughes, "Compensation for Executed Slaves," Port Gibson (Miss.) *Herald*, June 18, 1856, Hughes scrapbook, MDAH.

72. See DeBow, *Industrial Resources*, II, 233; Hughes, "Re-Opening of the Slave Trade," *Southern Reveille*, July 30, 1859, Hughes scrapbook, MDAH.

73. Moore, *Hughes: A Funeral Sermon*, pp. 9, 10, 17.

74. Ibid., pp. 30–31.

75. Ibid., pp. 13–14.

76. Genovese, *World the Slaveholders Made*, pp. 227–29, draws an interesting analogy between the Prussian state and the South, but South Africa may be a closer parallel. See George M. Fredrickson, *White Supremacy: A Comparative Study in American and South African History* (New York, 1981).

77. C. Vann Woodward, *The Strange Career of Jim Crow* (New York, 2nd rev. ed., 1966), pp. 111–12, 121–22.

78. Moore, *Hughes: A Funeral Sermon*, p. 35.

Common Right and Commonwealth:
The Stock-Law Struggle and the Roots
of Southern Populism

STEVEN HAHN

I T remains a commonplace of American political wisdom that the countryside in general and the family farmer in particular represent the mainstays of social order, if not of outright conservatism. Thomas Jefferson pinned his hopes for an alternative to the immiseration and disorder he saw in Europe on the abundance of "vacant land" and the character of independent cultivators. Nineteenth-century advocates of land reform pressed for cheap Western homesteads as a "safety valve" for urban discontent. New Dealers looked to agricultural resettlement programs as a partial response to poverty and displacement in the 1930s. Contemporary political analysts expect the farm belt to vote Republican as a matter of course. And yet, during the 1890s, thousands of small farmers in the West and South rallied to the banner of Populism, the greatest third-party movement in American history—a movement that historians increasingly view as a grassroots challenge to capitalist relations, institutions, and values.[1]

That political radicalism could win a mass constituency among erstwhile defenders of the status quo seems confounding, to say the least. Without fully confronting the enigma, the standard

Earlier versions of this essay were presented to the Regional Economic History Research Center's Joint Seminar at the University of Delaware (October 1979), to the annual meeting of the Social Science History Association in Rochester, New York (November 1980), and to the Department of History at the University of Chicago (February 1981). For helpful questions, criticisms, and suggestions, I should like to thank those in attendance, as well as Barbara J. Fields, Charles Flynn, Robert McMath Jr., Lawrence Powell, Jonathan Prude, and Armstead Robinson.

explanations rest heavily upon economic determinants: the dislocations and distress befalling rural America in the late nineteenth century.[2] The argument marshals considerable force, for agricultural depression reached severe proportions. Especially in the South, where Populism established its firmest foothold, the postwar years brought steadily deteriorating material conditions to most small landowners who entered the cotton market. Impoverishment, dependency, and ultimate dispossession were epidemic among the yeomanry, as cotton prices eventually dipped below the cost of production.[3] Economic tribulation, however, does not necessarily spark political insurgency. It just as easily may sap resistance, and it dispenses no inherent ideology to its victims. Hard times alone can scarcely account for the Populist vision of a democratic and cooperative alternative to the dominant structures of the Gilded Age.

The economic interpretation of Populism reflects a widely held assumption that yeomen farmers in the South, as elsewhere, were petty entrepreneurs whose possession of property served as a hedge against radical unrest. The outbreak of political protest, by extension, can only derive from some cyclically initiated "disequilibrium." The logic seems impeccable. Indeed, the association of property ownership with political moderation or conservatism has infused American historiography.[4] But, as a general principle, it cannot withstand closer scrutiny. Popular movements here and abroad, at least before the triumph of industrial capitalism, normally drew their strength from producers with skills and claims to productive resources, not from the poor and disadvantaged. The role of artisans in early labor radicalism already has been well documented,[5] and a similar phenomenon was evident in the countryside. The *petits propriétaires* or the so-called middle peasants, for example, have been the leading edge of populist, socialist, and communist movements in rural Europe and the Third World.[6] What matters is not the fact, but the kind, of property claims and the specific social relations such claims entail.

If, from this perspective, the Populist vision of cooperative commonwealth suggests that Southern yeomen were something other than entrepreneurial in behavior and outlook, it should not imply that convention be overturned and farmers deemed incipient radicals. Students of rural societies in other parts of the world have noted a paradox quite akin to that perplexing their

American counterparts. The most culturally conservative peasants are often the most likely to embrace radicalism.[7] A conceptual resolution may be found by recognizing that peasant movements have a dynamic rather than a categorical quality. They usually begin as defenses of customary rights, standards, and obligations threatened by new social forces—in the modern era, generally those of the marketplace and the state. Whether they simply seek a redress of grievances and thus remain anchored to the past, or chart novel and far-reaching courses, hinges on a number of historically discrete conjunctures: their social composition, heritage, leadership, and links with other local and supralocal groups; the character and relative strengths of the dominant classes; the nature, pace, and extent of economic developments; wider cultural and political currents. The roots of collective action lie in distinct relationships, traditions, and sensibilities, and in the experience of social change.

That experience is equally central to Southern Populism. For the white farmers who would fill the ranks of the People's party, most of whom resided in nonplantation areas, the common denominator was the process and repercussions of moving into the cotton economy and its attendant social relationships between 1865 and 1890. Yet, neither the process nor the repercussions were entirely uniform. Each locale traveled its own road, marked by episodes that provided focus and meaning for the broader experience.* One such episode in one such locale was a bitter conflict over grazing rights—the stock law—that erupted in the Georgia Upcountry during the 1880s. In microcosm, the conflict spoke to the profound social and economic transformations that occurred in this region, and others like it, after the Civil War; to the social divisions and tensions created by those transformations; and to the ways in which the divisions and tensions found cultural and political expression. Supporters of the stock law, which would eliminate common grazing rights, represented the interests of merchants, landlords, and the towns as well as the values of the "free market." They had taken control of and would stay loyal to the Democratic party. Opponents defended the claims of

---

* The Upcountry (Upper Piedmont), a group of piedmont plateau counties, stretches across the state just below the Mountains. Directly to the south and embracing much of central and southwestern Georgia is the Black Belt (Lower Piedmont). To the southeast, lie the Wiregrass and coastal plain.

yeomen and tenants in the countryside as well as the precepts of a "moral economy." Many would break with political orthodoxy and flock to the third party. The stock-law struggle thereby anticipated the dimensions of, and paved the Georgia Upcountry's road to, Populism.

I

When L. J. Jones, a Georgia hill farmer, learned of an impending stock-law election in 1885, he had no doubt about what was at stake. "We as poor men and negroes do not need the law," he cried, "but we need a democratic government and independence that will do the common people good."[8] Jones's challenge to the tenets of white supremacy marked an important departure, for Upcountry whites had a well-known reputation for racism. But his associating the stock law with class oppression and political misrule struck a responsive chord. Hundreds of small farmers and tenants, of both races, joined with Jones to protect the grazing rights the stock law threatened to abridge. For them, the law was the starkest instance of efforts by the emerging postbellum elite to cast petty producers into a state of dependency.

Common grazing, what was known as the "open range," had long prevailed in the South. From earliest settlement, farmers customarily fenced their crops and turned livestock out to forage.[9] Colonial assemblies and later state legislatures added the sanction of statute law, uniformly upheld by the antebellum courts. "Unenclosed lands," one judge announced in a typical ruling, "are to be treated as common pasture for the cattle and stock of every citizen."[10] Such practices can be traced to Celtic areas of Britain, whence came many migrants to the South, but were also widespread in continental Europe before capitalist agriculture fully penetrated the countryside. Everywhere they enabled smallholders and the landless to own draft animals, hogs, and sheep.[11]

The right of common pasture at once bolstered the sustenance of poor cultivators and complemented the social relations of an Upcountry economy devoted to semisubsistence agriculture and local exchange. During the pre-war period, this region in Georgia, as in other states of the Lower South, had a white majority and a preponderance of small owner-operated farms. Yeomen households, perhaps with the aid of a few slaves, grew food crops and occasionally some cotton, made much of their own clothing and furnishings, and raised substantial numbers of livestock.[12] Poor transport facilities and limited Plantation-Belt demand for grain left the area on the periphery of the staple economy, yet farm families were isolated neither from each other nor from a marketplace. Productive organization, while centering on the household, involved various forms of "swap work" within settlements, especially at harvest and other points in the year when labor proved most arduous and pressing.[13] The need for additional goods and services, moreover, brought yeomen into a network of trade characterized by direct transactions between different producers—farmers, artisans, hired hands—and governed by local custom. Some type of barter frequently served as the medium of exchange.[14] And the handful of merchants followed suit, extending low-interest credit and accepting "all kinds of country produce" to settle accounts.[15] General farming, household manufactures, and a community-wide division of labor contributed to a broad-based self-sufficiency.[16] Independence and interdependence, ownership of productive resources and "habits of mutuality," were linked intimately in this rural culture.

The years after 1865 saw the workings of a major transformation, fully unleashed by the Civil War, that drew the Upcountry into the cotton economy and, by 1890, made it the major cotton-growing area in Georgia. The expansion of rail lines made the transformation possible, but more important was the development of social relations and credit arrangements that impelled yeomen to cultivate greater quantities of cotton at the expense of foodstuffs.[17] Merchants, strengthened by the crop lien though facing uncertain prospects in the plantation districts, became the agents of the Upcountry's new order. Beginning in the 1870s, they streamed into proliferating towns and hamlets and took charge of the local marketplace.[18] Farmers wishing to purchase supplies on credit—the norm—now had to mortgage their crops as security, and storekeepers made plain their preference for cotton. By 1880, as a result of state constitutional reform, merchants could, and did, demand that real and personal property also stand as collateral.[19] And to enhance their leverage, they soon moved into ginning, marketing, and other services.[20] Through these means, merchants altered the structure of exchange and shifted producers' energies to commercial agriculture.

Under such a system, and in the context of declining cotton

prices which drove many farmers into debt, merchant control over exchange relations translated into control over production itself. Through foreclosures, storekeepers became landlords and reduced freeholders to tenants or croppers. Landlessness grew apace.[21] Even if foreclosure was not impending, mortgages on land, crops, tools, and livestock put productive property within the merchants' reach and gave them greater authority over patterns of cultivation on yeomen farms. Smallholders and tenants were turned into rural laborers—a status shared by Upcountry blacks—and merchants were turned into agricultural employers. One farmer, suffering under the burdens of debt and encumbrance, thus explained his desperate flight from a hounding creditor: "I just got tired of *working for* the other fellow."[22]

The stock-law controversy emerged in this struggle over social relations in the Upcountry's developing cotton economy, though its origins lay in the Plantation Belt, where the "labor question" first surfaced after Emancipation. Seeking to reestablish their command over the newly liberated slaves and believing black dependency to be the handmaiden of labor discipline, the planters moved to circumscribe the freedmen's access to the means of production and subsistence. The legal and extralegal actions taken by the planting elite to prevent blacks from owning land, to tie them to the plantation sector, and, with the rise of tenancy, to control their crops, were products of such an offensive—an offensive waged by large landowners throughout the Western Hemisphere and Europe in response to the emancipation of slaves and peasants.[23] Day-to-day matters of work rhythms, provisioning, and leisure also proved to be bones of contention. Freedmen, the traveler Edward King observed in 1874, "are fond of the same pleasures which their late masters gave them so freely—hunting, fishing, and lounging; pastimes which the superb forests, the noble streams, and the charming climate minister to very strongly."[24]

These "pleasures" may have been viewed as paternal indulgences by wealthy slaveholders; following abolition, as the old plantation forms of management dissolved, the "pleasures" were direct challenges to the planters' prerogatives and claims on the freedmen's labor time. Hence, when Georgia's landed elite regained political power after Reconstruction, they set their sights on remedying the problem. Commencing in 1872, a series of game laws, localized in nature, literally fanned out over the Plantation Belt. Citing a "wholesale and ill-seasoned destruction of deer, partridges, and wild turkeys," legislation established hunting seasons for a considerable assortment of animals and fowl, prohibited certain methods of entrapment, and, perhaps most important, restricted access to game on unenclosed private land—a right enjoyed by antebellum whites and privileged slaves despite some grumbling from the planters. As the decade closed, hunting and fishing had come under regulation in most of the plantation districts, and a process of defining absolute property had begun.[25]

Arising as a central feature of this process, the grazing issue similarly put conservation, as well as agricultural improvement, in the service of altering property rights. In Georgia, as elsewhere in the Lower South, planter organizations, such as local and state agricultural societies and the Grange, took the lead in agitation. Arguing that the "old habits" threatened the timber supply, exacted undue expense, and encouraged theft, they called for new laws requiring the fencing of livestock instead of crops.[26] And they received eager assistance from railroad companies liable for damages if locomotives struck animals straying on the tracks. The open range, one reformer scoffed, "impedes business" by slowing rail traffic.[27]

The planter class did not entirely close ranks on the fencing question. As with other matters bearing on social relations in the postwar South, some clung to the traditional ways. Representatives from many nonplantation counties, particularly in the cattle-raising Wiregrass region, also balked. But advocates mustered sufficient strength to see local-option legislation through, and "An Act Relating to Fences and Stock and for the Protection of Crops" won approval in 1872. It provided for a county-wide election when fifty freeholders submitted a petition to the county ordinary. All eligible voters, whether they owned property or not, were entitled to cast ballots, and if a majority favored the initiative, the law, which forced farmers to enclose their livestock and deemed land boundaries legal fences for crops, would take effect within six months.[28]

Traditionalist planters were not alone in opposing the new fence, or stock, law in the Black Belt. Small landholders and landless whites, along with the freedmen, properly saw the measure as a threat to their ownership of livestock, and in some counties

succeeded in defeating, or at least postponing, implementation.
As an indication of their growing power in the area, however,
promoters of the law achieved notable results in relatively short
order. By the early 1880s much of the central Plantation Belt had
the statute in operation, and it was being pressed vigorously in the
southwestern section of the state.[29] While sharing with traditional
planters the desire to keep the South "a cotton country," these
reformers inspired a significant metamorphosis in the character of
their class as a whole. For in accepting abolition and searching for
new means of labor control, they enabled the landowning elite to
withstand the demise of slavery and reassert their authority in
the realm of production. In so doing, they contributed to a larger
process through which the planters transformed themselves into
a type of agrarian bourgeoisie and market relations in agriculture
took hold.[30]

II

The fencing question elicited only scattered attention in the
Upcountry for some years after the enactment of local-option
legislation. With relatively few blacks, with cotton culture just
beginning to expand, and with political alignments being re-
fashioned in the area, the reform minded still lacked the economic
and political muscle to mount an assault on customary property
rights. Not until the late 1870s and early 1880s, when the threshold
of the new order had been crossed and the Independents went
into eclipse, was a campaign launched.[31] Spurred in part by the
deliberations of the State Agricultural Society, Upcountry landlords and merchants assumed the mantle of reform, hoping to
consolidate their control over the region's economy. Through
county newspapers, farmers' clubs, and associations linked to town
and commercial interests, they made the stock law a subject of
public discussion and, increasingly, acrimonious debate. Following the course charted by the General Assembly, they also provoked heated electoral contests.[32]

Upcountry supporters of the stock law trumpeted the refrains
of their counterparts in the Plantation Belt. "There is considerable interest manifested over the effort now being made in some
sections of the South, to abolish the old, unjust laws whereby each
farmer is compelled to fence his fields; and compel instead, the
owners of stock to confine them," Jackson County's Jefferson

Forest News reported in 1880, adding that "wherever intelligence becomes widely disseminated, the injustice and folly of the present law is recognized." Pointing to the high cost and strenuous labor involved in fencing, the paper believed it "sad evidence of old fogyism, general ignorance, and backwardness of agriculture . . . that such a law as that now in force can exist." Other proponents similarly styled the stock law a means of conservation and a requisite for agricultural "progress." They felt it "absolutely necessary . . . to have such a law . . . from the fact that timber is becoming scarce" and the country overrun "with useless, scrubby stock." Sound reason demanded fencing reform, they maintained, "for we have found that it takes less labor and less expense to fence our stock than it does our crops. . . ." Insisting that the "law would greatly improve both stock and land," they proclaimed that "we must learn to give way to the fittest, for by so doing we will keep prospering."[33]

European agricultural reformers said the same in support of enclosures and the abolition of common rights to forage, woodlands, and waste; in America the arguments melded comfortably with the dominant bourgeois currents of the late nineteenth century. But such logic failed to win much acceptance among either the peasantries of Europe or the farming population of Georgia's Upcountry.[34] However much stock-law promoters claimed to speak for the interests of Southern agriculturalists in general, their effusions on the benefits of "progress" fell on many deaf, if not hostile, ears. One Paulding County advocate admitted this when he moaned that "for some reason most men will not take the time to study the advantages in many new, important, and advantageous ideas."[35] Those who took the time to study the matter often found the "new, important ideas" less than "advantageous." They ridiculed the alleged timber shortage as fabrication, denied that it was more costly to fence crops than stock, and even questioned the desirability of improved animal husbandry. A Bartow County cultivator said that there was "a great deal of timber . . . on land which can be used for nothing else," while a Carroll County farmer exclaimed that he and others "would be deprived of . . . thousands of acres of land that give our stock pasture . . . if the fence law was passed." Gwinnett County's T. Ramsden, challenging the notion "that it is cheaper to fence in stock than crops," charged that in states like South

Carolina, which had the law in effect, "very few tenants, small landowners, and 'poor' people generally own milch cows and hogs," and that "pasturing runs down the land much faster than cropping." Another stock-law opponent felt that raising better breeds would quickly place livestock beyond the financial reach of the less well-to-do.[36]

The fencing debate, as these spokesmen made plain, reflected more than a mere quarrel over the merits of agricultural reform. Opponents of the stock law did not reject farm improvement *per se;* rather, they branded the statute a direct attack on the rights and economic welfare of small producers. "[T]he law would benefit the extensive landowners," a disgruntled Gwinnett countian wrote, and as one of his neighbors warned, it "would be the greatest curse to the poor laboring men that ever befell them."[37] Petty proprietors often had little besides cropland, they argued, for "it requires perhaps all of [their] land to make a support for . . . [their] family," and many whose farms included unimproved acreage "have not a drop of water on it." "What will they do for water for their stock?" they asked. T. Ramsden suggested that these farmers might be forced to sell out: "A man owning 65 acres in a stock law county rented a three-horse crop in this county . . . because he had not enough land to tend and pasture both." The measure threatened to divest yeomen free-holders of the means of production and subsistence and, therefore, undermine their "independence." "The stock law will divide the people . . . into classes similar to the patricians and plebeians of ancient Rome," a man who farmed 125 acres in Carroll County grimly predicted, while James W. Andrews of Gwinnett County concluded that "it would be proof of insanity for a poor man that don't own as much as 100 acres of land to vote for [the stock law]."[38]

Tenants and laborers seemed even clearer losers should fencing reform be effected. As a Jackson County correspondent reported, "We have yet to find a poor man of much intelligence who advocates 'no fence'* while it is justly regarded by tenants, or non-landowners, as a measure calculated seriously to injure their

---

* The term "no fence" also refers to the stock law, reflecting the wording in the 1872 local-option statute.

rights and privileges." Access to forage enabled landless whites and blacks to raise work animals and other livestock of their own. With a horse or mule, a cow and some hogs, a tenant could strike a better contract and meet part of his family's basic needs. The stock law, then, spelled nothing but trouble. In the opinion of one Carroll County inhabitant, "no fence . . . is ultimately going to be the ruin of the people and especially the poor people that have no where to keep their stock [and] . . . are entirely dependent on the landowners for pasture." He was not alone in forecasting that if the new statute became operative, "not one man out of ten will let them have pasture room free of rent," and in all likelihood landlords would "charge them more than double what their milk and cow is worth." Few laborers could absorb the expense and they soon would be dispossessed.[39]

Stock-law advocates readily conceded that the issue divided Upcountry Georgians along class lines, but argued that the split stemmed from misapprehensions. "Three classes" oppose fencing reform, a Gwinnett County proponent complained: blacks; tenants and croppers who "from some conjectured up fallacy of a reason will vote with Africa"; and "men that have land" yet "were born under a fence [and] can't rise above their raising no matter how things and circumstances have changed." Scoffing at the idea that "the stock law would benefit the rich and oppress the poor," they insisted that the statute required landowners to provide pasture, that only minimal fees would be charged for its use, and, indeed, that tenants would be the beneficiaries.[40] Jackson County's "Progress," convinced that what was good for landlords was good for laborers, found it difficult to believe that poor whites and blacks risked victimization. "The income of tenants and the wages of hirelings will be regulated by the profits of the land owners," wrote this devotee of liberal economics.[41]

Although an occasional tenant voiced agreement, even to the point of suggesting that fencing reform would extend landowner-ship,[42] most had nothing but contempt for such reasoning. "It is said there never was anything that brought more relief to the tenant and laborer than the stock law," one noted sarcastically. "We agree with him there, as they are relieved of the privileges our fathers established. They will be relieved of the care and use of the cow, the hog, and . . . all the necessities, only as they are furnished by the landholders." Carroll County's John Stogner put in historical perspective what he, too, saw as a ploy:

We were told in 1859 [sic] that secession was the greatest thing the South could do, so it was to lead her into destruction. It was a rich man's war and a poor man's fight, so will the stock law be a benefit to a few landlords who have plenty of water on their land, while nine-tenths of the people will be in a deplorable condition.

"God makes the grass the mountains crown and corn in the valley grow," he concluded, "so let's not try to deprive our poor neighbors from receiving his blessing. . . ."[43]

Stogner's use of religious injunction as a counterpoint to political deception was not simply a polemical device. It bespoke a significant line of controversy running through the fencing debate. For if adversaries crossed swords over what appeared to be purely economic concerns, they imbued the concerns with deeper cultural and ideological meaning. What underlay contention over the material consequences of the stock law were considerably different, and increasingly antagonistic, ideas about social relations and property rights—ideas that would infuse the conflicts of the 1890s.

Thus, after parading the inconveniences he attributed to the traditional system of grazing, a contributor to the Jefferson *Forest News* set forth a maxim eagerly embraced by the supporters of reform: "The land outside a farm is as much the property of the farmer as that he may cultivate, and truly in essential justice no stock of others has any right thereon without express permission." Other stock-law proponents similarly lectured that "a farmer's corn is just as much his property as his timber, and as his neighbor is prohibited from entering on the land and cutting down his trees, so he should be required to prevent his stock straying to devour and trample down the corn." These spokesmen found the open range a manifestation of "custom" rather than "law." They acknowledged that "when the land belonged to the government it was right for all to pasture" it, but once "the government transferred those lands to different individuals" no one had the "right to trespass on another man's land." "Before a man buys a horse, cow, or hog," a Jackson County advocate prescribed, "he should have something to feed them on."[44]

Regarding timeworn grazing practices as a custom dignified by little more than peculiar circumstances and hardheadedness, supporters of the stock law elevated absolute property to a moral, if not a natural, right. One contemptuously dismissed common foraging as a "privilege" or "favor" bordering upon theft: "My neighbor has as much right to pasture my enclosed land as he has my unenclosed, as his stock . . . robs it of its vegetable matter . . . making it poorer every day." J. M. Green of Carroll County held that the "idea of fencing a man's possessions against a neighbor's stock is a creation of local statute, and contrary to natural rights, nature, and common sense," adding flatly that the "border of a man's possessions is the supposed wall that protects them. . ." Rejecting any obligation to "feed another man's stock," the reformers bluntly proclaimed that "what is mine I have a right to do as I please with and no man has a right to graze my land whether enclosed or not."[45] Property, in short, was absolute in the individual, its ownership mediated solely by the market.

Stock-law men may have considered these arguments to be self-evident; others did not. As a Paulding County reformer grudgingly observed, "It is true that it is unlawful for the stock of one man to trespass on the domain of another, still the privilege has been in vogue so long . . . that to most men it would seem a species of tyranny to suddenly enforce the restraints of law." Indeed, opponents of "no fence" reserved their deepest indignation for the legal and moral side of the question. Unfurling the banner of "equal rights, equal liberty, and equal privileges," of "equal rights to all and special privileges to none," they elaborated a vision of the cooperative commonwealth and defended the claims of the community of producers.[46]

Stock-law opponents viewed local custom, not as an aberration, but as an expression of natural right. "The woods . . . were put here by our Creator for a benefit to his people," Carroll County's W. D. Lovvorn declared, "and I don't think it right to deprive a large majority to please a minority." Abner Nixon, another Carroll County farmer, also invoked higher authority in defense of traditional grazing practices: "The citizens of this county have and always have had the legal, moral, and Bible right to let their stock . . . run at large. We all knew this when we purchased our lands."[47] Echoing these sentiments, spokesmen from Gwinnett and Jackson counties argued that "a man has . . . a legal right derived from custom to the range," and reckoned that "our present system is . . . so old that it would seem cruel to attempt an innovation upon it. From long usage our people have become accustomed to it, and any change or abridgement of it will unquestionably work serious injury to a large number of our citizens."[48]

The force of custom evolved from its connection with an array of social relations and cultural norms that the open range epitomized in a particularly dramatic way. Common grazing was more than an expedient of frontier life: long before the 1880s the frontier passed well beyond the Georgia Upcountry. Common grazing embodied distinct ideas about labor, community, independence, and the role of the state—about commonwealth. A Jackson County correspondent, therefore, could say that advocates of the stock law were "men who never split but few, if any, rails" and that "I don't call a man a farmer until he does keep his fields fenced, and well fenced at that." Such a distinction, based upon the performance of manual labor, served as a key element of nineteenth-century producer ideology, and its meaning was deepened by a cooperative principle that challenged the tenets of bourgeois individualism and property, that challenged the hegemony of the marketplace. "L.F.L." made that clear in tersely expressing what he saw as the abiding logic of the open range: "While my cow is on my neighbor's land eating grass, his is on mine, that makes it all right."[49]

Looking to the state government as the protector of the public good, these rural folk had no doubt that common grazing rights received more than local sanction. A Carroll County yeoman farmer, wishing to "controvert [the] proposition [that] 'What is mine I have a right to do as I please with', " explained the fundamental principles. "No man can deny that all the land of this country was once common property, belonged to all the people of Georgia in common as public domain," he confidently stated; "all once had a perfect right to graze it in common." "How or when did any of them loose [sic] that right?" he asked rhetorically, finding less than persuasive the argument "that they lost it in that game of chance called a lottery, when the drawee became the owner . . . to do as he pleased with." "[T]he fence law was in force at that time and each drawee, if he raises crops on his land, was required to enclose it," the farmer reminded his audience. He believed this to be unmistakable proof "it was understood that all citizens of this country still retained the rights to let their stock run at large on all lands not so enclosed." And, in his eyes, "as citizens of this grand old commonwealth . . . they still . . . have that RIGHT."[50]

One landlord and stock-law supporter fitfully ascribed to such attitudes "the spirit of communism fully displayed."[51] Yet, the law's opponents hardly favored the abolition of private property. Like small producers elsewhere in the South and throughout the United States, they deemed property ownership the basis of freedom and independence and assailed fencing reform precisely because it threatened expropriation. The fiery L. J. Jones knew what he was about when he urged "every man [to] come and vote for fence if he wishes to be a free man."[52] From the vantage point of the late twentieth century this defense of both private property and common rights may appear peculiar if not contradictory; in the Georgia Upcountry of the late nineteenth century it was neither. Instead, it reflected a complex world view, rooted in persisting strains of preindustrial republicanism, that linked the individual and the collective through the medium of *productive* labor and *productive* property. The freedom to which Jones and others adhered was not merely that founded upon ownership of one's person and exchange in the marketplace, but that founded on control over productive resources, labor time, and subsistence which, in turn, could be realized only through membership in the commonwealth of producers.[53] The stock-law controversy set the moral economy of those producers against the economy of the free market—a conflict that would give Populism its grass-roots vitality.[54]

III

The fencing issue ultimately came down to being a matter of politics and political power, and elections brought no less determined a response than did the debate ringing through the newspapers. During the weeks preceding an election heated discussion spilled into public forums, political gatherings, and casual social meetings. Jackson countians assembled at the county seat of Jefferson one Saturday to hear "Mr. John Ross . . . [and] Capt. A. C. Thompson . . . give speech[es] on the stock law question . . .

one for and the other against the fence." In Carroll County the grand jury shifted attention from the dockets in the fall of 1881 to deliberate on the issue.[55] Candidates for the state legislature in Cherokee County felt compelled to stake out a position during the course of the campaign.[56] The Gwinnett *Herald* believed the "fence law . . . of much more importance to the people of this county than [who] . . . shall be nominated for Governor." And, apparently, that opinion was shared widely. "The stock law is being fiercely discussed by the farmers," one Upcountry paper reported, while another noted that "the feeling is bitter between the two sides and the excitement is up to a white heat."[57]

Considering that the local-option statute of 1872 required only thirty days' notice before polling and that contests normally occurred in July before crops were "laid by," election day brought impressive turnouts. Beginning in the early 1880s, Upcountry Georgians, white and black, marched to the ballot box in numbers approaching 80 percent of those eligible to vote. No other local issue, including prohibition, elicited such a response; it nearly matched that for national elections, which had the advantage of greater publicity and regular, post-harvest scheduling. In Jackson County the vote in an 1881 stock-law election in fact exceeded the vote in a congressional race the preceding year when the controversial Independent Emory Speer had his hat in the ring.[58] Thus, the Atlanta *Constitution* observed that the "contests in the counties over fence and no fence have been as exciting as contests usually are in which the pockets and muscle of the voter is [sic] concerned," and a local paper could marvel that an election drew "perhaps one of the largest crowds ever seen."[59]

The voting returns gave stock-law advocates no cause to rejoice and indicated the extent of popular resistance. In county after county, the law met resounding defeat, the margins being three or four to one. Within counties, however, some militia districts showed reform more favor. These districts were not distinguished clearly by their racial composition or land-tenure arrangements: the racial mix changed relatively little from district to district, and blacks generally threw their weight against the law; the proportion of landholders varied throughout the counties in no readily discernible pattern.[60] Rather, the districts lending the stock law its substantial support tended to have the closest links to market centers, the highest real-estate assessments and per capita wealth, and the greatest concentrations of land held by large land-owners. It was here that merchants, big landlords, and other commercial interests wielded most influence and authority. Poorer, rural districts having more evenly distributed landholdings, on the other hand, rejected the law overwhelmingly and, at times, with virtual unanimity. Here, small farmers had their best cultural foothold.[61]

When, for example, Carroll County voters went to the polls in 1882, they defeated fencing reform by 1,616 to 620. Yet two districts turned majorities for it: the Tenth District, which had the largest town of Carrollton, and the Second District, which contained the town of Villa Rica. Indeed, over half the county-wide votes for the stock law came from these two districts alone. The law also obtained some backing in the town and village districts of Temple, Bowdon, Roopville, and Whitesburg. Together these six districts provided the stock law with 80 percent of its votes. The eight remaining rural districts collectively spurned the statute by over six to one, with some delivering more than 90 percent of their votes to the retention of common grazing rights. Another election several months later brought a larger turnout but much the same results.[62]

The fencing contest had similar dimensions in Jackson County. First casting ballots in 1881, voters defeated the law by the wide margin of 1,379 to 478. Unlike Carroll County, not one of the districts registered majorities in favor of reform, but it is telling that over 60 percent of the votes received by the stock law came from the three districts in which the towns of Jefferson, Harmony Grove, and Pendergrass were located. When the town and village districts of Wilson and House are added, the total climbs to over 80 percent. Excepting the wealthiest, the rural districts rendered only 12 percent of their votes to support the statute, and in the two districts previously strongholds of Independentism, the law failed to win even 10 percent approval. Symbolizing larger class and cultural divisions, the countryside rallied against the towns.[63]

Electoral returns from other Upcountry counties gave further evidence of this configuration,[64] though disappointed stock-law advocates did not need statistics to comprehend the parameters of their failure. Finding it "simply . . . a question of Labor vs Capital," the Floyd County landlord John H. Dent declared that "agrarianism rules[,] the Niggers and white trash voting against

No Fence." Others reached the same conclusion with somewhat less passion and contempt. "Nonlandholders" in general and the "colored element" in particular stood "solid against the law," they insisted.[65] Discouragement, however, only steeled the reformers' determination, for the initial elections did not settle the issue. The statute of 1872 made additional contests possible, and proponents moved on several fronts to reverse their fortunes. They were, in the words of the Jackson *Herald,* "on track again and thoroughly in earnest."[66]

This time stock-law supporters launched a more organized drive. Using the machinery of the Democratic party, which they had come to dominate, and especially the vehicles of local agricultural clubs, they waged a campaign throughout the counties. One such club in Bartow County set the agitation of fencing reform as its first task when it formed during the early 1880s. The Norcross Agricultural Club of Gwinnett County, which had a longer history, resolved "to contribute articles on the advantages of the stock law" to the county newspaper, as did similar bodies elsewhere. Associations were founded, moreover, with the sole purpose of pressing for a popular mandate. One of these, the Apple Valley Stock Law Club of Jackson County, consisting primarily of prominent Democrats, county officials, merchants, and substantial farmers, met in the fall of 1885 and proceeded "to canvass the District in the interest of the" law.[67]

Electoral fraud and coercion, so familar to postbellum Southern politics, also came into play. Neither camp could claim innocence, to be sure. As one paper put it, there was "some tail pulling on both sides."[68] But opponents of the stock law issued most of the complaints, citing cases of bribery, threats, ballot-box stuffing, and the tossing out of votes. Manipulating the choices on tickets in an effort to confuse the electorate proved a common method of deception. The local-option statute prescribed that voters favor either "Fence" or "No Fence," the latter meaning the stock law—a choice hardly designed to foster clarity in any event. Returns sent in by the districts, though, often included a considerable array cf ballots. One Carroll County district reported: "For Stock Law 73," "For Fence 68," "Fence 30," "A Fence 2," and "The Fence 2." On another occasion several districts sent in almost 200 ballots marked "more fence and better fence." In each instance, the local official threw out a sizable number to the advantage of the stock-law forces.[69] Recognizing the impact of the black vote, reformers not infrequently "promised to pay [their taxes] if they would vote for no fence," while in one case promoters, attempting "to please the negroes," chartered them an excursion train to Atlanta—on the day of an election.[70]

These tactics brought only limited rewards. Despite drawing a greater percentage of the vote in county-wide elections as the 1880s progressed, the stock law continued to meet defeat as initial alignments generally persisted. Carroll County deliberated five separate times between 1882 and 1890. Each time the measure was rejected, each time support for reform came primarily from the town districts, and each time the margin of difference narrowed. In 1882, 73 percent of the voters opposed the law; three years later the figure dropped to 67 percent, and by 1890 it declined to 61 percent. It was a trend that held some promise for the elite, but one that certainly did not put victory close at hand.[71]

Indeed, frustrated stock-law advocates saw in these results the logic, as one said, of "pauper" democracy. As early as 1875, the state commissioner of agriculture, a leading fighter for reform, reasoned that "the present Act, which leaves the question of 'fencing stock' or 'fencing crops' to the *voters* of several counties, is unjust, since it allows non-freeholders, who generally constitute a majority of voters in every county, to decide a question of policy in which they have no direct interest." Hence, he explained that "the most equitable way of disposing of the question . . . is by legislative enactment leaving the decision to the *freeholders* of each county." A contributor to the *Dixie Farmer,* an agricultural journal, also believed that "in elections under the law . . . the voting should be restricted to freeholders, as they are the class upon whom the entire expense of keeping up fencing devol'es, and whose rights alone are involved in the question."[72]

Upcountry reformers soon joined the chorus. "I could not find where a man has any right to vote in matters where he has no interest," a correspondent to the Jackson *Herald* announced in 1885, adding that "the man who has no fence hasn't any interest in the matter and has no right to vote." A like-minded resident of Carroll County, acknowledging the opposition of "the non-landholders and the laboring class," bluntly stated, "None should be allowed to vote on this question except landholders." "[I]f the poor are going to hold this country back and be an impossible lump in the tube of progress," these men sneered, "build a poor-house like a palace . . . and send them there and feed them on cake and wine and let the country go on."[73]

Other members of the elite viewed the conflict as a product of a more pervasive dilemma. Arguing that the stock law "would be our best plan," but that the votes of "two thirds of our population [who] own no land but own on an average of one cow and two or three pigs" defeated it, John Dent drew a larger lesson. "Such show that capitalists and taxpayers of the country are at the mercy of a class of men whose only capital are their votes," he exclaimed. "Such is the result of the Constitution and laws of this country, and ever will be so long as the pauper class are allowed a vote, and nothing but a restriction on the voters qualifications will ever protect capital from such injustice and wrongs. . . ." A Carroll County advocate also attributed the nation's problems to the fact that "the negroes and one fourth of the whites have been allowed the privilege of going to the ballot box," and hoped he would "see the day, when none will be allowed to vote, who do not own so much property. . . ."[74] Although no movement to disfranchise the propertyless succeeded in this case, these sentiments help explain the antidemocratic tide that swept not only the South but the entire United States after Reconstruction.[75]

For the mass of Upcountry yeomen, tenants, and laborers, these blasts against democratic rights confirmed fears that the stock law threatened more than their economic welfare. One compared the law's promoters "to the Breckinridge ring of Democrats that seceded from the Democratic convention at Charleston" and warned that unless "every man has the right to be his own judge about casting his vote," the "common farmer" would be led into the same "trouble as they were in 1860." The "monied men" wished to lord it over the polity, another cried as he called upon "the poor people to open their eyes and come forward and stand up for their rights . . . and show [them] that they cannot have things their own way all the time." At stake was not merely economic independence, but the very survival of the democratic commonwealth of producers.[76]

As the fencing conflict wore on, the weight of numbers proved an increasingly poor match for the weight of superior resources. Having the support of landlords, merchants, and business interests throughout the state, holding sway in the local Democratic party, and enlisting the aid of county newspaper editors and office-holders, stock-law advocates marshaled considerable political clout. And success eventually came their way when they availed themselves of an amendment to the 1872 local-option statute that permitted implementation at the district level. Through identical procedures of petition and election, one district alone within a county could enact the measure, and beginning in the mid-1880s the districts became the centers of contention.[77] Not surprisingly, towns and wealthier districts stepped out front, but not without concerted effort. Other rural districts were more troublesome, and adversaries locked horns in a struggle that could engender lawsuits and violence.

Thus, in 1884 fifty-three residents of Carroll County's Carrollton district signed a petition requesting a stock-law election. Although they failed to achieve victory, two years later the town council passed an ordinance making it "unlawful for any cow, steer, bull, calf, heifer, pig, sheep [etc.] to run at large within corporate limits." The next year, by 353 to 251, voters extended the law's jurisdiction over the surrounding countryside.[78] The Villa Rica district had its first election in the fall of 1885. While returns had the stock law narrowly defeated, supporters charged irregularities and appealed to the county ordinary for a ruling. He found in the reformers' favor and awarded them the contest. By the end of 1887, Villa Rica and Carrollton were joined by the town and village districts of Temple, Roopville, Whitsburg, and Bowdon.[79]

The rural districts of Carroll County offered greater resistance. Voters in Fairplay rejected the stock law in 1885 by a margin of 85 to 56, although the results were overturned after a legal battle. So, too, in the Kansas district when local officials reversed an electoral majority against the law in 1887. The relatively well-to-do County Line district passed the measure that same year, but in poorer Cross Plains, Shiloh, and Lowell the stock law met defeat.[80] Gradually, however, even these areas of traditionally adamant opposition came into line: Shiloh approved the law in 1889, Cross Plains did so when it voted for a second time several months later, and the next year Flint Corner and Smithfield followed, the latter only after an initially disputed election. By 1891 all except the Lowell and New Mexico districts had abandoned the open range.[81]

The story was much the same throughout the Upcountry. After Jackson County voters turned down the stock law in county-wide elections of 1881 and 1883, reform agitation looked to the districts. Complaining that he "can't keep stock off the courthouse grounds," and that "the county can't afford to make a public pasture of her property in this way," the sheriff, and others of similar disposition, sought to "improve" at least their own locales. By virtue of a town ordinance or district balloting, Jefferson and Harmony Grove, along with three of the wealthier rural districts, put some form of the stock law into effect between 1885 and 1887.[82] Elsewhere in Jackson County recalcitrance was the order of the day; fencing reform made no inroads. It took a special legislative act, later ruled unconstitutional, to bring the entire county to heel by the end of the decade.[83] The years between 1885 and 1890 also saw districts in Paulding, Cherokee, Floyd, Forsyth, Gwinnett, Franklin, Hall, Milton, Douglas, Banks, and Heard counties accept the statute. Only in three Upcountry counties did the open range prevail throughout.[84]

That contested elections and legal battles commonly accompanied the stock law's district-level triumphs suggests that reform was not simply a product of voters' changing heart. Sympathetic officials overturned adverse results in every county from which direct evidence is available. In some instances returns shifted so dramatically from one election to another that opponents had little doubt that foul play was afoot. The Sugar Hill district in Gwinnett County, for example, defeated the law on two occasions by "good majorities," but a third contest brought it a narrow victory, prompting "great dissatisfaction . . . [on] the ground . . . that the election is illegally conducted and is therefore void."[85] When ballot-box tampering or official appeal proved ineffective, proponents of reform frequently petitioned the county to alter district boundaries in an effort to eliminate pockets of staunch resistance or attach pockets of strong support. In 1887 a group of Cherokee countians asked for such a change in "the district lines between Bells and Sixes district . . . [so that] about 40 voters will be cut off of Bells and into Sixes." "Although the petition did not state it," the local paper surmised "that the change is desired so that Sixes district may be able to adopt 'no fence.' " County officers acceded to the request, and the Sixes district did enact the stock law by a small margin within six months.[86]

Advocates of fencing reform had other advantages. Public noti-
fication of impending elections rested in the hands of county
officials and newspaper editors who recognized that large turnouts
spelled defeat. It was no accident, then, that as the 1880s wore
on the papers gave district elections little attention and sometimes failed to print the returns. As a result, the stock law's road
to victory was often paved by declining voter participation. In
Gwinnett County the number of ballots cast dropped by almost
60 percent between 1885 and 1891; in Carroll County it dropped
by almost 65 percent during the same period. The Gwinnett
Herald could then note in 1890 that a contest in the Harbins
district "passed off quietly" with the law winning by four votes.[87]
Further, as more and more districts within a county adopted the
law, it became increasingly difficult for holdouts, as inhabitants
would be liable for damages should their livestock cross district
lines and trespass in a stock-law district. One county newspaper,
admitting that some "districts have good ranges and it would . . .
suit the people better to let fences remain as they are," argued
that "as the stock must be kept out of the no fence districts, it is
quite probable that each of these districts will be forced to adopt
the stock law."[88]

The "wearing thin" of popular resistance reflected a larger and
more chronic problem as well. Unlike their reform-minded counterparts, stock-law opponents never developed an organizational
structure to mobilize their ranks and inspire confidence in their
numerical strength. The problem had its origins less in a tradition
of rugged individualism than in the social relations of Upcountry
farming settlements, which fostered collective endeavor among
neighboring families while nurturing a profound suspicion of
outsiders. Although promoting a cooperative ethos, these relations
circumscribed the formation of extracommunity ties and sustained
political activity. Yeomen and tenants could rise to defend customary rights but make no move toward organizing their forces.
Consequently, they found themselves highly vulnerable to fraud
and intimidation; their resistance slowly collapsed when confronted by the considerable power of their foes. And it was a
dilemma that would return to haunt them.

Yet, if by the early 1890s a substantial number of districts in
most Upcountry counties had formally adopted the stock law,
enforcement could be another matter. A veritable "war" erupted

in some areas after ratification as embittered farmers ripped down
newly constructed fences or simply ignored the statute, threatening summary punishment for anyone seeking to implement it.
The Carroll *Free Press* charged that "outlaws" lurked in "the
dead of the night when all gentlemen were asleep," breaking
fences and gates "to smash." "[T]he work of these rascals has been
kept up," the paper fretted, "until they have torn up five gates and
torn down 1200 panels of fence. . . ." Here and in sections of
other Upcountry counties, "the fence men [were] doing their best
to evade the law and warning that if any man takes up their stock,
they will turn their little guns on him."[89] The tide of social change
swept forcefully, but the embers of resistance still burned.

IV

For those who study peasant societies, the stock-law struggle
must strike a familiar rhythm: an expanding market economy and
market relations; an attack on traditional rights; popular indignation emboldened by customary notions of justice, order, and
obligation; an elite offensive; bitter skirmishes; resorts to threats,
manipulation, and coercion; failure of the rural masses to organize
effectively; and finally the erosion of popular resistance. Peasantries waged the battle through riots and risings, violent acts of
retaliation, land occupations, or, in rare cases, their votes.[90]
Georgia dirt farmers waged it at the ballot box, although they
drew upon traditional means of exacting popular retribution. If
nothing else, the stock-law controversy should suggest that Southern farmers, white and black, shared aspirations and sensibilities
with rural peoples in other parts of the world.

But there is more. Most episodes of rural unrest end rather
abruptly, bringing marginal concessions or categorical defeat.
Their dimensions are relatively narrow and their repercussions
limited, though they often are triggered by wider political events
and crises. Yet, there are moments when these episodes become
part of a larger tide, when traditional ideologies and cultural
forms serve to rally popular support and redirect collective behavior, when from the materials of scattered discontent a movement emerges. So it has been in nineteenth- and twentieth-century
Europe, Asia, and Latin America.[91] So it was in the nineteenth-

century South. Had the stock-law struggle occurred in isolation, it would have remained defensive, however rich in the language of class conflict its rhetoric. But the emergence of the People's party promised to transform defensiveness into a new and progressive force: by capturing the tenor of rural disaffection, linking the experiences of small producers throughout the South, and harnessing those experiences to a platform of mass political action and cooperative economic endeavor.

The full story of that transformation, with its attendant contradictions and ultimate failure, cannot be told here. Some of its aspects bear on the larger meaning of Populism, however, and deserve brief mention. For while the stock law did not become a major Populist issue,[92] there are good reasons, other than chronological proximity, to associate the two. First, local issues such as the stock law drove a wedge into chapters of the Southern Farmers' Alliance, which initially embraced a membership of large and small landowners as well as tenants—a wedge splitting not only richer and poorer farmers, but those opposing and those supporting a third-party effort. When, for instance, a Carroll County Allianceman called for implementing "the stock law all over the county" and wedded it "to the principles of the Farmers' Alliance," he provoked dissension in the order. A fellow member, in fact, blamed divisions in the ranks on such concerns as whether "somebody is too strong a stock law man." A similarly disgruntled Allianceman could thunder that the organization had fallen under the influence of men who "are not the working people . . . who [do not] toil with their hands . . . [who] are really nothing more nor less than Jay Goulds and Vanderbilts on a smaller scale," much to the detriment of the "real farmers of the country . . . [who] are tenants and men who own small farms . . . [with] mortgages over them."[93] He and other individuals actively opposing fencing reform tended to align with the Populists. Carroll County's W. D. Lovvorn, who penned stinging protests against the stock law during the 1880s, thus became a local Populist leader in the 1890s. Vocal supporters of fencing reform, on the other hand, tended to remain within the Democratic party. Such a list of stock-law advocates in Carroll County includes numbers of prominent Democrats.[94]

Election returns offer even more compelling evidence of the

connection between the conflicts of the 1880s and those of the 1890s. Upcountry Democrats, like stock-law proponents, had their base in the town districts. The Populists, like stock-law opponents, had their strength in the countryside and, particularly, in the poorer rural districts. In Jackson County only the three largest town districts maintained staunch Democratic allegiance: the Populists received about 30 percent of the votes there. But in the countryside, Populism reigned triumphant, amassing about 70 percent of the votes.[95] In Carroll County, Populists mustered around 40 percent of the votes in districts containing the towns of Carrollton, Villa Rica, Roopville, Bowdon, and Whitesburg, yet won over 70 percent of the votes in the rural districts of Turkey Creek, Kansas, New Mexico, Smithfield, Flint Corner, Lowell, and Shiloh, among the poorest in the county and having hoisted the stiffest resistance to the stock law.[96] Other Upcountry counties displayed similar patterns.[97]

Perhaps most important, the stock-law struggle illuminated an experience and ideology that lay at the heart of the People's party appeal and program, making more comprehensible the movement's ostensibly "forward and backward looking" features. When Southern Populists assailed the "money kings," the "speculative parasites," and the "capitalists," who "grow richer and richer . . . at the expense of those who produce," and linked the third-party cause to "liberty and independence, which can only be realized by giving equal rights to all and special privileges to none," they did not advance a version of political pluralism. They lent wider expression to a moral economy founded on social relations quite at odds with those becoming dominant in post–Civil War America. Attributing the concentration of wealth and power to the corruption of the political process, Populists did not wish to unfetter the "invisible hand" of the marketplace. They wished to protect a "liberty tree" rooted in petty ownership of productive resources. The People's party, they insisted, "is composed of the yeomanry of the country. The small landed proprietors, the working farmers, the intelligent artisans, the wage-earners, men who own homes and want a stable government."[98]

In its advocacy of the subtreasury system, the democratization of the money supply, and government ownership of the means of transportation and communication, Populism looked to building a producers' commonwealth through cooperative enterprise and public regulation of exchange. It was a vision informed by historical experience—by the structure and dynamic of the farm, the shop, and the local market; by notions of government as the repository of the public will and the defender of the public good—and tailored to the exigencies of an increasingly mass society. As one Carroll County cultivator could write, "Competition may be the life of trade, but it is death to the farmer." Not a proletarian movement, Populism spoke for men and women of "small means" who faced the specter of proletarianization, of "be[ing] forced to work at the pleasure of the money lords," of "be[coming] a nation of shylocks and serfs."[99] Although it would founder on internal weaknesses, political inexperience, and naked repression, this vision of cooperative commonwealth inspired a movement to the threshold of victory, a movement holding the potential of a humane and democratic alternative to the established road of American capitalism.

APPENDIX

TABLE 1 Militia Districts, the Stock Law, and Populism—Jackson County

	Stock Law[1] Districts	Anti-Stock Law[2] Districts
Per Capita Wealth	$1,081	$646
Percentage of White Population	74.7%	70.7%
Percentage of Landowners	49.3%	49.0%
Average Size of Landholding (acres)	169.1	159.4
Percentage of Land in Holdings of 500 or More Acres	24.7%	15.5%
Number of Holdings of 500 or More Acres	35	19
Number of Mercantile Firms	47	8
Percentage of Vote for Populists (six elections)	33%	70%

[1] Denotes districts most favorable to the stock law over several elections (over 40 percent of their votes for the law). Includes Jefferson, Harmony Grove, Wilson, Cunningham, and Harrisburg.

[2] Denotes districts most opposed to the stock law over several elections (under 20 percent of their votes for the law). Includes Clarksboro, Newtown, Chandlers, Santafe, and Randolph.

Source: Jackson County Tax Digest, 1890; Jackson *Herald*, July 8, 1881, September 14, 1883, October 14, 1892, November 11, 1892, January 6, 1893, October 12, 1894, November 9, 1894, January 4, 1895.

TABLE 2 Militia Districts, the Stock Law, and Populism—Carroll County

	Stock Law[1] Districts	Anti-Stock Law[2] Districts
Per Capita Wealth	$1,129	$617
Percentage of White Population	81.4%	96.0%
Percentage of Landowners	61.3%	60.3%
Average Size of Landholding (acres)	144.2	125.4
Percentage of Land in Holdings of 500 or More Acres	17.9%	11.6%
Number of Holdings of 500 or More Acres	26	10
Number of Mercantile Firms	57	2
Percentage of Vote for Populists (three elections)	42%	73%

[1] Denotes districts most favorable to the stock law over several elections (over 40 percent of their votes for the law). Includes Carrollton, Villa Rica, Temple, and Roopville.

[2] Denotes districts most opposed to the stock law over several districts (under 20 percent of their votes for the law). Includes Smithfield, Kansas, New Mexico, Lowell, Turkey Creek, Flint Corner, and Shiloh.

Source: Carroll County Tax Digest, 1890; Carroll County *Times*, January 11, 1882, September 9, 1882; Carroll *Free Press*, July 3, 1885, July 8, 1887, November 9, 1894, October 5, 1894, January 4, 1895.

NOTES

1. Lawrence Goodwyn, *Democratic Promise: The Populist Moment in America* (New York, 1976); Bruce Palmer, *"Man over Money": The Southern Populist Critique of American Capitalism* (Chapel Hill, 1980); Robert C. McMath, Jr., *Populist Vanguard: A History of the Southern Farmers' Alliance* (Chapel Hill, 1975).

These scholars have staked out new terrain in a long-standing debate over the meaning of Populism. Others are beginning to explore the movement's social bases through the use of quantitative techniques. Their findings, although presented in various forms, suggest that Populism drew its strength from rural areas with the deepest precapitalist traditions. For a review of the recent literature see James Turner, "Understanding the Populists," *Journal of American History*, 67 (1980), 354–83.

The Populist constituency was not wholly rural. Especially in the mountain West, the movement had substantial support among miners and timber workers. See James E. Wright, *The Politics of Populism: Dissent in Colorado* (New Haven, 1974); Thomas A. Clinch, *Urban Populism and Free Silver in Montana: A Narrative of Ideology in Political Action* (Missoula, Mont., 1970); David Montgomery, "On Goodwyn's Populists," *Marxist Perspectives*, 1 (1978), 166–73.

2. This line of argument runs through virtually all of the major treatments of Populism, whatever their particular assessments of Populist politics, beginning

with John D. Hicks, *The Populist Revolt: A History of the Farmers' Alliance and the People's Party* (Minneapolis, 1931).

3. C. Vann Woodward, *Origins of the New South, 1877–1913* (Baton Rouge, 1951), pp. 178–86; Roger Ransom and Richard Sutch, *One Kind of Freedom: The Economic Consequences of Emancipation* (Cambridge, 1977), pp. 104–05; Gavin Wright, *The Political Economy of the Cotton South: Households, Markets, and Wealth in the Nineteenth Century* (New York, 1978), pp. 158–80; Roger W. Shugg, *Origins of Class Struggle in Louisiana: A Social History of White Farmers and Laborers during Slavery and After, 1840–1875* (Baton Rouge, 1939), pp. 269–313; Michael Schwartz, *Radical Protest and Social Structure: The Southern Farmers' Alliance and Cotton Tenancy, 1880–1890* (New York, 1976), pp. 57–88; William Warren Rogers, *The One-Gallused Rebellion: Agrarianism in Alabama, 1865–1896* (Baton Rouge, 1970), pp. 222–24.

4. The role of property ownership as a buffer against radicalism has, for instance, been a central assumption informing most studies of social mobility in the nineteenth century. Even the major studies are too numerous to mention here, but one can begin with the pioneer, Stephan Thernstrom, *Poverty and Progress: Social Mobility in a Nineteenth Century City* (Cambridge, Mass., 1964).

5. Eric Foner, *Tom Paine and Revolutionary America* (New York, 1976); Bruce Laurie, *The Working People of Philadelphia, 1800–1850* (Philadelphia, 1980); Sean Wilentz, *Chants Democratic: New York City and the Rise of the American Working Class* (New York, forthcoming); and, of course, E. P. Thompson, *The Making of the English Working Class* (New York, 1963).

6. Eric Wolf, *Peasant Wars of the Twentieth Century* (New York, 1969); Tony Judt, "The Origins of Rural Socialism in Europe: Economic Change and the Provençal Peasantry, 1870–1914," *Social History*, 1 (1976), 45–65.

7. Manfred Hildermeier, "Agrarian Social Protest, Populism, and Economic Development: Some Problems and Results From Recent Studies," *Social History*, 4 (1979), 325; Hamza Alavi, "Peasants and Revolution," in Ralph Miliband and John Saville, eds., *The Socialist Register, 1965* (New York, 1965), pp. 241–77.

8. Carroll (County) *Free Press*, May 15, 1885.

9. Rupert P. Vance, *Human Geography of the South: A Study in Regional Resources and Human Adequacy* (Chapel Hill, 1932), pp. 146–47; Peter H. Wood, *Black Majority: Negroes in Colonial South Carolina from 1670 through the Stono Rebellion* (New York, 1974), pp. 29–30; Lewis C. Gray, *History of Agriculture in the Southern United States to 1860*, 2 vols. (Gloucester, Mass., 1958), II, pp. 836, 843.

10. Nashville and Chattanooga Railroad Company v. Peacock, 25 *Alabama Reports*, 229. Also see Vicksburg and Jackson Railroad Company v. Patton, 31 *Mississippi Reports*, 156; Macon and Western Railroad Company v. Lester, 30 *Georgia Reports*, 911. For state fencing statutes see Thomas R.R. Cobb, *A Digest of the Statute Laws of the State of Georgia* (Athens, 1851), pp. 18–19; David J. McCord, *The Statutes at Large of South Carolina* (Columbia, S.C., 1839), pp. 331–32; A. Hutchinson, *Code of Mississippi, 1798–1848* (Jackson,

1848), pp. 278–80; John J. Ormond, Arthur Bagby, and George Goldwaite, *Code of Alabama* (Montgomery, 1852), pp. 250–51; Williamson S. Oldham and George W. White, *A Digest of the General Statute Laws of the State of Texas* (Austin, 1859), pp. 217–18.

11. Forrest McDonald and Grady McWhiney, "The Antebellum Southern Herdsman: A Reinterpretation," *Journal of Southern History*, 41 (1975), 156–58; Jerome Blum, *The End of the Old Order in Rural Europe* (Princeton, 1978), pp. 123–25, 149–50; Marc Bloch, *French Rural History: An Essay on Its Basic Characteristics* (Berkeley, 1966), pp. 167–89, 205–13; J. L. Hammond and Barbara Hammond, *The Village Labourer, 1760–1832* (London, 1911), pp. 2–18.

12. For a more detailed discussion of Upcountry yeomen before and after the Civil War see Steven Hahn, "The Roots of Southern Populism: Yeomen Farmers and the Transformation of Georgia's Upper Piedmont, 1850–1890 (Ph.D. diss., Yale University, 1979), pp. 14–118, 189–283, and passim. Also see Steven Hahn, "The Yeomanry of the Non-Plantation South: Upper Piedmont Georgia, 1850–1860," in Robert C. McMath, Jr., and Vernon Burton, eds., *Class, Conflict, and Consensus: Antebellum Southern Community Studies* (Westport, Conn., forthcoming). Here, I shall use "Upcountry" and "Upper Piedmont" interchangeably.

13. Floyd C. Watkins and Charles H. Watkins, *Yesterday in the Hills* (Chicago, 1963), pp. 103–04; Reverend Lloyd C. Marlin, *A History of Cherokee County* (Atlanta, 1932), p. 83; Frank L. Owsley, *Plain Folk of the Old South* (Baton Rouge, 1949), pp. 104–17.

14. See, for example, Job Bowers Account Book, Hart County, 1832–1836, Georgia Department of Archives and History (hereafter cited as GDAH); Foster and King Mill Account Book, Cherokee County, 1857–1858, GDAH; Watkins and Watkins, *Yesterday in the Hills,* p. 59. Roughly 10 percent of free household heads in two Upcountry counties during the 1850s listed craft occupations.

15. Thomas Morris Store Ledger, Franklin County, 1847, GDAH; Fain Account Books, Floyd County, 1847–1852, GDAH; R. G. Dun and Company, Credit Reporting Ledgers of the Mercantile Agency, Georgia, V, 102–06, 110, 112, 115, Baker Library, Harvard University; Lewis E. Atherton, *The Southern Country Store, 1800–1860* (Baton Rouge, 1949), p. 49.

16. These social and economic patterns seem to have had parallels in parts of the rural North during the eighteenth and early nineteenth centuries. See Max Schumacher, *The Northern Farmer and His Markets during the Late Colonial Period* (New York, 1975); Clarence H. Danhof, *Change in Agriculture: The Northern United States, 1820–1870* (Cambridge, Mass., 1969), pp. 1–48; James A. Henretta, "Families and Farms: *Mentalité* in Preindustrial America," *William and Mary Quarterly*, 3rd series, 35 (1978), 3–32; Michael Merrill, "Cash Is Good to Eat: Self-Sufficiency and Exchange in the Rural Economy of the United States," *Radical History Review*, 7 (1977), 42–71; Christopher Clark, "Household Economy, Market Exchanges, and the Rise of Capitalism in the Connecticut Valley, 1800–1860," *Journal of Social History*, 13 (1979), 169–85; Robert E. Mutch, "Yeoman and Merchant in Preindustrial America: Massachusetts as a Case Study," *Societas*, 7 (1977), 279–98.

17. For the entire Upper Piedmont, per capita cotton production doubled between 1860 and 1890, while in some counties it more than quadrupled. Per capita corn production, on the other hand, dropped by as much as one-third during the same period. By 1890, the acreage planted in cotton considerably surpassed the acreage planted in corn. See *Eighth Census of the United States, 1860* (Washington, D.C., 1864), Agriculture, 22–29; *Tenth Census of the United States, 1880* (Washington, D.C., 1883), Report on the Productions of Agriculture, 183–84; *Eleventh Census of the United States, 1890* (Washington, D.C., 1892), Agriculture, 128–32, 202–04, 360–61, 393–94.

18. After a series of legislative skirmishes, Georgia landlords won superior lien rights for both rent and advances on the crops of their tenants in 1874. Factors and merchants could obtain first lien only on the crops of farm proprietors, although an 1875 law enabled landlords to transfer lien rights if they so chose. Since a majority of customers in the black belt were tenants or croppers (only 45 percent of the farm units were owner operated), this clearly restricted the operations of landless merchants and encouraged them to look to the Upcountry, where the majority of customers were proprietors (60 percent of the farm units were owner operated) and where the planter element was relatively weak. See Robert P. Brooks, *The Agrarian Revolution in Georgia, 1865–1912* (Madison, 1914), pp. 32–33; Enoch Banks, *The Economics of Land Tenure in Georgia* (New York, 1905), p. 47. Also see Woodward, *Origins of the New South*, pp. 180–81; Jonathan M. Wiener, *Social Origins of the New South: Alabama, 1860–1885* (Baton Rouge, 1978), pp. 77–102; Harold D. Woodman, "Post–Civil War Southern Agriculture and the Law," *Agricultural History*, 53 (1979), 327–29.

   In practice, of course, there was more variation, but the legal triumph of black-belt landlords doubtless contributed to the great influx of merchants into the Upcountry. Carroll County, for example, had only thirteen mercantile establishments in 1870; by 1880 it had forty-nine, and by 1885 it had seventy. See R. G. Dun and Company, *The Mercantile Agency Reference Books, 1870–1885* (New York, 1870–1885).

19. In Carroll County between 1875 and 1885, the number of property mortgages recorded annually soared from 18 to over 900. See Superior Court Deeds and Mortgages, Carroll County, 1875, GDAH; Mortgage Book, Carroll County 1885, Vols. B–C, Carroll County Courthouse. Also see Jackson (County) *Herald*, April 10, 1891. Before 1877, what was known as the "homestead exemption" protected a substantial amount of real and personal property from levy for debt. But at the planter-dominated state constitutional convention that year, the homestead's coverage was sliced, and, more important, debtors were permitted to waive its protection. Thereafter, waiving the homestead and mortgaging real and personal property in addition to crops became prerequisites for obtaining credit. See *Proceedings of the Constitutional Convention Held in Atlanta, Georgia, 1877* (Atlanta, 1877), pp. 451, 463–64.

20. Dun and Company, Credit Ledgers, Georgia, V, 116, 116E, 118, 121, 134, 138–39; XVIII, 31; *Report on Cotton Production in the United States*, 2 vols. (Washington, D.C., 1884), II, 170; Jefferson (Jackson County) *Forest News*, August 7, 1875; Jackson *Herald*, June 3, 1887; Carroll County *Times*, August 3, 1888; Thomas D. Clark, *Pills, Petticoats, and Plows: The Southern Country Store, 1865–1900* (New York and Norman, Okla., 1944), p. 43; Harold D.

Woodman, *King Cotton and His Retainers: Financing and Marketing the Cotton Crop of the South, 1800–1925* (Lexington, Ky., 1968), pp. 301–2. Growing merchant power in the marketplace reflected postwar economic integration and came at the expense of local artisans. In 1880 only 5 percent of household heads reported craft occupations, compared with 10 percent in 1860.

21. In 1880, the first year the federal census enumerated land tenure, 60 percent of Upcountry farms were owner operated. By 1890, only 48 percent were owner operated. While these figures are not distinguished by race, they point to a clear trend in an area with relatively few blacks and only a handful of black landowners, See *Tenth Census*, Agriculture, 40–45, 183–84; *Eleventh Census*, Agriculture, 128–32, 202–4, 360–61, 393–94.

22. Jackson *Herald*, February 26, 1892.

23. In a pioneering essay, C. Vann Woodward has demonstrated that emancipation in much of the Caribbean and Latin America, as in the South, ushered in new forms of labor coercion designed to maintain the viability of plantation agriculture. See "Emancipations and Reconstructions: A Comparative Study," *XIII International Congress of Historical Sciences* (Moscow, 1970). Also see Willemina Kloosterboer, *Involuntary Labour since the Abolition of Slavery* (Leiden, 1960).

The age of emancipation embraced not only the Western Hemisphere. Between the last quarter of the eighteenth and the third quarter of the nineteenth centuries, serfdom was abolished throughout continental Europe and Russia. Yet, in most areas, peasant emancipations were gradual, came with the grudging consent of the nobility, and were laden with persisting burdens of indemnification, customary obligations, and restricted mobility. See Blum, *End of the Old Order*, pp. 357–441.

24. Edward King, *The Great South: A Record of Journeys* (Hartford, Conn., 1875), pp. 274–371. For detailed accounts of the struggles between planters and freedmen see Michael Wayne, *Antebellum Planters in a Postwar South: The Natchez District, 1860–1880* (Baton Rouge, forthcoming); James L. Roark, *Masters without Slaves: Southern Planters in the Civil War and Reconstruction* (New York, 1977), pp. 156–209; Leon F. Litwack, *Been in the Storm So Long: The Aftermath of Slavery* (New York, 1979), pp. 336–449.

25. *Acts and Resolutions of the General Assembly of the State of Georgia, 1872* (Atlanta, 1872), p. 469; *Acts and Resolutions, 1873* (Atlanta, 1873), p. 235; *Acts and Resolutions, 1874* (Atlanta, 1874), pp. 389–401; *Acts and Resolutions, 1875*), (Atlanta, 1875), pp. 296–303. Similar game laws were enacted throughout the South during the same period. On antebellum practices see William Elliott, *Carolina Sports by Land and Water* (New York, 1859), pp. 254–60. On the development and meaning of absolute property see C. B. Macpherson, "Capitalism and the Changing Concept of Property," in Eugene Kamenka and R. S. Neale, eds., *Feudalism, Capitalism, and Beyond* (New York, 1975), pp. 112–13; Richard Schlatter, *Private Property: The History of an Idea* (New Brunswick, N.J., 1951), pp. 205–49 and passim.

26. *The Plantation*, 3 (1871), 323–24, 335; Memorial of the State Grange, Atlanta, February 4, 1871, Legislative Department, Petitions, Record Group 37/Series 12, GDAH. Also see E. Merton Coulter, *The South during Reconstruction, 1865–1877* (Baton Rouge, 1947), p. 288; Grady McWhiney, "The

Revolution in Nineteenth Century Alabama Agriculture," *Alabama Review,* 31 (1978), 3–32; William I. Garfinkel, "The Rejected Vision: J. Hendrix McLane and Independent Politics in South Carolina, 1878–1894" (Paper, Yale University, 1975), p. 19.

27. Carroll County *Times,* January 10, 1873; James C. Bonner, *Georgia's Last Frontier: The Development of Carroll County* (Athens, 1971), p. 140.

28. *Acts and Resolutions, 1872,* pp. 34–35.

29. Atlanta *Constitution,* November 11, 1883. Throughout the Lower South, stock laws first took hold in the black belt. I have explored the process in some detail in a paper presented to the Shelby Cullom Davis Center Seminar at Princeton University, "Hunting, Fishing, and Foraging: The Transformation of Property Rights in the Postbellum South." A revised version will appear shortly in the *Radical History Review.* Also see J. Crawford King, "The Closing of the Southern Range," *Journal of Southern History* (forthcoming).

30. Southern historians recently have been engaged in a debate over the character of the postwar South and its ruling class. The discussion might be enhanced by a closer examination of changing property relations bearing on production and exchange. For an excellent survey and critique of the main points of contention see Harold D. Woodman, "Sequel to Slavery: The New History Views the Postbellum South," *Journal of Southern History,* 43 (1977), 523–54. Also see Jonathan M. Wiener, "Class Structure and Economic Development in the American South, 1865–1955," *American Historical Review,* 84 (1979), 970–92, and the comments by Harold Woodman and Robert Higgs that follow. Woodward's *Origins of the New South* still serves as the point of departure.

31. As commercial agriculture penetrated the Upcountry during the 1870s, local politics also underwent a significant transformation. The growing market towns increasingly came to dominate the Democratic party and then the county offices. The Independent movement of the 1870s, especially strong in the Upcountry, had its roots in this development. Only when Independentism went into decline did the region's elite agitate for the stock law. See Hahn, "Roots of Southern Populism," pp. 284–330; C. Vann Woodward, *Tom Watson: Agrarian Rebel* (New York, 1963), pp. 68–69; George L. Jones, "William H. Felton and the Independent Democratic Movement in Georgia" (Ph.D. diss., University of Georgia, 1971).

32. Carroll County *Times,* February 22, 1878, March 3, 1882; Jackson *Herald,* September 25, 1885; Agricultural Club of Bartow County, No. 3, Minutes, 1883, GDAH.

33. Jefferson *Forest News,* April 23, 1880; Cherokee (County) *Advance,* April 21, 1880; Carroll County *Times,* September 1, 1882. Also see Jackson *Herald,* March 20, 1885; Carroll County *Times,* September 8, 1882, August 4, 1882; Cottage Home Farm Journal, Floyd County, January 14, 1878, John H. Dent Papers, GDAH.

34. Blum, *End of the Old Order,* pp. 262–71; Hammond and Hammond, *Village Labourer,* pp. 12–14; Bloch, *French Rural History,* pp. 197–213.

35. Paulding (County) *New Era*, April 19, 1883.

36. Cartersville *Express*, June 21, 1880; Carroll County *Times*, June 7, 1878, September 8, 1882; Gwinnett (County) *Herald*, October 18, 1882. Also see Carroll *Free Press*, May 1, 1885; Gwinnett *Herald*, June 29, 1885.

37. Gwinnett *Herald*, September 20, 1882, June 29, 1885. Also see Carroll *Free Press*, June 19, 1885, June 26, 1885; Jackson *Herald*, June 17, 1881; Carroll County *Times*, May 17, 1878; Cartersville *Express*, June 21, 1880.

38. Gwinnett *Herald*, June 29, 1885, October 18, 1882, September 20, 1882; Carroll County *Times*, August 25, 1882.

39. Jackson *Herald*, June 17, 1881; Carroll *Free Press*, June 19, 1885. Also see Gwinnett *Herald*, June 29, 1885; Jackson *Herald*, January 14, 1881, August 21, 1883; Carroll County *Times*, May 17, 1878; Carrol *Free Press*, June 5, 1885. Tax records from Upcountry counties demonstrate that most landless whites and blacks owned a few head of livestock during the 1880s. In Jackson and Carroll counties, for example, 60 percent of the blacks had livestock. See Jackson County Tax Digests, 1880–1890, GDAH; Carroll County Tax Digests, 1880–1890, GDAH.

40. Gwinnett *Herald*, August 18, 1885, April 12, 1882; Cartersville *Express*, June 29, 1876; Carroll *Free Press*, May 1, 1885; Carroll County *Times*, September 1, 1882.

41. Jackson *Herald*, June 24, 1881.

42. Cherokee *Advance*, July 1, 1882; Jackson *Herald*, June 17, 1881, August 3, 1883. Also see Carroll *Free Press*, May 15, 1885.

43. Carroll County *Times*, September 8, 1882; Carroll *Free Press*, June 26, 1885.

44. Jefferson *Forest News*, April 23, 1880; *The Plantation*, 2 (1871), 388; Jackson *Herald*, April 3, 1885.

45. Jackson *Herald*, May 27, 1881; Carroll County *Times*, January 6, 1882; Carroll *Free Press*, May 8, 1885. Also see Jackson *Herald*, June 17, 1881; Gwinnett *Herald*, August 30, 1882; Carroll County *Times*, June 7, 1878.

46. Paulding *New Era*, April 19, 1883; Carroll County *Times*, June 21, 1878.

47. Carroll *Free Press*, June 5, 1885, June 25, 1885.

48. Gwinnett *Herald*, October 18, 1882; Jackson *Herald*, June 17, 1881.

49. Jefferson *Forest News*, January 14, 1881; Carroll *Free Press*, n.d.

50. Carroll *Free Press*, May 8, 1885.

51. Cottage Home Farm Journal, Floyd County, November 17, 1886, Dent Papers.

52. Carroll *Free Press*, May 15, 1885.

53. The import and legacy of eighteenth-century republicanism is receiving growing attention, particularly regarding the culture and world view of petty producers in both the cities and the countryside. I believe that much of the

social and political conflict of the nineteenth century, including Populism, can be reinterpreted fruitfully as a struggle over the meaning of the Revolutionary republican heritage. Lawrence Goodwyn hints at this in *Democratic Promise,* but does not fully develop it. A number of outstanding studies treat the significance of republicanism in an urban, working-class context, but with far-reaching implications. See Foner, *Tom Paine;* Wilentz, *Chants Democratic;* Leon Fink, *Workingmen's Democracy: The Knights of Labor in Local Politics* (Urbana, Ill., forthcoming); David Montgomery, *Beyond Equality: Labor and the Radical Republicans, 1862–1872* (New York, 1967). For a provocative treatment of the impact of republicanism in the antebellum South see J. Mills Thornton III, *Politics and Power in a Slave Society: Alabama, 1800–1860* (Baton Rouge, 1978). It is worth noting that Tom Paine attempted to distinguish between uncultivated land, which, he believed, belonged to all in common, and improved land, which belonged to the producer. See Schlatter, *Private Property,* p. 175. The distinction between productive and unproductive property also influenced the single-tax plan of Henry George.

54. On the confrontation between the moral economy of commoners and the free-market economy see Thompson, *Making of the English Working Class,* pp. 62–76; E. P. Thompson, "The Moral Economy of the English Crowd in the Eighteenth Century," *Past and Present,* no. 50 (1971), 76–136. On moral economy and republicanism in Revolutionary America see Foner, *Tom Paine,* pp. 145–82.

55. Jackson *Herald,* September 22, 1882; Carroll County *Times,* October 14, 1881. Also see Carroll *Free Press,* March 27, 1885, June 12, 1885; Cherokee *Advance,* March 11, 1882.

56. Cherokee *Advance,* July 10, 1884, September 4, 1884, September 18, 1884.

57. Gwinnett *Herald,* June 29, 1885, October 14, 1884; Cherokee *Advance,* November 24, 1883.

58. Jackson *Herald,* July 8, 1881; Jones, "Felton and the Independent Democratic Movement," p. 170 fn.

59. Atlanta *Constitution,* November 11, 1883; Jackson *Herald,* July 1, 1887.

60. See Appendix, Tables 1 and 2, for the relevant statistics from two counties. Interestingly, while very few blacks owned land in the Upcountry, the proportion of black landowners tended to be higher in districts that most strongly opposed the stock law. In Carroll County as a whole, for instance, fewer than one black in ten owned land, but more than three blacks in ten owned land in the rural districts of Kansas, Shiloh, and Flint Corner, where the stock law was defeated by about 90 percent of the votes.

61. See Appendix, Tables 1 and 2.

62. Carroll County *Times,* January 11, 1882, January 18, 1882, September 9, 1882.

63. Jackson *Herald,* July 8, 1881.

64. Cartersville *Express,* July 15, 1880; Gwinnett *Herald,* July 14, 1885.

65. Cottage Home Farm Journal, Floyd County, December 15, 1881, October 24, 1883, Dent Papers; Carroll *Free Press*, September 10, 1886; Carroll County *Times*, September 1, 1882; Jackson *Herald*, June 10, 1881.

66. *Acts and Resolutions, 1872*, 36; Jackson *Herald*, July 20, 1883.

67. Agricultural Club of Bartow County, No. 3, Minutes, June 1884; Gwinnett *Herald*, August 9, 1882; Jackson *Herald*, September 25, 1885. Also see Jackson *Herald*, December 25, 1885.

68. Jackson *Herald*, September 2, 1887.

69. *Acts and Resolutions, 1872*, p. 36; Jefferson *Forest News*, November 19, 1880; Carroll *Free Press*, March 18, 1887; Carroll County *Times*, September 23, 1881, October 7, 1881. See also Carroll *Free Press*, June 19, 1885, April 8, 1887, April 15, 1887; Gwinnett *Herald*, January 13, 1891.

70. Carroll County *Times*, September 23, 1881, October 7, 1881.

71. Ibid., January 13, 1882, September 9, 1882; Carroll *Free Press*, July 3, 1885, July 8, 1887, June 4, 1890; Jackson *Herald*, July 8, 1881, September 14, 1883; Gwinnett *Herald*, July 14, 1885, July 7, 1891.

72. Georgia Department of Agriculture, *Annual Report of Thomas P. Janes, Commissioner of Agriculture of the State of Georgia for the Year 1875* (Atlanta, 1876), p. 66; *Dixie Farmer*, quoted in Jefferson *Forest News*, September 10, 1880.

73. Jackson *Herald*, April 3, 1885, June 24, 1885; Carroll County *Times*, May 3, 1878.

74. Cottage Home Farm Journal, Floyd County, January 14, 1878, Dent Papers; Carroll County *Times*, June 7, 1878.

75. The disfranchisement of Southern blacks in the late-nineteenth and early twentieth centuries is familiar enough to historians. But as J. Morgan Kousser has recently argued, suffrage restriction was directed against the poor of both races, and it stood as only the starkest manifestation of a general national trend. See Kousser, *The Shaping of Southern Politics: Suffrage Restriction and the Establishment of the One-Party South, 1880–1910* (New Haven, 1974), pp. 52–53 and passim. Also see Woodward, *Origins of the New South*, pp. 321–49, and *The Strange Career of Jim Crow*, 3rd ed. (New York, 1974), pp. 82–93. We still know very little about developments during the Gilded Age in the North, but for some suggestive evidence see Walter Dean Burnham, "The Changing Shape of the American Political Universe," *American Political Science Review*, 59 (1965), 7–28; Leon Fink, "Class Conflict in the Gilded Age: The Figure and the Phantom," *Radical History Review*, 3 (1975), 56–73. Michael McGerr of Yale University will make a significant contribution to the social and political history of this period with his forthcoming doctoral dissertation, "The Decline of Popular Politics: Connecticut, 1876–1926." I am indebted to him for his sharing his research and ideas with me.

76. Carroll *Free Press*, June 5, 1885, June 19, 1885.

77. *Acts and Resolutions, 1880–1881*, pp. 79–81.

78. Carroll *Free Press,* July 4, 1884, March 26, 1886, April 1, 1887.

79. Ibid., September 4, 1885, March 18, 1887, April 1, 1887, September 9, 1887, September 23, 1887. Also see Bonner, *Georgia's Last Frontier,* pp. 141–42.

80. Carroll *Free Press,* September 4, 1885, April 1, 1887, April 15, 1887, June 3, 1887, June 24, 1887, December 16, 1887, September 10, 1889; Bonner, *Georgia's Last Frontier,* pp. 141–42.

81. Carroll *Free Press,* March 1, 1889, August 2, 1889, July 18, 1890; Bonner, *Georgia's Last Frontier,* pp. 142–43.

82. Jackson *Herald,* March 27, 1885, July 1, 1887, September 2, 1887, November 11, 1887.

83. Ibid., March 12, 1886; *Publications of the Georgia Department of Agriculture* (Atlanta, 1889), XV, 117–23.

84. Ibid.; Gwinnett *Herald,* October 17, 1883, September 23, 1884, October 14, 1884, September 27, 1887, February 12, 1889; Cherokee *Advance,* April 16, 1886, October 22, 1886, November 4, 1887, November 30, 1888, August 8, 1890, August 29, 1890; Paulding *New Era,* August 30, 1889; Franklin County Records, Elections, 1889–1893, GDAH.

85. Gwinnett *Herald,* January 13, 1891, October 14, 1884, October 21, 1884; Carroll *Free Press,* n.d.

86. Cherokee *Advance,* August 26, 1887, November 11, 1887. Also see Carroll *Free Press,* October 31, 1890.

87. Gwinnett *Herald,* July 14, 1885, July 7, 1891, April 29, 1890; Carroll *Free Press,* July 3, 1885, June 4, 1890.

88. Cherokee *Advance,* August 21, 1891; Gwinnett *Herald,* September 27, 1887; Bonner, *Georgia's Last Frontier,* pp. 142–43.

89. Carroll *Free Press,* July 12, 1889, March 26, 1886. Also see ibid., April 23, 1886, February 3, 1888, March 4, 1890.

90. Henry A. Landsberger, ed., *Rural Protest: Peasant Movements and Social Change* (London, 1973), pp. 1–64; Roland Mousnier, *Peasant Uprisings in Seventeenth Century France, Russia, and China* (New York, 1970); E. J. Hobsbawm, "Peasant Land Occupations," *Past and Present,* no. 62 (1974), 120–52; Hildermeier, "Agrarian Social Protest," pp. 319–32; Judt, "Origins of Rural Socialism," pp. 45–65.

91. Wolf, *Peasant Wars;* Landsberger, ed., *Rural Protest,* pp. 158–93; James C. Scott, *The Moral Economy of the Peasant: Rebellion and Subsistence in Southeast Asia* (New Haven, 1974); Barrington Moore, Jr., *Social Origins of Dictatorship and Democracy: Lord and Peasant in the Making of the Modern World* (Boston, 1966).

92. Although virtually every Georgia Upcountry county had a Populist newspaper, none is extant. The Democratic papers do not mention the stock law as a local Populist issue. But it should be noted that in Alabama the stock-law controversy did continue into the 1890s. See Marie B. Owen, *Alabama: A Social and Economic History* (Montgomery, 1938), p. 102.

93. Carroll County *Times,* March 30, 1888; Carroll *Free Press,* July 5, 1889; Atlanta *Southern Alliance Farmer,* n.d., in James T. McElvaney Papers, GDAH; Bonner, *Georgia's Last Frontier,* p. 145.

94. Carroll *Free Press,* July 25, 1890; Carroll County *Times,* November 4, 1892.

95. In Jefferson, Minishes (Harmony Grove), and Wilson (Maysville), the Populists never received a majority in six elections; the Populist vote totaled 29 percent. When we add the village district of Cunningham (Pendergrass) and the wealthiest rural district of Harrisburg, both of which leaned toward the stock law, the Populist-vote total in six elections climbs to 33 percent. The five rural districts most strongly opposed to the stock law went solidly Populist. See Appendix, Table 1.

96. Carrollton, Bowdon, and Roopville voted Democratic in all three of the elections for which returns are available; Villa Rica and Whitesburg went Populist once. In total, they gave only 37 percent of their votes to the Populists. The Temple district, which leaned toward the stock law, did side with the Populists. But the combined vote of all the districts inclined to the stock law (Carrollton, Villa Rica, Roopville, and Temple) left the Populists with 42 percent. The rural districts most opposed to the stock law gave the Populists 73 percent of their votes. See Appendix, Table 2.

97. Carnesville (Franklin County) *Enterprise,* November 1, 1892; Paulding *New Era,* October 7, 1892; Gwinnett *Herald,* October 2, 1894; Cherokee *Advance,* October 7, 1892, November 11, 1892.

98. Atlanta *People's Party Paper,* January 14, 1892; Gracewood (Georgia) *Wool Hat,* July 22, 1893.

99. "The Omaha Platform," in George B. Tindall, ed., *A Populist Reader* (Gloucester, Mass., 1976), pp. 90–96; Carroll *Free Press,* March 2, 1888; Gracewood *Wool Hat,* July 27, 1892.

Of the Man at the Center:
Biographies of Southern Politicians
from the Age of Segregation

ROBERT DEAN POPE

I N 1937 an article in the *Journal of Southern History* called for
a new assessment of the leadership of the South since the 1890s.
Pointing to a record of considerable achievement by figures
generally known to the literate public only for their outrageous
political behavior, Daniel M. Robison rejected the theory that a
new class of leadership had sprung from the ignorance and bigotry
of the South and argued that these new leaders might in fact be
more the true heirs to the Old South tradition than their more
staid opponents. Robison attempted no lengthy analysis of the
Southern "demagogues," but he did call for biographies that
would treat the leaders of the New South as more than just the
natural result of an electorate populated by characters from
Tobacco Road.[1]

Professor Robison must have been gratified when in the next
year, 1938, C. Vann Woodward published his first book, *Tom
Watson: Agrarian Rebel*.[2] Woodward's story was a fascinating one,
replete with excitement and personal tragedy. It featured an
entertaining, able, and often execrable figure who in recent
memory had been seen as a running sore on the body politic.
Before Woodward's book, many people were likely to remember
only the Watson who had inspired the lynching of Leo Frank, an
episode that was made into a movie in 1937, and to thoughtful
people outside the South he represented the dark, sinister forces
of bigotry.

In *Tom Watson* Woodward set forth themes and raised questions to which he would frequently return. He explored the

nature of Populism and the degree of class consciousness in the South. *Tom Watson* showed surprising contrasts. It detailed the transformation of a young crusader who protected black fellow Populists into an aging bigot spewing forth hatred against blacks, Catholics, and Jews that was virulent even by the standards of the time. The book won immediate praise as a classic of its kind, and its reputation has endured. Structured as a conventional biography, it unobtrusively argued that Watson was very much a product of his own times and of forces that "thwarted at every turn his courageous struggle" and "led him into the futility and degeneration of his later career." Although *Tom Watson* was Woodward's doctoral dissertation, he never made the mistake, so common in dissertation-biographies, of subjecting his readers to the trivial details of his subject's life. On the other hand, Watson—not the South or Georgia or Populism—was the subject. He was alive; he was a person, a part of his time and not merely a reflection of it.

The ease with which *Tom Watson* "reads" makes it tempting to believe that it was easy to write. Drama abounds in every chapter as we follow the fortunes first of a very appealing and earnest young Tom Watson and then of a vicious and unhappy old man who forfeited almost all of his rights to sympathy or understanding. Perhaps inspired by the excitement of the story he found, Woodward often used extravagant phrases, and his description of "Southern masses . . . on the march" occasionally suffers from a Marxist diction that doesn't quite ring true. At times one is also suspicious that the evidence supporting the great drama of the story is somewhat overstated, in particular in Woodward's description of Watson's commitment in the early 1890s to racial justice.[3] Yet Woodward's energy, his clear-headed point of view, and his use of evidence, structure, and a consistently interesting style carry even the reluctant reader toward Woodward's own conclusions. In this respect he was indeed a model biographer.

Woodward never returned to biography, and one cannot help suspecting that he knew he would never find a subject so peculiarly suitable to a writer of his talents. We ought to ask, however, why Woodward has had so few distinguished followers. To be sure, there have been some excellent biographies of Southern politicians in the Age of Segregation, that period running from the final elimination of the Negro from political participation at the end of the nineteenth century to the period just after World War II when segregation came under serious attack.[4] By and large, however, biography has not been a popular genre, especially for professional historians of the South. One reason must surely be the wider trend in recent years toward social history—toward a concern with classes, social forces, and ideas. There has been a great and fruitful concentration of scholarly effort in determining whether the South is distinctive and, if so, why. Historians have been endlessly concerned with groups—Redeemers, New Departure Men, Persistent Whigs, Bourbons, Populists, and Progressives —and therefore less concerned with individuals. Biographies, like all history, reflect the age in which they are written. So, too, is the age reflected in the degree of interest in biography. In reviewing a book on biography in nineteenth-century Britain, the *Economist* observed that biography "is par excellence the literary product of the Protestant ethic—the idea of individual autonomy, the idea of rigorous intellectual honesty, the idea of 'progress' and of a living past, the deification of rationalism, and, above all, the idea that the ineffable can be comprehensively described in terms as concrete as those used to define a brick or a table."[5] The popularity of such sentiments in American society generally and in history departments particularly is obviously not what it was in nineteenth-century Britain.

Another reason for the dearth of first-rate biographies is the simple fact that writing biography is difficult. "Biography," wrote Boswell, "occasions a degree of trouble far beyond that of any other species of literary composition." Most definitions of biography have recognized its dual nature—as historical research and as literary art. A successful biographer must first be a successful historian who assembles his facts with care and resists the temptation to stress those facts that make his story easier to tell—or more exciting when told. On the other hand, he must also be a writer of imagination who brings his subject to life and tells a tale that has a unity and purpose. It is difficult to imagine any life of importance or interest that would not create a tension between the biographer's impulses as a literary artist and his duties as an historian. For the best biographers this conflict creates a beneficial stalemate, with the artist uniquely qualified to make leaps of imaginative interpretation but always restrained by the single person best able to see the fallacies in his interpretations, the biographer as historian. If either side in the conflict routs the other, the results are unsatisfactory—either careless theorizing that ignores available evidence or a dull litany of facts that is even more obviously a failure than is a dull monograph.

Another clue to the underdeveloped state of biography is found in the common observation that most biography begins, in one sense or another, in praise. The literary biographer Robert Gittings has refined this argument by asserting that the biographer must at least have enthusiasm for his subject, as Boswell clearly did for Dr. Johnson and, in a different way, Woodward did for Watson.[6] Southern political figures of the Age of Segregation are by and large not an attractive group to modern biographers. Dr. Johnson stated that a man would have to eat and drink with his subject in order to write a proper biography of him. One suspects that many historians would not embrace the opportunity to sit at the table with most of the Southern politicians of this period.

The subjects themselves have not been cooperative. Few kept diaries or unburdened themselves to thoughtful, literate friends. If they did not burn their letters in order to thwart their biographers, they also did not write very many. Information about their childhoods is usually scant, and it is often suspect because of its self-serving usage in political campaigns. Accurate accounts of political speeches are often difficult to obtain because of distorted or sketchy press coverage of rural political rallies.

Hanging over the biographical approach to Southern history is the image of the Southern demagogue. Woodward criticized the use of the term in his introduction to *Tom Watson*, written at a time when Bilbo, Talmadge, and "Cotton Ed" Smith were active and successful politicians and the demagogue was, in the popular mind, at least outside the South, symbolic and symptomatic of the region's politics and society.

The pervasiveness of this image was shown in an ideologically overburdened book published in 1939, *Dixie Demagogues,* which made the expected enlightened statements about the wickedness of the race baiters but tried to tar their more civilized colleagues with the same brush.[7] The book in effect defined as demagogues all Southern politicians except Hugo Black and Claude Pepper, described the South as "a region where democracy has never had a chance to work," denied the claims of Vardaman and Bilbo to progressivism, and saw the specter of fascism rising in the region.

It appeared to the authors that the people of the South could be freed from their prejudices only if they would consistently elect candidates who shared all the views of the authors.

Two years later, in 1941, there appeared a much more important book.[8] W. J. Cash's *The Mind of the South* was not history in the traditional sense, but it has worked its way into most history courses on the South as well as into the minds of most Southern historians. Citing Cash, if only to disagree with him, is almost de rigueur for writers on the modern South. Cash put forth nothing less than a theory of Southernness, and he wrote with an eloquence and painful personal involvement that enhanced his credibility. The "man at the center" of Cash's South was a colorful contradiction—a romantic "hell of a fellow," honorable, short-tempered, and addicted to the "vastly ego-warming and ego-expanding distinction between the white man and the black."

When Cash's man at the center turned to politics, he naturally embraced the demagogues. There was no need for any special explanation of men like Cole Blease or Talmadge or Bilbo; they were the natural expression of the people who elected them and who looked to politics as a theater "for the play of the purely personal, the purely romantic, and the purely hedonistic." According to Cash, the politics of the South in the Age of Segregation had almost nothing to do with meaningful social and economic issues. "I think," wrote Cash, "the demagogues would have appeared if Populism and economic and social irritations had never been heard of."[9]

Although Cash talked much about the importance of individualism in the South, he said very little about individuals. Preoccupied with the distinctiveness of the South and convinced of the existence of a Southern character, Cash offered no inspiration for biography.

The first major biography to appear after *The Mind of the South* was Francis Butler Simkins's *Pitchfork Ben Tillman: South Carolinian*.[10] Like *Tom Watson*, it is scholarly, comprehensive, thoughtful, and open-minded, and it partially confirmed Professor Robison's suggestion that the reputations of the "demagogues" would undergo considerable favorable revision if considered in the context of their time. Simkins shows that Tillman was violent, hardheaded, egocentric, and bitterly devoted to the suppression of political rights of blacks. But he also shows that he was honest, occasionally creative, and a man of considerable integrity. Simkins took his subject as he found him. He analyzed him, empathized with him, and occasionally sympathized with him, while never losing his ability to judge him for sins major and minor. Simkins is particularly skillful at drawing verbal pictures of Tillman, standing, for example, before a rural crowd and using his striking appearance and striking rhetoric to convince his listeners that he was a strong man who would use his strength for them. Simkins also partially accepts Tillman's claim to have "educated" the Yankee on the race issue, thus, in Simkins's words, fostering "the modern reaction against the Negro."

Simkins accepts that Tillman's life was not all drama and, like most, had no great climax. He shows the last years of an old man who increasingly gave in to self-pity, self-righteousness, and their frequent concomitant, self-deception. Simkins recognizes that Tillman never was a radical, grew more conservative, and became almost, but not quite, the candidate of the gentry against the common man. He recognizes the importance of simple political inertia in Tillman's last years, when he survived politically because he was, or had been, an effective senator, because of what he had been to the white masses, and because those who had first opposed him finally realized what he was not. Tillman, however, could never have become the political force that he was without the strength of personality and the political will that Simkins recognizes as his most important political characteristics.

Tillman's successors in South Carolina, Cole Blease and "Cotton Ed" Smith, have not yet attracted biographers, but scholars have turned their attention to the "demagogues" of Mississippi, South Carolina's greatest rival as the home of peculiarly Southern politics. *The Man Bilbo,* written by a professor of English at the University of Mississippi, is a short, impressionistic book that describes a figure right out of W. J. Cash's South.[11] A. Wigfall Green pictures Bilbo as a master of politics as entertainment, whose poor white constituents took delight in his ability to offend the sensibilities of decent people within and without Mississippi.[12] Although Green does not deny Bilbo's accomplishments as governor, he also does not analyze them. Neither does he probe very deeply into Bilbo's racism, which he simply says "stemmed from his background and his profession." While Green notes that the two primary foci of Bilbo's Senate years were his racism and his support of New Deal legislation that had the purpose and effect of improving the conditions of the Negro, he does not pursue the irony of this theme.[13]

William F. Holmes's biography of James K. Vardaman has the opposite virtues and vices to those of Green's book on Bilbo.[14] The book is carefully researched, comprehensive without being excessively long, and a valuable source of information on Mississippi politics. It suffers from occasional lapses in logic, especially in its discussion of racism, but as a biography its greatest shortcoming is its failure to capture and convey the vividness that was critical to Vardaman's success. Like Tillman, whom he admired, and Joseph Chamberlain, who was a force in British politics at the same time, Vardaman was a man whose ability to convey a sense of strength and purpose was essential to his political success.

The problem was not that Holmes did not recognize the importance of this highly subjective, unquantifiable quality. Clearly he did, and he ends his narrative of the White Chief's life by quoting a revealing and admiring comment on Vardaman's "ability to stir the masses," made upon his death by a longtime enemy, the editor of the Jackson *Daily News*. The failure is not one of understanding but of description. It is a major failure, however, because it leaves us with only rather wooden descriptions of Vardaman's appeal and gives us little help in sensing the personal tragedies of Vardaman's career, as when failing health crippled his political ability and left him, like Chamberlain in similar circumstances, vulnerable to lesser men whom he knew to be far weaker than he had been. The disappointment is with Holmes the writer rather than Holmes the historian, a disappointment that reminds us how much biography depends on literary ability.

A better understanding of both Vardaman and Bilbo can be found in *Revolt of the Rednecks: Mississippi Politics, 1876–1925,* a monograph published in 1951.[15] Like Woodward in *Tom Watson,* Albert D. Kirwan puts his individual politicians firmly in the context of their time and place but does not overlook their strengths and weaknesses as individuals. Kirwan shows the racism of Vardaman and Bilbo, not as something at war with their progressive politics, but rather as a dimension of their political appeal that allowed them to succeed where their predecessors in the

Populist era had failed. We cannot know which of their most striking characteristics, their progressivism or their racism, was more important to their success. It does seem, however, that the enthusiasm generated by their blatant racism gave them a competitive edge in politics and indeed provided the margin of success that enabled them to institute reforms.[16]

While Vardaman and Bilbo have now been recognized as the progressives they in fact were, not even a sympathetic biographer could do much for the reputation of Eugene Talmadge. *The Wild Man from Sugar Creek* shows Talmadge as the perfect Cashian demagogue, a rabble-rouser who stirred up the masses with rhetoric and entertainment but offered them little else.[17] As Woodward did with Watson, William Anderson describes Talmadge as a "prisoner," but Woodward's book was a success whereas Anderson's was not. Part of the reason is undoubtedly the subject, for if Watson was a prisoner, he was a prisoner who struggled, who several times escaped, and who, even if he ultimately gave in, had considerable knowledge as to what had happened to him. Anderson could not make Talmadge into more of a man than he was, but one does not have to share Dr. Johnson's belief that almost every life could be the subject of a useful biography to suspect that there was more to Talmadge than Anderson presents.

Governor Sidney J. Catts of Florida had many of Talmadge's characteristics—meanness, bigotry, and the ability to appeal to the "them against us" mentality. Catts and Talmadge even appear to have adopted the same rallying cry. Anderson apparently assumed that Talmadge was exercising his gift for original rhetoric when he claimed that the "poor dirt farmer ain't got but three friends on this earth: God Almighty, Sears Roebuck, and Gene Talmadge," but according to a source cited by his biographer, Wayne Flynt, Catts used essentially th. same phrase years before Talmadge did.[18] Flynt's biography is a competent and thoughtful work that sometimes catches the tone of Catts's appeal and recognizes the role of Baptist theology in the development of Catts's politics.

Catts was not particularly important because he was a failure as a politician. Elected only once, he had no gift for organization and, except as a stump politician, inspired neither loyalty nor fear. Flynt concludes that Catts's "bigotry and cavorting" were neces-

sary for the election of a "reformer" in Florida, and he describes
Catts's failure as in part the "inevitable" result of a "movement
which focused on one charismatic, flamboyant man instead of a
consistent reform credo or even a reform faction within the
party."[19] That conclusion, however, overlooks the fact that many
long, successful political careers in the South have been based on
one charismatic, flamboyant personality rather than on any reform
credo or faction.

While Sidney Catts was a failure as a politician, E. H. Crump
was undoubtedly a success. First elected mayor of Memphis in
1909, he dominated that city's politics until his death in 1954.
Long a power in statewide politics, he was the undisputed king-
maker in Tennessee between 1930 and 1948. Crump was no
rabble-rousing demagogue. Instead of eliminating black voting,
this Mississippi-born son of a Confederate cavalry officer used
black voters not to control local elections, which were never in
doubt, but instead to increase his power in the statewide Democratic primary.[20]

Crump's only biographer to date, William D. Miller, came to
Memphis as a college professor during Crump's last years and even
participated in the generally unsuccessful local opposition to
Crump.[21] It is obvious that Miller was fascinated, indeed charmed,
by Crump. *Mr. Crump of Memphis* is not quite the whitewash it
is sometimes made out to be, but it is needlessly long on the details
of Crump's personal life and short on the more controversial episodes in his political career. Miller never gives us a very convincing picture of how Crump's organization worked or how it
changed over the years, and he deals only superficially with the
intriguing question of how much Crump's rule became one of
actual consent by the citizens (at least the white citizens) of
Memphis, who knew that Crump's power to deliver their votes
gave Memphis greater power at the state level.

Although some of Crump's personal magnetism is conveyed,
we long to know more about how Crump dealt with his subordinates and how much he kept them divided among themselves.
There is much more to be told about state politics and about
Crump's relationship with Senator Kenneth D. McKellar, his most
important and consistent ally, and his relationship with Mc-
Kellar's political friends in East Tennessee.

Miller's failures are particularly irritating because Crump is a remarkably attractive subject for a biography. He had character, personality, and ability. A genuine progressive on many issues, he was a master of machine politics. A self-disciplined puritan who abstained from alcohol, tobacco, and profanity, he came to political prominence in the "murder capital of the world," allied himself with saloon keepers in fighting prohibition, and for a while tolerated a controlled red-light and gambling district. A master manipulator of black votes, he openly advocated increased public services for blacks at a time when few others did, but broke with the national Democratic party in 1948 to support the Dixiecrats. He courageously stood up for Al Smith in 1928 against local religious leaders and recruited Roman Catholics and Jews into his organization, but he disastrously tried to link Estes Kefauver with communism in 1948. A man of genuine personal charity who scrupulously avoided mixing his own business with politics, he once had his hand-picked mayor try to ruin a local editor's career by accusing him of homosexuality. Endowed with a stern sense of public morality that permeated all but the lowest levels of his very efficient machine, Crump became increasingly unable to see any honesty or decency in those who opposed him.

Like *Mr. Crump of Memphis,* T. Harry Williams's *Huey Long* shows considerable sympathy for its subject.[22] Long is a formidable figure for any biographer. He was a showman but obviously not the clown he often played in public. His administration brought reforms to Louisiana that were sorely needed, yet his imposition of one-man rule and his treatment of the opposition were brutal and repulsive. He had national ambitions and the drive and intelligence to realize them. Williams's lengthy (876 pages) work is unsatisfying, not because it is sympathetic to its subject, but rather because it defines Long almost exclusively in terms of his enemies. Williams's thesis often seems to be that Long's methods were justified by the viciousness of his enemies and that the excesses of his regime came only in response to the excesses of his opponents.

Such a view is not an irrational one, Williams marshals considerable evidence on its behalf, and certainly Long cannot be understood apart from the governments that preceded him and the enemies who fought him. Too often, however, Williams's arguments are labored, and he grasps at bits of evidence to argue, for instance, that Long was not a coward or that he required undated resignations from his appointees only to ensure that his policies could be carried out. The opposition, however, is treated as a wicked monolith, mindlessly opposed to Long. Williams is inconsistent in explaining this opposition's motivation. Several times he describes it as politically reactionary, yet elsewhere he says it was "fundamentally social and personal." He claims that "aristocratic" Louisianians might have tolerated Long's radicalism and corruption "if he had come from the right class and had 'belonged.' " Furthermore, Williams sees the opposition as not only monolithic but unchanging. Long, on the other hand, realized "the lengths to which the conservatives would go to destroy anyone who proposed change" only after he was very nearly expelled from office. There is little recognition that the excesses of the opposition arose in part from Long's increasingly dictatorial rule and unprecedented destruction of local government rights. One did not have to be an antidemocratic reactionary to see in Huey Long a threat to democratic government.

Harnett T. Kane's *Louisiana Hayride* provides an interesting contrast to *Huey Long*.[23] An impressionistic work without formal documentation, *Louisiana Hayride* was written by a reporter with a scholarly bent who had lived through the regimes of Long and his paltry successors. Although most of the book is about the scandals that followed Huey's death, Long is indicted for both provable and unprovable charges. His enemies appear only at the end of the story to help toss out the venal successors who had little of Huey's ability or progressivism. On a number of points Williams is more convincing than Kane, especially in claiming that by any standard Long's political principles were progressive in their economic outlook. The tone of Williams's book, however, is that of special pleading. It reminds us of how many biographers —Simkins on Tillman, Miller on Crump, even Holmes on Vardaman—have found that their subjects were not the ogres they first suspected and have developed an affection that made them sometimes defensive about their subjects. This is not surprising—or a bad thing in itself. Few men who succeed in politics are without either virtue or ability, and one of the tasks of the biographer is to see a man by his own lights as well as by those of others. Judgment, however, is also one of the biographer's tasks, and Williams is curiously unassertive in judging Huey Long.

That same sort of surprised affection can also be seen in the delightful *The Earl of Louisiana,* a rambling book that is about,

among other things, Huey's younger brother Earl.[24] Derived from
several articles in the *New Yorker,* the book is not a biography,
but it is several things that a biography of a Southern politician
ought to be. A. J. Liebling brought to his observations of the
1959 gubernatorial primary in Louisiana the eye and ear of a
muckraker, yet he came away impressed with Earl and convinced
that he was "the only effective Civil Rights man in the South."
The book is about the era immediately following the Age of
Segregation, and Liebling works a little too hard in propounding
his theory that Southern Louisiana constitutes an exotic Medi-
terranean outpost in a dull Anglo-Saxon nation. His book ought
to be read, however, by anyone undertaking the life of a Southern
politician, not as a model, but rather as a reminder that colorful
politicians are best described with colorful prose.

The aspiring biographer ought also to read Marshall Frady's
Wallace, again, not as a model, but because it reminds us that
a book is more likely to enlighten if it entertains.[25] George
Wallace was not a politician of the Age of Segregation, but Frady's
biography is worthy of note if only because it is written so consciously as a Southern political biography. *Wallace* is unabashedly
in the muckraking style, unconcerned about documentation, overly
devoted to the clever phrase, and much more interested in
vulgar form than in substance. Frady has almost a pornographer's
instinct for the grotesque detail, and like all true addicts of
Southern politics, he cannot resist the extravagant phrases and
gestures that were the stock in trade of Wallace and many before
him.

One is reminded by the careers of the Longs and of Wallace
that despite the educational deficiencies of the South and despite
the fact that politics in the South sometimes seemed downright
anti-intellectual, those who succeeded in Southern politics had
uncommon intelligence, even if they sometimes tried to disguise
it. Although few were rich, most had been raised in respectable
circumstances. They were also to a remarkable extent well educated, some by self-education but most through at least a few
years of college or law school. A number of thoughtful, sympathetic, but generally pedestrian biographies of quite civilized and
intelligent Southern politicians are useful in reminding us that
men succeeded in the South politically for many of the same reasons that men succeed anywhere, because of their ability, attrac-

tiveness, and decisiveness in political battle.[26] One of the earliest biographies of this period, George Coleman Osborn's *John Sharp Williams,* is one of the most sympathetic, but despite its lack of analysis, it demonstrates that notions of honor and duty, ideas not talked about much today, were important in the lives of some Southerners.[27]

It is also apparent that in the early twentieth century it was almost impossible to find an influential Southern white man who did not want blacks removed from the political process. All the revisionist writings about Reconstruction and the period immediately thereafter, about interracial experiments and the persistence of black voting, have not changed the fact that the disfranchisement of blacks was ultimately accepted without meaningful exception by Southern whites and that a remarkably large portion of thoughtful men actively supported it. Most of the political figures in this era experienced childhood and/or young manhood in the years immediately after the Civil War, and their revulsion against Reconstruction and the imposition of even limited black influence on the political South was genuine, deep, and in some cases overwhelming. For a historian writing in 1944 the intensity of these feelings was easier to accept than it is today. Ben Tillman, according to Simkins, "was firmly convinced that Reconstruction was one of the most horrible experiences recorded in history." Similar sentiments were expressed by almost every Southern political figure from this age, and the honesty of the sentiment can hardly be doubted.[28] This feeling could of course combine with different goals in different people. For Tillman, disfranchisement of blacks may have been a way to assert himself against both the potentially dangerous Negro and the hated Yankee, but it was also a way of gaining political success. For A. J. Montague of Virginia, Hoke Smith of Georgia, and scores of lesser politicians, the permanent removal of blacks from politics was both desirable in itself and also necessary for the modest but meaningful political reform generally associated with the "progressive era." Montague told an audience at the University of Chicago in 1909 that the disfranchisement of blacks had freed his region from an era in which "all questions gravitated to the control of the local government by the white race, and all other questions [were] subordinated." In the same speech Montague implied that someday a black electorate might develop and that at such

time the South, having made many of the reforms that Montague
supported, would be in a better position to accept the existence
of that electorate.[29] Such a view was not callous; in fact it may
have been one of the few accurate predictions about the South
made in the decade in which it was spoken.

Not surprisingly one comes away from a review of these biographies feeling that the racial views of his subject present the most
difficult issue for the modern biographer. Biography "is inextricably linked with the priorities and assumptions of the age
which produced it," and the priorities and assumptions of the
present age discourage sympathy for and sometimes even understanding of the South's politicians in the Age of Segregation.[30]

The combination of progressive politics and racist demagoguery
is especially difficult for the modern historian to understand, and
one result has been the tendency to damn the opponents of the
"demagogues," both for their lack of progressivism and for quietly
sharing the racist assumptions that the demagogues shouted out
loud. The demagogues, the argument goes, were no more racist
than their opponents, and they brought in progressive measures
even if they offended public sensibilities. "Vardaman's view of
the Negro," Holmes writes, "actually differed little from that of
most white southerners; his appeal to white supremacy aroused
concern chiefly because of the blunt and dramatic way he presented it, not because of what he said." Vardaman's opponents, he
argues, "believed he used racism as a cheap political tool and in
so doing encouraged lynch mobs and other forms of racial lawlessness." Furthermore, "another aspect of the problem frightened
some even more: his harsh racial utterances might awaken the
conscience of northern whites and result in actually strengthening the Negro's cause. The surest way to keep the Negro from
voting and to keep him segregated was to soft-pedal the question
and thus avoid rekindling sectional animosity."[31] What is unfortunate is not Holmes's speculation on this but his inability to
decide whether Vardaman's particular brand of racism made any
difference. Holmes admits that Vardaman "intensified Negrophobia in Mississippi and encouraged racial lawlessness" and that
more than any other man he "instilled a blatant brand of racism
into Mississippi politics that plagued the state into the late
twentieth century," yet he is unable or unwilling to see one of
the important distinctions between Vardaman and men who did

not regularly incite crowds to a pitch of racial fury. Holmes
piously concludes that Vardaman was a failure because his racism
was inconsistent with his progressive goals. Vardaman, he writes,
"failed to realize that it was impossible to elevate the whole state
while at the same time trying to suppress more than half of its
population."[32] All of this may be true, but Holmes does not offer
any evidence that it is so. Instead he takes it as self-evident that
meaningful improvement in the condition of poor whites could
not come until there was improvement in the conditions of
blacks. This may be good Keynesian, consumer-oriented economics, but there are plenty of other examples in Southern Africa,
in nineteenth-century Britain, and elsewhere that show it is not
necessarily true.

In dealing with the less "progressive" Talmadge, William
Anderson makes the same kind of mistake. "The thing that differ-
entiated a so-called racist from a 'good man,' " he writes, "was
one's willingness to verbalize his feelings against blacks. Good
white folks just didn't say much about the Negro. But they did
less for him."[33] Nonsense. Some demagogues in fact did more for
the black man. Others, like Talmadge, did not. Holmes and other
historians have apparently assumed that there is an objective body
of "progressive politics" that is good, that the economic policies
of people like Vardaman and Bilbo were a part of that objective
body but that racism was not. Consider the following confused
comment by Holmes: "To view Vardaman only as an advanced
liberal would be a grave distortion, for he added open racism
to his Jeffersonian and progressive convictions, resulting in an
unusual political *ménage à trois*."[34]

Because by current standards substantially all white Southerners were hopeless racists, it is easily assumed today that there is
no point in distinguishing between them, except perhaps to show
how they used the race issue to further their other political goals.
The meaningful distinctions must therefore be on other, certainly
important, issues—roads, schools, social services. It is appropriate
to judge politicians on these issues and to relate them to the
conditions of black people in the South, but we will overlook the
only significant difference among white Southerners on the race
issue if we do not distinguish between those segregationists who
opposed violence and favored a degree of protection to blacks,
totally inadequate to modern eyes, and those who would deny

blacks the most primitive rights and indeed encouraged immediate threats to their lives and property. Vardaman was a political
progressive. He was also a virulent racist whose behavior set back
race relations in his time and therefore in our time. The view
put forth by Anderson and hinted at by Holmes is in effect that
it did not make any difference that black people by and large did
not get lynched in Virginia whereas the risk to blacks in Mississippi was considerably greater. It would be foolish to claim that
the differences between Vardaman and A. J. Montague explain
why there was substantial racial violence, including murder, in
Mississippi in the 1960s, but not in Virginia; but it would be
irresponsible to blind ourselves to the possibility that the tone of
politics in the two states made an important difference.[35] It is
difficult to believe that racial justice in the South has not been
slowed in coming because of racial demagoguery in politics and
that it has come slowest of all in those areas where such demagoguery was most openly and successfully practiced. And it is also
difficult to believe that the black resentment against whites that
affects race relations today is not greater than it would have been
if there had been no race baiters.

   This is not to deny the basic racist views of almost all Southern
whites or to claim that such racism was not important. The
difference between those who said "never" to the black man and
those who said "not in the foreseeable future" may not seem very
important today, but it was important in what has happened in
the South in recent decades. Biography ought to help us find out
where along the continuum of racism in the South individuals
placed themselves and if and why they moved, however slightly,
on that continuum. Such an examination of the lives of many
men would require an examination of their religious views. Unfortunately very little that is helpful has been written on the role
of religion in the postbellum South. It is easy for us to view the
Bible-quoting Southern politicians as mere hypocrites who used
the mellifluous phrases of the Authorized Version simply for their
political appeal, but in doing so we almost certainly would be
wrong.

   The dominance of the race issue is manifestly one reason why
the Age of Segregation was an age of singular politicians. To be
sure, Southern politicians were not exclusively the publicly out-

sized men who traveled the road of political success with outrageous behavior that was not nearly so common in the South in the period before or after the Age of Segregation, but their conduct distinguished the South from the rest of the nation. Were these extravagant Southerners really outsized men or simply "normal" American politicians forced to play a particular role and, like all good politicians, warming to the role? Did the times produce such men? Did it instead merely elevate such men? Biography ought to help us find the answers.

One of the striking things about a review of the biographies of this period is that even though it was the age of spectacular politicians who specialized in the creation of political drama on the hustings, we rarely find in biographies the moments of high drama that are the stuff of great biographies, of men struggling with tragic pressures. Is this more a fault of the biographers or a reflection of the region? Was Cash correct in seeing in Southern politics a stifling conformism that masqueraded as the much vaunted Southern individualism? Were there no men for whom there were agonizing choices as they faced the dominant social and political pressures of the day? Were such men naturally inclined to avoid politics in favor of the different challenges of business or the law or to migrate to the political and academic climates of the North?

There were, nonetheless, moments of drama and irony in the lives of Southern politicians. Woodward found them in the life of Watson, in his frustration with the race question. William Jennings Bryan, Watson wrote, "had *no everlasting and overshadowing Negro Question to hamper and handicap his progress*: I HAD."[36] By and large, however, the biographies produced have not risen to the task of capturing such moments. Surely there is challenge in trying to paint the picture of Vardaman, having brought in progressive government riding on the back of racial bigotry, as he faces political ruin in 1918 because of a pro-war hysteria as mindless as his own prejudice. And there is more than the passing irony Bilbo's biographer recognizes in Bilbo's loyal support of New Deal programs that helped bring an end to the Age of Segregation and in his finding himself the most damned enemy of those forces in Washington that voted with him most consistently on economic issues.

There are also the painful conflicts in men more conventional and admirable, like Montague, who wrote to Walter Hines Page in 1908:

The Southern Democracy seems a dead sea. . . . The South now seems wholly given over to the detail of politics, the genius of which is office-getting, not office-serving. . . . [O]ur one party . . . has driven a great people from the orbit of national responsibility and national opportunity until we in the South are outside of the great currents of the republic and of the world as well.[37]

Surely there are compelling biographies to be written of men like Montague, who perceived this state of affairs but who either could not change it or were unwilling even to try.

Southern biography should also be important for the same reasons that biography generally is. It should help not only to protect us from the glib generalities that can be put forth with such ease in the age of social history but also to test new theories about classes and other groups. Several historians have suggested that Professor Woodward's work has done nothing less than alter the basic interpretation of Southern history, and it is no denigration of this accomplishment to suggest that the task of writing a biography of Tom Watson led him to ask the questions that produced in his own later work an improved understanding of the New South. In undertaking biography, the historian has before him a single life responding to the pressures of conflicting forces. If he has assembled his evidence properly, he will be forced to consider influences and theories that he might well have ignored in any approach other than biography.

Biography ought also to be an important stimulus to literary excellence in Southern history. Biography is more self-consciously literary than any other kind of history, although admittedly many Southern politicians offer little literary inspiration to those who chronicle their lives. The biographer of a Disraeli or a Lincoln must write in salutary fear that his every sentence will be compared with the style of his subject. What kind of fear is instilled in the biographer by Oscar Underwood, who wrote abominably, or by Eugene Talmadge, who hardly wrote at all? Professor Woodward once told a group of his students that he had always felt a

greater affinity for Southern novelists than for Southern historians. Unfortunately, such affinity is rarely encouraged in history
departments. The teaching of the writing of history is more difficult than the teaching of history generally, and it is certainly more
time-consuming. How many papers are returned to undergraduate
and graduate students to be rewritten? How many courses rely on
examinations that judge a student exclusively on what can only
be a rough first draft of a proper answer and never expect him or
help him to produce a second draft? Until literary excellence is
encouraged far more than it is today, poor writers of history will
not become good writers and those with a gift for literary excellence will not be pressed to refine it.

Another problem is that modern biography, especially historical biography, currently has no real sense of purpose. In the nineteenth century, hagiography, always a natural impulse in biography, reached its peak in an age with a taste for, indeed a belief
in, hagiography. But if hagiography was for many years the enemy,
that enemy has now been routed. The problem following its defeat is that nothing has replaced it. In order to find a sense of
purpose again for biography, historians need to examine why it
is popular in all times. In fact, few modern biographies, especially from the academy, offer what every biography should produce—moments upon which the reader pauses at a scene in a
man's life, feels the presence of that man's personality, and con-
templates, in Dr. Johnson's words "the parallel circumstances and
kindred images to which we readily conform our minds."

Perhaps modern academic historians have rejected these scenes
as unimportant and distracting from the larger issues. After all,
why should we pause to view the personal affairs of a not altogether attractive individual when our task is to understand the
forces that produced good or evil for millions? For several reasons.
Biography, in Allan Nevins's phrase, "humanizes the past" and
therefore makes it easier for both the writer and the reader to
come to grips with the problems of the times discussed. The primary function of historians is to teach history, not to each other,
but to others. The public taste for biography is demonstrated
annually in the bookstores, and professional historians have a
responsibility to take advantage of such a popular pulpit. As a
number of recent works in British and European history show, a

book with footnotes is not necessarily dull and unpopular. After all, as Dumas Malone has observed, "[n]ot even a professor can rightly object if a biography turns out to be a corking story."[38]

To historians of the South in the Age of Segregation, biography offers an opportunity to come to grips with peculiarities of the time and the region. It is in the lives of men that decency and indecency mix and that each tempers and shapes the other. The decencies and indecencies of the early-twentieth-century South are easily listed. On the one hand we find a tradition of political democracy, a system that valued and respected individual efforts, a social system that, whatever its faults, created genuine ideals of honor and community obligation and meaningful personal contact even across racial lines, and a powerful religion that taught, among other things, Christian charity. On the other hand we find provincialism, economic stagnation, violence, cruelty, and of course racism. In weighing these factors, measuring them, comparing them, and seeing how they mix, we should look primarily at the lives of people. To the modern historian, the South of a half century ago seems in many ways to be an alien world, yet it was a world populated by people with many of the same values and experiences that people have today. In examining biography, Dr. Johnson noted the importance of the common capacity for good and evil. Biographies, well researched, well thought out, and above all well written, can help us to reflect on that capacity and understand better how Southerners in the Age of Segregation thought and acted. We will not understand the Age of Segregation unless we understand the segregationists, and we will not understand the segregationists unless we look at them, as Woodward did at Watson, as living individuals more like us than we usually admit, rather than as mere "symptoms of the past" or reflections of the self-interest that can be found in the lives of all men. We cut ourselves off from any real understanding of racism in the American South if we deny that racial views offensive to us could be—and can be—held by intelligent and decent people. Through the work of a biographer who has entered into the personality of his subject we can grasp the complexity of an individual's moral decision making. And in doing so perhaps we can learn something about moral decision making today, especially as it relates to the problems that we have inherited from the South of not very long ago.

NOTES

1. Daniel M. Robison, "From Tillman to Long: Some Striking Leaders of the Rural South," *Journal of Southern History*, 3 (1937), 289.

2. C. Vann Woodward, *Tom Watson: Agrarian Rebel* (New York, 1938; available in paperback).

3. Charles Crowe has argued that in order to make his "Jekyll and Hyde" story of Watson work, Woodward had to invent an enlightened Dr. Jekyll. Because of Watson's "life-long devotion to white supremacy" and his failure "to grasp rare historic opportunities," Watson's "few token concessions" to blacks were, in Crowe's view, just part of his "eccentric leftist dabbling." One does not have to accept Crowe's hyperbole or his rather patronizing ad hominem arguments to conclude that Woodward sometime overstated both the extent and sincerity of Watson's appeals to black voters. Like any good biographer, and unlike Crowe, Woodward viewed Watson in the context of his time. Even if he sometimes exaggerated Watson's "enlightened viewpoint," his assertion that Watson was "perhaps the first native white Southern leader of importance to treat the Negro's aspirations with the seriousness that human strivings deserve" is hardly undercut by the completely unsurprising facts that Watson revered the memory of the Confederacy, opposed the Lodge "Force Bill," and professed opposition to "social equality and miscegenation." See Crowe, "Tom Watson, Populists, and Blacks Reconsidered," *Journal of Negro History*, 55 (1970), 99.

4. The Louisiana State University Press has played a leading role in encouraging biography from this period. The new editor of its Southern Biography Series is William J. Cooper, Jr., who succeeded the late T. Harry Williams.

5. *Economist*, February 23, 1974, p. 113. The book reviewed was A. O. J. Cockshut, *Truth to Life: The Art of Biography in the Nineteenth Century* (New York, 1974; available in paperback).

6. Robert Gittings, *The Nature of Biography* (Seattle, 1978), pp. 16–19.

7. Allan A. Michie and Frank Ryhlick, *Dixie Demagogues* (New York, 1939).

8. W. J. Cash, *The Mind of the South* (New York, 1941; available in paperback).

9. Ibid., pp. 38, 50–52, 247. Although Cash claimed to be writing about all Southern history, the bulk of the book is about the Age of Segregation, and, as Professor Woodward has pointed out, Cash's view of a stable South was encouraged by the fact that he wrote toward the end of the longest and most stable of the "successive orders" of the South, the one lasting from 1877 to the 1950s—in other words, the Age of Segregation. C. Vann Woodward, "The Elusive Mind of the South," in *American Counterpoint: Slavery and Racism in the North-South Dialogue* (Boston, 1971).

10. Francis Butler Simkins, *Pitchfork Ben Tillman, South Carolinian* (Baton Rouge, 1944; available in paperback).

11. A. Wigfall Green, *The Man Bilbo* (Baton Rouge, 1963).

12. Bilbo and to a lesser extent Long and Blease succeeded in part because they demonstrated to their poor white constituents that at least one ostensibly poor white man had successfully thumbed his nose at the respectable world. The most strikingly analogous figure from the North was Adam Clayton Powell, Jr. Though located in New York, his often Southern-born constituents shared with the poor whites of the South a common religious experience, educational and economic deficiencies, and anger at a system that left them poor and despised. Powell's career contained many of the same things that characterized Bilbo's career—biblical rhetoric, titillating episodes outside the conventional morality, financial pocketlining, and irrational appeals. Powell was loved by his constituents as a black man who beat the system, who outdid the white man at his own game. One is reminded of William Alexander Percy's assertion that Bilbo was loved by the poor whites because he was a "slick little bastard." "He was one of them and he had risen from obscurity to the fame of glittering infamy—it was as if they themselves had crashed the headlines." William Alexander Percy, *Lanterns on the Levee: Recollections of a Planter's Son* (New York, 1941; available in paperback), p. 148.

13. Bilbo, T. Harry Williams has observed, "meets the test for admission to the liberal heaven, a straight New Deal voting record." Several years after Bilbo's death an elderly black woman who had lived through Bilbo's career told a friend that she didn't believe he hated Negroes. "[H]is works contradicted his words. He certainly did more for the Negro during his administration as Governor of Mississippi than had been done before his time." T. Harry Williams, "The Gentlemen from Louisiana," *Journal of Southern History*, 26 (1960), 20; private manuscript.

14. William F. Holmes, *The White Chief: James Kimble Vardaman* (Baton Rouge, 1970).

15. Albert D. Kirwan, *Revolt of the Rednecks: Mississippi Politics: 1876–1925* (Lexington, 1951; available in paperback). Obviously the book does not cover the later years of Bilbo's career.

16. J. Morgan Kousser's statistics show that it was only in 1907 and 1911 that Vardaman split the state along "class" lines, and Holmes describes Vardaman as giving little attention to racism in his 1911 campaign. None of this proves that Vardaman's racism, apparent in all of his campaigns, was not crucial to his political success. The 1902 primary law, in Holmes's words, "initiated a new era in Mississippi politics" and encouraged the kind of campaign in which Vardaman could mix race baiting and economic issues quite effectively. Vardaman's victory in 1911 was undoubtedly the result of several causes—the weakness of his opponent, his ability to exploit the secret caucus issue and, I believe, a popularity among poor whites that the race baiting in his previous campaigns had helped to create. The value of Vardaman's race baiting cannot be quantified, but certainly the Populists, who previously had tried to divide the state along class lines without exploiting the race issue, had failed where Vardaman succeeded. For Kousser's contrary view, see J. Morgan Kousser, *The Shaping of Southern Politics: Suffrage Restriction and the Establishment of the One-Party South, 1880–1910* (New Haven, 1974; available in paperback), esp. pp. 231–37.

17. William Anderson, *The Wild Man from Sugar Creek: The Political Career of Eugene Talmadge* (Baton Rouge, 1975; available in paperback).

18. Wayne Flynt, *Cracker Messiah: Governor Sidney J. Catts of Florida* (Baton Rouge, 1977), p. 79.

19. Ibid., pp. 340–41.

20. Crump could usually turn in 50,000 to 60,000 of the approximately 300,000 votes cast in the statewide Democratic primary. In 1936, with Crump's backing, Gordon Browning was elected governor, carrying Shelby County (Memphis) by a margin of 59,874 to 825. Two years later Browning, having broken with Crump, received around 9,000 votes (a total that seemed surprisingly large to local observers) while his successful opponent got approximately 57,000.

21. William D. Miller, *Mr. Crump of Memphis* (Baton Rouge, 1964).

22. T. Harry Williams, *Huey Long* (New York, 1969).

23. Harnett T. Kane, *Louisiana Hayride: The American Rehearsal for Dictatorship, 1928–1940* (New York, 1941).

24. A. J. Liebling, *The Earl of Louisiana* (New York, 1961; available in paperback).

25. Marshall Frady, *Wallace* (New York, 1968; available in paperback).

26. Dewey W. Grantham, Jr., *Hoke Smith and the Politics of the New South* (Baton Rouge, 1958; available in paperback); William Larsen, *Montague of Virginia: The Making of a Southern Progressive* (Baton Rouge, 1965); John Robert Moore, *Senator Josiah William Bailey of North Carolina: A Political Biography* (Durham, N.C., 1968); Joseph L. Morrison, *Governor O. Max Gardner: A Power in North Carolina and New Deal Washington* (Chapel Hill, 1971); Martha H. Swain, *Pat Harrison: The New Deal Years* (Jackson, Miss., 1978); Evans C. Johnson, *Oscar W. Underwood: A Political Biography* (Baton Rouge, 1980).

27. George Coleman Osborn, *John Sharp Williams: Planter-Statesman of the Deep South* (Baton Rouge, 1943). For a thoughtful assertion that the dignity, honor, and sense of duty of the "Southern gentleman" were not mere fiction, see Robert Penn Warren's sympathetic essay on another Mississippian who served in the Senate, Jefferson Davis. Robert Penn Warren, *Jefferson Davis Gets His Citizenship Back* (Lexington, 1980), originally published in the *New Yorker,* February 25, 1980.

28. The most common current fallacy in discussions of Reconstruction is that the outrage expressed against Reconstruction must have been feigned because Reconstruction was not outrageous. This overlooks several important points. First, white Southerners viewed Reconstruction as bad per se because it was rule, or partial rule, by a combination of aliens (Yankees) and those simply unfit to rule (blacks). Second, white Southerners were behaving quite normally in being more outraged by both real and alleged "crimes" of Reconstruction than by the homegrown white corruption that followed. One does not expect members of the Palestine Liberation Organization or the Irish Republican Army to be objective about Israeli rule on the West Bank or the government

of Northern Ireland. And finally, accurate or not, the view of Reconstruction as outrageous became so commonly accepted in the South—and the North—that even a very few years after it was over, it would have taken an extraordinary combination of research, scholarship, and objectivity for an individual white Southerner even to consider revising his view of Reconstruction.

29. Larsen, *Montague of Virginia*, p. 154. For Tom Watson's view that removing the "bugaboo of negro domination" would allow each white man to vote "according to his own conscience and judgment," see Woodward, *Tom Watson*, p. 371.

30. The quotation is from Alan Shelston, *Biography* (London, 1977), p. 15.

31. Holmes, *The White Chief*, pp. xi, 109, 114–15, 205.

32. Ibid., p. 388.

33. Anderson, *The Wild Man from Sugar Creek*, p. 225.

34. Holmes, *The White Chief*, p. 270.

35. Holmes makes a point of the fact that Vardaman as governor attempted to stop racial violence. Such conduct while in office is not surprising, but it could hardly diminish the effect of Vardaman's public defense of "mob law." Montague's stands as private citizen and public servant were consistent. White Mississippians were not likely to believe the public stance against mob violence of a man who once told a crowd that although as governor he might send troops to protect "a negro fiend," "if I were a private citizen I would head the mob to string the brute up, and I haven't much respect for a white man who wouldn't" (Holmes, *The White Chief*, p. 109). See Larsen, *Montague of Virginia*, pp. 122–23, 250.

36. Woodward, *Tom Watson*, p. 220.

37. Larsen, *Montague of Virginia*, p. 252.

38. Dumas Malone, "Biography and History" in Joseph R. Strayer, ed., *The Interpretation of History* (Princeton, 1943), p. 132. Recent examples of scholarly best-sellers include Robert K. Massie, *Peter the Great: His Life and World* (New York, 1980; available in paperback); Antonia Fraser, *Royal Charles: Charles II and the Restoration* (New York, 1979; available in paperback), and Giles St. Aubyn, *Edward VII: Prince and King* (New York, 1979). The gulf between popular and scholarly biography, which is to the credit of neither genre, can be blamed in part on Lytton Strachey, whose *Eminent Victorians*, published in 1918, encouraged talented writers to elevate style and imagination over research and logic. This led to a reaction among serious historians like Allan Nevins, who defended "conventional" biography against those who were "substituting cleverness for profundity" (Allan Nevins, *The Gateway to History* (New York, 1938), pp. 332–41). See also Bernard DeVoto, "The Skeptical Biographer," *Harper's*, January 1933, p. 181.

Race and Region in American Historical Fiction: Four Episodes in Popular Culture

WILLIE LEE ROSE

N EARLY every scholar who has asked himself Crèvecœur's famous query "What then is the American, this new man?" has come sooner or later to an explanation that rests on a peculiarly American view of experience that has little to do with the past, much to do with the future. The most widely recognized formulation of this idea is R. W. B. Lewis's *The American Adam*, an influential study that regards the authentic American as a "figure of heroic innocence and vast potentialities, poised at the start of a new history."[1] Lewis based his conception on an insightful reading of the great writers of the nineteenth century, particularly those of the first half, and he clearly identified a theme in American letters that has a continuing if diminishing currency. But it surely does no harm to point out that Lewis's concentration on the "articulate thinkers and conscious artists" means that a large area of popular thought was left out of consideration, a matter of some concern to the social historian.

Perhaps this mattered little in the eighteenth century, when what was distinctly American about our experience was still comparatively new, and most expressions of that experience were limited to the "articulate thinker." But by the second quarter of the nineteenth century the level of literacy in American began to rise sharply, along with a wider than ever spread of political participation. The invention of the steam press provided the technology to produce plentiful reading matter for the new popular taste. As a consequence, it would seem that cultural historians may be missing important clues in not studying more carefully the best-seller lists when they attempt to assess that elusive item the "national character."

The historian interested in the influence of popular preferences and political action may find food for thought, for example, in the curious coincidence that four of the most popular reading-viewing events in all American history—they might even be called public celebrations—have been about the great twin problems in American political life. One is the Civil War and its causes. The other, so closely related to it, is slavery and race in that conflict and the Reconstruction period that followed.

For a people uninterested in the past, this coincidence must at least raise some question whether the vast middle reach of American intellectual activity that fills the space between the lower levels of academia and the upper levels of folk culture is very much concerned to discuss our history, to argue points, strike compromises, and justify the past in the enjoyment of historical fiction, in print and in drama. The "authentic" American may be irritatingly prone to assuming a posture of innocence on account of our new start in a new land. But he is not dismissing two aspects of our past: race and region. Few critics have taken seriously even one of the four astonishing publishing successes I have in mind. These works have nevertheless in one form or another (more often both book *and* drama) traveled around the world. They have given a vocabulary to American mythologies and demonologies that is generally understood at home and abroad; and in each case they have been recognized immediately as important statements explaining a point of view in the ongoing discussion of race and region in American history. They endure.

I do not mean to be mysterious. The sequence of reading-viewing events I have in mind begins with Harriet Beecher Stowe's famous book *Uncle Tom's Cabin,* published in 1852.[2] *Uncle Tom* was dramatized promptly by George Aiken and has run almost continuously somewhere in some form ever since. The list continues with the trilogy of works on Southern Reconstruction, especially *The Clansman,* published in 1905, by Thomas Ryan Dixon.[3] *The Clansman,* as a book, is virtually unread today, but it was fabulously successful in its time—and the motion picture by D. W. Griffith from the Dixon text, called *Birth of a Nation,* has brought the lurid story through to our own time. This moving picture may have been seen by more persons than any other ever made. *Birth of a Nation* was the first truly modern feature film, and surely the most controversial ever shown.

More recently, *Gone With the Wind,* written between 1926 and 1929 and published in 1936, was Margaret Mitchell's enduring contribution to the fictionalized Civil War. It has sold over 20 million copies and still (forty years later) sells 40 thousand per year at hardback prices, and perhaps ten times that number in paperback. For the first forty years this makes an average of over 500 thousand copies per year.[4] The classic moving picture made by David O. Selznick is one of the most popular films of all time; CBS television has paid $35,000,000 for the exclusive right to show it once per year for twenty years.[5] This princely payment may have some relationship with the fourth event which set my mind back along the direction described.

Alex Haley's fabulously successful book called *Roots* was published in late 1976; its author refers to it as his bicentennial gift to his countrymen. Some are referring to *Roots* as the black *Gone With the Wind,* in part because it had much the same astonishing and instant recognition, and was quickly turned into a dramatic television marathon that ran for eight successive evenings in the January following the autumn publication. It quickly appeared that this work, which sold a million copies in six months, was viewed by a larger television audience than any previous show, even including *Gone With the Wind.* Perhaps as many as 135 million Americans watched one or more episodes. Surely, if numbers participating count, author Haley provided the most outstanding cultural event of the American bicentennial.[6]

Haley's book purported to trace his family's lineage back to its African origins in a village near the Gambia River in West Africa. He achieved this feat with the aid of linguists expert in the Mansdinka language spoken in contemporary Gambia. Certain "strange" African words, passed down in the Haley family, turned out to be code words for rich African natural phenomena.[7] Further assistance from a griot of the village of Juffure convinced Haley that he had found the very home of his ancestor Kunta Kinte, captured at the age of sixteen in 1767 and transported to Annapolis in Maryland aboard the slaver the *Lord Ligonier.* This griot from Juffure, Kebba Fofana, it turned out, had stored in his memory bank the key story about how the young warrior Kunta Kinte had been out in the woods carving out a drum when he was captured. It was the very story, Haley marveled, that his grandmother Cynthia had told him when he was a boy.

That Kebba Fofana was no true griot, but a song-and-dance man, a popular entertainer, was bound to come out sooner or later. No nonmythical anecdotes concerning individuals are entered in *any* griot's memory bank going back so far as the eighteenth century. Surely none would be there concerning a relatively unimportant personage sixteen years old in a society that values age. Haley had simply let out what he wanted to hear, and Fofana had responded. But the outcry that arose when *Sunday Times* (London) reporter Mark Ottaway opened this information to the general public, along with several other incriminating items, showed that the number of Americans, white as well as black, who had taken Kunta Kinte into their hearts was very large.[8]

The 135 million or so who had seen the television series had willingly suspended disbelief to follow the young hero out of his contrived but beautiful African Garden of Eden into the hell of slavery in North America. His name, along with that of Uncle Tom (whom he did not in any way favor), had entered the vocabulary of race relations. Haley was sitting down to talk things over with the contemporary descendants of his ancestor's first owners, and was on television nearly every other morning to discuss, promote, and defend the authenticity of his research. Following reporter Ottaway's charges, Haley's distant relatives from West Africa were flown over to claim kinship on the air.[9]

All this had something of the style of promotion, something of the style of celebration; it clearly demonstrated that *Roots* had gone down where grass roots are, and on some things the general public does not care for an expert opinion. Haley had insisted on the accuracy of his genealogical researches, but admitted freely that beyond *that* he had improvised at will to give a character and human relationships to Kunta Kinte and his African parents, and to his American connections. Haley called this contact between fact and fiction "faction" and insisted at least on the spiritual accuracy of the *faction*. There is much in the spiritual department that might be challenged about *Roots*, as book and especially as television. The anachronisms on details are so plentiful as to arouse distrust on more important matters in which it is essential to have full faith; the characterizations lack depth, especially those of the white persons in the plot, and the women in general. But since the work was "faction," reviewers of "fiction' could say they supposed the *history* was good enough, and those historians who reviewed it could call it fiction, and applaud its "spiritual truth."[10]

Actually Haley promised to clear up the historical difficulties by producing another book, and was perhaps unaware how neatly he was falling into the pattern already established by his predecessors in the Tom–Klan–Wind–Roots saga. When similarly called to account, Harriet Beecher Stowe produced the famous *Key to Uncle Tom's Cabin* (1853), and when he was challenged on the accuracy of his romantic and exculpatory history of the Ku Klux Klan, T. R. Dixon said he'd get a committee from the American Historical Association to referee and pay $1000 to anyone who could prove an error. Margaret Mitchell simply answered an incredible number of letters, reeling out her citations. Not one of the four authors has yet said it doesn't matter, as a few professional historians did in the wake of the *Roots* phenomenon.[11]

Actually in most instances the writers in this sequence could offer some kind of factual authority for the historical background in their works. However, the common fault of selective omission runs through all of them, accounting for the dramatic story line, the simplicity of the emotional appeal, and the literary accessibility through so wide a range of readers. This may in fact be the historical interface of the division that exists between popular culture and high culture.

Accounting for Haley's success, Haley's comet, as one wit has it, may be hazardous. On the hunch that the appeal of *Roots* touches some of the primary chords that its predecessors played on, it is an observable fact that Haley's story, like all the others, is at bottom a story about the family. It celebrates the strength flowing from the cultural lifeline for blacks.

Although historians of not too many years ago seemed agreed that Afro-American culture owed little or nothing to Africa, most recent scholars who have worked this field have returned a different verdict. *Roots* serves to dramative this change of view, in keeping with the favor now accorded Swahili, dashikis, and the "natural" hairstyle.

Another aspect of common currency among these spectacular publishing events is that we have in *Roots* a *success* story. The family is victorious over slavery, just as Uncle Tom has a spiritual victory over his oppressors, and as the Southern whites "redeem" their region from the presumed tyranny of carpetbaggers and evil blacks in Dixon's story. Like Scarlett O'Hara, who becomes rich and saves her plantation home, Haley is a Horatio Alger millionaire who has, in celebrating his roots, come right out from the story as its own triumph, an example to all, of a black man who made it, and not in athletics, either. Overnight Haley became a folk hero, and the day the television series ended, more than three thousand persons, mostly teenagers, lined up outside a Los Angeles bookstore to wait for the author to sign their copies of *Roots*. Those who take note of these matters informed the public that newborn babies all over America were being named after Kunta Kinte and his American-born daughter Kizzie.[12]

Haley shared with his predecessors another signal attribute: he had an overt didactic purpose. Haley believed Afro-Americans needed a Garden of Eden and Innocence to look back upon, and so he created a highly romanticized West Africa that owed more to modern anthropology than to history. Here was an African Dixie "before the war." Looking back on the success of the book and the television series, Haley concluded that it was more than his own perseverance that had at last got his book finished, after more than a decade of struggle. "However this sounds," Haley said, "it was one of those things that God in his infinite wisdom and in his time and way decided should happen. I feel that I am a conduit through which this is happening. It was just something that was meant to be. I say this because there were so many things that had to happen over which I had not control."[13]

Leaving Haley in order to slip backward in time, we learn that Harriet Beecher Stowe was equally modest about her part in the writing of *Uncle Tom's Cabin,* once telling an enthusiastic pilgrim who had come to shake the famous hand that wrote it that she had only taken dictation; God had written *Uncle Tom.*[14] In light of President Abraham Lincoln's famous and often quoted remark of her, that here was the little woman who had caused the great American Civil War, Mrs. Stowe may have had a special reason for wishing to share honors with Higher Authority. But it is also true that there is no understanding the phenomenon of Stowe's book without the moral impulse behind it. The work appeared in serial installments in the *National Era* between June 5, 1851, and April of the following year, when the book was published in two volumes and began its spectacular rise. The last episode of the story was actually the one written first, and the real key to the motivation of the plot.[15]

One Sunday during communion at her church in Brunswick, Maine, Stowe's imagination divined a scene set somewhere in faraway Louisiana, where a black man was writhing in anguish under the lashes of two fellow slaves who were beating this black Christian to death at the behest of their cruel owner, the villain who became the infamous Simon Legree.[16] As he lay dying, Uncle Tom, the martyr, brought his black persecutors to a saving knowledge of Christ, and forgave his enemies. When Uncle Tom prayed for victory he was asking for the strength to refrain from betraying others in an escape attempt, and of him his creator writes, "The brave, true heart was firm on the Eternal Rock. Like his Master, he knew that, if he saved others, himself he could not save; nor could utmost extremity wring from him words, save of prayer and holy trust." That Tom's martyrdom is intended as atonement and that he is meant to be the Christ figure is left in no doubt, for in death he calls on God in Jesus' words: "Into thy hands I commend my spirit."[17]

From Mrs. Stowe's decision regarding Tom's character the rest of the action flowed toward this conclusion she had already written. Studying antislavery tracts and narratives of fugitive slaves, and putting these together with a visit she had once made into slaveholding Kentucky some years before, Stowe developed a galaxy of characters and events as alive today as they were a century ago. Her plot has been much criticized, for it is full of extravagant coincidences, surprise endings, and not a little preaching to the dear reader, but it nevertheless served to get Tom to his martyrdom within the year. It drove home Mrs. Stowe's main point relentlessly, with illustration after illustration, from Upper South to Lower South, under all sorts of masters, that slavery could never be ameliorated as a social system so long as slaves were objects of *trade*. The kindness or goodwill of individual owners availed nothing when slaves might be taken for debts.

Indeed two of Tom's successive owners are generous to a fault, and Stowe refers to "good-humored indulgence" of masters and mistresses, and "affectionate loyalty" of slaves on some plantations, but it is only to add:

So long as the law considers all these human beings, with beating hearts and living affections, only as so many *things* belonging to a master,—so long as the failure, or misfortune, or imprudence, or death of the kindest owner, may cause them any day to exchange a life of kind protection and indulgence for one of hopeless misery and toil,—so long it is impossible to make anything beautiful or desirable in the best regulated administration of slavery.[18]

Mrs. Stowe's specific target and immediate impulse for writing her novel was the enactment of a new fugitive-slave law as a part of the famous sectional compromise of 1850, a law more stringent and difficult to evade by antislavery men and women who were engaged in aiding fugitive blacks escaping from the South. The enormous and instantaneous success of Stowe's book came in large part because concern about this law was reflected across a far wider spectrum of public opinion than the abolition movement. Stowe's own family had not been in the front of any movement in that direction before this time, and even as she spoke out in the most unequivocal terms against oppression in her novel, she conceded enough to the Southern argument to suggest that she might have hoped to win a few converts there.[19] Of the three successive owners of Uncle Tom, only the last, Simon Legree, is vicious. Mrs. Stowe makes him a pushing, driving Northerner. The other two are Southern-born and easygoing. The failing of the first is that he had let himself get into debt; the second only that he did not live long enough to render his emancipation of Tom effective in the courts. It is in fact through *this* owner of Uncle Tom, the charming, slightly Byronic Augustine St. Clare, that Harriet Beecher Stowe makes a major sectional concession to the South, and a rebuke, if you will, to her fellow Northerners. The slavery question is frequently discussed between St. Clare and his angular New England cousin Miss Ophelia, who has come South to help look after St. Clare's small daughter, the Little Eva of legend. Miss Ophelia is a woman of conscience, who is, says Mrs. Stowe, a bond slave to the word "ought," but St. Clare notices that as trenchant as she is in her observations against slavery and slave-holding, his cousin flinches with displeasure to see Uncle Tom and Little Eva in physical contact with one another. Miss Ophelia shudders. "Confess it, cousin," St. Clare presses her,

I know the feeling among you Northerners well enough. Not that there is a particle of virtue in our not having it; but custom does with us what Christianity ought to do,—obliterates the feeling of personal prejudice. I have often noticed, in my travels north, how much stronger this was with you than with us. You loathe negroes as you would a snake or toad, yet you are as indignant at their wrongs. You would not have them abused; but you don't want to have anything to do with them yourselves. You would send them to Africa, out of your sight and smell, and then send a missionary or two to do up all the self-denial of elevating them compendiously. Isn't that it?

And Miss Ophelia admits thoughtfully that "there may be some truth in this."[20]

By conceding racial prejudice to the woman who otherwise speaks the views of the author, Mrs. Stowe was conceding a significant point to the proslavery argument. She did not convert the South, but she did write a book around which all shades of anti-slavery opinion could rally. One of her favorable reviewers even seemed to believe that her book reopened the hope that some form of gradual emancipation might yet be undertaken, or some amelioration of the system effected by favorable legal reform.[21] There were even reviewers who believed that the great success of the book was rather in spite of its antislavery than because of it, holding that it was the religious faith of Uncle Tom and his small charge, Miss Eva, that swayed the public.[22] The impact of the book surely owes something to religion and family, but Mrs. Stowe placed these in the service of her main theme, which was the terrible suffering caused by the internal slave trade. Few were the young mothers who could not identify with the beautiful mulatto Eliza Harris, who flies from the clutches of the slave-trader with her little boy in her arms, chancing a wintry dash across the frozen Ohio River in her attempt to avoid separation from her child. Few young fathers could help sympathizing with George Harris, the mulatto husband of this brave girl; few could blame him for despairing at the thought of losing Eliza, for choosing life in Liberia over America, for saving his sympathies for

his mother's race and not his father's, for saying he wished himself
two shades darker rather than two shades lighter.

By playing splendidly on the deepest instincts of her readers,
Mrs. Stowe wrote the most effective of all tracts against slavery,
so that an English reviewer claimed that *Uncle Tom,* especially
after it was put on stage and was being played everywhere in the
middle and late fifties, had in effect repealed the Fugitive Slave
Act.[23] The same reviewer thought the process was a remarkable
transformation that had little to do with rational analysis. Referring to the pandemic racial hostility throughout the North,
particularly among working-class people, he pointed out that
Uncle Tom ran 150 consecutive nights in New York alone, and
that George and Eliza Harris had converted "the sovereign people" while audiences cheered them on. The impact of *Uncle Tom*
on the coming of the Civil War has never been properly evaluated,
but it was great. Surely the fact that Simon Legree could be found
cracking his whip in six London theaters at once in the late fifties
made it unlikely that the public opinion there would readily
yield to Southern desires for recognition once the Emancipation
Proclamation had introduced antislavery as a Northern war
objective.[24]

Dramatic art is more vulnerable than written literature to the
impact of change in popular choice or preference, and the degradation of *Uncle Tom's Cabin* in the late decades of the nineteenth
century is a particularly sad example of that truth. So long as the
idealism of the best aspirations of the Civil War era retained some
vigor, the old melodrama retained a certain amount of dignity,
however badly played it was in country towns across the land.
But soon there was no barrier to making Uncle Tom a poor
parody of the brave Christian of the original, and as a traveling
road show the play gave rise to the miserable stereotype of shuffling
cowardice that has caused Tom's name to become an epithet of
derision in the twentieth century. Live bloodhounds to enhance
the drama of Eliza's flight, real angels to gather around Little Eva
as she died her beautiful death, these all but eclipsed the real
meaning of the original book and play.[25]

Fortunately the book, as distinct from the play, with all its
flaws, read and imagined, remained an internationally recognized
American classic and is now regarded by several highly perceptive critics as being very serious literature indeed.[26] Nobody ex-

pressed better the reason this should have happened in time than Henry James did many years ago. As he remembered it,

> We lived and moved . . . with great intensity, in Mrs. Stowe's novel . . . There was, however, I think for that triumphant work no classified condition; it was for no sort of reader as distinct from any other sort, save indeed for Northern as differing from Southern; it knew the large felicity of gathering in alike the small and the simple and the big and the wise, and had above all the extraordinary fortune of finding itself, for an immense number of people, much less a book than a state of vision, of feeling and of consciousness, in which they didn't sit and read and appraise . . . but walked and talked and laughed and cried . . . in a manner of which Mrs. Stowe was the irresistible cause . . . .[27]

However ludicrous *Uncle Tom* became at its worst, his was too realistic and compassionate a story to lend itself to the vicious hate-inciting characterizations of blacks that became increasingly common as the nineteenth century neared its close. In time the moving-picture industry would favor blacks and restore much of the original dignity of Uncle Tom, but that development had to wait many years. In fact the most successful movie of the era of silent film was David Wark Griffith's *Birth of a Nation,* a brilliant piece of technology in the development of a new art form, and a drama that gave evidence of the very nadir of race relations and the badly deteriorating images of blacks. The classic picture was released in 1915, and it continues to be seen regularly in spite of its characterizations of blacks as beastly savages, in part because of its historical position in the development of silent film, in part because, at the time it appeared, the National Association for the Advancement of Colored People secured the removal of some of the more shocking scenes. They have been lost, but what remains sums up the clichés for an unhappy epoch in American life and suggests how harsh the excised footage must have been.[28]

The movie was an adaptation of a best-selling novel called *The Clansman,* by Thomas Ryan Dixon, a native of North Carolina, who was brought up in poverty in the shadow of the Civil War and Reconstruction years.[29] Dixon shared some characteristics with his Georgian contemporary Thomas Watson, whose sudden onslaught of racist bigotry at the end of the century is explained by his biographer, C. Vann Woodward, as being born of frustration that reflects a souring of his hopes as a Populist leader working for political cooperation across the color line.[30] Though Dixon was not a Populist, he had been in the decade of the 1890s a highly influential Baptist minister preaching in an unfashionable section of New York, who packed in great crowds to hear his Social Gospel message. He was admirably solicitous of the poor and the immigrants. The words he had for blacks in those days were encouraging and favorable to their progress since emancipation. But, for reasons not entirely clear, the Reverend Mr. Dixon had concluded by 1902 that the Negro was a "menace." Some writers have suggested that America's entry into the scramble for empire combined badly with Dixon's unabashed Darwinism and caused him to turn against blacks; it is true that just at the time this change on race is registered, Dixon began fulminating jingoistic attacks on the Spanish.[31] For his own part Dixon explained that his decision to write a set of novels that would set the Civil War and Reconstruction in a true perspective had come to him when he saw a 1901 revival of *Uncle Tom's Cabin*. In his anger he restrained the impulse to jump up and denounce the play, but decided to "make a merciless record of the facts" instead.[32]

In the first of the triology, *The Leopard's Spots,* Dixon called for complete separation of the races, or the expulsion of blacks from the country, claiming, in the words of one of his characters, "in a democracy you cannot build a nation inside a nation of two antagonistic races. . . ."[33] Not so subtly Dixon introduced a few of the characters from *Uncle Tom's Cabin* to make his argument. Now George Harris reappears, still a mulatto, still a well-educated one, but now he is in love with a daughter of a prominent Northern political leader, who instantly sees the error of his ways when Harris asks for her hand. This routine became a cliché in the language of racist argumentation for two generations. Dixon always denied having any but "the friendliest feelings and the profoundest pity" for blacks, and maintained that his book was "the most important moral deed of my life. There is not a bitter or malignant sentence in it." Dixon's brother, A. C. Dixon, who was also a minister, accused him of writing his book for profit, and the aging father once reproached his son for being too hard on the black man, who had too much to bear in any case.[34]

The Clansman followed in 1905 and was used a decade later as the main plot for Griffith's famous film. This novel was openly aimed to redirect sympathies on the main events of the postwar Reconstruction, which it described in lurid detail. There were political aspects surrounding its appearance and reception that indicated the time was ripe for the North to take a more Southern point of view. The central figure of the story is a Southern war hero named Ben Cameron, who has returned home to the Southern Piedmont after convalescing from a serious wound in a Washington, D.C., hospital. He has, of course, fallen madly in love with his attractive nurse, a Northern girl who happens to be the daughter of the United States senator Austin Stoneman. Stoneman is a very, very thinly veiled impersonation of Thaddeus Stevens, whose grim countenance has long graced the American-history textbooks with the appropriate indication beneath identifying him as the chief of the "Vindictives" in Congress, those who wished to impose a severe punishment on the South after the end of the war.

Few scholars today would accord Congressman Stevens that importance, and all would be aware that there was much more at stake in Reconstruction than punishing the South. But in Dixon's story the wicked forces of vengeance in Congress are released by the assassination of Lincoln, for Radical leaders are able to blame the South for this terrible deed, and they employ it to impose a reign of terror on the prostrate Southern states. This is accomplished by the simple expedient of disenfranchising all the white people who have had anything to do with the war, and enfranchising the slaves.

There are significant changes in the film version, but in both book and film black voters are manipulated by wicked Northerners who have come south to humiliate Southern whites, especially the old owners, who suffer many indignities before they resort to violence. Insults were endured by a law-abiding people, but once the safety of pure white womanhood was in danger they did not hesitate, and the hero of the action, Ben Cameron, becomes the leader of the Ku Klux Klan, organized to punish perpetrators of rape. This secret organization, the real centerpiece of Dixon's story, became in his hands the saving instrument of Southern civilization. That it was connected in some way with the rise in the 1920s of the modern Klan is hard to dispute, though Dixon tried to dissociate them altogether, and disapproved of the new Klan.[35] Throughout the story there are many history lessons. One is given by young Ben Cameron when he courts Senator

Stoneman's daughter. Elsie Stoneman "began to understand why
the war, which had seemed to her a wicked, cruel, and causeless
rebellion, was the one inevitable thing in our growth from a loose
group of sovereign states to a United Nation. Love had given her
his point of view."[36]

Actually the nation itself was having a kind of love feast, celebrating over these years the fiftieth anniversary of the beginning
and close of the Civil War. A new, highly symbolic interpretation of the conflict and its close was being worked out, not, of
course, by Ben Cameron and Elsie Stoneman alone, but by serious
scholars, including Woodrow Wilson, the future president. While
ready to pay tribute to the heroism of the Confederate soldiers,
and the sacrifices to the lost cause, the South should be glad that
the North had won and ended slavery, he said, for its was "ener-
vating our Southern society and exhausting our Southern energies."[37] This new view could arrange a classic historiographical
quid pro quo between North and South on the basis of agreement
on both sides that the North had been right about the Civil War,
that secession had been wrong, and that through the suppression
of secession had come the end of slavery, which was a good thing,
especially for white people.

On the other hand, the Northern leaders had been much
mistaken in their Reconstruction policy—"damnable cruelty and
folly," Woodrow Wilson had called it—and their attempt to
enforce equal rights for the former slave had been a grave
injustice to Southern white people. The sensationalism of Dixon's
demonology cast a lurid glare over his fictional history, but many
respectable persons, some of them scholars of repute, shared his
views if not his style. The images of bestial sexuality and yellow
eyes gleaming in the jungle, and the apelike characterizations in
the picture seared themselves into the minds of the thousands who
saw the film. That these parts were played by whites blacked up
with burnt cork completed the irony.[38]

After Dixon's books and the Griffith film the South commanded
center court on Reconstruction history for many years. One of the
early reviewers of *The Clansman* asked why this should be. There
were some questionable matters of historical detail, but more
significant was "the apparent ease with which the author makes a
decidedly plausible presentation for his defense of the Southern
attitude, and the apparent readiness of the Northern mind to

receive that defense in unruffled patience, if not with positive favor." He commented that only a few years earlier such ideas would have been rejected instantly, for American orators were praising political equality as "the immediate jewel of our national soul."[39] The reviewer saw the answer: it was that the idea of political equality was "dangerous and ill-defined," and that "whether it was formerly so or not, the North must now bear with the South its equal share of responsibility for those dangers."[40]

The author might have added that the increased immigration from southern Europe caused many old friends of freedom in the North to wonder if the South hadn't been right in opposing equal franchise. The growth of urban political machines and the power of political bosses over these people whose appearance and languages were strange seemed to threaten the world they had understood.[41] And so the steady march of segregation in the South went largely unopposed. With *Plessy* v. *Ferguson* in 1896 the Supreme Court gave approval to the doctrine of separate but equal. Only one dissenter, the Kentucky-born John Marshall Harlan, reasoned that separate facilities were inherently unequal and designed to fill the excluded with self-contempt; it would be fifty years before a new Supreme Court would see that he was right.

The dominant view of the Civil War epoch popularized at the turn of the century remained powerful down to World War II, when it was at last challenged to its roots by the Nazi holocaust. Then the hypocrisy of maintaining so great a struggle in the name of democracy so badly abused at home smote the consciences of thoughtful citizens. But even before that time the Dixon demonology was much abated, almost directly in proportion to the degree to which the black man was rendered insignificant in the ballot box and invisible at the soda fountains.

After World War I the black image in books and plays is muted and more often assumed than it is explained and illustrated. Dixon's success is registered in this quiet acceptance. The classic example of this tendency was Margaret Mitchell's *Gone With the Wind,* which appeared in 1936, and launched the greatest publishing-viewing extravaganza of all time.[42]

The point to remember about this work was that it had the same power to sweep its readers and audiences into the state Henry James described in the *Uncle Tom* experience. It became a state of mind and as much a part of the late years of the depression as *Uncle Tom* had been in the 1850s. On June 30, 1936, the day of publication, 100 thousand copies were in print; in three months the figure had nearly quadrupled; and within six months the then unheard-of figure of one million had been sold. The naughty heroine, Scarlett O'Hara, has had the international appeal of Uncle Tom, and as soon as the David O. Selznick movie plans became known, casting the main characters of the story became a favourite parlor game. There were important differences between the book and the play, but together they registered completely the national state of mind about race and region.

Margaret Mitchell had read Dixon's books early in life, and had as a girl-playwright actually adapted one of them for a neighborhood theatrical for her playmates to enact. Miss Mitchell acknowledged this influence in a graceful letter thanking the aging Dixon for writing her a fan letter. She acknowledged Dixon further, and less directly, by using his view of the rise of the Ku Klux Klan to explain the phenomenon in her book.[43] But on the whole the picture of race relations in Margaret Mitchell's work is more paternalistic, and the "good darkies" are highly significant elements of the plot. It is the reverse of the case in *The Clansman,* where the "bad niggers" are important to the action, and the good ones merely background. Mammy is essential to *Gone With the Wind,* and Hattie McDaniel's grand execution of her role in the movie won her an Oscar. She made even more of "Mammy" in the film than Miss Mitchell had in her book, and in doing so disarmed much black criticism that might otherwise have come upon the plantation stereotypes the modern Negro had begun so much to hate.[44]

It was a step forward, if a very small one, to see what a great black actress could make of the stock figure of the plantation mammy. For the most part the rendering of blacks as the happy, carefree plantation darkies was the natural consequence of Mitchell's celebration of the romantic plantation legend. Until the image of black as beast was thrust aside it made no sense to paint a picture of a period of peace and plenty, white columns and peacocks, cotton and serenity back before the war. Dixon had not tried it, and contented himself with some rather simple conclusions about the affectionate, God-fearing life pursued by his Scots-Irish ancestors in the Upcountry of the western Carolinas.

One reason for *Gone With the Wind*'s success was that it became the first fully realized film version of the traditional plantation romance. But it had enough realism, just enough, to make it credible. There is a recognition of economic force in historical explanation totally absent from Dixon. The renegade aristocrat Rhett Butler is Scarlett's supremely realistic romantic foil; he tells the young Southern cavaliers so anxious to get into war that they cannot win. Why not? Not enough munitions plants and woolen mills. What if there should be a blockade, as there surely would be?[45] It was quite as though Miss Mitchell had been reading Charles Beard's economic interpretation of American history. After the heroine returns to the ruined plantation near the end of the war and faces starvation, she becomes frenetic in her pursuit of security. Her trouble has been great, to be sure, and after a dramatic gesture choking on a raw turnip she has devoured to assuage her great hunger, outlined against a red sky, she pledges that she will never be hungry again.

Scarlett solves her problems, essentially by doing what her folks would have called "outyankeeing the Yankees." She goes into trade, and gets for herself a store in booming postwar Atlanta, and then a lumber mill. Her search for security becomes sheer greed, and her shabby dealings in business are meant as a personal characterization of the city of Atlanta itself, and by extension the New South. This is what Margaret Mitchell contributed to the growing legend. Here was a brash young city, burned out in war, rising from its ashes, a country-cousin kind of town when compared with stately, refined places like Charleston and Savannah. By implication these gentle old cities could no more cope with the crude necessities of the postwar world than Scarlett's more aristocratic friends and relatives. "Atlanta," on the other hand, it seemed, "must always be hurrying, no matter what its circumstances might be." Of course, "it was ill-bred and Yankeefied to hurry. But Atlanta was more ill-bred and Yankeefied (after the war) than it had ever been before or would ever be again." The identification of Scarlett's character and the city is quite explicit: "Atlanta was of her own generation, crude with the crudities of youth and as headstrong and impetuous as herself."[46]

What that city became was what Scarlett herself became, and the cost of success to character in overcoming defeat is Miss Mitchell's second important theme. Atlanta celebrates the vulgarity of new wealth in the accumulation of ugly mansions with massive furniture in the dark, rich, and cloying interiors rendered so faithfully in the Selznick film. In character Scarlett is a match for this crass materialism, fulfilling her pledge that she'll never go hungry again by laying up treasures on earth through the exploitation of convict labor and many other shabby, immoral acts. Her character is meant to illustrate the cost of survival. Gentle people who represent the best of the past fare poorly, and are like Ashley Wilkes, in Rhett Butler's description of him. Such people "have neither cunning nor strength, or having them scruple to use them. And so they go under. . . ."[47] The New South creed was torn between the realism of facing the future with the spirit of Yankee enterprise and comforting its sense of loss with a new devotion to the myth of the lost world of serenity, peace, and plenty.

Therefore Margaret Mitchell was of two minds about the capacity of old aristocrats to endure. For all the Ashley Wilkeses who are going down because they lack some vital force, there are others like his wife. Melanie, who derive strength from the traditional past, who are ready to pay the price in contemporary terms for maintaining the standards of decency and honorable relations that they learned in happier times. They do not go under; but they do not get rich either. The author is almost dividing the personality of the New South between Scarlett and Melanie, for there were both aspects to the face of survival. The value the author assigns to family loyalty and the abiding devotion to land and place and people is important not only in explaining Melanie Wilkes, but also in explaining how Scarlett began her sordid life in commerce. Whatever she is, or is to become, Scarlett holds the family together, forces all to work as hard as she does, and does not scruple to lie or steal, even to sell herself, in order to raise the money that will save her father's plantation from the tax collectors.

Margaret Mitchell's fictional New South of the 1870s was influenced to a considerable degree by the experience of the 1930s' Depression. Themes of hardship and survival had special appeal to the Depression generation, who could understand without prompting how it was to be penniless and confused in the middle of a rich and fallow land. There had to be a little bit of Scarlett and a little bit of Melanie in those who came through that

troubled time. Margaret Mitchell had worried ahead of publication that the South would reject the materialism of her work;
indeed, Scarlett's survival owes nothing to religion, however much
nostalgia she may feel for that lost religion of her good mother.
But Miss Mitchell need not have concerned herself. There was
the comforting image of what people liked to think their world
had once been, in a time of peace and plenty, and any good
Southerner could see what a great impression the work was making
north of the Mason-Dixon line.

The North was going to adopt the plantation South before the
war as its *own* Garden of Eden, and if Atlanta looked and behaved
a lot like many New England towns and cities in the Gilded Age
and after, then why not regard these qualities at a safe distance?
A fully romantic vision of the Old South *and* the New served
emotional appeals in both sections. The critics, like Malcolm
Cowley and Bernard DeVoto, might rail to their heart's content
against the false vision, and they could assail the damaging effects
of a belief in the plantation myth as much as they liked, but Miss
Mitchell and her friends professed themselves to be amused, and,
like Haley later on, could see from the sales that there was a good
market for myths, of however recent vintage.[48]

How good are these works? It would not surprisre me greatly
if *Gone With the Wind* eventually arrives with its strong survival
credentials and wins the respect of the more discriminating critics,
as *Uncle Tom's Cabin* has now shown signs of doing. *The Clansman* never will, and it is too soon to predict anything about *Roots.*
There is good writing and bad in it. But it seems beside the point
to assess these works as high culture, as *art,* for they do not need
to be. They serve as vehicles for celebration of shared convictions,
the public vehicle of new agreements on what to believe, at the
growing point of American myth. It doesn't really matter whether
some of us like it and some of us do not.

In conclusion may I say that I have seriously searched for other
such popular reading-viewing successes that have sustained themselves for so long, and contributed to the shorthand visual images
and vocabulary of the American experience in section and race as
these have done. I cannot find them. It seems there must therefore
be certain characteristics that have marked these books-turned-
drama for special favor from the time of their initial appearance.
High inspiration, didactic purpose (in all save *Gone With the*

Wind): these, plus the shared theme, pull them together. The major setting of each is the South, except for the African parts of *Roots*. Celebratory effects, mass participation, an *insistence* on sharing the experience, these are the universal style of these events. Each in its own way has positive things to say about family and affirms the force of cultural continuity. Each has appeared at just the moment when a new synthesis was forming concerning the American Civil War and race in America.

This combination of circumstances emboldens me to suppose that somewhere around the year 2000 some such thing may occur again. Whether it will be a good thing or a bad thing I do not feel obliged to guess, but that there are cautionary signals against too free a use of history as national or sectional or ethnic therapy ought to be plain enough. Popular culture, as distinguished from high culture, is widely accessible at some level to a multitude who may or may not be equipped to place what is seen in a perspective. The modern pop culture relies more on pictures than on words, and ambiguities may be lost in the impact of living color and violent action. The advent of television has opened potential problems undreamed-of in Harriet Beecher Stowe's time, when literacy first began to outstrip real education. Reading is in some degree an arranged match between reader and book; if he doesn't understand the words the reader will discard the book.

Thomas Ryan Dixon, in a successful ploy to defuse criticism of his controversial film, invited a very distinguished company of senators, congressmen, and the Supreme Court to a private viewing; and while they watched *Birth of a Nation,* he watched them: "that we had not only discovered a new universal language of man, but that an appeal to the human will through this tongue would be equally resistless [irresistible] to an audience of chauffeurs or a gathering of a thousand college professors."[49] There were few even then who could be at once as appreciative and objective as the poet Vachel Lindsay, who wrote of the film that it was a "picture of crowd splendor" in which the "Ku Klux Klan dashes down the road as powerfully as Niagara pours over the cliff" with "mobs splendidly handled, tossing wildly and rhythmically like the sea." Alas, thought Lindsay, that D. W. Griffith had put this art in service to "the Reverend Thomas Dixon's poisonous hatred of the Negro."[50]

Dixon's father and brother had more detachment than most,

when they criticized him for inciting hatred for personal gain. President Woodrow Wilson called it "history written in lightning," and thought it "all too true." He had been a college professor, it is worth remembering, and had picked up some Aryan notions of his own in the same school where Dixon studied briefly.[51] If the college professors of tomorrow are to prove Dixon wrong about their own inability to resist the blandishments of "history written in lightning" they have a very large order; if they are to help others to bring a detached capacity to discern, the order is much larger. It will involve at the very least teaching more history more effectively to more students. The good teacher will be suspicious of the trendy, but sufficiently modest to recognize that what is apparent may also be real. Modesty is the appropriate reading-viewing style.

NOTES

1. R. W. B. Lewis, *The American Adam: Innocence, Tragedy, and Tradition in the Nineteenth Century* (Chicago, 1955), p. 1. The genesis of this essay was my review of Alex Haley's *Roots* done for the *New York Review of Books* (November 11, 1976). At the time it seemed to me a part of an ongoing process of myth making, and in a lecture given at the State University of New York at Brockport I made a connection between the four writers discussed here and their works. I placed more emphasis at that time on the technological advances. I am much indebted to Mr. William Harris of the Department of History at the Johns Hopkins University for rounding up many obscure reviews and articles on the four works I discuss in this essay; he also proved a most stimulating conversationalist on the subject, offering many suggestions that were useful. I should also like to thank Mr. John d'Entremont for serving as a clipping agency for notices of *Roots* and "Roots" on his own research trips during the winter and spring of 1977.

2. The publication phenomenon of *Uncle Tom's Cabin* is recounted in many places. An excellent summary of the event is found in James D. Hart's *The Popular Book* (New York, 1950), pp. 111–12. Hart points out that the sales at the end of 1852 within the United States stood at 305,000 copies, which would be for the population of that time about equivalent to a sale of three million in the population of the country as it stood in 1947; when one considers that the sales south of the Potomac must have been very small, the popular success of *Uncle Tom's Cabin* is all the more remarkable. It was even more astounding in England. A manufacturer of parlor games quickly devised a new one to show with pawns "the continual separation and reunion of families," while far out on the frontier California miners were renting copies "for two bits a day." Hart, p. 111.

3. *The Leopard's Spots: A Romance of the White Man's Burden* (New York, 1901); *The Clansman: A Historical Romance of the Ku Klux Klan* (New York, 1905); *The Traitor: A Story of the Fall of the Ku Klux Klan* (New York, 1907). The last book was not as successful as the first two. It detailed the dissolution of the Klan after the founders saw the abuse to which it was put in the hands of unworthy leaders. Needless to say, most modern scholars have recognized that the Klan was never free of political impulses, and Allen Trelease in *White Terror: The Ku Klux Klan Conspiracy and Southern Reconstruction* (New York, 1971) emphasizes the Klan's objectives as being the removal of blacks from political life and the return of the Democratic party to majority status.

4. Richard E. Harwell, in his editorial "Introduction" to *Margaret Mitchell's "Gone With the Wind" Letters, 1936–1949* (New York, 1976), p. xxvii. The figure of 21 million is given for hardback and paperback sales since 1936 in "Why 'Roots' Hit Home," *Time*, February 14, 1977. Other figures have been deduced from James D. Hart, *The Popular Book*, p. 263.

5. BBC radio news bulletin of April 6, 1978.

6. The phenomenon is perhaps still too fresh for the establishment of accurate data, but the most authoritative accumulation of reasonable statistics is in David Gerber's essay-review "Haley's *Roots* and Our Own: An Inquiry into the Nature of a Popular Phenomenon," *Journal of Ethnic Studies*, 5 (1977), 87–111. The television showing of the drama occurred in the United States on eight consecutive evenings between January 23 and 31. For sales, see "Why 'Roots' Hit Home," *Time*, February 14, 1977.

7. Alex Haley, *Roots: The Saga of an American Family* (New York, 1976), pp. 568–70. Kunta Kinte called the guitar a "ko," and a river in Virginia (probably the Rappahannock) the "kamby Bolongo"—very likely "Gambia" River.

8. Mark Ottaway, "Tangled Roots," *Sunday Times*, April 10, 1977; and personal correspondence from Africanist field workers in author's possession.

9. ABC had frequent interviews on their morning show with Haley, the actors, and members of the production team of "Roots" during the week of the television series and for some weeks afterwards, especially in the period following April 10, when Mark Ottaway's article appeared.

10. See Willie Lee Rose, "An American Family," *New York Review of Books*, November 11, 1976; "Root's Errors Held Unimportant," Baltimore *Sun*, April 10, 1977; "New York Panel Digs at 'Roots'," New York *Post*, April 14, 1977; Israel Shenker, "Some Historians Dismiss Charge of Factual Mistakes in 'Roots'," New York *Times*, April 10, 1977; Walter Goodman, "Fact, Fiction or Symbol?," editorial page, New York *Times*, April 15, 1977.

11. Harriet Beecher Stowe, *A Key to Uncle Tom's Cabin* (Boston, 1853). Raymond Allen Cook, *Fire from the Flint: The Amazing Careers of Thomas Dixon* (Winston-Salem, N.C., 1968), p. 142, quoting the Charleston *News & Courier*, October 19, 1905. See Harwell (ed.), *Mitchell's Letters*, especially Mitchell's letter of July 30, 1937, to Miss Ruth Tallman of Lakefield, Minnesota, pp. 160–2, where eight points are taken up individually, and to Alexander

L. May of Berlin on July 22, 1938, where Mitchell lists a bibliography of works on the Civil War and Reconstruction, pp. 215–17.

12. There is another reward too that pleases Haley: black children see him as a model for success. One stiff-braided little girl, brought with her class to meet Haley at a Los Angeles bookstore, said matter-of-factly, "I'm going to write a bigger book than you." Replied Halty: "Come on, honey, and do it." *Time*, February 14, 1977, p. 51.

13. Ibid.

14. Frank Luther Mott recounts the incident without citation in *Golden Multitudes: The Story of Best Sellers in the United States* (New York, 1947), p. 15.

15. Essay-review, "Uncle Tomitudes," *Putnam's Magazine*, I (January 1853).

16. Catherine Gilbertson, *Harriet Beecher Stowe* (New York, 1937), pp. 140–42. Mrs. Stowe gives this account of her inspiration in her preface to the 1878 edition of *Uncle Tom's Cabin*.

17. *Uncle Tom's Cabin* (Cambridge, Mass., 1962), edited with an Introduction by K.S. Lynn, pp. 422, 424, 425. This edition will be used throughout for citations from the text.

18. Ibid., p. 12.

19. Harriet's brother, Edward, and his wife, Isabel Hooker Beecher, were becoming increasingly involved in abolition, and the entire family was more disturbed by the slavery question after the passage of the Fugitive Slave Act of 1850, but before that time their course had been moderate, little in advance of the position the Congregational churches had taken. As head of Lane Seminary, Lyman Beecher had been unsympathetic to the radical position of the young orator Theodore Dwight Weld, one of the students at Lane and leader of a famous series of debates that concluded slaveholding was a sin. Weld led a student exodus to Oberlin College, which became an avowed center of anti-slavery activity.

20. *Uncle Tom's Cabin*, p. 184. The Byronic characteristics of St. Clare have often been pointed out, but nowhere more effectively than by Kenneth S. Lynn in his introduction to the edition used here.

21. The reviewer-essayist for the *North American Review*, 77 (1853), 466–93, took this position, arguing that "No one worthy a reply" would demand that the Negroes of the South should be given a "share of political power" (p. 481), and he believed that in most instances free blacks of the North were "properly" denied such rights. He pointed out that women and children were also denied full freedom and for the same reason. They were subject to authority "for their own good and the good of society." The author thought blacks to be much inferior to whites, and that slavery "is necessary to the repose, prosperity, and safety of the white race in the South, because of the numbers and degraded condition of the negroes," and that it was "also essential to the well-being of the negro, because of his incapacity to govern and take care of himself, and because experience shows that he is by nature fitted for this

relation and that he thrives and is happy in it." He calmly pointed out that some persons believed such a social relationship should be set up for the governance in the Northern states of "the swarms of emigrants who crowd our shores, many of them equally degraded by ignorance, poverty, and vice and equally needing care, guidance and government." He admitted that he was "not sure" himself that this was a desirable measure, but went on to explain that it was not slavery that was wrong, but rather the consideration of a slave as property. The evils of slavery flowed from the laws and practices of the South that declared a slave to be property, and without these slavery could be what it claimed to be, a system "of domestic relations" (pp. 483–84). The writer indulged in unrealistic hopes that ownership of the slave's labor and not his person would serve to preserve the slave from separation from family by sale, from the brutality of wicked owners, and from the nonslave-holders, who were, he said, "a wretched population, idle, vicious, and poor, such as grows up where free industry is degraded by slavery, and robbed by it, also, of employment and reward," who were "the worst enemies of the slave" and "the greatest obstacle to any scheme for his benefit" (pp. 488–89). The review was thoroughly racist and elitist to the core, and the author plainly believed that Mrs. Stowe's book demonstrated the wisdom of his proposals, and had intended nothing more. His view is an excellent illustration of the cause for fear among many working-class Northerners that some form of peonage might be pressed upon them by Northern supporters of the "Slave Power Conspiracy."

22. Mott, *Golden Multitudes,* p. 122.

23. *American Slavery* (London, 1856), p. 29. This pamphlet is an enlargement and reprinting of an article on *Uncle Tom's Cabin* appearing in no. 206 of the *Edinburgh Review*. The author was Nassau W. Senior.

24. "But it is in England where Uncle Tom has made his deepest impact," wrote the author of "Uncle Tomitudes" in *Putnam's Magazine* (January 1853). "Such has been the sensation produced by the book there, and so numerous have been the editions published, that it is extremely difficult to collect the statistics of its circulation with a tolerable degree of exactness. But we know of twenty rival editions in England and Scotland, and that millions of copies have been produced" (p. 99). The reviewer pointed out that the copyright laws did not protect Mrs. Stowe's work, and suggested that Lord Carlisle should have restrained his criticisms of slavery in the introduction to the Routledge edition until the publisher paid the author for the use of her text! The readers of *Uncle Tom's Cabin* in England and Scotland were taking up a penny subscription as a testimonial to reimburse the author. Dicken's work had been the victim in America of the same abuse owing to inadequate copy-right protection. This fact was brought to my attention by H. G. Nicholas, Rhodes Professor, Oxford University. Forrest Wilson, *Crusader in Crinoline: The Life of Harriet Beecher Stowe* (Philadelphia, 1941), p. 351, quotes the remark of Charles Sumner, that Lincoln could not have been elected in 1860 without the effect of *Uncle Tom's Cabin* on public opinion.

25. Thomas L. Cripps, *Slow Fade to Black: The Negro in American Film, 1900–1942* (New York, 1977), pp. 16–17. The role as played by James Lowe in 1927 marked the beginning of a more favorable trend toward the restoration of admirable characteristics to the hero.

26. In *Patriotic Gore: Studies in the Literature of the American Civil War* (New York, 1962), Edmund Wilson has a distinguished essay on Harriet Beecher Stowe and her achievement. Kenneth S. Lynn's introduction to the John Harvard Library edition (see n. 17) praises her characterizations, "shockingly believable," and compliments Stowe on her "penetrating and uncompromising realism. . . ." Leslie Fiedler has also taken Mrs. Stowe very seriously. See Edward C. Wagenknecht, *Harriet Beecher Stowe: The Known and the Unknown* (New York, 1965), p. 3, for others. Needless to say, these tendencies have appeared only in the last two decades.

27. Henry James, "A Small Boy and Others," pp. 92–93, in *Henry James' Autobiography*, ed. Frederick W. Dupré (London, 1956).

28. Reconstructing the acceptance of *Birth of a Nation* by the public is complicated by the fact that some parts were edited out for showing in one locality, while different sections were deleted in others. For the NAACP the most objectionable parts were the original scenes showing blacks running amok in the town of Piedmont, pursuing white women into dark alleys with all too obvious intentions (footage now gone), and the actions of Senator Stoneman's mulatto mistress, writhing in a perfect passion of mingled lasciviousness and anticipated revenge for a social insult, from none other than Senator Charles Sumner! Other objectionable scenes were the attempted rape of Flora Cameron and Silas Lynch's assertion of independence from Senator Stoneman. Kenneth Paul O'Brien, "The Savage and the Child: Images of Blacks in Southern White Thought, 1830–1915" (Ph.D. diss., Northwestern University, 1974), pp. 219–20, 223. I read this dissertation in Microfilm Publications.

29. Raymond Allen Cook, *Fire from the Flint: The Amazing Careers of Thomas Dixon*, has limitations from the point of view of the social historian, but it is the only biography available, though there are interesting treatments of Dixon in the context of his work in Maxwell Bloomfield, "Dixon's *The Leopard's Spots:* A Study in Popular Racism," *American Quarterly*, 16 (1964), and in O'Brien.

30. C. Vann Woodward, *Tom Watson: Agrarian Rebel* (New York, 1938, also issued as a paperback in 1963).

31. O'Brien, "Savage and Child," pp. 197–98. Dixon claimed to be a radical and a socialist. Bloomfield points out that Dixon justified his Negrophobia on scientific and humanitarian grounds. "He used liberal arguments to buttress a reactionary creed, and therein lay his appeal to a reform-minded generation." Bloomfield, "Dixon's *The Leopard's Spots*," p. 396.

32. Cook, *Fire from the Flint*, p. 105.

33. *The Leopard's Spots*, the Reverend John Durham speaking, quoted in Cook, *Flint*, pp. 119–20.

34. Cook's biography makes use of family letters in private custody. Brother Clarence's criticisms are described on p. 116.

35. Kenneth T. Jackson, *The Ku Klux Klan in the City, 1915–1930* (New York, 1967), explains the rise of the twentieth-century Klan.

36. Dixon, *Clansman*, p. 149.

37. Thomas J. Pressly, *Americans Interpret Their Civil War* (New York, 1965), pp. 199–200, quoting a speech made by Wilson at the University of Virginia. Cripps and others have stressed the importance of the Golden Jubilee years of Civil War in promoting the new synthesis of the history of the epoch, and so it is interesting to find Wilson speaking the substance of the quid pro quo so early.

38. Cripps, *Slow Fade,* p. 27: "This metaphor of Southern tragedy which he [Griffith] developed and with which he infused his epic, *The Birth of a Nation*, helped to firmly etch the outlines of Negro character in film long after its fidelity to American realities had passed." This was particularly unfortunate in its consequences for the North, especially the nonurban North, for contacts with blacks were infrequent, and there were few correctives. This accounts in part for the ready acceptance of the same view as it reappears in less melodramatic form in *Gone With the Wind* twenty years later.

39. W. H. Johnson, reviewing *The Clansman* in *Critic,* 46 (1905), 278.

40. Ibid.

41. The development of the "tragic era" interpretation of Reconstruction is associated with the work of William R. Dunning and his students who wrote monographs on the individual Southern states during Reconstruction, and it finally achieved a popular expression almost as melodramatic as Dixon's *The Clansman* in Claude Bowers's *The Tragic Era,* which was not to appear until 1929. Dunning's teachings might have influenced the young novelist, and ideas circulating at the Johns Hopkins Historical Seminar under Herbert Baxter Adams no doubt had their influence on Dixon. But Dunning's own *Reconstruction, Political and Economic* had not appeared when Dixon wrote *The Clansman,* and it is perhaps realistic to see this classic historiographical bargain between North and South as being of gradual development. Indeed, the pieces were there lying around from the beginning, and one will find an excellent prospective view of it in Herman Melville's supplement to his *Battle Pieces,* a collection of poems he published in 1866, just after the war, and before the installation of the program of military reconstruction. He is pleading from moderation on the part of the North, asking that consideration for blacks should not cause the North to be "hostile to [white] communities who stand nearer to us in nature . . ." and arguing further that the great problem, the "grave evil," was the necessity of interracial coexistence. He pointed out that the misguided defenders of the Southern cause could not be convinced they were wrong simply because they were defeated, and that the heroes of the Confederacy would remain heroes in spite of defeat. Just as Burns and Scott honored "the memory of the gallant clansmen ruined through their fidelity to the Stuarts," so would the South remember her own, and Melville strongly suggests the North will too. Thus, before the event of Radical Reconstruction, ingredients of the turn-of-the-century peace were at present: the South wins points on Robert E. Lee, and the North, on Lincoln and Union.

42. Harwell, ed., *Mitchell Letters,* introd., p. xxvii.

43. Margaret Mitchell to Thomas R. Dixon, August 15, 1936, in Harwell, ed., *Mitchell Letters,* pp. 52–53.

44. Cripps, *Slow Fade,* pp. 361–66.

45. In an important letter to Alexander L. May, July 22, 1938, Margaret Mitchell recommends that her correspondent read Robert S. Henry's *The Story of the Confederacy* and his *The Story of Reconstruction* (Harwell, ed., *Mitchell Letters,* pp. 215–17).

46. *Gone With the Wind,* chaps. VIII, XXXVII.

47. Ibid., chap. XLI. Henry Steele Commager singled out this passage to compliment the author in the review he wrote for the New York *Herald Tribune Books,* July 5, 1936. In a grateful response Margaret Mitchell said that this idea was the genesis of her work, that her mother had told her she would very likely have to work very hard herself, and would be expected to struggle for her existence as those whose burned-out houses stood along the Jonesboro Road out of Atlanta had struggled. The connection between those who faced the Depression in their young adulthood as Margaret Mitchell did and the post–Civil War generation is implied, but not developed. Paul M. Gaston in *The New South Creed* explains the importance of the Old South myth as a comfort to the New South, hustling along under the self-deception that the "progress" the new factories and mines seemed to represent was really progress. The blatant Darwinism of Rhett Butler's speech on Ashley Wilkes did not go down easily, and required the accompaniment of memory. The Old South is thus to a considerable degree a creation of the New. Mitchell's generation did not create it, but those she wrote of in postwar, late-century Atlanta did.

48. Harwell, ed., *Mitchell Letters,* passim.

49. Cook, *Fire from the Flint,* p. 173.

50. Quoted in Cripps, *Slow Fade,* p. 55.

51. Cook, *Fire from the Flint,* pp. 50–53.

Race

Ideology and Race in American History

BARBARA J. FIELDS

T HE notion of race has played a role in the way Americans think about their history similar to that once played by the frontier and, if anything, more durable. Long after the notion of the frontier has lost its power to do so, that of race continues to tempt many people into the mistaken belief that American experience constitutes the great exception in world history, the great deviation from patterns that seem to hold for everybody else. Elsewhere, classes may have struggled over power and privilege, over oppression and exploitation, over competing senses of justice and right; but in the United States, these were secondary to the great, overarching theme of race. U. B. Phillips once wrote that the determination to preserve a white man's country was the central theme of Southern history.[1] Today, chastened by the failed hopes of the civil-rights era and genuinely appalled at the ironic turn of events that has seemed at times to give the Ku Klux Klan as much standing in California and Michigan as in Georgia or Mississippi, many humane individuals would re- gretfully extend Phillips's dictum. The determination to keep the United States a white man's country, they would say, has been the central theme of American, not just Southern, history. Racism has been America's tragic flaw.

Questions of color and race have been at the center of some of the most important events in American experience, and Americans

I completed this essay while a guest scholar at the Woodrow Wilson International Center for Scholars, Smithsonian Institution. During that period I was supported by a fellowship from the Ford Foundation.

For their comments on the manuscript I would like to thank the following people: Ira Berlin, David Brion Davis, Karen E. Fields, Eugene D. Genovese, Steven Hahn, Thomas C. Holt, James Horton, James A. McPherson, Sidney Mintz, Joseph P. Reidy, Richard Stites, Laurance Whitehead, and Harold D. Woodman.

continue to live with their ugly and explosive consequences. It would be absurd and frivolously provocative to deny this, and it is not my intention to do so. It is my intention to suggest that Americans, including many historians, tend to accord race a transhistorical, almost metaphysical, status that removes it from all possibility of analysis and understanding. Ideologies, including those of race, can be properly analyzed only at a safe distance from their terrain. To assume, by intention or default, that race is a phenomenon outside history is to take up a position within the terrain of racialist ideology and to become its unknowing—and therefore uncontesting—victim.

The first false move in this direction is the easiest: the assumption that race is an observable physical fact, a thing, rather than a notion that is profoundly and in its very essence ideological. A recent newspaper article about the changing composition of the population of Washington, D.C., included the following statement: "The Washington area's population of races other than white or black, meaning mainly Asians, tripled between 1970 and 1977. Recent statistics equivalent to those for racial groups are not available for Hispanics, *who are an ethnic group rather than a separate racial category.*"[2] What makes Hispanics an ethnic group, while blacks, whites, and Asians are racial groups? Presumably, the fact that, while they share a language (no one, surely, would suppose that Hispanics all share a single culture), they do not comprise a single physical type and they originate from different countries. But, on that reasoning, black and white Americans constitute an ethnic group: they are originally from different countries, they certainly do not all look alike, but they share a language.* What about Asians? They are not of a single physical type and they, too, come from different countries. Adhering to common usage, it is hard to see how they can be classed as either a single race or a single ethnic group: they do not all share either a language or a culture.

Then what about blacks? They do not look alike; they came originally from different countries, spoke different languages, and had different cultures. In the heyday of the Atlantic slave trade, both traders and their customers understood that the cargoes of

---

* There comes to mind in this connection the marvelous line in the movie *Little Big Man,* when the old Indian speaks of the freedmen as "the black white men."

the slave ships included Africans of different national, cultural, and linguistic backgrounds. Slave-buying planters talked in voluble, if no doubt misguided, detail about the varied characteristics of Coromantees, Mandingoes, Foulahs, Congoes, Angolas, Eboes, Whydahs, Nagoes, Pawpaws, and Gaboons. Experienced buyers and sellers could distinguish them by sight and speech, and prices would vary accordingly.[3] Black people, in other words, were initially no more a racial group than Hispanics. In the era of the slave trade a social fact—that these people all came from the same exotic continent and that they were all destined for slavery—made the similarities among them more important, in principle, than the differences. Their subsequent experience in slavery, particularly in its mainland North American form, eventually caused the similarities to overwhelm the differences in reality as well.[4]

The fallacy of regarding race as a physical fact may be more likely to receive open expression in the columns of a newspaper than in careful scholarly work, but in moments of mental relaxation, historians often embrace it tacitly. Few, perhaps, would be as bald in this regard as Harmannus Hoetink, who speaks of "somatic norm images" as a psychosocial force that determines human behavior.[5] Still, in discussing the earliest contact between Englishmen and Africans, Winthrop Jordan lays great stress on the Englishmen's reaction to the Africans' color: "Englishmen actually described the Negroes as *black*—an exaggerated term which in itself suggests that the Negro's complexion had powerful impact upon their perceptions. Even the peoples of northern Africa seemed so dark that Englishmen tended to call them 'black' and let further refinements go by the board. Blackness became so generally associated with Africa that every African seemed a black man."[6] There is no reason to doubt that such a striking contrast in color would arrest the attention of Englishmen encountering it for the first time. But surely other circumstances account more powerfully than the psychological impact of color as such for the fact that the English did not tarry over gradations in color. Not the least was the fact that with all their variations in appearance, these people were all inhabitants of the same strange and distant continent. Jordan's own statement concerning the North Africans suggests that the Englishmen's generalization was based as much on geography as on color. Jordan returns to much firmer ground when he remarks: "The Negro's color . . . . served as a highly visible label identifying the natives of a distant continent which for ages Christians had known as a land of men radically defective in religion."[7] Had some of these same dark-skinned, exotic strangers been indigenous to, let us say, a remote corner of Europe upon which Englishmen suddenly and inadvertently stumbled after their first visits to Africa, the difference in geographic origin alone would probably have led the English to attach significance to—and therefore take verbal notice of—variations in appearance that, in the context of the African continent, seemed to them insignificant.

Ideas about color, like ideas about anything else, derive their importance, indeed their very definition, from their context. They can no more be the unmediated reflex of psychic impressions than can any other ideas. It is ideological context that tells people which details to notice, which to ignore, and which to take for granted in translating the world around them into ideas about that world. It does not bother Americans of the late-twentieth century that the term "black" can refer to physically white people, because an ideological context of which they are generally unaware has long since taught them which details to consider significant in classifying people. And the rules vary. Everyone knows, or at least every black person knows, that there are individuals who would be unhesitatingly classified as black in Louisiana or South Carolina and just as unhesitatingly "mistaken" for white in Nebraska or Idaho or the Upper Peninsula of Michigan. According to a story that is probably apocryphal but nonetheless telling, an American journalist once asked the late Papa Doc Duvalier of Haiti what percentage of the Haitian population was white. Duvalier's answer, astonishingly enough, was "Ninety-eight percent." The startled American journalist was sure he had either misheard or been misunderstood, and put his question again. Duvalier assured him that he had heard and understood the question perfectly well, and had given the correct answer. Struggling to make sense of this incredible piece of information, the American finally asked Duvalier: "How do you define white?" Duvalier answered the question with a question: "How do you define black in your country?" Receiving the explanation that in the United States anyone with any black blood was considered black, Duvalier nodded and said, "Well, that's the way we define white in my country."

Even in the limiting case of the earliest contacts between Europeans and Africans, when by definition the context was least elaborated, people made use of whatever reference points fell readily to hand in assimilating the new experience. To this process Biblical tradition, folk superstition, and the lore of the ages certainly contributed. But the key reference points are most immediately given by the social circumstances under which contact occurs. People are quicker than social scientists sometimes believe to learn by experience, and much slower than social scientists usually assume to systematize what they have learned into logically consistent patterns. They are thus able to "know" simultaneously what experience has taught and what tradition has instilled into them, even when the two are in opposition.[8] The proposition that attitudes are "discrete entities" that can be isolated from each other and analyzed on their own is the bane of attempts to understand the reaction of people to one another (and, for that matter, of attempts to understand much else in the realm of human affairs).[9]

The late Walter Rodney's study of the upper Guinea coast demonstrates that the Portuguese who wanted to do business in the area had to and did come to terms with the sovereignty of the African potentates they encountered. In other words, they came to terms with the Africans' actual superiority from the standpoint of political power—that most fundamental of realities. Learning to live and function in a world dominated by that reality, they also of necessity eventually learned to appreciate some of the cultural nuances of societies in which they were fully aware of being tolerated guests. Even if they were capable of speaking, then or in retrospect, in terms of superiority over their African hosts, they knew better. Or, more accurately, they simultaneously believed and did not believe in their own superiority, and were not greatly troubled by the contradiction. They were capable, as are all human beings, of believing things that in strict logic are not compatible. No trader who had to confront and learn to placate the power of an African chief could in practice believe that Africans were docile, childlike, or primitive. The practical circumstances in which Europeans confronted Africans in Africa make nonsense of any attempt to encompass Europeans' reactions to Africans within the literary stereotypes that scholars have traced through the ages as discrete racial attitudes.[10]

The Portuguese engaged in early missionary activities among the Africans, understandably taking special pains with those leaders whose cooperation was essential. (In attenuated form this activity continued in the context of the slave trade.) Europeans whose contact with Africans occurred on a different basis—and the Portuguese as their basis changed—naturally made a different synthesis of their contradictory notions about Africans. Though the comparison with the Portuguese might have warned him against such a conclusion, Winthrop Jordan takes the absence of early missionary activity by the English in Africa to be a consequence of color. To emphasize the point, he contrasts Englishmen's missionary ambitions with respect to the American Indians with their indifference toward missionary work among the Africans. Passing rather lightly over the very important differences in the social context within which Englishmen confronted Africans in Africa and Indians in America, he concludes that "the distinction which Englishmen made as to conversion was at least in some small measure modeled after the difference they saw in skin color."[11]

It would of course be foolhardy to argue that the Englishmen failed to notice the difference in color and general appearance between Africans and American Indians. The question, however, is whether it is proper to consider this a cause of their different course with respect to the one people and the other. The fact is that when Englishmen eventually went to Africa on an errand similar to that upon which they arrived in America—namely, settlement, in direct collision with the territorial and political sovereignty of African peoples—they engaged in missionary activity far more grandiose than anything they had directed at the hapless Indians. And the results were far more momentous.[12] In this case the difference is attributable, not to attitudes about color, but to a notable difference between the nineteenth century and the seventeenth. For by the nineteenth century the colonial endeavor involved plans for the African populations that would have been seriously compromised by their extermination; specifically, the creation of zones of imperial influence that would exclude rival European powers, the creation and enlargement of markets for the output of metropolitan industry, and the provision of wage labor for mines and estates. These plans would be better served by the annexation of African sovereignty than by its obliteration.[13] Thus the field for missionary work was not prematurely foreclosed by the disappearance of the potential targets.

The idea one people has of another, even when the difference between them is embodied in the most striking physical characteristics, is always mediated by the social context within which the two come into contact. This remains true even when time-honored tradition provides a vocabulary for thinking and talking about the other people that runs counter to immediate experience. In that case, the vocabulary and the experience simply exist side by side. That is why travelers who knew Africans to come in all colors could speak of "black" Africans; why traders who enjoyed "civilized" amenities in the compounds of their African patrons could speak of "savage" Africans; why missionaries whose acquaintance included both Muslim and Christian Africans could speak of "pagan" Africans; and (later) why slave owners who lived in fear of insurrection could speak of "docile" Africans. An understanding of how groups of people see other groups in relation to themselves must begin by analyzing the pattern of their social relations—not by enumerating "attitudes" which, endowed with independent life, are supposed to act upon the historical process from outside, passing through it like neutrinos to emerge unchanged at the other end.

The view that race is a biological fact, a physical attribute of individuals, is no longer tenable. From a scientific standpoint, race can be no more than a statistical description of the characteristics of a given population—a description, moreover, that remains valid only as long as the members of that population do not marry outside the group.[14] Any attempt to carry the concept further than that collapses into absurdity: for example, a child belonging to a different race from one of his parents, or the well-known anomaly of American racial convention that considers a white woman capable of giving birth to a black child but denies that a black woman can give birth to a white child. With a few well-publicized exceptions, no one holding reputable academic credentials overtly adheres to the view that race is a physical fact. But echoes of this view still insinuate themselves into writing on the subject. Perhaps scholars assume that since the lay public has historically considered race to be a physical fact, this is therefore a good enough working definition to use when trying to understand their ideas and behavior. A telltale sign of the preoccupation of historians, sociologists, and others with a physical definition of race is the disproportionate concern of the field of comparative race relations with the incidence and treatment of mulattoes, as though race became problematic only when the appearance of the people concerned was problematic. While it is undeniable that this line of inquiry has yielded some useful information, it is also not hard to sympathize with Marvin Harris's impatient comment upon the obsessive attention given it by some scholars.* Important as these questions may be in their own right, concentration upon them becomes an obstacle to clearer understanding if it obscures the fact that race is a complicated and far from obvious concept, even when—perhaps especially when—it appears most physically precise.

Let us admit that the public, composed by and large of neither statisticians nor population geneticists, cannot have held a scientific definition of race. But neither can they, being human (that is, social) creatures, have held a notion of race that was the direct and unmediated reflex of a physical impression, since physical impressions are always mediated by a larger context, which assigns them their meaning, whether or not the individuals concerned are aware that this is so. It follows that the notion of race, in its popular manifestation, is an ideological construct and thus, above all, a historical product. A number of consequences follow. One of the more far-reaching is that that favorite question of American social scientists—whether race or class "variables" better explain "American reality"—is a false one. Class and race are concepts of a different order; they do not occupy the same analytical space, and thus cannot constitute explanatory alternatives to each other.[15] At its core, class refers to a material circumstance: the inequality of human beings from the standpoint of social power. Even the rather diffuse definitions of applied social science—occupation, income, status—reflect this circumstance, though dimly. The more rigorous Marxian definition involving social relations of production reflects it directly. Of course, the objective core of class is always mediated by ideology, which is the refraction of objective reality in human consciousness. No historical account of class is complete or satisfying that omits the ideological mediations. But at the same time, the reality of class can assert itself independently of people's consciousness, and sometimes in direct opposition to it, as when an artisan who considers himself a cut above the work-

---

* "It is time that grown men stopped talking about racially prejudiced sexuality. In general, when human beings have the power, the opportunity and the need, they will mate with members of the opposite sex regardless of color or the identity of grandfather." *Patterns of Race in the Americas* (New York, 1964), pp. 68–69.

ing class is relegated to unskilled labor by the mechanization of his craft, or when a salaried technocrat who thinks he is part of the bourgeoisie suddenly finds himself thrown out of work by the retrenchment of his enterprise.

Race, on the other hand, is a purely ideological notion. Once ideology is stripped away, nothing remains except an abstraction which, while meaningful to a statistician, could scarcely have inspired all the mischief that race has caused during its malevolent historical career. The material circumstance upon which the concept purports to rest—the biological inequality of human beings—is spurious: there is only one human species, and the most dramatic differences of appearance can be wiped out in one act of miscegenation. The very diversity and arbitrariness of the physical rules governing racial classification prove that the physical emblems which symbolize race are not the foundation upon which race arises as a category of social thought.[16] That does not mean that race is unreal: All ideologies are real, in that they are the embodiment in thought of real social relations. It does mean that the reality underlying racial ideology cannot be found where the vocabulary of racial ideology might tempt us to look for it. To put it another way, class is a concept that we can locate both at the level of objective reality and at the level of social appearances. Race is a concept that we can locate at the level of appearances only. A material reality underlies it all right, as must be true of any ideology; but the underlying reality is not the one that the language of racial ideology addresses. Since this distinction has important implications for understanding the role of race in American history, I shall return to it later in more detail. But the general theoretical point bears emphasizing: because class and race are not equivalent concepts, it is erroneous to offer them as alternatives to each other; and because any thorough social analysis must move simultaneously at the level of objective reality and at that of appearances, it is self-defeating to attempt to do so.

For the moment, let us notice a more obvious consequence of recognizing race to be an ideological and therefore historical product. What is historical must have a discernible, if not precisely datable, beginning. What is ideological cannot be a simple reflex of physical fact. The view that Africans constituted a race, therefore, must have arisen at a specific and ascertainable historical moment; and it cannot have sprung into being automatically at the moment when Europeans and Africans came into contact with each other. Contact alone was not sufficient to call it into being; nor was the enslavement of Africans by Europeans, which lasted for some time before race became its predominant justification.[17] Prejudice and xenophobia may be transhistorical, but their subsumption under the concept of race is not. As Christopher Lasch pointed out many years ago, the idea of the Negro took time to become distinct "from related concepts of nationality and religion —from the concepts of African, heathen, and savage." It was, he argued, "at the very point in time when large numbers of men and women were beginning to question the moral legitimacy of slavery" that the idea of race came into its own. [18]

There is surely disturbing matter to ponder in the simultaneous appearance of antislavery sentiment and racialist ideology. But the roots of this grim coincidence are not to be sought in the exclusive realm of race relations.[19] They are rather to be sought in the unfolding of bourgeois social relations, and the ethos of rationality and science in which these social relations were ideologically reflected. Bourgeois "rationality" tore loose from "natural" categories the task—which all societies carry out in some form—of identifying and classifying differences among people. The latter had to be recreated from scientific first principles, with the enterprise of classification and identification now subordinated to the practical business of disciplining—and, if need be, institutionalizing—deviance and nonconformity. Not race alone, but a whole edifice of "forms of institutionalized segregation" arose: the asylum, the school (a place of isolation for children, now defined as radically distinct by nature from the adult population), and the bourgeois family itself (redefined as a refuge from society and built around an "exaggerated consciousness of sexual roles").[20] Race is a product of history, not of nature. And as an element of ideology, it is best understood in connection with other elements of ideology and not as a phenomenon sui generis. Only when set next to contemporary ideas having nothing to do with race can ideas about race be placed in the context of the ideological ensemble of which they form a part.

To treat race as an ideology, and to insist upon treating it in connection with surrounding ideologies, is to open up a vast realm of further complications. Ideologies offer a ready-made interpretation of the world, a sort of hand-me-down vocabulary

with which to name the elements of every new experience. But
their prime function is to make coherent—if never scientifically
accurate—sense of the social world. Therefore, new experience
constantly impinges on them, changing them in ways that are
diabolically difficult for the detached observer, let alone the
engaged participant, to detect. The standard and now nearly
automatic formula according to which ideas "have a life of their
own" needs to be handled with caution. Ideas live only in the
minds of men and women and cannot escape the contagion, so to
speak, of the material world these men and women inhabit. They
seem to have a life of their own in that, providing a ready-made
vocabulary for the interpretation of new experience, they subtly
(and sometimes grossly) prejudge the content of the interpretation.
But new experience constantly exerts a reciprocal influence. A
vocabulary stays alive only to the degree that it names things
people know, and, as Michael T. Taussig has recently remarked,
to the extent that these things are ritually verified in day-to-day
social practice.[21] There would be no great problem if, when the
things changed, the vocabulary died away as well. But far the more
common situation in the history of ideologies is that instead of
dying, the same vocabulary attaches itself, unnoticed, to new
things. It is not that ideas have a life of their own, but rather that
they have a boundless facility for usurping the lives of men and
women. In this they resemble those creatures of horror fiction who,
having neither body nor life of their own, take over the bodies and
lives of human beings. The history of racialist ideologies provides
excellent examples. Take the case of an antebellum planter whose
sense of racial superiority over the slaves embraced the belief that
they could not survive—would literally die—outside the tutelage
of the master class. Emancipation was bound to change such an
individual's ideology fundamentally, even if it failed to change the
language in which he expressed that ideology. He could not fail
to notice that the freedmen were not dying out, either figuratively
or literally. Whether or not he took explicit cognizance of the fact,
his consciousness would reflect the reality that what had once
seemed a necessary and immutable relation—slavery—had now in
fact changed. But since he would continue to speak the language
of racial superiority, an incautious historian might easily infer
that the ideology had not changed, and might even extrapolate all
manner of unwarranted conclusions to the effect that the planter's

ideology was independent of the institution of slavery. It would be only a short slide from there to central themes, and the start of race on a full metaphysical career.

Of course there are complications within the complications. Since attitudes are not discrete entities and people have no innate compulsion toward logical consistency, it would not be hard to show that the same planters who believed in their slaves' incapacity also knew—and believed—the contrary.[22] Precisely because ideologies consist of contradictory and inconsistent elements, they can undergo fundamental change simply through the reshuffling of those elements into a different hierarchy. Ideological change that occurs in this fashion may easily pass undetected, with very serious consequences. Failure to attach due importance to exactly this kind of change accounts for recent erroneous assertions that Southern society has, in its fundamentals, experienced no important discontinuity.[23] Just in itself, the change in the way planters compelled the labor of their black subordinates—and thus, necessarily, in their view of these subordinates—signaled a momentous discontinuity; and that is to say the least and to speak of only one part of the Southern population.[24]

There is something profoundly unsettling in the contemplation of a change immense in scope and purchased at great cost, yet so ambiguous that it is impossible to say with full conviction whether it is a change for the better or for the worse. This probably accounts for historians' great reticence about recognizing that the abolition of slavery worked an important change in racialist ideology. Once recognize that a change took place, and the disheartening next step is to realize that what replaced the racialism of slave society was, in its different way, just as repulsive—perhaps more so. It may be marginally comforting to assume that racialist thinking must be one of those primordial flaws of the human psyche, a sort of background noise of the mind, against which even revolutionary upheavals may not prevail. The search for some such slender refuge seems to be the unspoken basis of so many historians' slowness in seeing that although there was no appreciable decline or mitigation of racialist thinking, there was a decisive shift in its character. There is, after all, a profound difference in social meaning between a planter who experiences black people as ungrateful, untrustworthy, and half-witted slaves and a planter who experiences black people as undisciplined,

irregular, and refractory employees.[25] Such a significant change
in reality as experience could not but be recorded in reality as
consciousness. Was it an improvement? That question is a very
blunt instrument to employ in a situation calling for delicate
tools. The view that the slaves could live only in slavery implied
both a radical devaluation of their human dignity and the
acceptance of an obligation to provide them a minimum of
subsistence and animal comfort. The collapse of this view represented at once a grudging, backhanded concession to the freedmen's human dignity and the transfer of their subsistence to the
realm of violence and social warfare. Something was gained; but,
just as surely, something was lost.

It is easy enough to demonstrate a substantial continuity in
racial "attitudes."[26] But doing so does not demonstrate continuity
of racial ideology. Attitudes, as I have already argued, are
promiscuous critters and do not mind cohabiting with their
opposites. Indeed, they sometimes seem to be happier that way.
Thus, a historian looking for continuity in attitudes is likely to
find it regardless of the set of attitudes selected, provided he is
sufficiently imaginative in his construction of what constitutes
evidence for the existence of an attitude. A text proposing that
Negroes, being the product of a separate creation, are not human
may be taken as evidence of one sort of attitude. But laws holding
slaves morally and legally responsible for their own criminal
conduct must be taken as evidence of a contrary attitude.[27] In the
end we cannot resolve the problem quantitatively, by the addition
of example and counterexample. We can resolve it only by posing
the question "What kind of social reality is reflected—or refracted
—in an ideology built on a unity of these particular opposites?"

Of course in any society more complex than the primal horde,
there cannot be a single ideology through which everyone appre-
hends the social world. In any event, what might appear from a
distance to be a single ideology cannot hold the same meaning for
everyone. If ideology is a vocabulary for interpreting social experience, and thus both shapes and is shaped by that experience,
it follows that even the "same" ideology must convey different
meanings to people having different social experiences. To suppose
otherwise is to take another false step onto the terrain of racialist
ideology. To suggest, for example, that classes of people whose
position in, relation to, and perception of the world and society

differ in every other fundamental have a common bedrock of ideological assumptions about black people is to betray the illusion that beliefs about race are a biological product rather than the creation of men and women in society. Historians ask us to do something very like this when they call upon us to believe that great planters, small land- and slaveholding farmers, nonslavehold-ing yeomen, poor whites, town merchants and artisans, and urban factors all shared a belief in "white supremacy," which thus constitutes the central theme of Southern history.[28]

White supremacy is a slogan, not a belief.[29] And it is a slogan that cannot have meant the same to all white people. Those who invoke it as a way of minimizing the importance of class diversity in the South overlook this simple but basic point. In fact, the unity of Southerners' belief in white supremacy is more often taken for granted than argued in its own right, because it cannot withstand serious analysis. To the extent that white supremacy summarized prejudices of color, how can it have meant the same for different classes of whites, who had different experiences with blacks? A planter's deep conviction of superiority over his slave— so deep that it seldom required actual statement—permitted him to regard with casual indifference a level of intimacy with his house and body servants that might have shocked the fastidious-ness of a New England abolitionist ostensibly believing in the equality and brotherhood of man. On the other hand, a hill-country white farmer, superficially sharing the same conviction of superiority, might feel insulted to the point of homicide upon finding himself unexpectedly jostled by a slave in a crowded market square. And white artisans who petitioned local and state authorities for the exclusion of slaves and free blacks from craft employment made a more ambiguous comment than they realized or intended upon the dogma of white superiority.

But white supremacy was not simply a summary of color prejudices. It was also a set of political programs, differing accord-ing to the social position of their proponents. Prejudices fed into them, naturally; but so far from providing a unifying element, they were as likely as not to accentuate the latent possibilities for discord. After all, Northern free-soilism and proslavery expan-sionism might both be regarded as expressions of white supremacy: the one wishing to keep blacks where white farmers need not come in contact with them, the other wishing to keep blacks where white

masters could have ready access to them when needed. It is clearly
fruitless to think of racial prejudice as the common denominator
of action when that prejudice led one group of whites to insist
heatedly on their right to take black slaves wherever they wanted
to, and another to insist just as heatedly on their own right to set
limits on the areas where black slaves could be taken.[30]

Obviously, the free-soil movement as such had no significant
following in the South. But it had a counterpart. The Southern
back country was full of independent yeoman whites who had no
use for slaves or their owners. Many were from families that had
moved into the back country to escape the encirclement of the
plantation and create a world after their own image. That image,
we are beginning to learn, was vastly different in most important
respects from the one after which the planters created their world,
and the yeoman surrendered it only with great reluctance and
after a bitter struggle.[31] In spite of the potential power of their
numbers in a formally democratic polity, they did not challenge
the effective dominance of the planters as long as they were largely
left alone to live their own life in their own way. But, according
to one scholar, the great planters' apprehension lest these people
discover an affinity with the free-soil Republicans was the central
dynamic of the secession movement in Georgia. It is at all events
beyond question that they were everywhere slow to support secession and quick to evince disaffection with the war.[32]

The slogan of white supremacy was never sufficient to place the
social and political ideology of the yeomen and poor whites at one
with that of the planter class. From the democratic struggles of
the Jacksonian era to the disfranchisement struggles of the Jim
Crow era, white supremacy held one meaning for the back-country
whites and another for the planters. To whites of the back country, it meant the political predominance of white-county whites
or their spokesmen—in other words, the political predominance
of their own kind. To the planters, it meant the predominance of
black-county whites—in other words, of their own kind. The tension between these diametrically opposed positions might at times
be dormant, but never absent, for it arose from political aspirations that the two groups did not share. In the antebellum era the
tension might surface over the issues of ad valorem taxation or
the apportionment of representation in state legislatures. During
and after Reconstruction, it was likely to surface over such ques-

tions as public schools, laborers' liens, fencing reform, debtors' relief, and homestead exemption. In North Carolina, for example, conservatives dared not make a frontal assault on the Reconstruction constitution, because of the popularity of many of its provisions among ordinary whites. Nor could they publicly display their private grounds of opposition to the constitution: its "tendency . . . to put the powers of government into the hands of mere *numbers.*"[33]

It is, of course, the job of the politician to advance a slogan that conceals underlying differences of ideology· or program in the interests of electoral victory. To some extent the Southern Democratic party succeeded in doing this with its slogan of white supremacy. But this has to be stated carefully and with much qualification. Independent challenges to the Democrats' power remained endemic in the South until the end of the nineteenth century, when the disfranchisement movement put a stop to them. At that moment, the Solid South came into being. In no sense, however, did its emergence represent a harmonization of the planters' standpoint with that of the yeoman and poor whites. To the contrary, it represented a political victory of the former over the latter. Poorer whites tended to oppose disfranchisement, despite the trappings of white-supremacist ideology with which it was proclaimed. They understood that they were to be its unstated secondary victims; and so they became.[34]

It would be silly and unproductive to pose the issue here as one of deciding whether class or race factors were more powerful. Each class of whites had its particular variety of racialist ideology. Moreover, the superficial resemblance among them—namely, the fact that in all of them, blacks were the victims—made it easier for the Democrats and their spokesmen to forge them into a spurious ideological unity. But racial ideology constituted only one element of the whole ideology of each class. And it is the totality of the elements and their relation to each other that gives the whole its form and direction; not the content of one isolated element, which in any case is bound to be contradictory. The racialism of the rich black-belt Democrats was annexed to an elitist political ideology that challenged—sometimes tacitly and sometimes openly—the political competence of the subordinate classes as a whole.[35] And it was armed with the political resources, violent if need be, to carry its program into effect. The racialism

of yeomen and poor whites was annexed to political ideologies
hostile to the elitist pretensions of the black-belt nabobs and, at
least potentially, solvent of some of the grosser illusions of racialism. The moments, rare though they are in comparison with the
entire sweep of Southern history, when such whites managed to
accept temporary alliances with blacks, testify to the potential.
But arrayed against the superior wealth, education, connections,
and technical sophistication of the black-belt patricians, these
whites needed the greatest possible unity of all the potential forces
of opposition. The objective situation alone threw up formidable
obstacles to the necessary unity.[36] Racialism threw up others.

The most important of these obstacles is not the one that comes
most readily to mind: a mental block in the path of actions that
violated the conventional color line. Racial prejudice is sufficiently fluid and at home with contrariety to be able to precede
and survive dramatic instances of interracial unity in action.[37]
The most important obstacle thrown up by racialism is the fact
that it formed a narrow one-way bridge, which allowed potential
support to straggle over to the side of the Democrats while offering little scope for movement in the opposite direction. Patricians
stood a better chance of attracting support among the common
people than the common people did of attracting support from
the patricians. The racialism of the black-belt elite, after all,
carried with it the luster of victory. That of the white common
people became ever more tightly bound up with the rancor of
hard blows and final defeat, as they watched the basis of their
proud independence eroded by economic and social forces with
which they were finally unable to cope. Their rancor became
pervasive in the cultural atmosphere of the South and lent itself
to demagogic manipulation by politicians seeking to turn it to
electoral advantage. But it could never be fully assuaged; quite
the contrary. Arising from a bleak day-to-day experience to which
the slogans and rituals of white supremacy offered no material
solution, that rancor only grew larger the more it was fed.

White supremacy, once disentangled from metaphysical and
transhistorical trappings, cannot be the central theme of Southern
history. It never was a single theme, and it never led to consensus
on a single program. Accepting that does not require dismissing
race as an ideological delusion which is therefore unreal: once
acted upon, a delusion may be as murderous as a fact. Nor does

it require entering into a tendentious and ultimately empty dis-
putation as to the relative benignity or malignity of various
racialist ideologies, or into the quantitative assessment of their
degree of racism. A racialist ideology harnessed to a ruling-class
will, intention, and capacity to dominate both blacks and whites
may be characterized by a patronizing tolerance, while that of a
rednecks' movement to unseat their white masters may be virulent
and homicidal.[38] Naturally, the victims cannot be neutral between
two such ideologies or their human representatives, and neither
can the historian. But practical choice and historical explanation
are not the same. Historical analysis cannot distinguish these
positions as "more" and "less" racist. Rather, they represent the
different shape of the space occupied by racialism in different
ideological ensembles. To think of them as different quantities
of the same ideological substance is fundamentally mistaken.

At the same time, the historian cannot afford to abdicate critical
judgment when confronting the unattractive cultural forms of
those who are themselves victims of exploitation. Refusing to
brand the rednecks' culture as more racist than the planters' does
not mean that one should ignore its ugly consequences out of
deference to its dissident or oppositional undertones. There may
be charm in quilting bees and logrollings, in the various traditions
of mutuality and reciprocity, and (for some) in country music.
But there is also a somber side to that culture, not unrelated to
the first: for example, the personal violence and the do-it-yourself
justice of the necktie party. Those inclined to romanticize, senti-
mentalize, or take vicarious comfort in the flowering of cultural
forms among the oppressed which challenge their subordination—
as if, somehow, what has been lost politically has been regained
on a higher (cultural) level—would do well to remember that
these autonomous cultural forms need not be gentle, humane, or
liberating. Where they develop apart from a continuing challenge,
politically articulate and autonomous, to the real structure of
power, they are more likely to be fungi than flowers.

If white supremacy is not the central theme of Southern, let
alone American, history, there remains the task of accounting for
the prominence of questions of race and color in so many of the
most important events in American history. The question becomes simpler and less susceptible to mystification once the ideo-

logical essence of the notion of race is clear. Ideologies are the eyes through which people see social reality, the form in which they experience it in their own consciousness. The rise of slavery, its growth and dispersal, and its eventual destruction were central events in American history. The various ideologies in which race was embodied became the form in which this central reality found distorted reflection in people's consciousness.

A number of circumstances collaborated to bring this about. The rise of slavery itself on the North American mainland was not in essence a racial phenomenon, nor was it the inevitable outcome of racial prejudice.[39] But it was a problem. As David Brion Davis memorably demonstrated in the first of his volumes on the subject, slavery has always been a problem, for it is based on a self-evident existential absurdity: that one human being can be a simple extension of the will of another.[40] And, as Davis has demonstrated yet more memorably in the second of his volumes on the subject, slavery became even more of a problem in the Age of Revolution. The way societies think about compelling labor develops along with the modes in which they actually do compel labor, both responding to those ways and helping to define, and thus change, them. The view that no one will work for someone else unless compelled to by force arises authentically in a society in which those who work for others in fact do so under direct compulsion. The view that people will not only work for others voluntarily, but work more efficiently for having volunteered, arises authentically only in a society in which people are, first of all, free to volunteer, and second, "free" of the material resources—land, tools, guaranteed subsistence—that might permit them to refuse without going hungry. (This is the famous "double freedom" by which Marx ironically defined the condition of the proletarian.) By the Age of Revolution, English society and its American offspring fell somewhere between the two: the assumption that the individual is the proprietor of his own person was not so all-pervasive as to appear the very bedrock of common sense, but it had advanced sufficiently to make bondage a condition calling for justification and to narrow the basis on which such a justification might rest. Slavery by then could be neither taken for granted nor derived from self-evident general principles. Pro-slavery and antislavery publicists, Davis argues, unconsciously collaborated in localizing that basis to the slaves' presumed incapacity for freedom, an incapacity that crystallized into a racial one with all its subsequent pseudobiological trappings.[41]

Slavery thus became a "racial" question, and spawned an endless variety of "racial" problems. Race became the ideological medium through which people posed and apprehended basic questions of power and dominance, sovereignty and citizenship, justice and right. Not only questions involving the status and condition of black people, but also those involving relations between whites who owned slaves and whites who did not were drawn into these terms of reference, as a ray of light is deflected when it passes through a gravitational field.[42] The great federal compromise, embodied in the new Constitution, placed slavery at the head of the nation's agenda; and there it remained, try as statesmen would to displace it, until its abolition. As long as it remained, so did the racial form of the social questions to which it gave rise. And when the hour eventually struck for its abolition, that set of questions, too, inevitably arose in racial form. Having defined blacks as a race, contemporaries could not think through problems involving them in any other terms. And, having built the institution of slavery around that definition, contemporaries could not resolve the problems of slavery and its liquidation except by confronting the definition.

It follows that there can be no understanding the problems arising from slavery and its destruction which ignores their racial form: recognizing that race is an ideological notion and that not all white Americans held the same ideology does not mean dismissing racial questions as illusory or unreal. It does not follow, however, that attention to the racial form alone will shed light on the ulterior substance of these problems. There is perhaps no better illustration of this fact than Reconstruction. If ever a period seemed in its very essence to concern race relations, it is Reconstruction. The most obvious embodiment of its work—the constitutional amendments abolishing slavery, admitting black people to citizenship, and forbidding the denial of suffrage on the basis of color or previous condition—might, in a sense, have been designed to define the race problem out of existence.

But the problem that has plagued the study of Reconstruction, at least since the "Birth of a Nation" school lost pre-eminence, has been to explain why these amendments failed to accomplish some of the simplest things that their plain language seemed to entail. The Thirteenth Amendment ended slavery, but not coercion: peonage flourished well into the twentieth century.[43] The Supreme Court soon interpreted the Fourteenth Amendment out of existence, at least insofar as the rights of black people were concerned. The Fifteenth Amendment functioned for a time—imperfectly— in those states that underwent congressional Reconstruction. But the Supreme Court eventually discovered that while forbidding the denial of suffrage, the amendment did not require its extension.

The American legal system works in large part on casuistry, and courts and lawyers had little trouble proving, at least to their own satisfaction, that the original intent of the Reconstruction amendments was exactly what they had reduced it to by the turn of the century. But the problem is not so easily resolved. Congressional Republicans as a group no more intended the Fourteenth Amendment to protect corporations from the beginning than they counted on the distinction between forbidding the denial of something and mandating its extension. The fact is that, divided and contentious, they provided a clumsy, undermanned, underfinanced, and finally inadequate machinery to accomplish a task whose limits they themselves could not clearly define. But historians have the benefit of hindsight. If, employing hindsight, we consider the actual accomplishments of the Reconstruction amendments—as opposed to the noblest hopes and intentions of those who fought for their enactment—we may be able to specify the limits of that task in a way that contemporaries could not. The Reconstruction amendments asserted the supremacy of the national state and the formal equality under the law of everyone within it. In so doing, they eliminated competing bases of sovereignty (such as the relation of master and slave) and set forth in the organic law that there was one and only one source of citizenship, that citizenship was to be nationally defined, and that the rights, privileges, and immunities deriving from citizenship arose from the federal Constitution.

Such were the formal accomplishments of Reconstruction and such, I would contend, the substance of its historic task. This task may seem a limited one in human terms, but it was by no means small or unimportant. It involved defining the nature of the United States as a nation-state.[44] In short, it was the representation in legal form of an enterprise of national unification—the same one that was taking place nearly simultaneously in other nations of what was to become the capitalist world: Japan, Germany, Italy. And it was an enterprise of bourgeois democracy, the establishment of national unification on the basis of a system of formally free labor mediated through the market.[45] In nineteenth-century America, any such enterprise would necessarily be racial in form: the obstacles to be cleared away derived from the attempted secession of a region in which a society founded upon racially defined slavery claimed separate sovereignty. The problems of black people occupied center stage for a time both because the institutions to be swept away involved them and because those doing the sweeping away discovered that they needed the freedmen's help in order to accomplish their ends.

But the ends of Reconstruction were not necessarily those of the freedmen themselves. It was much more fundamental to the historic task of Reconstruction to define the proper relation of the Southern states to the national government, and of the citizen to the national government, than it was to supervise relations between the ex-slaves and the ex-masters. (The Freedmen's Bureau thus closed up shop well before the formal end of Reconstruction.) Abraham Lincoln said as much openly and insistently at the beginning of the war, when he forswore any intention of tampering with slavery and rebuffed those among his generals who seemed to move beyond this position. Later, of course, it became clear that tampering with slavery was the only way to achieve the more limited objective. That in turn came about in no small part because, by their own determined actions—running to Union lines, serving in the army, or simply slowing down the pace of work— the slaves placed their freedom on the agenda. The Republican party provided the machinery through which the nationalist task of Reconstruction was accomplished: those scholars who have argued that the chief motivation behind most of what the Republicans did was partisan advantage reveal no more than this. By the usual processes of jockeying, trimming, and yielding to expediency, the system of partisan politics itself taught Republicans which parts of the freedmen's agenda were essential to their own, and which were not.

Republicans eventually discovered that their objectives did not necessarily entail revolutionizing relations between the freedmen and their former masters. But those are not the terms in which this discovery usually presented itself to their consciousness. What they typically experienced—that is to say, the way ideology usually interpreted their experience to them[46]—was that the freedmen had disappointed them by failing to live up to their responsibilities. They were shiftless, were not dependable wage workers, failed to respond like civilized people to wage incentives. They were the dupes of unscrupulous allies and the helpless victims of murderous opponents, and in either case were to blame for their own victimization. As often as not, perhaps more often than not, racial incapacity was the explanation for these supposed failures. Persuaded finally that the freedmen had proven unworthy of freedom, the Republicans contented themselves with the formal accomplishments of Reconstruction and left the freedmen to make the best deal they could with their former masters. Only a few outnumbered voices consistently (and ineffectually) demanded full, forcible protection of the freedmen's substantive rights; and the few abortive efforts along these lines—for example, the Lodge Election Bill of 1890—were pitifully disproportionate to the magnitude of the force arrayed against the freedmen.[47]

However the Republicans may have perceived the situation through the veil of racial ideology, their frustration with the freedmen had nothing to do with color. Complaints about undependable work habits echo and re-echo in the sources concerning the freedmen—and, for that matter, the antebellum free blacks. But they have also appeared again and again, in every part of the world, whenever an employer class in process of formation has tried to induce men and women unbroken to market discipline to work in exchange for a wage.[48] The planters, indeed, made the same complaints about the people whom they contemptuously labeled crackers, rednecks, sandhill tackeys, and the like. Northern employers made similar complaints about the behavior of their immigrant employees, and frequently accounted for that behavior in racial terms—a practice that eventually acquired academic respectability.[49]

Those Northerners who became missionaries, teachers, Freedmen's Bureau agents, and—perhaps most important of all—planters in the South after the Civil War[50] believed very genuinely that, in offering the freedmen a chance to become free wage laborers, they were offering them a wonderful boon. But the freedmen knew what they wanted, and it was not to substitute one kind of master for another. They wanted their own land and the right to farm it as they chose. And their choice was likely to disappoint those eager to reconstitute the staple economy: most found bizarre the white folks' preoccupation with growing things that no one could eat.[51] A deep misunderstanding, which reflects a real if at the time unappreciated difference in class standpoint, caused the authors of Reconstruction to offer with a great flourish a gift that the freedmen did not want, and to interpret as perversity or racial incapacity the latters' refusal to accept the gift with gratitude.

While the freedmen were being hustled into the market economy at the well-intentioned (though not always disinterested) initiative of various groups of Yankees, the white yeomanry was also being drawn into that economy: in their case, through a combination of indebtedness and complex changes in law and social usage that followed in the wake of the Civil War. Both groups, as more and more studies make clear, would have preferred a different outcome.[52] Secure tenure of land and peace in which to pursue essentially self-sufficient farming, with only incidental resort to the market, would have suited their desires more than conscription willy-nilly into the world of commercialized agriculture, with its ginners, merchants, storekeepers, moneylenders, and crop liens. There never was much chance that they would get the kind of world they wanted. Since neither the planters nor the various Northerners who collaborated in designing Reconstruction had reason to promote such a result,[53] it could have arisen only through the united efforts of the white yeomanry, the poor whites, and the freedmen. That sort of unity would have required as a minimum precondition the very material circumstances to. which it was prerequisite.[54] Moreover, resting as it would have had to on a much more thorough expropriation of the planters than actually occurred, such a result would have exacted a high cost in violence and suffering, though not necessarily, as Eugene D. Genovese has recently pointed out, a higher cost than had to be paid as it was.[55] Needless to say, it is not a course of events that would invite the endorsement of a modern development economist. The resulting proliferation and entrenchment of smallholdings would have created an even more durable obstacle to the capitalist "rationalization" of Southern agriculture than that created by landlordism and a captive labor force. For this rationalization eventually required the concentration of land and capital and the expulsion of thousands from the land.[56]

An outcome favorable to the black and white common people is, in short, a might-have-been that probably could not have been. Even so, we may well pause for a moment to consider why not. To do so is to remind ourselves that the "race problem" took its form, not from discrete attitudes, but from the circumstances under which ordinary people had to make their choices. When the Republicans left the freedmen to their own devices, they left them sufficiently detached from their former masters to be largely bereft of the latters' self-interested protection, but not sufficiently detached to bridge the gap between themselves and the yeomen and poor whites. Their vulnerability to economic manipulation and intimidation by landlords made them suspect as political allies of the back-country whites, thus ratifying and reinforcing racialist suspicions. And, still more important, their reduction closer and closer to the status of wage laborers set their political-economic agenda at odds with that of the back-country whites. The latters' grievances were by and large those of farmers whose land and livelihood were threatened by the vicissitudes of debt-ridden commercial agriculture in an era of world depression.

A program combining land distribution with debtors' relief might have permitted both freedmen and yeomen whites to live, for a time, in the essentially self-sufficient peasant manner that both groups seem to have preferred. In time, that life would have been disrupted, though probably not as early as some have assumed. Had the planters lost both possession of their land and control over black labor, there could have been no reorganization of the plantation economy. That, in turn, would have given more breathing space to the white yeomanry. Not just the personnel of Southern agriculture, but its entire economic, social, and political structure would have been rearranged. If black and white yeomen had been free to choose substantial self-sufficiency or production for local markets, they would not necessarily have been sucked at once into the agrarian depression of the 1870s and 1880s which, as E. J. Hobsbawm has pointed out, was "essentially a depression of the staple national and international food-crops."[57]

With a sounder material basis for political cooperation and with their grievances more in phase with each other, the yeomen and the freedmen might have been able to build a workable alliance. In all likelihood, they would have eventually gone down to joint defeat. But the experience itself would have had to affect racial ideology, acting as it would have upon other elements in the ideology of which race was a part. Prejudice would no doubt have remained. But prejudice is as promiscuous as any other attitude and can make itself at home within a variety of ideologies and political programs. There is just a chance that, set in a context which allowed for a less stunted and impoverished existence for both groups and which provided a basis for political cooperation, it might have taken a less virulent and overwhelming form. And it might one day have mellowed into the sort of ritualized rivalry that allows the French and the English, despite centuries of murderous tribal antagonism, to twit each other with stereotypes that may often wound, but now seldom kill. Speculation, perhaps tainted by wishful thinking, suggests that the racialism of ordinary Southern whites might have changed for the better. Sober and dispassionate logic insists that, at the least, it would have been different.

And, had it been so, where would historians have located the central theme of Southern history? Perhaps they would not then have been beguiled into that fruitless quest in the first place. History does not provide us with central themes—with motors such as "racial attitudes" that propel the historical process forward from without. History provides us only with outcomes; and these, as long as the historical process goes on, must remain provisional. Each new stage in the unfolding of the historical process offers a new vantage point from which to seek out those moments of decision in the past that have prepared the way for the latest (provisional) outcome. It is the circumstances under which men and women made those decisions that ought to concern historians, not the quest for a central theme that will permit us to deduce the decisions without troubling ourselves over the circumstances.

Race is neither the reflex of primordial attitudes nor a tragically recurring central theme. It became the ideological medium through which Americans confronted questions of sovereignty and power because the enslavement of Africans and their descendants constituted a massive exception to the rules of sovereignty and power that were increasingly taken for granted. And, despite the changes it has undergone along the way, race has remained a predominant ideological medium because the manner of slavery's unraveling had lasting consequences for the relations of whites to other whites, no less than for those of whites to blacks. There are no tragic flaws or central themes in which to take shelter, however reluctantly. There are only acts and decisions of men and women in a society now past, and a responsibility which, because the outcome remains provisional, we are obliged to share with them.

NOTES

1. Ulrich B. Phillips, "The Central Theme of Southern History," *American Historical Review*, 34 (1928), 30–43.

2. Washington *Post,* June 17, 1980 (emphasis added).

3. U. B. Phillips still spoke in their accents when he wrote *Life and Labor in the Old South* (Boston, 1963), pp. 188–90 (orig. pub. 1929).

4. The process took time, however, and was neither automatic nor even. Ira Berlin explores some of the intricacies of this unevenness in "Time, Space, and the Evolution of Afro-American Society in British Mainland North America," *American Historical Review*, 85 (1980), 44–77.

5. Harmannus Hoetink, *The Two Variants in Caribbean Race Relations,* trans. Eva M. Hooykaas (London, 1967), pp. 120–60. A statement whose crudeness contrasts oddly with the sophistication of the analysis that follows it appears in Philip D. Curtin, *The Image of Africa: British Ideas and Action, 1780–1850* (Madison, Wisc., 1964), p. 28: "At one level, there is the simple and unavoidable fact that major racial differences are recognizable. In every racially mixed society, in every contact between people who differ in physical appearance, there has always been instant recognition of race: it was the first determinant of inter-group social relations." The last statement cannot withstand either historical or ethnographic scrutiny. The first two account for a phenomenon by taking it eternally for granted. When Inuit (Eskimos) distinguished themselves by appearance from Aleuts, or Sioux from Cheyenne, or Chagga from Kikuyu, did this count as "instant recognition of race"? Which differences in physical appearance qualify as "major racial differences"? Any endogamous population will, over time, show physical characteristics enabling others to identify it by appearance. To call all such distinctions racial is to extend the concept so far that, in covering everything, it covers nothing.

6. Winthrop D. Jordan, *White over Black: American Attitudes toward the Negro, 1550–1812* (New York, 1977), p. 5 (emphasis in original).

7. Ibid., p. 20.

8. The fact that the everyday thought of human beings is quite at home with contradiction is readily accessible to commonsense observation. Nevertheless,

some scholars, particularly those of neo-positivist inclination, continue to
deny it on principle, often invoking individualistic psychological theories
like that of cognitive dissonance. However, no serious observer of human
beings in society has been able to avoid confronting the reality, indeed the
necessity, of contradiction. Max Weber, a product of the positivist tradition,
is explicit: "Neither religions nor men are open books. They have been
historical rather than logical or . . . psychological constructions without
contradiction. Often they have borne within themselves a series of motives,
each of which, if separately and consistently followed through, would have
stood in the way of the others or run against them head-on." H. H. Gerth and
C. Wright Mills, eds., *From Max Weber: Essays in Sociology* (New York,
1946), p. 291. A warning along the same lines from writers in the phenomeno-
logical tradition may be found in Alfred Schutz, "The Problem of Rationality
in the Social World," *Economica,* n.s. 10 (1943), 130–49, and Harold Garfinkel,
"The Rational Properties of Scientific and Common Sense Activities," in
Garfinkel, *Studies in Ethnomethodology* (Englewood Cliffs, N.J., 1967). In the
historical-materialist tradition, the classic statement, unlikely to be surpassed,
is Marx's sardonic discussion "The Fetishism of the Commodity and Its
Secret," in *Capital,* trans. Ben Fowkes (London, 1976), I, 163–77. A discussion
of the same point holding considerable interest appears in Norman Geras,
"Marx and the Critique of Political Economy," in Robin Blackburn, ed.,
Ideology in Social Science (New York, 1973).

9. "I have taken 'attitudes' to be discrete entities susceptible of historical
analysis. This term seems to me to possess a desirable combination of precision
and embraciveness." Jordan, *White over Black,* p. viii.

10. Walter Rodney, *A History of the Upper Guinea Coast, 1545–1800* (Oxford,
1970). The same point emerges in more general terms in Curtin, *Image of
Africa,* esp. chap. 2.

11. Jordan, *White over Black,* pp. 21–22.

12. By this should be understood not simply numbers of converts, but also
consequences of conversion. These, in turn, are not confined to those con-
ventionally adduced—for example, the spread of literacy and education and
the rise of a class of nationalist *evolués* who could challenge the colonialists
on their home ground. An article by Karen E. Fields, "Christian Missionaries
as Anti-Colonial Militants," *Theory and Society,* 11 (1982), 95–108, demonstrates that the most important consequence of conversion was that it put an
intolerable strain on the colonial regime at its weakest point: the intersection
of colonial authority and indigenous legitimacy.

13. This question receives explicit treatment in Karen E. Fields, "Political
Contingencies of Witchcraft in Colonial Central Africa: African Culture in
Marxian Theory on the State," *Canadian Journal of African Studies,* 16
(1982), forthcoming.

14. Jordan sets this point forth in exemplary fashion in his "Note on the
Concept of Race," in *White over Black,* pp. 583–85.

15. Fixation on this artificial dichotomy vitiates the otherwise interesting
analysis of William J. Wilson, *The Declining Significance of Race* (Chicago,
1978). A recent vacuous example of the consequences of pursuing this

dichotomy is Manning Marable, "Beyond the Race-Class Dilemma," *Nation,* April 11, 1981, an essay that fails to advance beyond the race-class dilemma.

16. The emblems that symbolize race are not always physical. The Lumber River Indians of North Carolina today differ only subtly in appearance from the descendants of the Scots who settled in the same area, though, according to prevailing social usage, the two groups belong to different races. But the Indians adopted English a century before the Scottish immigrants arrived and therefore learned an older form of the language. Today, as a result, "a person's speech sometimes gives a clearer indication as to which racial community he belongs [to] than does his physical appearance." W. McKee Evans, *To Die Game: The Story of the Lowry Band, Indian Guerrillas of Reconstruction* (Baton Rouge, 1971), pp. 30–31. Nothing could more precisely demonstrate that the symbols of race are not its substance, since, whatever anyone may say about physical characteristics, no one can believe that speech patterns are anything but a historical product.

17. David Brion Davis has persuasively located the historical moment when race assumed this role in the Age of Revolution, and has traced with great subtlety the ideological processes through which it did so. See *The Problem of Slavery in the Age of Revolution* (Ithaca, 1975), passim and esp. pp. 299–306.

18. Christopher Lasch, "Origins of the Asylum," in Lasch, *The World of Nations* (New York, 1974), p. 17. The essay dates from 1968.

19. George M. Fredrickson, *The Black Image in the White Mind* (New York, 1971), ponders this coincidence in great depth, but remains largely in the realm of race relations.

20. The quoted phrases are from Lasch, "Origins of the Asylum," whose argument is closely related to those of Philippe Ariès, *Centuries of Childhood: A Social History of Family Life,* trans. Robert Baldick (New York, 1962), and Michel Foucault, *Madness and Civilization: A History of Insanity in the Age of Reason,* trans. Richard Howard (New York, 1965); *Discipline and Punish: The Birth of the Prison,* trans. Alan Sheridan (New York, 1978); and *The History of Sexuality,* trans. Robert Hurley (New York, 1978). Perhaps no one has given more specific and detailed attention to the unfolding of bourgeois "rationality" than Max Weber. But, writing from the terrain of this ideology, he vacillates between according rationality a capital R and questioning it with inverted commas. The tension between these two is one of the most enduring sources of interest in his work. For example, see "The Social Psychology of the World Religions," in Gerth and Mills, eds., *From Max Weber,* chap. 11.

21. Michael T. Taussig, *The Devil and Commodity Fetishism in South America* (Chapel Hill, 1980), p. 230.

22. The entire argument of Eugene D. Genovese's *Roll, Jordan, Roll: The World the Slaves Made* (New York, 1974) provides an eloquent demonstration of why this was, and had to be, true.

23. For example, Carl N. Degler, *Place over Time: The Continuity of Southern Distinctiveness* (Baton Rouge, 1977).

24. A sensitive treatment of the importance of this change to the masters' view of themselves and of the ex-slaves may be found in James L. Roark, *Masters*

without Slaves: Southern Planters in the Civil War and Reconstruction (New York, 1977), esp. chaps. 3 and 4. See also Genovese, *Roll, Jordan, Roll*, pp. 97–112.

25. Harold D. Woodman has developed this position with exemplary persistence and eloquence. See "Sequel to Slavery: The New History Views the Postbellum South," *Journal of Southern History*, 43 (1977), 523–54; "Comment" in American Historical Review Forum, "Class Structure and Economic Development in the American South, 1865–1955," *American Historical Review*, 84 (1979), 997–1001; "Post–Civil War Southern Agriculture and the Law," *Agricultural History*, 53 (1979), 319–37; and "The Revolutionary Transformation of the South After the Civil War" (Paper presented at the University of Missouri-St. Louis Conference, February 1978, on the First and Second Reconstructions). It is scarcely possible to overstate the importance of Woodman's forthcoming book, on which the last-named paper is in effect a progress report.

26. Fredrickson, *Black Image*, pp. 321–22, sets forth a list of attitudes on which "widespread, almost universal, agreement existed" from the 1830s on, going so far as to call these attitudes a "creed" accepted by "all but a tiny . . . minority of white spokesmen."

27. In trying to prove that racism was the core of the slaveholders' ideology, Fredrickson lays heavy stress on the prevalence of the first sort of attitude, but totally ignores the second. Genovese demonstrates brilliantly that it is not the one attitude or the other, but precisely the fact of their contradictory coexistence, that constitutes the essence of the slaveholders' ideology, as of their society itself. Fredrickson, *Black Image*, chaps. 2 and 3; Genovese, *Roll, Jordan, Roll*, pp. 25–49.

28. The concept of "herrenvolk democracy" has the curious quality of recognizing the gulf between the world view of the great planters and those of the yeomen and poor whites, only to dismiss it with a shallow formula. The gulf was the product of vastly different social circumstances and was bound to persist as long as these circumstances differed. Political contest determined whose viewpoint prevailed at the level of actual government institutions. Eugene D. Genovese and J. Mills Thornton III have examined this contest and reached opposite conclusions as to which side won. But neither suggests that the gulf itself was or could be conjured away at the stroke of a slogan. See Fredrickson, *Black Image*, p. 68; J. Mills Thornton III, *Politics and Power in a Slave Society: Alabama 1800–1860* (Baton Rouge, 1978); and Eugene D. Genovese, *The Political Economy of Slavery* (New York, 1965), and "Yeomen Farmers in a Slaveholders' Democracy," *Agricultural History*, 44 (1975), 331–42.

29. The distinction is not that a slogan is bogus while a belief is genuine. A slogan has the purpose of summarizing different beliefs in such a way as to provide a basis for common political action among those holding these beliefs, in spite of their differences. A slogan that precisely and explicitly stated a particular belief would not be an effective slogan, since it would isolate those holding that belief from potential allies. For example, "Cut government spending and balance the budget" is a slogan that may unite into a coalition those wishing to abolish welfare, those wishing to curtail the military, and

those wishing to dismantle the space program. But the slogan "Cut military spending" would immediately separate the coalition into its constituent parts.

30. Fredrickson has attempted to show that these opposite views actually derive from the same impulse: both bespeak a "desire for racial homogeneity." Free-Soilers sought to accomplish it in reality, while slaveowners sought to accomplish it symbolically, by defining the slaves as outside the human species. *Black Image*, pp. 130–32. A conflict of views which ends in a Civil War leaving 600,000 dead demands discussion at the level of real politics, not symbolism. In any case, Fredrickson appears to have abandoned the attempt; see "Masters and Mudsills: The Role of Race in the Planter Ideology of South Carolina," *South Atlantic Urban Studies*, 2 (1978), 44.

31. A sophisticated, imaginative, and growing body of literature, much of it as yet unpublished, has now established this point in rich detail. Recent examples include Steven Hahn, "The Yeomanry in the Non-Plantation South: Upper Piedmont Georgia, 1850–1860," in Orville Vernon Burton and Robert C. McMath, Jr., eds., *Class, Conflict and Consensus: Antebellum Southern Community Studies* (Westport, Conn., 1982); and Hahn's, "The Roots of Southern Populism: Yeomen Farmers and the Transformation of Georgia's Upper Piedmont, 1850–1890" (Ph.D. diss., Yale University, 1979); John Schlotterbeck, "Orange and Greene Counties, Virginia, 1850 to 1880: A Case Study of the Impact of Civil War and Emancipation in an Upper South Community" (Paper delivered at OAH annual meeting, San Francisco, April 1980); Grady McWhiney, "The Revolution in Nineteenth-Century Alabama Agriculture," *Alabama Review*, 31 (1978), 3–32.

32. Genovese, "Yeomen Farmers"; Michael P. Johnson, *Toward a Patriarchal Republic: The Secession of Georgia* (Baton Rouge, 1977). The ambiguity of the yeomen's attitude toward both the Confederacy and the war is well documented in such older works as J. G. Randall and David Donald, *The Civil War and Reconstruction*, 2nd ed., rev. (Boston, 1969), chap. 14; and Clement Eaton, *The Freedom-of-Thought Struggle in the Old South* (New York, 1964), chap. 14, and *A History of the Old South: The Emergence of a Reluctant Nation*, 3rd ed. (New York, 1975), chap. 25. A forthcoming book by Armstead L. Robinson, *Bitter Fruits of Bondage: Slavery's Demise and the Collapse of the Confederacy*, deals systematically with the position of the white yeomanry in an effort to specify the social reasons for the South's defeat in the Civil War.

33. Otto H. Olsen, "North Carolina: An Incongruous Presence," in Otto H. Olsen, ed., *Reconstruction and Redemption in the South* (Baton Rouge, 1980), pp. 167, 185–86 (emphasis in original). Also see Steven Hahn, "Merchants, Farmers, and the Marketplace: The Transformation of Production and Exchange in the Georgia Upcountry, 1860–1890" (Paper delivered at AHA Annual Meeting, Washington, D.C., December 1980); and Hahn's essay in this volume.

34. J. Morgan Kousser, *The Shaping of Southern Politics: Suffrage Restriction and the Establishment of the One-Party South, 1880–1910* (New Haven, 1974), esp. chaps. 8 and 9.

35. Ibid., pp. 250–57.

36. As when, for example, the Colored Farmers Alliance and the white National Farmers Alliance found themselves on opposite sides in a strike, the

former organization comprising the employees of the latter. See David Montgomery, "On Goodwyn's Populists," *Marxist Perspectives*, 1 (spring 1978), 171–72; Robert McMath, Jr., "Southern White Farmers and the Organization of Black Farm Workers: A North Carolina Document," *Labor History*, 18 (1977), 115–19.

37. For instance, New Orleans witnessed a dramatic interracial general strike and a murderous race riot within eight years of each other. C. Vann Woodward, *Origins of the New South, 1877–1913* (Baton Rouge, 1951), pp. 231–32, 351.

38. By the same token, when an upper class loses confidence or feels threatened in its capacity to dominate, it may set aside tolerance and become virulent and homicidal as well. Examples from the anti-abolition mobs to the Ku Klux Klan and other terrorist organizations of the Reconstruction period demonstrate that when circumstances warranted, patricians were fully prepared either to carry out violence themselves or to hire it done. See Leonard L. Richards, *'Gentlemen of Property and Standing': Anti-Abolition Mobs in Jacksonian America* (New York, 1970), and Allen W. Trelease, *White Terror: The Ku Klux Klan Conspiracy and Southern Reconstruction* (New York, 1971).

39. Edmund S. Morgan has shown that plantation slavery was the eventual answer to a social crisis that afflicted colonial Virginia. The origin of that crisis was the planters' loss of control over the white laboring population. See *American Slavery, American Freedom: The Ordeal of Colonial Virginia* (New York, 1975).

40. David Brion Davis, *The Problem of Slavery in Western Culture* (Ithaca, 1966). Much of the book, as also much of Eugene D. Genovese's *Roll, Jordan, Roll,* may be read as a sustained reflection on the way in which the very efforts of slaveholders to affirm this proposition ended by admitting its negation.

41. David Brion Davis, *Problem of Slavery in the Age of Revolution.* The breadth, subtlety, and delicacy of Davis's argument resists hasty or ham-fisted summary. I hope this brief sketch does rough justice, in particular, to the prefatory comments on ideology (pp. 14–15) and to the section "Race and Reality" (pp. 299–306).

42. The furor launched in the South by Hinton Rowan Helper's racialist antislavery tract, which claimed to speak on behalf of the nonslaveholding whites, provides a good illustration.

43. See Pete Daniel, *Shadow of Slavery: Peonage in the South, 1901–1969* (Urbana, 1972).

44. Charles and Mary Beard's argument to this effect provided a generation of scholars with material for hostile review and contemptuous dismissal. Nevertheless, it contains a strong underlying element of truth. The Beards' error was twofold. First, they unwarrantably identified the motives and intentions behind Reconstruction with its ultimate consequences. Second, they understood ideology to be a simple tool for the manipulation of one class by another, rather than what it is: a distorted reflection of social reality that

deceives the supposed manipulator as much as the putative manipulee. Charles and Mary Beard, *The Rise of American Civilization* (New York, 1930), esp. chap. 18.

45. David Montgomery takes the nationalist content of Reconstruction as primary, and demonstrates that Reconstruction politics largely revolved around different groups' interpretations of and reactions to that nationalism. *Beyond Equality: Labor and the Radical Republicans, 1862–1872* (New York, 1967), esp. chap. 2. Eric J. Hobsbawm, *The Age of Capital, 1848–1875* (London, 1975), discusses, from a global standpoint, the process of consolidating large territorial nation-states and of abolishing the remaining instances of coerced labor.

46. Lawrence N. Powell, *New Masters: Northern Planters during the Civil War and Reconstruction* (New Haven, 1980), offers a revealing look at the moment in which frustrated Yankees acquired that experience at first hand. John G. Sproat, *'The Best Men': Liberal Reformers in the Gilded Age* (New York, 1968), provides a good critical treatment of the ideology into which that experience typically metamorphosed.

47. Not all Republicans took the low ground of race in justifying the abandonment of the freedmen. Some explained the freedmen's failure to respond as expected by reference to their lack of education, and proposed to remedy this by the provision of schools. However, the assumption that once properly schooled, the freedmen would adopt the Yankees' view of the world was scarcely more realistic than the expectation that the same thing would happen automatically upon emancipation. And the political conclusion thereby deduced was the same as that which others reached by a less well-intentioned route: that the struggle for equality should be postponed until the freedmen were "ready" for it. "Time, education, moral suasion . . . a 'natural' division of southern whites into two parties, [and] bi-racial progress through the economic growth of a 'New South'": these "abolitionist prescriptions for Negro advancement," to use the phrase of the abolitionists' most persuasive partisan, amount to abandonment when stacked against the stark forms of intimidation, exploitation, and brutality to which the freedmen fell victims. James M. McPherson, *The Abolitionist Legacy: From Reconstruction to the NAACP* (Princeton, 1975), makes perhaps the strongest case that can be made for the abolitionists.

48. No one has made this point more elegantly than E. P. Thompson, "Time, Work-Discipline, and Industrial Capitalism," *Past and Present*, no. 38 (1967), 56–97.

49. Herbert G. Gutman, "Work, Culture, and Society in Industrializing America," in Gutman, *Work, Culture, and Society in Industrializing America* (New York, 1977). See also John Higham, *Strangers in the Land: Patterns of American Nativism 1860–1925* (New York, 1970), esp. chap. 6.

50. Powell, *New Masters*, pp. xii–xiii, estimates that Northern planters were one of the most numerous of the groups active in Reconstruction.

51. Freedmen on the Sea Islands, who did for a time have their own land, showed a reluctance to devote themselves to the production of cotton, something the Yankee entrepreneurs expected them to do automatically. Some

Northerners understood the importance of land to complete the ex-slaves' freedom. But their view did not prevail. See Willie Lee Rose, *Rehearsal for Reconstruction: The Port Royal Experiment* (New York, 1964), esp. chap. 13; and Eric Foner, "Thaddeus Stevens, Confiscation, and Reconstruction," in Foner, *Politics and Ideology in the Age of the Civil War* (New York, 1980). In any case, it is doubtful that many of these Northerners would have approved of the freedmen's intentions had they fully understood them. It was one thing for the freedmen to have their own land; it was another for them to refuse to grow cotton.

52. Rose, *Rehearsal for Reconstruction;* Hahn, "Merchants, Farmers, and the Marketplace"; Joseph Reidy, "The Unfinished Revolution: White Planters and Black Laborers in the Georgia Black Belt, 1865–1910" (Paper delivered at OAH annual meeting, San Francisco, April 1980). The view that responsiveness to the incentives of the competitive market is an innate characteristic of human behavior stands as an article of faith among many scholars. In fact, such behavior has been a phenomenon limited in both historical time and geographic space. And even where it appears, it does not necessarily take the form predicted by the assumptions of neoclassical market rationality. An important theoretical discussion of this point appears in Witold Kula, *An Economic Theory of the Feudal System,* trans. Lawrence Garner (London, 1976), pp. 41–44. This work dealing with Polish feudalism has wide relevance for scholars specializing in neither Poland nor feudalism.

53. A few Republicans understood that allowing the freedmen to follow their inclination would probably bring adverse economic consequences, and were prepared to accept this. For example, see Foner, "Thaddeus Stevens," pp. 137–38. Few went as far as the *Nation* editorial that, in admitting that its prescriptions would probably lead to "a great falling off in the cotton crop," warned against "the notion that the great mission of the American people . . . is the production of goods for the market." *Nation,* November 9, 1865. Leslie Rowland kindly brought this item to my attention.

54. According to Jack P. Maddex, one reason for the defeat of the Radical Republicans in Virginia was that because the yeoman whites and the freedmen were in such different material circumstances, their grievances matured at different times. They were therefore unable to function as a purposeful coalition. "Virginia: The Persistence of Centrist Hegemony," in Olsen, ed., *Reconstruction and Redemption in the South,* pp. 113–55.

55. Eugene D. Genovese, "Reexamining Reconstruction," New York *Times Book Review,* May 4, 1980.

56. The appalling human and social costs of this "rationalization," and some of the mechanisms by which it eventually came about, receive consideration in Pete Daniel, "The Transformation of the Rural South, 1930 to the Present," *Agricultural History,* 55 (1981), 231–48.

57. Eric J. Hobsbawm, *Age of Capital,* p. 178. The death of the family farm may well have been inevitable (the view expressed by David Potter in *Division and the Stresses of Reunion, 1845–1876,* (Glenview, Ill., 1973, pp. 186–87); but the timing of its demise has always depended on the economic weight, and thus the political leverage, of the large-scale, commercialized

capitalist sector. Considering the stubborn persistence of agrarian independence and dissidence in a South whose balance of power favored large landowners and their partners and allies, it would be hazardous to belittle the political prospects of a black and white yeomanry possessed of land in a South not dominated by plantations and their economic and political appurtenances.

Othello in America:
The Drama of Racial Intermarriage

TILDEN G. EDELSTEIN

A RECENT historian of nineteenth-century race relations claims that pre-Victorian Americans so feared racial intermarriage and amalgamation that they "found it difficult to sit through a performance of *Othello*." Given the history of American race relations such difficulty hardly seems surprising. Paradoxically, despite its racial and sexual elements, *Othello* has been one of the most frequently performed Shakespearean plays in a nation that has watched more Shakespeare than it has the works of any other playwright.[1] Shakespeare encompassed art, culture, and the wisdom of Western civilization; and for American actors and audiences *Othello*'s volatile racial, sexual, and class themes provided drama surpassing the dimensions of the stage. Engrossing drama, exemplified by *Othello,* communicates symbolically, simultaneously presenting the recognizably concrete event with verbal and physical images transcending material reality. Two centuries of American *Othello* performances dramatized some of this country's racial reality and its racial fantasies.

A standard Shakespearean reference source warns that *Othello* was "not intended as a problem of miscegenation American style, because Othello was an aristocrat of royal birth." A writer in the *Shakespeare Quarterly* argues that "it is not important that he happened to be full-blooded, or part-blooded Arab, Moor, Negro,

For their helpful criticism and suggestions, I am indebted to the editors of this volume, to Richard P. McCormick, David R. Weimer, and my colleagues in the Rutgers University History Department's Social History Seminar. The Rutgers University Research Council has provided necessary funding for my work on miscegenation and racial intermarriage.

Blackamoor, or whatever. These are just names." Even the distinguished historian of American culture Louis B. Wright stresses
that "Shakespeare was *not* trying . . . to emphasize any racial
differences between the hero and the heroine." But Wright concedes that the generations after Shakespeare may have perceived
the play in racial terms.[2] Obviously fundamental to perception in
the theater is the direct visual sense of the action—you go to *see* a
play—and so, regardless of what Shakespeare intended, if *Othello*
is perceived in racial terms, this will affect the acting and reception of the play and even its very meaning.

From the eighteenth century to the present, changing American
racial, sexual, and class attitudes necessitated the periodical alteration of characterization, costuming, makeup, and even dialogue.
These changes, of course, functioned reciprocally: they both reflected and promoted revealing responses to the play from audiences and critics. What is revealed are societal tensions found in
pervasive and changing American views about race, sex, and class.
Especially important is the conclusion of a recent American
theater historian who notes that, particularly in the first half of
the nineteenth century, "closeness of audience control made the
drama, more than any art form, the theater as much as any social
institution, immediately sensitive to public opinion." These audiences, he writes, were a pluralistic mix of classes, colors, and sexes.[3]

The colonists' distrust of the theater, primarily motivated by
Puritan moral prescriptions against idleness and frivolity, delayed the first American performance of *Othello* until the mid-
eighteenth century. At Newport, Rhode Island, in 1765, it was
performed in a tavern and advertised as a "Moral Dialogue in
Five Parts," since local law banned both plays and theaters. The
playbill didactically noted the moral lessons taught by each character, including the "dreadful passion of jealousy" demonstrated
by the "noble and magnanimous Moor." Brabantio's rejection of
Desdemona's marriage to black Othello also had a moral: her
father "is foolish enough to dislike the noble Moor . . . because
his face is not white, forgetting that we all spring from one root.
Such prejudices are very numerous and very wrong." The playbill further embellished the racial moral with a couplet:

> Fathers beware what sense and love ye lack.
> 'Tis crime, not color, makes the being black.

But class insubordination was not tolerated. Emilia was a faithful attendant and a good example "to all servants, male and female, and to all persons in subjection." Accepting the prevailing single-origin theory of evolution did not mean conceding class equality. Neither menial servant nor slave, but a black man of royal birth, Othello, in this era, was qualified by class to marry Desdemona. Only the racially prejudiced could disagree.[4]

In this production, as in others of the seventeenth and eighteenth centuries, a white actor played Othello wearing heavy black makeup, and the most renowned Othellos toured major American Northern and Southern cities. The white American actor James Quin, a big, black Othello, wore a white wig, an all-white British officer's uniform, and white gloves. As a result of the visual impact of contrasting colors, high drama occurred when Quin peeled off his white gloves to reveal his black hands.[5] Shakespeare, the actor David Garrick argued, had depicted jealous white men before, but in *Othello* he sought to disclose this passion in all its violence and so chose an "African in whose veins circulated fire instead of blood."[6] Men's passions, in the Age of Reason, were a central concern; in *Othello* the passion of jealousy is magnified by the character of the black African. His white British uniform further linked Othello to his white audience, making visible the idea that black was not entirely separate from white.

Similarly, John Adams, writing in 1760, judged the play's moral to be how love turns to hatred and revenge when a man feels betrayed. He quoted Othello: "Arise, black Vengeance, from the hollow Hell."[7] Adams, whose thought was indebted both to the Enlightenment and to Puritan moral didacticism, emphasized human frailty, not distaste for racial intermarriage. Yet by accepting Shakespeare's linking of black with irrational vengeance, and the Newport production's view that crime was "black," Adams's opinion confirms Winthrop Jordan's suggestion that a negative color consciousness emerged before racist theory fully developed.[8] Nevertheless, moral questions rather than racial ones dominated Adam's thought as it did that of other eighteenth-century American intellectuals.

Seeing *Othello* performed in London in 1786, Abigail Adams perceived none of the racial-equality themes stressed by the 1765 Newport production. Her response also contrasted with her husband's observations of 1760. Mrs. Adams's perceptions were too close to the era's racial views to be dismissed as exemplifying only her unique view. Massachusetts, which had abolished slavery in 1783, re-enacted its law against racial intermarriage in 1786 while eliminating legal prohibitions against interracial fornication. Abigail Adams admitted that she was disturbed by "the sooty appearance of the Moor . . . I could not separate the African color from the man, nor prevent that disgust and horror which filled my mind every time I saw him touch the gentle Desdemona; nor did I wonder that Brabantio thought some love potion or some witchcraft had been practiced to make his daughter fall in love with what she scarecely dared to look upon."[9] Here were fundamental issues for Mrs. Adams and her contemporaries: the paramount importance of black indelibility and revulsion against physical contact between a black man and a white woman. Her perception that it requires evil black magic for a white woman to succumb to the love for a black man suggests a growing awareness of women's will in relationships with men. Inability to see beyond Othello's blackness obstructed comprehension of any deeper meaning, she admitted: "I lost much of the pleasure of the play. . . ." Othello's color did not magnify a human trait like vengeance but compelled her to distinguish him from any white lover of a white woman.

Observing that the renowned Sarah Siddon, who played Desdemona, was pregnant, Mrs. Adams expressed comfort that the actress's brother, John Phillip Kemble, acted Othello "so that both her husband and the virtuous part of the audience can see them in the tenderest scenes without once fearing for their reputation."[10] Obviously, racial intermarriage, *not* any thoughts of incest, caused Mrs. Adams's repugnance for Othello. Knowledge that a white man in black makeup was playing Othello seemed obscured to her in the context of America's struggle to reconcile freedom and slavery, equality and racism. The aristocratic compatibility of Desdemona and Othello would no longer compensate for their racial differences.

Although a Natchez editor called Othello a "dirty Moor" and suggested that had any other playwright "laid such a plot and made such an ill-assorted match it would have damned him," it was not merely reverence for Shakespeare that accounted for ante-

bellum Americans' continuing to attend *Othello* productions—
and nowhere more than in the South. Charleston witnessed most
performances, and it played as often in New Orleans as in Philadelphia.[11] Fascination with the racial and sexual themes remained,
but major adjustments were needed to make the play more acceptable to early-nineteenth-century audiences. For the next 125 years
American audiences could not accept the credibility of a "noble
Moor" of aristocratic and royal birth whose skin color was black.
How, then, to get audiences to feel the tragic power of *Othello?*

Edmund Kean, after having played the part in traditional black
makeup, greatly lightened that coloring by 1820 and thus inaugurated the so-called bronze age of *Othello*. Most free blacks in
the North and South were mulattoes, who were accorded higher
status than blacks.[12] An actor playing Othello now had the advantage, explained a Southern newspaper, of "not being so dark
as to obscure the expression of his countenance."[13] Light makeup,
it has been argued, was demanded by poor stage illumination
and by a new romantic acting style emphasizing facial expressions.[14] Underlying the view that black skin hides expression,
however, were the clichés that all black faces looked the same and
were expressionless. Such anonymity ill suited the unique personality Shakespeare created and the play's dramatic impact.

The gradual decline of the Enlightenment belief in environmental causes of black character and the growing acceptance by
Americans of the theory that blacks were closer in origin to animals than to men made blacks appear inherently unequal to
whites and therefore subject to different treatment. In the South,
until about 1850, only the mulatto, thanks to some white blood,
would be viewed as a black not limited by animal traits.[15] Also
contributing to the play's credibility was the nineteenth-century
tradition that the actors playing Othello and Iago exchanged roles
at different performances. Audiences thus were reminded that
Othello was a play and not reality.

Samuel Taylor Coleridge is as revealing as Abigail Adams in
explaining why makeup changed and how the British, for a time,
shared American views. Shakespeare, said Coleridge, was not "so
utterly ignorant as to make a barbarous *negro* plead royal birth. . . .
It would be something monstrous to conceive this beautiful
Venetian girl falling in love with a veritable negro." After seeing

the great Edmund Kean playing Othello in light makeup, Coleridge exuberantly concluded that it was "like reading Shakespeare by flashes of lightning."[16]

Further "lightening" of Othello soon occurred in the United States. After Kean's last American performance as Othello in the 1820s, a young Philadelphian, Edwin Forrest, appeared on the New York stage with the makeup of an octoroon. Tragic octoroons, looking white but having a trace of black blood and some telltale Negroid features that condemned them to slavery or prevented their marrying whites, were frequent figures in sentimental antebellum fiction. Until about 1840, Forrest had played a robust Othello, a blinded giant who killed Desdemona by seizing her "with illimitable rage." This characterization, so close to popular fears about animallike free blacks, Forrest distinctly muted by deleting lines dealing with racial amalgamation; and he moved further away from portraying Othello as a black and closer to a "warrior Moor . . . the descendant of a long illustrious line of ancestry."[17] Thus another step had been taken to whiten Othello. An English critic observed that the American actor looked more like a Shawnee or a Mohican than a Moor.[18] To have an Indian, or, even better, a man who only looked like one, marry your daughter was obviously less repulsive to many Americans than the prospect of a black son-in-law.

During the Jacksonian era, John Quincy Adams's views about *Othello* reveal the continuing difficulties, despite Forrest's lightening efforts, that color-conscious Americans were having with the play, especially in the 1830s and 1840s, when emerging racist thought was denying human characteristics to blacks or seeing them unequal to whites, and when the number of state laws prohibiting racial intermarriage was increasing.[19] In the very years when Adams was heroically defending slaves who had mutinied aboard the *Amistad* and was fighting the "gag rule" in Congress against antislavery petitions, he wrote in his diary about Desdemona, "whose sensual passion I thought over ardent, so as to reconcile her to a passion for a black man; and although faithful to him, I thought the poet has painted her as a lady of easy virtue. . . ."[20] A few years later Adams revealed how much beyond his mother, Abigail Adams, he had traveled in perceiving the play principally in racial and sexual terms and how much more troubled even a thoughtful American had become about racial intermarriage, miscegenation, and female sexuality. Now a published theater critic, John Quincy Adams abandoned the privacy of his diary to publish two articles about *Othello*. Dwelling upon what he interpreted as the wanton character of Desdemona, he wrote:

. . . she not only violates her duties to her father, her family, her sex and her country, but she makes the first advances. . . . The great moral lesson of *Othello* is that black and white blood cannot be inter-mingled without a gross outrage upon the law of Nature; and that, in such violations, Nature will vindicate her laws. . . . Upon the stage her fondling of Othello is disgusting. Who, in real life, would have her for a sister, daughter or wife. . . . she is always deficient in deli-cacy. . . . This character takes from us so much of the sympathetic interest in her sufferings that when Othello smothers her in bed, the terror and the pity subside immediately to the sentiment that she had her just deserts.[21]

Adams noted in another essay, "I must believe that in exhibiting a daughter of a Venetian nobleman of the highest rank eloping in the dead of night to marry a thick-lipped, wool-headed Moor, opening a train of consequences which lead to her own destruc-tion by her husband's hands, and to that of her father by a broken heart, he [Shakespeare] did not intend to present her as an exam-ple of the perfection of female virtue. . . ."[22] A thick-lipped, wooly-headed Moor hardly was identical to the portrayal of an eighteenth-century aristocratic African king. Yet as disturbing as Othello's race were Desdemona's exaggerated female character-istics, which moved her to make the first advances, elope, and remain a loving wife in alleged defiance of her father, family, sex, country, and class. To Adams, she seemed to have uncontrolled sexual passions instead of feminine warmth; instead of being sweetly innocent she seemed devastatingly gullible; and instead of showing unquestioning filial loyalty she appeared a woman dog-gedly enslaved to her black husband. Only by seeing Desdemona as wanton and the play as a lesson against racial intermarriage could Adams accept the credibility of even a bleached Othello and a Desdemona who betrays her race and class.

Still another way to make the play plausible to antebellum American audiences was to cast Desdemona as an innocent blond victim, blondness being the characteristic attribute of the virtuous female until the 1920s, when it began to connote the very opposite of innocence. Desdemona became a childlike blond who tragically strayed too far from her English teas, domestic needle-work, polite music, and proper dancing. As either a wanton woman or an innocent victim, Desdemona thus exemplified a view of the play in which the race issue eclipsed not only the question of jealousy but just about everything else. Only after the subsequent casting of Edwin Booth as an Othello who bore no resemblance to a black African, either as African king or thick-lipped wooly-headed Moor, would Desdemona be characterized as both a virtuous and rational woman.

Booth, who played Othello for the first time in 1849, sought to expunge from the play any taint of miscegenation by becoming the lightest-skinned Othello ever, thus eliminating visually any liaison between a black man and a white aristocrat's daughter. (Even after electricity illuminated the stage in 1878 and the alleged problem of black makeup hiding facial expressions no longer could be defended, Booth never became black.)[23] Wearing robes of glittering Oriental splendor, he was transmogrified into Desdemona's Persian suitor. With studied gestures, such as hold-ing above his purple-and-gold turban a scimitar forming a cres-cent, Booth made his costume, makeup, and manner identify Othello. At times he wore a long, hanging, Tartar like mustache to emphasize that Othello was "Arabian, not African." His con-fessed purpose was to raise Othello's character above that of a "brutal blackamoor."[24]

Portraying, moreover, chivalrous love devoid of onstage em-braces, Booth presented a genteel Othello. (One critic complained of Booth's acting like a "young Jesuit student" or like an "elderly schoolboy.") To Ellen Terry, one of his most famous leading ladies, he vowed: "I shall never make you black." When he touched her, Booth shielded her fair skin from his tan makeup with his costume. His characterization allowed Desdemona to be cast as "a true woman with a mind of her own."[25] Once Othello ceased being black, Desdemona no longer had to be viewed as a wanton woman or an innocent child lured sexually to love a black man.

Booth's Othello was popular throughout much of the post–Civil War era, suggesting the continuity of racial and sexual atti-tudes from 1850 to 1880 in the North, as he continued to expunge lines that explicitly emphasized race. American audiences demanded whitewashed Othellos, so it was understandable that Henry Irving, the great English Shakespearean actor, never played the part in any of his eight American tours. Irving had a reputation for acting Othello in black makeup and besmirching his leading ladies with it.[26] American audiences, on the other hand, had the reputation, according to an antebellum critic, of considering "actors as public slaves . . . bound to be obedient victims of their caprice."[27]

Until the 1850s the South welcomed productions of *Othello*. But when the lines separating North and South grew more distinct, Southern cities witnessed a declining number of *Othello* performances. In Macon, Georgia, a Shakespearean company was informed that the play displeased many of the town citizenry and that no actor could portray a black Othello. To avoid a disturbance, said one leading man, "I played him nearly white." As the South moved toward secession and the issue of miscegenation became central to the slavery debate, Joel Williamson has written, another Othello admitted being "afraid of the negro part." The period of Booth's greatest popularity coincided with the strong fear of mulattoes that initially affected the South in the decade before the Civil War, and then spread through all America once emancipation came.[28] Despite the whitening and orientalizing of the main character, that fear of one drop of black blood in the men whom white daughters married continued to haunt and fascinate Americans with the tenacity of a morbid compulsion.

Issues that audiences have difficulty confronting directly are often presented, as we know, by the indirectness of parody. Through satire and ridicule, parodies of *Othello* both evaded and capitalized on miscegenation tensions. In parody the continuing demands for plausibility could be ignored. Of all Shakespearean plays, it was *Othello* that was most frequently parodied in nineteenth-century America, and always the parody assured the audience of the absurdity of racial intermarriage. Among the parodies were *Dars de money, Old Fellow, or the Boor of Vengeance,* and *Desdamonium.* The most popular parody was performed by the Christy Minstrels.[29] Suggesting that Othello married for money, it included this speech by Desdemona:

> For you I've run away from pap,
> But I don't care a snap for that. . . .

I love you and you love me,
And all our lives we'll merry be . . .
With you I'll sport my figure . . .
Although you are a nigger.

One Othello not requiring dark makeup was the New York–born black actor Ira Aldridge. A celebrated Othello in Europe, Aldridge received enthusiastic acclaim for his London performance of 1833. Here at last, said a European drama critic, was an Othello whose complexion did not need "licorice juice or coffee grounds, or steeves of chocolate colored meat. He had the right skin already. . . . Consequently his appearance on the scene was magnificent . . . his eyes half shut as if dazzled by an African sun . . . that easy negro gait which no European can imitate." European audiences watched Aldridge enclose Desdemona's hand in his, but while the Europeans appeared less fearful about racial intermarriage and miscegenation than Americans did, they were not equalitarian in racial thought. Black men, explained a European who saw Aldridge as Othello, believe that black women are licentious and therefore distrust all women.[30]

Aldridge never performed in the United States. Not only was it unprecedented for black actors to appear with whites; Aldridge's life hardly recommended him to Americans. He was married to a white woman while simultaneously fathering children by his Swedish mistress.[31] A black Othello, James Hewlett, had appeared on the New York stage in 1821 but with an all-black cast and audience, and not at a major theater. Only after the Civil War did black actors even perform in minstrel shows; those who looked mulatto wore burnt cork in the tradition set by white minstrels.[32]

Black actors remained excluded from major *Othello* productions, and well into the decades after the Civil War most audiences continued to see light-skinned Othellos. However, in 1873, a touring Italian actor, Tomasso Salvini, brought to America a new conception of the part. Wearing makeup shaded between copper and coffee, Salvini was the darkest Othello Americans had seen since early in the nineteenth century. His acting style also contrasted with Booth's fastidiousness and studied diction and elocution. Salvini spoke only Italian and often performed with a cast of his countrymen. A lurid and terrifying Othello, he "fiercely swept into his swarthy arms the pale loveliness of Desdemona. . . . Passion choked, his gloating eyes burned with the mere lust of the 'sooty Moor' for that white creature of Venice." Emile Zola hailed Salvini as the "champion of modern realism."[33] But one era's realism can be another era's stereotypes. Salvini's Othello was frequently likened to a tiger or a lion.[34] Before he murdered Desdemona he paced back and forth

with long strides, like a caged lion, his head sunk upon his breast. . . . convulsed with fixed and flaming eyes, half-crouched, [he] slowly circled the stage toward her, muttering savagely and inarticulately as she cowered before him. Rising at last to his full height with extended arms, he pounced upon her, lifted her into the air, [and] dashed with her across the stage. . . . You heard a crash as he flung her on the bed, and growls as of a wild beast over his prey.[35]

Of course that savage and inarticulate muttering might simply have been Salvini's speaking Italian to an uncomprehending audience. To murder Desdemona brutally (Booth had acted as if it were a sacrificial religious rite) and then repeatedly hack at his own throat with a short scimitar previously concealed in his belt portrayed the frenzied behavior of a dangerous, lower-class foreigner, not a royal British officer with white gloves. Salvini explained that he had Othello stab himself because it was an African custom. And by adding the epithet "cruel tiger" for Emilia to shout at Othello, Salvini enhanced the animal and jungle imagery. When he acted Othello in the 1880s, accompanied by an English-speaking cast, few actresses were willing to be Desdemona and submit to the physical fury of his attacks.[36]

Salvini exhilarated most critics, and audiences rushed to see him in New York, Boston, Philadelphia, Chicago, and New Orleans. Except for New Orleans, with its long tradition of miscegenation, the South, however, no longer would tolerate performances of *Othello*. At a time when many Americans increasingly feared the social impact of Italian immigration, Salvini's acting reached a tremulous emotional level as the fair Desdemona married not only a black man but one who was Italian. The producer had a great drawing card "in the Anglo-Italian idea," acknowledged one newspaper reporter. While responding favorably to Salvini's performance, Henry James, never one to lose his sense of proportion, concluded: "The pathos is perhaps a little crude." He also conceded: "There is a class of persons to whom Italians and Africans have about equally little to say."[37]

Emma Lazarus, soon to welcome Europe's huddled masses in her poem enshrined on the Statue of Liberty, wrote that Salvini's Othello "won our love, our admiration, our pity, our horror, and in the end our active sympathy." Disagreeing, however, were those who had admired Booth and rejected a lower-class black Othello. One critic commented: "Salvini's Moor excited no sympathy with him. . . . You hate him and are impatient for his death, as you might be for the death of a mad dog let loose in the streets of a crowded city. . . ." Even when Salvini eliminated some tiger leaps in response to those who found them un-Shakespearean, the reporting of a Chicago performance reveals the prevailing image of Othello as a barbarian, and the barbarian as a cannibal. Salvini "looks as if he could eat up Booth . . . in a single meal, then go on and play the Moor as if he were hungry for another banquet of light weight tragedians."[38] By contrast with John Quincy Adams's day, when a white Desdemona was blamed for irrationally succumbing to a black man and thus deserved to be murdered, by the 1880s it was the aggressive black man's character as tiger, lion, mad dog, or cannibal that warranted being killed. Worrying less about their daughter's wantonness than about the emancipated slaves' physical aggressiveness, playgoers, in keeping with late-nineteenth-century racial thought, at last found a plausible black Othello—but only if he was deprived of his aristocratic class and the ability to speak the language of his American audiences, as well as being portrayed as a wild beast. The "Noble Moor" had disappeared entirely. In his place was an example of the new realism, of a fascination with repulsive characters and events.

The 1880s saw the height of *Othello*'s popularity in post–Civil War America. An all-black cast performed it in Greenwich Village, ironically having Desdemona played by an octoroon. It was an era when that word was seriously treated in fiction, and also by the 1890 census takers, who sought to count the numbers of octoroons along with blacks, mulattoes, and quadroons in America. A racially integrated performance of *Othello* occurred in 1890 but only because an American Indian played the title part.[39] Subsequent efforts to copy Salvini's style or makeup were not well received. When another Italian actor played Othello, his graphic murder of Desdemona caused several women to leave the theater and the men to hiss. Thomas Kean's attempt to appear Negroid by emphasizing Othello's gleaming teeth moved one critic to comment that he looked as if he were going to bite Desdemona. And when Tomasso Salvini's son, Alexander, played the part in the 1890s he was praised for not being "offensively swarthy." Declaring that his father had been wrong for choosing very dark makeup, the young Salvini said: "Desdemona could not have loved a man of such dark skin, no matter how noble his other qualities, so I resolved to make him as attractive as possible, despite his necessary color."[40]

From 1890 to 1920, during the Jim Crow era, with heightened national fear about "mongrelization" of the white race and about increased miscegenation, the play declined in popularity and was seldom staged. When an all-black cast played it in 1910, a Boston critic called the performance enjoyable although the black cast was "less dextrous with rapiers than members of their race have the reputation of being with other sharp implements of more frequent use." When the same cast, headed by Edward Sterling Wright, performed before a predominantly black audience in New York, a newspaper critic suddenly discovered "proof of an unsuspecting histrionic genius in the colored race."[41]

A record fifty-seven Broadway performances of *Othello* occurred in 1925 with Walter Hampden as the lead, but without any change from the light makeup. Othellos were praised for not being "so black skinned as to be taken as escaped from a minstrel show." As one critic explained, "if we are to believe that Desdemona, the fine spirited daughter of a patrician Venetian household, was a normal woman and not an erotic pervert, only such an Othello could, to twentieth century imaginations, have plausibly won her."[42] Calling a white woman an "erotic pervert" for marrying a black man is different from John Quincy Adams's suggesting that Desdemona revealed "over ardent sensual passions." Yet the degree of difference does not warrant the assertion made by the historian George Frederickson that opposition to miscegenation lacked the sexual tone during the antebellum era that it acquired in the post–Civil War era.[43] The difference might simply have been the addition of the language, lacking in antebellum America, of Krafft-Ebing and Freud.

About the only group in which an Othello in black makeup performed with a white cast in the 1920s was New York City's Yiddish Art Theatre Company, known for exploring the anguish of distorted family relationships. But here the director added a silent character: a young daughter of Emilia and Iago. Her complexion was dusky and her features resembled Othello's.[44] Iago now had compelling conjugal reasons for seeking Othello's destruction.

Paul Robeson made his debut as Othello in London in June 1930. With a fine sense of poetic justice, he acknowledged receiving help in preparing for the part from the daughter of Ira Aldridge, herself named Ira Aldridge. American critics attending Robeson's performance left convinced that "by reason of his race" he had been "able to surmount difficulties" in playing Othello because he belonged to "a race whose characteristic is to keep control of its passions only to a point and after that point to throw control to the winds." Said Robeson in an interview: "I think there is no question that he [Othello] must be of a different race, in order to make his jealousy credible." And now with a black Othello and racially liberal ideas becoming evident, Desdemona seemed a brave pioneer rather than a passive victim. The New York *Tribune*'s drama critic enthusiastically predicted that the production would come to New York during the next season.[45]

Twelve years later Robeson appeared for the first time in the United States as Othello. Cautiously opened during a summer tryout in Cambridge, Massachusetts, this historic wartime performance ended with the whole cast joining the audience to sing the national anthem. Like those wartime movies which often depicted the ethnic and racial diversity of Americans, here was Robeson's popular *Ballad for Americans* on the Shakespearean stage.

Othello arrived on Broadway in October 1942. American fears about interracial marriage had not vanished. While Robeson obviously relished being Othello, he was very conscious of the likely public response to a black man's marrying and making love to a white woman. "For the first two weeks in every scene I played with Desdemona," he recalled, "that girl couldn't get near me, I was backin' away from her all the time. I was like a plantation hand in the parlor, that clumsy. But the notices were good. I got over it."[46]

Robeson's good notices emphasized the importance of his race: "He convinces you that he is a man of a different race from the woman he marries, a man who, for all his heroic virtues, is set apart by his color and origins from those whose equal he has become through virtue of his personal achievements." Otherwise Othello "swallows a series of preposterous lies and murders his wife on evidence that would not convince an observant child." In contrast to a response to his 1930 performance, Robeson now could not be criticized for being unstately, for walking stooped over, and for appearing too humble and apologetic. In order to stress Othello's heroic virtues he changed the way he played the epileptic scene in London, and the way Salvini had played it, by ceasing to froth at the mouth. Robeson represented the thrust to integration during World War II by the black intelligentsia and sympathetic white liberals. After 400 Broadway performances, he took Othello on an American tour in 1944, but refused to appear in any theater that practiced racial discrimination, sharply reducing the number of places where he could perform. Othello, it was predicted, would unlikely ever be played again by anyone but a Negro.[47]

Subsequently, Earle Hyman, Canada Lee, and James Earl Jones were the leading black actors to cross the racial barrier Robeson had breached as Othello. But it was the English performance of Sir Laurence Olivier, reaching America on film in 1966, that was as revolutionary as Robeson's original American appearance. Olivier reflected the growing American disillusionment with both the image of the innocent and poetic black man and the idealization of interracial marriage. He abandoned a noble and sensitive Othello by transforming him into a dangerous and self-satisfied fool. Olivier's Othello, suggested one American critic, was like some neophyte diplomat representing a new African nation in the United Nations General Assembly. Rather than needing each other, Desdemona and Othello, in a post-Freudian world, were a modern couple needing a psychiatrist.[48] On the other hand, by wearing makeup that made him look blacker than Robeson, Olivier had returned to the Othello tradition of the seventeenth and eighteenth centuries, a tradition that accepted Othello's deep blackness as an intrinsic part of the play. Abandoned was the more recently developed racial notion that only a man born black was capable of acting Othello successfully.

Throughout its American stage history, *Othello* stimulated actors, directors, and audiences to use the play as a forum for their attitudes about miscegenation and racial intermarriage, to display them from the physical and psychological distance that the theater allowed. Shakespeare's accepted authority as a sage and spokesman of culture required that *Othello*, unlike many other controversial fictional works, not be ignored or dismissed as racially and sexually unpalatable; instead it had to be transformed by actors and directors, and perceived by audiences in ways harmonious with changing racial, sexual, and class attitudes. In the very process of transformation and perception, the play itself probably contributed to shaping the views of performers and audiences.

It remained popular because the real tragedy of America's racial history found a suitable stage on which to be observed and played. Much of the play's power was readily evident, but that power also stemmed from the play's implications, for it avoided what was more common in America, the illicit sexual relationship between a white man and a black woman. Instead, it enacted what was least practiced and most feared: the legal marriage of a black man and a white woman. What Claude Wauthier has said about miscegenation fiction was made even more graphic in the performances of *Othello:* "There are few literary subjects where crime and love, blood and sex are so morbidly interwoven."[49] *Othello*, it appears, helped American audiences define their own racial morality and vicariously experience their own imaginings.

NOTES

1. Linda K. Kerber, "Abolitionists and Amalgamators: The New York City Race Riots of 1834," *New York History*, 48 (1967), 28. The popularity of Shakespeare is surveyed in Esther C. Dunn, *Shakespeare in America* (New York, 1939); David Grimsted, *Melodrama Unveiled: American Theater and Culture, 1800–1850* (Chicago, 1968); and Charles H. Shattuck, *Shakespeare on the American Stage: From the Hallams to Edwin Booth* (Washington, D.C., 1976). Also see William B. Carson, *Theatre on the Frontier Stage* (Chicago, 1932).

2. Oscar J. Campbell and Edward J. Quinn, *The Reader's Encyclopedia of Shakespeare* (New York, 1966), p. 599; Arthur H. Wilson, "Othello's Racial Identity," *Shakespeare Quarterly*, 4 (April 1953), 209; Louis B. Wright, ed., *General Reader's Shakespeare* (New York, 1957), p. xiv.

3. Grimsted, *Melodrama Unveiled*, p. 62.

4. Hugh F. Rankin, *The Theater in Colonial America* (Chapel Hill, 1960), pp. 2–7; Alfred Westfall, *American Shakespeare Criticism, 1607–1865* (New York, 1939), pp. 56–57; Robert A. Law, "Shakespeare in Puritan Disguises," *Nation*, November 23, 1916, p. 486.

5. Marvin Rosenberg, *The Masks of Othello* (Berkeley, 1971), p. 38; John S. Kendall, *The Golden Age of the New Orleans Theater* (Baton Rouge, 1952), pp. 5, 6, 49, 153, 163, 243, 269, 524; R. P. McCutcheon, "Shakespeare in Antebellum Mississippi," *Journal of Mississippi History*, 5 (1943), 28–37.

6. George W. Stone, Jr., "Garrick and *Othello*," *Philological Quarterly*, 45 (1966), 305; the quotation is from Carol Carlisle, *Shakespeare from the Greenroom* (Chapel Hill, 1969), p. 188.

7. John Adams to Josiah Quincy, summer 1759, in Lyman H. Butterfield, ed., *Diary and Autobiography of John Adams*, 4 vols. (Cambridge, Mass., 1961), I, 114.

8. Winthrop Jordan, *White over Black* (Chapel Hill, 1968), pp. 4–11.

9. Abigail Adams to Mrs. Shaw, March 4, 1786, in C. F. Adams, ed., *Letters of Mrs. Adams, the Wife of John Adams* (Boston, 1840), p. 125.

10. Ibid., p. 126.

11. Quoted in James Dormon, *Theater in the Antebellum South, 1815–1861* (Chapel Hill, 1967), p. 276; Grimsted, *Melodrama Unveiled*, p. 252.

12. Carlisle, *Shakespeare from the Greenroom*, pp. 191–92; Joel Williamson, *New People: Miscegenation and Mulattoes in the United States* (New York, 1980), p. 15.

13. Virginia *Herald* [1819], in Harvard University Theatre Collection.

14. Carlisle, *Shakespeare from the Greenroom*, p. 190.

15. George M. Fredrickson, *The Black Image in the White Mind* (New York, 1971), pp. 1–5, 13, 172–73; William Stanton, *The Leopard's Spots* (Chicago, 1960), pp. 19–22; Williamson, *New People*, pp. 15–19.

16. Quoted in Gino J. Matteo, "Shakespeare's *Othello*: The Study and the Stage, 1604–1904" (Ph.D. diss., University of Toronto, 1968), p. 275; Barbara Alden, "Differences in the Conception of Othello's Character as Seen in the Performances of Three Important Nineteenth-Century Actors on the American Stage" (Ph.D. diss., University of Chicago, 1950), p. 29.

17. Howard H. Furness, *A New Variorum Edition of Shakespeare* (Philadelphia, 1886), VI, 406; Shattuck, *Shakespeare on the American Stage*, p. 79; New York *Dramatic Mirror*, November 26, 1836, October 26, 1889; Jean F. Yellin, *The Intricate Knot* (New York, 1972), pp. 84–85, 171–72; Jules Zanger, "The 'Tragic Octoroon' in Pre–Civil War Fiction," *American Quarterly*, 18 (1966), 63–70.

18. Richard Moody, *Edwin Forrest* (New York, 1960), p. 225.

19. Frederickson, *Black Image,* pp. 176–81; David Fowler, "Northern Attitudes towards Interracial Marriage: A Study of Legislation and Public Opinion in the Middle Atlantic States and the States of the Old Northwest" (Ph.D. diss., Yale University, 1963), pp. 155–57, 163–69.

20. November 1831, in Alan Nevins, ed., *The Diary of John Quincy Adams, 1794–1845* (New York, 1928), p. 424; Frederickson, *Black Image,* pp. 46–58, 132.

21. "Misconceptions of Shakespeare upon the Stage," *New England Magazine,* 9 (1835), 252.

22. "The Character of Desdemona," *American Monthly Magazine,* 1 (1836), 151.

23. Carlisle, *Shakespeare from the Greenroom,* p. 205; Alden, "Othello's Character," pp. 210, 325; New York *Herald,* September 13, 1869.

24. Edwina Booth Grossman, *Edwin Booth* (New York, 1894), pp. 21–22, 210; Boston *Evening Transcript,* March 6, 1878.

25. Alden, "Othello's Character," pp. 179–80; Shattuck, *Shakespeare on the American Stage,* p. 141; Booth to Howard H. Furness, May 12, 1885, in Grossman, *Edwin Booth,* pp. 285, 304.

26. Laurence Irving, *Henry Irving* (New York, 1952), pp. 272, 377, 709, 715, 716; Matteo, "Shakespeare's *Othello,*" p. 297.
27. Quoted in Grimsted, *Melodrama Unveiled,* p. 64.

28. Quoted in Dormon, *Theater in the Antebellum South,* p. 276; Frederickson, *Black Image,* p. 49; Williamson, *New People,* pp. 65–100.

29. Ray B. Browne, "Shakespeare in American Vaudeville and Negro Minstrelsy," *American Quarterly,* 12 (1960), 384, 387–88; George W. Griffin, *"Othello": A Burlesque* (New York, 188[?]), p. 4.

30. Newspaper clipping, April 1883, Stead Collection, Vivian Beaumont Library Theatre Collection; Rosenberg, *Masks of Othello,* p. 118; Hermann Burmeister, *The Black Man* (New York, 1853), p. 18; *Blackwood's Magazine,* 57 (1850), 484. Also see Christine Bolt, *Victorian Attitudes to Race* (London, 1971), pp. 23, 209, 295.

31. Herbert Marshall and Mildred Stock, *Ira Aldridge: the Negro Tragedian* (New York, 1958), pp. 79, 219, 295.

32. Edith Isaacs, *The Negro in the American Theatre* (New York, 1947), p. 19; George Odell, *Annals of the New York Stage,* 15 vols. (New York, 1927–1949), XII, 305.

33. Boston *Transcript,* May 16, 1861; New York *Dramatic Mirror,* April 17, 1880; Alden, "Othello's Character," p. 428; Zola quoted in ibid., p. 347.

34. Henry James, "Salvini's Othello," *Atlantic Monthly,* 51 (March 1883), 377–86; *Othello* Scrapbooks, Folger Library.

35. John Ranken Towse, *Sixty Years of the Theater* (New York, 1916), pp. 93, 162–63; Clara Morris, *Stage Confidences: Talks about Players and Play Acting* (Boston, 1902), p. 240.

36. Alden, "Othello's Character," pp. 275, 420; Tomasso Salvini, "My Interpretation of Othello," *Putnam's Magazine*, 3 (October 1900), 27; New York *Dramatic Mirror*, December 4, 1880; Arthur Hornblow, *A History of the Theatre in America* (New York, 1919) II, 229.

37. "Tomasso Salvini," *Century*, 23 (November 1881), 413; New York *Times*, December 14, 1880; New York *Dramatic Mirror*, December 4, 1880; James, "Salvini's Othello," p. 380.

38. New York *Dramatic Mirror*, November 4, 1882; Newspaper clipping, October 27, 1885, Harvard University Theatre Collection; New York *Tribune*, April 27, 1886; Boston *Evening Transcript*, May 11, 1886; Chicago *Herald*, January 7, 1890; Alden, "Othello's Character," pp. 439-40.

39. Odell, *Annals of the New York Stage*, XII, 125, and XV, 34; Robert A. Bone, *The Negro Novel in America* (New Haven, 1965), pp. 22-23.

40. Odell, *Annals of the New York Stage*, XV, 325; New York *Dramatic Mirror*, November 5, 1881; Boston *Traveller*, May 19, 1886; Boston *Globe*, May 19, 1886; [May 1886], February 12, 1914, January 27, 1898, Harvard University Theatre Collection; Boston *Evening Transcript*, March 5, 1907.

41. Macon *Telegraph*, November 4, 1897; Philadelphia *Public Ledger*, April 5, 1916; newspaper clippings, January 1898, May 9, 1916, Harvard University Theatre Collection; New York *Tribune*, April 24, 1916.

42. Boston *Herald*, September 11, 1944; Boston *Evening Transcript*, March 5, 1907; newspaper clipping, February 12, 1914, and New York *Telegram*, January 3, 1923, Harvard University Theatre Collection.

43. Fredrickson, *Black Image*, pp. 276-77.

44. New York *Tribune*, January 26, 1929.

45. Newspaper clipping, June 9, 1930, Harvard University Theatre Collection; Boston *Transcript*, New York *Tribune*, June 29, 1930.

46. Boston *Herald*, August 11, 1942; Edwin P. Hoyt, *Paul Robeson: The American Othello* (Cleveland, 1967), p. 53; New York *Times*, June 6, 1943.

47. Newspaper clipping, May 19, 1930, Harvard University Theatre Collection; New York *Times*, January 16, 1942, October 24, 1943, July 3, 1944; Boston *Herald*, September 26, 1943; *New Yorker*, October 20, 1943, p. 38; New York *Tribune*, October 17, 1943.

48. Boston *Record American*, February 17, 1965; New York *Tribune*, October 14, 1964; *Newsweek*, January 17, 1965, p. 85.

49. *The Literature and Thought of Modern Africa*, trans. Shirley Kay (New York, 1967), p. 183.

Sam Williams, Forgeman:
The Life of an Industrial Slave in the Old South

CHARLES B. DEW

WILLIAM WEAVER was the leading ironmaster in Rockbridge County, and perhaps in the entire Valley, when he died at his home at Buffalo Forge, Virginia, in March 1863. During his eighty-three years he had built up a legendary fortune which, at the time of his death, included his iron-making facilities and rich farmlands centered at Buffalo Forge, over 20,000 additional acres of land scattered across three Virginia counties, and a force of seventy slaves—twenty-six men, fourteen women, and thirty children—that made him the largest slave owner in the county.[1] The inventory of his estate provided a detailed listing of his personal property—his "goods and chattels," in the language of the law—and along with entries for items like feather beds, rocking chairs, farm implements, and draft animals was a careful enumeration and appraisal of his slave holdings.[2] The lengthy list evaluating Weaver's slaves included the following brief notations:

One male slave	Sam Williams	$2,800.00
One male slave	Sam Williams Senior	0 000.00
One female slave	Sally	500.00
One female slave	Nancy	1,500.00
One female slave	Lydia	2,000.00
One female slave	Caroline and two children	2,500.00
Two female slaves	Mary Caroline and Julia	600.00

These entries constituted one of the rare instances when the name of Sam Williams and the names of his father (Sam Williams,

199

Senior), his mother (Sally), his wife (Nancy), two of their children (Lydia and Caroline), and two of their grandchildren (Mary Caroline and Julia) appeared on a legal document. And it is symbolic of the status of slaves as property that two of Sam and Nancy Williams's grandchildren—Caroline's "two children" in the appraisal—were not even identified by name on this occasion. The public record, in short, is sparse indeed on the life of Sam Williams and his family.

As might be expected, Sam Williams did not leave letters, diaries, journals, or other manuscript materials behind, either— the kind of documentary evidence that Weaver and his family left in abundance. Like most slaves in the American South, Sam Williams never learned to read or write; the closest thing we have to a document written by him is an "X" he made over his name on a work contract he entered into in 1867.[3] No member of the Williams family, as far as we know, ever talked to an interviewer from the Federal Writers' Project or from Fisk or Southern University when their invaluable oral histories of slavery were being compiled in the nineteen-twenties and thirties.[4] Yet it is possible to discover a great deal about Sam Williams and his family, and I would offer that they are, on many grounds, eminently worth knowing. They deserve our attention not only because they were people caught up in the American system of human bondage and thus illustrate something of the nature of the antebellum South's most significant institution. They also warrant our best efforts at understanding because, if we look carefully, we can catch at least a glimpse of them as men and women who lived out human lives despite the confines and cruelties of their enslavement. Their love and affection, their joys and sorrows, their times of trial and moments of triumph come through to us —imperfectly, to be sure, but visibly nonetheless, in spite of their inability to speak to us through traditional historical sources. This essay will attempt, in some small measure, to speak for them.

William Weaver became an ironmaster, a slave owner, and a Virginian almost by accident. He was born in 1781 on a farm near Philadelphia, and he spent most of his first forty or so years in and around that city, where he developed a series of successful business enterprises. As a merchant, miller, and textile manufacturer, Weaver began accumulating enough surplus capital to look elsewhere for profitable investments, and the War of 1812 seemed to create some excellent prospects in the Valley of Virginia.[5] The brisk wartime demand for iron prompted him to form a partnership in 1814 with Thomas Mayburry, another Philadelphia merchant, who had several years' experience in the Pennsylvania and Maryland iron business. The firm of Mayburry & Weaver purchased two iron properties in the Valley in the summer of 1814: Union Forge (which Weaver later renamed Buffalo Forge), located on Buffalo Creek some nine miles south of Lexington in Rockbridge County, Virginia; and Etna and Retreat furnaces, two charcoal blast furnaces approximately eighteen miles southwest of Union Forge in neighboring Botetourt County.[6] Retreat Furnace was abandoned rather quickly, but the firm launched extensive rebuilding projects at Etna Furnace and Union Forge and soon had both properties in full operation.[7]

Weaver did not move to Virginia immediately, however. Mayburry came down to manage the ironworks and supervise renovations at both installations, but Weaver remained in Philadelphia to raise needed capital and look after his business interests there. Over the next few years, Weaver sank close to $40,000 into the Virginia iron-making venture.[8] Among the more valuable acquisitions made with this money during the early years of Mayburry and Weaver's partnership was a growing force of slaves at both Etna Furnace and Union Forge.

The first slaves acquired by the firm were purchased in the fall of 1815. The seller was John S. Wilson, one of the Virginia ironmasters from whom Weaver and Mayburry had bought their furnaces and forge the previous year. Wilson had a number of slaves he wished to dispose of, and Mayburry wanted and needed these hands, but the two men could not agree on a price. Wilson apparently grew tired of dickering with Mayburry and decided he might be better off talking directly to the man who controlled the firm's finances.

In late October 1815, he journeyed north to Philadelphia, and there he and Weaver completed the deal. Weaver paid $3,200 for eleven slaves, divided into two very distinct groups. The first parcel consisted of an ironworker named Tooler, his wife, Rebecca, and her four children, all boys: Bill, seventeen, Robert, seven, Tooler, four, and Joe, two. The father and the oldest son, Bill, promised an immediate return to the firm since their services would be available without delay. It would be several years before Robert, Tooler (Jr.), and Joe could enter the work force, but since they were all boys, there was a strong likelihood that they might also be productive furnace or forge hands at some future point.

The second group of slaves Weaver bought from Wilson, however, contained no males at all. This parcel was made up of a slave woman named Mary and her four daughters: Sally, thirteen, Amey, ten, Louisa, six, and Georgianna, two.[9] In this instance, Weaver appears to have been looking toward the future labor needs of his ironworks in a far different way from the way he did with the acquisition of Tooler and his family. By securing the ownership of Mary and her daughters, Weaver was, in effect, seeking to ensure that his slave force could be built up, at least to some extent, by natural increase. Mary clearly seems to have been, in Weaver's eyes, a "breeding woman," to use a phrase Weaver himself employed on another occasion to describe a similar situation.[10] The sale papers contain no mention of Mary's husband, and there is no indication in the surviving records that he was ever acquired by Weaver or Mayburry. He may have lived near Etna Furnace or Union Forge, so the sale of his wife and daughters to Weaver might not have separated the family. Since Mary had several more children after Wilson sold her, there is a strong possibility that her husband lived close by, but there is no way to be sure. One thing is certain, however. In obtaining Mary and her daughters, Weaver made an investment that was to pay rich dividends. In the years that lay ahead, this slave family would play a monumental role in shaping the fortunes of Weaver's iron-making venture in Virginia, a role that was in many ways as significant as that of Weaver himself.

Mary and her children settled at Etna Furnace. There, probably in 1817 when she was fifteen years old, Sally—Mary's oldest daughter—married a man named Sam Williams, who was one of the skilled slave ironworkers Weaver and Mayburry were constantly seeking to add to their labor force. Sam and Sally Williams had their first child, a girl, in 1817, and they named her Mary, undoubtedly for her grandmother. Three years later, Sally gave birth to another child, a boy this time, and she and her husband named their new baby after his father, Sam Williams.[11]

Very little is known about Sam Williams, Sr., because most of the records dealing with Weaver's early iron-making activities in Virginia have not survived. According to a slave register compiled at Buffalo Forge during the Civil War, Sally's husband was born in 1795, but that date was probably a rough approximation.[12] The appraisal of him at the time of Weaver's death in 1863— "no value"—suggests that he was physically or mentally incapacitated and unable to perform useful work at age sixty-eight or so, an assumption reinforced by the fact that other slave men of similar age had values of $200 to $300 beside their names on the 1863 estate inventory. Other fragmentary evidence indicates the cause of his disability. In 1832 when one of Weaver's managers was in desperate need of a skilled worker to fill in temporarily for a sick hand, he spoke to Sam about taking a turn at the forge. Sam refused; "he objects [because of] . . . his eyes (which is in fact a very great objection might in all probability loose [sic] them if continued in the forge)," the manager told Weaver.[13] Ironworkers, both black and white, were in constant danger of eye injuries from sparks and flying bits of red-hot metal, and Sam Williams, Sr., seems to have suffered such an injury, or perhaps a series of them. Clearly his eyes were badly damaged while he was still a relatively young man; he would have been in his middle or late thirties in 1832 and, if sound, still in his most productive years as a slave—a "prime hand," in the language of the trade. He may well have been blind by 1863, when the county appraisers examined, itemized, and evaluated "the goods and chattels of William Weaver deceased" and entered a string of zeroes after the name Sam Williams Senior.

Toward the end of 1823, when Sam and Sally Williams's boy, Sam, was three years old, Weaver took up residence at Union Forge. Weaver's presence in Virginia was the result of the floundering financial condition of his iron-making enterprise there. Despite the substantial amount of capital that he had poured into the blast furnace and forge operations since 1814—almost $40,000 —Mayburry & Weaver had still not returned a profit on their investment (which seems to have consisted largely of Thomas Mayburry's rather limited managerial skills and William Weaver's money). With that much money at stake, Weaver felt that he had no choice but to move to the Valley and try to pull things together.[14] Not long after his arrival at the forge, he renamed the property after the creek that supplied water power to the works.

The name Union Forge had not brought much luck to the two Yankees who made up the firm of Mayburry & Weaver; perhaps Buffalo Forge would do better.

A year's experience of working firsthand with Mayburry apparently convinced Weaver of something he had suspected for some time—that his partner was incompetent. As a result Weaver moved early in 1825 to dissolve their partnership and divide the assets of the firm.[15] Prominent among these assets were the "Wilson negroes," the name that both Mayburry and Weaver regularly used to describe the first slaves bought by the partnership in 1815. Their argument over the ownership of the "Wilson negroes"— Tooler and his wife and children, and Mary and her children (including Sally Williams) and grandchildren (including Sam Williams, Jr.)—soon brought to light an interesting fact, one that revealed a great deal about Weaver and his business practices. When Weaver purchased these slaves from John Wilson in 1815, he took title to them in his own name, not in the name of the firm of Mayburry & Weaver. He had done this, he assured Wilson at the time, only because he feared that Mayburry "might have some religious scruples" about owning slaves.[16] Mayburry did not discover Weaver's delicate concern for the health of his soul until Weaver moved to dissolve their association in 1824, nine years after these slaves had been purchased, and demanded that Mayburry surrender the entire Wilson slave force. Mayburry, who was living at Etna Furnace, where a number of these slaves worked, refused to do so, on the quite reasonable grounds that Weaver had duped him in the original transaction. Their clash over these slaves was one of a series of heated disputes between the two men that led to Weaver's filing suit against Mayburry and throwing the entire matter into the tortuously slow machinery of the Virginia chancery courts.[17] It was eleven years before the two former partners finally reached a compromise (in the form of an out-of-court settlement) that brought a measure of satisfaction to both men. Their settlement, made in the summer of 1836, also brought with it the seeds of bitter anguish for many of the slaves involved.

In their article of agreement signed on August 3, 1836, Weaver and Mayburry agreed to a division of the "Wilson negroes." On January 1, 1837, Mayburry was to turn over to Weaver the bulk of these slaves still in his possession. Since Weaver already had

Tooler and his wife and children at Buffalo Forge, that family remained intact under Weaver's ownership. Mary's family was not so fortunate, however. Mayburry still had Mary and her children and grandchildren at Etna Furnace, and his share of the human assets of the firm was to include Mary and three of her younger children: two boys, John, born in 1816, and Hamilton, born in 1823, and her youngest child, a daughter, Ellen. Two of Mary's older daughters, Sally Williams and Louisa, along with their children, were to pass into Weaver's possession on New Year's Day, 1837.[18]

The division took place as scheduled at the beginning of 1837. Mayburry surrendered Sally and Louisa and their children to Weaver at Buffalo Forge; he retained, as their agreement stipulated, Mary and John, Hamilton, and Ellen. When Mayburry left the vicinity shortly thereafter to take up a new iron-making venture in northern Rockbridge County, he took Mary and her three young children with him.[19] As a result, Mary's family was broken in order to provide Mayburry and Weaver with a fair division of the property belonging to their former partnership. Mary—young Sam Williams's grandmother—had been stripped of a substantial portion of her family, but subsequent events were to show that she and the children who went with her were not forgotten by those who were left at Buffalo Forge early in 1837.

Sam Williams would turn seventeen sometime during that year, and this birthday would occur at a new home under a new master. But he could take some comfort from the knowledge that his immediate family would be there with him. Sam Williams, Sr., had been under Weaver's control for a number of years prior to 1837, as the 1832 letter regarding his deteriorating eyesight indicates, and his mother, Sally, had, of course, come to Weaver in the division, along with young Sam's brothers and sisters. The family had grown substantially during the last few years and now included at least four children: Sam; his older sister, Mary; a younger sister, Elizabeth, born in 1825; and a younger brother, Washington, born in 1827.[20] The birthplace of Sally Williams's sons was indicated clearly in the Buffalo Forge records as they entered Weaver's labor force; their names were recorded as "Sam Etna" and "Washington Etna."[21] The reason for this seems clear. It simply was easier to write "Sam Etna" than "Sam Williams, Jr." whenever an entry had to be made under his name, and it identified him clearly as one of the "Wilson negroes" born and raised at Etna Furnace. And if you were going to refer to one brother that way, why not do it for both of them? From the master's point of view, it made perfectly good sense. Sam Williams took quite a different view of the matter, however. He knew who he was, and he did not like being called "Sam Etna." It would take him a long time, but eventually he would get his name back.

To be precise, it took sixteen years. On a page in the Buffalo Forge ledgers covering his work for the year 1853, his name appears two ways: as "Samuel Etna" and as "Sam ·Williams."[22] The most logical explanation for the change is that Sam himself wanted it made. By the 1850s he was important enough to Weaver's operations to get his way, particularly since his request must have struck Weaver as a fairly minor matter. One suspects that Sam viewed the subject in quite a different light. From this point on, as far as the records were concerned, he was "Sam Williams" at Buffalo Forge; his father was "Sam Williams Senior."[23]

Since the early Etna Furnace records have not survived, there is no way to trace young Sam Williams's life prior to his arrival at Buffalo Forge in 1837. If his youth was spent like that of most slave boys who grew up at iron-making facilities in the South, he probably had no regular duties until he reached age eight or so, when he would have been expected to assume some light chores, such as helping to look after the younger slave children during the day. By age twelve or fourteen, he would have entered the regular work force, perhaps as a furnace boy doing odd jobs or as a leaf raker at the charcoal pits.[24] The elder Sam Williams's failing eyesight probably prevented him from training his teenage son in his ironworking skills, a method of transmitting knowledge and expertise that occurred frequently at Virginia furnaces and forges in the nineteenth century.[25] He may have been untrained when he arrived at Buffalo Forge as a sixteen-year-old youth on New Year's Day, 1837, but William Weaver could clearly see that Sam Williams's boy had the potential for forge work.

His assets were several. First of all, he came from a family that produced good mechanics. Intelligent Southern iron men looking for slave recruits for critical furnace and forge jobs paid close attention to things like heredity, and Weaver was certainly no fool when it came to the iron business. He seemed to feel about black ironworkers the same way he felt about white ironmasters. You had to have "the proper head for it," Weaver told his nephew-in-law, Daniel C. E. Brady, when he was trying to persuade Brady and his wife to move to Buffalo Forge during the 1850s. "Training alone will not [do] as nature must do something, in order to make a good Iron Master."[26] Nature seemed to have done a great deal for Sam Williams. He had the necessary size and strength; he stood five feet ten inches tall when he achieved his full stature, which made him one of the tallest slave hands at Buffalo Forge. And his color suggested to white Southerners of that place and time that he was likely to possess intelligence and good judgment as well. A physical description of him drawn up during the Civil War listed his color as "yellow."[27] He had, at some point in his ancestry, a strong admixture of white blood.

Where this miscegenation occurred in the Williams family remains a mystery. Since he took the elder Sam Williams's name as his own, one assumes that both his father and mother were slaves, and that Mary, his grandmother, was also enslaved, as the property settlement signed with Mayburry in 1836 made clear. It could well be that his maternal or paternal grandfather was white, but there is no way to know. Whatever the case, Weaver obviously knew he had a likely candidate for his forge gang when Sam "Etna" came into his possession in 1837.

After a year in which the only work recorded for him at Buffalo Forge consisted of field labor with the farmhands, Sam entered the forge in 1838 at the age of eighteen.[28] Weaver undoubtedly had Sam go down to the forge and watch the black refiners and hammermen at their jobs before deciding whether he wanted to train as a forgeman. This was Weaver's usual practice with potential recruits for his ironworking crew, and there is no reason to suspect that he did things differently this time.[29] It was far better to have a willing apprentice than a surly, rebellious underhand who would turn out poor-quality work, try to escape, or perhaps sabotage the forge machinery. As Sam walked in to the stone forge building that stood alongside Buffalo Creek, he would have seen an impressive, even awesome, sight: charcoal fires burning at white heat; slave refiners and their helpers working bars of pig iron in those fires until the iron turned into a ball of glowing, pasty metal, then slinging this semimolten mass of iron onto their anvils, where they pounded and shaped it under the rhythmic blows of their huge, water-powered hammers. Through successive reheatings and poundings, Weaver's refiners removed enough of the impurities in the pig iron to work it into something called an "anchony." Turning out high-quality anchonies was the most important single job in the forge, and that was what Weaver wanted Sam Williams to do.[30]

Weaver himself described an anchony in a court deposition he gave in 1840. It was a piece of malleable iron about six inches square weighing between 80 and 150 pounds, "with a blade of iron about the length of my cane," Weaver noted (his cane measured thirty-two inches); "one end of the blade has what is called the *tail end,* which contains iron enough generally to make a shovel mould, and out of which shovel moulds are generally made," he added.[31] Producing this rather strange-looking item was no easy task. The key point in the refining process was exactly when the pig iron heating in the refinery fire had reached just the right temperature and consistency for pounding and shaping on the anvil block. Bringing the pig iron "to nature," as this was called, was the most difficult forge skill to learn, and it could be acquired only by many months of apprenticeship to a master refiner.[32] If Sam Williams decided that he wanted to follow in his father's footsteps and became a refiner, he would have to start as an under-hand at the fires of men like Phill Easton, John Baxter, or the Hunt brothers—Harry and Billy—all of whom were skilled slave refinery hands at Buffalo Forge in the late 1830s.[33]

Pounding out anchonies was the most critical part of the forge operation, but it was only the first half of the manufacturing process. The final stage came when a second group of operatives, the hammermen, reheated the anchonies and worked them at another forge called a chaffery. The hammermen produced iron bars of various standardized shapes, sizes, and lengths—"merchant bars," in the language of the iron trade—which would be shipped to market and sold. Merchant bars kept the wheels of agriculture turning. Blacksmiths hammered these bars into the things needed on (or off) the farm that had to be made out of iron: horse and mule shoes, wagon tires, nails, tools, agricultural implements, and the like.[34] The slave hammermen at Buffalo Forge at the time of Sam Williams's arrival—Tooler (the son of the ironworker of the same name and one of the original "Wilson negroes"), his brother

Bob (another "Wilson negro"), and Garland Thompson—were, like the refiners, prize hands worth a substantial premium on the open market.[35]

Weaver was well aware of their value to him. Without his forge, and the slaves who ran it, William Weaver would have been just another valley farmer—a prosperous one, to be sure, but a farmer nonetheless. There would have been nothing wrong with that, of course; most of his Rockbridge County neighbors were farmers, and agriculture was certainly an honorable occupation in the Old South. But Buffalo Forge and his skilled crew of slave hands made him much more—they made him an ironmaster, a person of premier importance in the local economy and someone to be reckoned with, politically and socially, in the Valley. "Some of my Friends in Phila. wondered why I did not reside amongst them," he confided to a friend in Lexington in 1848. "I replied— At home I was but a small person—but that I was somebody—The people knew me—and in crowded Phila. I would be nobody."[36] Weaver was much more than "a small person" in Rockbridge County, and he knew very well where the source of his prestige lay. It lay in that stone forge building that stood beside Buffalo Creek—in the massive hammers and charcoal fires and in the black men who worked them so skillfully.

To retain his status, and the wealth that went with it, Weaver had to train and hold good slave artisans and replace those hands who were growing too old (like Billy Hunt) or were too infirm (like Sam Williams, Sr.) to work. One suspects that when young Sam Williams decided he wanted to be a forgeman, William Weaver could not have been happier.

The advantage of doing forge work would not have been unknown to Sam Williams, either. In making himself indispensable to Weaver's iron-making operations, he would be gaining a significant amount of influence over his own fate. There was no sure guarantee against punishment or sale; like all Southern masters, Weaver could do pretty much what he wished in the way of punishment, and if he should fall deeply into debt or die suddenly, his slave force could be dispersed either by sale or the division of his estate. Barring that sort of catastrophe, however, Sam would be in a much stronger bargaining position as a skilled forge hand than in any other occupation at Buffalo Forge. If he trained as a refiner and showed an aptitude for the work, he would have talents his owner would need and even be willing to pay him for.

Compensation for extra work was almost a universal feature of the labor system at slave-manned furnaces and forges in the Old South, and Buffalo Forge was no exception. Slaves had a daily or weekly task to accomplish, but they were paid for anything they turned out over and above that amount—"overwork," it was called.[37] The task for refiners at Weaver's forge and everywhere else in the Valley was a ton and a half of anchonies per week (the quota required of hammermen was a "journey" of 560 pounds of bar iron per day).[38] These amounts had been the customary tasks for years, and old traditions like this were hard to change. Slaves as well as masters knew what the tasks were, and any attempt by ironmasters to increase work quotas or to abolish compensation for overwork entirely would have been a very risky venture. It did not take much, for instance, to break a hammer "helve"—the huge wooden beams that supported the 500- to 600-pound cast-iron hammerheads in the forge. And every time a helve broke, the forge had to shut down for at least a day or two for repairs. Sabotage of this sort would be relatively simple to accomplish, and who could say whether it was deliberate? Helves did, after all, wear out and break in the normal course of forge operations. It was this sort of unspoken threat that gave slave forgemen considerable protection against an increase in their tasks and helped them preserve their right to earn compensation for themselves.

Payment for overwork came in several forms, and the option as to how this pay would be taken lay with the slave. The slaves at Buffalo Forge could take it in cash; they could take it in credit at Weaver's store and draw against it for items they wished to buy; they could use their overwork to secure time off from their regular duties; and finally, if Weaver permitted, they could attempt to purchase their own freedom.[39] This last option was almost never granted. In 1830, Weaver allowed an elderly slave forge hand whom he had purchased in the Lynchburg area to buy himself and return to his former home.[40] But this appears to be the only time Weaver made such a concession to any member of his slave force. Even without the opportunity to try to attain freedom, however, the overwork system had obvious advantages for the slave, as Sam Williams's life at Buffalo Forge would illustrate in rich and elaborate detail.

Sam's first year in the forge, 1838, was a year of apprenticeship. He served as an underhand to both John Baxter and Harry Hunt, and under their guidance he sought to master the refiner's art: learning to put up and maintain the special refinery fire, heating the pig iron and bringing it "to nature," and then pounding the red-hot metal under the huge hammer into those oddly shaped anchonies.[41] He undoubtedly cost Weaver some money that year in wasted pig iron and excessive use of expensive charcoal, but the only way to learn was by doing.

Sam had expert teachers. Harry Hunt, for instance, was fifty years old in 1838 and had been a refiner for well over twenty-five years. He, like many other slave ironworkers, had been born to the trade. In his case, this meant birth, youth, and young adulthood at the Oxford Iron Works in Campbell County, Virginia, not far from Lynchburg. His father had been a limestone miner at Oxford Furnace, and Harry and his brother Billy had been trained in the forge at Oxford. There they had refined for David Ross, one of the most famous Virginia ironmasters of the Revolutionary and post-Revolutionary eras. Ross's death in 1817 and the subsequent sale of his estate sent a number of his best ironworkers across the Blue Ridge Mountains and into the Valley, where the Virginia iron industry was moving during the early years of the nineteenth century and where ironmasters like William Weaver were eagerly seeking skilled furnace and forge workers.[42]

Harry Hunt knew his job, and Sam learned quickly. Before his first year was out, he had sufficiently mastered the techniques of refining to earn a modest amount of overwork: "½ ton over iron 2.00."[43] It was not a great deal of money, especially when compared to what some of the other skilled forgemen were able to put away for themselves. But it was a start toward something better, toward a life in which his skills could help make things a little more comfortable and perhaps a bit more predictable and secure. By 1840, he had added reason to be concerned about a more comfortable present and a more certain future.

Sometime during the year 1840, Sam Williams married. His wife was a slave woman named Nancy Jefferson, who was also owned by William Weaver. She was twenty-three years old that year, three years older than Sam, but the difference in age meant little.[44] Sam had finished his forge training by then and was now one of Weaver's master refiners.[45] His future was probably as secure as any slave's could ever be, and he was ready to assume the responsibilities of a husband and, soon, a father. Their marriage was not a legal one, of course. Slave marriages had no standing in Virginia law, or in that of any other Southern state. But time would clearly show that Sam Williams and Nancy Jefferson viewed themselves as man and wife. The date of their marriage was not recorded in the journals and papers kept at Buffalo Forge, but they knew the year was 1840 and they never forgot it.

The birth of their first child did appear in the Buffalo Forge records, however, and for good reason. The birth of a new baby in the slave quarters meant an addition to the master's wealth and potential work force. So, when Elizabeth Williams came into the world later that year, note was taken of the event.[46] Elizabeth, or Betty, as she was more frequently called, was undoubtedly named after Sam's younger sister, Elizabeth, who is mentioned in early legal documents dealing with the dispute over the "Wilson negroes."[47] This sister was not one of those children taken by Mayburry in the 1837 division, but there is no record that she came to Weaver, either. She may well have died before her name-sake was born to Sam and Nancy Williams in 1840. If she was living in that year, she would have been fifteen. The practice of naming children after older, and particularly lost, relatives would recur frequently in the Williams family in the years that lay ahead. Much of the family's history would be mirrored in those names.

Sam Williams's marriage and the birth of his daughter gave him added incentive to exploit the possibilities opened up by the overwork system. He had earned some relatively small amounts of money prior to 1840: a total of $3.00 in 1837, the same in 1838, and just over $4.50 in 1839.[48] He would not be content with earnings of this size in 1840, however. Early in the year, he began devoting a considerable amount of his spare time to "tar burning," as it was called. He would collect the heart of fallen pine trees from the woods around Buffalo Forge, stack it closely on a low, hard-packed mound of earth with gutters running out from the center, cover the resinous pine with dirt, and light it. As the wood smoldered, the gum would flow out as tar through the trenches cut in the earth.[49] Sam would collect this "tair," as it was spelled in the Buffalo Forge books, and sell it to his master. Weaver was willing to pay twenty-five cents a gallon for it—pitch and tar were always needed around installations dependent on water power—and Sam's long hours in the woods produced no less than fifty-nine gallons of tar before the year was out.[50]

He also did something else in the year he was married that he had not done during his three previous years at Buffalo Forge—he worked through the Christmas holidays. The break beginning on Christmas Day and ending with a return to work on New Year's Day was a traditional period of rest for Weaver's slave hands, as it was for most slaves throughout the South. The forge would close down for Christmas, but there were plenty of other things to do—stock to feed and water, roads and walks to shovel if it snowed, ice to cut from the forge pond and haul to the ice house if a cold snap hit. Sam worked five days out of the seven-day Christmas break in 1840 and earned $2.50 for his labor (fifty cents a day was the usual pay for anyone, white or black, who did common labor, so Sam was not paid "slave wages" for his holiday work). By his tar burning, forge overwork, and Christmas labor in 1840, he earned $22.42, well over four times what he had made for himself in any previous year at Buffalo Forge.[51]

There is no way of knowing why Sam worked so hard in 1840, but it seems safe to assume that his efforts were spurred by a desire to be able to do more for his wife and his new baby. This view is reinforced by the record of his purchases during the year: sugar and molasses (treats all three of them could enjoy), coffee for himself and Nancy, and crocks for her to use for household storage. Unfortunately, several of the larger expenditures he made in 1840 were not spelled out in the books, like his store "order" of $4.00 on March 7 and a similarly vague general entry on September 5 for $9.16.[52] These sizable store purchases probably included items for Nancy and Betty, but we cannot be sure.

Sam and Nancy Williams's family grew steadily over the next several years. In 1842, a second daughter, Caroline, was born, and she was followed by two more girls, Ann, born in 1843, and Lydia, born the next year.[53] Sam's overwork increased along with the size of his family. He continued his tar burning in 1841, but on a reduced scale. He concentrated more and more on his work at

the refinery forge in his effort to earn extra income for himself
and his wife and daughters. This made sense. As his skills improved, so did his chance to earn overwork pay by hammering
out extra pounds of anchonies. It was now easier for him to make
his task of a ton and a half of refined iron per week, and anything
he turned out above that amount meant money in his pocket or
credit at the Buffalo Forge store. He was paid $8.82 for pounding
out over two tons of extra iron in 1841, while his tar production
dropped off to thirty-six and a half gallons (which still earned
him $9.12). Once again, his purchases at Weaver's store suggest
that he was using his overwork compensation to buy things his
family could use—items like sugar, calico, ticking, drill, jeans
cloth, and trimmings. And a week before Christmas in 1841, he
spent $1.25 for a silk handkerchief.[54]

Sam's growing prowess as a refiner and his continued support
of his family are apparent in his overwork accounts during the
next few years. No records have survived for 1842 and 1843, but
he made a total of $31.00 in overwork pay in 1844, most of which
he earned at his forge. As a master refiner, he was paid for his
overwork at the same rate a white artisan would have been paid
for the same job—$8.00 per ton, with three-fifths of that going
to Sam as the refiner and two-fifths going to his underhand. Sam's
five tons of "over iron" in 1844 translated into a credit of $24.00
on Weaver's books. The debit side of the ledger is incomplete for
1844, but fortunately some of his purchases were listed, particularly
his holiday buying at the end of the year. One item he bought
early in 1844 is especially interesting: "10 yds. best silk" on
February 20. This certainly was a present for Nancy, and since
their daughter Lydia was born sometime during that year, this
gift of silk may have been to celebrate that occasion. As Christmas
approached, he made several additional purchases. On December
21, he bought four pounds of sugar for his mother, Sally, undoubtedly to give to her for Christmas (the cost was seventy-
seven cents). Three days later, on Christmas eve, he took $1.00 in
cash from his account, spent $2.00 for eight yards of calico, and
drew against his store credit for no less than $20.00 for a "Blue
Coat Fine." Whether this last item was for himself or Nancy is
not clear, but even after spending that sum (for what must have
been a very fine coat), he still had a balance to his credit of $5.21.
That amount was carried over on the books to the next year, which

was always done when one of Weaver's slaves had not spent his full earnings by the end of the year. And Sam almost invariably carried at least a small balance in his favor into the new year.[55]

During the next several years, Sam's overwork earnings continued to mount. By the early 1850s, he was regularly making over $50.00 per annum, and in 1855 and 1856, the last two years for which his complete accounts are available, his compensation reached even greater levels. In 1855, his overwork amounted to $92.23, and the next year, for the first time, it exceeded $100.00—$103.00, to be exact, $100.00 of which he made by refining twenty tons of "Over Iron."[56]

There is no need to make a detailed list of his purchases during this ten- to twelve-year period, but some of the things he did with his money suggest a good deal about this man and his attitudes and priorities. He supplemented Weaver's standard rations of pork and cornmeal with regular purchases of flour, sugar, coffee, and molasses, and he frequently bought cloth for Nancy to sew into garments for the family. His overwork kept him, and perhaps Nancy as well, supplied with tobacco. And his gifts to various members of his family continued. His mother received fifty pounds of flour from him in February 1845, and he gave his father a pound of coffee in April 1846—to cite two instances where the items were specifically identified in the records as going to his parents. Nancy, as might be expected, received a number of presents: a pair of buckskin gloves at Chritsmas in 1848; a shawl in May 1849; nine yards of silk in October 1851. One of his special purchases for his children was eight and three-fourths yards of cloth for a bedspread for Ann when she was ten years old.[57]

The most fascinating items of all that he acquired during these years were the articles of furniture he bought for the cabin that he, Nancy, and the girls shared. His major Christmas gift to the family in 1845 consisted of a table (at $3.00) and a bedstead (which cost $9.00), both of which he purchased at the Buffalo Forge store on Christmas eve of that year. He added significantly to the cabin's furnishings six years later when he apparently attended an estate sale held in the neighborhood. In April 1851, he made two acquisitions "at Blackford's Sale": a set of chairs, for which he paid $7.25, and, probably his most revealing purchase of the entire antebellum era, "1 looking glass," priced at $1.75.[58]

There are many reasons why any family would want to own a mirror—perfectly natural reasons, such as curiosity about one's appearance or a touch of vanity, perhaps. Sam and Nancy Williams had growing daughters, too. Betty was eleven, Caroline was nine, Anne was eight, and Lydia was seven, in 1851. But a *slave's* buying a mirror suggests something more. It would seem to indicate a strong sense of pride in one's self and one's family that transcended their status as slaves. Why else would Sam spend that kind of money on such a purchase? One dollar and seventy-five cents represented the sweat and sore muscles that went into several hundred pounds of overwork iron. One almost suspects that that looking glass, packed carefully in a wagon and hauled home from "Blackford's Sale," stood as a symbol of Sam and Nancy Williams's feelings about themselves and their children. And there were other signs of pride as well.

In 1849, Sam began making fairly frequently cash withdrawals against his overwork account. Some of this money he undoubtedly used to buy items at rural stores that dotted the nearby countryside, places like Saunder's Store, which stood just across Buffalo Creek from the forge. But he was not spending all of it in this way. The individual withdrawals were small at first, a dollar or two, generally, but they soon added up: $24.00 taken out in cash in 1849 (as opposed to $6.75 in 1848, $5.00 in 1847, and $1.50 in 1846); $23.25 in 1850; a jump to $41.16 in 1851, followed by a one-year fall-off to $16.00 in 1852; and then a sharp increase to almost identical sums of $51.00 in 1853, $57.00 in 1854, $56.87½ in 1855, and $57.81 in 1856. In 1857, the last year in which the withdrawals can be traced in full, he took out $25.50 in cash.[59] Part of the money that he pocketed during these years ended up in a rather remarkable place, as indicated by a letter written by Weaver's young forge clerk in 1855. On February 25 of that year, John A. Rex, a twenty-three-year-old nephew of Weaver's who had come down from Pennsylvania to help out at Buffalo Forge, described an incident that had recently occurred there. "I wish to ask you one question," he wrote James D. Davidson, a prominent lawyer in Lexington who served as Weaver's attorney: "whether Sam Williams can draw his money from the Savings Bank or if he cannot." Sam, it seems, had made a bet with a man named Henry Nash, a free black cooper who lived near Buffalo Forge and who made the barrels for Weaver's flour. Nash refused

to believe that Sam had a savings account in the bank in Lexington, and Sam had bet his watch (another impressive acquisition
for a slave) against Nash's watch that he did. "It is my opinion
that he can draw his money if he gives the Directors of the Bank
10 days notice," Rex continued. "After he receives the money he
wishes to show it to Henry Nash, and then he will return the
said money back to the Bank again." Rex closed the letter by
assuring Davidson that he "was witness to the said bargain."[60]

J. D. Davidson was an experienced attorney, but it is doubtful
that he had ever before had to give an opinion as to how a slave
should handle his savings account. The only thing he knew to do
was advise young Rex "to confer with Wm. Weaver" on the business.[61] Perhaps the master could decide how a man who was himself legally property should deal with his own property, in this
case a sizable account in a major Lexington financial institution.

There are several extraordinary things about this incident, not
the least of which is the episode of the white forge clerk's holding
the bet for a slave and a free Negro and serving as a witness to their
wager. But everyday life in the Old South was filled with
anomalies of this sort, so perhaps this part of the story was not so
remarkable after all. Sam Williams's possession of a savings
account was remarkable by any standard, however, and, given the
value of the dollar in the 1850s, his account was a large one. We
know the size of his savings because just over a year after Rex
wrote Davidson about the bet, the lawyer withdrew Sam's money
from the bank. It may have been that the bank directors felt
uneasy about holding, and paying interest on, a slave's money,
particularly after the wager brought up the subject. Or maybe
Weaver decided it would be better to handle these funds in some
other way. Whatever the reason, on April 22, 1856, Davidson rode
out to Buffalo Forge carrying Sam Williams's savings of $91.31.
He also brought with him $61.96 belonging to Sam's wife.[62]

Nancy Williams, it turned out, had a savings account, too, and
in her own name. Since she was in charge of dairy operations at
Buffalo Forge and did a good deal of housework at Weaver's
residence, she clearly had had opportunities to earn overwork pay
in her own right. The house account books have not survived, so
there is no way to discover exactly what she did to make money
for herself or to trace the precise amounts of her compensation.
But since her savings account was fully two-thirds the size of her

husband's, her earnings must have been substantial. Between them, Sam and Nancy had over $150.00 in cash.

What were they saving for? No evidence exists to show that Weaver had given them the right to buy their own freedom or that of their children, so self-purchase apparently was not the reason. The fact that they were saving anything at all suggests that they felt their material standard of living was adequate to the family's needs; if it had not been, they probably would have spent much more than they did on various food items and cloth. The most logical explanation for their extraordinary, and substantial, bank accounts would seem to be that they both had extra overwork funds and that they had simply put their money in a safe place where it would earn interest for them. This conclusion is rein-forced by the subsequent history of their accounts at Buffalo Forge.

William Weaver, in effect, replaced the savings bank as the holder of the Williamses' money and as the payer of interest on their accounts. Special entries were made under their separate names in a private ledger kept at the forge, and both Sam and Nancy placed their full savings with Weaver on April 22, 1856, the day Davidson brought their funds out from Lexington. Neither Sam nor Nancy made any withdrawals during the next twelve months, so exactly one year after their initial deposits, Weaver credited both accounts with interest on the full amounts. Sam's $91.31 earned him $10.96, and Nancy's $61.96 made $7.44 for her. The interest rate in both instances was 12 percent.[63]

In the years just ahead, Sam and Nancy would follow quite different courses in handling their savings. In the spring and fall of 1858, Nancy made fairly systematic cash withdrawals of $4.00 to $5.00, and in 1859 she used the remainder of her money for substantial purchases at Buffalo Forge and at two neighboring country stores. On October 27, 1859, she closed out her account by spending $4.82 at Saunder's Store. Sam, on the other hand, kept exactly $100.00 on deposit throughout these years and into the 1860s. He withdrew the interest each year, in either cash or goods, but kept the $100.00 principal fully intact. Weaver regularly credited him with interest on his $100.00, figured after 1860 at 6 percent, and Sam just as regularly drew off his $6.00 a year (for some reason, two interest payments were made in 1862, so Sam took out $12.00 that year). His account was not finally closed out until after the Civil War.[64]

The picture that emerges from this story of two slaves with savings accounts is by no means a simple one. On the surface, one might be tempted to argue that their behavior indicated a placid acceptance of their status and condition. Since they had to complete their required tasks before they could start earning money for themselves, they obviously were turning out a considerable amount of work for William Weaver—working like slaves, so to speak, and taking the bait the master offered to do a good deal more than they had to do. Yet they clearly were doing a great deal for themselves as well, and for their children. They were improving the material conditions under which all of them could live, and they were protecting themselves against the fearful threat that hung over them all—the breakup of the family through sale. Weaver would be very reluctant indeed to part with workers like this man and woman, who meant so much to the smooth running, and the success, of his iron-making and farming activities. Nor would he want to run the risks that would certainly occur if he tried to sell Sam and Nancy Williams's daughters off Buffalo Forge. Through their overwork, both Sam and Nancy could help to shield and provide for each other and for their children. The psychological importance of this to them—the added access it afforded Sam to the traditional responsibilities of a husband and father, and Nancy to the role of wife and mother—cannot be overemphasized. Their feelings and emotions can be shared by anyone who has ever tried to make a good and decent life with another person and has helped to bring children into a fragile and uncertain world.

The nature of Sam's attitude toward his work does not have to be left totally to the imagination, however. Thanks to the arrival at Buffalo Forge of a new manager in 1857 and his meticulous record keeping, we can follow Sam at his forge and in the fields for months on end. The insights to be gained from a close look at his daily activities during the late 1850s and early 1860s are revealing.

By the mid-1850s, Weaver was no longer capable of supervising the complex industrial and agricultural operations at Buffalo Forge by himself. He was in his seventies, his health was un-

certain, and just moving around the property was becoming more
and more difficult for him.[65] As a result, he began a campaign to
persuade his favorite niece and her husband to move down from
Philadelphia and take over the management of day-to-day affairs
at the house, the forge, and the farms. Weaver had brought a
number of young relatives down from Pennsylvania over the
years, but none had worked out to his full satisfaction. He had no
one in his immediate family to take over for him; he had not
married until 1830 when he was forty-nine, and his wife, a
Philadelphia widow named Elizabeth Newkirk Woodson, was only
four years younger than he was. She had died in 1850, and they
had had no children.[66] So he set his mind on persuading his niece
Emma Matilda Brady and her husband, a young Philadelphia
banker named Daniel C. E. Brady, to move to Buffalo Forge and
assume direction of things there.[67] "I am old, all but 75," Weaver
wrote to Daniel Brady in 1855, and he was worried about what
would happen after his death. "The great object with me is, that
my servants shall remain where they are, and have humane
masters," he went on. "This point is the only difficulty on my mind
in relation to my Estate. Giving them their freedom, I am satisfied,
would not benefit them as much as having good masters, and
remain where they are. You I presume understand my intentions,
—and if you get here I hope they will be carried out. The means
will be given you to do so," Weaver promised, an unmistakable
hint that Emma and Daniel Brady would inherit his considerable
estate if they and their three children moved permanently to
Virginia.[68]

Late in 1857, the Bradys closed up their affairs in Pennsylvania
and moved to Buffalo Forge. There were only two children with
them when they came: Anne Gertrude, who was nine, and Charles
Patrick, who was seven. Their younger son, William Weaver
Brady, had died in the spring of 1856, when he was only two and
a half years old. They gave their next baby the same name, but
he died the same day he was born, in August 1857. Perhaps the
loss of these two boys, as well as business reverses Daniel Brady
had recently suffered in Philadelphia, had something to do with
their decision to start a new life for themselves in the Valley of
Virginia.[69]

The arrival of the Bradys was an event of major significance
in the lives of the slaves at Buffalo Forge. It must have relieved

much of the anxiety that would have been growing in the quarters as Weaver's age advanced and his health deteriorated. Now there was a clear prospect that the Buffalo Forge slave community would remain intact after Weaver's passing, that families would not be broken and friends separated by a division of the master's estate. Weaver obviously had not consulted with his slaves about what arrangements they would prefer after his death. One suspects very strongly that if he had, he would not have continued to believe that they would rather have "humane masters" to succeed him than to have their freedom. But aside from manumission, there was probably nothing more important to these black men and women than the strong probability that they could all "remain where they are," as Weaver put it, after he was gone. The Bradys' coming (and the fact that they already had a son, seven-year-old Pat, who might also inherit the place one day) would have been the cause for some quiet rejoicing in the slave cabins that dotted the landscape around Buffalo Forge.

A historian seeking to reconstruct the lives of these slaves also has reason to celebrate the arrival of the Bradys. Daniel Brady was a remarkably careful and devoted keeper of records. Soon after his arrival, he began a regular daily journal in which he wrote down the work routine for each day—what the weather was like, which slaves were doing what jobs, how much work they did, who was sick, who was pretending to be sick. If some notable event occurred at or around Buffalo Forge, if a freshet interrupted forge operations or washed out roads and fences, if a snowstorm hit and prevented work, that information also went into his journal. The result is a running description of slave activities at Buffalo Forge that fills three neatly written volumes and covers a span of over seven years, from March 1858 to June 1865.[70] These years, perhaps the most critical in the entire history of the slave South, are the ones in which we can follow the life of Sam Williams in the greatest and most elaborate detail.

When Sam was putting in a routine day at his refinery forge, Brady simply noted "Sam at work" in his journal. And Sam was "at work" most of the time. He and his underhand, a slave named Henry Towles, were the steadiest pair in the forge, but they also had their own ideas about when they had worked long enough and hard enough to deserve a break. The summer of 1860 was such a time. Sam and Henry Towles manned their forge through some very warm days at the beginning of July, but by the middle of the month they had obviously had enough. Henry said he was too ill to work on Wednesday, July 18, and Brady apparently believed him. "Henry Towles sick," he recorded in his journal. Jim Garland, a slave who served as a swing hand between the field gang and the forge, was brought in to relieve Henry, and he and Sam put in a full day together. The next day, the temperature reached 100 degrees at one o'clock in the afternoon, and the heat in the forge must have been stifling. Henry did not show up for work that day, either. "Henry Towles sick i.e. loafing" was Brady's assessment. Sam and Jim Garland continued to work, so the forge had its supply of anchonies that day, but Sam was working under very trying conditions, and no one knew it better than he did. He and Jim finished out the week, however, with "Henry Towles loafing" both Friday and Saturday.[71]

On Monday, July 23, it was Sam's turn, and he may not even have made a pretense of being sick. Henry returned to work that day; he could handle Sam's job, with Jim Garland's help. Sam was now "loafing," according to Brady, and he stayed out "loafing" the entire week. Brady realized he had pushed his hands about as far as he could in the oppressive heat, and he probably was not surprised on Saturday when his two chaffery forgemen, Tooler and Harry Hunt, Jr., also took matters into their own hands. "Tooler & Harry drew a few pounds and then broke down to loaf," he wrote. He decided about the middle of the day that there was no sense fighting it any longer: "All hands had a ½ [day] holiday."[72] From Brady's vantage point, Saturday, July 28, had been a difficult day. The slaves undoubtedly took just the opposite view.

Sam's vacation was not over yet, though. He did not go back to work for three more weeks. From Monday, July 30, to Saturday, August 18, Brady noted with regularity that Sam was "loafing" each day.[73] Even the appearance on August 7 of J. E. Carson, a Rockbridge County slave trader, did not drive Sam back to his post. If Sam were going to be intimidated into returning to work, the slave dealer's visit to Buffalo Forge should have done it. Carson was no idle threat. In the spring of 1859, he had carried one of Weaver's slaves, a man named Lawson, to New Orleans and sold him, and Carson had purchased a slave woman and her children from Weaver several months later. Lawson had tried to run away; the woman had apparently disrupted the quarters by her licentious behavior.[74] Weaver, as was his custom, simply got rid of unruly slaves. But Sam's extended period of "loafing" was not enough to convince Weaver that he should part with his most valuable forgeman. Carson did buy a slave from Weaver on August 7. When he left after dinner on that day, he took away a runaway field hand, Bill Greenlee, in handcuffs.[75] Sam did not return to his forge until Monday, August 20. He had been off the job four full weeks.[76]

Sam returned to work as if nothing had happened. Jim Garland went back into the fields, and Sam and Henry Towles took up where they had left off a month or so earlier. As far as we know, neither Weaver nor Brady attempted to do anything to coerce him back to work earlier. If they did, Brady made no mention of it in his journal. Carson's trip out to the forge was not staged for Sam's benefit. The slave trader had captured Bill Greenlee, the runaway, and was bringing him back to Buffalo Forge in shackles to haggle with Weaver over his price. Sam's vacation, if that word fits the occasion, seems to have been something he felt was due him. He had worked hard that year up to his four weeks of "loafing." His overwork accounts unfortunately do not go beyond 1858, but Weaver's cash books show a number of payments to him between late 1859 and the summer of 1860:[77]

December 24, 1859	To Sam	$10.00
February 11, 1860	"	5.00
March 25, 1860	"	10.00
May 10, 1860	"	1.00
July 10, 1860	"	5.00

It had taken a lot of extra pounds of iron to make this kind of money. And a month after he returned to work, he began receiving cash payments from Weaver again, a strong indication that he was working overtime after he rejoined Henry Towles at the refinery forge:[78]

September 24, 1860	To Sam	$2.50
November 13, 1860	"	1.00
December 1, 1860	"	5.00

Perhaps most significant of all, his savings account, which Weaver was holding, was not touched during or after his month-long absence from his job.

What this fascinating incident suggests is that Sam was fully aware of the power he possessed and the quite distinct limits of that power. He knew that his skills were critically important to his master and that this gave him a considerable amount of leverage in his dealings with Weaver and Brady. In his view, he deserved some time off, and he chose the hot, muggy dog days of July and August 1860 to take it. It was probably no accident that he did not leave his forge until Henry Towles returned. This kept the situation from assuming potentially dangerous and threatening dimensions. Since they were off one at a time, Jim Garland could come in to spell each one of them temporarily, and forge operations could continue. Iron making would not grind to a complete and costly stop because Henry was feigning illness and Sam was "loafing" back at his cabin. Thus Weaver and Brady would not be backed into a corner where they would be forced to crack down on their two refinery hands. Sam knew just how far he could go with his resistance, and he was careful to keep the situation under control.

At the same time, he had enough pride in himself to insist, through his actions, that there was a line beyond which he would not allow himself to be pushed. Months of steady labor, followed by forge work in temperatures reaching 100 degrees, was one step over that line. He took off for a month, and there were certainly risks attendant on that. But they would probably be manageable risks, and that was the way things turned out. By tolerating his absence, Weaver and Brady tacitly recognized that Sam had the power to force reasonable, limited, and temporary changes in his work regimen; they also silently acknowledged that, in a certain sense, he was justified in what he was doing. None of this fits the classic definition of what Southern slavery was supposed to be: total dominance by the white master and total subservience by the black slave. But social institutions have a way of getting fuzzy around the edges, especially when they are as complex as the institution of human bondage.

Sam Williams won this confrontation, probably because of who he was and because his challenge to the system was guarded and oblique and had a limited objective—rest from work. Bill Green-lee's case was quite a different matter. He was twenty-eight years old and a "prime field hand," but he was, from the perspective of Weaver's labor needs, still only a field hand.[79] Even more important, his defiance of the slave regime was open and direct and had an objective that no slaveholder could tolerate—freedom. Not surprisingly, Weaver brought the full force of the system swiftly and brutally down on him. The example of the unsuccessful runaway's being taken off in chains was immediately before the eyes of Sam Williams and every other slave at Buffalo Forge, and that was undoubtedly the way Weaver wanted it. Even Sam's status as a master refiner probably would not have protected him if he had carried his resistance as far as Bill Greenlee did his.

Bill's attempt to escape and Sam's much more limited protest raise one of the ultimate questions about American slavery. What, in fact, was the better part of valor for a slave? Should one fight, confront, resist openly, run away, do everything one could to bring the system down? Or should one maneuver as best one could within the system, stay with one's family and try to help and comfort them, and attempt to carve out the best possible life, despite the physical and psychological confines of enslavement? These were questions each slave had to decide; they were not easily answered then and they are not easily answered now. But most, like Sam Williams, chose the latter course. To have done otherwise would have placed almost everything he loved in jeopardy. And Sam—husband of Nancy, father of Betty, Caroline, Ann, and Lydia, and son of Sally and Sam Williams, Sr.—had a great deal to lose.

The exact date when Sam and Nancy Williams's oldest daughter married was not entered in the Buffalo Forge records, but it was probably sometime in 1857. Betty was seventeen then, and she and a man named A. Coleman, who apparently belonged to a neighboring slaveholder, became husband and wife.[80] On February 18, 1858, she gave birth to her first child, a boy, and they named him Alfred Elliott Coleman.[81] The baby may well have been named for his father, but since we know only the initial of his father's first name, we cannot be sure. Sam and Nancy were grandparents now, and Sam had just that much more reason to try to shelter his family from the worst aspects of the slave regime.

Perhaps nothing was more indicative of the precariousness of their existence than the events of December 1859. Daniel Brady was away on a cattle drive to Richmond during the first part of the month, but one of the clerks took note of the events that were pressing in on the black men and women there. On Friday, December 2, 1859, "John Brown of Ossawatiamie [*sic*] Noteriety to [be] hung at Charlestown Va. to day, for Insurrection," he wrote in Brady's journal.[82] The day was unusually warm and sultry for December, a sign that something worse was on the way. The rains came the next day, Saturday, and enveloped Buffalo Forge in a cold, biting drizzle that continued from early morning until well into the night. It was not the best day for a wedding, but it was the day Caroline Williams and Andrew Reid, a slave teamster who lived nearby, had chosen to be married. Caroline, like her older sister Betty, was seventeen at the time of her marriage, and, again like her sister, had taken for her husband a man who was not one of Weaver's slaves. Another slave girl at Buffalo Forge, fifteen-year-old Amy Banks, was getting married at the same time; her husband-to-be, James Carter, belonged to Charles H. Locher, who operated the cement works at Balcony Falls on the James River, a few miles south of Weaver's place.[83] A double wedding, with both grooms coming from off the property, meant a large gathering of slaves; and the timing—the day after John Brown was hanged —was undoubtedly the reason why a distinctly unwelcome group of uninvited guests turned up at Buffalo Forge that day. On Saturday, December 3, the Rockbridge County slave patrol came calling.[84]

Something akin to panic had swept over much of the South in the wake of John Brown's October raid on Harper's Ferry, and the Valley of Virginia was no exception. The only way to prevent slave rebellions, whites argued, was through an overwhelming show of force and the immediate suppression of the slightest hint of insurrectionary activity.[85] It was not work for the squeamish. We do not know what, if anything, Weaver's slaves said about John Brown, but one of them apparently said or did something the patrol did not like. The hated "paddyrollers," as the blacks called them, left Buffalo Forge after the wedding party broke up on Saturday, but they were back the next day.

Overnight the temperature plunged and the first snow of the season fell at Buffalo Forge. Sunday dawned bright and clear, one of those magnificent early-winter days in the Valley when the air is crisp and fresh and the cloudless sky forms a stunning contrast to the snow-covered Blue Ridge. The tranquility of this December day was soon shattered by the clatter of horses' hooves, as the slave patrol rode up the hill to Weaver's house. Perhaps a snide remark had been directed their way the day before, the day of the wedding, and had festered in the patrollers' minds during the night. Maybe it was nothing more than rumors of some loose talk among the slaves at the forge. It did not take much to set off the paddyrollers in the overheated atmosphere brought on by John Brown's raid. Whatever the reason may have been, their return visit resulted in an ugly incident that struck close to Sam Williams. The patrol singled out Henry Towles, Sam's helper at the refinery forge, for punishment; the twenty-three-year old forge hand was taken out, stripped, and whipped.[86] Towles, whose wife, Ann, and three young children lived with him at Buffalo Forge, did not return to work until December 15.[87] It had taken him ten days to recover from the beating administered by the Rockbridge County patrol.

Two weeks later, as the Valley lay under a new two-inch blanket of snow, a much happier event occurred at Buffalo Forge. At eight o'clock in the morning on December 29, Betty Coleman gave birth to her second child, and this time it was a girl. Both mother and daughter were fine.[88] Sam and Nancy Williams now had a granddaughter as well as a grandson at Buffalo Forge.

It had been a month of stark contradictions. The love and hope expressed in the marriage of two young people, followed by the pain and despair brought on by the brutal whipping of one of their own people, had been followed by the joy surrounding the birth of a healthy child. Those events spoke eloquently of the pleasure and anguish that mingled together in the lives of these black men and women, at Buffalo Forge and throughout the South.

Much of the history of American slavery could also be said to reside in the name of Betty Coleman's new baby. She and her husband called their newborn child Mary Caroline.[89] Her middle name was almost certainly given her in honor of her Aunt Caroline, who had celebrated her marriage just two weeks earlier. What better way could there be for Betty to show love and respect for her sister and, in the process of naming her new child, to demonstrate the transcendent importance of the family to them all? The baby's first name, Mary, went back much farther in the history of the family, back to little Mary's great-great-grandmother. That Mary, mother of Sally Williams, grandmother of Sam Williams, was the woman taken by Thomas Mayburry when he and Weaver divided the "Wilson negroes" over two decades before. Memories of her, it seems fair to say, were still alive in the minds of her descendants at Buffalo Forge, a family that in 1859 spanned four generations there.

John Brown's raid was a prelude to the war that would free them all, although many of them would not be there when emancipation came in 1865. William Weaver was also not there. His final illness set in on a bleak day in mid-March 1863, just over a week after he had celebrated his eighty-third birthday. He died on March 25, 1863, and, true to his word, he left most of his considerable fortune to Daniel and Emma Brady.[90] "As I have kept the great bulk of my estate together partly to provide for the comfort of my servants I desire that they should be treated with kindness and humanity," he had written in his will.[91] The Bradys, from all we can tell, honored his wishes. Only one of his former slaves was put on the block after Weaver was gone. Bill Comiskey, a woodchopper, came in from the coalings with syphilis late in October 1863; a month later he was sold.[92] It was death, not the auctioneer's hammer, that took so many from Buffalo Forge before the day of freedom arrived.

The years of the Civil War were a time of mounting expectations among slaves everywhere in the South, and we can be reasonably sure that such was the case at Buffalo Forge. The Rockbridge Grays, a company in Stonewall Jackson's legendary brigade, had been recruited from the area right around the forge and had drawn off most of the young white men from that section of the county.[93] Even the most isolated slave could see the significance of that fact. And then the refugee families had come streaming past Weaver's place, sometimes spending the night in the big house, while their slaves took their rest in the quarters—and undoubtedly passed on the latest news to the black men and women there.[94] In Sam and Nancy Williams's case, however, the joy and hope inspired by the prospect of freedom must have been tempered by the grief and sorrow they had to live with during these years.

By the fall of 1862, their family had grown significantly. Their daughter Caroline had given birth to her first child, Mary Martha Reid (yet another Mary in the Williams family tree) in October 1860, and Betty Coleman had had her third baby, Julia, in November 1861. Less than a year later, in September 1862, Caroline had delivered another healthy child, a boy, William John Reid (one of Mary's children taken by Mayburry in 1837 had been named John).[95] But that September was also the month when death had begun stalking the Williams family at Buffalo Forge.

Caroline's boy, William John Reid, was born on September 5, 1862. Nine days later, Betty Coleman's four-year-old son, Alfred Elliott, complained of a sore throat. When Daniel Brady examined the boy, he saw unmistakable signs of impending disaster at Buffalo Forge. Alfred Elliott Coleman had diphtheria. Since immunization and effective treatment were not available, it was bound to spread quickly, and no one, black or white, would be safe from its ravages. In rapid succession, Betty, Caroline, and Lydia, three of Sam and Nancy Williams's four daughters, came down with the disease.[96]

When death came to Betty Coleman, it must have been a relief from terrible torment. The first signs of her diphtheria appeared on September 19, and it was clear from the large yellow streaks extending deep into her throat that she had a severe case, much worse than her son's. When a membrane formed at the top of her throat, Brady cauterized it, and she vomited up large, leathery pieces of tissue. She died late in the afternoon on Wednesday, September 24.[97] She was twenty-two years old and the mother of three small children, one of whom, Alfred Elliott, was fighting his own struggle against diphtheria. Her father and his forge helper, Henry Towles, dug her grave in the slave cemetery at Buffalo Forge the next morning, and that afternoon, under a clear, cool autumn sky, she was buried. Brady gave all hands the afternoon off so that they could be present at her funeral. Sam was not asked to return to his forge until the following Monday.[98]

For over two months, diphtheria lingered at Buffalo Forge, and before it ran its course, fifteen of Weaver's slaves contracted the disease. Alfred Coleman, Caroline Reid, and Lydia Williams gradually recovered, although the caustic and turpentine with which their throats were treated must have caused them enormous pain. Daniel Brady was also stricken. He was confined to his bedroom for several weeks, but his case did not turn out to be one of the fatal ones. Three more slaves at Buffalo Forge did die of diphtheria following Betty's fatal attack, however, and before October had ended, her son was also dead. Alfred Elliott Coleman, perhaps weakened by his bout with diphtheria, died on October 31, 1862. Brady listed the cause of his death as an infestation of worms.[99] In the space of six weeks, Sam and Nancy Williams had lost their firstborn child and their oldest grandchild.

More grief was in the offing. Sam Williams was at his forge on May 5, 1864, when news came that his mother was dead. Brady noted that she died of "paralysis," probably a stroke. Sam and a number of the older slaves were released from their duties on the morning following her death, and later that day, Friday, May 6, a beautiful spring day in the Valley, she was buried in the slave cemetery at Buffalo Forge.[100] The cemetery, which stood in a grove of locust trees on a hill behind the mansion, commanded a magnificent view of the Valley—the pale haze of the Blue Ridge, the dense green forests of oak, hickory, walnut, and cedar, the rich fields of wheat, oats, and corn, the waters of Buffalo Creek freshened by the spring thaw. There her wooden coffin was lowered into the earth, and a plain, uncarved shaft of limestone was set up to mark her grave.[101] She had been among family and friends in the last days of her life, and they were doubtless there for her funeral: Sam Williams, Sr., in frail health but still alive; her son Sam; her daughter-in-law Nancy; her grandchildren and great-grandchildren; and her friends of many years' standing. Not the least of the comforts that came to the enslaved was represented by that gathering of black men, women, and children on a hilltop overlooking Buffalo Forge in the spring of 1864—the solace and strength that came from family and community in times of trial and sadness.

Sam and Nancy Williams's time of troubles was still not over. Tragedy seemed to haunt them in late 1864 and early 1865 as the end of the war and the moment of freedom drew closer and closer. In the fall of 1864, their twenty-year-old daughter Lydia, who was unmarried, contracted typhoid fever. On October 7, 1864, as her condition worsened, her older sister, Caroline Reid, gave birth to her third child, a girl. The baby was named Lydia Maydelene Reid in honor of Caroline's stricken sister. Two days later, on Sunday, October 9, Lydia Williams died. Sam's forge was idle on

Monday as he spent the day with his family. On Tuesday morning, the black families of Buffalo Forge once again climbed the dirt road behind the big house to the locust grove on the hill. There Sam and Nancy laid their youngest child to rest.[102]

It was not finished even then. By early 1865 it was clear that a third Williams daughter was gravely ill. Caroline Williams Reid had "consumption," or tuberculosis, and there was no cure. She died on Thursday, January 12, 1865; she was twenty-three years old and the mother of three small children. Sam remained at home that day, and he would have been sorely needed by Nancy, by his one remaining daughter, Ann, and by his grandchildren. Betty Coleman had left two young children behind when she died in 1862, and now there were Caroline's three: Mary Martha, three years of age, William John, two, and Lydia Maydelene, who was only three months old.[103] If ever there was a time when a man and woman, slave or free, black or white, needed to be with each other and with their own, this was surely such a time. Sam and Nancy Williams were there, together.

They were also there when freedom came to Buffalo Forge in the spring of 1865. Brady's matter-of-fact entries for three days in late May tell the story:[104]

Friday May 26, 1865	Declared free by order of military authorities.
Saturday May 27, 1865	All hands quit work as they considered themselves free.
Monday May 29, 1865	Commenced work on free labor.

Sam and Nancy Williams were among those who signed three-month contracts on May 29, Sam as master refiner at the forge and Nancy as head dairymaid.[105] Sam continued refining until 1867, when outside competition finally forced Brady to abandon iron making at Buffalo Forge.[106] Sam shifted to farming on Brady's land in that year and, not surprisingly, became the most successful sharecropper, black or white, on the place.[107] And when he and Nancy finally moved off the property in 1874, they went only a short distance away—to an adjoining farm, owned by one of Brady's neighbors, where many of Sam's friends lived and where he found employment as an agricultural laborer.[108]

Space does not permit a full discussion here of Sam and Nancy
Williams's life in freedom, but a few points that shed light on
their experience in slavery deserve at least a brief mention. Their
marriage and their family, so critically important to their survival
in former times, was no less vital to them now. We can catch a
glimpse of this at two poignant moments. One occurred in 1866
when they entered the office of the Freedmen's Bureau in Lexington. They had come to register their marriage, to legalize that
slave union which had taken place twenty-six years before.
"Samuel Williams and Nancy Jefferson as man and wife since
1840," the clerk recorded. Sam correctly listed his age at forty-six,
Nancy as forty-nine; their only surviving child, their daughter
Ann, was twenty-four.[109]

Fourteen years later, in 1880, there is another revealing moment,
this one at the time when the census taker was making his rounds
in southern Rockbridge County. He reported that Samuel Williams, farmhand, age sixty-one, and Nancy Williams, housewife,
age sixty-three, lived in the same household in the Natural Bridge
section of the county. Checks placed in the appropriate boxes
indicated that neither could read or write. There was a third
member of the family, however. Living with them, the census
taker noted, was Lydia Maydelene Reid, their granddaughter.
The baby who had been only three months old when her mother
had died in 1865 was now a girl of fifteen.[110]

How long Sam and Nancy Williams lived on after 1880 is
unclear. Lydia married in January 1882 and left the household
to begin raising a family of her own. Her husband was a young
man named Charles Newman, and their first child, a girl, was
born in November 1882; they named her Mary Ann Newman.[111]
We do not know exactly when Sam and Nancy died—it was
sometime before 1900—but we can be reasonably sure where they
are buried.[112] Shortly after the Civil War, the black men and
women at Buffalo Forge organized their own church. For a
nominal sum, Daniel Brady sold the church trustees a small tract
of land just a mile south of the forge; among the trustees of the
Buffalo Forge Colored Baptist Church (soon renamed the Mount
Lydia Church) was one Samuel Williams.[113] The freedmen erected
a wooden church and schoolhouse and laid out a cemetery on this
land in 1871.[114] The church building has long since disappeared,
and today the cemetery site is covered with trees and a heavy

growth of underbrush. But if one looks closely enough back among the trees and under the dense carpet of honeysuckle, one can discern small, uncarved, triangular-shaped pieces of limestone. Almost certainly, one of these simple limestone markers stands over the grave of Sam Williams. It is equally certain that a similar stone on the grave nearest his marks the final resting place of Nancy, his wife. The points of all these stones face in the same direction—toward the sky.

NOTES

1. Weaver's property was located in Rockbridge, Botetourt, and Amherst counties. On the quantity of land held by Weaver, see his property-tax receipts in James D. Davidson Papers, McCormick Collection, State Historical Society of Wisconsin, Madison (hereafter cited as Davidson Papers, McCormick Collection); articles of agreement between William Wilson and Thomas Mayburry and William Weaver, July 30, 1814, Jordan and Irvine Papers, ibid. (hereafter cited as Jordan and Irvine Papers, McCormick Collection); entries for William Weaver in Manuscript Census of Agriculture, 1860, Virginia (microfilm copy, Virginia State Library, Richmond). Weaver's slave holdings at the time of his death are given in "An appraisement of the goods and chattels of William Weaver, deceased," June 1, 1863, William Weaver Papers, University of Virginia Library, Charlottesville, Va. (hereafter cited as Weaver Papers, Virginia).

2. "An appraisement," June 1, 1863, Weaver Papers, Virginia.

3. "Article of agreement . . . between Danl. C. E. Brady . . . and Sam Williams (Freedman)," January 1, 1867, Weaver-Brady Papers in the possession of T. T. Brady, Richmond, Va. (hereafter cited as Weaver-Brady Papers, T. T. Brady). I would like to thank Mr. Brady for kindly granting me access to these papers and for his generous assistance on numerous occasions when I needed help on points relating to Buffalo Forge and the Weaver and Brady families.

4. See Charles L. Perdue, Jr., et al., eds., *Weevils in the Wheat: Interviews with Virginia Ex-Slaves* (Charlottesville, 1976), and George P. Rawick, ed., *The American Slave: A Composite Autobiography,* 41 vols. (Westport, Conn., 1972, 1977, 1979).

5. "Weaver Family: Memo and Historical Notes," Weaver-Brady Family Record Book, Weaver-Brady Papers, T. T. Brady.

6. Articles of agreement between William Wilson and Thomas Mayburry & William Weaver, July 30, 1814, Jordan and Irvine Papers, McCormick Collection.

7. Mayburry to Weaver, September 15, October 18, 1815, February 4, 1816, in Case Papers, Weaver v. Mayburry, Superior Court of Chancery Records, Augusta County Court House, Staunton, Va. (hereafter cited as Case Papers, Weaver v. Mayburry).

8. Statement of Thomas Mayburry, October 1, 1821, ibid.

9. John S. Wilson to Weaver, October 24, 1815, ibid. All ages given on the bill of sale were approximations.

10. See deposition of James C. Dickinson, August 15, 1836, in Case Papers, Weaver v. Jordan, Davis & Co., Superior Court of Chancery Records, Rockbridge County Court House, Lexington, Va. (hereafter cited as Case Papers, Weaver v. Jordan, Davis & Co.).

11. Bond of Mayburry for the forthcoming of slaves, December 20, 1828, Case Papers, Weaver v. Mayburry; "An appraisement," June 1, 1863, Weaver Papers, Virginia.

12. "Names, births & c: of Negroes," Weaver-Brady Papers, T. T. Brady.

13. W. W. Davis to Weaver, July 7, 1832, William Weaver Papers, Duke University Library, Durham, N.C. (hereafter cited as Weaver Papers, Duke).

14. Mayburry to Weaver, October 18, November 10, December 19, 1817, March 29, July 16, 1818, September 22, 1819, August 19, 1821, June 15, November 14, 1822, Case Papers, Weaver v. Mayburry; deposition of William Weaver, December 10, 1840, Case Papers, Alexander v. Irvine's Administrator, Superior Court of Chancery Records, Rockbridge County Court House (hereafter cited as Case Papers, Alexander v. Irvine's Administrator).

15. "Articles of agreement . . . between Thomas Mayburry and William Weaver," February 9, 1825, Weaver Papers, Duke.

16. John S. Wilson to Mayburry, March 1, 1825, Case Papers, Weaver v. Mayburry.

17. See deposition of Thomas Mayburry, April 22, 1839, Case Papers, Weaver v. Jordan, Davis & Co.

18. "Article of agreement . . . between Thos. Mayburry & Wm. Weaver," August 3, 1836, Weaver Papers, Duke.

19. Ibid.; deposition of Thomas Mayburry, April 20, 1839, Case Papers, Weaver v. Jordan, Davis & Co.

20. Bond of Thomas Mayburry for the forthcoming of slaves, December 20, 1828, Case Papers, Weaver v. Mayburry; "Names, births & c: of Negroes," Weaver-Brady Papers, T. T. Brady; Buffalo Forge Negro Books, 1830–40, 1839–41, 1844–50, 1850–58, Weaver-Brady Records, University of Virginia Library, Charlottesville (hereafter cited as Weaver-Brady Records, Virginia).

21. Buffalo Forge Negro Books, 1830–40, 1839–41, 1844–50, 1850–58, Weaver-Brady Records, Virginia.

22. Ibid., 1850–58.

23. "An appraisement," June 1, 1863, Weaver Papers, Virginia.

24. See Charles B. Dew, "David Ross and the Oxford Iron Works: A Study of Industrial Slavery in the Early Nineteenth-Century South," *William and Mary Quarterly*, 3rd ser., 31 (1974), 197–98.

25. Ibid., pp. 197, 210–11; "List of Slaves at the Oxford Iron Works in Families and Their Employment, Taken 15 January 1811," William Bolling Papers, Duke University Library, Durham, N.C. (hereafter cited as Bolling Papers, Duke).

26. Weaver to Brady, March 4, 1856, Weaver Papers, Duke.

27. "Descriptive List of Negroes hired . . .," Confederate States Nitre and Mining Service, 1865," Weaver-Brady Papers, T. T. Brady.

28. Buffalo Forge Negro Book, 1830–40, Weaver-Brady Records, Virginia.

29. Weaver to James D. Davidson, November 4, 1849, Davidson Papers, McCormick Collection.

30. See Arthur Cecil Bining, *Pennsylvania Iron Manufacture in the Eighteenth Century*, 2nd ed. (Harrisburg, Pa., 1973), pp. 72–73.

31. Deposition of William Weaver, December 10, 1840, Case Papers, Alexander v. Irvine's Administrator; Weaver's cane is in the possession of Mr. D. E. Brady, Jr., Buffalo Forge, Va.

32. Samuel Sydney Bradford, "The Ante-Bellum Charcoal Iron Industry of Virginia" (Ph.D. diss., Columbia University, 1958), p. 134; Bining, *Pennsylvania Iron Manufacture*, pp. 72–73.

33. Buffalo Forge Negro Books, 1830–40, 1839–41, Weaver-Brady Records, Virginia.

34. Bining, *Pennsylvania Iron Manufacture*, pp. 73–74.

35. Buffalo Forge Iron Book, 1831–62, Weaver-Brady Records, Virginia; Moses McCue to Weaver, July 3, 1829; Weaver Papers, Duke; deposition of William Weaver, December 10, 1840, Case Papers, Alexander v. Irvine's Administrator.

36. Weaver to Davidson, June 12, 1848, Jordan and Irvine Papers, McCormick Collection.

37. See Buffalo Forge Negro Books, 1830–40, 1839–41, 1844–50, 1850–58, Weaver-Brady Records, Virginia. The best general discussions of the overwork system are Robert S. Starobin, *Industrial Slavery in the Old South* (New York, 1970), pp. 99–103, and Ronald L. Lewis, *Coal, Iron, and Slaves: Industrial Slavery in Maryland and Virginia, 1715–1865* (Westport, Conn., 1979), pp. 119–27.

38. Depositions of John Doyle, February 5, 1840, Anthony W. Templin, January 24, 1839, John Jordan, July 22, 1836, and Henry A. Lane, February 5, 1840, Case Papers, Weaver v. Jordan, Davis & Co.

39. Buffalo Forge Negro Books, 1830–40, 1839–41, 1844–50, 1850–58, and Etna Furnace Negro Book, 1854–61, Weaver-Brady Records, Virginia.

40. Wm. C. McAllister to Weaver, February 22, 1830, Weaver Papers, Duke.

41. See entries for Sam Etna, John Baxter, and Harry Hunt in Buffalo Forge Negro Book, 1839–41, Weaver-Brady Records, Virginia.

42. See "List of Slaves at the Oxford Iron Works . . . 1811," Bolling Papers, Duke; Dew, "David Ross and the Oxford Iron Works," pp. 189–94, 222–24.

43. Buffalo Forge Negro Book, 1839–41, Weaver-Brady Records, Virginia.

44. Marriage Register for Rockbridge County, Sub-district "A," 6th District, Virginia, Records of the Bureau of Refugees, Freedmen, and Abandoned Lands, Record Group 105, National Archives, Washington, D.C. (hereafter cited as Marriage Register for Rockbridge County, Freedmen's Bureau Records, RG 105, NA).

45. As indicated by his entries in Buffalo Forge Negro Book, 1839–41, Weaver-Brady Records, Virginia.

46. "Names, births & c: of Negroes," Weaver-Brady Papers, T. T. Brady.

47. Bond of Thomas Mayburry for the forthcoming of slaves, December 20, 1828, Case Papers, Weaver v. Mayburry.

48. Buffalo Forge Negro Book, 1830–40, Weaver-Brady Records, Virginia.

49. For a description of this process, see W. McKee Evans, *Ballots and Fence Rails: Reconstruction on the Lower Cape Fear* (Chapel Hill, 1967), pp. 195–96.

50. Buffalo Forge Negro Book, 1839–41, Weaver-Brady Records, Virginia.

51. Ibid.

52. Ibid.

53. Marriage Register for Rockbridge County, Freedmen's Bureau Records, RG 105, NA; "Names, births & c: of Negroes," Weaver-Brady Papers, T. T. Brady.

54. Buffalo Forge Negro Book, 1839–41, Weaver-Brady Records, Virginia.

55. Ibid., 1844–50.

56. Ibid., 1850–58.

57. Ibid.

58. Ibid., 1844–50, 1850–58.

59. Ibid.

60. John A. Rex to Davidson, February 25, 1855, Davidson Papers, McCormick Collection.

61. Notation on reverse, ibid.

62. D. C. E. Brady Private Ledger, Weaver-Brady Papers in the possession of Mr. D. E. Brady, Jr., Buffalo Forge, Va. (hereafter cited as Weaver-Brady Papers, D. E. Brady, Jr.). I would like to thank Mr. Brady for kindly granting me access to these papers and for his generous assistance when I need help on points relating to Buffalo Forge and the Weaver and Brady families.

Without his aid and that of his brother, Mr. T. T. Brady, the research for this essay could not have been completed. I am deeply grateful for all they have done.

63. Ibid.

64. One can follow their accounts by tracing the entries under their names in: Buffalo Forge Ledger, 1851–59, Weaver-Brady Papers, T. T. Brady; Buffalo Forge Ledger, 1859–78, Weaver-Brady Papers, D. E. Brady, Jr.; Buffalo Forge Journal, 1859–66, Weaver-Brady Records, Virginia; and Buffalo Forge Journal, 1866–78, Weaver-Brady Papers, D. E. Brady, Jr.

65. Weaver to Brady, August 27, 1855, March 4, 1856, Weaver Papers, Duke.

66. Weaver family history compiled by D. E. Brady, Sr., October 28, 1951, Weaver-Brady Papers, D. E. Brady, Jr.; "Weaver Family," Weaver-Brady Family Record Book, Weaver-Brady Papers, T. T. Brady.

67. Weaver to Brady, August 27, 1855, March 4, 1856, and to Emma M. Brady, March 21, 1856, Weaver Papers, Duke.

68. Weaver to Brady, August 27, 1855, ibid.

69. "Brady Family" and "Gorgas Family," Weaver-Brady Family Record Book, and [D. C. E. Brady] to Davidson, July 27, 1867, Weaver-Brady Papers, T. T. Brady.

70. Daniel C. E. Brady, Home Journal, 1858–60, Weaver-Brady Records, Virginia; Daniel C. E. Brady, Home Journal, 1860–65, McCormick Collection (hereafter cited as Brady, Home Journal, Virginia; Brady, Home Journal, McCormick Collection).

71. Ibid., Virginia.

72. Ibid.

73. Ibid.

74. Ibid.; J. E. Carson to Weaver, March 12, May 30, June 27, 1859, Weaver Papers, Duke; Weaver to Carson, July 2, 1859, Buffalo Forge Letterbook, 1858–65, Weaver-Brady Records, Virginia; entries for June 9, July 30, 1859, Buffalo Forge Cash Book, 1849–62, ibid.

75. W. W. Rex to Weaver, August 15, 1860, Weaver Papers, Duke; entry for August 7, 1860, Buffalo Forge Cash Book, 1849–62, Weaver-Brady Records, Virginia; Brady, Home Journal, Virginia.

76. Brady, Home Journal, Virginia.

77. Buffalo Forge Cash Book, 1849–62, ibid.

78. Ibid.

79. "Names, births & c: of Negroes," Weaver-Brady Papers, T. T. Brady.

80. Ibid. Betty's husband's name was given at the time one of their children married in 1876; see marriage registration of Mary C. Coleman and Steward Chandler, July 27, 1876, Register of Marriages, Book 1A, 1865–89, Rockbridge County Court House, Lexington, Va. (hereafter cited as Rockbridge County Marriage Register, 1865–89).

81. "Names, births & c: of Negroes," Weaver-Brady Papers, T. T. Brady.

82. Brady, Home Journal, Virginia.

83. Ibid.; Ch. H. Locher to Weaver, December 3, 1859, Weaver-Brady Papers, T. T. Brady; "Names, births & c: of Negroes," ibid.; Marriage Register for Rockbridge County, Freedmen's Bureau Records, RG 105, NA. Caroline's husband's name was given at the time one of their children married in 1882; see marriage registration of Lydia Reid and Charles Newman, January 4, 1882, Rockbridge County Marriage Register, 1865–89.

84. Brady, Home Journal, Virginia.

85. Clement Eaton, *The Freedom-of-Thought Struggle in the Old South* (New York, 1964), pp. 102–3; Eaton's chapter "The Fear of Servile Insurrection" provides an excellent discussion of overall white attitudes. See also Charles B. Dew, "Black Ironworkers and the Slave Insurrection Panic of 1856," *Journal of Southern History*, 41 (1975), 327–33.

86. Brady, Home Journal, Virginia.

87. Ibid.; "Names, births & c: of Negroes," Weaver-Brady Papers, T. T. Brady.

88. Ibid.

89. "Names, births & c: of Negroes," Weaver-Brady Papers, T. T. Brady.

90. Brady, Home Journal, Virginia; Last Will and Testament of William Weaver, January 8, 1863, William Weaver Papers, Washington and Lee University Library, Lexington, Va. (hereafter cited as Weaver Papers, W & L).

91. Last Will and Testament, January 8, 1863, Weaver Papers, W & L.

92. Entry for October 24, 1863, Brady, Home Journal, McCormick Collection; "Names, births & c: of Negroes," Weaver-Brady Papers, T. T. Brady.

93. Oren F. Morton, *A History of Rockbridge County, Virginia* (Staunton, Va., 1920), pp. 126, 425–27; entry for April 20, 1861, Brady, Home Journal, McCormick collection.

94. Entries for March 7, April 28, 1862, Brady, Home Journal, McCormick Collection.

95. "Names, births & c: of Negroes," Weaver-Brady Papers, T. T. Brady.

96. Brady, Home Journal, McCormick Collection; see entries under "Diptheria & Sore Throat 1862," rear flyleaf, vol. 1, ibid.

97. Ibid.

98. Brady, Home Journal, McCormick Collection.

99. "Names, births & c: of Negroes," Weaver-Brady Papers, T. T. Brady; "Diptheria & Sore Throat 1862," Brady, Home Journal, McCormick Collection.

100. Brady, Home Journal, McCormick Collection.

101. Ibid. Mr. D. E. Brady, Jr., pointed out to me the site of this cemetery; a number of the gravestones are still there.

102. "Names, births & c: of Negroes," Weaver-Brady Papers, T. T. Brady; Brady, Home Journal, McCormick Collection.

103. Ibid.

104. Buffalo Forge Journal, 1859–66, Weaver-Brady Records, Virginia; Brady, Home Journal, McCormick Collection.

105. See entries under "Sam Williams" and "Nancy Williams," Buffalo Forge Negro Book, 1865–73, Weaver-Brady Records, Virginia.

106. Ibid., "Sam Williams"; "Account Sales Iron made by Rocke & Murrell," Lynchburg, Va., 1865, 1866, Weaver Papers, Duke.

107. "Article of agreement . . . between Danl. C. E. Brady . . . & Sam Williams (Freedman)," January 1, 1867, Weaver-Brady Papers, T. T. Brady; entries for Sam Williams and other sharecroppers in D. C. E. Brady, Home Journal, 1865–76, ibid. (hereafter cited as Brady, Home Journal, T. T. Brady).

108. The last entries for Sam Williams are dated 1874 in Brady, Home Journal, T. T. Brady; Manuscript Population Schedules, Rockbridge County, Va., Tenth Census of the United States, 1880, National Archives Microfilm Publications, T9.

109. Marriage Register for Rockbridge County, Freedmen's Bureau Records, RG 105, NA.

110. Manuscript Population Schedules, Rockbridge County, Va., Tenth Census of the United States, 1880.

111. See marriage registration of Lydia Reid and Charles Newman, January 4, 1882, Rockbridge County Marriage Register, 1865–89; birth registration of Mary Ann Newman, Birth Register No. 2, 1878–1896, Rockbridge County Court House, Lexington, Va.

112. A search of the index and population schedules for the 1900 Census failed to turn up the names of either Sam or Nancy Williams; Card Index (Soundex) to the 1900 Population Schedules, Virginia, National Archives Microfilm Publications, T1076; Manuscript Population Schedules, Rockbridge County, Va., Twelfth Census of the United States, 1900, National Archives Microfilm Publications, T623.

113. Deed between D. C. E. Brady, et al., and Samuel Williams, et al., October 9, 1871, Deed Book MM, Rockbridge County Court House, Lexington, Va.

114. "Col. Baptist Church of Buffalo Forge, Va.," account with D. C. E. Brady, 1871, Weaver-Brady Papers, T. T. Brady.

Red, Black, and White:
A Study in Intellectual Inequality

ROBERT F. ENGS

I

IN 1878 Reconstruction was over and the final conquest of the frontier was under way. At this juncture, the United States committed itself to two contradictory policies toward its most troublesome minorities, that is, the blacks and the Indians. American blacks had been thrown upon the mercy of their Southern white brothers and were being pushed with ever increasing vigor back toward a status of permanent inferiority. For the Indian, whites had chosen an opposite destiny. Under the "Peace Policy" initiated by President Grant in 1868, the nation proposed moving the native American toward civilization, citizenship, and assimilation.

An indispensable component of the "Peace Policy" was educating the Indians to the white man's beliefs and customs. Indians were to learn English; they were "to give up the blanket," or their traditional dress; they were to abandon communal life for individually owned farms; they were to acquire the white man's habits of working hard, taking individual initiative, and practicing Christian responsibilty.[1]

There was much debate about how this educational process could best be achieved. Many whites, especially those operating religious missions for the Indians in the West, believed that schools should be created on the reservations, so as not to remove students too far from their own people and so that the educated Indian could have maximum impact on his parents and peers. Others argued that to civilize the Indian, it was necessary to remove him entirely from the negative influences of family and tribe. Indian Commissioner Marble insisted that "the opportunity for teaching Indian children how to live as well as how to read and think is found only in the boarding school."[2] It was the advocates of this second viewpoint who, somewhat hesitantly, supported the creation of an Indian boarding school at Hampton Institute in 1878.[3] The Institute was a small school in southeastern Virginia, founded in 1868. Its purpose was to provide normal and agricultural education to black students, who were to become the teachers of Southern black masses.

At first glance, it may seem paradoxical that the federal government and advocates of its peace policy should support education of Indians at a school for the subjugated black man. This apparent contradiction disappears, however, when the distinction between government rhetoric and actual popular attitudes is made clear. Americans were far from being of a single mind about the wisdom or even the possibility of Indian assimilation. Westerners wanted Indian land, not Indian neighbors. Easterners were more inclined to support the equality of Indians in the abstract, *and* in the West, than they were to welcome them in Boston, New York, or Philadelphia. Hampton Institute, as will be seen, became a school for Indians by default. It was prepared to act when other Eastern schools were not. More important, Hampton had a proven record of training members of one "backward race" for useful participation in the dominant society. Hampton's principal and faculty were eager to try their methods on Indians as well.

It was under these circumstances that one of the most unusual efforts in multiracial education began at Hampton Institute in 1878. During the thirty-four years of black and red education that followed, all of the absurdities, hypocrisies, contradictions, and injustices inherent in American racial attitudes could be discovered at the Institute and in the lives of its Negro and Indian graduates. It is not that Hampton failed in its mission to "civilize" its students. Rather it was that American society refused to accept either blacks or Indians on the basis of equality, no matter how "civilized" they might be.

II

Failure to prepare students for the realities of American life seems an unlikely charge to level at Hampton Institute. The school's founder and first principal, General Samuel Chapman Armstrong, had been determined from the start not to educate his black students "out of sympathy with those they must teach and lead." The black man's future, Armstrong believed, lay in the South, and black graduates of Hampton must learn to accept both the limits and the possibilities that a society dominated by white Southerners permitted.[4]

Armstrong was the son of missionaries to Hawaii, a graduate of Williams College, and a commander of black troops during the Civil War. After two years' service as a Freedmen's Bureau sub-commissioner in Hampton, he founded the Institute with the assistance of the American Missionary Association. Armstrong brought to his work at Hampton all the idealism, Christian enthusiasm and dedication, self-righteousness, and conviction of his own superiority over those he would "serve" that is often evident in missionaries. For him, the problem of the South lay in the black man's "improvidence, low ideas of honor and morality, and a general lack of directive energy, judgment and foresight."[5]

To correct these deficiencies, Armstrong proposed a system of "tender violence" to teach blacks the habit of labor and to instill in them a strong moral character. They would be closely over-seen, sternly corrected for error, and lovingly encouraged when-ever their progress tended in the right direction.[6]

Hampton under Armstrong intended to teach blacks how to educate their own race, to provide them with Christian values, and to equip them with agricultural and mechanical skills by which they could support themselves during the months when school was not in session. They were to abjure politics and con-centrate on uplifting their race through hard work, thrift, and the acquisition of property.[7] Armstrong's program was hardly a blueprint for black equality or even rapid advancement. Its wide-spread adoption in the South by the end of the century helped retard black achievement in higher education for decades. Never-theless, his strategy, proposed in the 1870s, reflected the limited opportunities permitted to blacks in an abidingly racist South and an increasingly indifferent North.[8] Moreover, the Hampton strategy for Southern black progress seemed to work. Its graduates left with an intense sense of commitment to "uplift their race." They taught school and Sunday school, served as advisers and arbiters to their communities, and instructed blacks on fiscal and agricultural matters. The Institute staff collaborated in this success, maintaining a voluminous correspondence with graduates and ex-students, sending old newspapers and magazines for use by students of their graduates, and arranging gifts to help support struggling schools operated by alumni.[9] By 1880, Hampton's graduates were teaching over ten thousand Southern black schoolchildren.[10]

Armstrong firmly believed that his philosophy at Hampton could be applied to all "backward races." After all, the inspiration for Hampton had come from work done by his parents and other missionaries in Hawaii. Once the work with black students was well under way, he saw no reason why the school could not expand, to serve other similar groups. More than idealism and missionary zeal were involved, however. Despite its achievements, Hampton remained an unendowed school that was always short of resources. Armstrong was perpetually in search of reliable sources of income. Discussions of a new Indian policy inspired him. In 1872 he wrote playfully to his wife:

I am on the track of some more money—it will be necessary to prove that the darky is an Indian in order to get it: but I can easily do that you know. . . . Keep dark about it and send me your thoughts on the identity of the Indian and the darky—SAME THING, aren't they?[11]

It was six years later that Armstrong launched his Indian school, but the project had clearly been long on his mind. The school began despite widespread concern among Hampton trustees and advocates of Indian-assimilation policy; it operated under considerable criticism; and it ended amid claims that it was a failure and an insult to Indians. Whatever the justice in these charges, the story of Hampton's Indian school was more complex than its critics or supporters knew.

In 1874, some 150 Kiowa, Comanche, and Arapaho Indians who had participated in an uprising in the Indian Territory were incarcerated at Fort Marion, Florida. Their warden was Lieutenant Richard Henry Pratt, an army officer who had commanded black troops during the Civil War. The exiled Indians had been imprisoned without regard to actual degree of guilt in the uprising. Such injustice outraged Pratt. He barraged officials in Washington with letters begging for the release of those who were innocent and some provision for "civilizing" the others. Finally, in 1877, the Army and the Indian Commissioner, E. A. Hayt, agreed to the release of Pratt's charges and to their education in Eastern schools if they desired it.[12]

Pratt immediately began seeking Eastern schools that would accept his Indians. None could be found. Whatever the national policy on Indian assimilation, Eastern whites wanted no part of Pratt's partially tamed savages. In desperation, Pratt turned to Hampton Institute.[13]

Samuel Armstrong leaped at the opportunity—and at the money potentially to be had in Indian education. Hampton's trustees were more reluctant, but Armstrong, as always, brought them around. Ten of the younger Indian boys were accepted. On April 14, 1878, the prospective students arrived with Lieutenant Pratt and his family.[14] Armstrong was as optimistic and ambitious as usual. The day before he had written to his wife, "We expect the Indians next Monday. I want some Chinese and New Zealanders."[15] Two days later he wrote again, reporting that "the Indians so far have scalped nobody." They had been given "food and religious instruction and set to hoeing onions." "Do as well as our darkies," Armstrong claimed.[16]

Pratt had taught his Indians to speak English, made them wear white men's clothes, which were called "citizen's dress," and given them some religious instruction. Armstrong continued these policies, adding classroom instruction in reading and writing, and assigning the Indians to manual-labor tasks. Each Indian was also to be given a black roommate, in order to aid in the process of civilization. This took some time, however, because blacks also had their prejudices against Indians; they feared they might be attacked and scalped. It took Armstrong's persuasiveness and further proof that the Indians were disarmed and peaceable before enough black men volunteered to room with their new Indian classmates.[17]

Armstrong did not hesitate long once the Indians arrived. He intended that Indian education at Hampton become a permanent program, not an isolated, short-term venture. His assiduously cultivated contacts with powerful men while he was in the army proved very useful. Armstrong arranged to have President Hayes and Secretary of the Interior Carl Schurz visit Hampton to observe the Indian-education program. The ploy was effective. A government-financed program for 120 Indians a year at Hampton was approved and Lieutenant Pratt was assigned to go west to recruit more Indian students.[18]

This alliance between Pratt and Armstrong was short-lived. Pratt was a firm believer in the Indian's equality with the white man. He objected to their education among "inferior" Negroes. A personal incompatibility also came into play; the two men were both driving, aggressive, ambitious people, too much alike to work well together. Still, the brief alliance was fruitful. Armstrong got his Indians and a new, assured source of income; Pratt established the contacts with important government officials that enabled him to start the Carlisle Indian School in 1879.[19]

Indian students could not be admitted to Hampton in the same manner as black students were. The latter often simply appeared at the school, were tested and interviewed, and if qualified, were admitted on the spot to the normal or night schools.[20] Indians, of course, could not come to Hampton; Pratt's journey to the West in search of Indian students was only the first of those undertaken each year that Indians attended Hampton.

Pratt toured primarily the Sioux agencies in Dakota; most of these were supervised by the Protestant Episcopal church. The Episcopal church had never been a stalwart friend of the black man, and Pratt discovered that at one agency missionaries had discouraged students from going to a "colored institution." Pratt reported that he "found this prejudice more or less at several other agencies." This experience deepened his conviction that Indians should be educated in a school of their own.[21]

Despite this problem, the quota of forty students was readily filled. No record was kept of the proportion of full-blooded Indians in the total Indian group at Hampton, but Pratt's first recruits included many Indians with white ancestry. At Fort Berthold, of thirteen students, four were half-breeds, and two were quarter-breeds. Between 1878 and 1888, 301 of Hampton's 427 Indian students were Sioux. There were, in addition, some

56 Sac and Fox tribesmen from the Indian Territory, 70 from Nebraska, mostly Omahas and Winnebagos, and a Pamunkey Indian from Virginia. In all, some seventeen tribes were represented at one time or another, including three Negro Seminoles who were ex-slaves.[22]

Indian students did not come "straight from the warpath" to Hampton Institute, but they were considerably less accustomed to white culture than were their fellow black students. Most of them spoke little or no English on their arrival. Conditions at their home reservations were rapidly changing, but most tribesmen still dressed in traditional Indian fashion, insisted on maintaining tribal institutions, and continued to hold their land communally. All of this irritated Indian agents. One, William Courtenay at Fort Berthold in Dakota, offered an apt description of what Indian civilization meant to white men in the field:

Indians are essentially conservative and cling to old customs and hate all changes. Therefore the government should force them to scatter out on farms, break up their tribal organization, dances, ceremonies, and tomfoolery; take from them their hundreds of useless ponies which afford them the means of indulging in their nomadic . . . habits, and give them cattle in exchange, and compel them to labor or accept the alternative of starvation.[23]

From the beginning it was apparent that the Indians could not be given the same education as was given to the blacks at Hampton Institute. The Indians were entirely unprepared for the standard normal-school program. A separate Indian School had to be established that taught basic language skills. As described by Helen Ludlow, a Hampton English teacher, the first three years of the Indian-school program concerned "oral training in English," with the rudiments of writing. Only in the fourth year did the students actually begin to read books. History, mathematics, geography, and art were also included in the curriculum. The Indian students, she recalled, had particular difficulty with mathematical concepts. On occasion, they also objected to the one-sided view of American expansion in the West as portrayed in the standard history texts.[24]

The Indian-school program ran five years, at the end of which a student would be ready to enter the normal program. But the government Indian scholarships allowed only three years' study for each student. Thus an Indian "graduate" usually returned to his reservation with only the most rudimentary knowledge of English, reading, writing, and arithmetic. The overwhelming majority of the Indians went through this three-year program. Only ten to fifteen Indians a year were enrolled in the normal program; these were supported by private charity rather than by government funds.[25]

Indians, like the black students at Hampton, were required to attain manual as well as academic skills. Indians were assigned to the various shops along with the blacks. Regular Indian-school students spent half the day in the classroom and the other half in a shop. A few Indians enrolled in the night school and spent their full time in the trade departments. In 1884, Indian men were learning carpentry, tin-smithing, harness-making, and painting. Women students were studying homemaking, sewing, cooking, and laundering together with the black girls. Greater experience with Indian graduates, however, demonstrated that opportunities for Indian employment in a specific trade were rare on the frontier. In 1887 the trade program was revamped; Indians studied in a "technical shop" in which they received a modest amount of training in a variety of trades.[26] As an aid in the pursuit of a trade on his return home, each Indian student was given a toolbox and tools when he left Hampton. The tools were paid for out of withheld wages the Indians had earned during their time of study at Hampton.[27]

Samuel Armstrong's concept of the proper education for backward races had never been limited to the acquisition of academic and technical skills. "The difficulty with both races," he explained in 1880, "is not so much ignorance as weakness or deficiency of character; not lack of brains but of moral stamina. Both need drill throughout the range of living."[28] To get the "drill," Indians, like the blacks of Hampton Institute, lived a rigid, carefully supervised existence. Indians had to learn all the proper habits of civilized men, from how to make a bed to what clothes to wear. They also had to acquire the "proper" attitudes of respect for women—an area in which Indian braves were held to be notoriously deficient.

Armstrong began by giving each Indian student a black roommate, by making Indian boys walk while Indian girls rode in wagons, and by holding up the behavior of the blacks as an example for Indians to emulate. The difficulties were many. The black men had to convince their Indian roommates to sleep on top of rather than under their beds, and to remind them to put on *all* of their clothing before leaving the room. More seriously, by using the formal and deferential way in which black men treated Indian girls as the model for Indian braves, the school challenged the Indian concept of manliness and aggravated latent racial tensions between the two races.[29] These tensions soon forced the creation of separate living facilities for Indians. The "Wigwam" was constructed for the boys, and "Winona" (Big Sister) Lodge for the girls. Even further separation was required in the Wigwam. The Sioux students did not get along with members of other tribes, and there were great differences in the ages of the male students. The building was divided into three parts, connected only by the sitting room of the resident matron.[30]

In each dormitory a student janitor was appointed. Along with a teacher, he or she inspected each room daily. The Indian men were organized in separate companies of the school cadet corps and were inspected daily by student officers. As with Negro students, the process of teaching civilization continued into the evenings. Indian students attended their required study halls and participated in their own debate society, prayer meetings, temperance association, and social events in Winona Lodge. On special occasions, such as Founders' Day, they joined with the black students in social affairs.[31]

Religion was, of course, an important "civilizing" ingredient. Indian students from Episcopal agencies attended St. John's Church in the village of Hampton, participating in all church activities, including singing in the choir. Presbyterian or Congregational students attended the school chapel; Catholics were sent to mass at the Soldiers' Home next to the Hampton campus.[32]

Unlike black students, Indian students suffered from many health problems. The Hampton climate, humid and warm, contrasted sharply with that of the western highlands from which most Indian students came. Most of the early students were described as suffering from "weak lungs," and many of them contracted pneumonia and tuberculosis. Moreover, Indians had difficulty adjusting to the traditional Southern diet provided for Hampton's black students, and they were frequently plagued by

scrofula. It became necessary to provide a special Indian menu
including more fresh fruits and milk and replacing pork with
beef. Special diet and special preparations, in turn, required special separate kitchen and dining facilities. Even these precautions
were not entirely sufficient; of the 427 Indian students who attended Hampton between 1878 and 1888, 31 died. Another 111
had to be returned to their reservations because of poor health.[33]

Like the black students, Hampton's Indians sometimes broke
school rules and required punishment. "They have quick tempers," Armstrong noted, and "a few have had bad dispositions."[34]
But expulsion, "the all-sufficient, severest punishment" for recalcitrant black students, could not be used against the Indian.
It would have meant sending the Indian back to the reservation
without the benefit of civilization and perhaps with a greater
inclination to "make trouble." Indian students strongly disliked
being separated from their peers; thus, the common punishment
for minor infractions was exile to Shellbanks, a school farm five
miles from the campus. This means of discipline was also practiced with black students. A method for dealing with more serious
infractions, one used only for Indian students, was a guard room
established under the principal's office. It was an unlighted room
without furnishings. Although Armstrong was severely criticized
for resorting to solitary confinement as a punishment for Indians,
the room had the desired effect in eliciting confessions or reform-
ing a student's behavior.[35]

With its special discipline, separate classrooms, dormitories,
and dining facilities, and separate social activities, Hampton,
after 1878, was not a school for two races but rather two distinct
schools, one for the black race and one for the red. Even the few
Indians in the normal school participated with their fellow
Indians in out-of-class activities.

The policy of separation evolved, in part, from the peculiar
needs of the Indian students. More basic was the need to defer to
the national attitudes toward blacks and Indians and to the
prejudices existing on the campus itself. The black and red students simply did not care much for each other's company. Black
students claimed they were more civilized than were the Indians;
the Indians retorted that *they* had never been slaves. In 1890, the
Indian students in the Wigwam (the men's dormitory) petitioned
for the removal of R. R. Moton as supervisor. They argued,

"Many of the boys have spoken of disliking him here, not because they have any feelings against him personally but because they do not like to have a colored person over them." They pointed out that "colored boys" had no school officials resident in their dormitories and asked, "Why can't they trust us?"[36]

George L. Curtis, commandant of the cadet military corps at Hampton, understated the racial situation when he said, "There has been much pleasant intercourse, though little intimacy between them."[37] Helen Ludlow, in charge of the Indian school, was more candid about student attitudes and the fears of Hampton's faculty when she wrote in her first national publication on Indian education,

> General social intercourse between the races of opposite sexes is limited and guarded. Trouble might come of it. . . . The effort is to build up self-respect and mutual respect. And we believe that education of the mind and heart tends to individual morality and race purity.[38]

Miss Ludlow emphatically reassured those who were concerned that the large black population of Hampton village would "contaminate" the school's Indians. Hampton's Negroes were "the most thrifty and industrious remnant of the 'contrabands.' " The school's holiday was set on Monday to avoid the town-market day, "when there is more drinking and loafing." A former Indian student, Anna Dawson, wrote to add her reassurances. She was concerned about "considerable and unfavorable talk concerning the Negroes and their influence over the Indians at Hampton." She explained that Indians did not "come into contact with the Negroes as most people suppose"; they had separate dormitories, dining rooms, and classrooms.[39] Hampton was a school for the civilization, not the amalgamation, of the red and black races. The basic contact in the Institute was an educational one between white faculty and one of the two races, not between the two races themselves.

The segregation of black and Indian students was not merely an accommodation to hostilities between blacks and reds. Hampton's white faculty conceived of the two races as being different and felt that these differences required separate handling of each group. The essential difference was, of course, that the Indians could be candidates for amalgamation with the white race, while blacks could not. This did not make the aim of Hampton's education for Indians entirely different. The Institute, Armstrong explained, was "to give the Negro and Indian races what they need most . . . a class of intelligent, earnest teachers, practical workers and leaders."[40] But unlike their black counterparts, the Indian leaders had a specific goal to which they were to lead their race—amalgamation with the white race. The Indians, Helen Ludlow said straightforwardly, "like our foreign elements . . . are being absorbed into our common population. The Indian problem is likely to disappear in the next century for want of a distinguishable Indian race."[41] No one at Hampton ever postulated such a future for the black race.

This separate destiny for the Indian required that safeguards be established against romances between the black and red students. Racial purity apparently meant the absence of any taint of Negro blood in superior red and white men.[42] Miss Ludlow could speak glowingly of two of her "star" Indian girls who had married white men. There is no record that any marriages of black to white occurred; but if they had, Hampton's faculty certainly would not have praised the nuptials.[43]

Martha Waldron, the school physician, offered her own "scientific" evidence for the benefits of Indian-white amalgamation and the evils of Negro-white amalgamation. "The full-blood Indians have less endurance than the half of mixed bloods," she observed. "This is the reverse of the condition seen in the Negro race, in which pure bloods are less subject to phythisis than mulattoes and lighter shades." At present, Negroes had more physical stamina than Indians, "though much less than the Anglo-Saxon." On the other hand, the Indian race, "with all its weakness and wildness, possesses traits which would make no unworthy addition to the sum of American civilization."[44] A similar vision of the black future in America seemed inconceivable to Hampton's white teachers.

Samuel Armstrong, as principal of Hampton, was very vocal in attempting to define the differences between blacks and Indians. He had no question "as to the Indian's mind." It was "observing, shrewd, quick and persistent in directions where it had been trained for generations." The failures of Indian students, Armstrong argued, were "to be found not from innate causes but

from surrounding influences."[45] In this statement, he was referring to both the traditional culture of the Indian tribe and the
failings of white culture on the frontier as "surrounding influences." Strikingly, he had never been willing to condemn the
failings of the white culture of the South in regard to the blacks'
problems. Perhaps because the Indians were already "in the
family," it was possible to be more candid. A more likely explanation is the reality that the survival of the Institute depended on
maintaining the goodwill of Southern whites, while the survival
of the Indian program—in 1883—was relatively independent of
the attitudes of Western whites.

These efforts to build up the Indian by comparison with the
Negro were threatened by the indisputable fact that black men
were more acculturated to white society than were red men. In
attempting to circumvent this problem, Armstrong carried his
arguments to their logical extreme.

The submissive Negro . . . has not thrown a pauper upon the
nation. Of the proud Indians, about one-half are in the national
poorhouse. . . . The superior personality of the latter is in the body
whose habits are opposed to industry and whose weakness unfits him
so far for competition with any other people.

The severe discipline of slavery strengthened a weak race. Professed
friendship for a strong one has weakened it. . . .

Somehow, the Indian was stronger than the black even though,
admittedly, all evidence seemed to prove the opposite. In addition,
it was permissible to blame white men for the Indian's plight.
But far from being guilty for the black man's condition, white
men, by making the Negroes slaves, had actually helped them![46]

The tortuous logic by which Armstrong reached this conclusion
bothered him not at all. The advantage of prejudice, after all, is
that conclusion precedes information. The meaning of all ensuing
facts must be reordered to fit the pre-established conclusion.
Armstrong, like many other white Americans, started from the
premise that the Indian was a potential equal and that the black
was not. Given this premise, it was necessary to explain away the
contradictory reality of black men's greater degree of acculturation. Having done so, Armstrong went one illogical step further.
Coeducation of blacks and Indians could be a great advantage to

both races. Blacks would serve as models for red men. It seemed that once the Indian had caught up with the Negro, he could strike out on his own and participate in white society.[47]

The logic was one that many whites understandably had difficulty accepting. Why not let whites provide the model for Indian civilization? Armstrong had a ready answer. The "sentimentalists" of a New England–style college would fill the Indian with "useless knowledge." The Indian needed to be educated to aid his brethren back on the reservation. For the Indian as well as the black, civilization evolved in stages. At his present stage, the Indian must learn to live simply, to acquire the rudiments of knowledge, to study the Bible, and to obey orders. Hampton Institute could provide this training better than could any white school.[48] Less openly stated, but equally important to the cause of racial coeducation at Hampton, was Armstrong's own ambition to "civilize" as many backward races as possible. Not stated at all, but certainly of considerable importance, was the tremendous contribution that Indian education made to the fiscal and political security of the Institute. The school was guaranteed an annual government subsidy of $20,000 for its 120 Indian students. In addition, wider sources of philanthropic support were made available. Many persons who had not the least concern for the black man would give for Indian education. In publications after 1878, Armstrong placed more emphasis on the education of Indians at Hampton than was merited by their numbers alone. Indian education brought many new contributions to the school coffers, and greater fame and prestige to Hampton and its founder.[49]

Samuel Armstrong's defense of Indian education at Hampton did not convince everyone. The program came under intermittent attack throughout its existence. Some critics, particularly Westerners, were opposed to the whole idea of Indian education, no matter where it occurred.[50] Others, like Richard Pratt, were specifically opposed to Indian education at a school for Negroes. The most serious attack came in 1888 from the Reverend T. S. Child, inspector for the Board of Indian Commissioners. Child rejected the argument that the education of Indians and Negroes together was beneficial for both races. Hampton was fine for Negroes but not for Indians. Child found the health problem of Hampton Indians severe, their diet inadequate, their careful regimentation into military companies unnecessary, and the guardroom used for confining misbehaving students "a fearful place of punishment." The new technical shop for Indians, Child complained, prevented the development of competency in any trade rather than preparing Indians for whatever jobs they might find on the reservation. The inspection report concluded:

It is a question whether it may not be wise and right that Hampton should devote itself entirely to the work for which it was founded— the education of the colored race—while the Indian is removed to some institution where he may have equal educational advantages at less serious risk of life and health.[51]

Armstrong's reply to this attack was lengthy and systematic. Indians at Hampton, he argued, were as healthy as those at the Carlisle Indian School. Most of those who died had been sick when they arrived. He presented testimony from the school physician and from a doctor in the village that the diet for Indians was entirely adequate and carefully formulated. Armstrong professed himself shocked at Child's readiness to accept the Indian students' grievances at face value. "Indians," Armstrong explained, "are fickle, fertile in grievances, and often wish to change their work for no good reason." As for the guardroom, Armstrong presented evidence that the Commissioner of Indian Affairs had approved its use. The charge that Indians were only superficially trained in trades, Armstrong rejected flatly. Indians trained intensively in one trade while they studied more casually a wide variety of others. Superficiality, Armstrong said pointedly, was a characteristic of the inspector's report, not of Hampton's training program.[52]

Armstrong's defense was an able one, but his own cordial relations with the Board of Indian Commissioners, particularly with its chairman, General Fisk, seem to have been the decisive factor. E. Whittlesey and Albert Smiley of the board visited Hampton and reviewed the complaints of Inspector Child. Their tour included a visit to the now infamous guardroom. They had little defense against the charms of Samuel Armstrong; Child's recommendations were promptly reversed. In fact, it is unlikely that Child would have gone away so unhappy with Hampton had Armstrong himself been on campus to act as his host. Smiley and Whittlesey wrote to the board that to close the Indian school at

Hampton would be a "great calamity." "No other Indian school can show better results, no other has taken stronger hold of the people or done more to mold public sentiment in favor of Indian education."[53]

Armstrong won this particular battle over racial coeducation. But under a less adroit politician and publicist than Armstrong, Hampton was unable to justify the education of a race that was preparing for assimilation in a school for a race that would perpetually occupy a separate, inferior status. In 1912, pressure in Congress, particularly from congressmen of Indian ancestry, forced the removal of the government subsidy and the end of Hampton's Indian school.[54] Indians, though in much smaller numbers, continued to attend the Institute for another decade, supported by private charities.

Though the Institute perceived and responded to the withdrawal of the government subsidy as a particular slight against Hampton, that action is better understood as symbolic of broader changes in the American racial system. By 1912 it was simply no longer as easy as it had been for well-meaning white paternalists to prescribe what was best to do for "backward races" and then proceed to do it. Indian spokesmen demanded a form of education different from the one Hampton provided. Many of these were the "acculturated" Indians produced by the day and boarding schools created under the "Peace Policy." Unhappily, one aspect of their acculturation appeared to be adoption of the prevailing white antipathy toward blacks.

Spokesmen for black Americans likewise increased their criticisms of the educational philosophy of Hampton and Tuskegee Institute, demanding that able blacks receive a genuine college education rather than the normal and agricultural training of schools like Hampton. Armstrong's programs, whatever their merits in the 1870s, were under scathing attack from blacks, Indians, and their white allies by 1912. Had the Institute failed its black and red graduates?

III

To Samuel Chapman Armstrong, respectability was the most important characteristic of civilized man:

Respectability in a civilized society is in the air; it is a habit, we inherit it, it is the fashion, and it pays. Among savages, degradation is in the air and in the blood. . . . The civilized man is honest, not because it is good, but because it pays to be honest; but it took many generations to find it out.

Not till a race comprehends the practical bearing of integrity will it practice it.[55]

If the Institute is judged by this standard that Armstrong set, the criticisms made after 1900 seem unfair.

Hampton's faculty members were prodigious, if not particularly systematic, record keepers. They kept track of their graduates and periodically reported on their success or failure. A review of the records of these men and women demonstrates that Hampton was strikingly successful in instilling "civilized" values in its black students but less successful in achieving the same with its Indian students.

The problem did not lie in changing the values of Indian students while they were at Hampton. One Indian graduate wrote to his former teachers,

Before I came to Hampton school I thought it is not good to work. I think now it is better to work than do the Indian's way, because Indians are lazy and make the women work. . . . I used to think it is not good to stay in the same country. Now I think it is better to stay in one place so the children can go to school. . . . If Indians stay in one place near good white people, then they will learn good ways, and how to take care of everything.[56]

In 1886 the Indian graduates gave a performance at commencement that conveyed the same sentiments. The skit, written by a white teacher, reveals what "civilizing the Indians" meant to Hampton's faculty.

My friends I shake your hands! I'm ready
  to do the work I once despised,
I've thrown away my bow and arrow,
I've taken up the plough and harrow,
  I'm willing to be civilized! . . .

We want to be what you have told us,
We've thrown away the things we prized;
It's hard to turn as we are turning,
We're old to learn, and still we're learning,
Please help us to be civilized.[57]

Obviously Hampton's teachers had been doing considerable "form-ative work" with Indians as well as with blacks. The red man had learned to love the white man's ways and to reject his own culture.

The problem was rather that the white man's ways had little value on a frontier reservation. Thomas "Wildcat" Alford, a former student, wrote back from his reservation that there were "a great many obstacles in the way of returned Indian students." The most formidable of these was the temptation to give way to "his natural propensities" toward Indian culture, which had been "dormant" while he was at Hampton. Work, Alford said, was the "great remedy" to this problem. Then he added, "Here we come to the worst feature of the case. There is not enough work for them at the Agency or at home."[58]

Alford had identified the heart of the problem. Indian culture on the reservation remained so different from white society that even Hampton's avowed effort not to alienate the Indian from his people was insufficient. Hampton teachers who journeyed to the reservations each year to evaluate their former students com-plained of the same problems. Those who could find jobs with the reservation's Indian agent did well enough, but few had such opportunities. Usually the Indian student had to make some accommodation with the tribal structure from which he had come. The problem was particularly severe for returned Indian women. They found themselves bound to marry the mate selected by their parents. He was usually a man without the benefit of a Hampton education and with little patience for the ideas about the respect due women that Indian girls learned at Hampton.

Under such circumstances, the chief criteria used to evaluate the Indian students were whether they had "gone back to the blanket" and whether they had managed to stay aloof from other tribal customs. The record was mixed. Of those returnees who could be located, only 60 percent qualified for the classifications of "good" or "excellent." Of 460 returned Indian students, 143 were judged as "fair," "poor," or "bad." Three were "criminals against the law of the land."[59]

Whereas 90 percent of the school's black graduates taught school, only a small number of the Indian graduates did so. The paltry education they had received at Hampton left them unprepared to do so. Even those who had completed the normal school found themselves handicapped; there were few openings for Indian-school teachers, especially for Indian ones.[60] The vast majority of Hampton's Indian male graduates became subsistence farmers. An overwhelming majority of the women became simply the wives of such men and the mothers of their children.[61]

There were, to be sure, some spectacular success stories among Hampton's Indian graduates. Susan LaFlesche, an Omaha, was salutatorian of the class of '86. She went on to become the first Indian woman doctor and dedicated her life to treating patients on her home reservation in Nebraska. Anna Dawson, who continued a lifelong correspondence with Hampton, arrived at the Institute as a young child in 1878. She was of mixed parentage, white and Arikara. She graduated from the normal program in 1885 and taught at Hampton in the Indian and night schools. Dawson later enrolled in the normal school in Framingham, Massachusetts, and devoted her career to serving as an extension agent at the Sioux reservation in Nebraska, and later at her home agency in Fort Berthold, North Dakota. She married a graduate of Carlisle Indian School and spent the rest of her long life caring for her children and those she took in from others. She died in 1968 at the age of 101.[62]

Some Indian men also achieved distinction after graduation from Hampton. Thomas Sloan, who was one-eighth Omaha Sioux, entered Hampton in 1884 and graduated as valedictorian. He returned west to the Omaha-Winnebago reservation, read law, and was admitted to the Nebraska bar in 1892. He was active in Indian reform work and served as president of the Society of American Indians and as a member of the Committee of One Hundred. That committee's work led to the Merriam Report, which served as the basis of New Deal Indian policy. William Jones, also of mixed blood, is acclaimed as Hampton's most illustrious Indian graduate. After graduating from the Institute in 1892, he attended Phillips Andover Academy, Harvard, and

Columbia, from which he received a Ph.D in anthropology under Franz Boas. Tragically, his career was short-lived. He was murdered in 1909 by the "heart-eating" Ilongot tribe in the Philippines, with whom he had spent a year and a half doing research.[63]

The achievements of Indian graduates like LaFlesche, Dawson, Sloan, and Jones are genuinely impressive, but they need to be placed in proper perspective. There were more black Hampton alumni professionals in the village of Hampton alone than there were Indian alumni professionals in the West. Neither Hampton's Indian school nor the opportunities available to Indians in the West enabled most red men and women to duplicate the achievements of Dawson or Sloan.[64]

The success record of Hampton's Indian graduates as compared with that of the blacks was disheartening, but the reasons for this were inherent in the whole national scheme to educate them. Hampton created men and women prepared to live by the values of white America. But Hampton had no power to affect the societal circumstances in which the Hampton graduate would find himself. The Indian had been promised equality before entering Hampton and was encouraged to expect it while there. Unfortunately, no change occurred on the frontier, where the Indian was expected to live, that fostered this equality. Three years of elementary education were not enough to prepare the Indian to teach his own people. Few other opportunities existed for Indians, and, in any case, Indians on the reservations were far less willing to accept white culture than were Southern blacks. Most important, whatever the national policy regarding Indians and whatever the beliefs of Hampton's faculty about the future equality of the Indians, other whites had no intention of permitting the Indian to become equal.

Because Hampton's teachers and principal failed to understand both society's real attitudes toward Indians and the desires of Indians on Western reservations, they were able to do nothing to prepare the Indians for what they would find outside the school itself. Hampton could teach its students to be respectable, but it could not change the criteria by which Southern and Western white men judged "respectability." Samuel Armstrong's opinion to the contrary notwithstanding, the basic requirement was a white skin. Neither the black nor the Indian could qualify. Education could change values and styles of behavior, but it could not make a black man or a red man white.

Hampton Institute's black graduates fared considerably better than the red ones. This was in large measure because neither the Institute's faculty nor its black students had an idealized vision leading them to expect that they would be made equal to whites, and nothing at the Institute changed their minds. The curriculum and the advice that they encountered constantly reminded them of the trials that lay before them. For thirty-four years black students at Hampton were given even further evidence of their plight. They were asked to help teach the "backward" Indians the ways of the white man because they knew them better, while, at the same time, they were told that the Indian could become a valued addition to American society, whereas they themselves could not for generations to come.

Although tainted by accommodation to racism and compromised by paternalism, Armstrong's program for blacks had equipped them for survival in the late nineteenth century and given them the skills and motivation to provide leadership in the twentieth century. His similar program for Indians, though equally well intended, left red men and women adrift between two cultures, alienated in a nation still unable to define a role for its oldest residents. The fault, to be sure, was not entirely Hampton's. Yet the arrogance that defined nonwhite peoples as backward and presumed to "civilize" them by the inculcation of white values was surely articulated as clearly at Hampton Institute as at any place in America.

NOTES

1. Margaret R. Muir, "Indian Education at Hampton Institute and Federal Policy" (M.A. thesis, Brown University, 1970).

2. Ibid., pp. 20–21.

3. Ibid., pp. 57–59.

4. *Catalogue of the Hampton Normal and Agricultural Institute, Hampton, Virginia, 1870–71* (Hampton, 1870), pp. 19–20 (hereafter HNAI).

5. Robert F. Engs, *Freedom's First Generation: Black Hampton, Virginia, 1861–1890* (Philadelphia, 1979), pp. 142–43.

6. Ibid.

7. Ibid., pp. 144–46.

8. Ibid., pp. 139–60. For a more elaborate and critical interpretation of Armstrong's motivation and accomplishments, see Elizabeth Jacoway, *Yankee Missionaries in the South: The Penn School Experiment* (Baton Rouge, 1980), esp. pp. xiii–23. For two more positive appraisals of Armstrong's role, see Joseph W. Tingey, "Indians and Blacks Together: An Experiment in Biracial Education at Hampton Institute (1878–1923)" (Ed.D. diss., Teachers College, Columbia University, 1978), and Muir, "Indian Education at Hampton Institute."

9. Records of Graduates and Ex-students, Hampton Institute Archives. Hampton maintained a Department of Graduate and Ex-students with a file on every known individual who had attended the Institute. These largely unexplored files offer an invaluable record of life in the late nineteenth century.

10. Engs, *Freedom's First Generation,* p. 154.

11. Samuel C. Armstrong (hereafter SCA) to Emma Armstrong, June 5, 1872, Armstrong Papers, Williams College.

12. Everett A. Gilcreast, "Richard Henry Pratt and American Indian Policy, 1877–1906: A Study of the Assimilation Movement" (Ph.D. diss., Yale University, 1967), pp. 1–7, 17, 24.

13. Ibid., pp. 25–30.

14. Tingey, "Indians and Blacks Together," pp. 105–6; Francis Peabody, *Education for Life* (New York, 1918), pp. 148–49.

15. SCA to Emma Armstrong, April 13, 1878, Armstrong Papers.

16. SCA to Emma Armstrong, April 15, 19, 1878, ibid.

17. Gilcreast, "Pratt and American Indian Policy," pp. 12–14; Peabody, *Education for Life,* p. 156; Muir, "Indian Education at Hampton Institute," p. 80.

18. Gilcreast, "Pratt and American Indian Policy," p. 25; *Ten Years' Work for Indians at Hampton Institute* (Hampton, 1888), p. 12.

19. Ibid., pp. 31–38.

20. The best known such "test" is that of Booker T. Washington. He reputedly swept and reswept classroom floors as his entrance exam to Hampton. See Louis Harlan, *Booker T. Washington* (New York, 1972), pp. 55–56.

21. *The Annual Report of the Commissioners of Indian Affairs for the Year 1878* (Washington, 1878), p. 174 (hereafter *ARCIA*). The bulk of Hampton's Indian students in the years 1878–88 were Dakota Sioux from the Yankton, Crow Creek, Lower Burie, Standing Rock, and Cheyenne River agencies.

22. Ibid., p. 173; *Ten Years' Work,* p. 11; *ARCIA,* 1882, p. 73.

23. *ARCIA*, 1879, pp. 20–22, 30–33.

24. *ARCIA*, 1882, p. 181; *Ten Years' Work*, p. 31. It should be noted that in the final years of the Indian program, students arrived better prepared and were able to enter the normal program.

25. Ibid., p. 30.

26. Ibid., pp. 25, 20; HNAI, 1884, p. 20.

27. Muir, "Indian Education at Hampton Institute," p. 43.

28. *Hampton Annual Reports*, 1880, p. 6.

29. Ibid., pp. 12–16; *Ten Years' Work*, p. 13; SCA, *Indian Education at Hampton* (New York, 1881), p. 6.

30. Peabody, *Education for Life*, p. 154; *Ten Years' Work*, p. 33; Interview with Miss Eleanor Gilman, retired staff member of Hampton Institute, March 11, 1968.

31. *Ten Years' Work*, pp. 32–33.

32. Ibid., p. 25; *ARCIA*, 1882, p. 184.

33. Tingey, "Indians and Blacks Together," p. 274; *Ten Years' Work*, pp. 19–24; M. F. Armstrong, Helen Ludlow, and Elaine Goodale, *Hampton Institute, 1868–1885: Its Work for Two Races* (Hampton, 1885), p. 23. By 1900 the separate dining hall for Indians had been replaced by separate tables for Indians in the regular dining area.

34. *Annual Report of the Principal of Hampton Normal and Agricultural Institute, 1879* (Hampton, 1879), p. 13.

35. *Ten Years' Work*, p. 34; Tingey, "Indians and Blacks Together," p. 179; SCA to E. Whittlesey and A. K. Smiley, Board of Indian Commissioners, March 15, 1888, Hampton Institute Archives.

36. Tingey, "Indians and Blacks Together," pp. 198–200; Minutes of Meetings of Wigwam Council, 1890–1891, Hampton Institute Archives.

37. *Hampton Annual Report*, 1884, p. 54.

38. *Ten Years' Work*, p. 14.

39. Ibid., pp. 15, 58.

40. *HNAI*, 1884, p. 5.

41. M. F. Armstrong, Ludlow, Goodale, *Hampton Institute*, p. 22.

42. *Ten Years' Work*, p. 14.

43. M. F. Armstrong, Ludlow, Goodale, *Hampton Institute*, pp. 15, 19.

44. Ibid., p. 23; Peabody, *Education for Life*, p. 498.

45. *Ten Years' Work*, p. 30; SCA, *Indian Education at Hampton*, p. 4; *ARCIA*, 1883, 165.

46. *Annual Report of the Principal of Hampton Normal and Agricultural Institute, 1881* (Hampton, 1881), p. 7. It is not entirely clear whether Armstrong was speaking his mind or pandering to his Northern and Southern white benefactors in this statement. His private correspondence suggests that the view he expresses about blacks is a genuine (though mistaken) one. That same correspondence indicates that his comments about Indians were a conscious distortion, for fund-raising purposes, of his personal opinion. See Engs, *Freedom's First Generation,* pp. 139–60; Samuel Chapman Armstrong Letter File, Hampton Institute Archives.

47. SCA, *Indian Education at Hampton,* p. 5.

48. Ibid., p. 12.

49. In addition to the several books and pamphlets by Hampton faculty cited above, smaller promotional leaflets and pamphlets were printed frequently by the Institute. In all of them Indian education was heavily stressed, and in some the only mention of the black students on campus was that on infrequent occasions the Indian students met with them. Several of these pamphlets still exist in the files of Hampton Institute.

50. *Southern Workman,* 16 (February 1887), 19; Helen Ludlow, *Are the Eastern Industrial Schools for Indian Children a Failure?* (Philadelphia, 1886), pp. 4–6.

51. *ARCIA,* 1888, p. 13.

52. SCA to Whittlesey and Smiley, March 15, 1888, Hampton Institute Archives.

53. *ARCIA,* 1888, pp. 11, 13.

54. *Southern Workman,* 41 (October 1912), 547; Peabody, *Education for Life,* pp. 167–68.

55. SCA, *Indian Education at Hampton,* p. 13.

56. *Hampton Annual Report,* 1881, pp. 33–34.

57. Elaine Goodale, "The Indians of Today," *Anniversary Exercises of Hampton Normal and Agricultural Institute, Thursday, May 20th, 1886,* Hampton Institute Archives.

58. *Ten Years' Work,* p. 49.

59. Ludlow, *Eastern Industrial Schools,* p. 7; M. F. Armstrong, Ludlow, Goodale, *Hampton Institute,* pp. 17–18; *Twenty-Two Years' Work of the Hampton Normal and Agricultural Institute at Hampton, Virginia: Records of Negro and Indian Graduates and Ex-Students* (Hampton, 1893), pp. 295–96, 317–18, 487.

60. Ibid., p. 203.

61. *Hampton Normal and Agricultural Institute,* Department of the Interior, Bureau of Education, Bulletin no. 27 (Washington, 1923), p. 91.

62. Susan LaFlesche file, Anna Dawson file, Records of Graduates and Ex-Students, Hampton Institute Archives; Tingey, "Indians and Blacks Together," pp. 207–9.

63. Thomas Sloan file, William Jones file, ibid.; Tingey, "Indians and Blacks Together," pp. 213–16.

64. Ibid.; Engs, *Freedom's First Generation,* p. 156.

Booker T. Washington's
Discovery of Jews

LOUIS R. HARLAN

B OOKER T. WASHINGTON in his struggle up from slavery learned
many things the hard way, through experience. His discovery
of and understanding with American Jewry was no exception. It
began with a faux pas. In an early article in a black church
magazine, Washington told the success story of a Jew, only a few
months from Europe, who had passed through the town of Tuskegee, Alabama, four years earlier with all of his earthly possessions
on his back. Settling at a crossroads hamlet, the Jew had hired
himself out as a laborer, soon rented land to sublet to others,
opened a store, and bought land; "and there is not a man, woman
nor child within five miles who does not pay tribute to this Jew."
What Washington assumed to be the unexceptionable moral of
this story was that "the blackest Negro in the United States"
had the same opportunity to succeed in business, pure and simple,
as "a Jew or a white man." He added, "Of course the black man,
like the Jew or white man, should be careful as to the kind of
business he selects." Washington's article, entitled "Taking Advantage of Our Disadvantages," suggested that blacks should enter
the occupations that white prejudice had left to them.[1]

Washington's expression "a Jew or a white man" aroused the
wrath of Rabbi Isaac Mayer Wise of Cincinnati, editor of the
American Israelite and one of the founders of Reform Judaism.
Wise was particularly sensitive on this point, for he had been an
apologist for Southern slaveholders and a Copperhead during the
Civil War. What Washington needed was "a lesson in primary
ethnology," wrote Wise. Assuming that Washington was a clergyman because his article appeared in a church periodical, Wise

added, "All Jewish Americans are Caucasians and when the Rev. Prof. uses such an expression as 'a Jew or a white man' he commits a scientific blunder." Wise then committed his own racist blunder: "Possibly, however, the Rev. Prof. is only exhibiting the secret malice that invariably marks a servile nature seeking to assume a feeling of equality with something higher, which it does not possess."[2]

Fortunately, this contretemps with Rabbi Wise following Washington's first known reference to a Jew was only the prelude to his gradually unfolding knowledge and his fruitful collaboration not with Wise himself but with many other American Jews. Washington was not unique in bridging the cultural gap between these ethnically diverse peoples who shared a common experience of defamation, discrimination, and segregation. Many other black spokesmen, for example, suggested the Jewish model for the rising black businessman,[3] the Jewish demonstration of the value of group solidarity,[4] and the common black and Jewish experience of proscription, suffering, and achievement. The National Association for the Advancement of Colored People also represented a collaboration of Jews with blacks and other Gentiles. Washington's experience, therefore, is significant chiefly because it was representative, because it was an early example of collaboration between the two groups, and because Washington's Tuskegee Institute was unique among black educational institutions of his time in seeking and securing substantial aid from Jewish philanthropy.[5] As we shall see, Washington also encouraged Jewish millionaires to contribute to black public schools and smaller industrial institutes founded by Tuskegee graduates.

Washington's growing involvement with Jews was also a voyage of discovery. What began in the embarrassment of his exchange with Isaac Wise became a pragmatic alliance for the endowment of his school with the Jewish millionaires, mostly of German origin, and gradually grew into a sympathetic identity with the poor Jewish immigrants of the Lower East Side and the victims of the violent pogroms of Eastern Europe in the late nineteenth and early twentieth centuries. The richness of detail in Washington's voluminous private papers affords the reader a glimpse of the beginnings of a collaboration between Negro and Jew that later flowered in the civil-rights movement of the 1960s.

In addition to his confusion about the racial identity of Jews, Washington shared with other rural and small-town Americans of his day a rhetorical anti-Semitism that identified Jews with the crossroads storekeepers who exacted high prices for goods bought on credit and charged usurious interest for crop mortgages. The Populist movement that dominated farm politics in the South and West in the 1890s also in some degree partook of anti-Semitism.[6] Unfavorable references to Jews apparently colored some of Washington's early speeches, but in his effort to secure donations to his school in the Northern cities, it was in his interest to drop his prejudice. "I would leave out the Jew as distinct from others in cheating the people," his close white adviser, the Reverend Robert C. Bedford, wrote him as he planned a fund-raising effort in Chicago. "He [the Jew] may have started it but others were quick and eager learners. I have always admired your addresses because of their freedom from any personal or race attack. This little tradition about the Jew I notice once in a while creeps in."[7]

Washington had no particular love for the immigrants who poured into the United States during his lifetime, regarding them as labor competitors of the Negro, and also perhaps unconsciously as threats to the stability of a society dominated by the rich donors to Tuskegee. He made an exception of Jews, however, particularly of Jews with money. Since these wealthier Jews were usually the settled and culturally assimilated German Jews rather than the newly arrived, more "Jewish" Jews from Eastern Europe, it was easier for Washington to see them as potential benefactors of his school than as potential competitors of his race. Despite their foreign tongue, religion, and habits, Jews symbolized to Washington a shrewd attendance to business instead of politics and abstract rights. When Simon Marx, a Tuskegee merchant, ran for county sheriff, Washington and other Tuskegee Institute faculty members voted for him and rejoiced in his election.[8] "The Jew that was once in about the same position that the Negro is to-day has now complete recognition," Washington observed, "because he has entwined himself about America in a business or industrial sense. Say or think what we will, it is the tangible or visible element that is going to tell largely during the next twenty years in the solution of the race problem."[9]

Blacks had a more compelling reason, however, to emulate the Jews in their group solidarity and pride. In *The Future of the American Negro* (1899), which was the closest he ever came to expounding a coherent racial philosophy, Washington wrote, "We have a very bright and striking example in the history of the Jews in this and other countries. There is, perhaps, no race that has suffered so much, not so much in America as in some of the countries in Europe. But these people have clung together. They have had a certain amount of unity, pride, and love of race; and, as the years go on, they will be more and more influential in this country—a country where they were once despised, and looked upon with scorn and derision. It is largely because the Jewish race has had faith in itself. Unless the Negro learns more and more to imitate the Jew in these matters, to have faith in himself, he cannot expect to have any high degree of success."[10]

As news of the Russian pogroms filled the newspapers, Washington sympathized with Jews as victims of persecution. "Not only as a citizen of the American Republic, but as a member of a race which has, itself, been the victim of much wrong and oppression," he said in a statement for the Kishineff Relief League of Chicago in 1904, "my heart goes out to our Hebrew fellow-sufferers across the sea."[11] Washington could always find a cheerful aspect of any situation, however. Speaking to a mixed audience in Little Rock in 1905, he noted, "In Russia there are one-half as many Jews as there are Negroes in this country, and yet I feel sure that within a month more Jews have been persecuted and killed than the whole number of our people who have been lynched during the past forty years, but this, of course, is no excuse for lynching."[12]

Jews frequently reminded Washington of their common bond of victimization. Rabbi Alfred G. Moses of Mobile, who was spellbound by one of Washington's speeches, sent him works on Jewish history to give him "a new conception of the Jews."[13] The rabbi's brother in New York invited Washington to dinner at the East Side settlement house where he lived and worked at problems similar to those Washington was meeting in the South. "We have people here whose faults and peculiarities are the result of persecution, as is the case with the Negro," wrote J. Garfield Moses. "So surely as the Negro is persecuted and dealt unfairly with, so surely will the status and the security of the Jews be the next object of attack."[14]

Louis Edelman, a Jewish physician in Huntsville, Alabama, befriended Washington and Tuskegee Institute in a variety of ways. Spending two days on the campus in 1903, he worked with the school physician to treat, free of charge, all students with eye, ear, or nose troubles, his specialty. He gave a lecture to an audience of a thousand in the chapel on "The Jew: His Persecutions and Achievements."[15] Edelman also defended the school against its Southern detractors in letters to the editor of Southern newspapers, but in conservative terms that suggested that a Southern attack on Tuskegee would lead to Northern interference. When Washington sent a copy of one of Edelman's letters to the chairman of the Tuskegee trustees as an example of Southern white support, the trustee replied, "Glad to see the courage of the man, and of the paper to print it. Is he an American, or Hebrew?"[16]

Tuskegee Institute attracted many Jewish supporters, partly because of Washington's aggressive canvass for funds among them and his persuasiveness as an intergroup diplomat. The nondenominational character of the institution also, no doubt, appealed to Jews of goodwill who would hesitate to aid black schools affiliated with Protestant denominations. With Jews as with Unitarians, Washington never allowed his own nominal affiliation with the Baptist faith to inhibit his active cultivation of millionaires. For whatever reasons, Jewish commitment to Tuskegee grew, both among Southern Jewish neighbors and those in the Northern cities. By Washington's own account, in 1911 "the majority of white people who come here for commencement are composed of Jews."[17] Two Jewish merchants of nearby Montgomery who did business with the school, Selig Gassenheimer and Charles F. Moritz, donated small prizes to be awarded to students at commencement, and Gassenheimer also gave money for the erection of a small building on the campus.[18] In 1905 a rabbi for the first time delivered the commencement sermon.[19]

Tuskegee originally modeled itself after Hampton Institute, where Washington had received his own education, and appealed to the old Protestant wealth and the Sunday-school collections of New England for its support. Around the turn of the twentieth century, however, Washington shifted his Northern fund-raising headquarters from Boston to New York and came into closer contact with the new wealth of industry and finance. In the same period Jewish bankers and merchants began to figure more prominently among the donors. In 1904 the idea occurred to Washington of "inviting Mr. [Paul M.] Warburg or some Hebrew of his standing" to join the board of trustees. "I feel that we need to put new life into the Board," he wrote the board chairman. He thought of two New Englanders, one a small businessman and the other a retired clergyman, who "in some way ought to be gotten rid of," as "Neither of these are of very much value to us."[20] Washington persuaded the two New Englanders to resign for the good of the school and proposed Paul M. Warburg, the New York investment banker. He was unanimously elected, and took his seat on the board.[21]

At about the same time as Warburg's election, other wealthy Jews began or increased their support of Tuskegee. Jacob and Mortimer Schiff, James Loeb, and Felix Warburg, all members of Kuhn, Loeb and Company, Paul Warburg's banking firm, gave donations. So did the Seligmans, the Lehmans, Joseph Pulitzer, Jacob Billikopf, and Julian Mack. Even Joel E. Spingarn, a founder and officer of the NAACP, made a small annual contribution to Washington's school while opposing Washington's race leadership.[22] The immensely wealthy Jacob H. Schiff, another early supporter of the NAACP, had such confidence in Washington that in 1909 he made him his almoner for other black schools. Schiff wrote to Washington that he felt "entirely at a loss to know where to contribute properly and justly," and put $3,000 at Washington's disposal, one-third to go to Tuskegee, smaller amounts to four other schools, and the remainder to schools of which Washington approved.[23] He annually sent Washington a list of the schools he had aided the preceding year on Washington's advice and asked him to make any changes he desired. The contributions, mostly of $100 or less, went principally to industrial schools on the Tuskegee model.[24] Schiff continued this practice until Washington's death in 1915, when his total contributions had increased threefold. He said of Washington soon after the latter's death: "I feel that America has lost one of its great men, whose life has been full of usefulness—not only to his own race, but to the white people of the United States."[25]

Though Paul Warburg resigned from the Tuskegee board of trustees in 1909, two years later Julius Rosenwald, president of Sears, Roebuck and Company, was profoundly moved by reading Washington's autobiography. He visited Tuskegee and a few months later agreed to become a trustee.[26] Rosenwald promoted the school with the same enthusiasm that he simultaneously showed in conditional grants for constructing black YMCA buildings in several major cities. He interested members of his family, friends, and other Chicago capitalists in Tuskegee, brought several parties of distinguished and wealthy visitors to the school in his private railroad car, and annually sent to Washington lists of wealthy men, many of them Jews, whom he should approach for contributions. The most imaginative of Tuskegee's philanthropists, Rosenwald gave bonuses to the Tuskegee faculty, and even sent surplus and defective Sears shoes and hats to be sold at low rates to students.[27]

Rosenwald's enthusiasm spread to some of Washington's other interests. In celebration of his fiftieth birthday in 1912 he gave $25,000 to be distributed by Washington on a matching basis to schools that had grown out of Tuskegee or were doing similar work.[28] At Washington's urging he aided the all-Negro town of Mound Bayou, Mississippi, by investing in its most ambitious enterprise, a cotton-oil mill, and lending money to its bank, both of which failed in the hard times of 1914.[29] Rosenwald's most ambitious philanthropic enterprise, however, involved a plan Washington had presented to him for aid to country public schools for blacks. Washington suggested that Rosenwald offer a small amount of money if patrons of a school would match it in money, materials, or labor for the construction of a small schoolhouse.[30] Under this program, which was institutionalized under the Rosenwald Foundation after Washington's death, hundreds of Rosenwald schools sprang up in places where white school authorities had refused to provide school facilities for blacks, and ever since freedom the black rural schools had met on weekdays in the single rooms of black country churches. Washington's close personal partnership in philanthropy with Rosenwald was the high point of his efforts to enlist the support of wealthy Jews.

Washington was always the realist. Despite his growing regard for individual Jews, both Northern millionaires and the Southern middle class, he told Tuskegee's business agent to buy supplies for the school whenever possible from Gentiles. "In looking over our bills from Montgomery," he wrote, "I very much fear that we are getting our trade too much centered in the hands of a few Jews. Wherever we can get equally fair treatment in prices and quality of goods from persons other than Jews, I prefer to have our trade scattered among them. In creating public sentiment in favor of the institution the Jews cannot be of much service. . . ." That this was a realistic business judgment rather than anti-Semitism, however, is suggested by an exception he made. He told the business agent, "Where all things are equal with our giving trade to Jews, I hope you will bear in mind Mr. J. Loeb. Quite a number of years ago when other wholesale merchants refused absolutely to deal with us and were threatened by boycott by the town merchants in case they did deal with us, Loeb paid no attention to our want of money and threatened boycott in town and stood by us and sold us goods at wholesale prices. Of course, after he was brave enough to stem the tide for several months, others fell in line, but we owe him a great deal for helping us out in this way in our earlier days."[31]

Washington found parallels in the historical experiences of blacks and Jews that bound the two peoples together more deeply than did either Jewish philanthropy or the Jewish example of self-help. In his early childhood Washington's favorite part of the Bible was the story of Moses leading the children of Israel out of the house of bondage, through the wilderness, and into the promised land. He had first heard that story from his mother when they were both slaves. "I learned in slavery to compare the condition of the Negro with that of the Jews in bondage in Egypt," he wrote in 1911, "so I have frequently, since freedom, been compelled to compare the prejudice, even persecution which the Jewish people have had to face and overcome in different parts of the world, with the disadvantages of the Negro in the United States and elsewhere." He had seen the poor Jews of New York and London, but it was not until his tour of the Continent in 1910 that he learned how life in the ghetto really was. He had thought he knew Jews on the sidewalks of New York, but after seeing those of Poland he decided that the Jews he had known were already halfway toward being Americanized. Polish Jews had lived for a thousand years, Washington observed, "as exiles and, more or less, like prisoners. Instead of trying to become like the other people among whom they lived, they seemed to be making every effort to preserve and emphasize the ways in which they were different from those about them."[32]

Washington was puzzled by the changing character of anti-Semitic prejudice from place to place and by its often religious rather than racial nature.[33] In a book about his European tour, *The Man Farthest Down,* he took the rather complacent view that, compared with the other downtrodden peoples of the earth, the Negro in the United States and especially in the South was better off.[34] On the other hand the Jews, who in America and Western Europe were often wealthy, were in Russia and parts of Austria-Hungary among the poorest of civilized people. The Jews showed superiority not in wealth but in education. Not only in America did Jews rival the recently freed blacks in their "yearning for learning," but even in Russia, where they were burdened with educational restrictions, they outdid the rest of the population in literacy.[35]

Near the end of his life, when asked by the New York *Times* to name his favorite Shakespearean passage, Washington chose Shylock's speech in *The Merchant of Venice* that begins "I am a Jew."[36] Washington had begun his career full of misunderstandings about Jews, as illustrated by his controversy with Isaac M. Wise of the *American Israelite.* By the end of his life he had come to understand and appreciate Jews not only as exemplars of self-help and mutual help but as companions in travail and striving. "Hath not a Jew eyes? Hath not a Jew hands, organs, dimensions, senses, affections, passions? Fed with the same food, hurt with the same weapons, subject to the same diseases . . . ?" This passage from Shylock's speech was a parallel to the black man's plea to be treated as "a man and brother."

Through Washington's ceaseless journeys across the color line, many Jews learned to appreciate a black man's personal qualities. Rabbi Stephen S. Wise of the Free Synagogue in New York City, where Washington had spoken several times, wrote to Washington's widow on news of his death, "He was not only the guide and friend of one race but the servant and benefactor of two races."[37] In an obituary address at his synagogue, Wise said of the Black Moses: "He was more concerned about the Negro doing justice to himself than securing justice from the white race." Wise urged whites, however, to deal more justly with blacks than they had done, concluding with a statement that went to the heart of the race problem in America: "The inward memorial to Booker

Washington lies in a new and heretofore untried justness of attitude toward the Negro in remembering that he is not a problem
but a man, that the Negro is not a racial question but a fellow
human to be accepted and honored in the spirit of that justness
which is faith."[38]

Like Columbus, who discovered a new world but never reached
the mainland and died thinking it was Asia he had reached, Washington died unaware that he and Rabbi Stephen Wise were
present at the birth of brotherhood week. In his pursuit of the
rich Jew, Washington also never fully understood the masses of
the new immigrant Jews. He showed no awareness of Zionism, of
the sectarian rivalries within Judaism, of the tension between
Jewish assimilationism and nationalism, of the hold of unionism
and socialism on the Jewish working class, or even of the lynching
of Leo Frank, a Southern Jew.[39]

If Washington never reached the promised land, however, he
did move the blacks and the children of Israel far down the road
to the full partnership of the civil-rights movement. Even while
he was still alive, Jewish donors to Tuskegee found no incon-
sistency in also being the angels of the early NAACP. As Washington groped, through contacts with Jews, toward an understanding of both their differentness and their common humanity,
so many key figures in American Jewry in the early twentieth
century found in Booker T. Washington a bridge to understanding of America's deepest social problem. Paradoxically, it was
because of Washington's ordinariness—his conventional attitudes,
his intellectual mediocrity, his penchant for cliché—that he could
explain each group to the other in terms each could understand.

NOTES

1. Booker T. Washington (hereafter cited as BTW), "Taking Advantage of
Our Disadvantages," *A.M.E. Church Review*, 10 (1894), 478–83, reprinted in
Louis R. Harlan and Raymond W. Smock, eds., *The BTW Papers* (Urbana,
Ill., 1972–), III, 408–12.

2. *American Israelite*, 41 (July 26, 1894), 4. A sympathetic review of Wise's
views on slavery, abolitionism, and the Civil War is in James G. Heller,
Isaac M. Wise: His Life, Work, and Thought (New York, 1965), pp. 331–49.

3. This theme is developed in detail by Arnold Shankman, "Friend or Foe? Southern Blacks View the Jew 1880–1935," in Nathan M. Kaganoff and Melvin I. Urofsky. eds., *Turn to the South: Essays on Southern Jewry* (Charlottesville, 1979), pp. 109–14.

4. Ibid., pp. 115–16; "A Fellow Feeling Makes Us Wondrous Kind," editorial in Washington *Colored American,* May 6, 1899, p. 4; "A Few Lessons from Jews," Indianapolis *Freeman,* September 5, 1891, p. 1.

5. Lenora E. Berson, in *The Negroes and the Jews* (New York, 1971), pp. 63–79, noted that BTW made "the earliest recorded attempt" at active partnership with an American Jew, Julius Rosenwald. A more successful treatment of Jewish attitudes toward blacks, however, is Hasia R. Diner, *In the Almost Promised Land: American Jews and Blacks, 1915–1935* (Westport, Conn., 1977), which despite the dates of its title has much information on BTW's era. See also Robert G. Weisbord and Arthur Stein, *Bittersweet Encounter: The Afro-American and the American Jew* (Westport, Conn., 1970); Leonard Dinnerstein and Mary Dale Palsson, eds., *Jews in the South* (Baton Rouge, 1973).

6. On the historiographical controversy over the extent of Populist anti-Semitism, see particularly Oscar Handlin, "American Views of the Jew at the Opening of the Twentieth Century," *Publications of the American Jewish Historical Society,* 40 (1951); C. Vann Woodward, "The Populist Heritage and the Intellectuals," *American Scholar,* 29 (winter 1959–60), 55–72; Norman Pollack, "The Myth of Populist Anti-Semitism," *American Historical Review,* 68 (1962), 76–80; Norman Pollack, "Handlin on Anti-Semitism: A Critique of 'American Views of the Jew,'" *Journal of American History,* 51 (1964), 391–403; and Walter T. K. Nugent, *The Tolerant Populists: Kansas Populism and Nativism* (Chicago, 1963).

7. R. C. Bedford to BTW, January 14, 1896, Container 114, BTW Papers, Library of Congress. Documents from this collection will be referred to hereafter only by the container number, in parentheses.

8. William Jenkins to BTW, August 7, 1896, G. W. A. Johnston to BTW, August 13, 1896 (118).

9. BTW, "Industrial Training for the Negro," *Independent,* 50 (February 3, 1898), 146, in Harlan and Smock, eds., *BTW Papers,* IV, 373.

10. Reprinted in Harlan and Smock, eds., *BTW Papers,* V, 369–70. The Cleveland lawyer John P. Green expressed in 1895 a common black attitude in "The Jew and the Negro," Indianapolis *Freeman,* December 21, 1895, p. 3. He wrote, "We feel and think our lot in this so-called 'white man's country,' is a hard one; and in very truth it is . . . but when we scan the blood stained recitals of what the Jews have passed through since the destruction of Jerusalem, during the first century of our Christian era, and then note how conspicuous they are in all civilized communities for their real attainments along the lines of science, art, literature and finance, we may well cheer up and persevere along the same lines until victory crowns our efforts."

11. BTW to Mrs. A. F. D. Grey, ca. June 5, 1903, in Harlan and Smock, eds., *BTW Papers,* VII, 169. See also Arnold Shankman, "Brothers Across the Sea:

Afro-Americans on the Persecution of Russian Jews, 1881–1917," *Jewish Social Studies,* 37 (1975), 114–21.

12. Excerpt of address in Boston *Transcript,* December 4, 1905, clipping (27).

13. Alfred G. Moses to BTW, January 2 and 8, 1906 (328).

14. J. Garfield Moses to BTW, January 14, 1906 (809).

15. *Tuskegee Student,* 15 (May 9, 1903), 2; typescript of lecture, May 5, 1903 (257).

16. Birmingham *News,* September 5, 1903 (clipping), BTW to W. H. Baldwin, Jr., September 11, 1903, and Baldwin's marginal note (257).

17. BTW to Robert H. Terrell, April 4, 1911 (443).

18. A. R. Stewart to BTW, June 14, 1909, BTW to Selig Gassenheimer, June 16, 1909 (734).

19. A. J. Messing of Montgomery, Ala., in *Tuskegee Student,* 17 (June 17, 1905), 1.

20. BTW to W. H. Baldwin, Jr., May 20, 1904 (18). See also BTW to Baldwin, June 2, 1904 (18).

21. Marcus M. Marks to BTW, May 24, 1904, in Harlan and Smock, eds., *BTW Papers,* VII, 512; minutes of adjourned meeting of the Tuskegee Institute board of trustees, June 23, 1904 (18).

22. Spingarn to BTW, December 24, 1909 (736).

23. Schiff to BTW, June 16 and July 7, 1909 (47).

24. BTW to Schiff, March 6, 10, 16, and 17, 1910 (51).

25. Schiff to W. H. Holtzclaw, in Cyrus Adler manuscript, microfilm reel 677, Jacob H. Schiff Papers, American Jewish Archives, Hebrew Union College.

26. BTW to Ruth S. Baldwin, January 25, 1912 (916).

27. Julius Rosenwald to BTW, May 31, 1912 (56); William C. Graves to BTW, December 30, 1912 (66); BTW to Rosenwald, February 8, April 2, and September 19, 1913 (66); Morris S. Rosenwald to BTW, April 2, 1912 (755); BTW to Julius Rosenwald, undated draft, ca. May 1915 (78). For a survey of Jewish philanthropy and Tuskegee, see Diner, *In the Almost Promised Land,* pp. 166–72.

28. Rosenwald to BTW, August 5, 1912 (56).

29. A detailed account is August Meier, "Booker T. Washington and the Town of Mound Bayou," *Phylon,* 15 (1954), 396–401, reprinted in Meier and Elliott Rudwick, *Along the Color Line* (Urbana, Ill., 1976), pp. 217–23.

30. BTW outlined his plan in letters to Rosenwald, June 21 and September 12, 1912 (62).

31. BTW to Lloyd G. Wheeler, October 17, 1904 (551). BTW also urged a liberal order of stationery from one of the school's Jewish benefactors, Selig Gassenheimer. BTW to E. T. Attwell, April 4, 1911 (610).

32. BTW, "Race Prejudice in Europe," typescript, December 5, 1911 (957).

33. Actually, racial anti-Semitism, as represented by the writings of Houston Stewart Chamberlain, was on the increase in Europe and the United States in the late nineteenth and early twentieth centuries.

34. (New York, 1912), with Robert E. Park.

35. See Meyer Weinberg, "A Yearning for Learning: Blacks and Jews through History," *Integrated Education,* 7 (1969), 20–29.

36. Later he changed his favorite quotation to the passage in *Julius Caesar* that begins "There is a tide in the affairs of men." BTW to the editor of the New York *Times,* April 15, 18, 1914 (525).

37. Stephen S. Wise to Margaret M. Washington, November 15, 1915 (952).

38. Stephen S. Wise, "Booker Washington: American," *Southern Workman,* 45 (1916), 382–83, an abstract of his address.

39. Washington's silence may be explained by the fact that a black janitor testified he had helped Leo Frank to remove the body. If the Jew was found innocent, the black man was the logical suspect. Jonah Wise, who succeeded his father, Isaac M. Wise, as editor of the *American Israelite,* at first thought Frank guilty because he doubted that a Southern white jury would convict on the "unsupported testimony of a low type of negro," but after Frank was lynched he concluded that the real murderer was "the vicious and criminal negro." Wise's only consistency was his racism. Quoted in Eugene Levy, " 'Is the Jew a White Man?': Press Reaction to the Leo Frank Case, 1913–1915," *Phylon,* 35 (1974), 218–19.

Reconstruction

"An Empire over the Mind":
Emancipation, Race, and Ideology in the British West Indies and the American South

THOMAS C. HOLT

T HE first half of the nineteenth century was preeminently an
era of revolutions—in social and political thought, in social
and economic relations. We now know that the problem of slavery
was a vital nexus for the ideological transformations of the era
and that slave emancipation figured prominently in its political
and military upheavals. Beginning with Haiti at the turn of the
century and ending with Cuba and Brazil during its final decades,
slave-labor systems in the Western Hemisphere were eroded and
finally swept away in successive waves of slave revolt, wars of
national liberation, and internal conflicts between social classes.
Concurrent with and linked to the dramatic transition from slavery to free labor was the maturing of industrial capitalism and
the liberal democratic ideology that purported to explain and
justify the new bourgeois economic order.[1]

But while antislavery agitation was closely intertwined with
the rise of bourgeois ideology in the early decades of the century,
actual emancipation exposed the difficulty of applying that ideology to radical transformations in the social relations of culturally
different populations. In the wake of these developments, the late

Research and an early draft of this paper were completed while the author
was a fellow at the Center for Advanced Study in the Behavioral Sciences at
Stanford, California. I am grateful to the Center, the National Endowment
for the Humanities, the Andrew Mellon Foundation, and the Social Science Research Council for their support of the larger research and writing
project on which this essay is based. I am also much indebted to Rebecca Scott,
Peter Railton, and Barbara Fields for their thoughtful comments on the
manuscript.

nineteenth century witnessed the rise of an explicitly racist ideology that gained a hitherto unprecedented intellectual and social
legitimacy, clashed with critical premises of liberal democratic
thought, and undermined the promise of black emancipation.
Indeed, there appear to have been subtle relationships and inter-
actions between the social transformations occasioned by slave
emancipation and this subsequent racist reaction. Early social
reformers had posed the problem of slavery in a way that justified
a particular concept of freedom in the emerging capitalist social
order; by the late nineteenth century what one might call "the
problem of freedom" in former slave societies confronted many
of these same thinkers with difficulties inherent in liberal democratic thought. Racism appears to have been, in part, a means of
evading that confrontation.

The confrontation was most compelling in the British and the
American emancipation experiences. In ideological as well as
diplomatic terms, abolition in the British West Indies and in the
southern United States were major turning points in the international antislavery struggle. The emancipation of approximately
three-quarters of a million British West Indian and four million
American blacks eliminated well over half the entire slave population in the Western Hemisphere.[2] Furthermore, only in Haiti
was the emancipation process more rapid than that under British
and American auspices; in both places the process was completed
over a four-year period. Of course, in the British West Indies
this "gradualism" was by design, while in the United States it was
caused by the vicissitudes of war. Hundreds of thousands of
American slaves fled to Union lines from the commencement of
the Civil War in 1861; their quest for freedom was accelerated
by the Emancipation Proclamation in 1863 and completed with
the Thirteenth Amendment in 1865. British West Indian planters,
however, were paid compensation totaling £20 million sterling
for their slave property and enjoyed an official four-year transition period between the abolition of legal slavery on August 1,
1834, and the complete emancipation of their workers on August
1, 1838. During this so-called apprenticeship period, the freedmen
were required to remain on the plantations and to work much
as they had before. They could not be subjected to corporal
punishment by their former masters, however, and part of their
week was reserved for their own use, preferably to work for wages.

Special magistrates, whose duties and recruitment were similar to those of the American Freedmen's Bureau agents, were appointed to supervise the transition and to protect the freedmen from abuse; however, they could and did order physical punishment to force recalcitrant freedmen to work.[3]

It was not simply the size and political significance of emancipation in the British possessions and the United States that affected other slaveholding powers; American and British policy debates shaped the terms of discussion if not the actual policies pursued elsewhere. For example, in July 1839, Alexis de Tocqueville completed a study of the British West Indian experience and recommended an emancipation plan for the French islands to the Chamber of Deputies. Following the British precedent, he suggested that a special transition period separate the ending of formal slavery and complete emancipation. This period, he thought, was "the most favorable moment to found that empire over the minds and habits of the black population" that was essential to preserving social order. Moreover, he proposed that during this transition period the French must be prepared, if necessary, to "compel the laborious and manly habits of liberty." Drawing attention to Tocqueville's remarks, C. Vann Woodward has observed that the problem of reconciling force with freedom, and liberty with necessity, represented a "paradox that lay at the heart of the problem of emancipations and reconstructions everywhere in the world."[4]

The political systems of Great Britain and the United States differed radically, and the British West Indies and the American South were politically, economically, and demographically distinct. Nevertheless, policymakers at the White House and in Whitehall posed the problem of emancipation in strikingly similar political and philosophical terms and wrestled with the same paradoxical issues. These similarities exist no doubt because the terms of their policy discussions were derived from the broader ideological presuppositions that British and American policymakers shared. The task of compelling the "voluntary" transformation of slaves into wage laborers, the crux of the problem of formulating emancipation policy everywhere, found precedents in the ongoing transformation of white agricultural workers into an industrial working class. Yet, the fact that such a transformation would pose an intellectual "problem" is comprehensible only in the context of the prevailing liberal democratic ideology of the emancipators, that is, the paradoxical situation of having to compel people to be "free" was rooted in the character of the "freedom" espoused.[5]

Defining freedom was the beginning of the difficulty. David Brion Davis has revealed how social reformers used slavery as a curious negative referent with which to define the otherwise elusive concept of freedom. For none was this difficulty more poignant than for English Quakers, the vanguard of British industrial development as well as of the abolitionist movement. For them slavery helped define the meaning of freedom within a capitalist economy and a liberal political state. Slavery, being clearcut and concrete, could be used to symbolize "all the forces that threatened the true destiny of man." Freedom, being abstract and liable to misuse, was more difficult to define in substance. Thus slavery helped locate the outer boundaries of freedom; it was the antithesis of freedom. Slavery meant subordination to the physical coercion and personal dominion of an arbitrary master; freedom meant submission only to the impersonal forces of the marketplace and to the rational and uniform constraints of law. Slavery meant involuntary labor for the master's benefit; freedom meant voluntary contracts determined by mutual consent, which theoretically should guarantee that one received the value of one's labor. Slavery meant little, if any, legal protection of property, person, or family; freedom meant equal protection of the laws. Historians might empirically determine that slavery and capitalism were compatible, but to contemporaries of the reform era, slavery was logically synonymous with irrational monopoly power in both labor markets and commodity markets. The power of the abolition movement in this era derived in large part from the fact that slavery was such a convenient foil for free markets, free labor, and free men.[6]

Moreover, the abolitionists and those men who fashioned and implemented emancipation policies were all heirs to a historically unique set of concepts about human behavior, about the sources of social action, and about the nature of political and economic justice. First, there was a materialist assumption regarding man's nature: man is a creature of insatiable material appetites, and all humans share an innate desire for self-improvement and personal gain. Second, it was assumed that in general men have a natural aversion to labor and that therefore material incentives are necessary to make them work. From these unquestioned assumptions was deduced a coherent view of political economy. Its key axiom was the notion C. B. Macpherson has called "possessive individualism"—namely, that society consists of an aggregation of individuals each of whom is proprietor of his own person and capacities, for which he owes nothing to society. Consequently, social action (at least beyond the bounds of the family) is reducible to exchange relations between these individual proprietors. The mainspring of the entire socioeconomic and political system is "that men do calculate their most profitable courses and do employ their labour, skill, and resources as that calculation dictates." Political order exists merely as "a calculated device for the protection of this property and for the maintenance of an orderly relation of exchange." In such a social order human freedom is defined as autonomy from the will of others, except in relations entered into voluntarily with a view to one's own interest, that is, self-interested contractual relations. But autonomy also means that whether one eats or starves depends solely on one's individual will and capacities. In the liberal democratic state, social relations—in their political as well as their economic dimensions—are ultimately self-regulating, impersonal, and therefore just.[7]

The efforts of British and American policymakers to define a framework for the transition from slavery to freedom reveal the force of these ideas. The essential difference between freedom and slavery, as Viscount Howick lectured the members of Parliament during the debate on British West Indian emancipation in 1833, was that free men worked "because they are convinced that it is in their interest to do so." Theirs was a rational calculation of the relative advantages to be gained from industry over the privation to be expected if they "indulge in their natural inclination for repose." Slaves worked out of fear of punishment and for the benefit of others.[8]

Three decades later, Americans echoed Howick's sentiments. "The incentive to faithful labor," advised the Boston *Advertiser* in 1865, "is self-interest." This pithy rule confirmed sentiments articulated earlier by the men and women who had gathered at Port Royal, South Carolina, to conduct the first experiment with black free labor in the American South. One of them, William Gannett, declared, "Let all the natural laws of labor, wages, competition,

&c come into play—and the sooner will habits of responsibility, industry, self-dependence & manliness be developed." His colleague Edward Philbrick added, "Negro labor has got to be employed, if at all, because it is *profitable,* and it has got to come into the market like everything else, subject to the supply and demand." Upon returning from Port Royal in May 1862, John Murray Forbes, a pre–Civil War abolitionist and postwar investor in Southern cotton, assessed the South Carolina situation for readers of the Boston *Advertiser:* "All those engaged in the experiment will testify that the negro has the same selfish element in him which induces other men to labor, and that with a fair prospect of benefit . . . he will work like other human beings." Elsewhere Forbes put the matter more bluntly: "The necessity of getting a living is the great secret of providing for sheep, negroes and humans generally."[9]

It was not so simple as all that, however. While it was true that "sheep, negroes and humans generally" work to keep from starving, it did not follow that freedmen would apply themselves to the production of plantation staples or that their labor would be disciplined and reliable. The problem was not merely to make ex-slaves work, but to make them into a working class, that is, a class that would submit to the market because it adhered to the *values* of a bourgeois society: regularity, punctuality, sobriety, frugality, and economic rationality.

One of the more thoughtful examinations of this central problem of freedom, from the liberal point of view, was written in 1833 by Henry Taylor, a middle-level bureaucrat in the British Colonial Office. In colonies like Jamaica, wrote Taylor, where the population density was low and large areas of the interior had not been devoted to plantation staples, the problem of getting the freedmen to work on the sugar estates would be formidable. Jamaican planters had encouraged their slaves to grow foodstuffs on interior lands to supplement their weekly rations of salt fish and corn. They allocated garden plots either on the plantation itself or on land leased from others. By custom, Jamaican slaves had come to treat these so-called provision grounds as their private property. They sold their surplus produce in the weekend markets of nearby villages and towns and retained the profits for themselves. Taylor noted that testimony before the House of Commons had shown conclusively that freedmen could earn their accustomed subsistence needs by working these provision grounds for little better than one day a week. The key question, therefore, was "What, except compulsion, shall make them work six?"[10]

Taylor brushed aside abolitionist testimony that the slaves' industry on their provision grounds showed they would continue to work on plantations after emancipation. Slaves who worked one or two days to purchase necessities would not necessarily work five or six more days for superfluous luxuries. They could be expected to expand their workweek sixfold only if their needs and wants were likewise expanded; this was an "extremely improbable" occurrence in the foreseeable future. "It is true that the wants and desires of mankind are indefinitely expansive," wrote Taylor, echoing a basic premise of Adam Smith's *Wealth of Nations,* "but when the habits of a whole population are concerned, the expansion must be necessarily gradual. Their habits cannot be suddenly changed." For the moment, one had to expect that the freedmen would strive merely for the possessions they were accustomed to, or for those which persons of slightly higher status—that is, the black headmen and estate artisans—possessed. It would be reasonable to assume that "it will only be in the long course of years and progress of society that their wants will creep up the scale of luxury, and be characterized by that exigency in the higher degrees of it which might suffice to animate and prolong their labours."[11]

Taylor thought that the dangers implicit in the proposed West Indian emancipation and the subsequent needs of the colonial economy would not permit such delay. It was necessary that industrious habits be inculcated in some manner; work discipline must be internalized by the freedmen without the normal spur of necessity or desire. The problem, therefore, was to overcome the legacy of slavery. "The state of slavery if it implies much injustice, implies also much ignorance and want of moral cultivation," Taylor concluded. Being "ignorant, destitute of moral cultivation, and . . . habituated to dependence," slaves required "both a sense of subordination in themselves, and the exercise by others over them of a strict and daily discipline." But there was reason to believe that under "disinterested instructors" they would advance in civilization. Once it had been thought that blacks were intellectually inferior, but the preponderant evidence presented to Parliament revealed striking cultural progress. Under the tutelage of missionaries, the slaves showed a strong desire to learn and were "a quick and intelligent race of people." Of course, some racial differences remained. Taylor rejected one witness's testimony that the blacks possessed "shrewd" intellects; he thought their mental character might be better described as rash, volatile, and somewhat shallow, "the intelligence, in short, of minds which had neither discipline nor cultivation, and nothing but natural vivacity to enlighten them."[12]

Given their character and the absence of sufficient incentives to work for wages, freedmen were likely to relapse "into a barbarous indolence" if suddenly or completely emancipated. Experience showed that where population density was low, people have a "strong propensity to scatter themselves" and to live in the wild as hunter-gatherers. A society must be "condensed" to be civilized, otherwise a situation develops wherein "capitalists [will be] shorn of their profits by the want of labour, and . . . those who *should be* labourers, turning squatters and idlers, and living like beasts in the woods."[13]

Given this situation, then, the government's objective should be "to devise a system of civil government" that would redeem West Indian communities from barbarism. An emancipation measure must be drafted "which shall preserve the frame-work of the present system of society in the West Indies, whilst it calls into immediate operation a power calculated to place that system substantially in the state of rapid transition." Taylor's plan, consciously modeled after the Spanish system of *coartación*, or gradual self-purchase by the slave, was designed to achieve this end. "On this plan," he recalled years later, "I conceived that before [the slave's] bondage ceased, he would have acquired habits of self-command and voluntary industry to take with him into freedom, by which *he* would be saved from a life of savage sloth and the planter from ruin."[14]

Taylor's plan provided that the value of all slaves between six and seventy years of age would be calculated and the British government would purchase one-sixth of their time, that is, one day. Thereafter the slave could use the earnings of that "free" day to purchase another day, and so forth, until he was entirely free. The key feature of the system was that the slave would earn his freedom by his own industry. Thus "the operation of the measure would be in accordance with the great moral principle of the government of men, which would call their own powers and virtues into action for their own profit and advantage; and bring home to them the consciousness of a moral agency and responsibility, by making the good and evil of their lives a result of their own conduct."[15]

Taylor's plan was not adopted by the British government. In trying to reconcile liberal democratic principles with the pragmatic needs of the plantation economy on the one hand and the political needs of the Whig government on the other, the plan stumbled over internal contradictions that radical abolitionists were quick to point out. The notion of earning one's freedom was antithetical to their (and Taylor's) basic premises about the nature of man, society, and social justice. Nevertheless, the apprenticeship system actually adopted was subject to the same errors and attracted similar criticism. Part of the planters' compensation, after all, was the forty and one-half hours per week that West Indian apprentices were forced to work on the estates without pay. Taylor and his political critics espoused the same basic principles and concepts; they differed only on details of implementation. Taylor's plan drew the most fire because it unwittingly exposed the blatant contradictions in all these schemes to reconcile black freedom with the planters' continued prosperity, but it was also the clearest statement of capitalist ethics and liberal values.

Taylor's attention focused on the laboring portion of the slave's day, week, or life; one's status as free or slave and, moreover, one's value were defined exclusively in terms of one's economic relationships. Thus freedom was parceled out into six equal parts congruent with the six-day workweek. After the first day had been purchased for him, the slave's access to freedom would be determined solely by his own desire for self-improvement and capacity for hard work. Taylor recognized that any inequalities in the circumstances as well as the character of the slaves would enable some to achieve freedom sooner than others, but such inequities—of industriousness, physical power, and local environment—exist naturally and justly "amongst men at all times and under every system of society." The able and worthy slaves would quickly gain their freedom, "leaving only an idle and spendthrift residue, whose liberation from arbitrary control would be duly retarded." Those who refused or were unable to embrace the values of capitalist society were to remain slaves.[16]

The problem that Taylor's memorandum highlights is that the necessity that leads men to work is culturally defined and therefore varies from culture to culture. Thus Taylor recognized that the remaking of slaves into a working class involved remaking the slaves' culture. As long as the freedmen limited their material aspirations to goods they had received as slaves, their interest in working for wages would be insufficient to maintain the production of plantation staples. Therefore, the physical coercion of slavery must be replaced by more subtle stimuli. Those insatiable material appetites that all humans were alleged to be blessed with needed to be awakened in the freed slaves.

British policymakers were quick to see the connection between stimulating the consumer desires of the freedmen and the economic health of the plantations. Special Magistrate John Daughtrey made the connection explicit in an 1836 report to the Colonial Office about conditions in Jamaica. "It is quite overlooked, that compulsion may exist without coercion, but of a rational, that is, of the highest and strongest kind, a moral compulsion arising from the presence of felt wants, whether natural or artificial." To create artificial wants the colonial secretary, Lord Grey (formerly Viscount Howick), urged Jamaican authorities to adopt low import duties, thereby encouraging blacks to purchase imported foodstuffs and clothing rather than to produce them at home. Such a fiscal policy, the colonial secretary wrote the Jamaican governor, "tends to encourage the laborer to form tastes for the gratification of which he must earn money by working for hire."[17]

Americans were also aware of the connection between black consumer desires and the larger economic and social order. John Miller McKim returned to Philadelphia in 1862 from Port Royal, waxing eloquent about the greatly expanded market for Northern goods in the South in the postwar period. "They [the Negroes] begin to demand articles of household use also such as pots, kettles, pans, brushes, brooms, knives, forks, spoons, soap, candles, combs, Yankee clocks, etc." In 1866 the New York *Herald* praised the role of business-minded people in managing freedmen's affairs in the South and made explicit the links between material consumption, education, and the preservation of social order. "Negroes will unquestionably be made better members of society, less subject to the influences of the enemies of social order, more industrious, because more ambitious to have the comforts and luxuries of life, if they can be thoroughly educated, than if they were allowed to remain in ignorance. A negro with no needs beyond a slave's allowance and a couple of suits of osnaburg a year, has far less motive to exert himself than one who sports a gold watch and fine clothes." The New York *Independent* expanded upon this theme. "Families that once fed out of the pot in which their hominy was cooked—the pot being their only utensil, and the hominy the only article of food—now breakfast, dine and sup as do other people, sitting down at a table, with food before them varying in character and decently served."[18]

Almost thirty years before, Special Magistrate Richard Chamberlain, a coloured Jamaican native, had voiced similar sentiments as he lectured the Jamaican freedmen on the "duties and responsibilities of a rational and unfettered freedom."

You are not going to be satisfied with the osnaburgh and rontoon clothing, which you have heretofore been accustomed to receive; you are not now, much less will you be hereafter, contented with a pot of coco soup and a herring tail for your dinners. Your wives and daughters will require their fine clothes for their chapel, churches, and holidays. You will visit your friends with your coat and your shoes, and you will require your dinners prepared for you with some respect to comfort and cleanliness; your soup will be seasoned with beef and pork; and in order to obtain these, the comforts and necessities of civilized life, you will have to labour industriously—for the more work you do, the more money you must obtain, and the better will you be enabled to increase and extend your comforts.[19]

Furthermore, Chamberlain added, even if the freedmen could achieve all these consumer comforts by working only two days each week, they should still insist upon working the other four in order to accumulate savings "for the winter of your days, when you will have no master's bounty or humanity to appeal to."

The state papers produced by Americans—though generally less full or articulate than Taylor's memorandum—expressed identical propositions about human behavior, the principles of social action, and the significance of race. In the spring of 1863, Secretary of War Edwin M. Stanton assigned three social reformers—Robert Dale Owen, Samuel Gridley Howe, and James McKaye—the task of studying the problems involved in the transition from slavery to free labor and recommending appropriate policies and programs. The report of this Freedmen's Inquiry Commission formed the basis for the establishment two years later of the U.S. Freedmen's Bureau, which like the British Special Magistracy was charged with overseeing the immediate transition from slavery.

Although the commissioners specifically rejected the unsuccessful British apprenticeship system as a model for American policy, they strongly recommended a very similar "guided" transition from slavery to free labor, during which the federal government would act as the temporary guardian, protector, and educator of the freedmen. In the first instance, they felt, the freedmen had to be taught that "emancipation means neither idleness nor gratuitous work, but fair labor for fair wages." The commissioners urged that the freedmen be given "a fair chance," but no more than that. There should be no compulsory contracts to labor, no statutory rate of wages, no interference between the hirer and the hired, and, except for antivagrancy legislation, no regulation of workers' movements. Thus freedom was defined in terms of wage labor, and wage labor meant competition in a market regulated only by "the natural laws of supply and demand."[20]

Freedom to compete did not imply equality, however. The commissioners were confident that "the African race . . . lacks no essential aptitude for civilization," but they did not expect blacks in general to equal whites in the race of life. Like Henry Taylor, they found blacks intelligent but different. They were "a knowing rather than a thinking race"; their intelligence was that of "quick observation rather than comprehensive views or strong sense." It was not, the commissioners felt, "a race that will ever take a lead in the material improvement of the world; but it will make for itself, whenever it has fair play, respectable positions, [and] comfortable homes." The freedman would become "a useful member of the great industrial family of nations. Once released from the disabilities of bondage, he will somewhere find, and will maintain, his own appropriate social position."[21]

The commissioners made clear that freedom of opportunity was not expected to lead to equality of condition, and they made racist assessments of black character and ability. But these should not distract us from the essential thrust of their report. Blacks were judged to have the same innate nature and potential desires and appetites as whites and were expected, therefore, to respond to the same market incentives. Consequently, they required neither perpetual guardianship nor special privileges. The import of such propositions and the subtlety of the distinctions were not lost on George King, a South Carolina freedman. "The Master he says we are all free, but it don't mean we is white. And it don't mean we is equal. Just equal for to work and earn our living and not depend on him for no more meat and clothes."[22]

The Freedmen's Bureau was established to implement the policy recommendations of the Inquiry Commissioners. Bureau officials carefully instructed freedmen and planters alike in the principles of a market economy. First of all, labor power—rather than the laborer—was now the commodity to be exchanged for wages. The rates of exchange would vary solely according to supply and demand. Neither the Bureau nor combinations of planters would be allowed to set wage prices artificially. Accordingly, General Clinton B. Fisk, the Bureau Commissioner for Tennessee, declared in a circular that labor would be "free to compete with other commodities in an open market." Similarly in Florida, T. W. Osborn, in later years a radical Republican politician, declared that "labor is a commodity in the market and that the possessor of it is entitled to the highest market value."[23]

Other Bureau officials expressed confidence in the freedmen's successful adoption of market values. Wages would induce thrift, J. W. Alvord, the Bureau's inspector of schools, assured General Oliver O. Howard. "The wants and opportunities of freedom show the worth of money, and what can be done with it." The South Carolina Bureau commissioner Rufus Saxton, after urging the freedmen to grow more cotton, the "regal crop," explained in phrases reminiscent of Special Magistrate Chamberlain the transformation he expected to observe in them. "In slavery you only thought of to-day. Having nothing to hope for beyond the present, you did not think of the future, but, like the ox and horse, thought only of food and work for the day. In freedom you must have an eye to the future, and have a plan and object in life."[24]

But it was clear to British and American authorities that the re-education and resocialization of the freedmen would require more formal institutions than the Freedmen's Bureau or the British Special Magistracy. In both instances religious and secular missionaries seemed best suited to achieve the desired transformation in ex-slave cultures and characters. Education seemed to offer the paradoxical possibility of encouraging greater material and moral aspirations as well as inculcating social restraint and acceptance of the status quo in social relations. "It was education which made us free, progressive, and conservative," declared the Boston cotton merchant Edward Atkinson in 1861, "and it is education alone which can keep us so." In a field report to President Andrew Johnson, Carl Schurz reiterated the conservative role of education. "The education of the lower orders is the only reliable basis of the civilization as well as of the prosperity of a people." Moreover, it was "the true ground upon which the efficiency and the successes of free labor society grows"; it was the means for making the freedman "an intelligent co-operator in the general movements of society." Similarly, a special magistrate reporting to the Jamaican governor insisted that "in infant schools we at once get over the obstacle to regulated thought and action in the negro's cottage."[25]

In the 1840s, Lord Elgin, the Jamaican governor, urged an even more directly targeted education program. The Jamaican sugar industry would revive only if planters adopted more technically innovative and scientific agricultural methods, he insisted. Therefore, Elgin organized agricultural fairs to encourage such innovations and urged planters to give cash rewards to blacks who had learned to plow or to use other labor-saving equipment efficiently. But the linchpin of his program would be industrial schools in which laborers would be taught modern methods of farming. The governor sought to overcome black resistance to innovation as well as to plantation work generally by attaching the adjective "scientific" to the manual education he wished the ex-slaves to embrace. Such a policy, he informed the Colonial Office, would "tend to redeem the pursuits of the [agricultural] husbandman from the discredit into which they had fallen as the vocation of slaves." Anticipating Samuel Armstrong of Hampton and Booker T. Washington of Tuskegee by several decades, Elgin urged the establishment of a school of industry "to connect the vocation of husbandman with subjects of intellectual interest," and "to create . . . a feeling favorable to the subject by presenting it to the Public in its most attractive guise as connected with questions of scientific and practical interest."[26]

Thus it was that missionaries and schoolmasters were dispatched to the British West Indies and the defeated Confederacy. Ex-slaves had to be taught to internalize the discipline and materialist psychology required in a free, but not equal, society. One should not lose sight of the fact, however, that fundamental to these emancipation policies was the belief that blacks shared the innate nature, desires, and psychology of white men. This is not to say that the emancipators were without racial bias; the point is that those biases were less salient in shaping their policies than were other propositions about human behavior which constituted their larger ideological commitments.

Ideally the freedmen would have access to economic, political, and social opportunities on the same basis as whites, as long as they conformed to the behavior patterns of whites. Should they fail to imbibe these cultural values and adhere to these norms, should education, religion, and consumerism fail to take, the freedmen would be remanded to the same types of social institutions used to discipline white deviants. In the harsh words of Henry Taylor, those who did not conform to the new order would be considered "an idle and spendthrift residue, whose liberation from arbitrary control would be duly retarded." In the liberal democratic state, when the market failed to achieve the appropriate discipline, these "arbitrary controls" were exercised by penal and reformatory institutions in various guises—workhouses, asylums, poorhouses, and penitentiaries.[27]

Of course, the emancipators assumed that such deviance would be the exception rather than the rule and that these institutions would act not simply to coerce but to reform their inmates. They were prepared for the fact that slavery had unfitted both the planter and the freedmen for the roles they would have to play in the new economy, and they anticipated the need to re-educate the master as well as the slave. But nowhere were they prepared for the depth and breadth of the resistance actually encountered from both former masters and ex-slaves.

A major obstacle to the attempt to transform slave societies into liberal states was the planter. In his 1865 tour of the Southern states, Carl Schurz found uniform and pervasive among white Southerners the belief that blacks would not work without physical compulsion. The planters rejected the free-labor system, one student of the period concludes, "not because it had been tried and failed, but because it contradicted fundamental assumptions." Clearly, the defense of slavery had left a legacy of racism that would not be easily surrendered. A Southern planter summarized the viewpoint of his class succinctly: "Northern laborers are like other men, [but] southern laborers are nothing but niggers, and you can't make anything else out of them. They're not controlled by the same motives as white men, and unless you have power to compel them, they'll only work when they can't beg or steal enough to keep from starving." A Louisiana planter declared that "the nature of the negro cannot be changed by the offer of more or less money, all he desires is to eat, drink and sleep, and perform the least possible amount of labor." The Alabamian Hugh J. Davis, Jr., declared, "Negroes will not work for pay, the lash is all I feel that will make them."[28]

That the planters clung to racist views of their black work force is clear, but the extent to which racial perceptions as opposed to perceptions of the requirements of the plantation regime governed their behavior is yet unclear. Putative racial deficiencies provided a justification for maintaining a highly coercive labor discipline, but the crux of the problem was the need for labor discipline regardless of the racial character of the work force. "Authority and control," George Beckford reminds us, "are inherent in the plantation system." After all, the raison d'être of slavery in the first place was the plantation's need for a docile, subservient, and immobile labor force. Arguing against free labor, Hugh W. Pugh, a Louisiana sugar planter, insisted that he needed "thorough control of ample and continuous labor." During the Civil War, planters in Union-occupied Jefferson Parish, Louisiana, expressed their willingness to accept "free" labor but wanted one or two military guards stationed on each plantation to "compel the negroes to work." Alabama planters meeting in 1867 resolved "that when we hire freedmen they concede to us the right to control their labor as our time and convenience requires." Historian Lawrence Powell has observed with appropriate sarcasm that "when the old masters talked of free labor, they really meant slave labor, only hired not bought."[29]

The freedmen also proved reluctant to accept the new economic order as defined by the emancipators. In the British West Indies as well as in the American South, most blacks had been born into slavery and few had experienced freedom. Nevertheless, ex-slaves had their own ideas about the meaning of freedom. They shared with their emancipators the notion that freedom involved some measure of personal autonomy, the ability to make choices about one's life and destiny. Initially, autonomy and control seemed to refer primarily to limitations on white action against them. They wished to be free from physical abuse, especially whipping. They wished to maintain the integrity of their families against forced separation by slave owners. In Jamaica and America freed women and children abandoned field labor for other economic endeavors and education, respectively. It was of such matters as these that they sang during the days of jubilee: no more "peck o'corn," "no more mistress' call," no more stocks and chains, no more driver's lash, no more auction block. But the act of singing itself points up the fact that autonomy was not simply personal, that it embraced familial and community relationships as well. In the American South freedmen withdrew from white churches and formed their own; in Jamaica they expanded their Christian congregations but returned to African rituals and beliefs.[30]

But the freedmen clearly recognized the bearing that economic relationships had on other social arrangements. When informed that the federal government would return to the planters lands temporarily confiscated during the war, a Georgia freedman declared, "Damn such freedom as that." After the war Southern freedmen everywhere resisted the Union policy of evicting them from those confiscated plantations, even when resistance brought them musket to musket against veteran federal troops.[31] Freedmen in Edisto Island, South Carolina, expressed their incredulity at a government policy that rewarded its erstwhile enemies and punished its loyal supporters; in the process they also revealed their understanding of the essence of freedom.

we are at the mercy of those who are combined to prevent us from getting land enough to lay our Fathers bones upon. We Have property In Horses, cattle, carriages, & articles of furniture, but we are landless and homeless, from the Homes we Have lived In In the past we can only do one of three things Step Into the public *road or the sea* or remain on them working as In former time and subject to their will as then. We can not resist It In any way without being driven out Homeless upon the road. You will see this Is not the condition of really freemen[.][32]

Other Afro-Americans and Afro-Jamaicans were jealous of their rights as they understood them and quick to defend against any infringement of those rights, even when defense required violence against planters and legal authorities. For example, efforts by planters and special magistrates in Jamaica to impose extra work on the apprentices or to reduce their compensation were met by determined resistance. There were work stoppages, sit-down strikes, and arson on Jamaican plantations. Likewise, in Louisiana during the Civil War, General Nathaniel Banks's forced-labor policies were resisted with strikes and work stoppages by black field hands.[33]

In certain ways the freedmen learned their new economic roles too well, in the view of some whites. They learned to bargain with and to discriminate among potential employers. They learned quickly to place a money value on their time and to demand overtime pay for work beyond normal hours. As one exasperated planter described the situation, "If he goes to the house for an axe he is to be paid extra for it. It's well enough to pay a man for all he does, but who can carry on a farm in such a way as that?" Jamaican planters voiced similar complaints about the freedmen's allegedly overscrupulous attention to the monetary value of time.[34]

The dramatic increase in market activity and thrift among Jamaican and American freedmen immediately following emancipation encouraged missionaries, Bureau officials, and special magistrates to report favorably on their apparent adjustment to the new order. As one American Missionary Association agent reported from the South Carolina Sea Islands: "In temporal things, the colored people of these islands, are mainly doing well. I do not think it would be for their good, at the present time, to increcis [sic] their facilities for getting money. Most of them have ample means for gaining property fast, by their industry & shrewdness; they have become owners of land to a considerable extent, & are raizing [sic] cotton, as they say for 'old nigger him-self,' & not fo 'massa.' "[35]

Despite this evidence, however, metropolitan authorities were disturbed by the tendency of freedmen everywhere to devote themselves to economic activities other than the cultivation of plantation staples. Both in Jamaica and in the American South many blacks showed a preference for raising food crops rather than cotton or sugar, just as Henry Taylor had feared they might. No doubt this was due in part to the fact that the labor require-ments were much less rigorous for food gardening than for staples, especially for sugar. And on occasion, particularly in Jamaica, provision crops could be more remunerative than plantation wages. But there probably existed more profound causes than these. Jamaicans were not averse to growing sugar, and American blacks grew cotton—on their own account. It was not the crop but the mode of labor organization that they seemed to object to. In both societies freedmen strongly resisted working for wages, preferring task systems and tenant arrangements that left them in apparent, and sometimes substantial, control of their labor.[36]

Of course, the freedmen's views of political economy are less accessible than are those of their emancipators and the planters; we can only infer their "ideology" or world view from their behavior. But one might begin with the hypothesis that because they issued from a radically different set of social relations, they embraced a radically different vision of what man, work, and society should be. In both the British West Indies and the American South many slaves had participated in a market econ-omy, hiring their "own time" and keeping part of the proceeds of their labor, raising and marketing food crops, and so forth. In Jamaica, slave provision grounds fed an extensive and well-developed internal marketing system. But this market experience had to be very different from that envisioned by classical econ-omists, simply because slaves were not subject to the market's full rigor. One needs to distinguish between mere participation in exchange relationships, as in the case of peasants and small landowners who sell their surpluses to buy "luxuries," and com-plete absorption in and loss of autonomy to the market, as in the case of planters, wage workers, and others whose *primary* purpose is to produce for exchange.[37]

In an attempt to clarify the inherent difficulties in liberal democratic thought, C. B. Macpherson describes a hypothetical simple market society, which he contrasts with a possessive market society like that of nineteenth-century Britain and America. In the former there is an exchange of goods and services that is regulated by the market (supply and demand, etc.), but labor itself is not a commodity. It is presumed that productive resources, such as land, are available to all in such a society. All members of the society retain control over their own resources, including their labor, and exchange only goods and services; consequently no person's gain comes at the expense of another. No person can accumulate more than he produces with his own hand. Although there can be a division of labor in a simple market economy and people are motivated by gain, according to Macpherson one maximizes gains only by greater exertion and more product exchanges and not by converting another man's labor power to one's own use. The difference between what one would earn as a dependent wage laborer and one's earnings as an independent producer—raising subsistence crops and selling the surplus in the market—is likely to be less than "the satisfaction of retaining control of one's labour," that is, one's autonomy. Presumably any inequities that might develop in such a society arise only because of differences in individual will and effort and not because of an unequal distribution of productive resources.[38]

Macpherson defines a possessive market society as one in which labor itself is a commodity. One man's conversion of another's labor power to his own use quickly leads to a society divided by class—one group controlling the means of production and another left without resources. Ultimately such a division undercuts the ostensible benefits of a free economy and liberal democratic political order, argues Macpherson, as one class loses its "powers" and its freedom of action not only in the marketplace but in political and social spheres as well.

It would appear that the ex-slaves, by their own lights, of course, recognized this danger. In Jamaica many withdrew into the hills and raised food crops, laboring on the sugar estates only during the time they could spare from their provision grounds or when natural and man-made disasters forced them back to the plantations. In the American South, given the relative lack of access to land, freedmen made the best deal they could to avoid the wage system—sharecropping. In retrospect, of course, we recognize that sharecropping degenerated into a system of in-kind wages, but this was not self-evident as the system evolved. Indeed, such a development was probably less the result of inevitable economic tendencies than a consequence of the collapse of black political power.[39]

In whatever way one might interpret the freedmen's behavior, it is clear that it disappointed many of the emancipation advocates and played an as yet uncharted role in the racial backlash of the late nineteenth century. It was not so simple a matter as racist ideas appearing where there had been none before. Racist ideas had been there all along; what was new was the willingness to express them, the use to which they were put, and the policies they appeared to justify. People like Henry Taylor, Carl Schurz, and Samuel Gridley Howe had always believed that blacks were inferior to whites in some respects, but their somewhat contradictory belief that blacks had the same basic innate character as whites had leeched their racism of many of its most poisonous consequences. But when released from slavery, blacks did not appear to respond in the ways predicted by the emancipators' other, more powerful ideas about human behavior. Thus racial explanations of the freedmen's behavior—by placing them in a different category of humankind—allowed the reformers to maintain their faith in their liberal democratic ideology which justified the bourgeois world they had created.

The irony, of course, is that the ex-slaves' response to freedom was in accord with many of the tenets of the liberal reformers as to "rational" self-interested behavior. Freedmen were motivated by gain. They worked hard, saved their money, built churches and schools, and tried to improve themselves materially and morally. But as long as they had choices—and possession of or access to land was the major factor creating choice—freedmen resisted working for wages on the plantations. It could be argued, of course, that higher pay, better working conditions, and greater security could have overcome this resistance (or as economists would put it, their "high reserve price" for plantation work). But plantations have traditionally, if not inherently, required cheap and docile labor forces. In any case, to improve conditions was not the way most planters dealt with the situation. American cotton planters adopted sharecropping, which along with crop liens and political coercion helped insure a subservient labor force. Sugar planters turned to indentured workers and mechanization. Where they monopolized the land and controlled the political system, the retooling of their industry proceeded without undue strain on themselves and often with indirect subsidies from their laborers.[40]

The pattern of events following emancipation, then, should have alerted the emancipators to the inconsistencies in their own ideology—namely, that inequality was a precondition for the economic and social system they envisioned. Given their three centuries of experience, the planter class saw this clearly. As long as they were unable to monopolize resources and alternatives, especially land, plantations required slavery or something very much like it. To give, sell, or allow freedmen to squat on land to any significant degree was to surrender the whole plantation system. Furthermore, conceding effective political power to ex-slaves, whereby they might redirect society's resources, threatened a similar disaster.

Their inability to grasp what the planters saw so well contributed to the emancipators' policy difficulties and inconsistencies. For example, in the final year of the British apprenticeship system, Lord Glenelg, the colonial secretary, distributed a circular to all West Indian governors boldly proclaiming that the entire object of British policy was to ensure freedom for the ex-slaves "in [that] full and unlimited sense of the term in which it is used in reference to other subjects of the British Crown." In another circular, however, he noted that whereas slaves could be compelled to labor on plantation staples, freedmen must be attracted to such work by making it in their material interest to do so. This circular, drafted no doubt by Henry Taylor, reiterated the arguments of his 1833 memorandum. Given the demographic imbalances in the colonies, the "natural" effect of complete emancipation would be a general desertion of the estates to cultivate food crops. Eventually the growth of population might right this imbalance, but the plantations would be destroyed in the meantime. Thus the government must interdict the freedmen's natural—and, one might add, rational—proclivity to abandon the plantations. The government's policy, Glenelg concluded, should be to *unnaturally* elevate the price of public lands so as to keep it "out of the reach of persons without capital." This extraordinary effort to confound the "free enterprise" initiatives of the freedmen was rationalized as a necessary function of the government's "civilizing" mission in the colonies.[41]

Society, being thus kept together, is more open to civilizing influences, more directly under the control of Government, more full of the activity which is inspired by common wants, and the strength which is derived from the division of labour; and altogether is in a sounder state, morally, politically and economically, than if left to pursue its natural course.

By this policy, Glenelg insisted with tortured logic, the government was not favoring one class over another, and it was not attempting to force the freedmen to stay on the plantations by depriving them of alternative employment; its object was "merely to condense and keep together the population in such manner that it may always contain a due proportion of labourers."

A proposition requiring both the attainment of genuine freedom (self-possession) for the ex-slaves and the health of the plantation economy was an antinomy. Most liberal reformers, like Glenelg, failed to recognize the difficulty. They saw only inadequacies in the victims of their policies, and the need for "a civilizing mission" to create what Tocqueville had called an "empire sur l'esprit."[42]

By the late 1860s and 1870s disillusionment with the progress of the freedmen was pervasive among emancipation advocates and policymakers of the preceding decades. The sighs of despair of an A.M.A. missionary in Jamaica, reflecting on the poverty and irreligion of his congregants, summed up the sentiments of many of his British and American colleagues:

In speaking thus of the straitened circumstances of our people, I cannot in truthfulness attribute it to causes altogether independent of themselves. For while they are not given to vicious habits which tend to impoverish those who indulge them, yet they lack qualities of heart & mind which are essential to success in undertakings of any kind. They are not indolent, yet they are not industrious after the manner of our countrymen, making the most of precious time. They are not extravagant, but neither are they wisely economical. They lack forethought, reflection & practical wisdom in the management of their affairs. They possess little or nothing of the spirit of enterprise & are especially lacking in that indomitable pluck which grapples with difficulties & scorns to succumb to adverse circumstances.[43]

Henry Taylor, who had composed most of the key policy documents relevant to West Indian emancipation during his tenure of more than a quarter of a century, retired from the British Colonial Office convinced that emancipation had failed. In 1865 he wrote the infamous "Queen's Advice" to the Jamaican freedmen, a policy document that urged them to abandon all aspirations for independent landownership and farming and to work for wages on the plantations. This befuddled response to the growing unrest among the Jamaican peasantry contributed materially to a major uprising at Morant Bay in the fall of 1865. The Morant Bay riot occurred on the eve of American Reconstruction—in fact at about the same time that Southern freedmen were being evicted from confiscated plantations—and it was interpreted by proponents as well as opponents of emancipation as an indication of the failure of the British experiment with free black labor.[44]

Henry Taylor strongly endorsed the draconian repressive measures taken by Jamaican authorities following the riot, and he oversaw the process by which Jamaica was subsequently deprived of self-government and ruled directly from Britain. It is probable that the idea of establishing a "benevolent guardianship" over coloured peoples was implemented first in Britain's former slave colonies. Certainly it was an idea that gained ready assent from other policymakers in late-nineteenth-century Britain. Lord Stanley, who as colonial secretary had shepherded the British Abolition Act through Parliament in 1833 and, at that time, had expounded at length on the innate fitness of blacks for freedom, declared in 1865 that the British had done enough for and spent enough resources on former slaves who seemed content with "a merely animal existence."[45]

In America many of the liberal reformers of the 1860s formed the core of the Liberal Republican movement in the 1870s and the Mugwumps of the 1880s and 1890s. Having urged a thorough reconstruction of Southern society earlier, one including civil and political rights for blacks, they came to revise their assessments of blacks and of the policies to be pursued. They now expressed disappointment with black progress since emancipation, opposed legislation favorable to the civil and political rights of blacks, and urged that such matters be returned to the control and discretion of Southern whites.[46]

One could interpret these reversals of racial attitudes as mere expressions of personal idiosyncrasies or group pathologies. But the strange ideological career of British and American emancipators suggests a different interpretation. Their racial attitudes and beliefs were not autonomous, discrete entities unrelated to other ideas and events; during the emancipation era racial attitudes were shaped by events even as they shaped events in turn. Thus these beliefs must be treated as a part of, and not abstracted from, the broader ideological and historical context in which they occurred.

Perhaps there are implications here for the general treatment of race and racism in American history. Historians often tend to treat racism as more or less constant in effect over time, undifferentiated in content, and disconnected from other developments —in short, as unresponsive to the processes and forces of history itself. Given such treatment, racism becomes a phenomenon that is *a*historical or, as another author has written, "*trans*historical." As such, racial phenomena are almost beyond the scope of historical analysis. It might be more fruitful to approach such ideas as integral to the larger world view of the protagonists we study and to evaluate them in the context of their ideas about human behavior generally.[47]

And, perhaps, it is precisely at this juncture that contemporary historians confront the difficulty that we are also heirs to that broader nineteenth-century ideology, even if not necessarily to its particular racist component. Our notions of the responsibilities of freedom and of appropriate human behavior are no less experientially and historically unique than were those of the nineteenth-century emancipators. Most of us would have difficulty defining innate human character and aspirations in other than our own Western cultural terms. The question of what terms ex-slaves would have used—their world view—is yet to be fully explored. But while we await that exploration, we must recognize the nature and limitations of our own presuppositions and resist imposing them upon people whose experience was by definition quite different. We are heirs of nineteenth-century liberal democratic thought; often we are its prisoners as well.

NOTES

1. David B. Davis, *The Problem of Slavery in the Age of Revolution, 1770–1823* (Ithaca, 1975).

2. Only Cuba, with 370,220 slaves in 1861, and Brazil, with 1.5 million in 1873, were comparable slave powers by the middle of the nineteenth century. The survival of slavery in both of these nations was adversely affected by emancipation in the British West Indies and the United States. The first casualty was the international slave trade that had depended upon British and American carriers; the second was the intellectual as well as political isolation of Cuba and Brazil as unprogressive social backwaters with anachronistic social systems. For population figures see David W. Cohen and Jack P. Greene, eds., *Neither Slave Nor Free: The Freedman of African Descent in the Slave Societies of the New World* (Baltimore, 1972), pp. 288, 314, 335–39.

3. The fact that the "gradual" transition from slavery to freedom in the British West Indies was a formal process while that in the U.S. was largely inadvertent may distract one from the striking similarities. In the South Carolina and Georgia Sea Islands, in the Mississippi Valley, in Hampton, Virginia, and in Louisiana, several hundreds of thousands of slaves came under Union control during the first years of the war. In Louisiana, General Benjamin Butler organized a contract labor system in which freedmen were forced to remain on the plantations working ten hours a day for twenty-six days each month. Military authorities also physically disciplined workers and controlled their movements. These and other initiatives were not unlike those of the British apprenticeship system.

4. "Il ne voit pas encore dans le magistrat un maître, mais un guide et un libérateur. C'est le moment où il est le plus aisé au gouvernement de fonder son empire sur l'esprit et les habitudes de la population noire, et d'acquérir l'influence salutaire dont il aura bientôt besoin de se servir pour la diriger dans la liberté complète." "Rapport fait a la Chambre des Députés, . . . relative aux esclaves des colonies," *Études économiques, politiques et littéraires*, ed. Calmann Lévy, 2nd ed. (Paris, 1878), pp. 227–64 (quote on p. 259). Of course, Tocqueville actually was very critical of the British apprenticeship system and called for complete and immediate emancipation. Nevertheless, his plan was generally indebted to the British model; the difference was that the state would assume a more powerful and active role during the transition period. See also C. Vann Woodward, "Emancipations and Reconstructions: A Comparative Study" (Paper presented to the XIII International Congress of Historical Sciences, Moscow, August 16–23, 1970), p. 8.

5. My use of the terms "emancipators" and "policymakers" is a deliberate, though cumbersome, attempt to distinguish the subjects of this study from "abolitionists" in general. That is, the cohort I am primarily concerned with had some direct influence on the formulation and implementation of policy. Even within this limitation I contend, not that they were the most influential or powerful figures in their respective governments—though some obviously were in the British case—but merely that they were critical spokesmen or

articulators of policy initiatives and their underlying premises in the dominant ideology. A more detailed exposition of the relationship between British ideology as applied to slave emancipation and the making of its own white working class will be made in the author's forthcoming study "The Problem of Freedom: the Political Economy of Jamaica after Slavery."

6. Davis, *The Problem of Slavery*, p. 41.

7. C. B. Macpherson, *The Political Theory of Possessive Individualism: Hobbes to Locke* (Oxford, 1962), pp. 1–4; and idem, *Democratic Theory: Essays in Retrieval* (Oxford, 1973), pp. 3–23, 185–94. Of course, these concepts were espoused primarily by the secular rather than the evangelical contingent among the emancipators. And although there is evidence, especially for the Jamaican missionaries, that the evangelicals shared many of the basic materialistic premises of the secular thinkers, I am not prepared at this juncture to say precisely how these were reconciled with their religious idealism. For a discussion of the values and objectives of missionary educators in the American South which emphasizes their idealism, see James M. McPherson, "The New Puritanism: Values and Goals of Freedmen's Education in America," in *The University in Society*, ed. Lawrence Stone (Princeton, 1974), II, 611–39.

8. *Hansard's Parliamentary Debates*, 3rd series, vol. 17, pp. 123–41.

9. Lawrence N. Powell, *New Masters: Northern Planters during the Civil War and Reconstruction* (New Haven, 1980), p. 76; Willie Lee Rose, *Rehearsal for Reconstruction: The Port Royal Experiment* (New York, 1964), pp. 218, 223; William H. Pease, "Three Years among the Freedmen: William C. Gannett and the Port Royal Experiment," *Journal of Negro History*, 41 (1957), 106.

10. [Henry Taylor], "Colonial Office, January 1833. Memo: for the Cabinet, pp. 45–47. C.O.884/I. (Hereafter cited as Taylor Memorandum.)

11. Ibid.

12. Ibid., pp. 7, 54, 55.

13. Ibid., pp. 54–55, 72. [Italics in original.]

14. Ibid., pp. 55, 67; Henry Taylor, *Autobiography of Henry Taylor, 1800–1875* (London, 1885), I, 127–28.

15. Taylor Memorandum, pp. 75–76.

16. Ibid., pp. 76–77.

17. John Daughtrey report in Marquis de Sligo to Lord Glenelg, July 9, 1836, Parliamentary Papers 1837 (521–I), LIII, 60–61; Earl Grey to Charles Grey, August 10, 1847, Richard Hart Collection, Jamaican National Library, Kingston, Jamaica. (Hereafter Parliamentary Papers will be cited as PP.)

18. Rose, *Rehearsal for Reconstruction*, p. 164; Henry L. Swint, "Northern Interest in the Shoeless Southerner," *Journal of Southern History*, 16 (1950), 463–64.

19. (Kingston, Jamaica) *Morning Journal*, August 17, 1838.

20. "Report of Secretary of War, communicating . . . Final Report of the American Freedmen's Inquiry Commission to the Secretary of War," May 15, 1864, 30th Congress, 1st sess., Senate Executive Document no. 53, pp. 13, 15, 110.

21. Ibid., pp. 20, 106.

22. Leon F. Litwack, *Been in the Storm So Long: The Aftermath of Slavery* (New York, 1979), p. 224.

23. "Freedmen's Bureau, Orders issued by Commissioners and Assistant Commissioners," 39th Congress, 1st sess., House Executive Document no. 70, pp. 45, 277.

24. Ibid., pp. 92, 347.

25. Rose, *Rehearsal for Reconstruction*, p. 229; "Message of the President of the United States communicating, . . . Report of Carl Schurz," 39th Congress, 1st sess., Senate Executive Document no. 2, p. 25; Barkly to Newcastle, February 21, 1854, PP1854 (1848), XLIII, 83.

26. Elgin to Stanley, August 5, 1845, Conf., C.O. 137/284. Cf. Douglas Hall, *Free Jamaica, 1838–1865: An Economic History* (New Haven, 1959), passim; Donald Spivey, *Schooling For the New Slavery: Black Industrial Education, 1868–1915* (Westport, Conn., 1978).

27. The literature touching this point is vast and growing, especially for England. See Joyce Oldham Appleby, *Economic Thought and Ideology in Seventeenth Century England* (Princeton, 1978); Michael Ignatieff, *A Just Measure of Pain: The Penitentiary in the Industrial Revolution, 1750–1850* (New York, 1978); J. R. Poynter, *Society and Pauperism: English Ideas on Poor Relief, 1795–1834* (London, 1969); David Rothman, *The Discovery of the Asylum: Social Order and Disorder in the New Republic* (Boston, 1971); and a thought-provoking review of Rothman's work by David B. Davis, "The Crime of Reform," *New York Review of Books,* June 26, 1980.

28. James L. Roark, *Masters without Slaves: Southern Planters in the Civil War and Reconstruction* (New York, 1977), p. 107; Litwack, *Been in the Storm So Long*, pp. 342, 365.

29. George L. Beckford, *Persistent Poverty: Underdevelopment in Plantation Economies of the Third World* (New York, 1972), p. 53; Louis Gerteis, *From Contraband to Freedmen: Federal Policy toward Southern Blacks, 1861–1865* (Westport, Conn., 1973), p. 92; Jonathan Wiener, *Social Origins of the New South: Alabama, 1860–1885* (Baton Rouge, 1978), p. 40; Powell, *New Masters*, p. 5. Beckford's point is being driven home by a growing number of monographs on postemancipation societies. See Alan H. Adamson, *Sugar without Slaves: The Political Economy of British Guiana, 1838–1904* (New Haven, 1972); Peter L. Eisenberg, *The Sugar Industry in Pernambuco: Modernization without Change, 1840–1910* (Berkeley, 1974); Frederick Cooper, *From Slaves to Squatters: Plantation Labor and Agriculture in Zanzibar and Coastal Kenya, 1890–1925* (New Haven, 1981); Rebecca J. Scott, "Slave Emancipation and the Transition to Free Labor in Cuba, 1868–1895" (Ph.D. diss., Princeton University, 1981).

30. For an insightful discussion of how Cuban slaves appear to have conceptualized emancipation in family and community rather than merely individualistic terms, see Rebecca J. Scott, "Slave Emancipation and the Transition to Free Labor in Cuba." Lawrence W. Levine has a stimulating discussion of changes in Afro-American music after emancipation in *Black Culture and Black Consciousness: Afro-American Folk Thought from Slavery to Freedom* (New York, 1977), pp. 136–89. The withdrawal of women and children from field work is examined for the United States and Jamaica, respectively, by Roger L. Ransom and Richard Sutch, *One Kind of Freedom: The Economic Consequences of Emancipation* (Cambridge, 1977), and Michael Craton, *Searching for the Invisible Man: Slaves and Plantation Life in Jamaica* (Cambridge, Mass., 1978). For changes in Afro-American and Afro-Jamaican religious life, see Joel Williamson, *After Slavery: The Negro in South Carolina during Reconstruction, 1861–1877* (New York, 1965), pp. 180–208; Thomas Holt, *Black over White: Negro Political Leadership in South Carolina during Reconstruction* (Urbana, 1977), pp. 87–91; Philip D. Curtin, *Two Jamaicas: The Role of Ideas in a Tropical Colony, 1830–1865* (New York, 1970), pp. 158–77.

31. Litwack, *Been in the Storm So Long*, p. 405; Holt, *Black over White*, pp. 68–69.

32. Henry Bram, Ishmael Moultrie, and Yates Sampson [Committee of Edisto, South Carolina, Freedpeople] to General [O. O. Howard], October 28, 1865, B–53(1865), Letters Received, Records of the Commissioner, Bureau of Refugees, Freedmen and Abandoned Lands, RG 105, National Archives. I am indebted to Leslie Rowland for bringing this letter to my attention.

33. Gerteis, *From Contraband to Freedmen*, pp. 77, 111–15; Powell, *New Masters*, p. 109; PP1837(521–I), LIII, 34–36; PP1835(177), L, 77–108.

34. Powell, *New Masters*, pp. 98, 103; Journal of Henry John Blagrove, 1841–42, Jamaica Archives, Spanish Town, Jamaica; Hearings before Committee of House of Assembly, October 31, 1834, November 6, 1834, enclosed with Sligo to Spring-Rice, November 29, 1834, December 29, 1834, PP1835(177), L, 53–108.

35. Holt, *Black over White*, p. 47. That freed people were avid savers is demonstrated by the history of the Freedman's Bank in America and by the history of local parish banks in Jamaica. On the former, see Carl R. Osthaus, *Freedmen, Philanthropy, and Fraud: A History of the Freedman's Savings Bank* (Urbana, 1976); for the latter, Holt, "The Problem of Freedom."

36. See Ransom and Sutch, *One Kind of Freedom.*

37. This slave marketing experience led to what Sidney W. Mintz has called "proto-peasantries." See *Caribbean Transformations* (Chicago, 1974), pp. 180–213; and "Slavery and the Rise of Peasantries," in *Roots and Branches: Current Directions in Slave Studies,* ed. Michael Craton, *Historical Reflections/Reflexions Historiques,* 6 (1979), 213–42. Of course, the phenomenon of peasant agriculture correlates not only with the prior marketing experience of the slave but also with the relative strength or weakness of the planters' political and economic control over other resources after slavery. For thought-provoking studies of peasants and yeoman farmers that explore market

orientations in which the emphasis is on a subsistence ethic or "safety-first" behavior, see James C. Scott, *The Moral Economy of the Peasant: Rebellion and Subsistence in Southeast Asia* (New Haven, 1976), and Gavin Wright, *The Political Economy of the Cotton South: Households, Markets, and Wealth in the Nineteenth Century* (New York, 1978).

38. C. B. Macpherson, *The Political Theory of Possessive Individualism*, pp. 51–60.

39. On the later devolution of sharecropping into an in-kind wage system, see Harold D. Woodman, "Sequel to Slavery: The New History Views the Postbellum South," *Journal of Southern History*, 43 (1977), 523–24.

40. The methods of domination used by sugar planters can be documented best in northeastern Brazil and Guiana, but I suspect they hold in general for other societies and crops. See Eisenberg, *Sugar Industry in Pernambuco* and Adamson, *Sugar without Slaves*. Technological development and concentration of ownership were generally accompanied by the "sharecropping" system characteristic of the sugar industry, that is, the development of central mills for grinding cane that was produced on lands leased or owned by small growers. Discussion of this system is beyond the scope of this paper, but it is important to note that the differences between sugar and cotton cannot be reduced to so simple a formula as that sugar required too great a capital investment to be grown by small producers. The large capital requirements were almost entirely related to the sugar mill, which could be and was separated from cane farming. Indeed, it is probable that in many areas sugar cane could be *grown* less expensively than cotton because it could be ratooned, i.e., successive crops could be harvested from a single planting.

41. Glenelg to governors of the West Indian Colonies, November 6, 1837, PP1837–38(154–I), XLIX, 9–11; Glenelg to governors of the West Indian Colonies, January 30, 1836, PP1836(166), XLVIII, 58–60. Similarly, Tocqueville observed in a series of articles in 1843 that desertion of the sugar estates was a "necessary consequence" of emancipation; the solution was to raise the price of land to prevent independent cultivation. Tocqueville, *Etudes économiques*, p. 285. Cf. Seymour Drescher, *Dilemmas of Democracy: Tocqueville and Modernization* (Pittsburgh, 1968), pp. 151–95.

42. The reluctance of the "liberals" to confront the contradictions within their ideological commitments may have to do with the emerging labor movement and political challenges from "the lower orders" generally. On this point, see David Montgomery, *Beyond Equality: Labor and the Radical Republicans, 1862–1872* (New York, 1967), and Douglas A. Lorimer, *Colour, Class, and the Victorians: English Attitudes to the Negro in the Mid-Nineteenth Century* (Leicester, Eng., 1978).

43. C.B.K—— to A.M.A., February 1871, American Missionary Association Archives, Jamaica File, roll 6, microfilm copy, F14391–F14394, Amistad Research Center, New Orleans, Louisiana.

44. See Forrest G. Wood, *Black Scare: The Racist Response to Emancipation and Reconstruction* (Berkeley, 1968), p. 121; Bernard Semmel, *Democracy versus Empire: The Jamaica Riots of 1865 and the Governor Eyre Controversy*

(New York, 1968), pp. 63–64; James McPherson, "Was West Indian Emancipation a Success? The Abolitionist Argument during the American Civil War," *Caribbean Studies,* 4 (1964), 26–34.

45. Taylor, *Autobiography,* vol. I; Lorimer, *Colour, Class, and the Victorians,* p. 124.

46. John G. Sproat, *"The Best Men": Liberal Reformers in the Gilded Age* (New York, 1968), pp. 31–38.

47. The full implications of this historiographical phenomenon are too complex to explore here; I merely want to suggest its relevance to studies of emancipation and to urge that historians become more aware of how often we invoke "racism" to explain the more difficult, apparently inexplicable problems of Afro-American history. Racism becomes a convenient caldron into which one tosses historical anomalies; or, a better metaphor might be a black box that explains without having itself to be explained. In this essay I argue that racism allowed the emancipators to avoid the difficulties inherent in their world view; I suspect it may have a similar purpose for contemporary historians. See Harold Woodman's "Sequel to Slavery" for incisive observations on this problem as it relates to the recent econometric literature. For a provocative description of how ideas about race fit into a larger system of ideas about human behavior and values, see Ronald T. Takaki, *Iron Cages: Race and Culture in Nineteenth-Century America* (New York, 1979); see also my review of Takaki's book in "Probing the American Dilemma," *Book & Arts,* November 23, 1979. For a more general discussion of race in American historiography (from which the term *"trans*historical" is taken), see Barbara J. Fields, "Ideology and Race in American History," in this volume.

The Politics of Livelihood:
Carpetbaggers in the Deep South

LAWRENCE N. POWELL

I is now beginning to dawn on historians of Reconstruction that Southern Republicans during those years were inordinately addicted to factional quarrels. In fact, the infighting probably had more than a casual bearing on the eventual collapse of Reconstruction, which makes it frankly bewildering and hard to explain.[1] Though the party was admittedly composed of wildly disparate elements, Southern Republicans had more reason to hang together than did any comparable group of politicians in American electoral history. Their political opponents, known variously as Conservatives or Democrats or Conservative-Democrats, were not a "loyal opposition" in any ordinary sense. They favored a "rule or ruin" policy and did not scruple to employ the methods of fraud, terror, and assassination in order to achieve their ends. But Southern Republicans were sometimes slow to catch on. At the very moment when their existence as a viable political party was at stake, they often seemed to devote less energy to fighting the opposition than to fighting one another. They appear to have been incapable of "*party discipline* and self control," to quote a typical complaint they made about themselves. What explains this puzzling failure of Republicans in the Reconstruction South to pull together in the face of common adversity? Why was the Southern wing of the party of emancipation unable "to create a political culture in which solidarity was a virtue?"[2]

A look at the experience of carpetbaggers provides a partial answer. Over the past twenty-odd years we have been taught to view these Northern Republicans in the South more objectively and charitably, and we have learned in addition a great deal that is informative about their background, their political creed, their voting behavior, and their typical constituency.[3] Yet few have taken the time to explore the question of why they entered and remained in Republican politics in the first place. The answer is revealing on several scores. Northern newcomers became Republican politicians in the South partly because they had to make a living that could not be easily earned at that time in the usual ways. That is to say, carpetbaggers[4] in the Lower South, which for the purposes of this essay includes Alabama, Florida, Georgia, Louisiana, Mississippi, and South Carolina (where most of them were concentrated),[5] were in a worse predicament than the ordinary American politician ever finds himself in. They relied on office not only for power and prestige but for economic survival. This dependence upon politics for their livelihood in turn greatly aggravated the factional weaknesses to which Southern Republicans were already prone.

No attempt is being made here to resurrect the Redeemer myth that the carpetbaggers were low-flung, penniless adventurers who came South originally for the purpose of living off of office. Every modern study of Reconstruction politics demonstrates conclusively that the carpetbaggers scarcely fit the caricature of them that used to pass for historical truth. They were, as a class, fairly well educated, a large proportion of them having attended college, and they came from backgrounds that were solidly middle class. They were not the jetsam and flotsam of Northern society.[6] Nor did they come South strictly for the sake of office. The fact is, as Richard N. Current reminded us several years ago, the overwhelming majority of carpetbaggers arrived in the region well before congressional enactments in 1867 made Republican politics a live possibility and officeholding a thing to be pursued. The few Northern newcomers who did hunger after office during presidential Reconstruction soon learned that Andrew Johnson preferred Southern men for federal appointments, and that Southern men frowned on Northern men who meddled in local politics without an invitation. In short, most Northerners who later ended up as carpetbaggers did not anticipate this aspect of their careers at all. They came to the former Confederacy for reasons other than politics.[7]

Of course, what mostly attracted Northerners to the South, or tempted them to remain or return there after their discharges from the military, were the manifold opportunities of a business nature that the region held forth in the years just preceding and following Appomattox. Land speculators and developers from the Old Northwest were sure that the former Confederacy would be the next frontier to roll into vision. Merchants and jobbers were just as positive that their special talents would find full scope in the consumer market that emancipation had recently enlarged.[8] Lawyers for their part sensed that there might be "much litigation growing out of the Confiscation Act[s] of the U.S. Congress, [and] also out of the Sequestration Act of the late Confederate Congress and other matters connected with the war."[9] In addition to all these types were those countless Northerners, numbering possibly in the tens of thousands, who believed that cotton growing at prices then prevailing was the quickest way imaginable to secure a financial "competency" of the sort that most men in nineteenth-century America envied and aspired to.[10] In a word, economic, not political, motives impelled most carpetbaggers originally to move to the South. And it remains to say that the newcomers were scarcely impecunious when they first put in their appearance. They invested thousands of dollars in the Southern economy, and in all likelihood they brought more money into the former Confederacy than they took out.[11]

If carpetbaggers originally came South for financial reasons, and if some of them abandoned whatever political ambitions they had not long after arrival, why then did they become involved in the Southern Republican party at the time they did? What were those "conditions which none of [them] could control" and which before long caused them to find themselves "up to [their] eyes in politics"?[12] The answers that have been given by revisionist historians cannot be lightly dismissed. It is undoubtedly true that the enfranchisement of the former slaves in the spring and summer of 1867 brought with it not only "political opportunity" but "political responsibility" as well, and that more than a few carpetbaggers seized both the opportunity *and* the responsibility out of a sense of duty.[13] In fact, some carpetbaggers had to be called to the colors, if not by the freedmen then by the native whites or, more common still, by the military commanders who were charged with putting the congressional plan of Reconstruction into motion. Union generals were often unable to find white Southern natives who could take the Ironclad Oath, so they simply selected many of their voting registrars and judicial officers from among "the late volunteer officers of our army when it [was] practicable. . . ."[14] Though the summons to office caught a few by surprise, the newcomers usually overcame initial reservations about officeholding and concluded that it was their solemn duty to assist the government and the newly enfranchised in the grand experiment about to be launched.[15] No explanation of the origins of carpetbaggers can do full justice to the subject if it disregards the feelings of public altruism and patriotic duty that were awakened in many Northerners by the birth of the Southern Republican Party.

Yet there was another motive that tended to draw many Northerners into Republican politics. It often had little to do with idealism and civic-mindedness, though it was by no means inconsistent with these virtues. This other motive was the practical one of how to earn a living. It figured rather large in the calculations of many soon-to-be carpetbaggers. For although the majority of the carpetbaggers were anything but penniless at the time they arrived in the South, they were very nearly penniless at the time they became Republican politicians, which is more than partly why they chose that occupation when they did. They needed to secure a livelihood.

The truth is, the Southern Republican party was born in the midst of hard times, and the bitter circumstances of its birth profoundly affected the style of politics to which it would be prone. To understand why this was so we need only consider for a moment the experiences of Northern cotton planters. Practically all of them were financially strapped when Radical Reconstruction commenced in the South. Every year since 1864 they had been planning to make a fortune, and every year since that time they had been going broke, casualties of agricultural disasters that, like misfortune, never came singly. By the beginning of 1867 they were on the ropes; at the end of the year they were on the canvas, for the price of cotton had fallen to levels that did not cover the cost of cultivation. Individual losses commonly ran into the tens of thousands of dollars. Henry W. Warren, a Yankee planter who later became Republican speaker of the Mississippi House of Representatives, summed up cotton raising as "an occupation that proved disastrous."[16]

Being for the most part lessees rather than purchasers, most Northern planters returned home after the crop failures of 1866 and 1867. The homecoming was anything but pleasant. While it was hard to live down reminders of unfulfilled boasts that they would return as rich as Croesus, it was even harder to find gainful employment.[17] The business recession that overtook the free states in 1865 began to hit bottom just at the time most Northerners were bailing out of their plantation enterprises.[18] "Perfect apathy" seemed to reign in Northern business circles in 1865.[19] Commercial houses in Boston, for example, could pay only family expenses, and job inquiries were sometimes greeted with the advice "Stick to cotton planting."[20] But this was an alternative that had played out. Eventually the thousands of Northern refugees of the cotton failures did find remunerative work in the North, yet not without difficulty. After losing $26,000 on a plantation he had leased in Louisiana, Francis P. Blair, Jr., a former Republican congressman and Union general, "was forced to seek political positions with salaries attached in order to gain a livelihood for his large family."[21] Henry Thomas, the son of U. S. Adjutant General Lorenzo Thomas, landed in the same predicament. Following heavy losses on plantations that he and his family had been renting near Natchez, Mississippi, since 1864, young Thomas had to turn to clerking in his father's Washington office by 1868. "It is a position I should never [have] chose[n]," he lamented, "but we poor devils have to grab at anything."[22]

Most of the positions up for grabs at the time, however, were in the South, and they were political positions with the new regime. Yankees who had lost money at cotton growing and who had decided to stay around went after these positions with a will. Walter L. Fleming estimates that "many of the carpet-bag politicians were northern men who had failed at cotton planting."[23] On this score it is suggestive to note that more than one-third of the Northern-born Republicans from the Lower South who served in the national House and Senate during Reconstruction had some planting experience,[24] and that over 48 percent of the carpetbagger delegates to the "Black and Tan" constitutional conventions from the same region were or had been planters.[25] One of these latter was Horatio Jenkins, Jr., a former lawyer and Union colonel from Massachusetts. Around the time he was campaigning for a seat in the Florida Constitutional Convention of 1868 (of which he later became president), his plantation in Alachua County was being seized by one of his partners, and Jenkins himself was forced to "go into bankruptcy in order to settle with his other creditors, of whom there [were] a great many. . . ."[26]

One of the attractions of the subject at hand is that it is not always necessary to infer motives from behavior. Several Northern planters who came to grief were unusually frank about their reasons for entering public life in the South, or for wanting to do so. Albert T. Morgan, for example, the Republican sheriff and state senator from Yazoo County, Mississippi, said that he saw in the congressional plan of Reconstruction a means "for a restoration to ourselves" as well as an opportunity for securing to "the freed people the right to life, liberty and the pursuit of happiness." The restoration he had in mind was the $50,000 he and his brother had lost in the same area because of planting setbacks and political troubles with his landlord.[27] Moses Bates, a Democratic editor from Massachusetts, moreover, wrote Andrew Johnson that all of his personal "fortune [had] been lost in the Radical plan of re-construction, everything having been invested upon plantations when the War closed," and would the president please give him "some duty to perform in the South."[28] And then there was Jacob Hale Sypher, a former colonel of an Ohio regiment, who, despite holding on to his property, had to confess in 1867, "I'm *poor*. . . . all my means are tied up in my plantation," which could not have been producing much income at that time.[29] Sypher was fortunate enough eventually to be elected to Congress by Louisiana Republicans, yet he was not completely satisfied. Because he had to wait more than eight months for the U.S. House of Representatives to certify his disputed election credentials, he wondered whether he might not have to *"quit politics or be a beggar."* He did not propose to do either in any case. Officeholding seemed his only economic salvation. But it dismayed Sypher that his "claims were equal with some others who now hold positions of *'honor and profit,'* " while he was struggling to keep wolves from the door.[30]

Yankee planters were certainly not alone among carpetbaggers in viewing Republican politics in the South as a source of livelihood. They were only more conspicuous in this regard, having been heavy losers in the crop failures of 1866–67. Yet everyone in the Lower South, at least, felt the reverberations of these cotton losses, and most everyone had to adjust his plans accordingly. As one Indiana native explained of a fellow Mississippi carpetbagger in distress, "Like nearly all of us northern men in the South, he is broken up financially. . . ."[31] Individual instances of what he meant can be found in a variety of occupations. A Northern lawyer in Mobile, Alabama, for example, who counted several former Confederates among his personal friends, said his clients were so poor, "I can't make anything." He wanted to be appointed recorder of deeds and mortgages in New Orleans.[32] Attorneys for the freedmen were in financial straits just as dire, if not more so. John Emory Bryant, a former Freedmen's Bureau agent in Georgia who had tried without success to make a living as a lawyer for the ex-slaves, saw in the Republican party a future that might bring him "position and money."[33] Northern teachers in the South also had pecuniary motives for a change of occupation. "I am tired of the schoolroom," one of them wrote the commanding general in Alabama in 1867, "and I would like to have an appointment . . . which will pay me liberal wages."[34] Northern-born editors of Republican sheets likewise found themselves in "financial distress" and in need of political assistance. They would continue to find themselves in this predicament throughout Radical Reconstruction, for it was nearly impossible to support a Republican journal in the South during these years except by means of state or federal printing contracts.[35]

At a time when business in general was flat and decent prospects were lacking, the financial attractions of political positions in the South could not be taken for granted. The prosaic duty of registering voters under the military Reconstruction acts of 1867, for instance, paid a commission fee of thirteen to forty cents a voter and could bring in several thousand dollars in some districts. These were not low wages for the time, and several Northerners who actively sought out registrar appointments apparently sensed as much.[36] Fees available to sheriffs and tax collectors, moreover, often added up to more than pocket change; salaries of $5,000 to $20,000 a year were not unheard of.[37] State legislators were not paid so liberally, but ordinarily they could supplement their incomes with generous per diem and travel expenses, and in other ways.[38] State officers, on the other hand, from the governor on down, were usually—though not always—well remunerated, and federal officeholders were everywhere handsomely rewarded. To name one case, registers in bankruptcy, a newly created federal position that did a brisk business in the Reconstruction South, earned annual incomes that ranged from $5,000 to $12,000. George E. Spencer, a future carpetbagger U.S. senator, landed one of these for Alabama's fourth congressional district. The position made him feel, as he put it, "that my duty is to remain here and help reconstruct this God forsaken and miserable country."[39]

In fact, the attractions of Southern political office were great enough to induce more than one transient Northerner to make the region his permanent residence. Although he had been leasing plantations in Carroll Parish since 1864, John Lynch decided to sell his property in the North once he secured a seat in the Louisiana state senate in 1868. "Here now is my only home," he explained, "and *here I intend to remain*."[40] Sometimes officeholding inducements were sufficient to tempt Northerners to return to the South as well. Charles W. Lowell, a former Union colonel who had served as an attorney for New Orleans freedmen before returning to his native Maine, said the cold weather of New England inclined him to relocate in Shreveport, Louisiana. But a warmer climate was only a partial motive. He confessed he did not want to return "unless I could be assured of *some* appointment." He must have received assurances of sorts, because before long he was serving as Republican speaker of the Louisiana house, and he later became the United States postmaster of New Orleans.[41]

General Francis J. Herron was another carpetbagger who felt it was his duty to reconstruct a region where he hesitated to remain, and it is instructive to follow his checkered career for a moment. Descended from old wealth, this onetime Iowa banker had established a cotton factorage and commission business in New Orleans not long after presiding over the formalities of surrender in the Pelican State. At about the same time he became a financial partner in the extensive planting operations near Natchez, Mississippi, of journalist Whitelaw Reid. The fortunes of the house of Herron scarcely rose before they fell. Bank failures and U.S. Treasury defalcations in the Crescent City in the spring of 1867 had weakened him considerably by the time the cotton crops fell below expectations later that year and nearly ruined him completely. In August 1866 Herron had declined an invitation to represent Louisiana at the conservative National Union

Convention in Philadelphia, but in 1867 the political landscape looked much different, and he was now in earnest about staking a claim somewhere upon it.[42]

Herron first tried for the position of United States marshal for New Orleans (this was around the time of his initial financial embarrassments due to the bank failures), and he succeeded so far as to win the endorsement of both President Andrew Johnson and Senator Charles Sumner. But the competition was keen and Herron lost out.[43] He then joined in the Republican party counsels regarding the makeup of Louisiana's new congressional delegation, and he stood in high hopes of receiving one of the party's nominations for U.S. senator.[44] This political prospect also fell through, and by the end of 1868 Herron was forced to declare bankruptcy, confessing that he was "in a bad way, completely cleared out, and working for a new start." A promising beginning appeared to be the post of U.S. collector of customs at New Orleans. But the new president, Ulysses S. Grant, was an old enemy from the war days, and he preferred his own brother-in-law for the position.[45] Herron next set his sights on the office of sergeant-at-arms for the U.S. House of Representatives. He had heard "some marvelous stories as to the value of the place" to the occupant of the same office in the U.S. Senate, and by now Herron welcomed any opportunity "to get away from the South."[46] But President Grant's influence reached into Congress as well, and General Herron met with yet another reversal.[47] Persistence and party fidelity bore fruit for Herron in the spring of 1871. His political colleagues from Louisiana realized he was in great need of "some place for absolute support," and Henry Clay Warmoth, the carpet-bag governor, offered him the tax collectorship of the fourth district of New Orleans.[48] The position paid around $12,000 a year, and Warmoth promised "to do even better" by Herron before the fall. "I am much in hopes that our new arrangement will work to advantage, both politically and financially," he exulted of his new relationship with the governor.[49] Although Warmoth proved to be a man of his word, appointing Herron to be secretary of state a short while later, the arrangement apparently did not meet financial expectations. Herron the tax collector was later caught with short accounts.[50]

If the experience of Herron the office seeker tells us anything, it is that the politics of livelihood lasted well beyond the formative years of the Southern Republican party. In fact, the office-hungry style lasted at least for the duration of radical Reconstruction, if not longer. Northern entrepreneurs who had failed at some Southern enterprise, say, midway through Reconstruction, proved as likely to turn to politics in 1872 as they had been in 1867. Charles C. Puffer, a New York wool grower who had lost a good deal of money at cotton planting in South Carolina right after the war, resolved never to show his face at home again until he was "even with the world."[51] He did not immediately enter politics after his planting setbacks, instead trying his hand at lumbering and gold mining, but with little success. Straining under debts and lawsuits, his mining concern could not even meet its payroll save by furnishing supplies, and by 1872, his company near bankruptcy, Puffer was jockeying as a Republican for one of the Palmetto State's congressional seats. He thought his chances for the position were good, provided his mining embarrassments did not interfere. "My Boy, we shall not always be in hot water I trust," he assured a business associate in New York.[52] Puffer never received the Republican nomination, although some lesser honor from the party might have come his way. One of his Northern associates in the abortive mining concern expected to be appointed Republican treasurer of Union County, South Carolina. He would accept the position for familiar reasons. "I imagine that you will be somewhat surprised at this course I have taken, and wonder how I can content myself to live in this *blasted* country," he wrote in explanation to a friend at home. "My only answer is that I think it is . . . the best I can do. Everything is objectionable except the salary of the office which will be at least $2,000 a year."[53] For as long as the Southern Republican party remained in power, Northern newcomers in impressive numbers tended to regard political patronage as a sort of insurance policy against insolvency.

That this style of politics lasted for as long as it did was owing in large measure to the stark reality of Southern poverty, on the one hand, and the unpleasant reality of pervasive ostracism, on the other. The two realities seem to have worked in tandem to reinforce the attitude that political patronage was indispensable to personal financial well-being. The poverty can scarcely be exaggerated. Never during Reconstruction—or for the remainder of the century, for that matter—did the former Confederacy enjoy anything like true prosperity. The years 1868–72 saw a return of commercial health and a quickening of business energies, but this was a prosperous period only in comparison with the economic desperation of the immediate past and future. When the panic of 1873 struck, triggering a depression that reversed such small gains as had been registered since the surrender, cotton prices had already commenced a long-term, though fluctuating, decline that before it ended would further impoverish white yeomen and black freedmen and leave the planters more land poor than ever.[54] Added to these problems was the handicap the South faced in the form of inadequate banking capital and currency, which the National Banking Act and supplemental congressional legislation did much to create. After Appomattox the region hardly had a circulating medium worthy of the name. Greenbacks were usually hoarded, in accordance with Gresham's law, and what circulated was mostly a bewildering variety of badly depreciated state, municipal, and business scrip and warrants. The makeshift money system caused a great deal of inconvenience without easing the credit stringencies of a people who had to borrow money in order to move their crops to market. Agricultural interest rates as embodied in the crop lien were usurious even by today's standards, and everyone along the line appears to have been squeezing everyone below him in an effort to maintain a relative advantage that seldom left anyone opulent.[55] The widespread poverty set effective limits to what the Reconstruction governments could accomplish in the way of extending state services to the new black citizenry. Reform came at a time when Southerners could least afford to pay additional taxes, however minimal these levies might appear when judged against modern or contemporaneous Northern standards. In some states land forfeitures for nonpayment of taxes were extensive, though not always permanent.[56] On the whole, economic conditions in the postwar South were nasty, brutish, but not short, and they tended to strengthen the attitude that patronage had a usefulness beyond the strictly political.

Hardly less effective in reinforcing the same attitude was the ostracism to which carpetbaggers were subjected. The proscription of Northern Republicans was as prevalent as it was relentless, and it ranged in intensity from the cold shoulder and the audible insult to the coarser techniques of terrorism, bullyism, and plain assassination, which was favored by the Ku Klux Klan and similar groups.[57] Commercial ostracism was also popular, and sometimes went forward on an organized basis. A Democratic editor in Alabama recommended it as superior to violence. "STARVE THEM OUT!" was the advice he gave for bringing white Republicans to heel. "Don't put your foot in the doors of their shops, offices, and stores. Purchase from true men and patronize those of known Southern sympathies."[58] The effect was merely to add an extra weight to the burden of economic difficulties carpetbaggers were already shouldering in their efforts to make a living in the Reconstruction South, particularly if they were business and professional men or otherwise dependent on the goodwill of the surrounding community. Their only clientele, the freedmen, were the most poverty-stricken of all Southerners, which partly explains why one Northern physician in Florida found it necessary to moonlight as a clerk of court (the position paid $5,000 annually). Confessed one importunate office seeker in South Carolina: "Being a 'Yankee' I suppose I must starve, if some employment is not given me. . . ."[59] The grossest forms of persecution were generally reserved for Republican officeholders, who were bushwhacked with regularity in some localities, yet even Northerners who eschewed office and merely voted Republican sometimes felt the sting of proscription and exclusion. In order to carry on a successful law practice, a few of them apparently concluded, it was essential to secure a political position, which could bring in clients by signifying that the officeholder enjoyed influence with state, local, or federal authorities.[60] As a general thing, it was not easy for carpetbaggers to " 'hero in the usual callings of life' in the South."[61] If they often looked upon officeholding as employment of last resort, it was probably because relentless ostracism conspired with persistent poverty to make Republican politics seem like the only reliable source of income they had.

But even the financial security of political office in the South was not always a safe gamble. The Radical governments may have offered good salaries, but in truth these regimes were as poor as the people they represented. Their securities seldom sold at face value, yet on occasion they had to float bonds in order to meet current operating expenses. Their treasuries were usually bare, yet officials drew pay in warrants they were expected to redeem for greenbacks the government almost never had on hand. Governor Harrison Reed of Florida, for example, who was paid in state scrip, realized only $1,000 from his $3,500 salary.[62] This widespread indigence in both the private and public economy understandably tempted several carpetbaggers to supplement their incomes by less than honest means. Thus we find some new-comers participating in various Reconstruction bond and railroad rings, profiting from inside information on state finances, and using their connections to secure lucrative state contracts for their private internal-improvement companies. Thus, we discover still more Northerners padding expense accounts, liberalizing per diem allowances, mixing together public and private accounts, stealing school funds, and coming up with ingenious ways to speculate in warrants. If the official salary was not what it appeared to be, then one could always collect taxes or fees in greenbacks, settle accounts in depreciated scrip, and bank the difference. Several sheriffs and tax collectors used these methods to shore up their incomes, until state governments undercut them by making scrip acceptable in the payment of taxes.[63] The motive of the speculators was prob-ably financial need, though the means employed could stimulate financial greed as well. Unlike large spoilsmen in Washington and New York, the carpetbaggers as a class could at least plead the excuse of economic hardship for yielding to the easy morals of Gilded Age America.

But the major way that Southern poverty—and ostracism too—affected the carpetbaggers was not so much by tempting them into corruption as by strengthening one of their original reasons for entering politics. Their appetite for office seems to have soared under the stimulus of hard times. Indeed, it is nothing short of remarkable that men who had affirmed openly and repeatedly their indifference to politics before Radical Reconstruction ap-pear to have been satisfied with nothing less than all of the offices, or at least all of the good ones, during radical Reconstruction. To be sure, they never succeeded in exercising political dominance in any Southern state during Reconstruction, though they came close to it in Louisiana. Yet they were extraordinarily successful at cornering many of the more powerful and lucrative positions, and they enjoyed a political influence out of all proportion to their actual numbers in the voting population.[64] That they were so conspicuous in the politics of the period probably has some-thing to do with another practice at which they were successful—

the occupancy of several positions simultaneously. Plural office-holding was not only permissible during Reconstruction, it was practiced on an extensive scale. It was not at all uncommon to find carpetbagger legislators serving in county and federal positions concurrently.[65]

Nor was it unusual to find them practicing nepotism. Several congressmen had brothers or brothers-in-law who held state or county offices. At the local level, it was sometimes hard to tell where politics began and kinship left off. In Yazoo County, Mississippi, the Morgan brothers, Albert T. and William, were the dominant powers, while in Carroll Parish, Louisiana, it was the "Benham Party," headed by George C. and his brother, that pulled the wires. Grenada County, Mississippi, moreover, was under the control of William Price, who was a pluralist as well as a nepotist.[66] Often this nepotism merely reflected the fact that men who planted together sometimes politicked together as well. More than one joint plantation venture midwifed a pair or two of carpetbaggers, the Gordon colony in Florida alone delivering two Republicans of some stature, Leonard G. Dennis and Horatio Jenkins, Jr. But nepotism usually got mixed in with cronyism before long. Marshall H. Twitchell, for example, a Freedmen's Bureau agent who married into a Louisiana plantation before becoming a Republican state senator, imported many friends and relatives to staff the offices that fell under his control in Red River Parish, Louisiana. At one time or another, his biographer tells us, his family and associates "held practically every office in the parish" and occasionally "held as many as four jobs at once." His Northern planting partner, who served with Twitchell in the legislature, also had a brother who became deeply involved in parish politics after shifting his theater of operations out of Madison Parish. The Twitchell clan was about the closest thing to a Republican family dynasty the Reconstruction South pro-duced.[67]

Carpetbaggers were not without legitimate excuses for their tendencies toward cronyism, nepotism, and pluralism. It was ad-mittedly difficult to find qualified native whites who would accept Republican appointments and nominations, and even a number of old Unionists scouted the idea of affiliating with the party of black rights. Yet the reason carpetbaggers gave most frequently for their office hunger—at least during the period when it was insatiable—was the self-serving one that they were "much more temperate than the men around them," that they "would do as well as any old citizen," and that, things being what they were, "all the offices should go to Federal officers," or at the very minimum to men born and raised above the Ohio River.[68] In these assertions of special claims and qualifications there was a certain amount of sectional hostility, prejudice, and downright vanity. But reading between the lines we can discover something else as well: the recognition that two offices in combination paid better than one alone; and the knowledge that a family with more than one breadwinner was financially more secure than a family with only one.

It is admittedly misleading, not to say unfair, to stress the pecuniary preoccupations of the carpetbaggers to the exclusion of other motives. The Southern Republican party had more than its share of Northerners who became carpetbaggers not because they loved money less, but humanity more. After all, Albert T. Morgan and his brother entered Republican politics not simply to secure to themselves a financial "restoration," but also to secure to the freedman "the right to life, liberty and pursuit of happiness."[69] Who is to say which motive was the controlling one? In the case of Albert Morgan, who kept faith with his principles long after it was popular or safe to do so, it was probably the idealistic motive that was dominant. He once passed up an opportunity to be sheriff of Yazoo County, a position "worth in fees and commissions six to ten thousand per year," because he wished to remain in the state legislature, where he thought he would "be able to do more good."[70] And what are we to make of the fact that Albion Tourgée ran for a seat in the North Carolina Constitutional Convention and later welcomed a state judgeship because his private business affairs were in disarray and he needed the money? Surely to say this about him is to leave a lot unsaid.[71] To the list of high-minded carpetbaggers should be added the names of John Emory Bryant in Georgia, Reuben Tomlinson in South Carolina, Leonard G. Dennis in Florida, and that skillful nepotist himself, Marshall H. Twitchell in Louisiana.[72] They and many like them were all committed to the proposition that racial and social justice were things worth dedicating one's life to. Their motives may have been complex, even contradictory at times, but this is no argument against either their integrity *or* their accomplishments, which were real and considerable.[73] It is no part of wisdom to sneer at sincere purpose even when it is difficult to dissociate from economic motivation.

But one of the tragedies of the Reconstruction period is that most carpetbaggers usually found it impossible to divorce economic and idealistic motives, altogether. Albert Morgan himself was eventually compelled to campaign for the post of sheriff in part because he needed more money to satisfy his clamorous creditors.[74] Having been obliged to enter politics in order to secure a livelihood, many carpetbaggers soon discovered they had to remain in politics in order to protect that livelihood. The bitter economic circumstances of the birth of the Southern Republican party did not ease with time, as we have seen, and the social and commercial ostracism to which several newcomers were subjected only made them more desperate to find some position that would pay or, having obtained this much, another position that "will pay better."[75]

Which brings us back to the subject of Southern Republican factionalism. A substantial amount of it appears to have originated in the financial weaknesses of the organizational leadership; otherwise there is no explaining why Southern Republicans fought about nothing so much as the loaves and fishes of office. By all accounts patronage was usually *the* issue over which the Reconstructionists quarreled the most. To be sure, a certain degree of internecine feuding was to be expected in a party composed of former slaves and former slaveholders, wealthy landlords and impoverished tenants, former Whigs and former Democrats, wartime Unionists and original secessionists, black-belt planters and hill-country yeomen, blacks and whites, and, not least, the victor and the vanquished. Once the Reconstructionists in the Deep South wrote into law their minimal reform agenda, these incongruent elements began to war among themselves over who should run the party and in whose interests. Did more need to be done in the way of racial integration and black economic uplift, or did wisdom dictate slighting the black vote in order to enlarge the white vote? If the latter was the case, which whites should be appealed to, the masses or the classes? And what of reform in general? Should it be in the direction of greater economic democracy or diversified economic development? Over the question of leadership the debate often became sulfurous. Many carpetbaggers, as we have

seen, believed they had special claims to dominance. Several scalawags, as native white Republicans were called, replied that they
were "opposed to newcomers occupying prominent positions either
in the State or general government." They felt they deserved pre-
eminence by virtue of their pre-war residence, wartime sufferings,
or high antebellum status, as the case might be, or in recognition
of the fact that they had sometimes been the first to come forward
as party organizers in their respective states.[76] Black Republicans
also excelled at special pleading, especially in the latter phases of
Reconstruction. Since they supplied the bulk of the votes, they
reasoned they should receive a fair share of the offices. Especially
hard words were exchanged between quondam Whigs and Democrats, and the recriminations that ex-Confederates and persistent
Unionists hurled at one another could not always be repeated in
polite company.[77] Factionalism along these lines and over these
issues was altogether natural, and when and where Southern
Republicans enjoyed comfortable legislative and electoral majorities, it thrived nearly unchecked.

Yet, what gave these antipathies of race, class, section, and party
an edge they might not otherwise have had was the financial
indigence of so much of the rank-and-file Republican leadership.
The simple truth is that carpetbaggers were by no means alone
in their reliance upon political office for a livelihood. Numerous
scalawags appear to have been in similar straits. Several pre-war
officeholders in Mississippi, for instance, converted to Republicanism largely for economic purposes. "I am in need of employment which would give me some remuneration," one of them
confessed. J. Madison Wells, the Johnsonian governor of Louisiana
who later joined the Republican party, offered this explanation
as to why his son should receive a federal appointment: "All
things being equal, I think preference should be given to those
'of the manor born' and who have lost everything by the war."[78]
A desire to secure a steady income was admittedly not the only—or
even the major—reason many scalawags identified with the party
of black rights. Their motives for becoming Republicans were
probably more mixed than were those of the carpetbaggers,
ranging from reform to revenge and including opportunism of
the broadest kind.[79] But poverty and proscription worked upon
native white Republicans with particular severity; in Alabama,
at least, "scalawags were much more bitterly hated than carpet-

baggers," and the financial effects of persecution caused many wartime Unionists to scurry for Republican appointments.[80] Of course, no class of Republican politician was more financially needy than were black officeholders. As we now know, many were artisans and small tradesmen and thus singularly vulnerable to the economic reprisals the white community was especially prone to bring down upon maverick black citizens. W. McKee Evans explains their situation best: "Once a Negro acquired the reputation of being a politician, for better or for worse, he became dependent upon political jobs for a livelihood."[81] Negro and native white Republicans also felt constrained to employ the various unethical means carpetbaggers relied on to supplement their incomes. Honest and dishonest graft were not a Northern import but generally selective adaptations for survival in the hostile Southern environment.

In short, here was a party that was financially hard pressed from head to toe and unusually wedded to political patronage for economic sustenance and well-being. Its leaders may not have pursued office entirely for financial reasons, but they soon discovered they had to stay in office largely for such reasons. The poverty of Southern life in these years made Republican offices peculiarly attractive; the commercial and social ostracism that most Republicans suffered made those same offices things that could not be gladly given up. Thus, Republican politicians intrigued and conspired, libeled and slandered and occasionally assassinated one another, and even bolted their party often for no loftier purpose than to get an office, hold on to an office, recover an office, or vent their anger at having lost an office. As one South Carolina Republican complained, "Anyone who is defeated swears, abuses all the rest, and bolts the action."[82] The only wonder about the defections is that there were not more of them (which is another way of saying that the courage and commitment of Republicans should never be lost sight of). Since nearly every Republican had made great personal sacrifices on behalf of the party, nearly every single one of them had a compelling argument as to why he should be rewarded with patronage. And if a paying office was not forthcoming, what good reason was there to remain within the Republican fold and thus continue enduring the proscription that was a sure guarantee lean times were around the corner?[83] The bolting was understandable, and so was the factionalism. It was as though the entire Southern Republican party was composed of so many newspaper editors who had to get up little quarrels with their competitors in order to obtain the public printing contracts that often meant the difference between survival and insolvency. The multiplication of offices beyond the requirements of even the modern state barely improved the situation. Nor was relief provided by granting to various governors appointive power over many local offices heretofore elective. The demand for office always exceeded the supply. The scalawag governor James L. Alcorn of Mississippi lamented early in his term that there were usually twenty applicants for every position at his disposal. At one time he controlled over one thousand appointments.[84]

Indeed, as Reconstruction wore on, the quarreling that grew out of office seeking began increasingly to cut across the other fault lines that rent the Republican party. Factional distinctions based on race, section, and party broke down or blurred around the edges. Carpetbaggers joined hands with scalawags, blacks with whites, in shifting, almost kaleidoscopic patterns, ostensibly for no larger purpose than personal convenience and private gain. As Adelbert Ames, the Northern-born governor of Mississippi, later recalled, "If one's own kind could not or would not meet a demand for office, an alliance would be made with another kind."[85] And so it went during most of Radical Reconstruction in the Deep South. Even ideological divisions showed great fluidity, or at least lost much meaning. Conservatives one day might become Radicals the next, and vice versa, as many of the internal struggles within the Republican party soon reduced themselves to naked struggles for spoils between the ins and the outs, the hopefuls and the disappointed. Everywhere it seemed the same. Jerrell Shofner's description of Republican politics in Florida gets at the heart of what was taking place elsewhere in the Lower South at the time: "There were many possible coalitions among the various groups in Florida, . . . but they were never clearly divided along racial lines and they were not static."[86] Nor were they always ideologically clear-cut. As Joel Williamson remarks of South Carolina, "many political contests . . . were merely fights between Republican factions standing on the same program and principles, the real issue being personal." "Such politics also produced strange electoral bedfellows," Williamson goes on to observe. By the same token, they gave rise to a host of personal political machines on both the state and local levels, for ring politics usually flourish where patronage for its own sake assumes unusual importance.[87]

Inasmuch as Republican feuding often boiled down to struggles for political jobs that paid, it should come as no surprise that one of the most durable forms of Republican factionalism was that between state and federal officeholders. Many of the rings and bosses lined up across this divide, generally falling in behind the state or federal machine. The former was always headed by the governor, if for no other reason than his vast appointive power, while tradition commonly gave federal patronage over to the care of one or both United States senators and an occasional congressman. Louisiana was exceptional in that the collector of customs was supreme because of his family relationship to the president.[88] Actually the personalities were usually secondary. In the Reconstruction South patronage was the thing, and the rivalry was in truth between competing forms of patronage or, to be more precise, between quantity and quality. State patronage imparted power to its dispenser because there was more of it and because it often served as the basis of local electoral strength. But federal patronage commanded allegiance because it paid higher salaries and paid them in greenbacks. The ideal arrangement for a Republican politician was to hold each type of position simultaneously (as many did). The one strengthened his hand at the local level, the other strengthened his bank account. But what if a hateful choice had to be made between the two? It requires no suspension of disbelief to imagine that the average Republican politician, pressed on all sides as he was by the threat of poverty and the lash of proscription, would in all likelihood place financial security above local political strength in any utilitarian calculus of personal well-being. Hereon hangs much of the tale of Reconstruction politics. Those in control of federal patronage were in an uncommonly strong position to mount serious challenges to the state machine, which is why the various governors were always complaining of their lack of control over federal appointments. The federal organization could easily bore from within the rival state organization by coupling policy appeals (to conservatives or radicals, as the case might be) with hints and promises of lucrative appointments. It could also put together a bigger campaign chest than could the state machine, because it could realize more money from the voluntary contributions of its employees. Even in its facilities for distributing campaign literature, mobilizing the vote, and organizing the party, the federal machine was often better situated than its state counterpart. A federal agency such as the Internal Revenue Service had collectors and assessors in nearly every county of the South, which provided it with an invaluable network of communications in a region where the means of transportation were but poorly developed.[89]

There were in fact few limits to the mischief the dispenser of federal patronage could cause if he put his mind to it. So as to enhance his re-election prospects, U.S. Senator Spencer from Alabama, the carpetbagger who felt it was his duty to reconstruct a region he did not like, actively intrigued to help elect a Democratic legislature and governor in 1870. His goal was to eliminate his carpetbag rival in the U.S. Senate and his scalawag rival in the statehouse, in order to give himself complete control over all Republican patronage, which would be only federal in nature if his scheme succeeded. He thought he "could use the men for whom he secured appointments and the money they controlled to eliminate any Democratic competition in 1872," when he stood for re-election. The scheme worked, more or less, though it left the Alabama Republican party in a shambles from which it never recovered,[90] testimony to the power that federal patronage possessed to destabilize a party with a weak social base and an economically pressed leadership class.

There was admittedly one group within the Southern Republican party that was not financially dependent upon officeholding, but it is the exception that proves the rule. These were the conservative Republicans, composed for the most part of former Whig planters and merchants and relatively well-to-do carpetbaggers. The latter usually resided in urban centers, in places like Jacksonville, Florida, and Vicksburg, Mississippi, but where they could be found in the rural districts they were almost always large landowners who were resentful of the high land taxes, frightened and annoyed by the labor instability caused by Reconstruction, and embarrassed by the corruption and factionalism that plagued their party. Conservative Northerners in the South especially craved respectability, which they believed their wealth entitled them to. In short, there was a rough correspondence between wealth and conservatism within Republican ranks, as seen in the extreme example of impecunious carpetbaggers who defected to the Democrats as soon as they accumulated some property.[91] Whether in town or country, moreover, conservative Republicans were very eager to encourage economic development through an alliance between government and business, and they hoped to give their party respectability and strength by attracting to it Democrats and Southern conservatives of the better sort. That patronage would have to serve as the means of conversion posed no threat to conservative Republicans, since they did not have to rely on office for any considerable portion of their livelihood. Republican governors of conservative leanings were forever courting Southern Democrats with the zeal of a young suitor, and in the name of reform often pledged to make their party into something better than a mere spoils agency by distributing patronage on the basis of merit. It must be admitted that Southern Democrats were very adroit at encouraging Republican overtures merely for the purpose of fostering Republican dissension. Democrats played their hand with consummate skill. Conservative Republicans could not broaden the base of the party without robbing Peter to pay Paul, without depriving some needy loyal Republican of his job in order to give it to some flirtatious but insincere Democrat, and without therefore plunging their party into factional patronage quarrels that in many states made the Republicans peculiarly vulnerable to Redeemer assaults.[92] The Republican rank and file were simply too financially indigent and dependent upon office to survive attempts by their leaders to build bridges to the political opposition.

In fact the party of emancipation could not even easily enact so-called good-government reforms, which conservative Republicans deemed essential to their strategy and which several Republican administrations late in Reconstruction found it necessary to press forward. Only at the risk of disrupting party unity could one correct even the most obvious abuses. When Governor Harrison Reed of Florida, for example, moved to put a stop to plural officeholding, he made himself the target of an impeachment effort engineered by the very carpetbag state senators against whom his reform was directed. The impeachers could afford to legislate a reduction in their state salaries, which they did do, but they could not sacrifice one of their county offices, which might have accounted for half of their income. In Mississippi, by contrast, after the panic of 1873 began to be felt, Republican law-makers refused even to cut their salaries or reduce expenditures and printing contracts, despite loud demands from various tax-payers' conventions that they do so.[93] It bears repeating that Republican politicians in the Deep South during Reconstruction were probably not more greedy than the average American politician, only more needy, and this fact doubtless explains in large measure the ruinous factionalism that plagued the Southern Republican party during the years of its ascendancy, and beyond as well.

In their motives for seeking office, in their reasons for holding on to office, and in their methods of living off of office, carpet-baggers in the Deep South illustrate a tragic truth about Republican Reconstruction that is unpleasant to acknowledge. If several carpetbaggers went into politics in order to secure a livelihood, if they grabbed for as many offices as they could in order to protect that livelihood, and if they tried by factionalist means to retain those offices because public and private poverty and economic and social ostracism made it necessary for them to do so, the Northern newcomers only throw into sharp relief the formidable handicaps that the Reconstructionists were up against. Those handicaps were the colonial economic status that the defeated Confederacy was sliding into, the weak social base of the party that the abandon-ment of land reform did nothing to strengthen, and the utter unwillingness of the conquered to concede legitimacy, not to mention fellowship, to the party of black rights. Between the poverty that resulted from the former two handicaps and the economic coercion that resulted from the latter, Southern Republi-cans could find little room to maneuver save by cannibalizing one another in patronage fights that they could ill afford. The experi-ence of carpetbaggers in the Lower South makes the factionalism that brought the Republicans to grief a little more comprehensible.

NOTES

1. For a good overview of the problem of Republican factionalism, see Otto H. Olsen's introduction to *Reconstruction and Redemption in the South,* ed. Otto H. Olsen (Baton Rouge, 1980), pp. 8–11.

2. John M. Morris to William E. Chandler, September 14, 1868, Chandler Papers, Library of Congress; Thomas H. Holt, *Black over White: Negro Political Leadership in South Carolina during Reconstruction* (Urbana, Chicago, and London, 1977), p. 175.

3. The seminal revisionism on carpetbaggers includes Otto H. Olsen *Carpetbagger's Crusade: The Life of Albion Winegar Tourgée* (Baltimore, 1965); David H. Overy, Jr., *Wisconsin Carpetbaggers in Dixie* (Madison, Wis., 1961); Jack B. Scroggs, "Carpetbagger Constitutional Reform in the South Atlantic States, 1865–1868," *Journal of Southern History*, 27 (1961), 475–93; and two important contributions by Richard N. Current: *Three Carpetbag Governors* (Baton Rouge, 1967) and "Carpetbaggers Reconsidered," in David H. Pinkney and Theodore Ropp, eds., *A Festschrift for Frederick B. Artz* (Durham, N.C., 1964), pp. 139–57. Some more recent additions to the published literature also deserve mention. They are William C. Harris, "The Creed of the Carpetbaggers: The Case of Mississippi," *Journal of Southern History*, 40 (1974), 199–224; Allen W. Trelease, "Republican Reconstruction in North Carolina: A Roll-Call Analysis of the State House of Representatives, 1868–1870," *Journal of Southern History*, 42 (1976), 319–44; Richard L. Hume, "Carpetbaggers in the Reconstruction South: A Group Portrait of Outside Whites in the 'Black and Tan' Constitutional Conventions," *Journal of American History*, 64 (1977), 313–30; and Peter Kolchin, "Scalawags, Carpetbaggers, and Reconstruction: A Quantitative Look at Southern Congressional Politics, 1868–1872," *Journal of Southern History*, 45 (1979), 63–76. There is also much useful information regarding carpetbagger voting behavior in Holt's *Black over White*.

4. My definition of "carpetbaggers" closely follows the sensible one outlined by Richard Current: "White Northerners who went South after the beginning of the Civil War and Reconstruction and, sooner or later, became active in politics as Republicans." See his "Carpetbaggers Reconsidered," p. 144.

5. See Hume, "Carpetbaggers in the Reconstruction South," p. 315; and Kolchin, "Scalawags, Carpetbaggers, and Reconstruction," pp. 67–68. The exception, of course, was Georgia, where, as C. Mildred Thompson pointed out, "The big plums of office went to Republicans or to Northerners who came South before the war." *Reconstruction in Georgia: Economic, Social, Political, 1865–1872* (New York, 1915), pp. 216–17.

6. Current, "Carpetbaggers Reconsidered," p. 146; Harris, "Carpetbagger's Creed," p. 201; Joel Williamson, *After Slavery: The Negro in South Carolina during Reconstruction, 1865–1877* (Chapel Hill, 1965), pp. 375–76; and Lawrence N. Powell, *New Masters: Northern Planters during the Civil War and Reconstruction* (New Haven, 1980), pp. 8–18, 160–62.

7. Current, "Carpetbaggers Reconsidered," pp. 144–49, 150–51; Powell, *New Masters*, pp. 8–34. One important exception was George E. Spencer, who arrived in northern Alabama in 1862 as a colonel in an Iowa regiment and a short while later raised a Union calvary regiment among white Unionists there. Not long after Appomattox, Spencer began to intrigue in Alabama politics. "When you get out of the army," he wrote his friend and patron General Grenville M. Dodge, "I wish you would come South and operate. We are bound to succeed ultimately and if we can't any other way we can by

'negro suffrage.' I have been figuring with the radicals & think I am in the ring. As I am in business with Gov. [William] Sprague I can get his & the Chase influence. . . ." At the same time, Spencer was also trying to secure federal appointments in the South for his friends in Iowa, and a few months earlier he had been pressing to have William H. Smith, Alabama's first Republican chief executive, appointed military governor, though without success. He tried, too, to interest Dodge in a scheme to buy a controlling interest in the Mobile and Ohio Railroad, whose stock in 1865 was selling at only five cents on the dollar. (George E. Spencer to Grenville M. Dodge, August 1, 1865 [for the quotation], May 25, 1865, October 14, 1865, G. M. Dodge Papers, Iowa State Department of History.) For more on Spencer and his subsequent political career, see Sarah Van V. Woolfolk's "Carpetbaggers in Alabama: Tradition versus Truth," *Alabama Review*, 15 (1962), 133–44; and "George E. Spencer: A Carpetbagger in Alabama," *Alabama Review*, 19 (1966), 41–52. See also Sarah W. Wiggins (the same author), *The Scalawags in Alabama Politics, 1865–1881* (University, Ala., 1977), passim.

8. Overy, *Wisconsin Carpetbaggers*, pp. 14–27, passim; Current, "Carpetbaggers Reconsidered," 148–49; Henry L. Swint, "Northern Interest in the Shoeless Southerner," *Journal of Southern History*, 16 (1950), 457–71; and Powell, *New Masters*, pp. 19–20, 88.

9. John Pettit to Governor William L. Sharkey, July 27, 1865, vol. 70, Governor's Correspondence, Mississippi Department of Archives and History. The writer was a former United States congressman and senator from Indiana.

10. Powell, *New Masters*, pp. 18–24.

11. Ibid., pp. 38–54, 145–50.

12. Henry Clay Warmoth, *War, Politics and Reconstruction: Stormy Days in Louisiana* (New York, 1930), p. 30.

13. Current, "Carpetbaggers Reconsidered," p. 151.

14. E. O. C. Ord to Major General John A. Rawlins, March 27, 1867, *Senate Executive Documents*, no. 14, 40th Cong., 1st sess. (Ser. 1308), 136. See also Henry W. Warren, *Reminiscences of a Mississippi Carpetbagger* (Holden, Mass., 1914), p. 97; Joe Gray Taylor, *Louisiana Reconstructed, 1863–1877* (Baton Rouge, 1974), pp. 130–31, 143; Ruth Currie McDaniel, "Georgia Carpetbagger: John Emory Bryant and the Ambiguity of Reform during Reconstruction" (Ph.D. diss., Duke University, 1973), pp. 102–6, 116–17, 122–24; and Jimmy G. Shoalmire, "Carpetbagger Extraordinary: Marshal Harvey Twitchell, 1840–1905" (Ph.D. diss., Mississippi State University, 1969), pp. 74–75.

15. [George C. Benham], *A Year of Wreck* (New York, 1880), p. 431; Warren, *Reminiscences*, pp. 34, 49.

16. Ibid., p. 52. On the failure of Yankee cotton planters, see Powell, *New Masters*, pp. 145–50.

17. [Benham], *A Year of Wreck*, p. 460; Albert T. Morgan, *Yazoo: Or, On the Picket Line of Freedom* (Washington, D. C., 1884), pp. 132–33.

18. Rendig Fels, *American Business Cycles, 1865–1897* (Chapel Hill, 1959), pp. 92–96.

19. George G. Klapp to James D. Waters, March 21, 1868, Box 11, folder 8, Waters Family Papers, Essex Institute, Salem, Mass. See also George D. Holyoke to James D. Waters, October 6, 1866, in ibid.

20. Mary Loomis to Eben Loomis, January 26, 1867, Box 9, Todd Family Papers, Yale University.

21. William E. Smith, *The Francis Preston Blair Family in Politics,* 2 vols. (New York, 1969), II, 334–35. Actually, Blair was one of those new planters in the South who tried to advance his interests along two fronts at once. "My affairs at the plantation are getting on very well," he wrote his father in May 1866. "I hope to have a good crop—I am going now to try for a political crop also & will plant good seed. I hope I may win on one string or the other." (Francis P. Blair, Jr., to Francis P. Blair, Sr., May 6, 1866, Box 8, Blair Family Papers, Library of Congress.)

22. Henry C. Thomas to James D. Waters, December 20, 1868, Box 11, folder 8, Waters Family Papers, Essex Institute.

23. Fleming, *Civil War and Reconstruction in Alabama* (New York, 1905), p. 718n. See also James L. Garner, *Reconstruction in Mississippi* (Baton Rouge, 1968), p. 136; Current, "Carpetbaggers Reconsidered," p. 150; Holt, *Black over White,* pp. 12–13.

24. They were Charles W. Buckley, Benjamin W. Norris, and Willard Warner, in Alabama; Chester B. Darrall, John S. Harris, John E. Leonard, James McCleery, Frank Morey, John P. Newsham, George A. Sheridan, and Jacob H. Sypher, in Louisiana; A. R. Harris, George C. McKee, and H. R. Pease, in Mississippi; and S. L. Hoge, in South Carolina, who was a cotton planter in Alabama before shifting his theater of operations to the Palmetto State. Derived from Current, "Carpetbaggers Reconsidered," p. 147n, who estimates there were sixty-two carpetbagger congressmen in the entire ex-Confederacy, forty-three of whom were from the Deep South alone. See also Kolchin, "Scalawags, Carpetbaggers, and Reconstruction," pp. 65–69, whose numbers are slightly smaller because he focuses only on the Fortieth through the Forty-third congresses.

25. This has been calculated from Richard L. Hume's "The 'Black and Tan' Constitutional Conventions of 1867–1868 in Ten Former Confederate States: A Study of Their Membership" (Ph.D. diss., University of Washington, 1969), esp. the table on pp. 464–65. My estimate differs markedly from his. He finds that only 15 percent of the "outside" delegates to the conventions in all of the ex-Confederate states were planters or farmers; his figure for the states of the Lower South is slightly higher. The discrepancy in our estimates partly has to do with his definition of "outside whites," which in his study includes foreigners and men from the border states. But it is mainly owing to the advantage I enjoyed of having to study only Northern immigrants and not the more numerous native whites and Northern and Southern blacks. My biographical information about some of the carpetbagger delegates is understandably more complete than his, a fact that reflects no discredit on his important study. We are in substantial agreement on one thing. Though

composing only 15 percent of the total, "the 'typical' outside white elected to a seat in the 'Black and Tan' conventions," Hume reports (p. 661), "was a native of a Middle Atlantic or New England State who became involved in agricultural pursuits in the South after leaving the Union army." See also his "Carpetbaggers in the Reconstruction South," p. 323.

26. Garth W. James to his parents, October 17, 1868, and November 11, 1868 (where the quotation appears), Garth W. and Robertson James Papers (typescript), in possession of Prof. William Childers, University of Florida. See also Jerrell H. Shofner, *Nor Is It Over Yet: Florida in the Era of Reconstruction, 1863–1877* (Gainesville, 1974), pp. 175, 183–84. Jenkins was a member of the Gordon colony, a settlement of Northern planters that included the younger brothers of Henry and William James and Leonard G. Dennis, another prominent Florida carpetbagger. (Powell, *New Masters*, p. 29.)

27. Morgan, *Yazoo*, p. 132.

28. Moses Bates to Andrew Johnson, November 1868, series 1, reel 35, Andrew Johnson Papers (microfilm), Library of Congress. Bates was unusual among Northern newcomers in seeking a Democratic appointment. Of the 123 non-Republican congressmen and senators (chiefly Democratic) from the former Confederacy during Reconstruction, only 6 were recent Northern arrivals, none of whom had been a planter. Most newcomers clearly preferred the Republican party. This was partly because they sensed that there was little officeholding room for them within the Southern wing of the Democratic party. Said one newcomer in Alabama of the Democrats in his state: "It is hard for a Northern man to get a position here as the people . . . are so poor themselves that they *go for everything in sight*." (Quoted in Current, "Carpetbaggers Reconsidered," p. 151.) But the main reason Northerners in the South overwhelmingly affiliated with the Republican party is that they frankly found that party's principles and programs more compatible with their own convictions—which is another way of reiterating that the monetary motive was by no means the only thing influencing the political conduct of these men.

29. J. H. Sypher to Henry Clay Warmoth, October 18, 1867, Warmoth Papers, Southern Historical Collection, Chapel Hill.

30. J. H. Sypher to H. C. Warmoth, December 5, 1869 and December 25, 1869 (where the quotation appears), in ibid.

31. Peter B. Bailey to William E. Chandler, August 10, 1868, Chandler Papers, Library of Congress.

32. [?] Turner to H. C. Warmoth, April 6, 1868, Warmoth Papers, Southern Historical Collection, Chapel Hill.

33. McDaniel, "Georgia Carpetbagger," pp. 128–29.

34. W. E. Connelly to Wager Swayne, April 12, 1867, Reconstruction Correspondence of Wager Swayne, Alabama State Department of Archives and History.

35. Albert Griffen to Gov. William H. Smith, September 3, 1868, Governor's Correspondence, Alabama State Department of Archives and History. See also Joseph Logsdon, "An Illinois Carpetbagger Looks at the Southern Negro,"

Journal of the Illinois State Historical Society, 62 (1969), 56; Taylor, *Louisiana Reconstructed*, p. 199; Elizabeth Nathans, *Losing the Peace: Georgia Republicans and Reconstruction* (Baton Rouge, 1968), pp. 24–25.

36. Henry H. Russell to Wager Swayne, April 12, 1867; W. V. Dimmitt to W. Swayne, May 14, 1867; Charles Mayer to Col. Smith, June 11, 1867; and M. H. Gibson to William H. Smith, May 7, 1867, all in Reconstruction Correspondence of W. Swayne, Alabama State Department of Archives and History. Also Shofner, *Nor Is It Over Yet*, p. 163.

37. Garner, *Reconstruction in Mississippi,* pp. 305–6. Even clerks in the state circuit courts could earn as much as $5,000 annually. See William J. Purman to James Finlayson and family, June 28, 1926, W. J. Purman Papers, University of Florida.

38. See, for example, James Graham to Henry C. Warmoth, July 27, 1870, Warmoth Papers, Southern Historical Collection. See also Taylor, *Louisiana Reconstructed*, p. 201; Williamson, *After Slavery*, pp. 388–91; Garner, *Reconstruction in Mississippi*, pp. 316–19; Shofner, *Nor Is It Over Yet*, pp. 198–224.

39. George E. Spencer to Grenville M. Dodge, October 22, 1867, Iowa State Department of History.

40. John Lynch to Henry C. Warmoth, June 10, 1868, Warmoth Papers, Southern Historical Collection; and application of John Lynch & Company, March 1 and 3, 1864, in "Applications for Lease of Abandoned Plantations" (Entry 2383), Records of the Bureau of Refugees, Freedmen, and Abandoned Lands, National Archives.

41. C. W. Lowell to Henry C. Warmoth, April 5, 1867 (for the quotation), and James Graham to Warmoth, July 27, 1870, Warmoth Papers, Southern Historical Collection. Also C. W. Lowell to John A. Andrew, October 1, 1867, Andrew Papers, Massachusetts Historical Society; and Taylor, *Louisiana Reconstructed,* pp. 212, 214–16.

42. On Herron's Southern commercial activities, see Francis J. Herron to Edward Atkinson, June 5, 1866, Atkinson Letterbooks, Massachusetts Historical Society; Herron to Benjamin F. Flanders, April 19, 1866, B. F. Flanders Papers, Louisiana State University; Herron to Whitelaw Reid, November 12, 1868, Reid Papers, Library of Congress; W. Reid to Anna E. Dickinson, May 27, 1867, August 18, 1867, Dickinson Papers, Library of Congress; and the classified section of the Boston *Daily Advertiser,* June 18, 1866. See also H. A. Stuart, *Iowa Colonels and Regiments* (Des Moines, n.d.), pp. 201–206.

43. New Orleans *Times,* April 15, 1867; Boston *Daily Advertiser,* April 20, 1867.

44. Herron to W. Reid, January 29, 1868, February 5, 1868, June 30, 1868, Reid Papers, Library of Congress.

45. Herron to Reid, November 12, 1868, Reid Papers, Library of Congress. See also William P. Kellogg to Henry C. Warmoth, July 23, 1868, Warmoth Papers, Southern Historical Collection.

46. Herron to Reid, November 21, 1870, Reid Papers, Library of Congress.

47. Lionel A. Sheldon to Henry C. Warmoth, March 5, 1871, Warmoth Papers, Southern Historical Collection. See also Herron to Warmoth, February 10, 1871, March 4, 1871; J. W. Fairfax to Warmoth, February 13, 1871; J. R. West to Warmoth, February 23, 1871, March 6, 1871, all in ibid. Also Herron to Reid, December 13, 1870, February 15, 1871, February 24, 1871, Reid Papers, Library of Congress.

48. J. R. West to H. C. Warmoth, March 6, 1871 (for the quotation), Warmoth Papers, Southern Historical Collection; Francis W. Binning, "Henry Clay Warmoth and Louisiana Reconstruction" (Ph.D. diss., University of North Carolina, 1969), p. 254; Warmoth, War, Politics and Reconstruction, p. 266. Warmoth's concern for Herron's well-being was not strictly altruistic. The governor saw some political value in Herron's close friendship with Whitelaw Reid, who as managing editor of the New York Tribune was in a position to prevent "the attacks upon [Warmoth] which occasionally appear[ed] in the Tribune." After his appointment as tax collector, Herron asked Reid to let him serve as the New Orleans correspondent of the Tribune. (Herron to Reid, April 2, 1871, Reid Papers, Library of Congress.)

49. Herron to Reid, April 2, 1871, Reid Papers, Library of Congress.

50. Antoine Dubuclet to H. C. Warmoth, September 4, 1872, October 30, 1872, Governor's Correspondence, Louisiana State University; Herron to Warmoth, April 30, 1873, Warmoth Papers, Southern Historical Collection; Warmoth, War, Politics and Reconstruction, p. 266; Binning, "Henry Clay Warmoth," p. 258; Taylor, Louisiana Reconstructed, pp. 242–44.

51. Charles C. [Puffer] to William [Markham], December 1, [no year], Markham-Puffer Papers, Cornell University. Puffer had been a leading light in the United States Cotton Company, one of the large Northern planting syndicates that operated in the South in the years just preceding and following Appomattox. See Powell, New Masters, pp. 15–17.

52. C. C. Puffer to William Markham, February 19, 1872 (for the quotation), June 20, 1872, June 29, 1872, Markham-Puffer Papers, Cornell University.

53. George E. Tuxbury to William Markham, November 10, 1872, Markham-Puffer Papers, Cornell University.

54. William C. Harris, Day of the Carpetbagger: Republican Reconstruction in Mississippi (Baton Rouge and London, 1979), pp. 3–4, 23–32, 274–77, 371–75; Roger L. Ransom and Richard Sutch, One Kind of Freedom: The Economic Consequences of Emancipation (Cambridge, 1977), pp. 191–93; Gavin Wright, The Political Economy of the Cotton South: Households, Markets, and Wealth in the Nineteenth Century (New York, 1978), pp. 97–102, 164–76; Taylor, Louisiana Reconstructed, pp. 314–63; and Shofner, Nor Is It Over Yet, pp. 201–2; Michael Stuart Wayne, "Ante-Bellum Planters in the Post-Bellum South: The Natchez District, 1860–1880" (Ph.D. diss., Yale University, 1979), pp. 104–40; Steven Hahn, "The Roots of Southern Populism: Yeomen Farmers and the Transformation of Georgia's Upper Piedmont, 1850–1890" (Ph.D. diss., Yale University, 1979), pp. 189–283.

55. C. Vann Woodward, *Origins of the New South, 1877–1913* (Baton Rouge, 1951), pp. 180–85; Ransom and Sutch, *One Kind of Freedom*, pp. 128–31; Taylor, *Louisiana Reconstructed*, pp. 348–50; Harris, *Day of the Carpetbagger*, pp. 36–37, 291–94.

56. Harris, *Day of the Carpetbagger*, p. 295; Wayne, "Ante-Bellum Planters in the Post-Bellum South," pp. 115–17, 132–38.

57. For a sampling of the terror tactics, see Allen W. Trelease, *White Terror: The Ku Klux Klan Conspiracy and Southern Reconstruction* (New York, 1971).

58. Quoted in Sarah Woolfolk Wiggins, "Ostracism of White Republicans in Alabama during Reconstruction," *Alabama Review*, 27 (1974), 58.

59. Andrew Vredenburgh to Gov. Robert V. Scott, July 22, 1868, Gov. Scott Papers, South Carolina Archives; W. J. Purman to James Finlayson, June 28, 1926, W. J. Purman Papers, University of Florida; Wiggins, "Ostracism," p. 61.

60. Hiram R. Steele to Henry Clay Warmoth, October 19, 1871, Warmoth Papers, Southern Historical Collection; M. F. Conway to John A. Andrew, November 6, 1865, Andrew Papers, Massachusetts Historical Society; Charles Nordhoff, *The Cotton States in the Spring and Summer of 1875* (New York, 1876), pp. 11, 81; and McDaniel, "Georgia Carpetbagger," p. 178.

61. Ibid., p. 159.

62. Taylor, *Louisiana Reconstructed*, pp. 193, 260–61; Shofner, *Nor Is It Over Yet*, pp. 201–2, 218, 272; Joe M. Richardson, *The Negro in the Reconstruction of Florida, 1865–1877* (Tallahassee, 1965), pp. 203–6, 209; Williamson, *After Slavery*, p. 390. Williamson's description of the economic vicissitudes faced by the typical black legislator in South Carolina applies to most Reconstruction lawmakers, irrespective of race or nativity: "Throughout the session, he was plagued by a lack of money and by a worrying uncertainty whether he would be able to collect his pay at all, regardless of how much he voted himself, and whether he would realize from his nominal salary enough cash to meet his debts in Columbia and his obligations at home, familial and otherwise." Ibid., p. 392.

63. One reason some Reconstruction governments authorized the use of warrants in tax transactions is that the practice would improve the premium at which those warrants were exchanged, thereby raising the salaries of state officeholders, who frequently had to sell the scrip on the open market. William P. Kellogg to William E. Chandler, January 31, 1873, Chandler Papers, Library of Congress; Williamson, *After Slavery*, pp. 382–91; Shofner, *Nor Is It Over Yet*, pp. 201, 251–53; Wiggins, *Alabama Scalawags*, pp. 43–45; Taylor, *Louisiana Reconstructed*, pp. 199–201, 206; Current, *Three Carpetbag Governors*, pp. 63–64; Shoalmire, "Carpetbagger Extraordinary," pp. 90–93, 123–28.

64. Carpetbaggers were more powerful and prevalent in the states of heavy black populations in the Lower South, where, as Peter Kolchin tells us, "they appropriated most of the key offices to themselves when victory was likely." Congressional seats and federal appointments were the chief areas of their officeholding strength. In Congress alone they accounted for 48 percent of

the total number of terms served by Republicans from the Deep South during Reconstruction. Computed from Kolchin, "Scalawags, Carpetbaggers, and Reconstruction," p. 66; the quotation is on p. 73. See also Wiggins, *Alabama Scalawags*, p. 40; Taylor, *Louisiana Reconstructed*, p. 138.

65. Richardson, *The Negro in the Reconstruction of Florida*, p. 213; Taylor, *Louisiana Reconstructed*, pp. 201, 266; Shofner, *Nor Is It Over Yet*, p. 289; Garner, *Reconstruction in Mississippi*, p. 314.

66. A. T. Morgan to Adelbert Ames, February 10, 1874, Gov. Correspondence, Mississippi Department of Archives and History; "Report of The Committee on the Condition of the South," *House Reports*, 43rd Cong., 2nd sess., No. 261 (ser. 1660), III, 237; Garner, *Reconstruction in Mississippi*, pp. 314–15n. For further evidence of nepotism see Emerson Bentley to Henry C. Warmoth, December 8, 1871, and J. H. Sypher to Warmoth, February 13, 1871, Warmoth Papers, Southern Historical Collection; Sypher to Thaddeus Stevens, March 15, 1867, vol. 9, Steven Papers, Library of Congress; Charles W. Buckley to William H. Smith, April 23, 1867, Reconstruction Corr. of Wager Swayne, Alabama Dept. of Archives and History.

67. Shoalmire, "Carpetbagger Extraordinary," pp. 102–3, 132 (for the quotation), 163; George P. DeWeese to Henry C. Warmoth, April 25, 1868, Warmoth Papers, Southern Historical Collection; Taylor, *Louisiana Reconstructed*, p. 287.

68. The quotations appear respectively in "Report . . . on the Condition of the South," p. 385; C. W. Keating to Henry C. Warmoth, September 16, 1869; and George P. DeWeese to Warmoth, April 25, 1868, Warmoth Papers, Southern Historical Collection. A Northern merchant in Alabama elaborated: "I take it that no man who has been born & raised South & remained here throughout the existence of the Confederacy, *harmless*, cannot help (to say the least) to have his prejudices in favor of the South . . . & will act accordingly." G. W. Graham to Wager Swayne, May 17, 1867, Reconstruction Correspondence of W. Swayne, Alabama Dept. of Archives and History.

69. Morgan, *Yazoo*, p. 132.

70. Ibid., p. 259. For an insightful appreciation of Morgan, see Joseph Logsdon, "Yazoo, Mississippi: Race Relations in the Deep South during Reconstruction" (Paper delivered at the conference on the First and Second reconstructions, University of Missouri, St. Louis, February 15–17, 1978).

71. Current, "Carpetbaggers Reconsidered," p. 151; Olsen, *Carpetbagger's Crusade*, pp. 73–75, 118.

72. McDaniel, "Georgia Carpetbagger," pp. 128–39; Williamson, *After Slavery*, pp. 364–69; Shoalmire, "Carpetbagger Extraordinary," p. 78.

73. In her sensitive treatment of John Emory Bryant, who had trouble separating personal ambition from racial idealism, Ruth Currie McDaniel poses this sensible question: "Does a complexity of motive in itself invalidate his contribution?" ("Georgia Carpetbagger," p. 85.)

74. Morgan, *Yazoo*, pp. 369–70.

75. Hiram Steele to H. C. Warmoth, October 19, 1871, Warmoth Papers, Southern Historical Collection.

76. W. G. Johnson to Gov. William H. Smith, June 26, 1868, General Correspondence, Alabama Dept. of Archives and History. See also M. M. Hale to William E. Chandler, Mar. 25, 1872, Chandler Papers, Library of Congress. Scalawags in Alabama complained the loudest of carpetbagger domination, even though most of the offices in the state were controlled by native whites. Wiggins, *Alabama Scalawags*, pp. 30, 46–48. See also William C. Harris, "A Reconsideration of the Mississippi Scalawags," *Journal of Mississippi History*, 32 (1970), 3–42; Otto H. Olsen, "Reconsidering the Scalawags," *Civil War History*, 12 (1966), 304–20; Carl Degler, *The Other South: Southern Dissenters in the Nineteenth Century* (New York, 1974), pp. 256–63.

77. Ibid., pp. 212–17; Holt, *Black over White*, pp. 105–6; Loren Schweninger, *James T. Rapier and Reconstruction* (Chicago, 1978), pp. 74–75; Shofner, *Nor Is It Over Yet*, pp. 275–76; Harris, *Day of the Carpetbagger*, pp. 419–23.

78. Quoted in Harris, "Reconsideration of the Mississippi Scalawag," p. 33; J. Madison Wells to William E. Chandler, May 18, 1867, Chandler Papers, Library of Congress. See also Degler, *The Other South*, pp. 207–8.

79. Wiggins, *Alabama Scalawags*, p. 135; Degler, *The Other South*, pp. 191–229; Harris, "Reconsideration of the Mississippi Scalawag," pp. 3–42; Olsen, "Reconsidering the Scalawags," pp. 304–20.

80. Wiggins, "Ostracism," p. 64; idem, *Alabama Scalawags*, p. 24.

81. W. McKee Evans, *Ballots and Fence Rails: Reconstruction on the Lower Cape Fear* (Chapel Hill, 1966), p. 157; Charles Vincent, *Black Legislators in Louisiana during Reconstruction* (Baton Rouge, 1976), pp. 48–58; Holt, *Black over White*, pp. 37–38, 112. A black barber in Fredericksburg, Virginia, reported that after he began campaigning for Grant, "My custom have left me. I have no surport [*sic*]. Benjamin F. Ross to [E. D. Morgan?], September 6, 1872, Chandler Papers, Library of Congress.

82. John M. Morris to William E. Chandler, September 14, 1868, Chandler Papers, Library of Congress. See also Harris, *Day of the Carpetbagger*, pp. 305–10, 617–19; Richardson, *The Negro in the Reconstruction of Florida*, pp. 190–92, 225–26; Shofner, *Nor Is It Over Yet*, pp. 202–3; Taylor, *Louisiana Reconstructed*, pp. 156–313; Holt, *Black over White*, pp. 197–99, 201–7, 220–24; Schweninger, *James T. Rapier*, p. 138; Wiggins, *Alabama Scalawags*, pp. 56–57, 76–78, 80–82, 88–89, 112–13; McDaniel, "Georgia Carpetbagger," pp. 175–76; and especially Evans, *Ballots and Fence Rails*, pp. 155–66, for a particularly fine analysis of the financial basis of Republican factionalism.

83. A Republican lawyer from Alabama gives this interesting account of what prompted the federal postmaster in Mobile to switch his allegiance to Horace Greeley in 1872. Frederick G. Bromberg, he wrote, "was appointed Postmaster at Mobile by General Grant in '69, occup[y]ing at the same time the lucrative offices of County Commissioner, City Councilman, & State Senator of his county. As long as the offices lasted he was all right but when he was removed from the Post Office to make room for a better man he suddenly discovered that Grant was a corruptionist and announced for Greeley." Mark

D. Brainard to William E. Chandler, May 28, 1872, Chandler Papers, Library of Congress. (I have taken the liberty of regularizing the punctuation.)

84. Evans, *Ballots and Fence Rails,* p. 160; Garner, *Reconstruction in Mississippi*, p. 315; Harris, *Day of the Carpetbagger,* p. 306; Richardson, *The Negro in the Reconstruction of Florida*, pp. 207–8; Shofner, *Nor Is It Over Yet,* p. 185; Taylor, *Louisiana Reconstructed,* pp. 175–76. Note what the Republican mayor of New Orleans had to say about patronage prospects in his city: "The public offices are full to full and hundreds are waiting on promises." Benjamin F. Flanders to William E. Chandler, February 2, 1872, Chandler Papers, Library of Congress.

85. Adelbert Ames to James Garner, January 17, 1900, Garner Papers, Mississippi Dept. of Archives and History.

86. Shofner, *Nor Is It Over Yet,* p. 165.

87. Williamson, *After Slavery,* pp. 396–97.

88. Richardson, *The Negro in the Reconstruction of Florida*, p. 226. The carpetbag-scalawag rivalry in Alabama had a lot to do with the fact that newcomers occupied many of the desirable federal positions. Wiggins, *Alabama Scalawags*, p. 40.

89. Volney Spalding to William E. Chandler, July 23, 1872, Chandler Papers, Library of Congress; Current, *Three Carpetbag Governors*, pp. 20–21; Holt, *White over Black*, pp. 116–20.

90. Wiggins, *Alabama Scalawags*, pp. 57, 76–78.

91. Nordhoff, *The Cotton States*, pp. 75, 77–78; Richardson, *The Negro in the Reconstruction of Florida*, pp. 226–27; Evans, *Ballots and Fence Rails,* pp. 124–25; Shofner, *Nor Is It Over Yet,* pp. 173–74; Holt, *White over Black,* pp. 193–94; "Report . . . on the Condition of the South," p. 390.

92. Holt, *Black over White,* pp. 180–92; Current, *Three Carpetbag Governors*, p. 20; Harris, *Day of the Carpetbagger,* pp. 301–4; Richardson, *The Negro in the Reconstruction of Florida*, pp. 200–201; Taylor, *Louisiana Reconstructed*, p. 210.

93. Shofner, *Nor Is It Over Yet,* pp. 203–4; Harris, *The Day of the Carpetbagger,* pp. 434–37, 608–10; Holt, *Black over White,* pp. 180–88.

Fiscal Policy and the Failure
of Radical Reconstruction in the Lower South

J. MILLS THORNTON III

O NE of the most pernicious difficulties afflicting the historiography of Reconstruction is that few historians of Reconstruction have done much research on the antebellum period that preceded it. White Southern voters who judged Reconstruction policies at the polls viewed those policies from the perspective of a lifetime's experience with their state government; history did not begin for them in 1867. But too many historians approach Reconstruction as the carpetbaggers at the time did: devoid of any thorough knowledge of what the earlier policies of Southern governments had been, relying instead on a few facts and hostile legends. This absence of an accurate conception of the antebellum context is arguably a principal reason that the carpetbaggers were so markedly unsuccessful in their efforts to hold the allegiance of native white voters. And it is the principal reason, I believe, that recent historians have so misunderstood the factors underlying white small farmers' desertion of the Republican cause.

In his first book, published more than forty years ago, Professor C. Vann Woodward laid much stress upon the necessity of appreciating the connections between antebellum political assumptions and postbellum discontent among white small farmers. He sought to show that the lines of descent in Southern history join antebellum policies and the attitudes of the Populists.[1] But that lesson has still not been learned. Recent historians of Reconstruction, displaying little sensitivity to the world view of nineteenth-century Southern small farmers, have therefore been unable to offer any compelling explanation for small farmers' behavior during the decade. Small farmers' increasing distrust of the Repub-

349

licans, and their eventual cooperation with the Redeemer Democrats in overthrowing Reconstruction, have been attributed simply to racism.[2]

I would certainly not wish to question the power of racial antipathies in shaping the course of Southern history. Racism cannot serve, however, as an all-purpose explanation for small farmers' electoral behavior. Another essential concern of the work of Professor Woodward has been his effort to demonstrate that lower-middle- and lower-class whites have often been willing to rise above their racial attitudes when presented, as in Populism, with a political or economic movement that offered real hope of ameliorating their hard lot.[3] As depicted in much of the recent historiography, Republicanism ought to have been just such a movement. Republicans, we are told, established or greatly increased support of public schools. They aided the building of railroads into the hill counties. They looked with favor on a wide variety of eleemosynary institutions. If white small farmers were not wholly averse to cooperating with blacks in the Populist effort to make the government the defender of the masses, one must wonder why their racism had so inhibited such cooperation only fifteen years earlier.

The answer, of course, is that Republicanism was not at all like Populism. One important difference between them, I should admit, reinforces the notion that racism was at the root of small-farmer behavior: the Populists did not take nearly so strong a stand in favor of legal guarantees of equal rights for blacks. But the Populist experience seems to me to indicate that small farmers might even have tolerated on practical political grounds the passage of state and federal civil-rights acts, if the Republican party had otherwise been vigorously espousing policies that promised small farmers important benefits. Far from promising them benefits, however, Republican policies may actually have seemed to be inimical to their interests. Many poorer whites did indeed support the Republicans early in Reconstruction, even though doing so meant working with blacks and Yankees. But the fiscal policies that the Republicans implemented, once in power, drove, I think, white small farmers into the arms of the Redeemers. And the final irony of this process is that many Republicans, particularly those who were carpetbaggers, never really comprehended why the small farmers were so hostile to these policies.

The explanation I would offer for the white small farmers' perception of Republican fiscal policies turns upon an understanding of the fiscal policies that they replaced. The principal source of tax revenue in all of the Lower South states during most of the antebellum period was the tax on slaves.[4] The slave tax constituted some 60 percent of the total receipts in South Carolina and 30 to 40 percent in the others. The substantial revenues from this source allowed the states to hold their land taxes at quite low levels. Even toward the end of the antebellum period, when the land tax rose somewhat to meet greatly increased expenditures, it generally remained under two mills on the dollar. In addition, the states levied a variety of specific taxes on luxuries and capital. Only the modest land tax and a small poll tax—a levy of from 25 cents to one dollar on white males between twenty-one and forty-five—were broad-based taxes. The result of this tax structure was in large measure to exempt poorer whites from direct taxation. It would appear that the wealthiest third of the citizenry in the Lower South paid at least two-thirds of its taxes.

The abolition of slavery brought dramatic changes to the Southern tax structure, as to all areas of Southern life. Reconstruction legislators turned to the land tax to make up for the loss of the slave tax; the land tax produced some two-thirds, and in a few cases an even larger proportion, of the state revenues during the decade. At the same time, disbursements rose far above those of antebellum levels. The greater reliance on the land tax and the increase in disbursements together forced extraordinary increases in the millage rates. In Mississippi, for instance, the tax rose from 1.6 mills near the end of the antebellum years, to 9 mills in 1871 and 12½ mills in 1873. Alabama taxed at a rate of 2 mills in 1860 and 7½ mills in 1870. In Louisiana the millage rate was 2.9 in 1860, but 20½ in 1872, and 14½ in 1874. In Florida the millage rate went from 1⅔ mills in 1860 to 7 mills in 1870 and 13 mills in 1874. These rates reflect only state taxes, of course. In Florida in 1874 the counties assessed an additional 11½ mills, for a total rate of 24½ mills. These large new taxes fell on every property owner. For the first time in Southern history the burden of taxation came home to the small farmer. Largely exempted from taxation throughout the antebellum years, he was suddenly called upon to support a very active government.

It might be said, of course, that in return for this new contribution the small farmer received much in disbursements for social-service programs. But such a contention would, I believe, misrepresent the small farmer's own perspective. Because the citizenry to be served had been virtually doubled by the emancipation of the slaves, and because the inflation of prices caused by the war required, until the panic of 1873, the expenditure of more money in order to purchase the same amount of goods and services, so that disbursements for many programs were apparently but not really larger, white small farmers had in many cases in the antebellum period actually received benefits equal to or greater than those they received during Reconstruction, and for a great deal less in taxes. Recent historiography, for instance, has emphasized Republican generosity to the public-school systems in the South. However, public-school expenditures per eligible child, measured in constant dollars, remained about the same in one state, rose in two, but still only to quite modest levels, and actually declined in two others.[5] I need hardly add that the freedmen, because they owned very little property, paid directly only a small proportion of the taxes: 2.3 percent of the property-tax receipts and 7.4 percent of the total tax receipts in Georgia in 1874, when they composed some 46 percent of the population. As the white small farmer could well have seen his situation, therefore, he was paying far more in taxes, but his contribution was in considerable measure state-enforced altruism; he was getting back little more in services than he had received earlier.

Having advanced these arguments in a preliminary way, I shall now turn to a more detailed examination of each of them. I shall then conclude with some remarks on the possible implications of my findings for Reconstruction politics.

I

In his inaugural address in 1841, Governor Benjamin Fitzpatrick of Alabama announced, "The essence of modern oppression is taxation. The measure of popular liberty may be found in the amount which is taken from the people to support the government; when the amount is increased beyond the requirement of a rigid economy, the government becomes profligate and oppressive."[6] This attitude was widely shared in the antebellum South, and as a result of it, both legislators and voters paid close attention to questions of tax policy. Historians who have failed to appreciate the extent of small farmers' political power in the antebellum South may be surprised at the extent to which taxes were borne by the wealthy. But if taxation was oppression, politicians could be counted on to know which of their constituents it was safe to oppress. Not only did planters pay almost all the slave tax and much of the land tax. In several states they were also faced with a variety of taxes on luxuries, directed at the external marks of their social position. Taxes were levied on pleasure carriages, race horses, private libraries, furniture worth more than $500 or so, gold watches, gold or silver plate worth over $50 or so, pianos, and similar property—which planters were likely, and poorer whites exceedingly unlikely, to own. These taxes were greater in both number and amount in the more Democratic states, but even Whiggish states taxed some of these items. At the other end of the scale, farmers' and mechanics' tools, livestock below a certain number, usually 100 head, and a variety of necessities were in most states exempted from taxation—and often also from execution for debt.

The Southern states generally also taxed capital. Money lent at interest or held in savings and capital invested in the stock of banks and corporations were taxed in all the states.[7] The practice of levying income taxes on professionals was not infrequent, though some states levied fixed license fees instead. There were also taxes on the gross receipts of insurance companies, on commissions received by factors and auctioneers, and, in Louisiana and Florida, on capital invested in steamboats. And trade was taxed in the form either of a percentage of total sales—that is, a sales tax—or of a percentage of the capital invested in merchandise offered for sale. These latter taxes were, presumably, borne indirectly by consumers.

All of the states levied poll taxes on free males. In all of them except Louisiana, the poll tax on free Negroes was substantially higher than that on whites, reflecting a conscious policy to discourage the settlement of free Negroes in the South. Because the poll tax was the one tax that reached those who did not own property as well as those who did, it was often in the later antebellum years—and always in the postbellum years—dedicated to the support of public schools. As a rule, only males between twenty-one and forty-five, that is, those likely to have children eligible for school, were subject to it. Georgia was the single state in this period that required the payment of the poll tax as a prerequisite for voting; that practice became universal only in the twentieth century.

These taxes—on land, slaves, luxuries, capital, trade, and polls —essentially constitute the limits of antebellum taxation. It was a tax structure whose principal result was to protect the less well-to-do from any but the most nominal exactions. As I have said, a crude estimate would indicate that the wealthiest third of the citizenry paid at least two-thirds of the taxes. In order to avoid misunderstanding on this point, I should enter two caveats. First, the total amount of taxes assessed by the Southern states in the antebellum years was small; indeed, the maintenance of a "rigid economy" was one of the articles of the antebellum creed. As a result, any redistributive effect this tax structure might otherwise have had was effectively nullified. It is, I think, one of the profoundest ironies of Southern Jacksonianism that while it succeeded in giving concrete expression to poor-white resentments through a tax structure directed at the rich, its fear of an active government at the same time prevented the levying of taxes sufficient to alter the distribution of wealth in the society.

Second, though the richest third of the citizenry paid fully two-thirds of the taxes, it may well have owned more than two-thirds of the region's total wealth. One scholar concludes, for instance, that owners of slaves held more than 90 percent of the Lower South's agricultural wealth, at a time when the value of farms and farm implements and machinery accounted for a bit less than a third of the total value of the area's real and personal property.[8] The fact that equity might have dictated an even more progressive tax structure, however, does not dim the significance of the fact that the tax structure was as progressive as it was.[9] Few, if any, states today can claim, I would venture, that their wealthiest citizens bear so large a proportion of the support of their government. The tax structure certainly points to important aspects of public sentiment and political reality in the antebellum South that are not always emphasized. And, material to our present purpose, it created for white small farmers a body of experience and assumption about public finance that was to receive a rude shock during Reconstruction.

Having said so much about the hostility to the wealthy—and particularly to planters—that the antebellum tax structure appears to reflect, I cannot leave the subject without noting an equally salient aspect of the story: the decline of the proportion of state revenue produced by the slave tax near the end of the antebellum period. I have elsewhere argued, in regard to one of the Lower South states, that the 1850s witnessed the emergence of planters as holders of a substantial—albeit still a minority—share of state legislative power for the first time.[10] The increasing legislative power of the planters in the South is, not surprisingly, the source of the relative decline of the slave tax. I shall not attempt to detail the process by which the decline occurred. I do want to give the outline of the story.[11]

South Carolina, Georgia, and Louisiana entered the depression of the 1840s with anachronistic methods of assessing the land tax, methods that had remained unchanged from the late eighteenth century. The values assigned to land in the various parts of the three states had doubtless at one time borne some relation to true prices, but by the mid-nineteenth century they were wholly arbitrary and discriminated particularly against the areas of the states that had been settled earliest. In the three younger states—Mississippi, Alabama, and Florida—the early antebellum tax laws reflected a much stronger effort to collect a land tax that was proportioned to real value. Land was divided into three or four grades by local assessors, the statutes fixed a value per acre to be assigned to land in each grade, and the tax was figured as a percentage of the value thus obtained.

However, though the classification method employed by Mississippi, Alabama, and Florida was vastly fairer than were the archaic nonmethods of South Carolina, Georgia, and Louisiana, the different practices of the six states had one thing in common: all held land values for tax purposes considerably below actual market values. This reality apparently fed the notion among slaveholders that their slave property was being taxed in a disproportionately heavy way, and during the depression of the 1840s it moved them to begin demanding the adoption of the ad valorem general property tax. On paper, slaves were not grossly disproportionately taxed in any state except Louisiana: the land tax in the other states was in the neighborhood of two mills; a two-mill tax on a slave valued at $300, an average value in the 1840s, is 60 cents, which is about what the slave tax per head was in most states. But it is not too hard to understand why many slaveholders did not see it that way. The slave tax, as a flat sum per head, was easily assessed and was evaded with great difficulty, and on the whole it was a not inaccurate reflection of market value. The land tax, on the other hand, was based on a value considerably below—in South Carolina, Georgia, and Louisiana, absurdly far below—market value. And the allegedly inequitable result of this system was clear for all to see in the larger total receipts from the slave tax compared with those from the land tax.

It is hardly surprising that nonslaveholding farmers looked with doubt and disfavor on the planters' proposals for ad valorem taxation. The controversy over these proposals was a main theme in Southern state politics in the late antebellum period, and the struggle became a principal testing ground for the emerging political power of the planters. The small farmers had on their side a long tradition of politicians' seeking to outdo each other in boisterous crusades against the machinations of the wealthy. But the final dozen years of the antebellum period saw the dawning of a new day in Southern politics. The planters had two powerful arguments on their side. The first was the seeming justice of their complaint. The second was that a great many of the young politicians of the 1850s desired their states to adopt social-welfare and internal-improvement schemes. Given the failure of many of the sources of nontax revenue after the panic of 1837, such schemes were feasible only if state tax receipts could be greatly increased; the general property tax gave promise of doing precisely that.

The first great triumph of the advocates of the ad valorem general property tax came in the Louisiana Constitutional Convention of 1846. The constitution produced by that body mandated both the adoption of an ad valorem general property tax and the establishment of a public school system; the state legislature complied with both of the mandates the next year. But in 1856 Louisiana retreated somewhat from the principle of the general property tax by, for all practical purposes, removing slaves from the ad valorem system. Slaves were divided by age into six categories, a value for each category was fixed by statute, and all tax assessors were required to use this statutory value, rather than the actual market value, in their assessments.

The tax provisions of both the constitution of 1846 and the statute of 1856 represented victories for the planters, at the expense of small farmers and of New Orleans capitalists. As a result of the ad valorem general property tax, Orleans Parish's share of state tax receipts rose from 18 to 38 percent. Tax revenues more than trebled. But nonslaveholding farmers saw their taxes increase even more than that; receipts from the land tax increased three and a half times, while receipts from the slave tax only doubled. The slave tax, half of all tax revenues in 1845, made up only 29 percent of them a decade later.

Alabama and Mississippi also fell under pressure to adopt the ad valorem general property tax in the 1840s. But both states— Alabama in 1847 and Mississippi in 1850—adopted instead a halfway conversion to the new system. Each abandoned classification in favor of ad valorem assessment for the land tax, but each retained specific taxes for all other objects of taxation, including slaves. Alabama made a bow in the direction of ad valorem taxation of slaves by erecting a variety of age classifications and by prescribing different head taxes in each category, the least for children and the elderly, the most for young adults. Mississippi quieted her planters more directly; it retained the flat-rate head tax but considerably reduced the amount. In Alabama, proceeds from the slave tax fell from 46 percent of the total tax receipts in 1849 to 39 percent in 1855 and 32 percent in 1860, at which point the land tax passed it as the state's principal source of revenue. In Mississippi, the slave tax fell from 40 percent of the tax revenue in 1850 to 34 percent in 1856 and 31 percent in 1859. But that percentage was too low for Mississippi's legislators to tolerate. Early in 1860, they increased the slave tax from 40 cents a head to 75 cents, a tax comparable to the two-mill land tax enacted at the same time.

The outcome, then, of the tax wars in Alabama and Mississippi —though not the clear planter victor found in Louisiana—appears to have been closer to a planter victory than not. In Florida and Georgia, however, the tax wars produced something of a draw. In Florida in 1850, the land tax and the slave tax were each producing 38 percent of the state's tax revenues. The land tax on rural property, however, yielded only 30 percent of the taxes; the additional 8 percent came from towns. The decade after statehood in 1845 saw the usual agitation for conversion to the ad valorem general property tax. Florida's legislators resisted, however, until the rapid escalation of slave prices and the considerable increase in the number of slaves in the state—an increase of more than 50 percent between 1845 and 1855—had greatly advanced the value of slave property. In 1855 Florida adopted an ad valorem general property tax, extending to slaves, just as Louisiana was about to remove slaves from the ad valorem assessment system. Florida thus became the only one of the six Lower South states making a real effort to assess slaves on a market-value basis at the outbreak of the Civil War. Unfortunately, no figures have survived that would allow the student to determine what percentage of the tax receipts was attributable to slaves after 1855. But a state census of 1855 reported that the value of slave property in the state was almost double that of land. And the federal census of 1860 reported that of the total assessed value of property in the state in that year, 68.5 percent was personal property and 31.5 percent real estate. It appears, therefore, that because Florida's legislators insisted on the inclusion of slaves in the general property tax, the adoption of ad valorem taxation in that state, uniquely, had the effect of greatly increasing the proportion of revenues derived from slaves.

In Georgia, planters had long wanted the abandonment of the state's outmoded tax system. In 1847, rural land produced only 18 percent of the tax revenue, while slaves produced 42 percent of it. And the assessment system was such that most of the land tax was paid by just a few areas of the state, particularly along the coast. But those who profited from this situation—especially non-slaveholders and inland residents—strongly resisted any alteration in it. Finally, in 1852, Georgia adopted a compromise. The legislature enacted a thoroughgoing ad valorem general property tax, as inclusive as Louisiana's. But it also provided that the taxpayer was to value his own property on oath, and it forbade any official to question the taxpayer's value. The functionary who in most states was called the tax assessor was in Georgia to be called simply, and accurately, the receiver of returns. It could hardly have been a surprise to anyone that this self-assessed ad valorem tax did not create in Georgia's tax structure the massive changes that the adoption of ad valorem taxation usually wrought. The general property tax had trebled Louisiana's receipts and would almost double Florida's, but in Georgia it increased receipts by only a third. The percentage of taxes derived from the tax on slaves declined slightly, from 42 percent to 40 percent, and the percentage derived from the tax on rural land rose from 18 percent to 24 percent. Most of the tax increase that occurred, however, resulted from the more inclusive taxation of capital. Taxes on capital were only 4 percent of tax receipts in 1847, but were 17 percent of them a decade later. Near the end of 1864, by which time it was much too late to matter, the legislature enacted a system to compel the assessment of slaves—but no other form of property—at true market value.

Only in South Carolina did agitation in favor of ad valorem taxation fail to develop. Progressive state officials sometimes called for reform, but there was no mass constituency favoring a change. The reason is close at hand. Residents of the backcountry in South Carolina escaped with virtually no taxation of their farms under that state's eighteenth-century assessments, and as a result they were not likely to seek any alteration in the system. Large slaveholders, and particularly those who resided in the coastal parishes, did indeed have to pay substantial taxes. But under an 1808 amendment to the state constitution, each parish and district received one member in the state house of representatives for each one-sixty-second part that its white population had of the total white population, and one member for each one-sixty-second part of the total state taxes that it paid. The coastal parishes, which had very small white populations, were thus rewarded for bearing a great part of the tax load by receiving a disproportionate voice in the state legislature. Under this arrangement, planters were also unlikely to seek a different tax structure. Though they could not use their legislative power to reduce their tax burden, they were in a position to protect their interests in other ways. And low-country legislators themselves were exceedingly unlikely to favor a change that would eliminate their legislative seats. South Carolina therefore retained her archaic tax laws throughout the antebellum period. The slave tax produced about 60 percent of tax revenues. The land tax produced between 20 and 25 percent of tax revenues, but only about 12 percent of tax revenues came from the tax on rural land; the remainder came from urban property.

The antebellum tax wars give clear evidence of the most important—and the least noted—single development in the political history of the time: the rise of planter political power during the final decade of the antebellum period. The increasing political influence of the planters in the 1850s has been so little noted because its earlier absence has been so seldom recognized. But the nature of tax policy before about 1847 and the strong efforts of the planters to alter that policy as soon as they gained the capacity to do so provide as strong evidence of the planters' earlier weakness as their subsequent successes do of the planters' emerging strength. Nor, of course, do the new tax systems adopted after 1847 indicate that planters were now able to dominate their political world. Rather, they indicate that nonslaveholders were still able to give planters a substantial battle. Although planters were able during the final antebellum years to reduce the portion of the tax load which they were compelled to bear to a level that seemed to them more nearly equitable, the slave tax nevertheless remained throughout the antebellum period one of the principal sources of state revenue. And each new tax act, to the very end of the period, meant the renewal of the war.

These observations bring us at last to the significance of the tax wars for the chief subject of this essay, Reconstruction. The general inattention to emerging planter power in the 1850s has inhibited historians from appreciating the true significance of the struggle over ad valorem taxation.[12] And the failure to appreciate its significance has led to a failure to emphasize its existence. It was thus easy for historians of Reconstruction, seldom also specialists in the antebellum period, to be unaware of the earlier importance of the question. But white small farmers were, of course, acutely aware of it. They entered Reconstruction painfully sensitive to the implications of tax policy, accustomed to thinking of taxation as a matter crucial to their political and social well-being, and prepared to listen with great respect to political leaders who stressed the subject.[13]

II

It does not seem to me that the recent historiography of Reconstruction has shown a sufficient awareness of just how large the receipts and disbursements of the Southern state governments during the decade were, in comparison with the figures from preceding and following years. They dwarfed the totals from the

U.S. Dollars

Receipts and Disbursements, Alabama, Actual Dollars

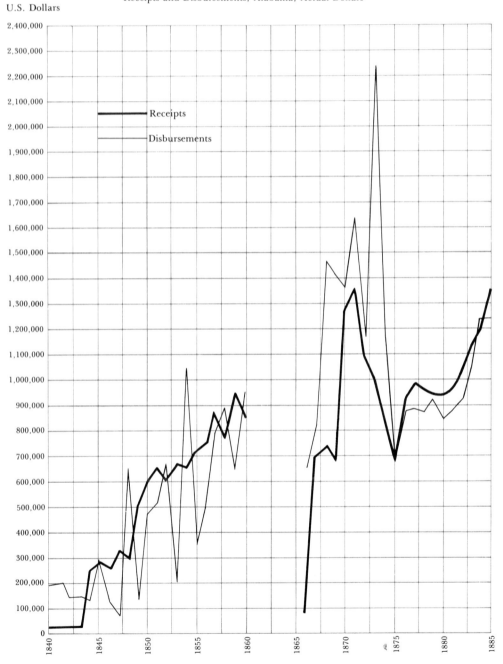

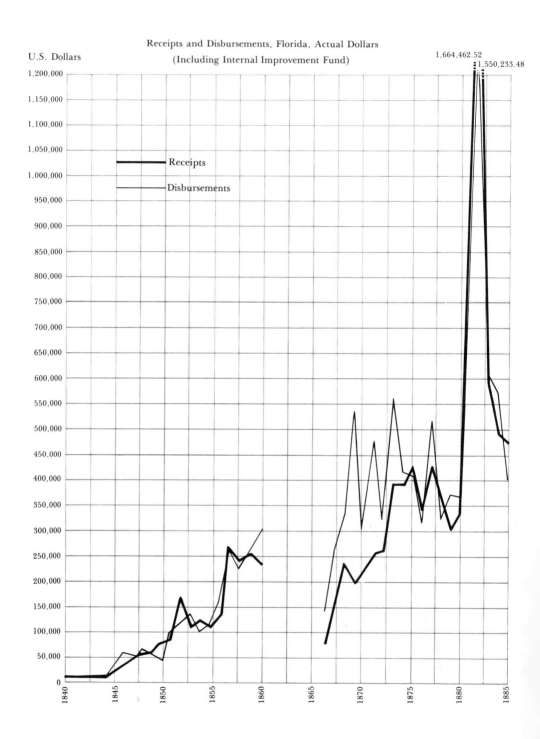

Receipts and Disbursements, Florida, Actual Dollars
(Including Internal Improvement Fund)

U.S. Dollars

1,664,462.52
1,550,233.48

Receipts
Disbursements

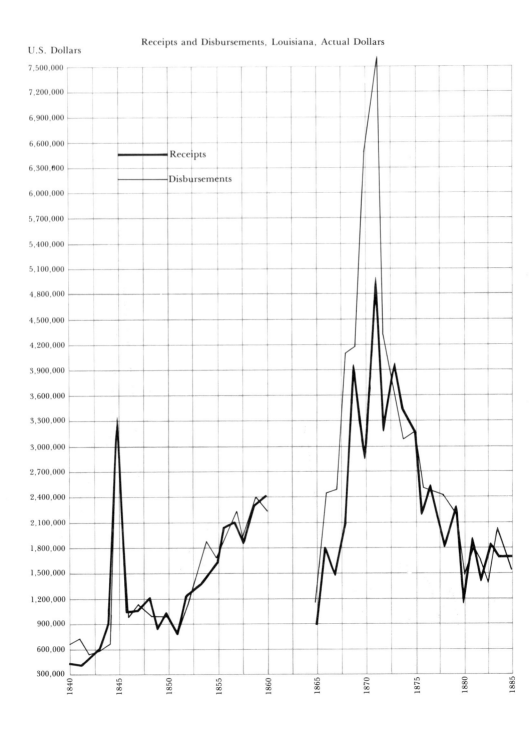

Receipts and Disbursements, Louisiana, Actual Dollars

U.S. Dollars

Receipts

Disbursements

U.S. Dollars　　　　　Receipts and Disbursements, Mississippi, Actual Dollars

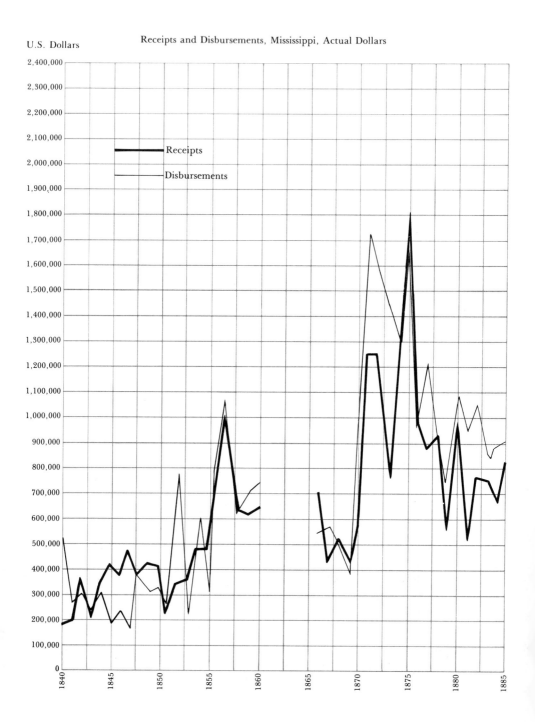

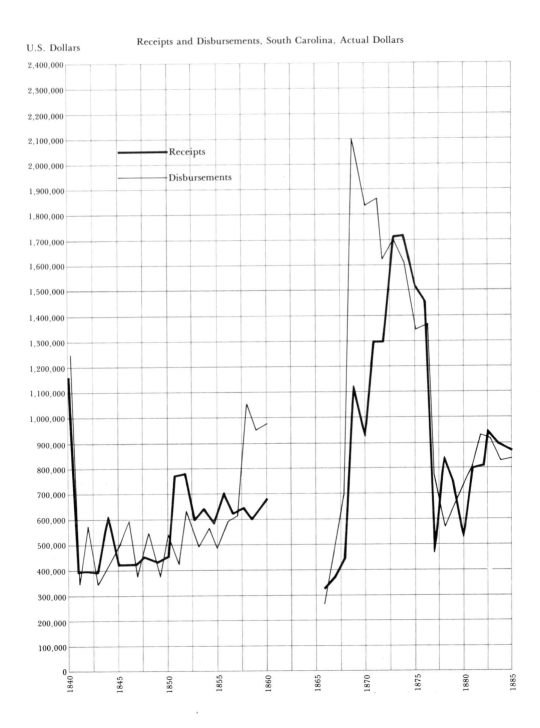

U.S. Dollars

Receipts and Disbursements, South Carolina, Actual Dollars

——— Receipts

——— Disbursements

1850s, though the 1850s had been a period of massive expansion in governmental activity in most of the Lower South states. The graphs on the following pages, showing state receipts and disbursements in actual (current) dollars between 1840 and 1885, illustrate clearly how much greater the Reconstruction totals are.[14] I do not, of course, mean to endorse the implicit assumption in much of the work of the Dunning school that the size of the figures is prima facie evidence of wastefulness. On the contrary, I believe that the heart of the Republicans' political dilemma, to which I shall return later in this section, is that the vast social needs of a devastated region peopled with millions of destitute citizens, black and white, clearly justified the states in undertaking expenditures on a scale equal to the problem. Indeed, one can make a persuasive argument that the expenditures, far from being excessive, were insufficient. But such an argument looks at the matter from the perspective of an administrator seeking to deal with the demands of a difficult situation. The reality of democracy demands that the politician look at matters from the perspective of the voter as well, and the two perspectives are by no means always congruent. In the case of Reconstruction, however great the social needs apparent from the capital may have been, it would not have been irrational for the white small farmer to have felt himself overtaxed and underserved by Republican policies. In the present section, I shall attempt to suggest what may have been his viewpoint on what was happening to him, as opposed to the viewpoint of his governors, which dominates the current secondary literature.

In the first place, it is necessary to underscore, as the graphs of rising receipts have already indicated, that taxes increased rapidly in this decade. I previously cited a sampling of Reconstruction millage rates, a sampling that shows increases over antebellum levels of from four- to eight-fold. I need not belabor this point further; it in any case is generally acknowledged. Far less often recognized is the apparent shift in tax incidence which accompanied the abolition of slavery. Slaves had, of course, been a very large part of the total wealth in the antebellum South. One index to their value is that in nine of the fifteen slave states in 1860, according to the federal census of that year, the assessed value of personal property exceeded that of real estate, whereas this situation obtained in only three of the nineteen free states.[15] Slaves were a form of property whose ownership was concentrated almost exclusively in the hands of wealthier citizens. And slaves were an obvious and readily assessable asset. The slave tax had therefore been chiefly responsible for the progressive features of the ante-bellum tax structure.

After the abolition of slavery, only intangible personal prop-erty—stocks, bonds, notes, money at interest—remained as a form of property whose ownership was essentially limited to the wealthy. A property tax on intangibles is, however, notoriously easy to evade, and intangibles did not constitute a substantial part of Southern wealth in any case. Nor is the property tax a very effec-tive method of taxing a business corporation. The Reconstruction statutes insisted that capital and the property of corporations had to be taxed, of course. But receipts from these sources were never very large, perhaps 15 percent of the totals. An additional 15 percent came from other personalty, including wagons, farming implements, furniture, and livestock. The poll tax usually con-tributed another 5 to 10 percent. It was not the taxes from these sources, however, that really sustained the rapidly expanding Reconstruction governments. Sixty percent or more of this burden fell on a single object of taxation—land.

In the antebellum period, the land tax had seldom exceeded a third of the tax receipts. The presence of the slave tax had allowed legislators to keep land-tax rates low. Just as governmental activity and the consequent need for revenue soared to levels unexampled in peacetime, however, the states faced a newly, and markedly, constricted tax base. It was the decision of Republican legislators to let the land tax alone bear the burden formerly divided be-tween the land and slave taxes.

Of course the value of real estate in the South during this unsettled period had declined markedly from the late 1850s, re-turning to the levels of the early 1850s. Therefore, the fact that tax rates increased by four to eight times does not imply that actual taxes rose so much. Still, the increase in taxes was steep enough. The following tables illustrate the taxes due on a 160-acre farm in Alabama and Mississippi in various years, assuming that the farm was worth the average assessed value per acre in the year. In Alabama, though the value per acre had declined by a third between 1860 and 1870, the tax on the farm had multi-plied by almost two and a half times, and the average tax in the

State Land Tax on a Farm of 160 Acres,
Valued at the Average per Acre, Alabama

Year	Average Value per Acre (dollars)	Tax Rate (mills)	Value (dollars)	Tax (dollars)
1848	3.71	2	593.60	1.19
1855	4.81	2	769.60	1.54
1860	6.41	2	1,025.60	2.05
1868	3.89	3	622.40	1.87
1869	4.08	7	652.80	4.57
1870	4.11	7.5	657.60	4.93
1871	3.84	5	614.40	3.07
1872	4.67	5	747.20	3.74
1873	3.52	7.5	563.20	4.22
1874	3.39	7.5	542.40	4.07
1875	2.81	7.5	449.60	3.37
1876	2.85	7.5	456.00	3.42
1877	3.09	7	494.40	3.46
1878	2.86	7	457.60	3.20
1879	2.32	7	371.20	2.60
1880	2.74	6.5	438.40	2.85

State Land Tax on a Farm of 160 Acres,
Valued at the Average per Acre, Mississippi

Year	Average Value per Acre (dollars)	Tax Rate (mills)	Value (dollars)	Tax (dollars)
1848	3.82	2.5	611.20	1.53
1850	4.54	1.25	726.40	.91
1852	5.70	1.6	912.00	1.46
1853	5.67	1.6	907.20	1.45
1854	5.57	1.6	891.20	1.43
1857	6.97	1.6	1,115.20	1.78
1871	4.38*	9	700.80	6.31
1872	4.33*	8.5	692.80	5.89
1873	4.26*	12.5	681.60	8.52
1875	4.01	7.25	641.60	4.65
1876	4.04	6.5	646.40	4.20
1877	4.03	5	644.80	3.22
1878	4.07	3.5	651.20	2.28
1879	2.72	3.5	435.20	1.52
1880	2.76	3	441.60	1.32

* Assuming the total taxable acreage of 1875.

State Land Tax on a Farm of 160 Acres,
Valued at the Average per Acre, in the One-Third of the Counties
with the Smallest Land-Tax Receipts, Alabama

Year	Average Value per Acre (dollars)	Tax Rate (mills)	Value (dollars)	Tax (dollars)
1848	2.81	2	449.60	.90
1855	2.63	2	420.80	.84
1860	3.64	2	582.40	1.16
1870	2.15	7.5	344.00	2.58
1871	2.04	5	326.40	1.63
1872	1.89	5	302.40	1.51
1873	1.60	7.5	256.00	1.92
1874	1.71	7.5	273.60	2.05
1875	1.55	7.5	248.00	1.86
1876	1.40	7.5	224.00	1.68
1878	1.41	7	225.60	1.58
1879	1.12	7	179.20	1.25

State Land Tax on a Farm of 160 Acres,
Valued at the Average per Acre, in the One-Third of the Counties
with the Smallest Land-Tax Receipts, Mississippi

Year	Average Value per Acre* (dollars)	Tax Rate (mills)	Value (dollars)	Tax (dollars)
1850	1.96	1.25	313.60	.39
1852	2.98	1.6	476.80	.76
1853	2.86	1.6	457.60	.73
1854	2.55	1.6	408.00	.65
1857	3.86	1.6	617.60	.99
1871	1.53**	9	244.80	2.20
1872	1.56**	8.5	249.60	2.12
1873	1.58**	12.5	252.80	3.16
1875	1.36	7.25	217.60	1.58
1876	1.42	6.5	227.20	1.48
1877	1.42	5	227.20	1.14
1878	1.42	3.5	227.20	.80
1879	.99	3.5	158.40	.55
1880	.91	3	145.60	.44

* Acreage of missing counties in various years is taken from lists of other years.
** Assuming the total taxable acreage of 1875, with two missing counties filled in from 1879.

Reconstruction years was double the level of 1860. In Mississippi, the tax in 1871 was three and a half times what it had been in 1857, and in 1873 it was almost five times the figure for 1857, though in 1873 the value of the farm was almost 40 percent less than in 1857.

It might be argued, on the other hand, that the actual tax, in dollar terms, was still a modest one. But such a contention misunderstands the situation of a small farmer operating on the edge of the cash economy. For him these taxes were indeed significant, because his cash income was so small. We may form a rough estimate of what the cash income of the owner of a 160-acre farm was in these two states. The federal censuses of 1860 and 1870 inform us that approximately two-thirds of the farm was unimproved acreage; let us assume that our farmer has 60 of his 160 acres in cultivation. Perhaps two-thirds of the improved acreage was given over to the growth of food crops for use by the farmer's family. On the remaining 20 acres, he might plant cotton to be marketed for cash. During Reconstruction, and we may assume also during the 1850s, the average yield of cotton was a bit less than four-tenths of a bale per acre. Thus our farmer marketed some eight bales. In the marketing years 1855–56 to 1860–61, the weighted average of ordinary-grade cotton sold at New Orleans was 8.445 cents a pound. In the marketing years 1870–71 to 1875–76, the comparable figure was 12.9 cents a pound. These figures, after we deduct 5 percent for factorage fees and transportation costs, produce a cash income for the farmer of about $257 a year in the late 1850s and about $392 a year in the early 1870s. The latter amount is, incidentally, less than 18 percent greater than the former one in constant dollar terms, because of the postwar inflation of prices. If these estimates are reasonable, then the state land tax alone represented 1 percent or more of the farmer's total cash income in Alabama during the Reconstruction years, except for the brief period in 1871–72 when the Democrats regained power. And it was some 1½ to 2 percent of his income in Mississippi during the period. The Alabama percentage is nearly double that for 1855 and 50 percent above that for 1860. The Mississippi percentage in 1873 is more than treble that for 1857.

To the state land tax must be added the county and school-district land taxes, the personalty tax on livestock, farm implements, and similar possessions, and the poll tax, which in Alabama was $1.50, and in Mississippi was $2.00 in 1870 but $1.00 in 1873. It is not at all unreasonable, therefore, to estimate that our owner of a 160-acre farm paid some 2 to 4 percent of his total cash income to the tax collector during Reconstruction. And when we reflect that a considerable part of the farmer's cash income necessarily went to pay the immediate expenses of his farming operation—to pay for seed, supplies, and, very probably, interest on his debts—then it becomes apparent that the taxes would have been an even larger percentage of his discretionary income. If a fourth of his cash income remained after the payment of unavoidable farming expenses, he would have paid some 8 to 10 percent or more of that remainder in taxes. Taxation at this level would most certainly not have been inconsequential for the small farmer. Nor are we reduced to mere speculation about its effect, in Mississippi at least. We need only note that by the spring of 1871, that state was reporting nearly 3,330,000 acres—14 percent of its entire taxable acreage—as having been forfeited to the government for nonpayment of taxes.

The abolition of slavery, then, because it moved so much of the burden of taxation to land, apparently brought about in the Lower South a marked shift in tax incidence downward in the social scale. At the same time, rapidly rising tax rates brought taxes to a level at which they became genuinely onerous to the small farmer. But, it might be said, if the small farmer was paying large taxes for the first time, he was also receiving substantial governmental services for the first time. Though at first glance this position looks very plausible, it does not, I think, accurately depict the small farmer's situation as he may well have perceived it. As an initial step toward understanding what I believe may have been the small farmer's own sense of the Reconstruction governments, let me offer a series of what may appear to be quite idiosyncratic graphs.

The graphs on the following pages portray Southern-state receipts and disbursements in an unusual way. In the first place, I have converted the figures into constant dollars, using the Consumer Price Index.[16] This conversion is essential for Reconstruction because, though prices remained fairly stable for much of the nineteenth century, in the years between the Civil War and the panic of 1873 prices maintained quite high levels. Thus the expenditure in 1870 of the same number of dollars disbursed in

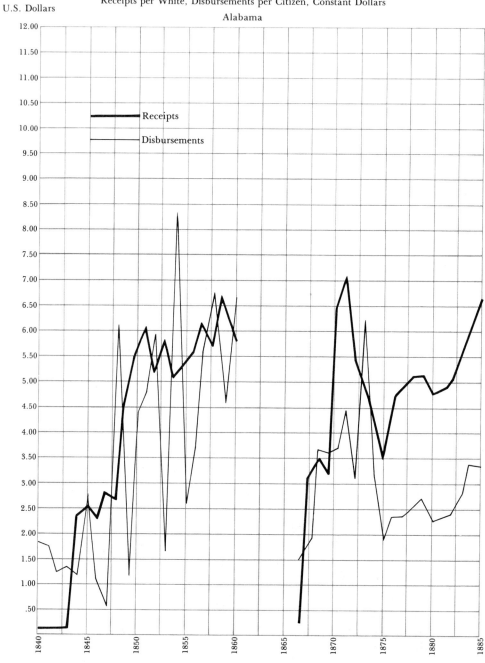

Receipts per White, Disbursements per Citizen, Constant Dollars
Alabama

U.S. Dollars

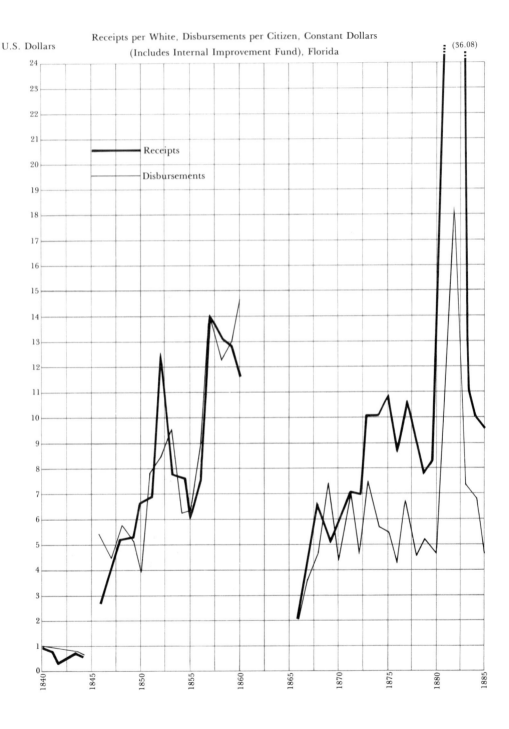

U.S. Dollars

Receipts per White, Disbursements per Citizen, Constant Dollars
(Includes Internal Improvement Fund), Florida

(36.08)

Receipts

Disbursements

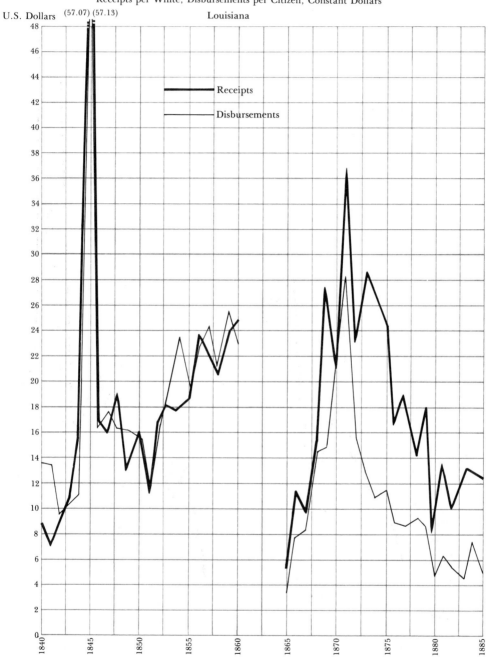

Receipts per White, Disbursements per Citizen, Constant Dollars

Louisiana

U.S. Dollars (57.07) (57.13)

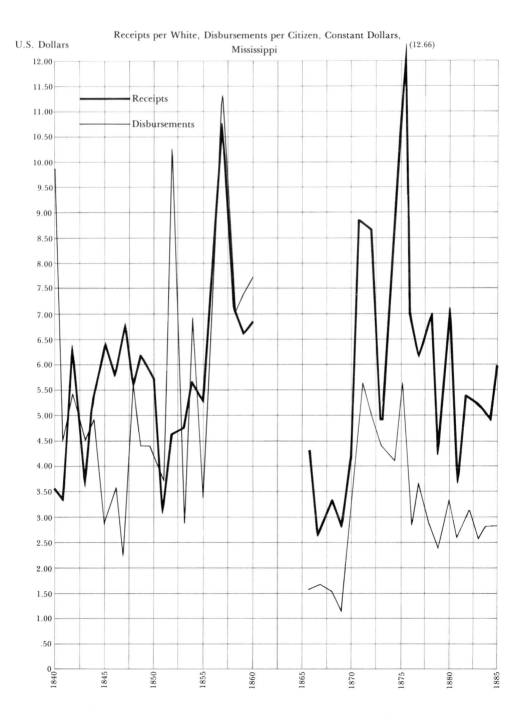

Receipts per White, Disbursements per Citizen, Constant Dollars, Mississippi

U.S. Dollars

Receipts

Disbursements

(12.66)

Receipts per White, Disbursements per Citizen, Constant Dollars,
South Carolina

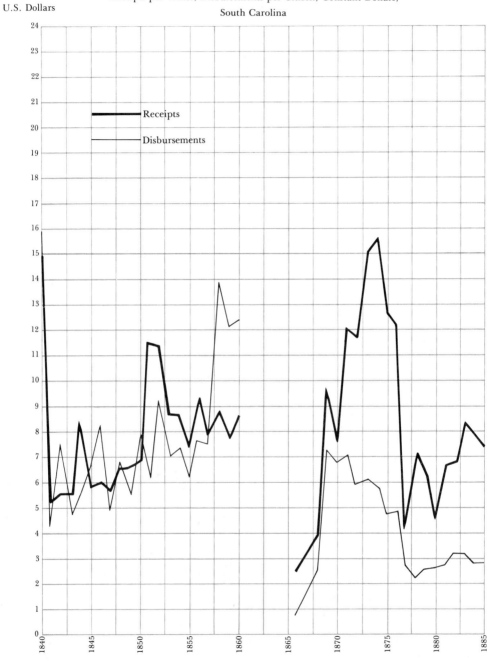

1860, would have purchased for the government significantly less in goods and services. Reconstruction legislatures could do nothing about this problem; just to maintain antebellum levels of services, they had to spend more, and fairness to them compels us to take account of this fact.

Having put the figures into constant dollars, I have then chosen to display them as I believe the white small farmers perceived them. Receipts are shown in constant dollars per white inhabitant. Whites paid almost all of the direct taxes both before and after the Civil War. In the antebellum period the only blacks who were taxpayers were, of course, the handful of free Negroes. But even after the war, the freedmen owned virtually no property, and therefore for all practical purposes they were subject directly only to the poll tax. Beginning in 1874 Georgia reported tax receipts segregated by race. The returns for 1874 indicate that blacks, who made up some 46 percent of the population in that year, paid only 2.3 percent of the property taxes. The addition of the poll taxes brings the black percentage of the total tax receipts to 7.4. Indeed, it was precisely the ability of the poll tax to extract a contribution from the propertyless that made it seem to Southern legislators—during Reconstruction, as before and afterward—the ideal tax for the support of the public schools. It was the one tax paid by a significant minority—and just after emancipation probably the majority—of the parents whose children used the schools. This attitude among the legislators is connected with the view general among white voters that they were being taxed to provide services to nontaxpayers. Now, this attitude was in part a misconception. Blacks who were renters or sharecroppers contributed to tax receipts indirectly by providing a part of the income out of which the white property owner paid the tax on the farm. But however unfair the attitude was, it was certainly real. After redemption, indeed, it produced a vigorous campaign throughout the South to expend on black schools only those school taxes actually paid by black citizens.

I thus come to my display of disbursements. I have shown them in constant dollars per white inhabitant until 1865, and in constant dollars per capita thereafter. It is essential to remember that while the number of taxpayers remained essentially constant after emancipation, the number of citizens needing state services was doubled at a stroke. Disbursements expressed in aggregate terms seem quite small in the antebellum era and much larger during Reconstruction. But the reality is almost the reverse. Because the citizenry was half as large before the Civil War, disbursements per citizen actually declined during Reconstruction. Republicans were well aware of this distinction; it was their standard reply to Democratic charges of profligate waste.[17] But we must note that it was the Democratic charge rather than the Republican reply which appears to have struck home with the white small farmer. As I have said, the Republican argument looked at the problem from the point of view of the administrators, of those in charge of the government. It was necessary for expenditures to expand rapidly even to maintain services at their former levels, they said, because prices were higher and because twice as many people had to be served. But such an explanation, however cogent it was in fact, would probably have seemed to the white farmer only an elaborate rationalization for a gross injustice. As the graphs indicate, the reality for the white farmer was a sharp increase in taxes and a decline in services. From this perspective, it was quite natural that the notion that the large new taxes were going into the pockets of corrupt officials—bolstered as the notion was by a number of cases of genuine corruption among the Republicans— was convincing. And even if it had not been, the simple fact of high taxes and small returns, produced by dividing the tax receipts between hard-pressed whites and "nontaxpaying" blacks, would probably have been damning enough.[18]

One striking example of the way in which small farmers experienced Reconstruction policies is found in state support for the public schools. It has become something of an article of faith in the recent historiography of Reconstruction that state-supported public school systems in the South were largely a product of the Reconstruction period. But such a contention distorts the actual story. State support for public schools had been considerable in the region even in the early antebellum period. Beginning in 1821, Georgia contributed approximately $40,000 annually to her schools and academies, and in 1837 created a full-fledged public school system. Alabama did likewise in the same year. In Louisiana after 1819 the state began distributing $45,000 a year in aid to the public schools. South Carolina adopted in 1811 a program under which it contributed $37,500 a year to public schools. The South Carolina aid continued without interruption into the 1850s, but the public-school programs in Georgia, Alabama, and Louisiana were all disrupted by the panic of 1837 and the depression that followed. Georgia and Alabama repealed their public-school acts, and Louisiana its state-aid act, in the early 1840s, and five or six years followed in which the schools were generally reduced to local support. With the return of prosperity toward the end of the 1840s, however, legislative attention once again focused on education.

Louisiana led this movement. As we have seen, the Louisiana constitution of 1846 had coupled the conversion to an ad valorem general property tax with the command to the legislature to create a state-supported public school system. The legislature of 1847 had complied, and by 1848 the state could claim to be funding its schools quite handsomely: at about $260,000 a year between 1848 and 1852, and at about $320,000 a year between 1853 and 1859. In 1859 the legislature increased the appropriation still further, to about $550,000 a year.

Other states followed Louisiana's example, though not on so lavish a scale. Alabama initially adopted a program of state payments to local schools that amounted to some $30,000 a year in the late 1840s and to more than $50,000 a year in the early 1850s. Then in 1854 Alabama created a state-supported public school system. The funding of this enterprise was placed on a solid foundation in 1856. The state was spending almost $225,000 a year in the middle of the decade and more than $280,000 a year by the end of it. Georgia, which was heavily involved in attempting to complete the state-owned Western and Atlantic Railroad, reinstated her program of state aid to schools quite hesitantly in the late 1840s. By the early 1850s Georgia was spending about $20,000 a year, and later in the decade the figure reached $30,000 a year. Then, at the end of 1858, when the Western and Atlantic was completed and paying dividends, the legislature finally adopted an extensive program of state school aid. State expenditures on public schools quintupled, from about $30,000 in 1859 to almost $150,000 in 1860. The Civil War, of course, cut short this promising new beginning.

Florida, which had entered the Union in 1845, at first sought to join the other Southern states in their interest in public schools. In 1849 it created a public school system, but one financed largely at the local level. In 1851, it offered to pay a sufficient amount from state funds to enable each school district to expend at least two dollars per eligible child, but in 1853 it pulled back from this commitment. In the later 1850s it devoted most of its slender resources to an extensive program of state aid to railroad construction. In the meantime, however, its common school fund, which was derived from the proceeds of public-land sales which had been invested in state bonds, had begun to produce income. Thus in the period from 1856 to 1860, Florida was able to distribute almost $5,000 a year in aid to local school districts—a modest sum but, given the state's small school-age population of 20,000 to 30,000, not an inconsequential one. South Carolina, thanks to the fact that the prudently managed Bank of South Carolina had weathered the panic of 1837, had been able to continue its annual school-aid payments throughout the 1840s. In 1854 legislators felt sufficiently confident of the state's financial position to double the annual appropriation, bringing it to $75,000. This doubling of funds increased the percentage of children in school who were receiving state aid from 23 percent to 41 percent.[19] Only in the case of Mississippi is the notion of antebellum state inactivity in regard to public schools a relatively accurate one. Mississippi, alone among the six Lower South states, had no program of regular state assistance to the schools. Even Mississippi, however, made several large distributions to local schools on a one-time basis in the early 1850s. If these distributions are averaged over the entire decade, they are the equivalent of aid at the rate of a bit less than $30,000 a year.

It is against this antebellum background, then, that we must judge Reconstruction efforts with the public schools. As a first step, we should emphasize the massive problems that war and emancipation created for the Southern public school systems. Reconstruction legislators did their best to meet these problems, but the fiscal barriers to their doing so were almost insuperable. In the two states, Louisiana and Alabama, that had established centralized state-financed public school systems before the Civil War, there was really no hope of duplicating antebellum levels of support. Expressed in constant dollars of 1967, Louisiana was spending an average of $11.53 per eligible child in the decade from 1850 to 1859, and $17.90 in 1860. In the six years from 1870 to 1875, Louisiana spent $4.86 per eligible child, on the average, measured in the same terms—which is less than a third of the final antebellum figure. In 1871, the single year in which disbursements approximated antebellum levels, the expenditures appear to have included a large sum to pay for deficits from previous years. Similarly, in Alabama, which was spending an average of $4.34 per eligible child, in 1967 dollars, during the late 1850s, and more than $4.90 in 1860, Reconstruction expenditures fell to an average of $2.85. In the early 1870s Alabama did for a brief time manage to regain antebellum levels of expenditure per child, but public discontent with the disbursements necessary to do so—between two and a half and three times the usual totals from the 1850s, in actual dollars—compelled reductions to more modest levels.

Even in the states that during the antebellum period had merely provided supplementary aid to local school districts, however, the quandary of Reconstruction legislators is evident. In South Carolina, state aid had averaged $2.52 per child, in constant dollar terms, in the years between 1854 and 1860. During Reconstruction, South Carolina gained a state-administered public school system. But constant-dollar expenditures per child in the years 1870 to 1876 rose one penny, to $2.53. In only three years, from 1873 to 1875, did expenditures per child exceed the average for the 1850s. And yet total disbursements for schools during Reconstruction were, on the average, treble those of the 1850s, and in two years were four and a half times the 1850s figure, in actual dollars. In Florida, school disbursements per eligible child, in constant dollars, averaged 65 cents in the years 1856 to 1860. The comparable figure for the years 1871 to 1876 is $1.74; if we exclude 1871, a year of abnormally high disbursements, we obtain an average of $1.44. Thus Florida school expenditures in constant dollars per child increased by a factor of between two and a quarter and two and two-thirds, a substantial growth. But the Reconstruction expenditure level remained distinctly modest. And to achieve it, Florida had to increase its total annual school expenditures, in terms of actual dollars, some eightfold. In Mississippi, the distributions made to local school districts in the early 1850s were the equivalent of an annual expenditure per eligible child in constant dollars of 86 cents. The comparable figure for the years 1871 through 1875 is $1.09, an increase of about a fourth. But as in the case of Florida, this level of expenditure is quite modest indeed, and achieving it required a nearly fourfold increase in total annual outlays, expressed in actual dollars.

These statistics bring the Reconstruction dilemma into sharp focus. Reconstruction legislators were correct in believing that the schools needed the money being spent on them. Indeed, given the demands being placed on the school systems, they were in most states clearly underfunded. But the white farmer-taxpayer was also correct in believing that he was paying much more in taxes, and was generally receiving no more—in fact, often less—in return than he had received before the war. For the Republicans, there was no way out. Black voters badly needed greater social services, and because they paid virtually no taxes, at least directly, they did not immediately feel the effects of the rising tax rates that were necessary to pay for the services; they therefore demanded more. White small farmers, living on the edge of the cash economy, found far more of their disposable incomes going to pay taxes and were unable to discern any increase in services for their greatly increased contribution; they demanded a reduction of

Expenditures on Public Schools per Eligible Child,
in Constant Dollars (CPI), Louisiana

1848	4.83	1858	10.12	1872	4.37
1849	20.11	1859	10.66	1873	4.10
1850	12.65	1860	17.90	1874	3.90
1851	11.94	1865	1.81	1875	3.92
1852	12.43	1866	1.59		
1853	14.38	1867	1.57	1877	2.57
1854	12.04	1868	1.53	1878	3.53
1855	9.66	1869	.70	1879	2.73
1856	10.74	1870	1.51	1880	1.38
1857	10.65	1871	11.38		

Expenditures on Public Schools per Eligible Child,
in Constant Dollars (CPI), South Carolina

1848	1.27	1856	2.62	1870	1.30
1849	1.40	1857	2.53	1871	2.26
1850	1.38	1858	2.64	1872	1.41
1851	1.31	1859	2.49	1873	3.81
1852	1.33	1860	2.44	1874	3.22
1853	1.76	1866	.05	1875	3.45
1854	2.53	1867	.26	1876	2.23
1855	2.37	1868	.13	1877	1.33
		1869	.56		

the tax rates and an explanation for the seeming disappearance of the state's receipts. And then, on the back of this acutely embarrassed camel was loaded one final straw—the panic of 1873.

The price of cotton had been falling throughout Reconstruction, placing greater and greater stress on the small farmer. The weighted-average price of ordinary-grade cotton sold at New Orleans declined from 18.743 cents a pound in 1871–72 and 15.306 cents in 1872–73 to 12.516 cents in 1874–75 and 9.162 cents in 1875–76. But it was a less obvious effect of the panic which was to prove crucial to the fortunes of Southern Republicans. The panic considerably exacerbated the problem of the public debt. At the outset of Reconstruction, several states issued bonds for state purposes, such as for the repair of levees in Louisiana and for an ill-fated land-redistribution scheme in South Carolina, and most of them agreed to endorse large amounts of the corporate bonds of railroads under construction, promising to pay them off if the railroads defaulted. One can easily understand the motives that moved the legislators to take these actions: the repair of the levees was essential; the completion of railroads in the South gave promise of restoring the devastated region to prosperity, and the bonds of an uncompleted railroad could not, of course, be sold at an acceptable interest rate without additional security. But the principal amounts issued quickly mounted to totals that were beyond the capacity of the fragile, essentially agricultural Southern economies to sustain—particularly if any substantial number of the railroad companies defaulted.

The day of reckoning as to the public debts was postponed in all the states except Louisiana. In Mississippi and in Alabama, the amount of the bonds issued for state purposes, and for which the states were responsible even before the panic, was comparatively small. In South Carolina and in Florida, the state debt became involved in litigation,[20] and the states essentially suspended the payment of all interest while the courts decided the questions at issue. In Louisiana, however, interest payments mounted quickly and alarmingly. Debt service had represented less than 10 percent of Louisiana's disbursements in the 1850s, amounting to an average of about $130,000 a year. But as early as 1869, Louisiana's debt service exceeded $400,000; it rose beyond $1,000,000 in 1870, and beyond $1,300,000 in 1871. In 1872, debt service represented 30 percent of the state's total disbursements.

This pattern was repeated a bit later in the other states. The settlement of the litigation in South Carolina and Florida was followed quickly by the panic and by the consequent defaulting of most of the railroads whose bonds had been endorsed. Mississippi, one of the most conservative of the Lower South states in issuing bonds, nevertheless saw its debt service leap from $110,000 in 1873 to $287,000 in 1875, when the amount was 16 percent of its disbursements. South Carolina's debt service rose from about $190,000 in 1871—and from only $10,000 in 1872 and $4,000 in 1873, years in which it had largely suspended interest payments—to $250,000 in 1875 and almost $300,000 in 1876, by which time debt service made up nearly 22 percent of its total disbursements. In Alabama, interest payments rose from $337,000 in 1871 to more than $540,000 in 1873, when they constituted some 28 percent of disbursements. In Florida, interest payments, including both those from the state and those from the internal-improvement fund, rose almost two and a half times between 1872 and 1876, to more than $100,000, or almost 32 percent of total disbursements.

In response to the rapid increases in debt service, Republicans in Florida, South Carolina, and Louisiana pioneered methods of debt reduction that subsequently became favorite devices of the Redeemers. In February 1873, even before the panic, Florida adopted a readjustment statute that swapped outstanding bonds for new ones at a lower rate but payable in gold; this statute repealed all taxes for interest on the older bonds, and in effect largely repudiated the massive endorsements of railroad bonds in which the state had indulged in 1870 by forbidding the swapping of railroad bonds for the new bonds. Under the terms of this act, the state negotiated a settlement with one of its largest creditors for 80 cents on the dollar of the face amount due.[21] After the panic, South Carolina and Louisiana took even more forceful action. In December 1873, South Carolina called in all of its outstanding bonds, exchanged them for new bonds bearing lower interest, at the rate of 50 cents on the dollar, and forbade the levying of any tax to pay for any of the older bonds; it thus reduced its state debt by half at one blow. In January 1874, Louisiana called in all its outstanding bonds and swapped them for new bonds at lower interest. It also amended the state constitution to authorize this action, to limit the state debt and total states taxes in the future, and to forbid deficit financing. And it repealed and forbade the collection of all taxes to pay for the older bonds. The next year, Louisiana sought to repudiate $14,000,000 of its bonds, though in the end the courts validated all of them except for one issue of levee bonds from 1866 that suffered from a technical imperfection. In 1876, Louisiana flatly repudiated some of its railroad bonds.[22]

Louisiana's maneuvers succeeded in reducing its annual debt service from more than $1,300,000 to about $800,000. But because South Carolina and Florida had ceased to pay interest in the early 1870s, the actual effect of their readjustments, as we have seen, was to divert 20 to 30 percent of their disbursements to debt service. And even in Louisiana, debt service was still some 26 percent of disbursements in 1875. For that reason the white farmer-taxpayer probably allowed the Republicans little credit for their efforts. From the perspective of Republican legislators, the re-adjustment doubtless represented a conscientious effort to put their states' financial house in order. From the perspective of the small farmer, however, it more likely seemed clear proof that the Republicans were beginning to tighten their belts in preparation for a long period of high expenditures to pay off the still outstanding state bonds. In all five of the Lower South states controlled by the Republicans, the period after the panic saw the levying of sizable taxes to meet substantial—and in most cases, substantially increased—interest payments, and the general reduction of disbursements for state services. These steps portended at least a decade, and probably more, of austerity.

The Democrats easily answered any claims the Republicans could make for their debt reduction. The repudiation of certain bond issues had forced the Republicans to acknowledge Democratic charges of corruption and mismanagement. The readjustment implicitly conceded that the issuance of so many bonds had been profligate and ill advised, just as the Democrats had argued. And as to the fact that the public debt and debt service had been reduced, the Democrats simply observed that if interest could be cut from $1,300,000 to $800,000, it could be cut still further, that if the face amount of the debt could be halved at a blow, it could be halved again. In the end, therefore, the Republicans' efforts appear merely to have focused the voters' attention even more sharply on the debt question, without blunting it.

The Redeemers' position on the debt has not always been accurately portrayed. During the 1880s they often devoted a large percentage of the sharply reduced state expenditures to paying interest on the sharply reduced public debts. As a result, the Dunning school of historians tended to depict them as honorable statesmen sternly committed to discharging in full, and at great sacrifice, the legitimate portion of the states' obligations. But the usual campaign pledge of the Democrats had been to repudiate as much of the debt as possible, to decrease the interest payments on the rest, and to reduce taxes to the lowest possible level; this was the same program with which their Jacksonian predecessors in many states had sought to meet the panic of 1837. Using highly dubious legal arguments, the Redeemers declared large segments of the outstanding bonds void. Only in South Carolina did a redemption government permit the bondholders to test these decisions in court—and the South Carolina courts rejected most of the Redeemers' rationalizations out of hand.[23] Following the precedents set by the Republicans themselves immediately after the panic, the Redeemers in several states also compelled the holders of the remaining bonds to exchange them for new ones at lower interest rates, by the simple expedient of repealing the taxes necessary to pay the interest on the older issues. The effect on the states' debt service was dramatic. In Louisiana, interest payments fell from $827,000 in 1877 to $174,000 in 1881. In Alabama, they fell from $540,000 in 1873 to $236,000 in 1878. Mississippi's interest payments fell from $287,000 in 1875 to $26,000 in 1878, and were eliminated altogether by 1881. South Carolina, under the compulsion of the state-court decision, became the single state in which debt service continued at an undiminished level.

The Redeemers also enacted substantial reductions in tax rates. In Alabama, the Democrats had captured the governorship and one house of the legislature in 1870, and almost their first action had been to reduce the tax rate from 7.5 mills to 5 mills. But when the Republicans returned to power in 1872, they promptly restored the 7.5 mill rate. After redemption in 1874, the Democrats both reduced the millage rate, to 6.5 mills by 1880, and, in compliance with the provisions of the new constitution of 1875, also cut assessments almost in half. The average assessed value per acre fell from $4.11 in 1870 and $4.67 in 1872 to $2.85 in

1876 and $2.32 in 1879. In Mississippi, assessments fell almost as much, from a $4.38 average per acre in 1871 and $4.01 in 1875 to $2.72 in 1879. And the millage rate fell precipitously, from 12.5 mills in 1873 through various stages to 3 mills in 1880. In Florida taxes were reduced from 13 mills in 1874 to 8 mills in 1878 and 4 mills in 1884. In Louisiana the Republicans had themselves reduced taxes from their high point of 20.5 mills to 12.5 mills, but the Redeemers slashed the rates even further, to 6 mills after the ratification of the constitution of 1879. And even in South Carolina, saddled as it was with the necessity of paying its Reconstruction debt, the Redeemers managed to reduce the tax rate from 12 mills in 1873 to 5 mills in 1880. This reduction was facilitated in several states by the Redeemers' efforts to diminish the Republicans' excessive reliance on the land tax for revenue. The addition of specific taxes, such as license fees for retailing liquor in Mississippi, produced a decline in the percentage of tax receipts derived from real estate. In Louisiana, for instance, real estate produced 77 percent of revenues, excluding the poll tax, in 1874, but 68.5 percent, with the same exclusion, in 1880. In Mississippi, the decline was quite significant, from 61 percent in 1872 to 51 percent in 1876 and only 33 percent in 1879.

The Redeemer governments of the late 1870s and the 1880s are firmly linked in historical literature—and for most states, deservedly so—with their extraordinarily niggardly fiscal policies.[24] But the extent to which these policies are a product of the Redeemers' ideological commitments may be overstated. In considerable measure the Redeemers were kept from increasing expenditures by the political necessity of maintaining the ground that they had assumed in the crusade against the Republicans during Reconstruction. There were laissez-faire ideologues among the Redeemers, of course, inflexibly dedicated to social Darwinist notions and hostile to any but the most minimal social services. But there also was a proto-Progressive element among them which persistently sought increased funding for educational and eleemosynary institutions. Most Redeemers occupied a middle ground between these extremes.

Because the Redeemers were divided in their attitudes toward governmental activity, the determining factor in the legislatures was very often the position of the Democratic party's agrarian wing. In the years immediately after Reconstruction the agrarians, badly scarred by Republican policies, were outspoken advocates of the Redeemers' efforts to repudiate Republican bonds and to reduce tax rates to the lowest possible level. Indeed, they sometimes sought to go further in the process of repudiation than the Redeemers thought wise. But in the late 1880s, after the memory of Reconstruction had faded a bit, the interest of many citizens, including many small farmers, in increased state services began to reassert itself. This development strengthened the hand of the proto-Progressives among the Redeemers. In the late 1880s and the 1890s, expenditures—and taxes—therefore edged upward again. The efforts of legislators to satisfy the demands of the Farmers Alliance and the Populists furthered this process. Although virtually the entire quarter of a century after 1875 is a period of comparatively low expenditures, the era of genuinely penurious disbursements thus spans no more than a decade. And the attitudes which produced that decade were a result of the political trauma of Reconstruction as much as they were a reflection of a consistent Redeemer ideology.

An interesting test case of this proposition is provided by the one Lower South state that Reconstruction had not really wounded, Georgia. The Republicans managed to hold legislative power in Georgia only for a single two-year term. During their brief tenure they had, as in other states, authorized the endorsement of a large quantity of railroad bonds. When the Democrats regained control of the legislature in 1871, they suspended, and subsequently repudiated, most of these endorsements. But bonds had also been issued to fund state operations and to meet outstanding debts, both by the Republicans and by the presidential Reconstruction legislature, and a considerable increase in the state debt was therefore unavoidable. Debt service accounted for a bit less than half of the state's total disbursements during the late 1870s and more than 60 percent of them in certain years. Moreover, Georgia, like South Carolina but unlike the other Lower South states, continued to bear large interest payments throughout the nineteenth century. In the period between 1880 and 1900, Georgia's interest payments amounted, on the average, to more than $600,000 annually.

These events—the shrill controversy over the railroad bonds and the continued burden of a large debt service—allowed Georgians to believe that their Reconstruction experience had been quite similar to that of their neighboring states. In truth, however, in all areas except that of the public debt, Georgia's Reconstruction was unique. The Republicans did not substantially modify the state's antebellum tax law, with its self-assessment provisions. Georgia established machinery to compel the assessment of property at market value only in 1874. And because the Republicans adopted no significant additional spending programs, they had no need to increase the state's millage rate. They passed a new public-schools act that, if they had remained in power, would eventually have cost a great deal of money. But before the law could go fully into operation, the Democrats recaptured the legislature and altered its provisions fundamentally.[25] Though the tax on slaves had accounted for 40 percent of the state's revenues at the end of the antebellum period, the loss of this tax was made up primarily, it appears, by taxes on urban property, not by ones on farm property.[26] In short, the features characteristic of Republican tax and fiscal policies elsewhere simply did not appear during the brief period of Radical rule in Georgia.

The implications for the pattern of Georgia's fiscal history of the brevity and mildness of her Reconstruction are unmistakable. The state's receipts and disbursements in the years before the Civil War show the developments common to all of the Lower South states. But their course after the war is sui generis. In the other states generally, the figures for the late 1860s and early 1870s reach extremely high levels, then plunge downward in the late 1870s and remain quite low through most of the 1880s. In Georgia, the figures remain relatively stable through the 1870s and actually show steady growth through the 1880s and 1890s. Redemption in most of the South had been preceded by years of fervid Democratic oratory attacking the Republicans' allegedly prodigal expenditures. The response of the electorate to these appeals had made parsimony a political necessity once the Democrats had gained power. But the ease of Redemption in Georgia meant that its Redeemers were not nearly so committed by their past to a niggardly attitude. Georgia's disbursements, measured in constant dollars per capita, remained well below those of any other Lower South state in the early 1870s. In large measure for that reason, there was much less resistance to relatively rapid increases in the 1880s and 1890s. At a time when South Carolina, Alabama, and Mississippi were still mired in penury,

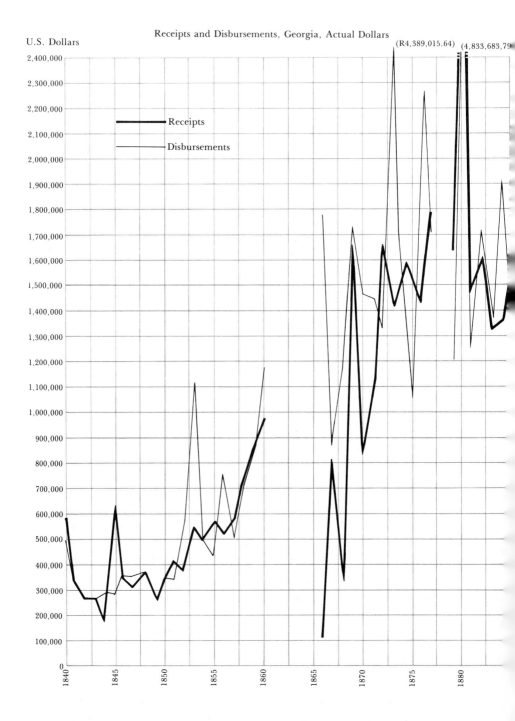

Receipts and Disbursements, Georgia, Actual Dollars

U.S. Dollars

(R4,389,015.64)   (4,833,683,79

Georgia already showed clear signs of moving toward more liberal policies.[27] The extent of the scars left by Reconstruction, then, appears to have been an exceedingly significant element in defining what was politically possible under the Redeemers.

I do not claim to have proven the validity of the explanation for the course of Reconstruction that I have here advanced, although the evidence offered in this paper is, I trust, at least suggestive. In order to establish the case beyond cavil, the student would need to explore the particular politics of the individual Southern states, to detail the precise manner in which fiscal issues were debated in each and to define the ways in which electoral constituencies responded to the various appeals. Such an enterprise is far beyond the scope of the present study. I have sought simply to draw attention to an aspect of the Reconstruction South which has heretofore attracted little attention, in the anticipation that I might move others to look into the matter further. It appears to me that Republican tax policy adversely affected the white small farmer and that Republican disbursement policies afforded him benefits that may well have struck him as incommensurate with his sacrifices. That the white small farmer was increasingly reluctant to support the Republicans does not, therefore, seem to me too difficult to understand. To my mind, these observations offer a persuasive explanation for small farmers' behavior during Reconstruction alternative to the explanation founded merely on unvarnished racism. But, lacking the evidence that meticulous investigations of this component of Reconstruction political warfare would provide, I must for the present rely on the plausibility of my account. It is my hope that its plausibility will prove sufficient to elicit such investigations.

NOTES

1. C. Vann Woodward, *Tom Watson: Agrarian Rebel* (New York, 1938).

2. Among the recent studies that are more or less enamored of the explanation of racism are Alan Conway, *The Reconstruction of Georgia* (Minneapolis, 1966); James Haskins, *Pinckney Benton Stewart Pinchback* (New York, 1973); Lillian A. Pereyra, *James Lusk Alcorn: Persistent Whig* (Baton Rouge, 1966); Joe M. Richardson, *The Negro in the Reconstruction of Florida, 1865–1877* (Tallahassee, 1965); Loren Schweninger, *James T. Rapier and Reconstruction*

(Chicago, 1978); Jerrell H. Shofner, *Nor Is It Over Yet: Florida in the Era of Reconstruction, 1863–1877* (Gainesville, 1974); Kenneth M. Stampp, *The Era of Reconstruction, 1865–1877* (New York, 1966); Joe Gray Taylor, *Louisiana Reconstructed, 1863–1877* (Baton Rouge, 1974); Vernon Lane Wharton, *The Negro in Mississippi, 1865–1890* (Chapel Hill, 1947). In a recent article, Prof. Michael Les Benedict states flatly that historians "now agree that racial rather than economic issues determined the course of Reconstruction" ("Southern Democrats in the Crisis of 1876–1877: A Reconsideration of *Reunion and Reaction*," *Journal of Southern History*, 46 (1980), 491).

3. Woodward, *Tom Watson;* idem, *Origins of the New South, 1877–1913* (Baton Rouge, 1951); idem, *The Strange Career of Jim Crow* (New York, 1955).

4. The states with which I shall deal are Alabama, Florida, Georgia, Louisiana, Mississippi, and South Carolina. All figures in this study are taken from the annual reports of the state treasurers, auditors, and comptrollers, unless otherwise stated.

5. In the sixth state, Georgia, the briefness of Republican rule creates a special case. I shall discuss it at the conclusion of this paper.

6. Alabama, *House Journal*, Sess. of 1841–42, p. 93.

7. The taxation of capital stock was more effective before the adoption of the general property tax. Throughout most of the antebellum years, the tax on capital stock was levied against the corporation and was borne by the stockholders only indirectly. After the adoption of the ad valorem general property tax, the individual stockholder was expected to report his stock as part of his personal property, and the opportunity for evasion was thus greatly increased.

8. Gavin Wright, *The Political Economy of the Cotton South: Households, Markets, and Wealth in the Nineteenth Century* (New York, 1978), pp. 35–36. On the question of the distribution of wealth in the antebellum South, however, the truth is still clouded; see ibid., pp. 24–42, and the works there cited.

9. I should say that I do not use the term "progressive" in its proper technical sense here. That is, the tax rates did not increase as the value of the property increased. I merely mean to characterize the social effect of the tax structure.

10. J. Mills Thornton III, *Politics and Power in a Slave Society: Alabama, 1800–1860* (Baton Rouge, 1978).

11. The following discussion is based on an examination of the session laws of the six states.

12. My account of this subject, for instance, differs considerably from that offered in George Ruble Woolfolk, "Taxes and Slavery in the Ante-Bellum South," *Journal of Southern History*, 26 (1960), 180–200.

13. In this connection, I might note that of the 490,601 potential white voters in the six Lower South states in 1870, almost 66 percent were old enough to have voted in 1860 and almost 42 percent were old enough to have voted in 1850.

14. Casting the figures in constant dollars would alter the pattern shown in the graphs, of course, but graphs of constant dollars per capita would restore the pattern revealed by actual dollars, as I shall shortly demonstrate. In order to emphasize the pattern under discussion, I have excluded from the graphs the abnormal figures from the war years. But perhaps I should say a brief word about receipts and disbursements during the war. These years saw relatively little experimentation with the states' tax structures, except in Georgia, which adopted a state income tax. Expenditures, however, even adjusted for inflation, rose to levels that would not be equaled again in the nineteenth century. The principal cause for these enormous disbursements was a massive program of relief for soldiers and their families. Because expenditures rose sharply and taxes lagged behind, the disbursements were necessarily financed by the creation of extremely large public debts. Later in the century, Democratic politicians founded careers on passionate denunciations of the large state debts created by the Republicans during Reconstruction. It is therefore an irony of considerable proportions that if the Confederacy had succeeded in winning its independence and the Southern states had thus been compelled to pay the debts created during the war, southern taxpayers would have incurred debt service far exceeding anything that Reconstruction produced.

15. *Preliminary Report of the Eighth Census,* p. 194 (table 35).

16. The Consumer Price Index for the nineteenth century may be found in U.S., Bureau of the Census, *Historical Statistics of the United States* (Washington, D.C., 1975), Series E 135–166, pp. 210–11. I should perhaps say a word about my choice of the CPI as the index for deflating the state budgets. Because the commodity composition of the CPI is heavily weighted toward food and housing, whereas the Wholesale Price Index gives more weight to, for instance, construction materials, it might be said that the CPI is the appropriate one for dealing with such components of state budgets as salaries but that the WPI should be used for expenditures on construction and related activities. This point is without doubt technically correct. Similarly, it might be noted that because there were real differences between regional price levels in this period, a national index may not accurately reflect the Southern situation. Again, the objection is well taken. Finally, it might be said that the Implicit Price Deflator would have been a better choice than either of the other two indices. Unfortunately, the IPD has never, so far as I know, been calculated for the first three-quarters of the nineteenth century. In any case, my answer to all three objections is that I believe that any broad index will serve the purpose of correcting for the major historical price swings. Therefore I do not believe that the CPI is misleading in the present instance. The WPI— and the IPD, for the years for which it is available—indicates essentially the same pattern as that which the CPI produces. I have benefited greatly from discussing these questions with my colleague Prof. Gavin Wright.

17. See, e.g., "Reply of the State Central Committee of the Union Republican Party of South Carolina to the Memorial of the Tax-Payers' Convention," in *South Carolina Reports and Resolutions of 1873,* pp. 983–90.

18. Of course it is by no means self-evident that the mass of the white electorate would have desired state services. For the years before about 1850, indeed, I would regard that notion as an anachronism, a product of our own

twentieth-century assumptions about the proper role of government. But beginning in the middle of the nineteenth century, the old hostility to governmental activity began to erode in the South, and by the end of the century a belief in at least certain doctrines of the positive state—particularly that it ought to provide schools—had gained widespread acceptance. Reconstruction was thus a time of transition in respect to these ideas. For my present purposes, however, the problem is not a crucial one. Those whites who continued to hold Jacksonian attitudes would have been hostile to Republican tax policies, and those who wanted increased state services would have found Republican efforts inadequate.

19. The state paid for the education of 9,122 children in 1849 and 18,915 in 1860. The federal census reported that 40,373 children attended school in 1850, and 46,590 in 1860.

20. Vose v. Reed, 28 Fed. Cas. 1298; Vose v. Internal Improvement Fund, 28 Fed. Cas. 1286; Morton, Bliss and Co. v. Comptroller General, 4 S.C. 430.

21. *Acts of Florida,* Sess. of 1873, pp. 12–15; Cheney and Wife v. Jones, 14 Fla. 587. In 1876, the Florida Supreme Court declared that the bulk of the railroad endorsements had been unconstitutional (Holland v. State, 15 Fla. 455).

22. *South Carolina Statutes at Large,* vol. 15 (1871–75), pp. 518–23; *Acts of Louisiana,* Sess. of 1874, pp. 39–43, 94–95, Sess. of 1875, pp. 110–12, Sess. of 1876, pp. 130–31; State ex rel. Forstall v. Board of Liquidation, 27 La. 577.

23. Walker v. State, 12 S.C. 200.

24. See, e.g., Woodward, *Origins,* pp. 58–66.

25. *Acts of Georgia,* Called Sess. of 1868, pp. 152–55; Sess. of 1869, pp. 159–61; Sess. of 1870, pp. 49–60, 506–7; 1st. Sess. of 1872, pp. 275–77, 279–83; 2nd Sess. of 1872, pp. 64–75; Sess. of 1874, pp. 108–9.

26. Statistics on the sources of taxation are not, unfortunately, available for Reconstruction proper. The statement in the text is based on a comparison of the sources of taxation in 1858 and in 1874. However, the tax laws in effect in 1874 are quite similar to those of Reconstruction.

27. Louisiana's expenditures at all times in the nineteenth century remained far above those of the other Lower South states, reflecting the presence of a great city within its borders. But in comparative terms its disbursements in the 1880s were as low as those elsewhere—no higher on a per capita basis, in fact, than they had been in the early antebellum period, and far below Reconstruction levels. In Florida, expenditures during the 1880s were sustained by a large source of nontax revenue, the proceeds from the sale of state-owned swamplands in the peninsula, which were first drained and brought into production during these years. I might note that as this nontax revenue declined in the 1890s, the growth of Florida's expenditures essentially ceased.

Amos T. Akerman:
The Lawyer and Racial Justice

WILLIAM S. McFEELY

"The Northern mind being full of what is
called progress runs away from the past."
Amos T. Akerman, 1871

T HEY fired the Georgian and that was the end of it. President
Ulysses S. Grant dismissed Attorney General Amos T. Akerman on December 2, 1871, and not only got rid of the only person
from the Confederacy to reach cabinet rank during Reconstruction, but also diminished the federal government's commitment
to an aggressive enforcement of civil-rights legislation. On January
9, 1872, Akerman, with meticulous care, disposed of pending
minor matters, sent copies of the annual report of the Justice
Department to the speaker of the house and the vice-president,
closed his letter book, and went home to Cartersville. Perhaps no
attorney general since his tenure—and the list of those who followed him is a long one that includes Ramsey Clark in the 1960s
—has been more vigorous in the prosecution of cases designed to
protect the lives and rights of black Americans.

The purpose of this essay, however, is not to recover a hero but
to examine what went into the making of a man who stood in
the center of Reconstruction and the struggle for a way of life he
valued in his adopted South. A Northerner come south and long
settled as a resident of Georgia, this Reconstruction Republican
was both carpetbagger and scalawag and, hence, neither; as usual
such labels do not explain much. There are, however, elements
in Akerman's past that suggest a possible explanation for the
actions he took. From his family and his New England he brought

a deeply considered belief in a sternly just God. There was no pale, effeminate, polite superficiality in Akerman's theology; there was, instead, an abiding faith and a sense of an almost legal duty. Instructing his children in the Ten Commandments, for example, he spoke of "the completeness of that law."[1]

But a commitment to religion, alone, was not enough to explain Akerman's stand against the Ku Klux Klan. There were, after all, many devout native Southerners, and many of them, along with some not so devout, were repelled by the terrorists' vicious cruelty. The difference for Amos Akerman was that both his profession and the office he held enabled him to do something about the Klansmen, other than let them have their way. He did not think it adequate to hope that they would desist once they had achieved the intimidation of the former slaves.

Akerman was, first and foremost, a lawyer. He was a profound scholar who also knew, from experience, the workings of the judicial system of the South. He had a fundamental belief in the rule of law, and he contended that it was a responsibility of government to govern—to protect its vulnerable citizens by holding everyone to strict compliance with the law. As attorney general, that responsibility was his.

He had not admired the vacillation of the federal government in the days just before the Civil War; he welcomed the firm, unequivocal law that he found in the Reconstruction amendments. And he welcomed this new law not at all as a punitive device; he sought to use it not to punish but to perfect the South. Akerman had a deep love for the region in which he had chosen to live. He wrote about the land both practically as a farmer and romantically as a man emotionally tied to it. Unlike such other able Reconstruction lawyers as Thomas Jefferson Durant and Benjamin Helm Bristow, Akerman did not forsake the South for lucrative practice in Washington or New York. Rich clients would not have been hard for a former attorney general to find in either city, but Akerman, once out of office, went straight back to his newly acquired house on a rise just outside town in Cartersville to resume his Georgian practice, keep his small farm, and raise his sons.

For his fight for racial justice Akerman had, then, his religion, his trust in the law, and his love for the South. He also had another asset. He was a bit of a maverick. To be sure he had been

a Whig, was a Presbyterian, and was no friend of economic un-
orthodoxy, but still he had a singular streak. For one thing he
was not very ambitious. He had not, at least until he was surprisingly propelled into the cabinet, done nearly as well with his
career as his teachers at Phillips Exeter Academy and Dartmouth
College had predicted. And after what he called his brief "notoriety" in Washington, he was content to be a small-town lawyer
again.[2] There was, for example, no trace of jealousy in the cognizance he took, from Cartersville, of the rise to power and
prominence of Benjamin Bristow, who had been his subordinate
in the Justice Department. In 1871 during the campaign against
the Klan, career did not for Akerman overwhelm cause. Not
ambitious, he was also not overly sensitive to the harsh words of
neighbors when he hewed to an unpopular line. Akerman had a
way too of becoming totally absorbed by an issue like the Ku Klux
menace. He was fascinated by the Klan's sadism, and, as quickly as
he felt its attraction, he repudiated it with a relentless determination to end the cruelties. What he did not do was turn his eyes
away from the ugly sights, as many gentlemen in Washington
chose to do.

In Amos Tappan Akerman, the Ku Klux Klan had a formidable foe, and yet few know of his enmity. Akerman was as obscure a man as any who has held an important cabinet post. When
the country pulled down the shades on the embarrassing postemancipation spectacle of the attempt to build something other
than a society based on racial subservience, it hid men like Akerman almost completely from view. And, to be honest, he was not
particularly visible even before the ideas he espoused were so
overwhelmingly repudiated. He was born in 1821 in Portsmouth,
New Hampshire, the ninth child of twelve of Benjamin and Olive
Meloon Akerman, and he died in 1880 in Cartersville, Georgia.
His mother died when he was fourteen, and the meager family
farm was mortgaged when he was sixteen.[3] How these severe blows
to a large family allowed the release of a boy old enough to work is
not clear, but Amos continued his studies at nearby Phillips Exeter
Academy. A part of the answer lies, no doubt, in Akerman's description of his father as "a man in humble condition, intelligent,
public-spirited, zealous in religion, anxious to raise his children
to a better condition, one of the old stock of the New England
middle classes, with a larger share of modern ways of thinking than

was accepted by his contemporaries."[4] There was, what's more, a grandmother—"a woman of uncommon energy of character." She was, he recollected, "stern and somewhat masculine" and not always "amiable," but one feels her force in his pressing on with his education.[5]

At Exeter, Akerman got a fine, thorough classical education, and his record was so strong that two of his schoolmates put up funds for his college education and his grandmother contributed one hundred dollars, after taking a note from the boy and his father.[6] His entrance examination, conducted orally as was the custom, won him a place in the sophomore class at Dartmouth. There he participated in a debating society, identified himself with the Whig party, and was elected to Phi Beta Kappa. As one of the editors of the literary magazine, the *Dartmouth,* he gave a commencement address entitled "The English Poets as Advocates of Liberty." He had had a splendid liberal education.[7]

What to do with such a luxury is not a problem limited to the twentieth century; a standard place in which to parry the question, then as now, was the classroom. Amos Akerman, however, chose a slightly unusual locale for a Yankee's first teaching job; he went south in 1842.[8] For a graduate of a Northern college to do so was not unprecedented; a remarkably large number of bright young students, female as well as male, went south to tutor in homes or teach in small schools.[9] Education was, after all, a leading New England commodity that ambitious Southerners were eager to import for their children. Curious and impecunious young Northerners went south not only to make a start on a career but also to see what that strange—and attractive—Southern world was all about. In October 1846, Akerman dismissed school "with good feelings for my students, and a pretty clear conscience concerning my endeavors to benefit them."[10] But, in truth, the teacher was restless. The preceding summer he had written in his diary, "I find I lose my temper in school more frequently than formerly."[11] He therefore welcomed the chance to move from Bath, South Carolina, to Savannah, where, in return for teaching his children, he could read the law under the auspicious tutelage of Judge John M. Berrien, who had been Andrew Jackson's attorney general. The phrase "read the law" meant exactly what it said, and Akerman read Blackstone and Story, Bacon and Bolingbroke, Virgil and

Kant, Kent's *Commentaries* and the Georgia *Reports;* he gave himself a thorough legal education.[12]

After having been admitted to the bar in 1850, he tried to establish a law practice in Peoria, Illinois, where his sister lived, but he soon returned to Habersham County, Georgia, where he had spent summers with the Berriens.[13] He started a practice and bought a farm; his diary suggests the quality of his life: "Today I drew up some interrogatories in an issue between Judge Hillyer and myself, . . . wrote a letter on business to John W. Martin in the Penitentiary, then went to Clarkesville, staid there about two hours, and after my return worked in the corn-field till night. Read in Blackstone on the subject of treason. The most striking reflection suggested by the subject is how strongly men are disposed to magnify crimes that are most odious to them."[14] In his judgment, the wild cruelties imposed on traitors in moments of passion were avoided in the United States because the Constitution "wisely defines this crime, and thus puts it out of the power of parties, in violent times, to punish their opponents under the charge of this offense."[15] Years later he took a similar view of the cruelties of the Klansmen who sought to impose their own justice on people they considered traitors to the Southern way of life.

Clearly the law held primacy with the bachelor lawyer, but the land had its own way of exacting claims. "I fear that I am doing myself an injustice by attending so much to the farm to the neglect of the law," he wrote on June 29, 1855. "But just now nature is active, my cornfields require work, and my force is small, laborers being hard to find, and so I am drawn into more work than I need for health or would choose for inclination."[16] His "force" consisted, of course, of slave laborers—whether hired or owned is not clear. Like other Southern landowners, he heeded the land's command that it be worked well, and his diary does not question the lawful use of slaves to do that work.[17]

Akerman came from the schools that had produced Daniel Webster, and there was nothing surprising in his being a Whig in New Hampshire or Georgia, but he saw politicians like Berrien and Howell Cobb move from party to party in an attempt to find a footing for themselves and the South in the mounting sectional crisis. That absence of a firm footing was felt acutely by Akerman at the time of secession. As he explained (or perhaps rationalized) to his Unionist sister a decade later, "I adhered to the Confederacy, having given up on the United States when its flag was fired on with impunity at Charleston in January [sic] 1861, and not feeling disposed to sacrifice myself for a government which showed no determination to assert its own rights."[18] The explanation for his allegiance is consistent with Akerman's view that there must always be a firm government, under the law. Slavery was a system of government and he respected it as such: "I recoiled from the horrors that we anticipated as the effect of emancipation."[19] He was surprised, after the war, that emancipation had not brought chaos: "I had no conception that slavery could be abolished as easily and safely as was actually done."[20]

Having gone with his adopted South in the secession crisis, Akerman, now practicing in Elberton, served in the Georgia State guard and was ordered into active service as a supply officer only when William Tecumseh Sherman invaded his state in the spring of 1864. On May 2, the day before he left for the front, Amos T. Akerman, aged forty-three, married Martha Rebecca Galloway, aged twenty-three.[21]

Matty Akerman, born in Saint Marys, Georgia, was the daughter of a Northern mother and Southern father. Her father, Samuel Galloway, born in Virginia, attended Princeton University and was ordained a Presbyterian minister.[22] He had churches in various towns in South Carolina and Georgia (including Cartersville).[23] Her mother died shortly after Martha was born, and her father, a man of "eccentric habits," took the children to Princeton to their maternal grandparents, Jacob and Hester Scudder, and went off to Texas.[24] Martha's grandparents and an uncle in Athens, Georgia, raised the children and sent two of the girls to Mount Holyoke Seminary, where they were taught a curriculum similar to the one Amos had known at Dartmouth.[25] In 1859, after one year of study—a conventional term, at the time—Martha followed her sister south to become a teacher. Mary was in Alabama, and Martha began her teaching in South Carolina, but during the Civil War she taught in her uncle's academy in Athens. It was there that she met and married Amos Akerman.[26]

Martha Akerman was a woman of strong character. She had been abandoned by a father and required to get a man's education by demanding uncles and grandfather, and she had, moreover, had the courage to carry that education back to where her difficult life had begun. She taught school and married a man twenty years older than she, only to have him go off to war. But once the marriage was resumed she met the demands of wife and mother with immense strength. She nearly died when she lost her first child in a breech birth, but went on to give birth to seven more sons.[27] Widowed when the youngest was an infant, she drove the boys relentlessly to education, even following one to Germany when work on a doctorate flagged. The product was a doctor, two lawyers, two professors, one black-sheep miner, and a tackle on the Princeton football team who became a popular postmaster in Cartersville.

Her strength had been critical to her hubsand, as well, in a way that illustrates a vital but neglected historical point. In a society in which the family is as central an institution as it was in nineteenth-century America, any judgment about people who make socially sensitive decisions should take into account the attitudes of their spouses. In the Akermans' America, women were certainly expected to follow the course of their husbands' career, but, in return, they exacted deference in matters of social mores. A man would be far more apt to trim on a public matter that might be expected to intrude into his private world than to force his wife to pay what seemed the stiff price of unconventionality. When the family was sacred, a husband broke with orthodoxy only if his wife concurred. Bachelors like Charles Sumner and Thaddeus Stevens could be unorthodox in the embarrassing business of championing equality for black people, but Amos Akerman could not have done so if Martha Akerman had not had the courage to face mockery and even physical danger. Her son told of a time when his father was away from home and a "crowd of hoodlums gathered outside shouting and threatening to burn the house." A sixteen-year-old boy, living with the Akermans, went to "the door with a shotgun and said that he would blow to pieces the first man who approached the house. The cowards slunk away."[28]

Earlier, just after the war, Akerman, "somewhat shattered in health and more broken in fortune," as he told his sister, had resumed his law practice in Elbert County.[29] He suffered from chronic dysentery (his health was a problem all his life). A year later, in 1866, times were still exceedingly hard, and it was difficult to make a living as a lawyer. In August 1866 he reported that his net worth dropped from $15,000 to $1,500: "Besides the losses by emancipation, there is a great loss, . . . a consequence of emancipation, to wit the loss of debts."[30] The lawyer was not being paid, and his wife was pregnant again. Benjamin was born in 1866, when the Akermans were living in a two-room house on three hundred acres of "very poor land" near Elberton.[31] Daily, Amos walked a mile cross-country to his law office. Once, while he was in court, the greater part of a winter's worth of meat was stolen from his smokehouse: "The rogues are supposed to be lazy negroes who prefer stealing to working."[32] Akerman predicted "a large exodus of our population, both black and white, next winter."[33] The poverty was severe, but Akerman began to regain his economic footing and, in 1866, to work to secure his region's political base as well. He refused to be embittered by the war: "When the end came, though a heavy sufferer, I was not shocked or enraged; for I had apprehended that result for two years. . . ."[34] He was ready to admit that his side had lost, and that things would change in the South. No longer slaves, the black people had to be something, and in Akerman's republican sense of things, they should be citizens.

With only the quickest backward glance at the lost cause, Akerman entered Reconstruction. "Some of us who had adhered to the Confederacy," wrote Colonel Akerman eleven years after the war, "felt it to be our duty when we were to participate in the politics of the Union, to let Confederate ideas rule us no longer. . . . In the great conflict, one party had contended for nationality and liberty, the other for state rights and slavery. We thought that our surrender implied the giving up of all that had been in controversy on our side, and had resolved to discard the doctrines of state rights and slavery. Regarding the subjugation of one race by the other as an appurtenance of slavery, we were content that it should go to the grave in which slavery had been buried."[35] In this instance, Akerman was writing to a Northerner, but he had spoken similarly at home when serving as a member of Georgia's constitutional convention of 1867–68. There he helped draft a constitution that replaced the one utilized by the white-supremacist government immediately after the war. The new document was designed to accept the participation of black Georgians in the electoral process.

"The extension of suffrage to colored men was at first an alarming imposition on account of the supposed ignorance of the class to be enfranchised," he wrote in 1876. "But on reflection we considered that if ignorance did not disqualify white men it should not disqualify black men. We considered that colored men were deeply interested in the country and had at least sense enough to know whether government worked well or not in its more palpable operations, and therefore would probably be safe voters."[36] This approach avoided high-flown rhetoric of equality and showed a practical appreciation of the needs of the black citizens for active participation in the politics of postwar Georgia. It reflects as well a deep conviction that political processes and the law mattered— that, indeed, they were all that mattered. Akerman seems never to have addressed the economic questions that confronted the black population of his state.[37] He took no stand in favor of land redistribution, and when, over his strong objections, debt repudiation was countenanced, he did not support the constitution he had helped draft. (This provision was later dropped.)

Akerman was dismayed when the black members of the legislature who had been elected under the new constitution were expelled from the state house in the fall of 1868: "We considered that those who most objected to their ignorance had opposed every proposition for removing it by public education, and that as a class they would never get education until they could force it by the ballot." Akerman argued for the readmission of the black legislators: "We saw that there would be strife as long as one part of this free people were denied rights which the other part enjoyed."[38] Akerman was also a lobbyist in Washington for the readmission of Georgia. He appealed for support with a line of argument similar to that taken by many confident Republicans in the capital. "We saw that it was idle for the South to seek prosperity now by the old means of involuntary labor or any thing akin to it, and that if she would prosper it must be as other parts of the country prosper, by the industry of those who broke the soil and those who voluntarily labor for others, encouraged by fair wages, by the protection of the law, by the hope of advancement, by the respect of the community, and by the ennobling presence of an equal voice in public affairs. These views," Akerman concluded, "reconciled us to the suffrage of colored men and carried us into the Republican Party."[39]

These politics also carried Amos T. Akerman into the cabinet of the Republican president. On the recommendation of Attorney General Ebenezer Rockwood Hoar, Akerman was named United States district attorney for Georgia. One of his chief responsibilities was to bring before the United States Circuit Court of Appeals cases of violators of the Civil Rights Act of 1866. Akerman was also part of the determined effort to build a strong Republican party in the South. Leading exponents of this Southern strategy, such as Senator Adelbert Ames of Mississippi and his father-in-law, Representative Benjamin F. Butler of Massachusetts, urged President Grant to ensure the already strong loyalty of the carpetbagger and scalawag senators by promising that their constituents would be protected against the growing depredations of the Ku Klux Klan. This, they argued, could be accomplished only with a far more aggressive campaign, directed by an attorney general more interested in racial matters than was Rockwood Hoar. The commitment to protect the lives of Southern Republicans would be underscored, they contended, if the man appointed was from the South. And, as usual in politics, there was a quid pro quo; Butler and Ames promised the president the votes of Southern senators for the annexation of the Dominican Republic if he would appoint an attorney general from a Southern state. Here Akerman's obscurity became an asset; many Southern Republicans in Washington were considered allies of Charles Sumner, Grant's chief opponent on the issue of Dominican annexation. When Hoar was dismissed for his allegiance to Sumner, Akerman, who was not known to care in the least about the Caribbean adventure, was, to everyone's surprise, named attorney general.

Akerman, alone, went to Washington and took rooms in the block behind the Willard Hotel and down the street from his office in the Treasury building.[40] Even less well known to the lawyers in the city than to the politicians, he assumed larger responsibilities than had any previous attorney general. That spring, Congress had voted to establish the Justice Department, in which all of the government's legal work was to be conducted. Before, private lawyers had been hired, at considerable expense, by cabinet departments when occasions for litigation had arisen. This enlargement of the attorney general's duties and staff coincided with a potentially vast increase in the number of cases that might be brought by the federal government if it were to enforce the Fourteenth and Fifteenth amendments to the Constitution. That it might do just that was suggested when Akerman established department headquarters in the handsome new Freedman's Savings Bank building.

Before the Civil War, Americans had looked to state courts to redress their private grievances; only with the Reconstruction amendments could people enter the federal courts to seek protection from violent neighbors. We are just beginning to get the studies we need of Reconstruction cases in the federal courts below the Supreme Court. We know, for example, how involuntary servitude was blocked from reappearance by the decision that Maryland's plan for enforced apprenticeship violated the Thirteenth Amendment, but major work remains to be done on the racial cases brought before those courts. When Akerman took office in June 1870, the hope persisted that stability would be achieved in the South and that with it would come voluntary compliance with the Thirteenth, Fourteenth, and Fifteenth amendments. In the fall of 1870, he reassured an anxious Millard Fillmore in Buffalo that there was "not a danger of a conflict of races at the South," and he predicted "probably harmony in the community . . . of white and colored people."[41] Indeed, Akerman's first year in office was not one of severe controversy. He spent much of his time working not on Reconstruction issues but on the nation's other preoccupation, railroad expansion. As attorney general he had to rule on the question of whether competing roads had complied with their agreements with the government and were entitled to lucrative land grants as a reward for expanding the nation's transportation system. The railroad lawyers quickly learned that Akerman had an exceedingly sharp eye. He required that the roads had truly been built and built where they were supposed to be; he was not long in making enemies among powerful railroad men like Collis P. Huntington and Jay Gould and their lawyers. They were particularly irritated when he indicated that he had matters more important than theirs to attend to.

In the spring of 1871, Akerman gave up any expectation of voluntary compliance with laws calling for the equal treatment of black former slaves. He had gone to Georgia to resettle the family in Cartersville, which was both safer than Elberton and accessible by railroad. Matty and the three children were more comfortable there, but, as her iconoclastic neighbor, Rebecca Latimer Felton, put it, only one prominent woman (probably

she) would call on the wife of the attorney general.[42] At Cartersville, Akerman learned firsthand and from letters from North and
South Carolina of the true intensity of the Ku Klux Klan. Already
strong, it seemed to be moving toward its goals of intimidating
black citizens and thus enforcing their subservience. There have
been times when both the power and the lethargy of a vast government have made anarchy attractive to thoughtful people, but
Amos Akerman did not find that the Reconstruction South provided such an occasion. Slavery, he might have argued, had provided a legal and relatively stable base for a society, but disguised
night riders taking the law in their own hands meant no law at all.

Akerman was not without resources for combating the Klansmen. We are so accustomed to the concept of Reconstruction as a
failure that we tend to forget that men like him were confident
they could succeed. Akerman was in the cabinet of a popular
president whom he trusted, and a Republican Congress had just
given him a strong law to enforce. The act of April 20, 1871,
contained the famous language making it illegal "to conspire
together, or go in disguise upon the public highway or upon the
premises of another for the purpose . . . of depriving any person
. . . of equal protection of the law."[43] The ugliness of Klan atroc-
ities, amply documented by congressional investigators in 1871
(and by Allen W. Trelease a century later) does not need rehearsal
here, but some examination is needed of the legal response to it.
The idea lingers that the only alternative to letting the Klan have
its way was for the federal government to send in troops. In
Akerman's view, there was another course. Martial law could be
avoided, not by the unacceptable expedient of giving in to the
Klan, but by the government's acting in a determined way truly
to govern. Murderous outlaws needed to be brought within the
law.

Suspects had to be identified by detectives, arrested by marshals, held for trial, and prosecuted by men eager to punish the
murderers. The trials had to be presided over by judges willing to
instruct juries to honor the law, not to ignore it. But even with
such determination to hew to a strong law, cases were hard to win.
Does the presence, for example, of Johnny Jones's inseparable and
identifiable old hound dog prove that the man in the sheet who
shot and killed Sam Smith was indeed Jones? The concept of the
presumption of innocence made the work of Akerman's lawyers

difficult, but, as the long and patient work of the lawyers of the Legal Defense and Education Fund in the twentieth century has taught us, the difficulty of holding a society to the law does not indicate that the effort to do so is wrong.

In his campaign against the Klan in 1871, Akerman had able allies. From North Carolina in June 1871, D. H. Starbuck, a determined United States district attorney, warned Akerman against false optimism. "While many persons are sincerely rejoicing at the prospect of the complete destruction of the Ku Klux conspiracy, I am compelled to think that its control has been so absolute in the minds of the whole community that public sentiment is not yet up to the point at which it would be wise for the government to show much leniency."[44] He was, nevertheless, not without hope of success. Judge Hugh Bond, who had a strong civil-rights record, was sitting in the case in question, and he had "manifested a determined purpose to go through with the trial of these men and bring them to justice as soon as possible."[45] Encouraged by the judge, Starbuck was on the other hand hampered a bit by an inefficient Justice Department. He asked Akerman, for a second time, for a copy of the law being contested; two months after its passage, he knew only what he had read in the papers.

There was some hope that the Klan could be contained in North Carolina; in South Carolina the situation was desperate. The Klan had been strong in the up-country region since 1868, and, after high black participation in the elections of 1870, it redoubled its efforts, particularly in Chester, Spartanburg, Union, and York counties. So severe and systematic were the murderous raids on black households, and so unavailing were Governor Robert K. Scott's efforts to use the state court system or the state militia to stop the terror, that federal troops were sent in. In March 1871, Major Lewis Merrill, who had "the head, face, and spectacles of a German professor and the frame of an athlete," arrived in charge of a detachment of troops in York.[46] Having warned the Klan to no avail, Merrill began making arrests, but witnesses to crimes often learned that what they told local law-enforcement officers resulted not in the conviction of the guilty party but in their own retaliatory punishment by the Klan. In July, congressional investigators arrived and confirmed that even with Merrill's diligent efforts, the state's legal system was not protecting the black people. It was then that Akerman went south to direct Merrill in bringing the cases into federal courts. He judged the Klan's activities to be so powerful as to constitute what he considered a rebellion. This gave the president constitutional grounds for the action, dangerous to democracy, of suspending the writ of habeas corpus so that Klansmen could be held for trial and not released by local judges. From Yorkville, he ordered Solicitor General Bristow to draft, and he advised the president to sign, an order suspending the writ in nine counties.[47] He was already working closely with the judges in scheduling trials and with the United States district attorneys who would prosecute them, as well as with Major Merrill. The use of army officers as marshals arresting, interrogating, and holding defendants in jail under the suspended writ of habeas corpus was the most criticized of Akerman's actions, and the precedent it set is not an attractive one.

Akerman kept a watchful eye on the complex process. On November 10, 1871, he ordered that "Deputy Marshals and all others concerned in making arrests should understand that they will be sustained in no unnecessary harshness." On December 1, he wrote, "I do hope that our friends will be cautious in prosecuting under these laws. . . . A prosecution which fails is apt to react unfavorably."[48] He was concerned here to criticize not only those opposed to harshness toward the Klan but those afraid the government was too lenient. In all instances he appears to have urged a stern fairness. He saw in the racial violence before him the need for a national constabulary, not to exercise military rule, but to enforce the law.

Perhaps because he loved his South, he understood its hatreds. In August he wrote to a friend, "A portion of our southern population hate the northerner from the old grudge, hate the government of the United States, because they understand it emphatically to represent northern sentiment, and hate the negro because he has ceased to be a slave and has been promoted to be a citizen and voter, and hate those of the southern whites who are looked upon as in political friendship with the north, with the United States Government and with the negro. These persons commit the violence that disturbs many parts of the South. Undoubtedly the judgement of the great body of our people condemns this behavior, but they take no active measures to suppress it."[49]

He favored active measures, and he was not always a patient man. To a friend at home he wrote, "I have been hoping that

Georgia would soon come out of the Confederate sulks." He had hoped his state "might be spared any severe handling by the government, . . . But if the friends of the government must suffer without law, or the foes of the government must suffer by law, I prefer the latter."[50]

Akerman's lawyers won a good many of their cases—over half those brought from 1870 to 1872, according to some authorities— but the belief that this action destroyed the Klan is not warranted.[51] Rather, the Klan went out of existence because its basic goal of white supremacy was being achieved by a host of psychological, economic, and political means in addition to those attacked by the Justice Department in Akerman's day. Akerman himself had been stopped in 1871 because men from the North as well as the South came to recognize, uneasily, that if he was not halted, his concept of equality before the law was likely to lead to total equality.

Much evidence points to the railroad men as the cause of Akerman's dismissal, but some doubt lingers as to whether they were Akerman's decisive enemies. For one thing Akerman, despite his austere railroad policy, had not become the muckraker of the Grant administration (that role was later played by Benjamin H. Bristow) and was therefore not hated by the president. For another, his letter-of-the-law rulings won him the grudging respect of some opposing lawyers. After he left office, Akerman, on trips to Washington, visited, cordially, with the chief of these, Rockwood Hoar. All the categorical statements that it was the railroad men who drove him out can be traced to Rebecca Latimer Felton's analysis, and Mrs. Felton found railroad barons to be the cause of all evil.[52] Akerman himself was guarded. In August 1871 he wrote Matty of the "new effort which I am satisfied is going on to oust me from office because I will not subserve certain selfish interests." "Selfish interests" sounds more like corporate foes than white supremacists, but he mentions no names. Somewhat disingenuously he claims he would not mind if no one but himself was affected, "but I have a delicacy on the point of exposing the President to annoyance and perhaps censure and dislike of powerful interests." It was a difficult time: "It is enough to contend against political opposition, but to be fighting for one's foothold against the machinations of professed friends, is too hard a life."[53]

It was getting harder and harder in cabinet meetings to receive a sympathetic ear on racial matters, and there appears to have been a coincidence of objectives between Secretary of the Interior Columbus Delano, the ally of the railroad people, and others close to Grant, who wanted Akerman's removal for his activities on the racial front. For months prior to the president's action, Hamilton Fish had been complaining in his diary. On October 31 he wrote, "Akerman made a long, long statement about the Ku Klux"; on November 24 his entry read, "Akerman introduces Ku Klux; he has it 'on the brain.' "[54] Fish was right; Akerman, trying hard to persuade Northerners to take the Klan seriously, wrote to a lawyer friend in Brooklyn about the difficulties of the cases and closed, "But I am chronically garrulous on the Ku-Klux."[55] Fish heard Akerman speak in a different voice: "He tells a number of stories, one of a fellow being castrated, with terribly minute and tedious details in each case. It has got to be a bore to listen twice a week to this same thing."[56]

Matty had come to Washington in the fall of 1871 and, with Mrs. Delano, had assisted Mrs. Grant as she received Grand Duke Alexis in the Red Room of the White House.[57] The Akermans were at the center of things, but rumors circulated that Amos would soon be replaced, if not by Solicitor General Bristow, then perhaps by John Marshall Harlan.[58] In the cabinet meeting on December 1, Akerman presented a request from the acting governor of Georgia for federal troops to help him hold his office, if his possession were to be contested. Fish, with sardonic pleasure, noted that Grant, while no lawyer, refused to answer a hypothetical question: "The President thinks (as anyone would suppose) that he has nothing to do with a speculative case of this kind."[59] The secretary of state's parenthetical remark was a slap at Akerman; he disliked any increase in federal-government interventions in the South and saw nothing but more requests if Akerman were to stay. Therefore, it was not without satisfaction that Fish noted in his diary on December 11, 1871, that the president had stepped into his room, as he often did when he was taking an action of which the secretary of state approved, and had said that he would "replace Akerman with Judge Williams of Oregon."[60] George H. Williams continued the prosecutions and achieved 456 convictions in 1872, 469 in 1873, and 102 in 1874, while Akerman had accomplished only 32 in 1870 and 128 in 1871.[61] But Williams did not claim a deep concern for the cases, and the greater credit for the successful prosecutions should probably go to the United States district attorneys in the courtrooms of the South. Williams's successors Edwards Pierrepont, in 1875, and Alphonso B. Taft, in 1876, were not interested in prosecuting civil-rights cases; bit by bit the federal government eased itself out of Reconstruction.

Back in the South, Akerman had no such escape. In 1874, on a train from Charlotte to Atlanta, "I heard one traveller say to another, pointing to a house, 'That is . . . where Tom Rountree was killed by the Ku Klux,' and they talked about the affair without an expression of horror. Rountree was a colored man, who was cruelly butchered in the latter part of 1870 by a band of disguised men." In his diary, he went on to reflect: "To persons who had not the strongest evidence of the facts, a history of the Ku Klux would be incredible. That any large portion of our people should be so ensavaged as to perpetuate or excuse such actions is the darkest blot on Southern character in this age."[62]

Akerman had pondered the character of his region, in its bright aspects as well as the dark, and though he had come to understand it a bit, he was philosophical about the lack of comprehension in the North. In 1871, he tried to explain his dismissal to a Georgian friend, Benjamin Conley: "The Northern mind being full of what is called progress runs away from the past."[63] Northerners had not wanted to face the South's ancient hatreds. In Georgia, race was the constant reminder that the past could not be run away from. And to another Georgian, Henry McNeal Turner, Akerman expressed his thinking about an attempt to close one's eyes to half of the racial equation: "A black man's party is just as wrong as a white man's party. The best man of the soundest principle should have your votes, without regard to his color."[64] Despite this advice, given in 1871, Akerman was not later interested in the social-equality goals of the Civil Rights Act of 1875. He considered the legislation a deflection from the basic need of black people—survival. "The measure is not required to secure justice to the negroes and will have the contrary effect by inflaming whites against them. What they need," he concluded somewhat flatly, "is something to protect them in independent suffrage. With this, they can get every other public right they ought to have. How a Congress which enacted this bill should have a scruple about the 'Force Bill' is surprising."[65] His sense of priorities was firm, but not inflexible, and he pursued a limited commitment to integration with a lecture to "students (colored) of Atlanta University" in June.[66]

But always he was the lawyer, practicing commercial and estate law in Cartersville and the surrounding region. (Toward the end of his life, it was generally expected that he would receive a federal judgeship.) As he traveled, he wrote of his work in his journal: "To Atlanta and back. To-night looking up law on a point of interest. This is the most pleasant part of my professional duty: to learn what has been pronounced to be law, is easier than to find out what law is by reflecting on what it ought to be, for much that we call common law is of the latter sort."[67] Early in September 1875 he had the occasion to test the law that was. The case was that of a black man accused of plotting an exposed "insurrection" in Washington County.[68] Akerman noted that when "panic arose, innocent acts were supposed to have criminal significance, and the mass of white people really believed themselves in danger. In this belief they were encouraged by a few demagogues who fanned the flame." He regarded the accusation as a "fabrication"—"I cannot believe them guilty . . . without stronger evidence than has yet appeared"—and went to Sandersville to defend Cordy Harris.[69] "The Judge was impartial and the jury rose above prejudice. The case was very weak under the evidence, and the only danger to the accused was in the odium attached to the alleged crime."[70] Harris was acquitted. "Considering the excitement in the community," Akerman noted calmly, "I think the result rather remarkable."[71] There had been those who thought they had stopped the lawyer when he had been fired in Washington, D.C., in 1871, but in Washington County, Georgia, in 1875, Amos Akerman showed them that that had not quite been the end of it.

NOTES

1. Amos T. Akerman, Diary, December 27, 1874, RHA. I am indebted to three descendants of Amos T. Akerman—Laura Love Yates, Joe A. Akerman, Jr., and Robert H. Akerman (a bit of a maverick in the manner of his great-grandfather)—for the loan of documents concerning him. Those cited are identified with their initials.

2. Amos T. Akerman, Diary, March 19, 1875.

3. "Notes by Joseph Akerman about his Father," undated typescript, JAA.

4. Amos T. Akerman, Diary, February 20, 1878, cited in Lois Neal Hamilton, "Amos T. Akerman and his Role in American Politics" (Master's thesis, Faculty of Political Science, Columbia University, 1939), p. 3. Akerman kept several diaries; Hamilton consulted at least one that I did not find.

5. Undated diary entry cited in Hamilton, "Amos T. Akerman," pp. 3–4.

6. Hamilton, "Amos T. Akerman," p. 7.

7. Ibid., p. 9.

8. Robert H. Akerman, "Amos Tappan Akerman," draft of entry for Kenneth Coleman and Steve Gurr, eds., Dictionary of Georgia Biography (Savannah, forthcoming).

9. David Brown, "In Another Country: Two Northern Women in the Slave South" (Honors thesis in American Studies, Amherst College, 1973).

10. Amos T. Akerman, Diary, October 30, 1846.

11. Ibid., July 18, 1846, cited in Hamilton, "Amos T. Akerman," p. 12.

12. Amos T. Akerman, Diary, November 5, 9, 1846, June 23, 26, 29, July 4, 1855, and June 8, 1861.

13. "Notes by Joseph Akerman."

14. Amos T. Akerman, Diary, June 22, 1855.

15. Ibid.

16. Ibid., June 29, 1855.

17. Later, in Elberton, he owned eleven slaves. Amos T. Akerman to Martha Rebecca Galloway Akerman, June 7, 1864, cited in Hamilton, "Amos T. Akerman," p. 34n.

18. Amos T. Akerman to his sister, July 17, 1870, JAA.

19. Ibid.

20. Ibid.

21. Amos T. Akerman to his sister, August 2, 1865, JAA.

22. Mrs. Alexander Akerman to Mrs. Albert Menard, July 31, 1946, JAA. Another source lists Jeffersonville, Georgia, as her birthplace.

23. Clipping from [Cartersville] newspaper, January 25, 1912.

24. Amos T. Akerman to his sister, August 2, 1865, JAA.

25. Mrs. Alexander Akerman to Mrs. Albert Menard, July 31, 1946, J.A.A.

26. Mary A. Galloway in Anna C. Edwards, ed., First Class Letter of the Lulasti: Mount Holyoke Female Seminary (Northampton, 1860) p. 7; Mrs. Alexander Akerman to Mrs. Albert Menard, July 31, 1946, JAA.

27. Amos T. Akerman to his sister, August 2, 1865, JAA.

28. Clement Akerman to Joe A. Akerman, Jr., May 24, 1969, JAA.

29. Amos Akerman to his sister, August 2, 1865, JAA.

30. Amos A. Akerman to his sister, August 19, 1866, JAA.

31. Ibid.

32. Ibid.

33. Ibid.

34. Ibid.

35. Amos T. Akerman to George W. Heidy [?], August 22, 1876, letter books of Amos T. Akerman, University of Virginia (U.Va.), microfilm.

36. Ibid.

37. Amos T. Akerman to "Dear Sir," October 9, 1867, quoted in Elberton *Gazette,* undated clipping [1880].

38. Amos T. Akerman to George W. Heidy [?], August 22, 1876, U.Va.

39. Ibid.; Laurie Mitchel, "The Short Career of Amos Akerman" (Seminar paper, Mount Holyoke College, 1979).

40. Amos T. Akerman to Martha Rebecca Galloway Akerman, July 17, 1870, JAA.

41. Amos T. Akerman, Diary, March 10, 1874, RHA.

42. Rebecca Latimer Felton, "Hon. Amos T. Akerman: A Biographical Sketch," Cartersville *Courant,* undated clippings [post 1880], LLY.

43. 17 U.S. Statutes 13.

44. D. H. Starbuck to Amos T. Akerman, June 17, 1871, Records of the Department of Justice, National Archives.

45. Ibid.

46. New York *Daily Tribune,* November 13, 1871, quoted in Allen W. Trelease, *White Terror: The Ku Klux Klan Conspiracy and Southern Reconstruction* (New York, 1971), pp. 369–70.

47. Hamilton, "Amos T. Akerman", pp. 74–76. Bristow's order specifying Marion County rather than Union County as one of the nine has often been cited as evidence of Akerman's incompetence. See, for example, the description of Akerman as a "lily-white" who made "incredible blunders" in Allan Nevins, *Hamilton Fish: The Inner History of the Grant Administration,* 2 vols. (New York, 1957), II, 591. The error was quickly corrected.

48. Amos T. Akerman, instructions of November 10, December 1, 1871, cited in Hamilton, "Amos T. Akerman," p. 80.

49. Amos T. Akerman, to J. H. H. Wilcox, August 16, 1871, U.Va.

50. Amos T. Akerman to W. H. McWhorter, November 14, 1871, cited in Hamilton, "Amos T. Akerman," p. 81.

51. Herman Belz, *Emancipation and Equal Rights: Politics and Constitutionalism in the Civil War Era* (New York, 1978), p. 130.

52. Felton, "Hon. Amos. T. Akerman."

53. Amos T. Akerman to Martha Rebecca Galloway Akerman, August 30, 1871, quoted in Felton, "Hon. Amos T. Akerman"; Judi M. Sanzo to the author, April 24, 1978.

54. Hamilton Fish, Diary, October 31, November 24, 1871, Library of Congress.

55. Amos T. Akerman to B. D. Silliman, November 9, 1871, U.Va.

56. Fish, Diary, November 24, 1871.

57. Ibid., November 23, 1871.

58. G. C. Wharton to B. H. Bristow, October 10, 1871, Bristow Papers, Library of Congress.

59. Fish, Diary, December 1, 1871.

60. Ibid., December 11, 1871.

61. Trelease, *White Terror*, p. 412; James Ford Rhodes, *History of the United States from the Compromise of 1850 to the Final Restoration of Home Rule of the South in 1877,* 7 vols. (New York, 1901–06), VI, 318.

62. Amos T. Akerman, Diary, April 9, 1874, RHA. In Allen Trelease, *White Terror,* pp. 363–64, the name is spelled Roundtree; other facts support Akerman's comments.

63. Amos T. Akerman to Benjamin Conley, December 28, 1871, U.Va.

64. Amos T. Akerman to Benjamin McNeal Turner, November 14, 1871, quoted in Laura Love Akerman, "The Life and Times of Amos Tappan Akerman: A Study of a 19th Century Georgian Politician" (Thesis, in possession of Laura Love Yates, McLean, Va.) p. 84, LLY.

65. Amos T. Akerman, Diary, March 6, 1875.

66. Ibid., June 26, 1875.

67. Ibid., August 16, 1875.

68. Ibid., August 20, 1875.

69. Ibid.

70. Ibid., September 6, 1875.

71. Ibid.

Rutherford B. Hayes and the Removal of the Troops and the End of Reconstruction

VINCENT P. DeSANTIS

IN the spring of 1877, President Rutherford B. Hayes removed the last of the federal troops protecting Republican state governments in the South and restored "home rule" to Southern whites. This action is usually cited as the formal ending of military Reconstruction and is so regarded by historians in their textbooks and scholarly studies. Actually, President Grant had already largely given up "bayonet rule" in the South by reassigning most of the federal forces supporting carpetbag governments even before Hayes assumed office. And Hayes really did not withdraw a single soldier from the South at the time but transferred the troops from the capitols at Columbia, South Carolina, and New Orleans, Louisiana, to their previous places of encampment. The troops went back to their barracks and after that were not used to support any state or local government in the South.

The whole United States Army, plus Indian scouts, chaplains, medical personnel, ordnance officers, quartermaster sergeants, and West Point cadets totaled only about 25,000 men in 1876–77, and most of them were busy fighting Indians on the Plains or protecting the Mexican and Indian frontier of Texas. When Texas is excluded, only 3,230 officers and men were on duty in the South at the end of the fiscal year 1876, and most of these were there mainly to aid revenue officers or to guard seacoast fortications. In Louisiana, for example, soldiers were widely scattered in sixty-two places. Hayes's order to remove the troops did not cause a single soldier to leave the South. Several companies later in the year were transferred from the South, but this was because of railroad strikes and Indian troubles in other parts of the country.[1]

Still, in withdrawing the troops, Hayes gained a reputation as a "statesman of reunion" and a "healer of strife." For some years he was praised by historians for doing this, even by those who connected his action with an agreement or bargain known as the Compromise of 1877 that allowed him to become president in the disputed election of 1876. But in recent years historians have been more critical of what Hayes did. Some have maintained that he abandoned the Southern Negro when he removed the troops, or at least curtailed the freedom of Negro suffrage in the South, and that he should have anticipated this result.[2] Others believe that the end of Reconstruction could have been achieved with more finesse, that Hayes confused conciliation with capitulation, that he appeased the Southern Democrats and transformed a defeat into a surrender, and that his pullback of the troops ended "any guarantee of free voting in the South and of any other reconstruction rights that the white southerners might choose to deny." And unfortunately the country accepted at the outset Hayes's one-sided conciliation efforts and this peace in the South without justice.[3]

Though the removal of the troops gave Hayes a reputation of a statesman and conciliator, he seldom received credit for having had sincere motives, because many, perhaps most, Americans in 1877 and thereafter believed that what he had done was in faithful accord with an agreement to make him president and that he had honored that part of the bargain calling for the withdrawal of the troops from the South. The public came to think this was so, because a number of newspapers at the time claimed that the president's action was prompted by an agreement made by him, or for him, by some of his Northern friends, with leading Southerners, to obtain their acceptance of the congressional canvass of the electoral vote making him president. Not many Southern Democrats in 1877, however, lavished praise on Hayes, because they thought he was trying to make a virtue of necessity. The Memphis *Appeal* may have spoken for many of them when it asked, "What credit, then, belongs to Hayes for doing what the Democrats have compelled him to do?"[4] Nevertheless, some Southern Democrats did express their gratitude to Hayes for recalling the troops "and trusting us for the observance of the constitution and the laws of the land."[5] As for Republicans, they were so split over Hayes's ordering the troops away that for a while it seemed that their party might suffer the same fate that the Whigs had suffered. Hayes was denounced by disappointed Republicans, especially the carpetbaggers and Stalwarts, who alleged they had been deceived, betrayed, and humiliated. But Hayes had a number of stout Republican defenders, and he appeared to carry the Republican party on the basis of what he had done.[6]

The popular belief that Hayes's decision concerning the troops was part of a bargain making him president was reinforced by historical perspective and scholarship. Paul L. Haworth, in his study of the disputed presidential election of 1876 a generation after the event, presented an account and explanation of what had happened then that ultimately became the standard account of this event and also became familiar to anyone taking a survey course in American history or reading an American-history textbook. At the height of the election crisis, according to Haworth, some close friends of Hayes reached an understanding with a group of Southerners in late February 1877, at the Wormley Conference, paving the way for Hayes's peaceful accession to the presidency. In this bargain the Republicans, while expressly disclaiming any authority to speak for Hayes, in effect guaranteed that Hayes as president would withdraw the troops from Louisiana and South Carolina and allow these two remaining Republican governments in the South to go over to Democratic claimants. They also agreed to try to persuade Grant to do the same thing before the end of his term. The Democrats, for their part, promised to defeat the filibustering that was holding up the electoral count, to assist in completing the count, and to see that Hayes was peacefully inaugurated president. Southern representatives also guaranteed protection of the law to whites and blacks alike and no retaliations for past political offenses.[7] This became the traditional account of the Bargain of 1877. In effect, the Republicans agreed to abandon the Republican state governments of Louisiana and South Carolina, and the Southerners agreed to abandon the filibuster and give up the presidency in exchange for the end of Reconstruction.

While Haworth maintained that a bargain had been made, he also argued that Hayes had not been a party to it and had steadfastly refused to authorize anyone to represent him. Furthermore, he contended, Hayes had already made up his mind to withdraw the troops, and he used as evidence for this contention a letter in which Hayes had written to Carl Schurz on February 4, 1877, in regard to the use of the military, as follows: "But there is to be an end to all of that, except in emergencies which I cannot think of as possible again."[8]

A decade later one of the country's leading political scientists, John W. Burgess, rejected the linkage of the removal of the troops with an agreement to make Hayes president.[9] Hayes's official biographer, Charles Richard Williams, in 1928 agreed with Burgess and argued that Hayes's Southern policy was simply the fulfillment of the promises he had made in his letter accepting the nomination for president.[10] Two years later, however, in the first critical biography of Hayes, H. J. Eckenrode affirmed Haworth's thesis of the removal of the troops and a bargain, and he even went beyond it by depicting Hayes as a party to the agreement. Bargain or not, Eckenrode like Haworth, argued that Hayes's actions "would have been much the same" without the agreement.[11]

Despite some dissent, such as that of Burgess and Williams, most American historians associated Hayes's removal of the troops with the Bargain of 1877 allowing him to become president. In 1951 C. Vann Woodward challenged this long-familiar account of the Compromise of 1877 by showing that the story behind it was more complex than the traditional account revealed. Woodward showed that the Compromise of 1877 was not arrived at in "two days of last-minute haggling. Instead, the negotiations stretched over a period of several months." They were not restricted to a settlement of the political problems of two Southern states but were involved with the economic, social, and political problems of the entire South, and the Wormley Conference was but one of many.[12]

The bulk of Woodward's book is devoted to explaining the "inadequacy" of the traditional account of the Bargain of 1877 and to placing "on record the large aspects it omits." It is a complicated analysis and is not easy to summarize, and there is much caution in its conclusions, but the following is a reasonable summary of it: in addition to the political aspects of the Wormley Conference, the "real" agreement, the one that brought the Southern Democrats around and resolved the electoral crisis of 1877, was reached before the Wormley meeting. It included the appointment of a Southerner to Hayes's cabinet, generous federal aid for internal improvements in the South, federal assistance for the completion of the Texas Pacific Railroad, Democratic control of federal patronage in the South, and the withdrawal of the troops from the South.

In passing, however, it should be noted that Woodward acknowledged that the purely political understanding may have been equal in importance to the economic ones. "It would be futile to attempt to decide at this late date [1951] . . . which of the 'two forces' was the more effective in winning the Southerners over and breaking the filibuster," he wrote. "They were complementary, sometimes closely interrelated, and occasionally indistinguishable." This was much the same as the judgment of General Henry Van Ness Boynton, one of the key and well-informed figures in the Compromise of 1877 when he wrote late in February 1877, "It is still difficult for me to judge which of these two forces [political and economic] has been the most potent element in the long fight. Both have been of the greatest consequences, and I have grave doubts whether either could have carried the day alone."[13]

Woodward's new interpretation of the Compromise of 1877 convinced most scholars and soon won "almost universal acceptance." His thesis was "widely reprinted and incorporated, virtually unchanged, in almost every major textbook of American history, achieving the status of the most influential monograph in its field." An even greater tribute to Woodward than the wide acceptance of his account has been its endurance. It continues in textbooks and is repeated in new scholarship. Recent college textbooks and monographic and synthetic works still accept Woodward's explanation of the 1876–77 electoral crisis.[14]

However, Woodward's version of the large matter of the Compromise of 1877 has been challenged in recent years. Joseph Frazier Wall contended that too little attention had been paid to the role of Northern Democrats and especially the "apostasy of the North" in resolving the electoral dispute of 1876–77. "Not only did the Northern Democrats furnish the numbers but also the leadership to stamp out the efforts at filibuster" to delay the electoral count. And according to Wall, "no special credit—or discredit—belongs to the South as a section for opposing the filibuster." Some analysis of the vote on each motion to recess or otherwise delay the electoral count shows that a larger proportion of the Southern and border-state congressmen voted for delay than did the Northern Democrats. Only on March 1, 1877, after Congressman William M. Levy of Louisiana, who had constantly voted with the filibusters, had informed his Southern colleagues that he had "solemn assurances" from Hayes's friends of a conciliatory policy toward the South, did the proportion of Southern congressmen favoring filibuster fall below that of Northern Democrats and even then only slightly. "In view of the generous promises made to the South in Hayes's name . . . and with due regard to the very real differences that existed between the Northern and Southern delegates," wrote Wall, "the surprising fact is not the number of Southerners who urged a speedy completion of the count, but rather the number of Southerners who continued to delay even after all hope was gone." If the South was under constant pressure from railroad men lobbying for Hayes, "the North was by no means free from pressure by business interests to end the crisis and allow Hayes to be inaugurated quietly and peacefully."[15]

Wall's position that too little attention had been given to the role of Northern Democrats appears well founded. Woodward himself acknowledged that Northern Democrats helped to break the filibuster on important roll calls, but the major point of his approach was to emphasize the machinations of opportunistic Southern politicians. But Wall did little in the way of systematic analysis of the filibuster votes, and his revision or challenge of Woodward's account has not had much effect on the historiography of this event.

Allan Peskin raised the more important question of whether there was a compromise at all in 1877, maintaining that a deal whose major terms were never carried out "appears suspiciously like no deal at all." Peskin was referring to the fact that when Hayes became president a number of these agreements of 1877 were not carried out. Since Peskin believed that none of the component parts of Woodward's alleged bargain of 1877 could explain the outcome of the contested election of 1876, he proposed that perhaps we could turn back for an answer to Ellis Paxson Oberholtzer's theory that the Republicans simply "outwitted and honeyfugled" their opponents at every step of the way. The Republicans held all the high cards—the Senate, the Supreme Court, the army, and the legal (or at least the recognized governments) in the disputed states. The Democrats held only two low cards—the threat of revolution and the House of Representatives. "Neither of them could take a trick." And once Tilden had been eliminated from consideration, "then and only then could southern Democrats negotiate for home rule. This part of the bargain, therefore, did not determine the outcome of the election. In fact, the raising of the issue merely confirmed the hopelessness of Tilden's cause."[16]

In reply to Peskin, Woodward agreed that Tilden's defeat "was not a result of the compromise," but the work of the Electoral Commission, the carpetbagger returning boards, "and all manner of ballot-box stuffers and bribers." Yet, Woodward maintained, an important bargain was made, with "home rule," "the supreme objective of the southern negotiators" and "the fundamental part" of it. "All else was incidental or contributory." "Home rule" meant, among many things, "the Republican party's abandonment of the Fourteenth and Fifteenth amendments in important respects and the civil-rights acts as well. Republicans had to abandon not only their moral obligations to the freedmen but political obligations to their loyal friends the carpetbaggers and scalawags as well as the ranks of black voters," continued Woodward. This compromise guarantee of "home rule" was fulfilled, and it lasted eighty years until the Little Rock crisis of 1957, when federal troops were ordered into action for purposes precluded by the Compromise of 1877. In this respect the Compromise was more than a "temporary understanding . . . barren of lasting results," as Peskin described it.[17]

Though the bargain on "home rule" enjoyed a long life span, many Republicans became dissatisfied with its results and sought to reverse it. Such Republicans came to oppose Hayes's policy of appeasing white Southerners and appointing Southern Democrats to office. These Republicans resumed the practice of bloody-shirt oratory, revived the old charges of Southern white disloyalty, and maintained that the Southern question and the matter of a Democratic South was not fully "settled." These Republicans also wanted the federal government to enforce the Fourteenth and Fifteenth amendments in the South, because Southern Democrats had nullified these constitutional provisions by a variety of methods and had thus oppressed the Negro and reduced or eliminated the Republican vote in the South.

Therefore, many Northern Republicans hardened their attitude toward the South in the 1880s and sought a way to annul the
bargain on "home rule." For instance, many of them criticized
the Supreme Court's decision in the *Civil Rights Cases* of 1883,
declaring illegal the Civil Rights Act of 1875. And when the
Republicans gained control of the presidency and both houses of
Congress together in the 1888 election for the first time since 1872
and were in a position to enforce the Fourteenth and Fifteenth
amendments, they almost did so by nearly passing the Lodge
Elections Bill of 1890, or the Force Bill, as it came to be known.
This measure provided for federal supervision of federal elections
and, had it been enacted, would have repealed the compromise on
"home rule" by again giving the national government control
over elections in the South, as had been the case during Reconstruction. But this effort failed, because enough Republicans in
the Senate would not support it, since they had a greater interest
in a high tariff and a silver measure in 1890 and since they also
feared that a revival of Reconstruction tactics would disrupt the
community of business interests that had developed between the
North and the South since the removal of the troops in 1877.[18]
So "home rule" remained intact until 1957.

Though Peskin's attack on Woodward's interpretation was a
vigorous one, he did not refute it or diminish its acceptance by
historians. Woodward's thesis continued to stimulate interest and
more investigation. Peskin did little to assess Woodward's evidence
or public opinion during the electoral dispute. And Peskin rested
his case on the question of whether there was a compromise on
the degree to which the component parts of the agreement were
fulfilled. But, as Woodward pointed out, the fulfillment of the
terms is not the test of whether a bargain was made. According
to this criterion, there was no Compromise of 1850, because its
terms were not carried out either. "The road to the mid-century
sectional truce like the road to reunion seems to have been 'paved
with broken promises,'" wrote Woodward.[19] In his response to
Peskin, Woodward strengthened his case for the existence of a
Compromise of 1877, especially on its "fundamental part" of
"home rule."

Keith Ian Polakoff also disputed Woodward's views on the
Compromise of 1877. He believed that Woodward "proposed a
misleading explanation about the peaceful resolution of the crisis,"

because "he accepted at face value the assertions made by Boynton and Kellar about the importance of their negotiations" and because he assumed a degree of central direction in national political parties "that subsequent scholarship has shown to be largely nonexistent." According to Polakoff, it was the very inability of party leaders to control their own organizations, even in a crisis demanding centralized direction that assured a peaceful, if blundering, solution to the electoral dispute. Polakoff maintained that the real compromise of 1877 was the creation of the electoral commission, and he further concluded that "the election dispute ended as it did because Hayes worked harder to hold the jealous factions of his party together in the crisis than did his Democratic adversary and because Tilden, after being outgeneraled, had the courage and grace to accept defeat." The Democrats acquiesced in the seating of Hayes, according to Polakoff, because there was nothing else they could do. And as for Hayes's promising to remove the troops, Polakoff, like other writers but with some modification, described it as "a policy to which he was all but publicly committed beforehand. With that the crisis ended. It would have ended on exactly the same terms if no understanding had been reached."[20]

Polakoff did not disprove Woodward's work. "After all, the negotiations he described did take place." But Polakoff questioned whether they settled the electoral dispute. He also questioned whether the parties to the Compromise of 1877 were in fact in control of events. His point that the major parties then had no national leaders and little national management and were rent with factionalism is well founded. Woodward concentrated on the maneuvers of William Henry Smith, general agent of the Western Associated Press and Hayes's closest friend, Andrew J. Kellar, editor of the Memphis *Avalanche*, and General Henry Van Ness Boynton, Washington correspondent of the Cincinnati *Gazette*, because "he was unaware that the factionalism within the Republican party was so serious or that Tilden conceded defeat so readily," wrote Polakoff. "He was frankly unconcerned with those Democrats and Republicans who did not participate in the 'compromise' negotiations." Thus, according to Polakoff, Woodward obtained "only a partial view of the complex pattern of events" making Hayes president. "When that pattern is seen in its entirety, however, it is clear that the diffusion of power in both major parties, and not the machinations of a handful of journalists, was instrumental in preserving the peace in 1877."[21]

Polakoff added a worthwhile dimension to our knowledge of the 1876–77 electoral crisis by his detailed analysis of the significance of the political considerations involved. But despite the important questions that he raised, the reservations that he had about the significance of the economic agreement, and the extensive evidence, except for newspapers, that he used, he did not discredit Woodward's claims. Neither did he weaken the hold of Woodward's thesis; it continued to be accepted by historians in their textbooks and in their studies of this period.

Michael Les Benedict, in a recent article on the same subject, contended that while Woodward described accurately a Republican effort to break down Democratic unity in the South, that effort had not been the determining factor in Democratic acquiescence in Hayes's inauguration. He also argued that Woodward "greatly overestimated" both the role Southern Democrats had played in resolving the electoral crisis and the part the railroads had played in influencing Southerners. Developing themes suggested by Peskin and Polakoff, Benedict attacked Woodward's reliance on the correspondence of the railroad lobbyists, pointing out that these people and others of the "Southern strategy" group overestimated or exaggerated the influence of their efforts. And elaborating on Wall's theme about Southern Democrats and the filibuster, Benedict in a systematic analysis of the filibuster votes showed there was no statistical correlation between Southern congressional support for internal improvements and Southern opposition to the electoral filibuster.

Benedict's analysis of the filibuster votes also demonstrated that northeastern Democrats were more involved in breaking the filibuster than were their Southern colleagues. Thus, according to Benedict, Hayes owed his peaceful inauguration "far more to the course of northern Democrats, particularly northeastern Democrats, than to that of the southerners." Northern Democrats were not going to fight very hard to make Tilden president. Afraid that Northern Democrats were going to abandon them as they had done in 1861 and were going to "fritter away Tilden's victory," Southerners began to talk to Hayes's friends in order to make the best deal they could get to preserve the "fruits of their apparent victory." Benedict also maintained that it was not the Wormley bargain—"and still less any deals involving patronage, the Texas and Pacific Railroad, or the Mississippi levees that broke the filibuster and guaranteed Hayes' inauguration." Yet one should not infer that economic matters played no role in the events of 1877, added Benedict. Fear of violence or instability played a large role in mitigating the belligerence of Democratic businessmen, "whose influence predominated in the northeastern wing of the party, as southern Democrats disgustedly recognized." Republican businessmen exerted similar pressure on their party. "But the outright bargain Woodward described did not take place," concluded Benedict, advancing Peskin's earlier claim, "and this eliminates the only evidence yet presented that there was a 'settlement' in 1877 specifically designed to secure the economic fruits of the Civil War at the sacrifice of its human achievements."[22]

Benedict pointed out there is no evidence of continued Republican–Southern Democratic discussions while Tilden still had a chance to win through the decision of the Electoral Commission. Not until the commission awarded Louisiana's votes to Hayes on February 16, 1877, "did negotiations begin in earnest." Democrats then knew they did not have majority support for the filibuster. If Hayes already knew he was going to win, why did he and his friends deal with the Southerners in the last days of February? Benedict agreed with Polakoff that it was in part because the Republicans were taken in by the Democrats' bluff and in part because Hayes had decided to commit himself to the reform wing of his party and to a new Southern policy. If Southerners had reinforced the filibuster, even in a hopeless cause, and had moved against the Republican government in Louisiana with force, the Republican regulars might have renewed their "bloody shirt" attacks on the Democracy, solidified the party against reformers, and forced Hayes to turn to the regulars for support. Thus, the "anti-climatic negotiations" culminating in the Wormley Bargain served the purposes both of Hayes's friends, who wanted time to carry out "by gradual process such methods as result in your full possession of the government," as they promised Louisiana Democrats, and of the Southerners, "who wanted definite, written assurances that Hayes would not double-cross them when he came under pressure from regulars."[23]

As for Hayes's actually gaining the presidency, Benedict's explanation relied on the one given by Henry Watterson of Kentucky, one of the Wormley House participants, who wrote as late as 1919 that "Hayes was already as good as seated. If the States of Louisiana and South Carolina could save their local autonomy out of the general wreck there seemed no good reason to forbid." A contemporary leading Southern newspaper correspondent, Lucius Quintus Washington, wrote in early 1877, rebutting "the silly charge of the bargain," "Southern Congressmen did not give away Mr. Tilden, nor could they do so . . . . the prize [was] . . . lost by the inaction and submission, or prudence—call it what you will—of our northern allies. They—not the South or her Congressmen—went back on Mr. Tilden." Washington's view is supported by Benedict's study, as already noted, and by his further assertions that the firm leadership opposing the seating of Hayes which Southern Democrats wanted from their Northern colleagues was never forthcoming, and that Southerners were receptive to the blandishments of Hayes's agents "primarily because of the 'timidity' of northeastern Democrats."[24]

Benedict's study, especially his analysis of the filibuster votes and his review of Woodward's "internal improvements" case adds new information to our understanding of the electoral crisis of 1876–77. And it is conceivable that, in the long run, when these views are better and more widely known and are more fully explored, they will weaken, or even break, the hold of Woodward's thesis. True, Benedict's study persuasively demonstrated that Southern Democratic votes were not the ones to break the filibuster and that railroad lobbyists exaggerated the strength of their lobby. But he was not able to show as convincingly that these two important pieces of information were that well known to the participants in the electoral crisis. Hayes and his friends believed that Southern Democratic congressional support was necessary to complete the electoral count and to inaugurate Hayes peacefully. This is how they perceived the situation, and why they maneuvered as they did to win Southern Democratic support. So, instead of proving there was no compromise in 1877, Benedict shows that the one that arose was the result of both Democratic bluffs and Republican miscalculations. Southern Democratic votes may not have been necessary to make Hayes president, but the Republicans nevertheless promised to give "home rule," patronage, and internal-improvements subsidies to obtain those votes.

Finally, William Gillette in his recent prize-winning study of Reconstruction concluded that the drama and timing of the disputed 1876 election had led many historians, including Haworth, Woodward, and Polakoff, to exaggerate the importance of its effect on Reconstruction. "Actually, the fact that Reconstruction was substantially at an end had shaped the outcome of the electoral dispute." Had Reconstruction "not been all but done for," Tilden would not have won almost the entire South and "there would not have been a close and disputed election," wrote Gillette. "If the Republican party had still considered the South politically important and had given high priority to the protection of Negro voters," Hayes would not have been the nominee, and the Republicans would not have conducted the campaign as they did, especially not in the South. "Neither would they have submitted to bipartisan arbitration and bisectional discussions; the stakes simply would have been too high. No matter who occupied the Executive Mansion," contended Gillette, "the troops at the two southern statehouses would have been withdrawn and the Democrats would have taken possession, for the southern Republican party was practically defunct. Hayes had known that and had been ready to accept the inevitable all along." And Gillette also maintained that Republicans did not abandon the Negro to gain the presidency, since he had been, in large part, deserted before 1876–77. Neither did the Southern Democrats give up Tilden's cause for their own, because his case had already been lost by the vote of the Electoral Commission.[25]

Gillette did not develop his views about the electoral dispute and the removal of the troops, and he offered little evidence in their support. They assume largely the form of conjectures, and they will probably have little discernible effect on the future of Woodward's interpretation. However, his point about Hayes's recognizing the inevitability of withdrawing the troops is an important one; as we shall see, that recognition influenced Hayes's decision on that matter.

But some of Gillette's other points are not convincing. The Republicans in 1876 still considered the South politically important, despite Gillette's assertion that they did not. They had not given up the fight in the South as hopeless, and in fact, as we know, they tried in a variety of ways over the ensuing years to break up the Democratic South and to rebuild their party in this part of the country on a strong and permanent basis. Neither did the Republicans give up the black vote in the South. They wanted and needed it as much as they had in Reconstruction, but they did not want to depend on it for their main strength in the South, because they hoped to win the esteem and support of Southern whites.

And the claim that Hayes would not have been the Republican standard-bearer in 1876 if the Republican party had still considered the South and the Negro vote politically important is speculative and not in accord with Hayes's views before he became president. As we shall see, Hayes supported the Radical plan of Reconstruction when he was in Congress and when he ran for governor of Ohio, and he encouraged a bloody-shirt campaign in his presidential campaign of 1876.

As I have already pointed out, Woodward's interpretation of the Compromise of 1877 won general acceptance among historians and became the standard account of the electoral crisis of 1876–77. This helped establish him as one of the premier historians of this period in American history. But a more important testimonial to Woodward's scholarship than the acceptance of his explanation of the Compromise has been its durability. As one of Woodward's most recent critics, Benedict, noted, "while historians have abandoned the postulates of economic determinism, while they have exploded the notion that Reconstruction-era Republicans fronted for northern capitalists, while they now agree that racial rather than economic issues determined the course of Reconstruction, Woodward's thesis seems to have weathered the storm."[26]

In saying this, Benedict probably meant that Woodward's thesis had weathered the storm of attacks on it before his own. But since he contends that the Republican effort to break down Democratic unity in the South as so "accurately" described by Woodward "was not the determining factor in Democratic acquiescence in Hayes's inauguration" and even more that "the outright bargain Woodward described did not take place," he believes he has shaken the hold of Woodward's thesis if he has not overturned it.[27] Gillette may also believe that he has done the same thing.

But since these two accounts questioning Woodward's interpretation have only recently appeared, it remains to be seen whether they have demolished Woodward's thesis. It may be some time before we know whether Gillette and Benedict, and especially the latter, have broken the persistence of Woodward's thesis in college textbooks and in new monographic and synthetic works. This could be the test of the acceptance of their views and the rejection or modification of Woodward's. Although one now has to take into account some of their questions and reservations, Woodward's account of the backstage maneuvering and bargaining in the disputed election remains, in my view, a more believable account of what happened at that time than those of his critics. And the fact that his explanation of the 1876–77 electoral crisis continues to be accepted by the latest editions of most leading college textbooks of American history and by monographic and synthetic works on Reconstruction attests to the wide and durable acceptance of *Reunion and Reaction.*

But the most important matter for this essay is that of the removal of the troops from the South, and not the larger issue of the electoral dispute and the Compromise of 1877, on which most of the controversy is focused. There is more agreement on the question of the removal of the troops than on that of the Compromise. Virtually every account of the electoral crisis, traditional and recent, maintains it would have ended in the same way if no agreement had been reached and that Hayes would have withdrawn the troops anyway, because he had indicated that he would. Even Woodward's account, the most influential one, holds to this view in pointing out "that at the time the Wormley Conference was held and the so-called Bargain struck the Southerners were already committed to the course they pursued and Hayes was already committed to a policy of conciliating the South."[28]

The question of the removal of the troops is of particular interest, says Woodward, because everyone took it for granted that the fall of the two remaining Republican state governments in the South and the succession of the Democrats—or "Redemption" and "Home Rule," as Southerners called it—would follow once the troops were withdrawn. "This has been presented as the critical point of the Wormley Conference and the *quid pro quo* of the Bargain from the Southern point of view," writes Woodward. But, he adds, a week before the Wormley negotiations opened, a way had been contrived to insure the removal of the troops in the event Hayes forgot his promises or could not carry them out. The Democrats in caucus on February 19, 1877, approved an amendment to the army appropriations bill, then pending, prohibiting the use of troops to support the claims of any state government in the South until it was recognized by Congress. A Democratic House approved this rider, but a Republican Senate rejected it, and Congress adjourned without providing any money whatever for the army.[29] In fact the army remained unpaid for seven months, until Congress finally changed its mind about the restricting clause.

Thus Woodward added another aspect to the question of the removal of the troops by arguing that the Democrats in the House could in any case have compelled withdrawal by eliminating appropriations for the army in Reconstruction efforts. For although he believed that Hayes had already been committed to a policy of conciliating the South, he maintained that the president's "hand had been forced by withholding of the Army appropriation." However, the Wormley Bargain "pledges of his friends may have assisted in smoothing the path for an early fulfillment of his policy."[30]

Both President Hayes and his wife seemed, in observations they made some months after the troops had been removed, to foretell what Woodward would say about the congressional restriction on the use of the army. "Why, what could Mr. Hayes do but what he did? He had no army," the president's wife reportedly told a friend. And the president himself, in a conversation with the same friend remarked, "In addition, the House was against me and I had no army, and public sentiment demanded a change of policy." Others as well blamed the Democratic House for forcing Hayes to recall the troops and to abandon the Republican governors in the South. Public sentiment demanding a change of policy, Woodward believed, was such a strong force that it made President Grant give up his own policy of forceful intervention in the South to prop up Republican governments.[31]

Hayes's recent biographers have not added much new information to the story of the removal of the troops. Harry Barnard contended that Hayes knew at the outset what he would do but that he did not take the direct course of issuing an immediate order barring the army from playing any further role in the affairs of South Carolina and Louisiana. This was because it took time to persuade Daniel H. Chamberlain and Stephen B. Packard, the Republican claimants to the governorship in these states, to accept the idea of giving way to the Democrats Wade Hampton and Francis T. Nicholls. It also took time to attempt to mollify Republican critics of a new Southern policy, to answer in part the allegations of a bargain with Southern Democrats and the charge of abandoning the Negro in the South, and to win from Hampton and Nicholls public pledges of protection for the constitutional rights of Negroes.[32]

Kenneth E. Davison emphasized Hayes's growing disillusionment with the Radical Republican policy in the South and his belief that the country and most white Southerners would welcome a policy of moderation and conciliation over that of coercion. With the benefit of hindsight, it is hard to see how Hayes might have acted differently in the situation he faced in March 1877, writes Davison. Grant had already terminated military occupation. Public opinion also favored the end of Reconstruction. And even if there had been a return to the policy of using military force in the South, there would have been no army to enforce it, because it was needed on the Indian frontier. Besides, Congress was not inclined to enlarge the army, let alone appropriate money for paying men already in the service.[33]

The argument of Woodward and Davison that Hayes had to remove the troops because Congress had not appropriated money for the army is not a persuasive one. It implies that federal troops would have been without provisions, pay, and transportation, and that under such circumstances the president might not have been able to depend on them to carry out his orders. Such reasoning supports Hayes's own contention that he had no army in the spring of 1877 or that he could not use it to enforce a return to military Reconstruction in the South if he had wanted to do this.

But when Hayes pulled the troops out, the army still had funds to use for more than two months before the end of the fiscal year; there was thus nothing to prevent him from keeping soldiers in the South, which he did when he had them transferred from the two state capitols to their nearby barracks. Federal troops could have been used to prop up the tottering Republican governments in Louisiana and South Carolina, even in the face of budgetary restrictions, just as they were employed to quell Indian and railroad-labor disturbances later in 1877. The issue of Hayes's continued use of federal troops to support Chamberlain and Packard involved political considerations, not financial ones. And if Hayes had little or no choice but to withdraw the troops, it was for political, not financial, reasons. The lack of funds for the army beyond the end of the fiscal year in 1877 did not keep the president from using the military when he wanted to do so. Woodward admitted this when he pointed out that Hayes was "compelled to rely upon unpaid and unhappy officers and men to suppress the violent labor upheavals in the several states in August 1877."[34] This action came at a time when the army was probably unhappier and shorter of money than it had been a few months earlier in the disputed-state-election controversy in the South.

Those Republicans who attacked Hayes's decision to withdraw the troops insisted that it came as a surprise to them and that it abandoned both the Negro and the hope of enforcing the Fourteenth and Fifteenth amendments in the South. Some even accused Hayes of selling them out, of displaying a "base ingratitude" to "those that elected him," of mistaking his duty "shockingly," and of abandoning the Republican party.[35] Even Hayes seemed to agree with some of these charges when he described his new policy as a "total departure from the principle, traditions, and wishes of the Republican party."[36] But there appear to be other reasons for making these allegations. Although the Republican platform of 1876 called for the "permanent pacification" of the South and for the removal of "any just causes of discontent on the part of any class," it also demanded the enforcement of the Fourteenth and Fifteenth amendments, and it resembled a bloody-shirt document in that it continued to associate the Democratic party with treason and warned Americans not to turn over the control of the country to the traitorous Democrats. Hayes's letter accepting the presidential nomination promised Southerners he would "cherish their truest interests" and would help them to obtain the "blessings of honest and capable local government," a statement they regarded as a pledge and looked to Hayes to fulfill, but he promised this only on the condition that Southern whites recognize the political and civil rights of the Negro.[37]

Hayes himself encouraged a bloody-shirt campaign in 1876, warning that "a Democratic victory will bring the rebellion into power," and that this would mean continued trouble, nullification of the Constitution, and "rebel" schemes and plans. "Our strong ground is dread of a Solid South, rebel rule, etc.," he told James G. Blaine, then starting out on a campaign tour of Ohio and Indiana. "It leads people away from hard times which is our deadliest foe." Republican leaders and newspapers followed the lead of their nominee, telling the country that a Democratic victory would re-enslave the Negro, put Southern Republicans at the mercy of "rope clubs," and compensate the South for the loss of its slaves. William E. Chandler, Republican leader from New Hampshire and one of the managers of his party's 1876 campaign, pointed out that "the bloody shirt, as it is termed, was freely waved, and Governor Hayes himself urged public men to put forward as our best argument, the dangers of 'rebel rule and a solid South.' "[38]

These were campaign documents and speeches made in an effort to win votes, and to what extent they reflected the personal opinion of Hayes and other Republican leaders is open to question. Still, the tenor of the 1876 Republican platform and campaign did not indicate the change in the Southern policy that Hayes would initiate. An exception, of course, was Hayes's letter of acceptance. In his inaugural address he again spoke to the South and repeated the assurances he had made in his letter. But once more, he said, while local government was an "imperative necessity" for the South, this local government had to guard the interests of both blacks and whites and to submit "loyally and heartily to the constitution and the laws."[39] Hayes's letter and inaugural statement were regarded at the time by many Southerners (and Northerners, too) as a pledge to eliminate federal interference in the South by withdrawing troops. And they have been so regarded by historians, which is why so many of them have contended that, with or without a bargain, Hayes would have removed the troops anyway. But these two public statements, considered widely at the time and subsequently as a prior commitment to end military Reconstruction, were no pledge to do this unless Southern whites agreed to recognize the political and civil rights of the Negro, a condition many of them would, as Hayes knew, find difficult to accept. Yet he was optimistic about the possibility of this acceptance, for, as he confided to his diary once he had ordered the troops away, "the result of my plan is to get from those States [in the South] by their governors, legislatures, press and people pledges that the Thirteenth, Fourteenth, and

Fifteenth Amendments shall be faithfully observed; that the colored people shall have equal rights to labor, education, and the privilege of citizenship."[40]

A number of leading Southern whites buoyed up Hayes's hopes when they promised to respect black civil rights. "We . . . will secure to every citizen, the lowest as well as the highest, black as well as white, full and equal protection in the enjoyment of all his rights under the Constitution," said Wade Hampton of South Carolina in the spring of 1877. His pledge was repeated by other prominent Southerners. But these promises were not kept. Hayes had urged Southern Negroes to trust Southern whites. But within a year and a half after having removed the troops, he was disillusioned, and he wrote in his diary following the 1878 elections, "By state legislation, by frauds, by intimidation, and by violence of the most atrocious character, colored citizens have been deprived of the right of suffrage . . . and to the protection to which the people of those States have been solemnly pledged."[41]

Why, then, did Hayes remove the troops? In doing so, he appeared to put aside his fears as to what would happen in the South and to the Negro with the restoration of "home rule" to this part of the country. On the day after the 1876 election, when he believed the Democrats had won, he told friends and newspapermen, "I do not care for myself, but I do care for the poor colored man in the South." If the Democrats were to regain control of the national government, then, according to Hayes, in the South the "Amendments will be nullified, disorder will continue, prosperity to both whites and colored will be pushed off for years." It seemed to him that he could do more "than any Democrat to put Southern affairs on a sound basis." He hoped that if he himself was in the White House, he could have Southern whites keep their pledges to protect blacks. But by restoring complete Democratic control to the South, which he did with the removal of the troops, he did not seem to be as apprehensive about this as he had been during the 1876 campaign, when he had promoted the idea that "a Democratic victory will bring the Rebellion into power" and that "the late rebels" would then "have the government."[42]

Hayes removed the troops and ended military Reconstruction for a number of reasons. Perhaps just one or two of these would not have been strong enough for him to act on, but their combined force caused him to make his decision. Most of these reasons are familiar to historians of this period, but this essay attempts to sum them up and to place them in their proper relation with the larger aspects of the problems and opportunities confronting President Hayes about the South in 1877. Because of the limits of this essay, it is not possible to elaborate on these reasons.

There are the bargains of 1877, of course, and they, especially the Wormley Conference, were much concerned about the restoration of "home rule" through troop withdrawals. This was an important issue, and even a crucial one at times, in the negotiations between Hayes's representatives and Southern Democrats in the winter of 1876–77. Whether President Hayes believed he was obligated by the terms of these agreements to withdraw federal military support from the two remaining carpetbag governments is a debatable matter. But both traditional and recent accounts, with few exceptions, indicate that these negotiated arrangements or understandings had something, possibly much, to do with Hayes's decision on the troops. Thus the bargains have to be considered one of the reasons.

But Hayes withdrew the troops for a different political reason, as well—probably the most important reason. He believed the policy of military intereference in the South had served only to thwart Republican hopes of success there. He therefore planned to build a new and strong Republican party in the South, not dependent on the Negro for its main support, and capable of winning the respect and backing of Southern whites. Hayes believed he could divide Southern whites on political and economic lines rather than on the race question. He hoped to do this by conciliating Southern conservative whites and former Whigs through a policy of friendship and nonintervention in their affairs. But the use of federal troops to support carpetbag regimes blocked such efforts, and Hayes recognized he had to remove this obstacle before he could begin to rejuvenate Southern Republicanism and to win white Southerners to its support.[43]

Another reason for Hayes's decision was his desire to "restore harmony and good feeling between [the] sections and races." He believed a complete reconciliation between the North and South was necessary for the moral and material prosperity of the South as well as for that of the nation as a whole. As for Negroes and whites in the South, only "by the united and harmonious effort of both races" could the difficulties afflicting both be remedied or removed.[44] But the presence of federal troops in the South galled Southern whites and blocked any real reconciliation of North and South, Negro and white. A former Negro congressman from Florida, J. Willis Menard, pointed out to Hayes as he pondered the question of troop removals "that inasmuch as troops and repressive laws have failed to establish permanent peace between the two races, we must seek . . . for a remedy."[45] Hayes himself thought that the public would not sustain the policy of upholding a state government against a rival government by the use of federal force. If this led to the overthrow of the de jure government in a state, the de facto government had to be recognized. Despite his bloody-shirt campaign, Hayes confided to his diary a few weeks after he became president, his policy toward the South would be one of "trust, peace, and to put aside the bayonet," and one that would no longer use "the national army . . . to decide contested elections in the States." He would not resort to intervention except to keep the peace.[46]

Hayes's decision regarding the troops was also influenced by the wide support he had among Republicans and in the country for a change of policy in the South. Hayes and those Republicans who so bitterly attacked his decision to withdraw the troops seemed to agree that it was a sharp departure from the policy the Republicans had largely followed in the South during Reconstruction and that it was at variance with the 1876 Republican platform. This appeared to be so when the new policy in the South, launched with the removal of the troops, was compared with the old policy in the South, and both Hayes and his Republican critics were aware of this.

But they were also aware that while the old policy was being carried out a change of attitude was beginning to occur in the country and among many Republicans toward Reconstruction, the South, and the freedman that helped to pave the way for a new policy in the South. To an increasing number of Republicans the old policy of propping up carpetbag governments in the South with federal troops was outmoded and out of step with the Republicanism of the 1870s, and in need of change. As Joseph Medill of the Chicago *Tribune* told Richard Smith of the Cincinnati *Gazette*, "we have tried for eight years to uphold Negro rule in the

South officered by Carpetbaggers but without exception it has ended in failure."[47]

Thus Republicans in the mid-1870s began to debate what was then probably a revolutionary idea for many of them—that of dropping the carpetbagger and the Southern Negro and changing from a policy of military interference to one of nonintervention in the South. The demand rose, not only from Southerners and Democrats, but from Northerners and Republicans as well, for the removal of the federal troops from the South.[48] While the *Nation* may not have been entirely correct in concluding, just a month before the troops were recalled, that "the great body of the Republican party is . . . opposed to the continuance at the South of the policy of military interference and coercion as pursued by General Grant,"[49] there were many Republicans who by then wanted a different policy in the South. But the sentiment within the party for change was not unanimous, for there was an element in the Republican party, especially among the regulars and many of the old leaders, that still favored the old policy toward the South.

Thus, while Hayes's policy was a departure from the Republican party's accustomed Reconstruction policy, it was also in line with an increasing public and Republican sentiment in the country for a change of policy. And, as already noted, Hayes was aware of this change in public sentiment and even listed it himself as one of the reasons he removed the troops.

Hayes's letter of acceptance led many Republicans, especially those who wanted a new policy in the South, and other Americans too, to believe that he had outlined a new policy for this section. And from all parts of the country they urged and encouraged him to take this step. The large number of letters that Hayes received on this question from the time of his nomination to the spring of 1877 clearly shows this sentiment for a change of policy and the wide support Hayes had within his party and in the country for his idea of restoring local government in the South.[50] Many Americans wanted the federal troops pulled out of the South and the carpetbaggers kicked out. An example of this kind of sentiment is in a letter to Hayes from a New Orleans Republican who wrote, "I am confident you will obtain the support of the whole people in every Southern State if you will keep the military away from them and let the military go after the Mexicans and Indians." Other examples include a letter from an Ohio friend who wrote Hayes, "Rutherford take a friends [sic] advice and kill our southern brethern with kindness," and one from an important Republican editor in the country, Whitelaw Reid, who pressed Hayes for "a policy that may retrieve the error and disgrace of Republican dealing with the South—precisely in accordance with the admirable tone of your letter of acceptance." Furthermore, Reid said, "We should not groan . . . by the downfall of such Southern State Governments as can only stand while propped up by bayonets."[51]

These are only some of the many letters that poured in on Hayes endorsing what he had said in his letter of acceptance and in his inaugural address about the Southern question.[52] This correspondence urged him to stand firm in the course he had charted for the South and told him that the "better class of men" supported him. "Your course is what we expected and heartily approve," wrote James Russell Lowell, Henry W. Longfellow, Charles W. Eliot, and C. E. Norton. "All good men heartily co-operate and sympathize with you," a Boston correspondent told Hayes. From Ohio came the counsel "Never forget that you are Captain," and from Pennsylvania the advice "Stand firm. Your policy meets the approbation of the people. They demand and will have it."[53] Hayes, as already noted, was quite aware of the sentiment in the country for a new policy in the South and was unquestionably influenced by it in his decision to remove the troops.

Even among some of the Republican leaders who later attacked the new departure taken by Hayes, there was support for a change of policy in the South. James G. Blaine, Republican leader from Maine, in conversations with Hayes and James A. Garfield during and after the 1876 campaign, expressed the opinion that the time had come for the Republican party to stop keeping state governments in power by the use of troops. Roscoe Conkling, Republican leader from New York, reportedly said that he did not object to the removal of the troops and that he did not find many Republicans who did.[54] Pressure for the removal of the troops also came from businessmen, Northern and Southern; for example, Marshall Jewell, a Connecticut businessman and future Republican national chairman, told Hayes that businessmen needed stable Southern governments and that these could be organized if the troops left and if the "best" white men returned to power in the South.[55] One cannot dismiss the influence of this pressure for a more moderate policy in the South.

Not only had much of the American public changed its mind about the South and military Reconstruction but so had Hayes, and this was another important reason why he withdrew the troops. Hayes had been in Congress (1865–67) when this body formulated a Reconstruction program for the South. While not in sympathy with Radical leaders like Thaddeus Stevens, Hayes supported the Radical plan of Reconstruction enacted by Congress, telling a close Southern friend it contained "the best terms you will ever get—and they should be promptly accepted . . . don't be deceived by Andy Johnson."[56] When he ran for governor of Ohio for the first time in 1867, he endorsed congressional Reconstruction although he believed that "no such absurdity and wrong" as preventing the South from participating in the national government "can be permanent."[57]

Hayes looked on Grant's election in 1868 as "a happy thing" and as having a good effect in the South and everywhere. He thought Grant had "begun the work of reconstruction in a masterly way and with marked success." Even by the early 1870s, Hayes was convinced that "the Administration is right on the South and the Democracy wrong" and that Grant was "faithful on the great question of the rights of colored people." It was Grant's quarrel with Senator Charles Sumner over Santo Domingo and not the problems of military Reconstruction that first raised doubt in Hayes's mind about Grant's renomination.[58]

But Hayes began to change his mind about the South and Reconstruction. He had kept up a correspondence with a college classmate, Guy M. Bryan of Texas, who urged a more moderate policy toward the South. Bryan pressed particularly for local self-government in the South.[59] His letters had a positive impact, as Hayes acknowledged when he told Bryan, "You will see in my letter of acceptance, I trust, the influence of the feeling which our friendship has tended to foster."[60]

While endorsing Grant and his Reconstruction policy, Hayes was outlining to Bryan what he would later do in the South as president.[61] By the mid-1870s he was not in sympathy with "a large share of the party leaders. . . . I doubt the ultra measures relating to the South." He had come full circle from his support of congressional Reconstruction when he privately wrote in 1875, "As to Southern affairs 'the let-alone policy' seems now to be the true course."[62] And Hayes expressed some of his changed views publicly. In launching his gubernatorial campaign in Ohio in 1875, he condemned the reopening of old issues that divided North and South and called for a complete reconciliation of the two sections. He repeated these themes in campaign speeches that year, and since they were widely published in newspapers, his views on the South should have been well known by the time he was nominated for the presidency.[63] Hayes's changing ideas on Reconstruction were a powerful influence on his decision to remove the troops— possibly as important as that of his effort to rejuvenate Southern Republicanism.

Hayes's decision to remove the troops also came from necessity. If he wanted to restore "home rule," he would have to order the troops away. Despite his seeming willingness to do this, he was concerned about the effect it would have on the Republican governments in South Carolina and Louisiana. At first he thought of adjusting the difficulties in these two states "so as to make one government out of two in each state but if this fails, if no adjustment can be made, we must then adopt the non-intervention policy, except so far as may be necessary to keep the peace."[64] He soon recognized that this compromise would not work.

Also confronting Hayes was the fact obvious to everyone that Republican state governments in the South had steadily lost strength and appeal during Reconstruction and that they were able to stay in office only with federal military support. As for the Republican claimants for governor in South Carolina and Louisiana in the disputed elections of 1876—Chamberlain and Packard—their cases had practically been decided adversely before Hayes took office. In the closing days of his presidency, Grant reversed himself on his earlier policy of intervention in the South. When Packard asked for the use of federal troops to settle the contested election in his state, Grant turned him down, telling him that "public opinion will no longer support the maintenance of a State government in Louisiana by the use of the military and he must concur in this manifest feeling."[65] Earlier, Grant had told Garfield that Packard could not be sustained but would be driven from the state as soon as the electoral count was decided. As for South Carolina, Grant believed the conflict there had reached such a point that "the whole army of the United States would be inadequate to enforce the authority of Governor Chamberlain." In an interview with the Associated Press, Grant expressed the opinion that "the entire people are tired of the military being used to sustain a State Government. If a Republican State Government cannot sustain itself, then it will have to give way. If a remedy is required, let Congress, and not the President provide it." Grant "had many advisers against" recognizing the last carpetbag governments, Alphonso Taft, the solicitor general, informed Hayes. "One consideration has had some weight with him," added Taft, "and that is, that he was not so well sustained by the Republican party when he recognized and upheld [William Pitt] Kellogg [in Louisiana] as he expected."[66]

Originally, Grant had intended to wait until Hayes was declared elected and then to recognize Packard and Chamberlain, but since this did not happen until the close of his presidency, he decided not to take a step not in accordance with Hayes's views.[67] Actually, Grant sent a telegram to New Orleans instructing General Augur to withdraw protection from Packard. But Secretary of War Donald Cameron stopped the order, and General Sherman directed General Augur to "go slow."[68] So, despite the Grant administration's having ended, for all practical purposes, the last phase of military occupation, the final decision was left to Hayes.

Also helping Hayes reach a decision on the troops was the encouragement he received from his cabinet. Hour after hour in the spring of 1877, the cabinet wrestled with this question. "All but [Charles] Devens [the attorney general] seemed indisposed to use force to uphold Packard's government and he is not decidedly for it," Hayes put in his diary. William Evarts, secretary of state, who had much influence with Hayes, advised the president against the use of the army to sustain one government against another in a contested election. The states must take care of these matters themselves.[69] Holding the same opinion, thinking "that the people will not now sustain the policy of upholding a State Government against a rival by the use of the forces of the United States," and keeping in mind all the influences at work on him, Hayes finally removed the troops.

Before he ordered the troops away, though, Hayes asked his old friend Guy M. Bryan to come from Texas to counsel him in these difficult hours. Bryan was Hayes's guest at the White House for more than three weeks during the settlement of the Louisiana and South Carolina disputes. Hayes explained to Bryan that it was not the president's duty but that of the state legislatures to determine questions "which circumstances bring here for my action. I am determined that the legislature shall not be trampled by the military, for the troops shall be removed as soon as I am informed the legislature is organized."[70]

While Hayes's contemporaries and historians have given different reasons for his decision to remove the troops, Hayes himself presented a variety of explanations for his action. Those included, as already noted, that the House of Representatives was against him, that he had no army, and that public sentiment demanded a change of policy. But he offered other accounts.

In a press interview in the same month during which he withdrew the troops, Hayes contended there should not have been any surprise about his Southern policy, since it had been foreshadowed in what he said in his Ohio gubernatorial campaign in 1875, in his letter of acceptance, and in his inaugural address. He also told the press that when he became president he was determined to carry out his policy.[71] In a speech Hayes gave in Cincinnati in October 1877, he maintained he had acted thus in the South, not because it was necessary, but because it was wise and right. "This is the true ground," he argued.[72]

Also in the same month, in a private gathering of friends, Hayes described how his Southern policy had come about. "The reconstruction plan of President Johnson was a failure, because the times were not ripe for it," he said. "The attempted reconstruction by the Democrats was a failure, as the people had no confidence in them," he continued. "General Grant, holding on to the Army, sustained a Southern policy for seven years, and a large portion of the Republicans in those states sloughed off, and he was finally compelled to let go; he came to the turn of the road. This was the condition when I came in as President," remarked Hayes, "so I had to act promptly."[73]

"The truth is, I had no confidants in regard to it," Hayes confessed about his policy in his diary. "My judgment was that the time had come to put an end to bayonet rule. . . . My task was to wipe out the color line, to abolish sectionalism, to end the war and bring peace. To do this, I was ready to resort to unusual measures, and to risk my own standing and reputation with my party and the country. . . . The army was withdrawn because I believed it a constitutional duty and a wise thing to do."[74]

In the last year of his presidency, before an audience at Yale, where he received an honorary degree, Hayes pointed out that before his inauguration, he had come to the conclusion that his paramount duty as president was the pacification of the country. To assure the nation that this was his first duty required, according to Hayes, some "distinct palpable act." Then he went on to say he had written President Theodore Dwight Woolsey of Yale about this matter and "then followed implicitly" Woolsey's advice. "All may not have followed as I hoped for," said the president, "but I do feel that, in that matter, I found the true key to the situation." Woolsey publicly denied that Hayes had written to him. What had happened was that Woolsey had communicated with a mutual friend of Hayes and that in this manner his ideas had reached the president. "I never knew what or how much influence my communication had," added Woolsey, "until the President was pleased to mention it in his recent visit."[75]

Thus we have seen how the traditional account of the Bargain of 1877 was challenged by Woodward and how in turn his long-dominant interpretation of it has been questioned. Those who have challenged Woodward's views are likely to have their own questioned. The recent literature about the Compromise of 1877 has probably not put an end to the controversy.

On the question of the removal of the troops there has been more agreement than on that of the Compromise. Virtually every account from Haworth's on has contended that Hayes would have withdrawn the troops with or without a bargain, because he had made up his mind to do it and had indicated he would do it. But the writers who advanced these views offered little or no evidence to support them. Likewise, they failed to take into consideration the various aspects of this matter and instead gave or emphasized a single reason for the withdrawal of the troops. Woodward, as an exception, alluded to reasons other than his main one for Hayes's decision, but he did not develop them very much.

In giving a broader and more complete account of the removal of the troops, this essay attempts to rectify the inadequacy of previous accounts and to explain the different aspects they omit. And it also endeavors to remedy the incompleteness in Reconstruction historiography of the end of military Reconstruction in which a bargain or Hayes's prior commitment to act is usually given as the reason for the withdrawal of federal military support from the remaining carpetbag governments in the South.

There is now a fuller account of the removal of the troops, one that brings President Hayes to the center of the deliberations. All this could bring a change in the customary Reconstruction story of the removal of the troops and in Woodward's long-accepted explanation of it. But Woodward's interpretation is still so implanted among historians that it is uncertain what present revisions will be able to do to it. A Rip Van Winkle who awoke from a thirty-year nap in 1981 would find the story of the removal of the troops in Reconstruction studies and in college textbooks not much different from the one he had read in Woodward's *Reunion and Reaction* in 1951.

NOTES

1. Clarence C. Clendenen, "President Hayes' 'Withdrawal' of the Troops— An Enduring Myth," *South Carolina Historical Magazine*, 70 (1969), 240–50; Kenneth E. Davison, *The Presidency of Rutherford B. Hayes* (Westport, Conn., 1972), pp. 137–38.

2. See, for example, Vincent P. DeSantis, *Republicans Face the Southern Question—The New Departure Years, 1877–1897* (Baltimore, 1959), pp. 73, 132; and DeSantis, "The Republican Party and the Southern Negro, 1877– 1897," *Journal of Negro History*, 45 (1960), 74.

3. William Gillette, *Retreat from Reconstruction 1869–1879* (Baton Rouge, 1979), pp. 346, 347, 360, 362.

4. Quoted in ibid., p. 345.

5. Charles Gayarre, historian of Louisiana, to Rutherford B. Hayes, April 21, 1877, in Rutherford B. Hayes Papers, Hayes Memorial Library, Fremont, Ohio.

6. For a full discussion of Republican dissensions and differences on what Hayes was doing in the South, see DeSantis, *Republicans Face the Southern Question*, pp. 104–32.

7. Paul L. Haworth, *The Disputed Presidential Election of 1876* (Cleveland, 1906), pp. 268ff; C. Vann Woodward, *Reunion and Reaction: The Compromise of 1877 and the End of Reconstruction* (Boston, 1951), pp. 6–8.

8. Haworth, *Disputed Presidential Election*, p. 270.

9. John W. Burgess, *The Administration of President Hayes* (New York, 1916), pp. 87–88.

10. Charles Richard Williams, *The Life of Rutherford Birchard Hayes*, 2 vols. (Columbus, Ohio, 1928), II, 67, 65.

11. H. J. Eckenrode, *Rutherford B. Hayes: Statesman of Reunion* (New York, 1930), pp. 223–24, 225, 227, 247.

12. Woodward, *Reunion and Reaction*, pp. 11–14.

13. Ibid., pp. 182–83.

14. Allan Peskin, "Was There a Compromise of 1877?" *Journal of American History*, 60 (1973), 63–64; Michael Les Benedict, "Southern Democrats in the Crisis of 1876–1877: A Reconsideration of *Reunion and Reaction*," *Journal of Southern History*, 46 (1980), 489–524. On pages 491–92, Benedict lists a number of recent college textbooks and monographs that still accept Woodward's thesis.

15. Joseph Frazier Wall, *Henry Watterson: Reconstructed Rebel* (New York, 1956), pp. 161–64. Wall does not directly say Woodward gave too little attention to the role of Northern Democrats, but he clearly implies it.

16. Peskin, "Was There a Compromise of 1877?" pp. 63–75.

17. C. Vann Woodward, "Yes, There Was a Compromise of 1877," *Journal of American History*, 60 (1973), 215–23.

18. Stanley P. Hirshon, *Farewell to the Bloody Shirt: Northern Republicans and the Southern Negro, 1877–1893* (Bloomington, 1962), pp. 45–62, 103–5; DeSantis, *Republicans Face the Southern Question*, pp. 182–226.

19. Woodward, "Yes, There Was a Compromise of 1877," p. 217.

20. Keith Ian Polakoff, *The Politics of Inertia: The Election of 1876 and the End of Reconstruction* (Baton Rouge, 1973), pp. x, xii, 313–14, 332.

21. Ibid., p. 314.

22. Benedict, "Southern Democrats in the Crisis of 1876–1877," pp. 492, 497, 502–3, 520.

23. Ibid., pp. 518–20.

24. Ibid., pp. 520, 501, 508.

25. Gillette, *Retreat from Reconstruction*, pp. 333, 427.

26. Benedict, p. 491.

27. Ibid., pp. 492, 520.

28. Woodward, *Reunion and Reaction*, p. 8.

29. Ibid., pp. 8–9.

30. Ibid., p. 11.

31. Ibid., pp. 9–10.

32. Harry Barnard, *Rutherford B. Hayes and His America* (Indianapolis and New York, 1954), pp. 420–32.

33. Kenneth E. Davison, *The Presidency of Rutherford B. Hayes* (Westport, Conn., 1972), pp. 136–44. Though Davison says that Grant had already terminated military Reconstruction, this was not so. Grant had reversed himself on his earlier policy of intervention in the South, but federal troops still occupied Columbia and New Orleans while Grant was president, and they were not ordered away until Hayes was president.

34. Woodward, *Reunion and Reaction*, p. 9.

35. See, for example, John A. Logan to his wife March 8, 1977, John A. Logan Papers, Library of Congress; New York *Tribune*, August 9, 1877; Ben Wade to Zachariah Chandler, August 9, 1877, Zachariah Chandler Papers, Library of Congress.

36. Diary entry of October 24, 1877, Charles R. Williams, ed., *Diary and Letters of Rutherford Birchard Hayes* (Columbus, Ohio, 1924), III, 449.

37. Kirk H. Porter, *National Party Platforms* (New York, 1924), pp. 94–98; Williams, *Life of Hayes*, I, 462.

38. DeSantis, *Republicans Face the Southern Question*, pp. 33–34.

39. Ibid., p. 71.

40. Diary entry of April 22, 1877, Williams, ed., *Diary and Letters*, III, 430.

41. Wade Hampton to Hayes, March 31, 1877, published in New York *Times*, April 4, 1877, quoted in Barnard, *Hayes*, pp. 426–27; Diary entry of November 12, 1878, Williams, ed., *Diary and Letters*, III, 510.

42. DeSantis, *Republicans Face the Southern Question*, pp. 34–35.

43. Vincent P. DeSantis, "President Hayes's Southern Policy," *Journal of Southern History*, 21 (1955), 476–94.

44. Diary entry of March 23, 1877, Williams, ed., *Diary and Letters of Hayes*, III, 429; James D. Richardson, *A Compilation of the Message and Papers of the Presidents* (Washington, D.C., 1911), VI, 4394–96.

45. Washington, D.C., *National Republican*, March 15, 1877.

46. Diary entries of March 14, 20, 23, 1877, Williams, ed., *Diary and Letters of Hayes*, III, 427–29.

47. Medill to Smith, February 17, 1877, Hayes Papers.

48. DeSantis, *Republicans Face the Southern Question*, pp. 24–56.

49. *Nation*, March 15, 1877, p. 156.

50. DeSantis, *Republicans Face the Southern Question*, pp. 57–62, 71–73.

51. Forrester Do Chonde to Hayes, March 1, 1877; J. B. Way to Hayes, March 8, 1877; Whitelaw Reid to Hayes, February 21, 1877, Hayes Papers.

52. There are very many such letters in the Hayes Papers, Hayes Memorial Library, Fremont, Ohio.

53. Lowell, Longfellow, Eliot, and Norton to Hayes, March 9, 1877; W. W. Kimball, Boston, to Hayes, March 9, 1877; W. W. Sloan, Port Clinton, Ohio, to Hayes, March 11, 1877; J. W. Gillespie, Harrisburg, Pennsylvania, to Hayes, March 12, 1877, Hayes Papers.

54. Diary entry of October 4, 1876, Williams, ed., *Diary and Letters*, III, 364; Garfield reported the substance of his talk with Blaine to George F. Hoar, *Autobiography of Seventy Years* (New York, 1903), II, 12; the Washington, D.C., *National Republican*, November 10, 1877, carried a story of a conversation that Conkling had with a reporter.

55. Marshall Jewell to Hayes, February 22, 1877, Hayes Papers.

56. Hayes to Guy M. Bryan, October 1, 1866, Williams, ed., *Diary and Letters*, III, 32–33.

57. Williams, *Life of Hayes*, I, 277–80, 292–327, 318.

58. Hayes to S. Birchard, his uncle, November 11, 1868; Hayes to Charles Nordhoff, March 13, 1871; Diary entries of March 16, June 12, 1871, Williams, ed., *Diary and Letters*, III, 56, 133–34, 135–36, 147.

59. E. W. Winkler, ed., "The Bryan-Hayes Correspondence," *Southwestern Historical Quarterly*, 25–30 (1920–1926); Robert C. Cotner and Watt P. Marchman, eds., "Correspondence of Guy M. Bryan and Rutherford B. Hayes: Additional Letters," *Ohio State Archaeological and Historical Quarterly*, 62 (1964), 349–77.

60. Hayes to Bryan, July 8, 1876, "Bryan-Hayes Correspondence," 26, p. 294.

61. Interview with Bryan in May, 1877, Galveston, Texas, *News*, May 27, 1877.

62. Diary entry of March 28, 1875; Hayes to Bryan, July 27, 1875, Williams, ed., *Diary and Letters*, III, 269, 286.

63. Hayes in an interview in April, 1877, referred to his speeches in the 1875 Ohio campaign to refute the charges that his new policy was a surprise. At the same time newspapers republished excerpts from his opening Ohio address. See, for example, New York *Tribune*, April 16, 1877; Louisville *Courier-Journal*, April 16, 1877; and New York *Times*, April 16, 1877.

64. Diary entry of March 23, 1877, Williams, ed., *Diary and Letters*, III, 429.

65. *Nation*, March 1, 1877, p. 124; New York *Times*, March 3, 1877; Louisville *Commercial*, March 3, 1877.

66. Garfield Diary, January 20, 1877, James A. Garfield Papers, Library of Congress; William E. Chandler to Hayes, January 13, 1877, Hayes Papers; *Nation*, March 1, 1877, pp. 127, 124; Alphonso Taft to Hayes, February 14, 1877, Hayes Papers.

67. Alphonso Taft to Hayes, February 19, 1877, Hayes Papers.

68. Barnard, *Hayes*, p. 420.

69. Diary entries of March 20, 23, 1877, Williams, ed., *Diary and Letters*, III, 428.

70. "Bryan-Hayes Correspondence," *Southwestern Historical Quarterly*, 29 (1925–1926), 302–3.

71. Chicago *Tribune*, April 16, 1877; New York *Tribune*, April 16, 18, 1877; New York *Times*, April 16, 1877.

72. *Harper's Weekly*, October 6, 1877, p. 779.

73. Entry of October 17, 1877, in "Memoirs of Thomas Donaldson," pp. 34–35. MS in Indiana State Historical Society, Indianapolis, copy in Hayes Library.

74. Diary entry of April 11, 1880, Williams, ed., *Diary and Letters of Hayes*, III, 594–95.

75. New York *Tribune*, July 2, 1880; Louisville *Commercial*, July 7, 1880.

The Published Writings of C. Vann Woodward:
A Bibliography

LOUIS P. MASUR

THE FOLLOWING BIBLIOGRAPHY of the writings of C. Vann Woodward includes books, articles, reviews, and miscellany, such as forewords, comments, and correspondence, published through the fall of 1981. A separate section of writings about Woodward is also included. The miscellaneous category is a partial listing; reprints and translations have been omitted. Citations within each category are in chronological order.

I. Books

Tom Watson: Agrarian Rebel. New York, 1938.
The Battle for Leyte Gulf. New York, 1947.
Origins of the New South, 1877–1913. Baton Rouge, 1951. 2nd ed. with new bibliographic essay by Charles B. Dew, 1971.
Reunion and Reaction: The Compromise of 1877 and the End of Reconstruction. Boston, 1951. Rev. ed. with new introd. and concluding chap. Garden City, N.Y., 1956.
The Strange Career of Jim Crow. New York, 1955. New and rev. ed., 1957; 2nd rev. ed., 1966; 3rd rev. ed., 1974.
The Burden of Southern History. Baton Rouge, 1960. Rev. ed., 1968.
The National Experience: A History of the United States, with John M. Blum, Edmund S. Morgan, Willie Lee Rose, Arthur M. Schlesinger, Jr., and Kenneth M. Stampp. New York, 1963. New and rev. ed., 1968; 2nd rev. ed., 1973; 3rd rev. ed., 1977; 4th rev. ed., 1981.
American Counterpoint: Slavery and Racism in the North-South Dialogue. Boston, 1971.

II. Pamphlets and Edited Works

The South in Search of a Philosophy. Phi Beta Kappa Series, no. 1. Gainesville, 1938.

American Attitudes toward History: An Inaugural Lecture Delivered before the University of Oxford on 22 February 1955. Oxford, 1955.

Ed., *Cannibals All! or, Slaves without Masters.* By George Fitzhugh. Cambridge, Mass., 1960. With an introd., pp. vii–xxxix.

Ed., *A Southern Prophecy: The Prosperity of the South Dependent upon the Elevation of the Negro (1889).* By Lewis H. Blair. Boston, 1964. With an introd., pp. xi–xlvi.

Ed., *After the War: A Tour of the Southern States, 1865–1866.* By Whitelaw Reid. New York, 1965. With an introd., pp. ix–xxi.

Ed., *The Comparative Approach to American History.* New York, 1968. With a pref., pp. ix–xi.

Ed., *Responses of the Presidents to Charges of Misconduct.* New York, 1974. With an introd., pp. xi–xxvi.

Ed., *Mary Chesnut's Civil War.* New Haven, 1981. With an introd., pp. xv–lviii.

III. Articles

"Thomas Edward Watson." In *Dictionary of American Biography.* Edited by Dumas Malone. Vol. 19. New York, 1936. Pp. 549–51.

"Tom Watson and the Negro in Agrarian Politics." *Journal of Southern History,* 4 (1938), 14–33.

"Bourbonism in Georgia." *North Carolina Historical Review,* 16 (1939), 23–35.

"Hillbilly Realism." *Southern Review,* 4 (1939), 676–681.

"Share-the-Wealth Movements." In *Dictionary of American History.* Edited by James Truslow Adams. Vol. 5. New York, 1940 and following editions. Pp. 64.

"Townsend Plan." In *Dictionary of American History.* Edited by James Truslow Adams. Vol. 5. New York, 1940 and following editions. P. 288.

"John Brown's Private War." In *America in Crisis.* Edited by Daniel Aaron. New York, 1952. Pp. 109–32.

"The Irony of Southern History." *Journal of Southern History,* 19 (1953), 3–19.

"Can We Believe Our Own History?" *Johns Hopkins Magazine,* 5 (1954), 1–6, 16.

"The Historical Dimension." *Virginia Quarterly Review,* 32 (1956), 258–67.

"The 'New Reconstruction' in the South: Desegregation in Historical Perspective." *Commentary,* 21 (1956), 501–8.

"Young Jim Crow." *Nation,* July 7, 1956, pp. 9–10.

"The Lowest Ebb." *American Heritage,* 8, no. 3 (1957), 52–57, 106–9.

"The Disturbed Southerners." *Current History,* 32 (1957), 278–82.

"The Political Legacy of Reconstruction." *Journal of Negro Education,* 26 (1957), 231–40.

"The Great Civil Rights Debate: The Ghost of Thaddeus Stevens in the Senate Chamber." *Commentary*, 24 (October 1957), 283–91.

"Toynbee and Metahistory." *American Scholar*, 27 (1958), 384–92.

"The Search for Southern Identity." *Virginia Quarterly Review*, 34 (1958), 321–38.

"Equality: America's Deferred Commitment." *American Scholar*, 27 (1958), 459–72.

"The South and the Law of the Land: The Present Resistance and Its Prospects." *Commentary*, 26 (November 1958), 369–74.

"The Populist Heritage and the Intellectual." *American Scholar* 29 (1959–60), 55–72.

"The Age of Reinterpretation." *American Historical Review*, 66 (1960), 1–19.

"Reflections on a Centennial: The American Civil War." *Yale Review*, 50 (1961), 481–90.

"The Antislavery Myth." *American Scholar*, 31 (1962), 312–28.

"The Unreported Crisis in the Southern Colleges." *Harper's Magazine*, October 1962, pp. 82–89.

"Our Past Isn't What It Used to Be." New York *Times Book Review*, July 28, 1963, pp. 1, 24–25.

"The Case of the Louisiana Traveler (Plessy v. Ferguson, 163 U.S. 537)." In *Quarrels That Have Shaped the Constitution*. Edited by John A. Garraty. New York, 1964. Pp. 145–58.

"Plessy v. Ferguson: The Birth of Jim Crow." *American Heritage*, 15, no. 3 (1964), 52–55, 100–3.

"The Question of Loyalty." *American Scholar*, 33 (1964), 561–67.

"Flight from History: The Heritage of the Negro." In *The State of the Nation*. Edited by David Boroff. Englewood Cliffs, N.J., 1965. Pp. 174–82.

"From the First Reconstruction to the Second." *Harper's Magazine*, April 1965, pp. 127–33.

"Southern Mythology." *Commentary*, 39 (May 1965), 60–63.

"After Watts—Where Is the Negro Revolution Headed?" New York *Times Magazine*, August 29, 1965, pp. 24–25, 81–89.

"Flight from History: The Heritage of the Negro." *Nation*, September 20, 1965, pp. 142–46.

"Seeds of Failure in Radical Race Policy." *Proceedings of the American Philosophical Society*, 110 (1966), 1–9.

"The North and the South of It." *American Scholar*, 35 (1966), 647–58.

"What Happened to the Civil Rights Movement?" *Harper's Magazine*, January 1967, pp. 29–37.

"The Comparability of American History." In *The Comparative Approach to American History*. Edited by C. Vann Woodward. New York, 1968. Pp. 3–17.

"The Test of Comparison." In *The Comparative Approach to American History*. Edited by C. Vann Woodward. New York, 1968. Pp. 346–58.

"History and the Third Culture." *Journal of Contemporary History*, 3, no. 2 (1968), 23–35.

"The Southern Ethic in a Puritan World." *William and Mary Quarterly*, 3rd ser., 25 (1968), 343–70.

"The Hidden Sources of Negro History." *Saturday Review*, January 18, 1969, pp. 18–22.

"The Uses of History in Fiction: A Discussion." With Ralph Ellison, William

Styron, and Robert Penn Warren. *Southern Literary Journal*, 1 (1969), 57–90.

"American History (White Man's Version) Needs an Infusion of Soul." New York *Times Magazine*, April 20, 1969, pp. 32–33, 108–14.

"Clio with Soul." *Journal of American History*, 56 (1969), 5–20.

"W. J. Cash Reconsidered." *New York Review of Books*, December 4, 1969, pp. 28–34.

"The Future of the Past." *American Historical Review*, 75 (1970), 711–26.

"Emancipations and Reconstructions: A Comparative Study." Paper presented at the XIII International Congress of Historical Sciences, Moscow, and published by Navka Publishing House, 1970.

"The Ghost of Populism Walks Again." New York *Times Magazine*, June 4, 1972, pp. 16–17, 60–69.

"History from Slave Sources." *American Historical Review*, 79 (1974), 470–81.

"That Other Impeachment." New York *Times Magazine*, August 11, 1974, pp. 9, 26–32.

"The Erosion of Academic Privileges and Immunities." *Daedalus*, 103, no. 4 (1974), 33–37.

"Collapse of Activism: What Became of the 1960's?" *New Republic*, November 9, 1974, pp. 18–25.

"Why the Southern Renaissance?" *Virginia Quarterly Review*, 51 (1975), 222–39.

"What Is the Chestnut Diary?" *In South Carolina Women Writers: Proceedings of the Reynolds Conference, University of South Carolina, October 24–25, 1975*. Ed. by James B. Meriwether. Spartanburg, S.C., 1979.

"The Graying of America: Reflections upon Our Most Enduring National Myth As We Put the Bicentennial Behind Us, and Move On." New York *Times*, December 29, 1976, p. 25.

"The Future of Southern History." In *The Future of History: Essays in the Vanderbilt University Centennial Symposium*. Edited by Charles Delzell. Nashville, 1977. Pp. 135–49.

"The Aging of America." *American Historical Review*, 82 (1977), 583–94.

"Segregation." In *Encyclopedia Americana: International Edition*. Vol. 24 Danbury, Conn., 1978. Pp. 523–24.

"The Price of Freedom." In *What Was Freedom's Price?* Edited by David G. Sansing. Jackson, Miss., 1978. Pp. 93–113.

"The Fall of the American Adam." In *New Republic*, December 2, 1981, pp. 13–16.

IV. Book Reviews

Hugh Russell Fraser, *Democracy in the Making*. In *New Republic*, January 4, 1939, p. 265.

Stanley F. Horn, *Invisible Empire: The Story of the Ku Klux Klan, 1866–1871*. In *New Republic*, July 26, 1939, pp. 341–42.

Elizabeth H. Davidson, *Child Labor Legislation in the Southern Textile States*. In *Journal of Southern History*, 5 (1939), 407–8.

Charles and Mary Beard, *America in Midpassage*. Howard Odum, *American Social Problems*. W. T. Couch, ed., *These Are Our Lives*. In *Virginia Quarterly Review*, 15 (1939), 632–36.

Gerald W. Johnson, *America's Silver Age: The Statecraft of Clay, Webster, Calhoun.* In *New Republic,* November 29, 1939, 176–77.

Josephus Daniels, *Tar Heel Editor.* In *New Republic,* January 1, 1940, pp. 27–28.

Allan Michie and Frank Ryhlick, *Dixie Demagogues.* Marquis James, *Mr. Garner of Texas.* Alfred Lief, *Democracy's Norris.* In *Virginia Quarterly Review,* 16 (1940), 129–34.

Eugene Tenbroek Mudge, *The Social Philosophy of John Taylor of Caroline.* In *North Carolina Historical Review,* 17 (1940), 273–75.

W. J. Cash, *The Mind of the South.* In *Journal of Southern History,* 7 (1941), 400–401.

William A. Mabry, *The Negro in North Carolina Politics Since Reconstruction.* In *North Carolina Historical Review,* 18 (1941), 82–83.

Josephus Daniels, *Editor in Politics.* In *Mississippi Valley Historical Review,* 28 (1941), 285–86.

Raymond B. Nixon, *Henry W. Grady: Spokesman of the New South.* In *Journal of Southern History,* 10 (1944), 114–15.

Charles W. Ramsdell, *Behind the Lines of the Southern Confederacy.* Edited by Wendell Stephenson. In *American Historical Review,* 49 (1944), 754–55.

Charles A. Beard, *The Republic.* Henry Steele Commager, *Majority Rule and Minority Rights.* Wilfred Binkley, *American Political Parties: Their National History.* In *Virginia Quarterly Review,* 20 (1944), 150–54.

Francis Butler Simkins, *Pitchfork Ben Tillman: South Carolinian.* In *North Carolina Historical Review,* 22 (1945), 378–79.

Katharine Du Pre Lumpkin, *The Making of a Southerner.* In *Mississippi Valley Historical Review,* 34 (1947), 141–42.

James A. Field, Jr., *The Japanese at Leyte Gulf: The Shō Operation.* In *American Historical Review,* 53 (1947), 82–84.

George Morgenstern, *Pearl Harbor: The Story of the Secret War.* In *American Historical Review,* 53 (1947), 188.

Frank O. Hough, *The Island War: The United States Marine Corps in the Pacific.* In *Pacific Historical Review,* 16 (1947), 459–60.

Arthur S. Link, *Wilson: The Road to the White House.* In *Pennsylvania Magazine of History and Biography,* 72 (1948), 97–98.

Russell Lord, *The Wallaces of Iowa.* In *Mississippi Valley Historical Review,* 34 (1948), 703.

William F. Halsey, *Admiral Halsey's Story.* In *American Historical Review,* 53 (1948), 898.

Richard Hofstadter, *The American Political Tradition and the Men Who Made It.* In *Mississippi Valley Historical Review,* 35 (1949), 681–82.

Samuel Eliot Morison, *History of United States Naval Operations in World War II: Coral Sea, Midway, and Submarine Actions, May 1942–August 1942.* In *Saturday Review of Literature,* October 29, 1949, pp. 20–21.

V. O. Key, Jr., *Southern Politics in State and Nation.* In *Yale Review,* 39 (1949), 374–76.

Stuart Noblin, *Leonidas Lafayette Polk: Agrarian Crusader.* In *American Historical Review,* 55 (1950), 1002–3.

Hodding Carter, *Southern Legacy.* In *Journal of Southern History,* 16 (1950), 381–82.

Samuel Eliot Morison, *History of United States Naval Operations in World War II: Breaking the Bismarck's Barrier, 22 July 1942–May 1944.* In *Saturday Review of Literature,* February 24, 1951, pp. 15–16.

William B. Hesseltine, *Confederate Leaders in the New South*. In *Journal of Southern History*, 17 (1951), 270–71.

Albert D. Kirwan, *Revolt of the Rednecks: Mississippi Politics, 1876–1925*. In *American Historical Review*, 56 (1951), 918–19.

Samuel Eliot Morison, *History of United States Naval Operations in World War II: Aleutians, Gilberts, and Marshalls, June 1942–April 1944*. In *Saturday Review of Literature*, November 24, 1951, pp. 14–15, 45.

Isaac F. Marcosson, *"Marse Henry": A Biography of Henry Watterson*. In *Journal of Southern History*, 18 (1952), 97.

Allen Johnston Going, *Bourbon Democracy in Alabama, 1874–1890*. In *Mississippi Valley Historical Review*, 38 (1952), 719–20.

Henderson H. Donald, *The Negro Freedmen: Life Conditions of the American Negro in the Early Years after Emancipation*. In *Saturday Review*, March 22, 1952, p. 40.

Ernest J. King and Walter Muir Whitehall, *Fleet Admiral King: A Naval Record*. In *Saturday Review*, November 22, 1952, p. 26.

Richard B. Morris, ed., *Encyclopedia of American History*. In *Saturday Review*, June 13, 1953, p. 45.

Mary C. Simms Oliphant et al., eds., *The Letters of William Gilmore Simms*. Vols. 1–2. In *American Historical Review*, 59 (1954), 466–67.

Frank Freidel, *Franklin D. Roosevelt: The Ordeal*. In New York *Herald Tribune Book Review*, January 31, 1954, p. 7.

James Dugan, *The Great Iron Ship*. In *Saturday Review*, February 6, 1954, p. 19.

Rayford W. Logan, *The Negro in American Life and Thought: The Nadir, 1877–1901*. Louis Ruchames, *Race, Jobs, and Politics: The Story of FEPC*. Lee Nichols, *Breakthrough on the Color Front*. In *Yale Review*, 43 (1954), 604–7.

John R. Lambert, *Arthur Pue Gorman*. In *American Historical Review*, 59 (1954), 1027–28.

Alice Nichols, *Bleeding Kansas*. In New York *Herald Tribune Book Review*, July 25, 1954, p. 3.

Howard K. Beale, ed., *Charles A. Beard: An Appraisal*. In New York *Times Book Review*, September 5, 1954, p. 9.

David Donald, ed., *Inside Lincoln's Cabinet: The Civil War Diaries of Salmon P. Chase*. In *Pennsylvania Magazine of History and Biography*, 79 (1955), 131–32.

Harry Barnard, *Rutherford B. Hayes and His America*. In *Nation*, May 28, 1955, p. 467.

John T. Trowbridge, *The Desolate South, 1865–1866*. In New York *Herald Tribune Book Review*, May 13, 1956, p. 4.

Joseph Frazier Wall, *Henry Watterson: Reconstructed Rebel*. In *Mississippi Valley Historical Review*, 43 (1956), 137–38.

Earl Schenck Miers, *Robert E. Lee: A Great Life in Brief*. In New York *Herald Tribune Book Review*, June 10, 1956, p. 3.

Thomas and Marva Belden, *So Fell the Angels*. In New York *Herald Tribune Book Review*, July 29, 1956, p. 3.

Daniel Guerin, *Negroes on the March*. Eli Ginzberg, *The Negro Potential*. In *Commentary*, 22 September 1956), 288–92.

Frank Freidel, *Franklin D. Roosevelt: The Triumph*. In New York *Herald Tribune Book Review*, September 9, 1956, p. 4.

John Hope Franklin, *The Militant South, 1800–1861*. In New York *Times Book Review*, September 23, 1956, p. 3.

Kenneth M. Stampp, *The Peculiar Institution: Slavery in the Ante-Bellum South*. In New York *Herald Tribune Book Review*, October 21, 1956, p. 6.

Willard Thorp, *A Southern Reader*. In *American Quarterly*, 8 (1956), 284–85.

Arlin Turner, *George W. Cable: A Biography*. In *Journal of Southern History*, 23 (1957), 133–34.

Arthur M. Schlesinger, Jr., *The Age of Roosevelt: The Crisis of the Old Order*. In *Saturday Review*, March 2, 1957, pp. 11–12.

J. C. Levenson, *The Mind and Art of Henry Adams*. Theodore Draper, *The Roots of American Communism*. Charles G. Sellers, *James K. Polk: Jacksonian, 1795–1843*. Broadus Mitchell, *Alexander Hamilton: Youth to Maturity, 1755–1788*. Hans Kohn, *American Nationalism: An Interpretive Essay*. Henry Pelling, *America and the British Left*. In *Key Reporter*, 22 (July 1957), 5.

Dexter Perkins, *The New Age of Franklin Roosevelt, 1932–1945*. In *Saturday Review*, July 6, 1957, p. 16.

Clement Eaton, *Henry Clay and the Art of American Politics*. In New York *Herald Tribune Book Review*, July 14, 1957, p. 9.

Bernard Baruch, *Baruch: My Own Story*. In *Saturday Review*, August 31, 1957, pp. 13–14.

Carl T. Rowan, *Go South to Sorrow*. In *Commentary*, 24 (September 1957), 271–72.

H. C. Peterson and Gilbert C. Fite, *Opponents of War, 1917–1918*. In *American Historical Review*, 63 (1957), 155–56.

Raymond Walters, Jr., *Albert Gallatin: Jeffersonian Financier*. Eugene H. Roseboom, *A History of Presidential Elections*. Philip Taft, *The A.F.L. in the Time of Gompers*. Robert D. Meade, *Patrick Henry: Patriot in the Making*. Otis A. Singletary, *Negro Militia and Reconstruction*. Amaury de Riencourt, *The Coming Caesars*. In *Key Reporter*, 23 (October 1957), p. 5.

James Jackson Kilpatrick, *The Sovereign States: Notes of a Citizen of Virginia*. In *Commentary*, 24 (November 1957), 465–66.

Mary C. Simms Oliphant et al., eds., *The Letters of William Gilmore Simms*. Vols. 3–5. In *American Historical Review*, 63 (1958), 529–30.

Carleton Putnam, *Theodore Roosevelt: The Formative Years, 1858–1888*. In New York *Times Book Review*, March 2, 1958, p. 22.

Leonard D. White, *The Republican Era, 1869–1901: A Study in Administrative History*. In New York *Times Book Review*, March 30, 1958, pp. 3, 26.

Wilma Dykeman and James Stokely, *Neither Black nor White*. Harry Ashmore, *An Epitaph for Dixie*. In *Virginia Quarterly Review*, 34 (1958), 292–94.

Marvin Meyers, *The Jacksonian Persuasion*. Bray Hammond, *Banks and Politics in America from the Revolution to the Civil War*. Howard Floan, *The South in Northern Eyes, 1831–1861*. Rexford Guy Tugwell, *The Democratic Roosevelt*. Frank E. Vandiver, *Mighty Stonewall*. In *Key Reporter*, 23 (April 1958), p. 4.

Arlin Turner, ed., *The Negro Question: A Selection of Writings on Civil Rights in the South. By George Washington Cable*. In New York *Times Book Review*, July 27, 1958, p. 6.

Thomas Wilkins, *Clarence King: A Biography*. George E. Mowry, *The Era of Theodore Roosevelt, 1900–1912*. Noble E. Cunningham, *The Jeffersonian*

Republicans: The Formation of Party Organization, 1789–1801. Edmund S. Morgan, *The Puritan Dilemma: The Story of John Winthrop.* In *Key Reporter,* 24 (October 1958), p. 7.

William D. Miller, *Memphis during the Progressive Era, 1900–1917.* In *American Historical Review,* 64 (1958), 200–201.

Henry Steele Commager and Richard B. Morris, eds., *The Spirit of 'Seventy-Six.* In New York *Herald Tribune Book Review,* November 2, 1958, p. 4.

James McBride Dabbs, *The Southern Heritage.* In *Nation,* November 15, 1958, p. 365.

Hodding Carter, *The Angry Scar: The Story of Reconstruction.* In New York *Times Book Review,* February 1, 1959, pp. 5, 33.

Glyndon G. Van Deusen, *The Jacksonian Era, 1828–1848.* In New York *Herald Tribune Book Review,* March 22, 1959, p. 4.

Ernest Samuels, *Henry Adams: The Middle Years, 1877–1891.* Richard N. Current, *The Lincoln Nobody Knows.* Forrest McDonald, *We the People: The Economic Origins of the Constitution.* Cushing Strout, *The Pragmatic Revolt in American History.* Samuel Eliot Morison, *Leyte, June 1944–January 1945.* In *Key Reporter,* 24 (April 1959), p. 6.

Samuel Eliot Morison, *John Paul Jones: A Sailor's Biography.* In New York *Times Book Review,* September 13, 1959, p. 3.

Nash Burger and John Bettersworth, *South of Appomattox.* In New York *Times Book Review,* September 20, 1959, p. 46.

Allan Nevins, *The War for the Union: The Improvised War, 1861–1862.* Jacques Barzun, *The House of Intellect.* Harold U. Faulkner, *Politics, Reform, and Expansion, 1890–1900.* R. L. Bruckberger, *Image of America.* In *Key Reporter,* 25 (autumn 1959), p. 6.

Fawn Brodie, *Thaddeus Stevens: Scourge of the South.* In New York *Times Book Review,* November 22, 1959, pp. 66–67.

Lester J. Cappon, ed., *The Adams-Jefferson Letters.* Vols. 1–2. R. R. Palmer, *The Age of the Democratic Revolution.* Vol. 1. Stefan Lorant, *The Life and Times of Theodore Roosevelt.* In *Key Reporter,* 25 (spring 1960), p. 7.

Henry F. May, *The End of American Innocence: A Study of the First Years of Our Own Time, 1912–1917.* In *American Historical Review,* 65 (1960), 637–38.

Eric McKitrick, *Andrew Johnson and Reconstruction.* In New York *Times Book Review,* September 25, 1960, pp. 3, 24.

Merrill D. Peterson, *The Jefferson Image in the American Mind.* Howard K. Beale, ed., *The Diary of Gideon Welles.* In *Key Reporter,* 26 (autumn 1960), p. 6.

Charles G. Sellers, Jr., ed., *The Southerner as American.* In *Journal of Southern History,* 27 (1961), 92–94.

Folke Dovring, *History as a Social Science: An Essay on the Nature and Purpose of Historical Studies.* In *American Historical Review,* 66 (1961), 1079.

William R. Taylor, *Cavalier and Yankee: The Old South and American National Character.* In New York *Times Book Review,* December 24, 1961, p. 6.

Edmund Wilson, *Patriotic Gore: Studies in the Literature of the American Civil War.* In *American Scholar,* 31 (1962), 638–42.

Robert F. Durden, *Reconstruction Bonds and Twentieth-Century Politics: South Dakota v. North Carolina.* In *American Historical Review,* 68 (1963), 840.

James MacGregor Burns, *The Deadlock of Democracy: Four Party Politics in America.* In *Commentary*, 35 (June 1963), 540–42.

John Thomas, *The Liberator, William Lloyd Garrison: A Biography.* In New York *Times Book Review*, June 30, 1963, p. 6.

Walter T. K. Nugent, *The Tolerant Populists: Kansas Populism and Nativism.* In *Mississippi Valley Historical Review*, 50 (1963), 516–17.

Page Smith, *The Historian and History.* Erich Kahler, *The Meaning of History.* In New York *Times Book Review*, July 26, 1964, p. 5.

James W. Silver, *Mississippi: The Closed Society.* In *New York Review of Books*, August 20, 1964, pp. 13–14.

Katharine Jocher et al., eds., *Folk, Region, and Society: Selected Papers of Howard W. Odum.* In New York *Times Book Review*, September 27, 1964, p. 48.

Frenise A. Logan, *The Negro in North Carolina, 1876–1894.* In *American Historical Review*, 70 (1965), 584.

James M. McPherson, *The Struggle for Equality: Abolitionists and the Negro in the Civil War and Reconstruction.* In New York *Times Book Review*, January 3, 1965, p. 6.

Edward N. Saveth, ed., *American History and the Social Sciences.* Werner Cahnman and Alvin Boskoff, eds., *Sociology and History: Theory and Research.* In New York *Times Book Review*, January 24, 1965, pp. 1, 44–45.

Robert Penn Warren, *Who Speaks For the Negro?* In *New Republic*, May 22, 1965, pp. 21–23.

Richard Hofstadter, *The Paranoid Style in American Politics and Other Essays.* In New York *Times Book Review*, November 14, 1965, pp. 3, 84.

David Donald, *The Politics of Reconstruction, 1863–1867.* In *American Historical Review*, 72 (1966), 315–17.

Barrington Moore, Jr., *Social Origins of Dictatorship and Democracy: Lord and Peasant in the Making of the Modern World.* In *Yale Review*, 56 (1967), 450–53.

David T. Bazelon, *Power in America: The Politics of the New Class.* In *Commentary*, 44 (July 1967), 92–95.

Alan Conway, *The Reconstruction of Georgia.* In *American Historical Review*, 72 (1967), 1502–3.

William Styron, *Confessions of Nat Turner.* In *New Republic*, October 7, 1967, pp. 25–28.

Joseph L. Morrison, *W. J. Cash: Southern Prophet.* In *New Republic*, December 9, 1967, 28–30.

Winthrop D. Jordan, *White over Black: American Attitudes toward the Negro, 1550–1812.* In New York *Times Book Review*, March 31, 1968, pp. 6, 43.

John Hammond Moore, ed., *Before and After: or, The Relations of the Races at the South.* By Isaac DuBose Seabrook. In *American Historical Review*, 73 (1968), 1255–56.

Neal R. Peirce, *The People's President: The Electoral College in American History and the Direct-Vote Alternative.* In *New Republic*, June 1, 1968, 33–34.

Barton J. Bernstein, ed., *Towards a New Past: Dissenting Essays in American History.* In *New York Review of Books*, August 1, 1968, pp. 8–12.

Aileen Kraditor, *Means and Ends in American Abolitionism.* Eugene Berwanger, *The Frontier against Slavery.* Lorman Ratner, *Powder Keg: Northern Opposition to the Antislavery Movement, 1831–1840.* V. Jacque Voegeli, *Free But Not Equal: The Midwest and the Negro during the*

Civil War. Forrest G. Wood, *Black Scare: The Racist Response to Emanci-pation and Reconstruction.* William S. McFeeley, *Yankee Stepfather: General O. O. Howard and the Freedmen.* In *New York Review of Books,* February 27, 1969, pp. 5–11.

Dan T. Carter, *Scottsboro: A Tragedy of the American South.* In New York *Times Book Review,* March 9, 1969, p. 5.

Allen W. Trelease, *White Terror: The Ku Klux Klan Conspiracy and Southern Reconstruction.* In New York *Times Book Review,* May 23, 1971, pp. 5, 28.

George M. Fredrickson, *The Black Image in the White Mind: The Debate on Afro-American Character and Destiny, 1817–1914.* Eugene D. Genovese, *In Red and Black: Marxian Explorations in Southern and Afro-American History.* In *New York Review of Books,* August 12, 1971, pp. 11–14.

Allan Nevins, *The War for the Union.* Vols. 3–4. In New York *Times Book Review,* December 26, 1971, pp. 5, 17.

Louis R. Harlan, *Booker T. Washington: The Making of a Black Leader, 1865–1901.* Louis R. Harlan, ed., *The Booker T. Washington Papers.* Vols. 1–2. In *New Republic,* November 11, 1972, 20–22.

William C. Havard, ed., *The Changing Politics of the South.* Chandler Davidson, *Biracial Politics: Conflict and Coalition in the Metropolitan South.* Albert Gore, *Let the Glory Out: My South and Its Politics.* In *New York Review of Books,* December 14, 1972, pp. 37–40.

Pete Daniel, *The Shadow of Slavery: Peonage in the South, 1901–1969.* In *Journal of American History,* 59 (1973), 1030–31.

Don E. Fehrenbacher and Carl N. Degler, eds., *The South and the Concurrent Majority.* By David M. Potter. In *Journal of American History,* 60 (1973), 123–24.

Daniel Aaron, *The Unwritten War: American Writers and the Civil War.* In *New York Review of Books,* February 21, 1974, pp. 26–29.

Carl N. Degler, *The Other South: Southern Dissenters in the Nineteenth Century.* In New York *Times Book Review,* March 10, 1974, p. 4.

Robert William Fogel and Stanley L. Engerman, *Time on the Cross: The Economics of American Negro Slavery.* Idem, *Time on the Cross: Evidence and Methods, A Supplement.* In *New York Review of Books,* May 2, 1974, pp. 3–6.

Eugene D. Genovese, *Roll, Jordan, Roll: The World the Slaves Made.* In *New York Review of Books,* October 3, 1974, pp. 19–21.

Shelby Foote, *The Civil War: A Narrative.* Vol. 3. In *New York Review of Books,* March 6, 1975, p. 12.

Allan Nevins, *Allan Nevins on History.* In *Reviews in American History,* 4 (1976), 25–26.

Bernard Sternsher, *Consensus, Conflict, and American Historians.* In *American Historical Review,* 81 (1976), 438–39.

Lawrence Goodwyn, *Democratic Promise: The Populist Moment in America.* In *New York Review of Books,* October 28, 1976, pp. 28–29.

Joe Gray Taylor, *Louisiana Reconstructed, 1863–1877.* In *Louisiana History,* 17 (1976), 97–98.

Thomas L. Connelly, *The Marble Man: Robert E. Lee and His Image in American Society.* In New York *Times Book Review,* April 3, 1977, p. 12.

John Hope Franklin, *Racial Equality in America.* In *Journal of American History,* 64 (1977), 776–77.

Robert Higgs, *Competition and Coercion: Blacks in the American Economy, 1865–1914.* In *Agricultural History,* 52 (1978), 194–95.

Howard N. Rabinowitz, *Race Relations in the Urban South, 1865–1890*. In *Journal of Southern History*, 44 (1978), 476–78.

David H. Donald, *Liberty and Union*. In New York *Times Book Review*, November 19, 1978, p. 13.

Don E. Fehrenbacher, *The Dred Scott Case: Its Significance in American Law and Politics*. In *New York Review of Books*, December 7, 1978, pp. 30–31.

Emory M. Thomas, *The Confederate Nation, 1861–1865*. In *New Republic*, March 17, 1979), 25–28.

David DeLeon, *The American as Anarchist: Reflections on Indigenous Radicalism*. James R. Green, *Grass-Roots Socialism: Radical Movements in the Southwest, 1895–1943*. In *New York Review of Books*, April 5, 1979, pp. 3–5.

J. Harvie Wilkinson III, *From "Brown" to "Bakke": The Supreme Court and School Integration, 1954–1978*. In *New Republic*, June 23, 1979, 27–29.

Leon F. Litwack, *Been in the Storm So Long: The Aftermath of Slavery*. In *New York Review of Books*, August 16, 1979, pp. 8–9.

Ronald T. Takaki, *Iron Cages: Race and Culture in Nineteenth-Century America*. In *New York Review of Books*, November 22, 1979, pp. 14–16.

Frances Fitzgerald, *America Revised: History Schoolbooks in the Twentieth Century*. In *New York Review of Books*, December 20, 1979, pp. 16–19.

Clark R. Mollenhoff, *The President Who Failed: Carter out of Control*. Bruce Mazlish and Edwin Diamond, *Jimmy Carter: A Character Portrait*. In *New York Review of Books*, April 3, 1980, pp. 9–11.

J. R. Pole, *Paths to the American Past*. In *Times Literary Supplement*, May 30, 1980, p. 609.

Merle Miller, *Lyndon*. In *New Republic*, November 1, 1980, 29–31.

William Gillette, *Retreat from Reconstruction, 1869–1879*. Otto H. Olson, ed., *Reconstruction and Redemption in the South*. In *New York Review of Books*, November 20, 1980, pp. 49–51.

Eric Foner, *Politics and Ideology in the Age of the Civil War*. In *New Republic*, November 22, 1980, 34–35.

George M. Fredrickson, *White Supremacy: A Comparative Study in American and South African History*. In *New York Review of Books*, March 5, 1981, pp. 26–28.

William S. McFeely, *Grant: A Biography*. In *New York Review of Books*, March 19, 1981, pp. 3–6.

Ray Allen Billington, *Land of Savagery, Land of Promise: The European Image of the American Frontier in the Nineteenth Century*. In *New York Review of Books*, June 11, 1981, pp. 33–35.

Dumas Malone, *The Sage of Monticello*. Vol. 6. Virginius Dabney, *The Jefferson Scandals: A Rebuttal*. In New York *Times Book Review*, July 5, 1981, pp. 1, 14.

Carol Bleser, ed., *The Hammonds of Redcliffe*. In *New York Review of Books*, Oct. 22, 1981, pp. 47–48.

V. Miscellany

"Statement in Favor of Abolishing Poll Taxes." *Congressional Digest*, 20 (1941), 309–10.

"Report on Current Research." *Saturday Review*, April 4, 1953, pp. 16–17, 48.

Monograph on the history of reconstruction in the South to brief for Oliver

Brown, *et al.*, v. Board of Education of Topeka, *et al.*, filed in the United States Supreme Court on November 16, 1953.

"Correspondence." *Commentary*, 25 (January 1958), 76.

Comment on "Outstanding Books, 1931–1961," *American Scholar*, 30 (1961), 628.

"Introduction" to *Life and Labor in the Old South*. By Ulrich B. Phillips. Boston, 1963. Pp. iii–vi.

"Reflections on the Fate of the Union: Kennedy and After." *New York Review of Books*, December 26, 1963, pp. 8–9.

"Introduction" to *Rehearsal for Reconstruction: The Port Royal Experiment*. By Willie Lee Rose. New York, 1964. Pp. xi–xiv.

"Foreword" to *Southern Negroes*. By Bell Irvin Wiley. New Haven, 1965. Pp. v–vi.

"Comments by Writers and Scholars on Books of the Past Ten Years." *American Scholar*, 34 (1965), 492.

"An Expert Pick of the Pack." New York *Times Book Review*, December 5, 1965, pp. 5, 52–54.

Comment on Eugene D. Genovese, "The Legacy of Slavery and the Roots of Black Nationalism." *Studies on the Left*, 6 (November–December 1966), 35–42.

"Letter: Adam Clayton Powell as Symbol." New York *Times*, January 18, 1967, p. 42.

"Race Prejudice Is Itself a Form of Violence" (comment for "Is America by Nature a Violent Society?"). New York *Times Magazine*, April 28, 1968, p. 114.

"Letter: Academic Freedom: Whose Story," With Edmund S. Morgan, *Columbia University Forum*, 11, no. 1 (1968), 42–43.

"Recommended Summer Reading." *American Scholar*, 37 (1968), 553–54.

"The Historian's Verdict on the Johnson Years." *Newsweek*, January 20, 1969, p. 19.

"Letter: Scottsboro: A Reply." New York *Times Book Review*, June 22, 1969, p. 34.

"Letter: Concern for Cambodia and Campus." With Felix Gilbert, Richard Hofstadter, H. Stuart Hughes, Leonard Krieger, Fritz Stern, and Gordon Wright. New York *Times*, May 10, 1970, IV, p. 17.

"Letter: On David Donald's 'Radical Historians on the Move.'" New York *Times Book Review*, August 30, 1970, p. 22.

"Richard Hofstadter, 1916–1970." *New York Review of Books*, December 3, 1970, p. 10.

"C. Vann Woodward." Interview in *Interpreting American History: Conversations with Historians*. Edited by John A. Garraty. Vol. 2. New York, 1970. Pp. 45–68.

Letter: "Indignity at Princeton's Institute for Advanced Study." New York *Times*, March 13, 1973, p. 38.

"Communication: Yes, There Was a Compromise of 1877." *Journal of American History*, 60 (1973), 215–23. (Reply to Allan Peskin, "Was There a Compromise of 1877?" *Journal of American History*, 60 (June 1973), 63–75.)

"Letter: *Time on the Cross*, A Reply." *New York Review of Books*, June 13, 1974, p. 41.

"Correspondence." *New Republic*, December 21, 1974, p. 25.

"Letter: On Forestalling Watergates." New York *Times*, June 26, 1975, p. 38.

"Reading, Writing, and Revolution: Comments by Historians on Books in American History." Washington *Post,* February 22, 1976, sect. E, pp. 1, 4.

"Comment: What Is a Liberal—Who Is a Conservative? A Symposium." *Commentary,* 62 (September 1976), 110–11.

"Letter." *New York Review of Books,* February 7, 1980, p. 53.

"Foreword" to *Mary Boykin Chesnut: A Biography.* By Elisabeth Muhlenfeld. Baton Rouge, 1981. Pp. xi–xii.

VI. About C. Vann Woodward

"Historian Scores New South Credo." New York *Times,* June 18, 1961, p. 48.

David Potter. "C. Vann Woodward." In *Pastmasters: Some Essays on American Historians.* Edited by Robin Winks and Marcus Cunliffe. New York, 1969. Pp. 375–407.

Eugene Genovese. "Potter and Woodward on the South." *New York Review of Books,* September 11, 1969, pp. 27–30.

Robert Coles. "In Black and White." *New Yorker,* April 15, 1972, 141–46.

Sheldon Hackney. *"Origins of the New South* in Retrospect." *Journal of Southern History,* 38 (1972), 191–216.

Michael O'Brien. "C. Vann Woodward and the Burden of Southern Liberalism." *American Historical Review,* 78 (1973), 589–604.

"Thank You, Mr. Chips" (the comments of seven retiring college professors), *Newsweek,* June 6, 1977, p. 90.

Larry Van Dyne. "Vann Woodward: Penetrating the Romantic Haze." *Chronicle of Higher Education,* May 8, 1978, 13–14.

Robert B. Westbrook. "C. Vann Woodward: The Southerner as Liberal Realist." *South Atlantic Quarterly,* 77 (1978), 54–71.

Dewey Grantham. "Comer Vann Woodward." In *The Encyclopedia of Southern History.* Edited by David Roller and Robert Twyman. Baton Rouge, 1979. P. 1358.

Michael Les Benedict. "Southern Democrats in the Crisis of 1876–1877: A Reconsideration of *Reunion and Reaction." Journal of Southern History,* 46 (1980), 489–524.

Richard H. King. "The New Southern Liberalism: V. O. Key, C. Vann Woodward, Robert Penn Warren." In *A Southern Renaissance: The Cultural Awakening of the American South, 1930–1955.* New York, 1980. Esp. pp. 256–77.

John H. Roper. "C. Vann Woodward's Early Career—The Historian as Dissident Youth." *Georgia Historical Quarterly,* 64 (1980), 7–21.